STUDENT'S SOLUTIONS MANUAL

BOB DAHL
Minnesota State University, Mankato

RANDY KRIEGER
Concordia University

TERRY A. KRIEGER
Winona State University

assisted by
BRYANT KRIEGER

to accompany

BEGINNING ALGEBRA WITH APPLICATIONS & VISUALIZATION

Gary K. Rockswold
Minnesota State University, Mankato

Terry A. Krieger
Winona State University

PEARSON
Addison
Wesley

Boston   San Francisco   New York
London   Toronto   Sydney   Tokyo   Singapore   Madrid
Mexico City   Munich   Paris   Cape Town   Hong Kong   Montreal

ISBN   0-321-20800-5

7 8 9 BRR 08 07

Table of Contents

Preface

This solutions manual is written as an aid for students studying the text *Beginning Algebra with Applications and Visualization* by Rockswold and Krieger. It contains answers and solutions to the odd-numbered exercises from each section as well as all solutions to the Checking Basic Concepts, Chapter Review and Chapter Test, Cumulative Review, and Extended and Discovery exercises.

This manual is consistent with the text and gives solutions that are accessible to beginning algebra students. The solutions are written in a clear format with hundreds of graphs and tables to help with the learning process. Solutions frequently include not only symbolic solutions but also graphical and numerical solutions to help students understand the problem completely. It is recommended that you make a genuine attempt to solve a problem before looking in this solutions manual for help. Regular class attendance is also recommended. Following these suggestions will promote insight and understanding of beginning and intermediate algebra.

It is the author's hope that you will find this manual helpful when studying the text *Beginning Algebra with Applications and Visualization*. Please email any comments or questions to tkrieger@mcleodusa.net. Your opinion is important. Best wishes for an enjoyable and successful beginning algebra course.

Terry A. Krieger

Chapter 1: Introduction to Algebra

1.1: Numbers, Variables and Expressions

Concepts

1. counting

3. 1

5. prime

7. factors

9. variable

Prime Numbers and Composite Numbers

11. The number 4 is a composite number because it has factors other than itself and 1; $4 = 2 \times 2$

13. The number 1 is neither a prime or a composite number.

15. The number 29 is a prime number because it's only factors are itself and 1.

17. The number 92 is a composite number because it has factors other than itself and 1; $92 = 2 \times 2 \times 23$

19. The number 225 is a composite number because it has factors other than itself and 1; $225 = 3 \times 3 \times 5 \times 5$

21. The number 149 is a prime number because it's only factors are itself and 1.

23. $6 = 2 \times 3$

25. $12 = 2 \times 2 \times 3$

27. $32 = 2 \times 2 \times 2 \times 2 \times 2$

29. $294 = 2 \times 3 \times 7 \times 7$

31. $300 = 2 \times 2 \times 3 \times 5 \times 5$

33. Yes, the population of a country could be described by the whole numbers because we cannot have a fraction of a person.

35. No, a student's grade point average could not be described by the whole numbers because a grade point average usually contains a decimal point.

37. Yes, the number of bytes stored on a computer's hard drive could be described by the whole numbers because computer bytes do not contain a fraction or a decimal point.

39. Yes, the number of students in a class could be described by the whole numbers because we cannot have a fraction of a person.

Algebraic Expressions, Formulas and Equations

41. The value of the expression $2x$, when $x = 5$, is $2x = 2(5) = 10$.

43. The value of the expression $8 - x$, when $x = 1$, is $8 - x = 8 - 1 = 7$.

45. The value of the expression $\dfrac{x}{8}$, when $x = 32$, is $\dfrac{x}{8} = \dfrac{32}{8} = 4$.

47. The value of the expression $3(x + 1)$, when $x = 5$, is $3(x + 1) = 3(5 + 1) = (3)(6) = 18$.

49. The value of the expression $\frac{x}{2} + 1$, when $x = 6$, is $\frac{x}{2} + 1 = \frac{6}{2} + 1 = 3 + 1 = 4$.

51. When $x = 5$ and $y = 4$, $x + y = 5 + 4 = 9$.

53. When $x = 8$ and $y = 4$, $4 \cdot \frac{x}{y} = 4 \cdot \frac{8}{4} = 4 \cdot 2 = 8$.

55. When $x = 5$ and $y = 7$, $y(x - 3) = 7(5 - 3) = (7)(2) = 14$.

57. When $x = 0$, $y = x + 1 = 0 + 1 = 1$.

59. When $x = 7$, $y = 4x = 4 \cdot 7 = 28$.

61. When $z = 12$, $F = z - 5 = 12 - 5 = 7$.

63. When $z = 6$, $F = \frac{30}{z} = \frac{30}{6} = 5$.

65. When $x = 3$ and $z = 15$, $y = x + z = 3 + 15 = 18$.

67. When $x = 9$ and $z = 3$, $y = \frac{x}{z} = \frac{9}{3} = 3$.

Translating Words to Symbols

69. If s is the cost of a soda, then three times this cost is $3s$.

71. If x is the number, $x + 5$ is five more than the number.

73. If n is the number, $3n$ is triple the number.

75. If p is the population of a town, $p - 200$ is two hundred less than the population.

77. If z is the number, $\frac{z}{6}$ is the number divided by 6.

79. If x is one number and y is another number, $\frac{x + 7}{y}$ is a number plus 7, all divided by another number.

Applications

81. See Figure 81. $F = 3y$ because there are three feet in one yard.

Yards (y)	1	2	3	4	5	6	7
Feet (F)	3	6	9	12	15	18	21

Figure 81

83. $P = 100D$ because there are one hundred pennies in one dollar.

85. $M = 50H$; M is miles and H is hours. If $H = 3$, then $M = 50H = 50(3) = 150$ mi.

87. $B = 70x$. If $x = 60$, then $B = 70x = 70(60) = 4200$ beats.

89. Each CD costs $12. Thus, $C = 12x$ where C is cost and x is number of CD's.

91. Since the area of a rectangle equals its length times its width, 22 ft. $\times$ 9 ft. = 198 square feet.

1.2: Fractions

Concepts

1. The person ate $\dfrac{3}{4}$ of the pie. $\dfrac{1}{4}$ of the pie remains.

3. The variable b cannot equal 0.

5. numerators

7. $\dfrac{a}{b} \cdot \dfrac{c}{d} = \dfrac{ac}{bd}$

9. The fractional part of half of a half is $\dfrac{1}{4}$.

11. $\dfrac{a}{b} \div \dfrac{c}{d} = \dfrac{a}{b} \cdot \dfrac{d}{c} = \dfrac{ad}{bc}$.

13. $\dfrac{a}{b} - \dfrac{c}{b} = \dfrac{a-c}{b}$.

15. The greatest common factor of 4 and 6 is 2 because 2 is the largest number that divides into both 4 and 6.

Lowest Terms

17. The largest number that divides into 4 and 12 is 4, so the GCF is 4.

19. The largest number that divides into 50 and 75 is 25, so the GCF is 25.

21. The largest number that divides into 100, 60 and 70 is 10, so the GCF is 10.

23. $\dfrac{3 \cdot 4}{5 \cdot 4} = \dfrac{3}{5} \cdot \dfrac{4}{4} = \dfrac{3}{5} \cdot 1 = \dfrac{3}{5}$

25. $\dfrac{3 \cdot 8}{8 \cdot 5} = \dfrac{3 \cdot 8}{5 \cdot 8} = \dfrac{3}{5} \cdot \dfrac{8}{8} = \dfrac{3}{5} \cdot 1 = \dfrac{3}{5}$

27. $\dfrac{4}{8} = \dfrac{1 \cdot 4}{2 \cdot 4} = \dfrac{1}{2} \cdot \dfrac{4}{4} = \dfrac{1}{2} \cdot 1 = \dfrac{1}{2}$

29. $\dfrac{5}{15} = \dfrac{1 \cdot 5}{3 \cdot 5} = \dfrac{1}{3} \cdot \dfrac{5}{5} = \dfrac{1}{3} \cdot 1 = \dfrac{1}{3}$

31. $\dfrac{10}{25} = \dfrac{2 \cdot 5}{5 \cdot 5} = \dfrac{2}{5} \cdot \dfrac{5}{5} = \dfrac{2}{5} \cdot 1 = \dfrac{2}{5}$

33. $\dfrac{12}{36} = \dfrac{1 \cdot 12}{3 \cdot 12} = \dfrac{1}{3} \cdot \dfrac{12}{12} = \dfrac{1}{3} \cdot 1 = \dfrac{1}{3}$

35. $\dfrac{12}{30} = \dfrac{2 \cdot 6}{5 \cdot 6} = \dfrac{2}{5} \cdot \dfrac{6}{6} = \dfrac{2}{5} \cdot 1 = \dfrac{2}{5}$

37. $\dfrac{19}{76} = \dfrac{1 \cdot 19}{4 \cdot 19} = \dfrac{1}{4} \cdot \dfrac{19}{19} = \dfrac{1}{4} \cdot 1 = \dfrac{1}{4}$

Multiplication and Division of Fractions

39. $\dfrac{1}{2} \cdot \dfrac{1}{3} = \dfrac{1 \cdot 1}{2 \cdot 3} = \dfrac{1}{6}$

41. $\dfrac{3}{4} \cdot \dfrac{1}{5} = \dfrac{3 \cdot 1}{4 \cdot 5} = \dfrac{3}{20}$

43. $\dfrac{5}{3} \cdot \dfrac{3}{5} = \dfrac{5 \cdot 3}{3 \cdot 5} = \dfrac{15}{15} = 1$

45. $\dfrac{5}{6} \cdot \dfrac{18}{25} = \dfrac{5 \cdot 18}{6 \cdot 25} = \dfrac{90}{150} = \dfrac{3 \cdot 30}{5 \cdot 30} = \dfrac{3}{5} \cdot \dfrac{30}{30} = \dfrac{3}{5} \cdot 1 = \dfrac{3}{5}$

47. $\dfrac{4}{1} \cdot \dfrac{3}{5} = \dfrac{4 \cdot 3}{1 \cdot 5} = \dfrac{12}{5}$

49. $\dfrac{2}{1} \cdot \dfrac{3}{8} = \dfrac{2 \cdot 3}{1 \cdot 8} = \dfrac{6}{8} = \dfrac{3 \cdot 2}{4 \cdot 2} = \dfrac{3}{4} \cdot \dfrac{2}{2} = \dfrac{3}{4} \cdot 1 = \dfrac{3}{4}$

51. $\dfrac{x}{y} \cdot \dfrac{y}{x} = \dfrac{xy}{yx} = \dfrac{xy}{xy} = \dfrac{x}{x} \cdot \dfrac{y}{y} = \dfrac{x}{x} \cdot 1 = \dfrac{x}{x} = 1$

53. $\dfrac{a}{b} \cdot \dfrac{3}{2} = \dfrac{a \cdot 3}{b \cdot 2} = \dfrac{3a}{2b}$

55. $\dfrac{1}{4} \cdot \dfrac{3}{4} = \dfrac{1 \cdot 3}{4 \cdot 4} = \dfrac{3}{16}$

57. $\dfrac{2}{3} \cdot \dfrac{6}{1} = \dfrac{2 \cdot 6}{3 \cdot 1} = \dfrac{12}{3} = \dfrac{4 \cdot 3}{1 \cdot 3} = \dfrac{4}{1} \cdot \dfrac{3}{3} = \dfrac{4}{1} \cdot 1 = 4$

59. $\dfrac{1}{2} \cdot \dfrac{2}{3} = \dfrac{1 \cdot 2}{2 \cdot 3} = \dfrac{2}{6} = \dfrac{1 \cdot 2}{3 \cdot 2} = \dfrac{1}{3} \cdot \dfrac{2}{2} = \dfrac{1}{3} \cdot 1 = \dfrac{1}{3}$

61. (a) $\dfrac{1}{5}$

   (b) $\dfrac{1}{7}$

   (c) $\dfrac{7}{4}$

   (d) $\dfrac{8}{9}$

63. (a) $\dfrac{2}{1}$

   (b) $\dfrac{9}{1}$

   (c) $\dfrac{101}{12}$

   (d) $\dfrac{17}{31}$

65. $\dfrac{1}{2} \div \dfrac{1}{3} = \dfrac{1}{2} \cdot \dfrac{3}{1} = \dfrac{1 \cdot 3}{2 \cdot 1} = \dfrac{3}{2}$

67. $\dfrac{3}{4} \div \dfrac{1}{2} = \dfrac{3}{4} \cdot \dfrac{2}{1} = \dfrac{3 \cdot 2}{4 \cdot 1} = \dfrac{6}{4} = \dfrac{3 \cdot 2}{2 \cdot 2} = \dfrac{3}{2} \cdot \dfrac{2}{2} = \dfrac{3}{2} \cdot 1 = \dfrac{3}{2}$

69. $\dfrac{4}{3} \div \dfrac{1}{6} = \dfrac{4}{3} \cdot \dfrac{6}{1} = \dfrac{4 \cdot 6}{3 \cdot 1} = \dfrac{24}{3} = \dfrac{8 \cdot 3}{1 \cdot 3} = \dfrac{8}{1} \cdot \dfrac{3}{3} = \dfrac{8}{1} \cdot 1 = 8$

71. $\dfrac{32}{27} \div \dfrac{8}{9} = \dfrac{32}{27} \cdot \dfrac{9}{8} = \dfrac{32 \cdot 9}{27 \cdot 8} = \dfrac{288}{216} = \dfrac{4 \cdot 72}{3 \cdot 72} = \dfrac{4}{3} \cdot \dfrac{72}{72} = \dfrac{4}{3} \cdot 1 = \dfrac{4}{3}$

73. $\dfrac{9}{1} \div \dfrac{8}{7} = \dfrac{9}{1} \cdot \dfrac{7}{8} = \dfrac{9 \cdot 7}{1 \cdot 8} = \dfrac{63}{8}$

75. $\dfrac{10}{1} \div \dfrac{5}{6} = \dfrac{10}{1} \cdot \dfrac{6}{5} = \dfrac{10 \cdot 6}{1 \cdot 5} = \dfrac{60}{5} = \dfrac{12 \cdot 5}{1 \cdot 5} = \dfrac{12}{1} \cdot \dfrac{5}{5} = \dfrac{12}{1} \cdot 1 = 12$

77. $\dfrac{9}{10} \div \dfrac{3}{1} = \dfrac{9}{10} \cdot \dfrac{1}{3} = \dfrac{9 \cdot 1}{10 \cdot 3} = \dfrac{9}{30} = \dfrac{3 \cdot 3}{10 \cdot 3} = \dfrac{3}{10} \cdot \dfrac{3}{3} = \dfrac{3}{10} \cdot 1 = \dfrac{3}{10}$

79. $\dfrac{a}{b} \div \dfrac{2}{b} = \dfrac{a}{b} \cdot \dfrac{b}{2} = \dfrac{ab}{2b} = \dfrac{a}{2} \cdot \dfrac{b}{b} = \dfrac{a}{2} \cdot 1 = \dfrac{a}{2}$

81. $\dfrac{x}{y} \div \dfrac{x}{y} = \dfrac{x}{y} \cdot \dfrac{y}{x} = \dfrac{xy}{xy} = 1$

Addition and Subtraction of Fractions

83. (a) $\dfrac{2}{3} + \dfrac{1}{3} = \dfrac{2 + 1}{3} = \dfrac{3}{3} = 1$

    (b) $\dfrac{2}{3} - \dfrac{1}{3} = \dfrac{2 - 1}{3} = \dfrac{1}{3}$

85. (a) $\dfrac{3}{2} + \dfrac{1}{2} = \dfrac{3 + 1}{2} = \dfrac{4}{2} = 2$

    (b) $\dfrac{3}{2} - \dfrac{1}{2} = \dfrac{3 - 1}{2} = \dfrac{2}{2} = 1$

87. (a) $\dfrac{5}{33} + \dfrac{2}{33} = \dfrac{5 + 2}{33} = \dfrac{7}{33}$

    (b) $\dfrac{5}{33} - \dfrac{2}{33} = \dfrac{5 - 2}{33} = \dfrac{3}{33} = \dfrac{1 \cdot 3}{11 \cdot 3} = \dfrac{1}{11} \cdot \dfrac{3}{3} = \dfrac{1}{11} \cdot 1 = \dfrac{1}{11}$

89. Prime factorizations are 5 and $10 = 5 \times 2$. The LCD is $5 \times 2 = 10$.

91. Prime factorizations are $9 = 3 \times 3$ and $15 = 3 \times 5$. The LCD is $3 \times 3 \times 5 = 45$.

93. Prime factorizations are 5 and $15 = 5 \times 3$. The LCD is $5 \times 3 = 15$.

95. Prime factorizations are $6 = 2 \times 3$ and $8 = 2 \times 2 \times 2$. The LCD is $2 \times 2 \times 2 \times 3 = 24$.

97. Prime factorizations are 2, 3 and $4 = 2 \times 2$. The LCD is $2 \times 2 \times 3 = 12$.

99. Prime factorizations are $4 = 2 \times 2$, $8 = 2 \times 2 \times 2$ and $12 = 2 \times 2 \times 3$. The LCD is $2 \times 2 \times 2 \times 3 = 24$.

101. $\dfrac{1}{2} + \dfrac{1}{3} = \dfrac{1}{2} \cdot \dfrac{3}{3} + \dfrac{1}{3} \cdot \dfrac{2}{2} = \dfrac{1 \cdot 3}{2 \cdot 3} + \dfrac{1 \cdot 2}{3 \cdot 2} = \dfrac{3}{6} + \dfrac{2}{6} = \dfrac{3 + 2}{6} = \dfrac{5}{6}$

103. $\dfrac{5}{8} + \dfrac{3}{16} = \dfrac{5}{8} \cdot \dfrac{2}{2} + \dfrac{3}{16} = \dfrac{5 \cdot 2}{8 \cdot 2} + \dfrac{3}{16} = \dfrac{10}{16} + \dfrac{3}{16} = \dfrac{10 + 3}{16} = \dfrac{13}{16}$

105. $\dfrac{1}{2} - \dfrac{1}{4} = \dfrac{1}{2} \cdot \dfrac{2}{2} - \dfrac{1}{4} = \dfrac{1 \cdot 2}{2 \cdot 2} - \dfrac{1}{4} = \dfrac{2}{4} - \dfrac{1}{4} = \dfrac{2 - 1}{4} = \dfrac{1}{4}$

107. $\dfrac{25}{24} - \dfrac{7}{8} = \dfrac{25}{24} - \dfrac{7}{8} \cdot \dfrac{3}{3} = \dfrac{25}{24} - \dfrac{7 \cdot 3}{8 \cdot 3} = \dfrac{25}{24} - \dfrac{21}{24} = \dfrac{4}{24} = \dfrac{1 \cdot 4}{6 \cdot 4} = \dfrac{1}{6} \cdot \dfrac{4}{4} = \dfrac{1}{6} \cdot 1 = \dfrac{1}{6}$

109. $\dfrac{11}{14} + \dfrac{2}{35} = \dfrac{11}{14} \cdot \dfrac{5}{5} + \dfrac{2}{35} \cdot \dfrac{2}{2} = \dfrac{11 \cdot 5}{14 \cdot 5} + \dfrac{2 \cdot 2}{35 \cdot 2} = \dfrac{55}{70} + \dfrac{4}{70} = \dfrac{55 + 4}{70} = \dfrac{59}{70}$

111. $\dfrac{5}{12} - \dfrac{1}{18} = \dfrac{5}{12} \cdot \dfrac{3}{3} - \dfrac{1}{18} \cdot \dfrac{2}{2} = \dfrac{5 \cdot 3}{12 \cdot 3} - \dfrac{1 \cdot 2}{18 \cdot 2} = \dfrac{15}{36} - \dfrac{2}{36} = \dfrac{15 - 2}{36} = \dfrac{13}{36}$

113. $\dfrac{3}{100} + \dfrac{1}{300} - \dfrac{1}{200} = \dfrac{3}{100} \cdot \dfrac{6}{6} + \dfrac{1}{300} \cdot \dfrac{2}{2} - \dfrac{1}{200} \cdot \dfrac{3}{3} = \dfrac{3 \cdot 6}{100 \cdot 6} + \dfrac{1 \cdot 2}{300 \cdot 2} - \dfrac{1 \cdot 3}{200 \cdot 3} =$

    $\dfrac{18}{600} + \dfrac{2}{600} - \dfrac{3}{600} = \dfrac{18 + 2 - 3}{600} = \dfrac{17}{600}$

115. $\dfrac{7}{8} - \dfrac{1}{6} + \dfrac{5}{12} = \dfrac{7}{8} \cdot \dfrac{3}{3} - \dfrac{1}{6} \cdot \dfrac{4}{4} + \dfrac{5}{12} \cdot \dfrac{2}{2} = \dfrac{7 \cdot 3}{8 \cdot 3} - \dfrac{1 \cdot 4}{6 \cdot 4} + \dfrac{5 \cdot 2}{12 \cdot 2} =$

$\dfrac{21}{24} - \dfrac{4}{24} + \dfrac{10}{24} = \dfrac{21 - 4 + 10}{24} = \dfrac{27}{24} = \dfrac{9 \cdot 3}{8 \cdot 3} = \dfrac{9}{8} \cdot \dfrac{3}{3} = \dfrac{9}{8} \cdot 1 = \dfrac{9}{8}$

Applications

117. Find the sum of the motor vehicle deaths and the firearms deaths as a fraction of all accidental deaths.

$\dfrac{31}{42} + \dfrac{31}{1260} = \dfrac{31}{42} \cdot \dfrac{30}{30} + \dfrac{31}{1260}$. It follows that $\dfrac{31 \cdot 30}{42 \cdot 30} + \dfrac{31}{1260} = \dfrac{930}{1260} + \dfrac{31}{1260} = \dfrac{930 + 31}{1260} = \dfrac{961}{1260}$.

119. Find the value of one-half of $64\dfrac{5}{8}$. First convert $64\dfrac{5}{8}$ to $\dfrac{517}{8}$. $\dfrac{517}{8} \div 2 = \dfrac{517}{8} \cdot \dfrac{1}{2} = \dfrac{517}{16} = 32\dfrac{5}{16}$ in.

121. Increase the amount of flour used because there are more people. The ratio of people is $\dfrac{12}{8}$.

Convert $3\dfrac{1}{2}$ to $\dfrac{7}{2}$ and multiply by $\dfrac{12}{8}$. $\dfrac{7}{2} \cdot \dfrac{12}{8} = \dfrac{7 \cdot 12}{2 \cdot 8} = \dfrac{84}{16} = \dfrac{21 \cdot 4}{4 \cdot 4} = \dfrac{21}{4} \cdot \dfrac{4}{4} = \dfrac{21}{4} \cdot 1 = \dfrac{21}{4} = 5\dfrac{1}{4}$ cups.

123. Convert the base of the triangle from $1\dfrac{2}{3}$ to $\dfrac{5}{3}$.

$\dfrac{1}{2} \cdot \dfrac{5}{3} \cdot \dfrac{3}{4} = \dfrac{1 \cdot 5 \cdot 3}{2 \cdot 3 \cdot 4} = \dfrac{15}{24} = \dfrac{5 \cdot 3}{8 \cdot 3} = \dfrac{5}{8} \cdot \dfrac{3}{3} = \dfrac{5}{8} \cdot 1 = \dfrac{5}{8}$ square yards.

125. Add the distance from Smalltown to Middletown and Middletown to Bigtown.

$3\dfrac{1}{2} + 4\dfrac{3}{4} = \dfrac{7}{2} + \dfrac{19}{4} = \dfrac{7}{2} \cdot \dfrac{2}{2} + \dfrac{19}{4} = \dfrac{7 \cdot 2}{2 \cdot 2} + \dfrac{19}{4} = \dfrac{14}{4} + \dfrac{19}{4} = \dfrac{14 + 19}{4} = \dfrac{33}{4} = 8\dfrac{1}{4}$ miles.

127. Multiply the fraction of the adult population by the fraction of the people aged 18 to 24 who smoked in 1995 to find the fraction of the entire adult population who were aged 18 to 24 and who smoked in 1995.

$\dfrac{1}{4} \cdot \dfrac{7}{25} = \dfrac{1 \cdot 7}{4 \cdot 25} = \dfrac{7}{100}$.

Checking Basic Concepts for Sections 1.1 & 1.2

1. (a) prime

   (b) composite; $28 = 2 \times 2 \times 7$

   (c) neither

   (d) composite; $180 = 2 \times 2 \times 3 \times 3 \times 5$

2. $\dfrac{10}{3 + 2} = \dfrac{10}{5} = 2$

3. $y = 6 \cdot 5 = 30$

4. $x + 5$

5. $\dfrac{17}{2} \cdot \dfrac{15}{1} = \dfrac{17 \cdot 15}{2 \cdot 1} = \dfrac{255}{2} = 127\dfrac{1}{2}$ square feet.

6. (a) $\dfrac{25}{35} = \dfrac{5 \cdot 5}{7 \cdot 5} = \dfrac{5}{7} \cdot \dfrac{5}{5} = \dfrac{5}{7} \cdot 1 = \dfrac{5}{7}$

   (b) $\dfrac{26}{39} = \dfrac{2 \cdot 13}{3 \cdot 13} = \dfrac{2}{3} \cdot \dfrac{13}{13} = \dfrac{2}{3} \cdot 1 = \dfrac{2}{3}$

7. $\dfrac{3}{4}$

8. (a) $\dfrac{2}{3} \cdot \dfrac{3}{4} = \dfrac{2 \cdot 3}{3 \cdot 4} = \dfrac{6}{12} = \dfrac{1 \cdot 6}{2 \cdot 6} = \dfrac{1}{2} \cdot \dfrac{6}{6} = \dfrac{1}{2} \cdot 1 = \dfrac{1}{2}$

   (b) $\dfrac{5}{6} \div \dfrac{10}{3} = \dfrac{5}{6} \cdot \dfrac{3}{10} = \dfrac{5 \cdot 3}{6 \cdot 10} = \dfrac{15}{60} = \dfrac{1 \cdot 15}{4 \cdot 15} = \dfrac{1}{4} \cdot \dfrac{15}{15} = \dfrac{1}{4} \cdot 1 = \dfrac{1}{4}$

   (c) $\dfrac{3}{10} + \dfrac{1}{10} = \dfrac{3 + 1}{10} = \dfrac{4}{10} = \dfrac{2 \cdot 2}{5 \cdot 2} = \dfrac{2}{5} \cdot \dfrac{2}{2} = \dfrac{2}{5} \cdot 1 = \dfrac{2}{5}$

   (d) $\dfrac{3}{4} - \dfrac{1}{6} = \dfrac{3}{4} \cdot \dfrac{3}{3} - \dfrac{1}{6} \cdot \dfrac{2}{2} = \dfrac{3 \cdot 3}{4 \cdot 3} - \dfrac{1 \cdot 2}{6 \cdot 2} = \dfrac{9}{12} - \dfrac{2}{12} = \dfrac{9 - 2}{12} = \dfrac{7}{12}$

9. Multiply $1\dfrac{2}{3}$ by 2. $\dfrac{5}{3} \cdot \dfrac{2}{1} = \dfrac{5 \cdot 2}{3 \cdot 1} = \dfrac{10}{3} = 3\dfrac{1}{3}$ cups.

1.3: Exponents and Order of Operations

Concepts

1. add

3. a^6

5. 6^2

7. 17, multiplication; addition

9. 4; left; right

11. No; $2^3 = 8$, but $3^2 = 9$

Natural Number Exponents

13. 2^5

15. 3^4

17. $\left(\dfrac{1}{2}\right)^4$

19. a^5

21. (a) $2^4 = 2 \cdot 2 \cdot 2 \cdot 2 = 16$

   (b) $4^2 = 4 \cdot 4 = 16$

23. (a) $6^1 = 6$

   (b) $1^6 = 1$

25. (a) $2^5 = 2 \cdot 2 \cdot 2 \cdot 2 \cdot 2 = 32$

   (b) $10^3 = 10 \cdot 10 \cdot 10 = 1000$

27. (a) $\left(\dfrac{2}{3}\right)^2 = \dfrac{2}{3} \cdot \dfrac{2}{3} = \dfrac{2 \cdot 2}{3 \cdot 3} = \dfrac{4}{9}$

   (b) $\left(\dfrac{1}{2}\right)^5 = \dfrac{1}{2} \cdot \dfrac{1}{2} \cdot \dfrac{1}{2} \cdot \dfrac{1}{2} \cdot \dfrac{1}{2} = \dfrac{1 \cdot 1 \cdot 1 \cdot 1 \cdot 1}{2 \cdot 2 \cdot 2 \cdot 2 \cdot 2} = \dfrac{1}{32}$

29. (a) $\left(\dfrac{2}{5}\right)^3 = \dfrac{2}{5} \cdot \dfrac{2}{5} \cdot \dfrac{2}{5} = \dfrac{2 \cdot 2 \cdot 2}{5 \cdot 5 \cdot 5} = \dfrac{8}{125}$

    (b) $\left(\dfrac{9}{7}\right)^2 = \dfrac{9}{7} \cdot \dfrac{9}{7} = \dfrac{9 \cdot 9}{7 \cdot 7} = \dfrac{81}{49}$

31. $8 = 2 \cdot 2 \cdot 2 = 2^3$

33. $25 = 5 \cdot 5 = 5^2$

35. $49 = 7 \cdot 7 = 7^2$

37. $1000 = 10 \cdot 10 \cdot 10 = 10^3$

39. $\dfrac{1}{16} = \dfrac{1}{2} \cdot \dfrac{1}{2} \cdot \dfrac{1}{2} \cdot \dfrac{1}{2} = \left(\dfrac{1}{2}\right)^4$

Order of Operations

41. Perform multiplication before addition: $5 + 4 \cdot 6 = 5 + 24 = 29$

43. Perform division before addition: $6 \div 3 + 2 = 2 + 2 = 4$

45. Perform division before subtraction: $100 - \dfrac{50}{5} = 100 - 10 = 90$

47. $10 - 6 - 1 = 3$

49. $20 \div 5 \div 2 = 4 \div 2 = 2$

51. $3 + 2^4 = 3 + 2 \cdot 2 \cdot 2 \cdot 2 = 3 + 16 = 19$

53. $4 \cdot 2^3 = 4 \cdot 2 \cdot 2 \cdot 2 = 4 \cdot 8 = 32$

55. $(3 + 2)^3 = 5^3 = 5 \cdot 5 \cdot 5 = 125$

57. $\dfrac{4 + 8}{1 + 3} = \dfrac{12}{4} = \dfrac{3 \cdot 4}{1 \cdot 4} = \dfrac{3}{1} \cdot \dfrac{4}{4} = \dfrac{3}{1} \cdot 1 = 3$

59. $\dfrac{2^3}{4 - 2} = \dfrac{2 \cdot 2 \cdot 2}{2} = \dfrac{8}{2} = 4$

61. $10^2 - (30 - 2 \cdot 5) = 10^2 - (30 - 10) = 10^2 - 20 = 10 \cdot 10 - 20 = 100 - 20 = 80$

63. $\left(\dfrac{1}{2}\right)^4 + \dfrac{5 + 4}{3} = \dfrac{1}{2} \cdot \dfrac{1}{2} \cdot \dfrac{1}{2} \cdot \dfrac{1}{2} + \dfrac{9}{3} = \dfrac{1}{16} + 3 = \dfrac{1}{16} + \dfrac{3}{1} \cdot \dfrac{16}{16} = \dfrac{1}{16} + \dfrac{48}{16} = \dfrac{1 + 48}{16} = \dfrac{49}{16}$

Translating Words to Symbols

65. $2^3 - 8 = 2 \cdot 2 \cdot 2 - 8 = 8 - 8 = 0$

67. $30 - 4 \cdot 3 = 30 - 12 = 18$

69. $\dfrac{4^2}{2^3} = \dfrac{4 \cdot 4}{2 \cdot 2 \cdot 2} = \dfrac{16}{8} = \dfrac{2 \cdot 8}{1 \cdot 8} = \dfrac{2}{1} \cdot \dfrac{8}{8} = \dfrac{2}{1} \cdot 1 = 2$

71. $\dfrac{40}{10} + 2 = \dfrac{4 \cdot 10}{1 \cdot 10} + 2 = \dfrac{4}{1} \cdot \dfrac{10}{10} + 2 = \dfrac{4}{1} \cdot 1 + 2 = 4 + 2 = 6$

73. $100(2 + 3) = 100 \cdot 5 = 500$

Applications

75. $1.44 \text{ MB} = 1.44 \cdot 2^{20} \text{ bytes} \approx 1{,}509{,}949 \text{ bytes}$

77. (a) Because $2^7 = 128$, $k = 7$.

(b) $\dfrac{128}{100} = \dfrac{32 \cdot 4}{25 \cdot 4} = \dfrac{32}{25}$. There were 32 males for every 25 females.

1.4: Real Numbers and the Number Line

Concepts

1. $-b$

3. b

5. rational

7. irrational

9. $\sqrt{2}$ is one example; *Answers may vary.*

11. approximately equal

13. 0

15. origin

17. $>$

19. $=$

Signed Numbers

21. (a) The opposite of 9 is -9.

(b) The opposite of -9 is $-(-9) = 9$.

23. (a) The opposite of $\dfrac{2}{3}$ is $-\dfrac{2}{3}$.

(b) The opposite of $-\dfrac{2}{3}$ is $-\left(-\dfrac{2}{3}\right) = \dfrac{2}{3}$.

25. (a) $-(-8) = 8$, so the opposite of 8 is -8.

(b) $-(-(-8)) = -8$, so the opposite of -8 is $-(-8) = 8$.

27. (a) The opposite of a is $-a$.

(b) The opposite of $-a$ is $-(-a) = a$.

29. The additive inverse of t is $-t$. $-t = 6$

31. The additive inverse of $-b$ is $-(-b) = b$. $b = \dfrac{1}{2}$

Numbers and the Number Line

33. $\dfrac{1}{4} = 0.25$

35. $\dfrac{7}{8} = 0.875$

37. $\dfrac{3}{2} = 1.5$

39. $\dfrac{1}{20} = 0.05$

41. $\dfrac{2}{3} = 0.\overline{6}$

43. $\dfrac{7}{9} = 0.\overline{7}$

45. 8 is a natural, whole and rational number, and is an integer.

47. $\dfrac{16}{4} = 4$ is a natural, whole and rational number, and is an integer.

49. 0 is a whole and rational number, and is an integer.

51. $-4.5 = -4\dfrac{1}{2} = -\dfrac{9}{2}$ is a rational number.

53. $\sqrt{11}$ is an irrational number.

55. $\dfrac{8}{4} = 4$ is a natural and rational number, and is an integer.

57. $-\sqrt{3}$ is an irrational number.

59. Number line from -5 to 5: (b) at -2, (a) at 0, (c) at 2.

61. Number line from -5 to 5: (b) at 0, (a) at 1, (c) at 2.

63. Number line from -5 to 5: (b) at -2, (c) at 1, (a) at $1\frac{1}{2}$.

65. Number line from -50 to 50: (b) at -20, (a) at -10, (c) at 30.

67. Number line from -5 to 5: (c) at -2, (b) at $1\frac{1}{2}$, (a) at $2\frac{1}{2}$.

Absolute Values

69. $|5.23| = 5.23$

71. $|-7| = 7$

73. $\left|-\dfrac{1}{2}\right| = \dfrac{1}{2}$

75. $|\pi - 3| = \pi - 3$

77. $|b|$, if b is negative, $= -b$

79. $5 < 7$

81. $-5 > -7$

83. $-\dfrac{1}{3} > -\dfrac{2}{3}$

85. $-1.9 < -1.3$

87. $-9, -2^3, -3, 0, 1$

89. $-2, -\dfrac{3}{2}, \dfrac{1}{3}, \sqrt{5}, \pi$

91. $-4^2, -\dfrac{17}{28}, -\dfrac{4}{7}, \sqrt{2}, \sqrt{7}$

Applications

93. (a) The percentage in 2000 was 16.5%.

   (b) *Answers may vary.*

   (c) The average percentage was $\dfrac{17.2 + 17.4 + 17.4 + 16.5}{4} = \dfrac{68.5}{4} = 17.125\%.$

Checking Basic Concepts for Sections 1.3 & 1.4

1. (a) $2^3 = 2 \cdot 2 \cdot 2 = 8$

   (b) $10^4 = 10 \cdot 10 \cdot 10 \cdot 10 = 10{,}000$

   (c) $\left(\dfrac{2}{3}\right)^3 = \dfrac{2}{3} \cdot \dfrac{2}{3} \cdot \dfrac{2}{3} = \dfrac{2 \cdot 2 \cdot 2}{3 \cdot 3 \cdot 3} = \dfrac{8}{27}$

   (d) $-3^4 = -(3 \cdot 3 \cdot 3 \cdot 3) = -81$

2. (a) $6 + 5 \cdot 4 = 6 + 20 = 26$

   (b) $6 + 6 \div 2 = 6 + 3 = 9$

   (c) $5 - 2 - 1 = 2$

   (d) $\dfrac{6 - 3}{2 + 4} = \dfrac{3}{6} = \dfrac{1 \cdot 3}{2 \cdot 3} = \dfrac{1}{2} \cdot \dfrac{3}{3} = \dfrac{1}{2} \cdot 1 = \dfrac{1}{2}$

   (e) $12 \div (6 \div 2) = 12 \div 3 = 4$

   (f) $2^3 - 2\left(2 + \dfrac{4}{2}\right) = 8 - 2(2 + 2) = 8 - 2(4) = 8 - 8 = 0$

3. $5^3 \div 3$, or $\dfrac{5^3}{3}$

4. (a) The opposite of -17 is $-(-17) = 17$.

   (b) The opposite of a is $-a$.

5. (a) $\dfrac{10}{2} = 5$ is a natural and rational number, and is an integer.

   (b) -5 is a rational number and is an integer.

   (c) $\sqrt{5}$ is an irrational number.

   (d) $-\dfrac{5}{6}$ is a rational number.

6.

7. (a) $|-12| = -(-12) = 12$

    (b) $|-a|$, if $a > 0$, $= -(-a) = a$

8. $-7, -1.6, 0, \dfrac{1}{3}, \sqrt{3}, 3^2$

1.5: Addition and Subtraction of Real Numbers

Concepts

1. 0

3. addends

5. difference

7. negative

9. addition

Addition and Subtraction of Real Numbers

11. The opposite of 25 is -25. $25 + (-25) = 0$

13. The opposite of $-\sqrt{21}$ is $\sqrt{21}$. $-\sqrt{21} + \sqrt{21} = 0$

15. The opposite of 5.63 is -5.63. $5.63 + (-5.63) = 0$

17. ; $1 + 3 = 4$

19. ; $4 + (-2) = 2$

21. ; $-1 + (-2) = -3$

23. ; $-1 + 3 = 2$

25. ; $-10 + 20 = 10$

27. ; $-50 + (-100) = -150$

29. $5 + (-4) = 5 - |-4| = 5 - 4 = 1$

31. $-1 + (-6) = -1 - |-6| = -1 - 6 = -7$

33. $\dfrac{3}{4} + \left(-\dfrac{1}{2}\right) = \dfrac{3}{4} - \left|-\dfrac{1}{2}\right| = \dfrac{3}{4} - \dfrac{1}{2} = \dfrac{3}{4} - \dfrac{1}{2} \cdot \dfrac{2}{2} = \dfrac{3}{4} - \dfrac{2}{4} = \dfrac{1}{4}$

35. $-\dfrac{6}{7} + \dfrac{3}{14} = \dfrac{3}{14} - \left|-\dfrac{6}{7}\right| = \dfrac{3}{14} - \dfrac{6}{7} = \dfrac{3}{14} - \dfrac{6}{7} \cdot \dfrac{2}{2} = \dfrac{3}{14} - \dfrac{12}{14} = -\dfrac{9}{14}$

37. $-\dfrac{1}{2} + \left(-\dfrac{3}{4}\right) = -\dfrac{1}{2} - \left|-\dfrac{3}{4}\right| = -\dfrac{1}{2} - \dfrac{3}{4} = -\dfrac{1}{2} \cdot \dfrac{2}{2} - \dfrac{3}{4} = -\dfrac{2}{4} - \dfrac{3}{4} = -\dfrac{5}{4}$

39. $0.6 + (-1.7) = 0.6 - |-1.7| = 0.6 - 1.7 = -1.1$

41. $-52 + 86 = 86 - |-52| = 86 - 52 = 34$

43. $8 + (-7) + (-2) = 8 - |-2| - |-7| = 8 - 2 - 7 = -1$

45. $\dfrac{1}{2} + \dfrac{3}{4} + \left(-\dfrac{1}{2}\right) + \left(-\dfrac{3}{4}\right) = \dfrac{1}{2} + \dfrac{3}{4} - \left|-\dfrac{1}{2}\right| - \left|-\dfrac{3}{4}\right| = \dfrac{1}{2} + \dfrac{3}{4} - \dfrac{1}{2} - \dfrac{3}{4} = \dfrac{1}{2} - \dfrac{1}{2} + \dfrac{3}{4} - \dfrac{3}{4} = 0 + 0 = 0$

47. $5 - 8 = 5 + (-8) = -3$

49. $-2 - (-9) = -2 + 9 = 7$

51. $\dfrac{1}{3} - \left(-\dfrac{2}{3}\right) = \dfrac{1}{3} + \dfrac{2}{3} = \dfrac{3}{3} = 1$

53. $\dfrac{6}{7} - \dfrac{13}{14} = \dfrac{12}{14} - \dfrac{13}{14} = \dfrac{12}{14} + \left(-\dfrac{13}{14}\right) = -\dfrac{1}{14}$

55. $-\dfrac{1}{10} - \left(-\dfrac{3}{5}\right) = -\dfrac{1}{10} + \left(-\dfrac{6}{10}\right) = -\dfrac{1}{10} + \dfrac{6}{10} = \dfrac{5}{10} = \dfrac{1}{2}$

57. $0.8 - (-2.1) = 0.8 + 2.1 = 2.9$

59. $-73 - 91 = -73 + (-91) = -164$

61. $-7 - (-6) - 10 = -7 + 6 - 10 = -11$

63. $10 - 19 = 10 + (-19) = -9$

65. $19 - (-22) + 1 = 19 + 22 + 1 = 42$

67. $-3 + 4 - 6 = -3 + 4 + (-6) = 4 - |-3| + (-6) = 4 - 3 + (-6) = -5$

69. $100 - 200 + 100 - (-50) = 100 + 100 - 200 + 50 = 200 - 200 + 50 = 50$

71. $1.5 - 2.3 + 9.6 = 1.5 + (-2.3) + 9.6 = 8.8$

73. $-\dfrac{1}{2} + \dfrac{1}{4} - \left(-\dfrac{3}{4}\right) = -\dfrac{2}{4} + \dfrac{1}{4} + \dfrac{3}{4} = \dfrac{2}{4} = \dfrac{1}{2}$

75. $|4 - 9| - |1 - 7| = |-5| - |-6| = 5 - 6 = -1$

77. $2 + (-5) = -3$

79. $-5 + 7 = 2$

81. $2^3 = 8$; the opposite of 8 is -8

83. $-6 - 7 = -6 + (-7) = -13$

85. $6 + (-10) - 5 = 6 + (-10) - 5 = 6 + (-10) + (-5) = -9$

Applications

87. Take the initial balance and then add to it the deposits and subtract from it the withdrawals.

    $358 - 45 + 37 + 120 - 240 = 358 + 37 + 120 + (-45) + (-240) = \$230$

89. The word height is in reference to sea level, the height of Mount Everest is 29,029 feet and the height of the

    Mariana Trench is $(-35,839)$.

    To find the difference take $29,029 - (-35,839) = 29,029 + 35,839 = 64,868$ feet.

1.6: Multiplication and Division of Real Numbers

Concepts

1. factors

3. negative

5. quotient

7. $\dfrac{1}{a}$

9. reciprocal or multiplicative inverse

11. positive

13. $\dfrac{-4}{-2} = 2$

Multiplication and Division of Real Numbers

15. $-3 \cdot 4 = -12$

17. $6 \cdot (-3) = -18$

19. $0 \cdot (-2.13) = 0$

21. $-6 \cdot (-10) = 60$

23. $-\dfrac{1}{2} \cdot \left(-\dfrac{2}{4}\right) = \dfrac{2}{8} = \dfrac{1}{4}$

25. $-\dfrac{3}{7} \cdot \dfrac{7}{3} = -\dfrac{21}{21} = -1$

27. $-10 \cdot (-20) = 200$

29. $-50 \cdot 100 = -5000$

31. $-2 \cdot 3 \cdot (-4) \cdot 5 = -6 \cdot (-20) = 120$

33. $-6 \cdot \dfrac{1}{6} \cdot \dfrac{7}{9} \cdot \left(-\dfrac{9}{7}\right) \cdot \left(-\dfrac{3}{2}\right) = -\dfrac{6}{6} \cdot \left(-\dfrac{63}{63}\right) \cdot \left(-\dfrac{3}{2}\right) = -1 \cdot (-1) \cdot \left(-\dfrac{3}{2}\right) = 1 \cdot \left(-\dfrac{3}{2}\right) = -\dfrac{3}{2}$

35. $(-1) \cdot (-1) \cdot (-1) \cdot (-1) = 1 \cdot 1 = 1$

37. $-10 \div 5 = -\dfrac{10}{1} \cdot \dfrac{1}{5} = -\dfrac{10}{5} = -2$

39. $-20 \div (-2) = -\dfrac{20}{1} \cdot \left(-\dfrac{1}{2}\right) = \dfrac{20}{2} = 10$

41. $-\dfrac{12}{3} = -4$

43. $\dfrac{39}{-13} = -3$

45. $-16 \div \dfrac{1}{2} = -\dfrac{16}{1} \cdot \dfrac{2}{1} = -\dfrac{32}{1} = -32$

47. $\dfrac{1}{2} \div (-11) = \dfrac{1}{2} \cdot -\dfrac{1}{11} = -\dfrac{1}{22}$

49. $-\dfrac{4}{5} \div (-3) = -\dfrac{4}{5} \cdot \left(-\dfrac{1}{3}\right) = \dfrac{4}{15}$

51. $\dfrac{5}{6} \div \left(-\dfrac{8}{9}\right) = \dfrac{5}{6} \cdot \left(-\dfrac{9}{8}\right) = -\dfrac{45}{48} = -\dfrac{15}{16}$

53. $-\dfrac{1}{2} \div 0 =$ undefined, because division by 0 is not allowed.

55. $-0.5 \div \dfrac{1}{2} = -\dfrac{5}{10} \div \dfrac{1}{2} = -\dfrac{5}{10} \cdot \dfrac{2}{1} = -\dfrac{10}{10} = -1$

57. $-\dfrac{2}{3} \div 0.5 = -\dfrac{2}{3} \div \dfrac{5}{10} = -\dfrac{2}{3} \cdot \dfrac{10}{5} = -\dfrac{20}{15} = -\dfrac{4}{3}$

Converting Between Fractions and Decimals

59. $\dfrac{1}{2} = 0.5$

61. $\dfrac{3}{16} = 0.1875$

63. Because $1 \div 2 = 0.5$, $3\dfrac{1}{2} = 3.5$

65. Because $2 \div 3 = 0.\overline{6}$, $5\dfrac{2}{3} = 5.\overline{6}$

67. Because $7 \div 16 = 0.4375$, $1\dfrac{1}{16} = 1.4375$

69. $\dfrac{7}{8} = 7 \div 8 = 0.875$

71. $0.25 = \dfrac{25}{100} = \dfrac{1 \cdot 25}{4 \cdot 25} = \dfrac{1}{4}$

73. $0.16 = \dfrac{16}{100} = \dfrac{4 \cdot 4}{25 \cdot 4} = \dfrac{4}{25}$

75. $0.625 = \dfrac{625}{1000} = \dfrac{5 \cdot 125}{8 \cdot 125} = \dfrac{5}{8}$

77. $0.6875 = \dfrac{6875}{10,000} = \dfrac{11 \cdot 625}{16 \cdot 625} = \dfrac{11}{16}$

Applications

79. $-220\left(\dfrac{3}{2}\right) = \dfrac{-220 \cdot 3}{2} = -330°\text{F}$

Checking Basic Concepts for Sections 1.5 & 1.6

1. (a) $-4 + 4 = 0$

    (b) $-10 + (-12) + 3 = -22 + 3 = -19$

2. (a) $\dfrac{2}{3} - \left(-\dfrac{2}{9}\right) = \dfrac{2}{3} + \dfrac{2}{9} = \dfrac{6}{9} + \dfrac{2}{9} = \dfrac{8}{9}$

    (b) $-1.2 - 5.1 + 3.1 = -1.2 + (-5.1) + 3.1 = -6.3 + 3.1 = -3.2$

3. $98 - (-46) = 98 + 46 = 144°F$ is the difference between these two temperatures.

4. (a) $-5 \cdot (-7) = 35$

    (b) $-\dfrac{1}{2} \cdot \dfrac{2}{3} \cdot \left(-\dfrac{4}{5}\right) = -\dfrac{2}{6} \cdot \left(-\dfrac{4}{5}\right) = \dfrac{8}{30} = \dfrac{4}{15}$

5. (a) $-5 \div \dfrac{2}{3} = -\dfrac{5}{1} \cdot \dfrac{3}{2} = -\dfrac{15}{2}$

    (b) $-\dfrac{5}{8} \div \left(-\dfrac{4}{3}\right) = -\dfrac{5}{8} \cdot \left(-\dfrac{3}{4}\right) = \dfrac{15}{32}$

6. The reciprocal of $-\dfrac{7}{6}$ is $-\dfrac{6}{7}$.

7. (a) $\dfrac{-10}{2} = \dfrac{-5 \cdot 2}{1 \cdot 2} = \dfrac{-5}{1} = -5$

    (b) $\dfrac{10}{-2} = \dfrac{5 \cdot 2}{-1 \cdot (2)} = \dfrac{5}{-1} = -5$

    (c) $-\dfrac{10}{2} = -\dfrac{5 \cdot 2}{1 \cdot 2} = -\dfrac{5}{1} = -5$

    (d) $\dfrac{-10}{-2} = \dfrac{-5 \cdot 2}{-1 \cdot 2} = \dfrac{-5}{-1} = 5$

8. (a) $\dfrac{3}{5} = 0.6$

    (b) Because $\dfrac{7}{8} = 0.875$, $3\dfrac{7}{8} = 3.875$

1.7: Properties of Real Numbers

Concepts

1. commutative; addition

3. associative; addition

5. distributive

7. identity; addition

9. $-a$

Properties of Real Numbers

11. $-6 + 10 = 10 + (-6)$

13. $-5 \cdot 6 = 6 \cdot (-5)$

15. $a + 10 = 10 + a$

17. $b \cdot 7 = 7 \cdot b$

19. $(1 + 2) + 3 = 1 + (2 + 3)$

21. $2 \cdot (3 \cdot 4) = (2 \cdot 3) \cdot 4$

23. $(a + 5) + c = a + (5 + c)$

25. $(x \cdot 3) \cdot 4 = x \cdot (3 \cdot 4)$

27. $4(3 + 2) = (4 \cdot 3) + (4 \cdot 2) = 12 + 8 = 20$

29. $a(b - 8) = ab - 8a$

31. $-1(t + z) = -1t - 1z = -t - z$

33. $-(5 - a) = -(1)(5) - 1(-a) = -5 + a$

35. $(a + 5)3 = 3a + (3)(5) = 3a + 15$

37. $(6 - z)(-3) = -18 + 3z = 3z - 18$

39. Commutative (multiplication)

41. Associative (addition)

43. Distributive

45. Distributive, Commutative (multiplication)

47. Distributive

49. Associative (multiplication)

51. Distributive

Identity and Inverse Properties

53. Identity (addition)

55. Identity (multiplication)

57. Identity (multiplication)

59. Inverse (multiplication)

61. Inverse (addition)

Mental Calculations

63. $(4 + 2) + (9 + 8) + (1 + 6) = 30$

65. $(45 + 43) + (5 + 7) = 100$

67. $129 + 49 = 178$

69. $379 + 98 = 477$

71. $178 - 99 = 79$

73. $6 \cdot 15 = 90$

75. $8 \cdot 102 = 816$

77. $\left(\frac{1}{2} \cdot \frac{1}{2} \cdot \frac{1}{2}\right) \cdot 2 \cdot 2 \cdot 2 = \left(\frac{1}{8}\right) \cdot 8 = 1$

79. $\left(\dfrac{7}{6} \cdot \dfrac{1}{2}\right) \cdot \left(\dfrac{1}{2} \cdot \dfrac{1}{2}\right) \cdot \dfrac{8}{7} = \left(\dfrac{7}{12} \cdot \dfrac{1}{4}\right) \cdot \dfrac{8}{7} = \dfrac{7}{48} \cdot \dfrac{8}{7} = \dfrac{56}{336} = \dfrac{1}{6}$

Multiplying and Dividing by Powers of 10 Mentally

81. (a) $10 \times 41 = 410$

    (b) $10 \times 997 = 9970$

    (c) $-630 \times 10 = -6300$

    (d) $-14{,}000 \times 10 = -140{,}000$

83. (a) $1000 \times 19 = 19{,}000$

    (b) $100 \times (-451) = -45{,}100$

    (c) $10{,}000 \times 6 = 60{,}000$

    (d) $-79 \times 100{,}000 = -7{,}900{,}000$

85. (a) $12.56 \div 10 = 1.256$

    (b) $9.6 \div 10 = .96$

    (c) $0.987 \div 10 = 0.0987$

    (d) $-0.056 \div 10 = -0.0056$

    (e) $1200 \div 10 = 120$

    (f) $4578 \div 10 = 457.8$

Applications

87. Because $100 + 75 = 75 + 100$, this shows the commutative property of addition.

89. Because 1 gallon is $10 \div 10$ gallons, divide 198 by 10 to get 19.8 miles.

91. (a) Because of the commutative property of multiplication, $500 \cdot 400 = 400 \cdot 500$. Thus, the number of pixels in an image 400 pixels wide and 500 pixels high is $400 \cdot 500 = 200{,}000$ pixels.

    (b) The commutative property of multiplication.

1.8: Simplifying and Writing Algebraic Expressions

Concepts

1. term

3. coefficient

5. like, unlike

Like Terms

7. The expression 91 is a term; it's coefficient is 91.

9. The expression $-6b$ is a term; it's coefficient is -6.

11. The expression $x + 10$ is not a term because it is the sum of two terms.

13. The expression x^2 is a term; it's coefficient is 1.

15. The expression $4x - 5$ is not a term because it is the difference of two terms.

17. The expression $-9xyz$ is a term; it's coefficient is -9.

19. The terms 6 and -8 are like because neither term contains a variable.

21. The terms $5x$ and $-22x$ are like because each term contains the same variable raised to the same power.

23. The terms $18x$ and $18y$ are unlike because the first term contains a different variable than the second term.

25. The terms x^2, $-15x^2$ and $6x^2$ are like because each term contains the same variable raised to the same power.

27. The terms xy, xz and $2xy$ are unlike because each term does not contain the same variables.

29. $3x + 5x = (3 + 5)x = 8x$

31. $19y - 5y = (19 - 5)y = 14y$

33. It is not possible to combine terms because the first term contains a different variable than the first term.

35. It is not possible to combine terms because the first term does not contain a variable and the second term does.

37. $5x^2 - 2x^2 = (5 - 2)x^2 = 3x^2$

39. $8xy - 10xy + xy = (8 - 10 + 1)xy = -1xy = -xy$

Simplifying and Writing Expressions

41. $5 + x - 3 + 2x = 5 - 3 + x + 2x = 5 - 3 + (1 + 2)x = 2 + 3x = 3x + 2$

43. $-\dfrac{3}{4} + z - 3z + \dfrac{5}{4} = z - 3z + \dfrac{5}{4} - \dfrac{3}{4} = (1 - 3)z + \dfrac{5}{4} - \dfrac{3}{4} = -2z + \dfrac{5}{4} - \dfrac{3}{4} = -2z + \dfrac{1}{2}$

45. $4y - y + 8y = (4 - 1 + 8)y = 11y$

47. $-3 + 6z + 2 - 2z = 6z - 2z - 3 + 2 = (6 - 2)z - 3 + 2 = 4z - 1$

49. $-2(3z - 6y) - z = -6z + 12y - z = -6z - z + 12y = (-6 - 1)z - 12y = -7z + 12y = 12y - 7z$

51. $2 - \dfrac{3}{4}(4x + 8) = 2 - \dfrac{3 \cdot 4}{4}x - \dfrac{3 \cdot 8}{4} = 2 - \dfrac{12}{4}x - \dfrac{24}{4} = 2 - 3x - 6 = 2 - 6 - 3x =$

$-4 - 3x = -3x - 4$

53. $-x - (5x + 1) = -x - 5x - 1 = (-1 - 5)x - 1 = -6x - 1$

55. $1 - \dfrac{1}{3}(x + 1) = 1 - \dfrac{1}{3}x - \dfrac{1}{3} = -\dfrac{1}{3}x + 1 - \dfrac{1}{3} = -\dfrac{1}{3}x + \dfrac{3}{3} - \dfrac{1}{3} = -\dfrac{1}{3}x + \dfrac{2}{3}$

57. $\dfrac{3}{5}(x + y) - \dfrac{1}{5}(x - 1) = \dfrac{3}{5}x + \dfrac{3}{5}y - \dfrac{1}{5}x + \dfrac{1}{5} = \dfrac{3}{5}x - \dfrac{1}{5}x + \dfrac{3}{5}y + \dfrac{1}{5} = \left(\dfrac{3}{5} - \dfrac{1}{5}\right)x + \dfrac{3}{5}y + \dfrac{1}{5} =$

$\dfrac{2}{5}x + \dfrac{3}{5}y + \dfrac{1}{5}$

59. $0.2x^2 + 0.3x^2 - 0.1x^2 = (0.2 + 0.3 - 0.1)x^2 = 0.4x^2$

61. $2x^2 - 3x + 5x^2 - 4x = 2x^2 + 5x^2 - 3x - 4x = (2 + 5)x^2 - (3 + 4)x = 7x^2 - 7x$

63. $\dfrac{8x}{8} = \dfrac{8}{8} \cdot \dfrac{x}{1} = 1 \cdot \dfrac{x}{1} = 1 \cdot x = x$

65. $\dfrac{-3y}{-y} = \dfrac{-3}{1} \cdot \dfrac{y}{-y} = -3 \cdot (-1) = 3$

67. $\dfrac{-108z}{-108} = \dfrac{-108}{-108} \cdot \dfrac{z}{1} = 1 \cdot \dfrac{z}{1} = 1 \cdot z = z$

69. $5x + 6x = (5 + 6)x = 11x$

71. $x^2 + 2x^2 = (1 + 2)x^2 = 3x^2$

73. $6x - 4x = (6 - 4)x = 2x$

Applications

75. (a) Let w be the constant width of the street in feet. The area of each street section equals it's length times it's width.

    The total area of the street is $400w + 350w + 220w + 600w = (400 + 350 + 220 + 600)w = 1570w$.

    (b) If the width $= 42$ feet, $w = 42$. Then, $1570w = 1570 \cdot 42 = 65{,}940 \text{ ft}^2$.

77. (a) Let x be the number of minutes. Then, $20x + 30x = 50x =$ the number of cubic feet of snow removed in

    x minutes.

    (b) Let $x = 48$. Then, the total number of cubic feet of snow removed in 48 minutes is $50x = 50 \cdot 48 = 2400 \text{ ft}^3$.

    (c) First, calculate how many cubic feet of snow the driveway contains. Volume equals length times width

    times height; thus, the driveway contains $30 \cdot 20 \cdot 2 = 1200 \text{ ft}^3$ of snow. If 50 cubic feet of snow is

    removed in 1 minute, then $\dfrac{1200}{50}$ cubic feet of snow is removed in 24 minutes.

Checking Basic Concepts for Sections 1.7 & 1.8

1. (a) $y \cdot 18 = 18y$

   (b) $10 + x = x + 10$

2. $5 \cdot (y \cdot 4) = 5 \cdot (4y) = 20y$

3. (a) $10 - (5 + x) = 10 - 5 - x = 5 - x$

   (b) $5(x - 7) = 5x - 35$

4. Because $5x + 3x = (5 + 3)x = 8x$, this equation illustrates the distributive property.

5. $-4xy + 4xy = (-4 + 4)xy = 0xy = 0$

6. (a) $32 + 17 + 8 + 3 = 60$

   (b) $\dfrac{5}{6} \cdot \dfrac{7}{8} \cdot \dfrac{6}{5} \cdot 8 = \dfrac{5 \cdot 7}{6 \cdot 8} \cdot \dfrac{6 \cdot 8}{5 \cdot 1} = \dfrac{35}{48} \cdot \dfrac{48}{5} = \dfrac{35}{5} \cdot \dfrac{48}{48} = 7 \cdot 1 = 7$

   (c) $567 - 199 = 368$

7. (a) $5z + 9z = (5 + 9)z = 14z$

   (b) $5y - 4 - 8y + 7 = 5y - 8y - 4 + 7 = (5 - 8)y - 4 + 7 = -3y + 3$

8. (a) $2y - (5y + 3) = 2y - 5y - 3 - (2 - 5)y - 3 = -3y - 3$

    (b) $-4(x + 3y) + 2(2x - y) = -4x - 12y + 4x - 2y = -4x + 4x - 12y - 2y =$

    $(-4 + 4)x - (12 + 2)y = 0x - 14y = -14y$

    (c) $\dfrac{20x}{20} = \dfrac{20}{20} \cdot x = 1 \cdot x = x$

    (d) $\dfrac{35x^2}{x^2} = 35 \cdot \dfrac{x^2}{x^2} = 35 \cdot 1 = 35$

Chapter 1 Review Exercises

Section 1.1

1. The number 29 is prime it's only factors are itself and 1.

2. The number 27 is a composite number because it has factors other than itself; $27 = 3 \times 3 \times 3$.

3. The number 108 is a composite number because it has factors other than itself; $108 = 2 \times 2 \times 3 \times 3 \times 3$.

4. The number 91 is a composite number because it has factors other than itself; $91 = 7 \times 13$.

5. $2x - 5$, when $x = 4$, is $2 \cdot 4 - 5 = 8 - 5 = 3$

6. $7 - \dfrac{10}{x}$, when $x = 5$, is $7 - \dfrac{10}{5} = 7 - \dfrac{2 \cdot 5}{1 \cdot 5} = 7 - \dfrac{2}{1} \cdot \dfrac{5}{5} = 7 - 2 \cdot 1 = 7 - 2 = 5$

7. $9x - 2y$, when $x = 2$ and $y = 3$, is $9 \cdot 2 - 2 \cdot 3 = 18 - 6 = 12$

8. $\dfrac{2x}{x - y}$, when $x = 6$ and $y = 4$, is $\dfrac{2 \cdot 6}{6 - 4} = \dfrac{12}{2} = \dfrac{6 \cdot 2}{1 \cdot 2} = \dfrac{6}{1} \cdot \dfrac{2}{2} = 6 \cdot 1 = 6$

9. $y = x - 5$, when $x = 12$, is $y = 12 - 5 \Rightarrow y = 7$

10. $y = xz + 1$, when $x = 2$ and $z = 3$, is $y = 2 \cdot 3 + 1 \Rightarrow y = 6 + 1 \Rightarrow y = 7$

11. Let c be the cost of the CD. Then, five times the cost of the CD is $5 \cdot c = 5c$.

12. Let x be the number. Then, five less than the number is $x - 5$.

13. Three squared increased by five is $3^2 + 5$.

14. Two cubed divided by the quantity three plus one is $2^3 \div (3 + 1)$.

Section 1.2

15. (a) $\dfrac{5 \cdot 7}{8 \cdot 7} = \dfrac{5}{8} \cdot \dfrac{7}{7} = \dfrac{5}{8} \cdot 1 = \dfrac{5}{8}$

    (b) $\dfrac{3a}{4a} = \dfrac{3}{4} \cdot \dfrac{a}{a} = \dfrac{3}{4} \cdot 1 = \dfrac{3}{4}$

16. (a) $\dfrac{9}{12} = \dfrac{3 \cdot 3}{4 \cdot 3} = \dfrac{3}{4} \cdot \dfrac{3}{3} = \dfrac{3}{4} \cdot 1 = \dfrac{3}{4}$

    (b) $\dfrac{36}{60} = \dfrac{3 \cdot 12}{5 \cdot 12} = \dfrac{3}{5} \cdot \dfrac{12}{12} = \dfrac{3}{5} \cdot 1 = \dfrac{3}{5}$

17 $\dfrac{3}{4} \cdot \dfrac{5}{6} = \dfrac{3 \cdot 5}{4 \cdot 6} = \dfrac{15}{24} = \dfrac{5 \cdot 3}{8 \cdot 3} = \dfrac{5}{8} \cdot \dfrac{3}{3} = \dfrac{5}{8} \cdot 1 = \dfrac{5}{8}$

18. $\dfrac{1}{2} \cdot \dfrac{4}{9} = \dfrac{1 \cdot 4}{2 \cdot 9} = \dfrac{4}{18} = \dfrac{2 \cdot 2}{9 \cdot 2} = \dfrac{2}{9} \cdot \dfrac{2}{2} = \dfrac{2}{9} \cdot 1 = \dfrac{2}{9}$

19. $\dfrac{2}{3} \cdot \dfrac{5}{11} \cdot \dfrac{9}{10} = \dfrac{2 \cdot 5 \cdot 9}{3 \cdot 11 \cdot 10} = \dfrac{90}{330} = \dfrac{3 \cdot 30}{11 \cdot 30} = \dfrac{3}{11} \cdot \dfrac{30}{30} = \dfrac{3}{11} \cdot 1 = \dfrac{3}{11}$

20. $\dfrac{12}{11} \cdot \dfrac{22}{23} \cdot \dfrac{1}{2} = \dfrac{12 \cdot 22 \cdot 1}{11 \cdot 23 \cdot 2} = \dfrac{264}{506} = \dfrac{12 \cdot 22}{23 \cdot 22} = \dfrac{12}{23} \cdot \dfrac{22}{22} = \dfrac{12}{23} \cdot 1 = \dfrac{12}{23}$

21. One-fifth of three-sevenths equals $\dfrac{1}{5} \cdot \dfrac{3}{7} = \dfrac{1 \cdot 3}{5 \cdot 7} = \dfrac{3}{35}$.

22. (a) The reciprocal of 8 equals the reciprocal of $\dfrac{8}{1} = \dfrac{1}{8}$.

    (b) The reciprocal of 1 equals the reciprocal of $\dfrac{1}{1} = \dfrac{1}{1}$.

    (c) The reciprocal of $\dfrac{5}{19} = \dfrac{19}{5}$.

    (d) The reciprocal of $\dfrac{3}{2} = \dfrac{2}{3}$.

23. $\dfrac{3}{2} \div \dfrac{1}{6} = \dfrac{3}{2} \cdot \dfrac{6}{1} = \dfrac{3 \cdot 6}{2 \cdot 1} = \dfrac{18}{2} = \dfrac{9 \cdot 2}{1 \cdot 2} = \dfrac{9}{1} \cdot \dfrac{2}{2} = 9 \cdot 1 = 9$

24. $\dfrac{9}{10} \div \dfrac{7}{5} = \dfrac{9}{10} \cdot \dfrac{5}{7} = \dfrac{9 \cdot 5}{10 \cdot 7} = \dfrac{45}{70} = \dfrac{9 \cdot 5}{14 \cdot 5} = \dfrac{9}{14} \cdot \dfrac{5}{5} = \dfrac{9}{14} \cdot 1 = \dfrac{9}{14}$

25. $8 \div \dfrac{2}{3} = \dfrac{8}{1} \cdot \dfrac{3}{2} = \dfrac{8 \cdot 3}{1 \cdot 2} = \dfrac{24}{2} = \dfrac{12 \cdot 2}{1 \cdot 2} = \dfrac{12}{1} \cdot \dfrac{2}{2} = 12 \cdot 1 = 12$

26. $\dfrac{3}{4} \div 6 = \dfrac{3}{4} \cdot \dfrac{1}{6} = \dfrac{3 \cdot 1}{4 \cdot 6} = \dfrac{3}{24} = \dfrac{1 \cdot 3}{8 \cdot 3} = \dfrac{1}{8} \cdot \dfrac{3}{3} = \dfrac{1}{8} \cdot 1 = \dfrac{1}{8}$

27. The least common denominator for the fractions $\dfrac{1}{8}$ and $\dfrac{5}{12}$ is 24, because 24 is the smallest number that both 8 and 12 divide into evenly.

28. The least common denominator for the fractions $\dfrac{2}{14}$ and $\dfrac{1}{21}$ is 42, because 42 is the smallest number that both 14 and 21 divide into evenly.

29. $\dfrac{2}{15} + \dfrac{3}{15} = \dfrac{2 + 3}{15} = \dfrac{5}{15} = \dfrac{1 \cdot 5}{3 \cdot 5} = \dfrac{1}{3}$

30. $\dfrac{5}{4} - \dfrac{3}{4} = \dfrac{5 - 3}{4} = \dfrac{2}{4} = \dfrac{1 \cdot 2}{2 \cdot 2} = \dfrac{1}{2}$

31. $\dfrac{11}{12} - \dfrac{1}{8} = \dfrac{11 \cdot 2}{12 \cdot 2} - \dfrac{1 \cdot 3}{8 \cdot 3} = \dfrac{22}{24} - \dfrac{3}{24} = \dfrac{22 - 3}{24} = \dfrac{19}{24}$

32. $\dfrac{6}{11} - \dfrac{3}{22} = \dfrac{6 \cdot 2}{11 \cdot 2} - \dfrac{3}{22} = \dfrac{12}{22} - \dfrac{3}{22} = \dfrac{12 - 3}{22} = \dfrac{9}{22}$

33. $\dfrac{2}{3} - \dfrac{1}{2} + \dfrac{1}{4} = \dfrac{2 \cdot 4}{3 \cdot 4} - \dfrac{1 \cdot 6}{2 \cdot 6} + \dfrac{1 \cdot 3}{4 \cdot 3} = \dfrac{8}{12} - \dfrac{6}{12} + \dfrac{3}{12} = \dfrac{8 - 6 + 3}{12} = \dfrac{5}{12}$

34. $\dfrac{1}{6} + \dfrac{2}{3} - \dfrac{1}{9} = \dfrac{1 \cdot 3}{6 \cdot 3} + \dfrac{2 \cdot 6}{3 \cdot 6} - \dfrac{1 \cdot 2}{9 \cdot 2} = \dfrac{3}{18} + \dfrac{12}{18} - \dfrac{2}{18} = \dfrac{3 + 12 - 2}{18} = \dfrac{13}{18}$

Section 1.3

35. $5 \cdot 5 \cdot 5 \cdot 5 \cdot 5 \cdot 5 = 5^6$

36. $\dfrac{7}{6} \cdot \dfrac{7}{6} \cdot \dfrac{7}{6} = \left(\dfrac{7}{6}\right)^3$

37. $3 \cdot 3 \cdot 3 \cdot 3 = 3^4$

38. $x \cdot x \cdot x \cdot x \cdot x = x^5$

39. (a) $4^3 = 4 \cdot 4 \cdot 4 = 64$

    (b) $7^2 = 7 \cdot 7 = 49$

    (c) $8^1 = 8$

40. $2^n = 32$; $2 \cdot 2 \cdot 2 \cdot 2 \cdot 2 = 32$, thus $2^5 = 32$ and $n = 5$

41. $7 + 3 \cdot 6 = 7 + 18 = 25$

42. $15 - 5 - 3 = (15 - 5) - 3 = 10 - 3 = 7$

43. $24 \div 4 \div 2 = (24 \div 4) \div 2 = 6 \div 2 = 3$

44. $30 - 15 \div 3 = 30 - (15 \div 3) = 30 - 5 = 25$

45. $18 \div 6 - 2 = (18 \div 6) - 2 = 3 - 2 = 1$

46. $\dfrac{18}{4 + 5} = \dfrac{18}{9} = \dfrac{2 \cdot 9}{1 \cdot 9} = \dfrac{2}{1} \cdot \dfrac{9}{9} = 2 \cdot 1 = 2$

47. $9 - 3^2 = 9 - 9 = 0$

48. $2^3 - 8 = 8 - 8 = 0$

49. $2^4 - 8 + \dfrac{4}{2} = (2 \cdot 2 \cdot 2 \cdot 2) - 8 + 2 = 16 - 8 + 2 = (16 - 8) + 2 = 8 + 2 = 10$

50. $3^2 - 4(5 - 3) = 3^2 - 4(2) = 9 - 8 = 1$

51. $7 - \dfrac{4 + 6}{2 + 3} = 7 - \dfrac{10}{5} = 7 - 2 = 5$

52. $3^3 - 2^3 = (3 \cdot 3 \cdot 3) - (2 \cdot 2 \cdot 2) = 27 - 8 = 19$

Section 1.4

53. The number 0 is a whole number and a rational number, and is an integer.

54. The number $-\dfrac{5}{6}$ is a rational number.

55. The number -7 is a rational number and is an integer.

56. The number $\sqrt{17}$ is an irrational number.

57. The number π is an irrational number.

58. The number 3.4 is a rational number.

59.

60. (a) $|-5| = 5$

    (b) $|-\pi| = \pi$

    (c) $|\sqrt{2} - 1| = \sqrt{2} - 1$

61. (a) $-5 < 4$

    (b) $-\dfrac{1}{2} > -\dfrac{5}{2}$

62. $-3, -\dfrac{2}{3}, \sqrt{3}, \pi - 1, 3$

Sections 1.5 and 1.6

63. $-1 + 2 = 1$

64. $-2 + (-3) = -5$

65. $5 + (-4) = 1$

66. $-9 - (-7) = -9 + 7 = -2$

67. $11 \cdot (-4) = -44$

68. $-8 \cdot (-5) = 40$

69. $11 \div (-4) = -\dfrac{11}{4}$

70. $-4 \div \dfrac{4}{7} = -\dfrac{4}{1} \cdot \dfrac{7}{4} = -\dfrac{4 \cdot 7}{4} = -\dfrac{28}{4} = -\dfrac{7 \cdot 4}{1 \cdot 4} = -\dfrac{7}{1} \cdot \dfrac{4}{4} = -7 \cdot 1 = -7$

71. $-\dfrac{1}{2} + \left(-\dfrac{3}{4}\right) = -\dfrac{1 \cdot 2}{2 \cdot 2} + \left(-\dfrac{3}{4}\right) = -\dfrac{2}{4} + \left(-\dfrac{3}{4}\right) = -\dfrac{5}{4}$

72. $-\dfrac{5}{9} - \left(-\dfrac{1}{3}\right) = -\dfrac{5}{9} + \dfrac{1}{3} = -\dfrac{5}{9} + \dfrac{1 \cdot 3}{3 \cdot 3} = -\dfrac{5}{9} + \dfrac{3}{9} = -\dfrac{2}{9}$

73. $-\dfrac{1}{3} \cdot \left(-\dfrac{6}{7}\right) = \dfrac{1 \cdot 6}{3 \cdot 7} = \dfrac{6}{21} = \dfrac{2 \cdot 3}{7 \cdot 3} = \dfrac{2}{7} \cdot \dfrac{3}{3} = \dfrac{2}{7} \cdot 1 = \dfrac{2}{7}$

74. $\dfrac{\frac{4}{5}}{-7} = \dfrac{4}{5} \div (-7) = \dfrac{4}{5} \cdot \left(-\dfrac{1}{7}\right) = -\dfrac{4}{35}$

75. $-\dfrac{3}{2} \div \left(-\dfrac{3}{8}\right) = -\dfrac{3}{2} \cdot \left(-\dfrac{8}{3}\right) = \dfrac{24}{6} = 4$

76. $\dfrac{3}{8} \div (-0.5) = \dfrac{3}{8} \div \left(-\dfrac{1}{2}\right) = \dfrac{3}{8} \cdot \left(-\dfrac{2}{1}\right) = -\dfrac{6}{8} = -\dfrac{3 \cdot 2}{4 \cdot 2} = -\dfrac{3}{4} \cdot \dfrac{2}{2} = -\dfrac{3}{4} \cdot 1 = -\dfrac{3}{4}$

77. $3 + (-5) = -2$

78. $2 - (-4) = 2 + 4 = 6$

79. $\dfrac{7}{9} = 0.\overline{7}$

80. $2\dfrac{1}{5} = 2.2$

81. $0.6 = \dfrac{6}{10} = \dfrac{3 \cdot 2}{5 \cdot 2} = \dfrac{3}{5} \cdot \dfrac{2}{2} = \dfrac{3}{5} \cdot 1 = \dfrac{3}{5}$

82. $0.375 = \dfrac{375}{1000} = \dfrac{3 \cdot 125}{8 \cdot 125} = \dfrac{3}{8} \cdot \dfrac{125}{125} = \dfrac{3}{8} \cdot 1 = \dfrac{3}{8}$

Section 1.7

83. Commutative (multiplication)

84. Associative (addition)

85. Distributive

86. Commutative (addition)

87. Identity (multiplication)

88. Associative (multiplication)

89. Distributive

90. Identity (addition)

91. Inverse (addition)

92. Inverse (multiplication)

93. $7 + 9 + 12 + 8 + 1 + 3 = (7 + 9) + (12 + 8) + (1 + 3) = 16 + 20 + 4 = (16 + 20) + 4 = 36 + 4 = 40$

94. $500 - 199 = 500 + (-199) = 301$

95. $25 \cdot 99 = (5 \cdot 5) \cdot (33 \cdot 3) = (5 \cdot 5) \cdot (11 \cdot 3) \cdot 3 = 5 \cdot 5 \cdot 3 \cdot 3 \cdot 11 = 2475$

96. $4581 + 1999 = 6580$

97. $54.98 \times 10 = 549.8$ because we move the decimal point to the right one place.

98. $4356 \div 100 = 43.56$ because we move the decimal point to the left two places.

Section 1.8

99. $55x$ is a term; it's coefficient is 55.

100. $-xy$ is a term; it's coefficient is -1.

101. $9xy + 2z$ is not a term because it is the sum of two terms.

102. $x - 7$ is not a term because it is the difference of two terms.

103. $-10x + 4x = (-10 + 4)x = -6x$

104. $19z - 4z = (19 - 4)z = 15z$

105. $3x^2 + x^2 = (3 + 1)x^2 = 4x^2$

106. $7 + 2x - 6 + x = 7 - 6 + 2x + x = 7 - 6 + (2 + 1)x = 1 + 3x = 3x + 1$

107. $-\dfrac{1}{2} + \dfrac{3}{2}z - z + \dfrac{5}{2} = -\dfrac{1}{2} + \dfrac{5}{2} + \dfrac{3}{2}z - z = \dfrac{-1+5}{2} + \left(\dfrac{3}{2} - 1\right)z = \dfrac{4}{2} + \left(\dfrac{3}{2} - \dfrac{2}{2}\right)z = 2 + \dfrac{1}{2}z = \dfrac{1}{2}z + 2$

108. $5(x - 3) - (4x + 3) = 5x - 15 - 4x - 3 = 5x - 4x - 15 - 3 = (5 - 4)x - 15 - 3 = x - 18$

109. $\dfrac{35a}{7a} = \dfrac{35}{7} \cdot \dfrac{a}{a} = \dfrac{35}{7} \cdot 1 = 5 \cdot 1 = 5$

110. $\dfrac{0.5c}{0.5} = \dfrac{0.5}{0.5} \cdot c = 1 \cdot c = c$

Applications

111. (a) Let x be the number of minutes. The first person then paints $3 \cdot x$. or $3x$, square feet in x minutes. The second person paints $4 \cdot x$. or $4x$, square feet in x minutes. working together the two people paint $3x + 4x = (3 + 4)x = 7x$ square feet in x minutes.

   (b) First convert hours to minutes; 1 hour = 60 minutes. Replace x with 60 to get $7x = 7 \cdot 60 = 420 \text{ ft}^2$.

   (c) First find the number of square feet the wall contains. The area of the wall is width times height. The area $= 8 \cdot 21 = 168 \text{ ft}^2$. Because the two people paint 7 square feet in 1 minute, $168 \div 7 = 24$ minutes.

112. The area of a triangle is $\dfrac{1}{2} \cdot$ base $\cdot$ height. The base of the triangle is 8 and the height is 4. Thus,

$$\frac{1}{2} \cdot 8 \cdot 4 = 16 \text{ ft}^2.$$

113. See Figure 113. Since there are 8 pints in 1 gallon, $P = 8G$, where $P =$ pints and $G =$ gallons.

Gallons (G)	1	2	3	4	5	6
Pints (P)	8	16	24	32	40	48

Figure 113

114. Because each CD costs 25 cents, $C = 0.25x$, where C represents cost and x represents the number of CD's purchased.

115. Find the fraction of the population that will be over the age of 65 but under the age of 85. Thus,

$$\frac{1}{5} - \frac{1}{20} = \frac{1 \cdot 4}{5 \cdot 4} - \frac{1}{20} = \frac{4}{20} - \frac{1}{20} = \frac{3}{20}.$$

116. Find the length of each piece when the board is cut into five equal lengths. Because the board measures

$$5\frac{3}{4} = \frac{23}{4}, \frac{23}{4} \div 5 = \frac{23}{4} \cdot \frac{1}{5} = \frac{23}{20} = 1\frac{3}{20} \text{ feet per piece.}$$

117. Add the individual lengths to find the total distance. Thus, $3\dfrac{1}{8} + 4\dfrac{3}{8} + 6\dfrac{1}{4} + 1\dfrac{5}{8} = \dfrac{25}{8} + \dfrac{35}{8} + \dfrac{25}{4} + \dfrac{13}{8} =$

$$\frac{25}{8} + \frac{35}{8} + \frac{50}{8} + \frac{13}{8} = \frac{25 + 35 + 50 + 13}{8} = \frac{123}{8} = 15\frac{3}{8} \text{ miles.}$$

118. Subtract the withdrawals and add the deposits to the initial balance.

Thus, $1652 - 78 - 91 + 256 - 638 = \$1101$.

119. The difference between the two temperatures is $108 - (-16) = 108 + 16 = 124°\text{F}$.

Chapter 1 Test

1. The number 56 is a composite number because it has factors other than itself and 1; $56 = 2 \times 2 \times 2 \times 7$.

2. $\dfrac{5x}{2x - 1}$, when $x = -3$, is $\dfrac{5 \cdot (-3)}{2 \cdot (-3) - 1} = \dfrac{-15}{-6 - 1} = \dfrac{-15}{-7} = \dfrac{15}{7}$

3. $4^2 - 3 = 16 - 3 = 13$

4. $\dfrac{24}{32} = \dfrac{3 \cdot 8}{4 \cdot 8} = \dfrac{3}{4}$

5. (a) $\dfrac{5}{8} + \dfrac{1}{8} = \dfrac{5 + 1}{8} = \dfrac{6}{8} = \dfrac{3 \cdot 2}{4 \cdot 2} = \dfrac{3}{4}$

   (b) $\dfrac{5}{9} - \dfrac{3}{15} = \dfrac{5 \cdot 5}{9 \cdot 5} - \dfrac{3 \cdot 3}{15 \cdot 3} = \dfrac{25}{45} - \dfrac{9}{45} = \dfrac{25 - 9}{45} = \dfrac{16}{45}$

   (c) $\dfrac{3}{5} \cdot \dfrac{10}{21} = \dfrac{3 \cdot 10}{5 \cdot 21} = \dfrac{30}{105} = \dfrac{2 \cdot 15}{7 \cdot 15} = \dfrac{2}{7}$

   (d) $6 \div \dfrac{8}{5} = \dfrac{6}{1} \cdot \dfrac{5}{8} = \dfrac{6 \cdot 5}{1 \cdot 8} = \dfrac{30}{8} = \dfrac{15 \cdot 2}{4 \cdot 2} = \dfrac{15}{4}$

6. (a) $6 + 10 \div 5 = 6 + 2 = 8$

   (b) $4^3 - (3 - 5 \cdot 2) = 64 - (3 - 10) = 64 - (-7) = 64 + 7 = 71$

   (c) $-6^2 - 6 + \dfrac{4}{2} = -36 - 6 + 2 = -40$

7. (a) Distributive

   (b) Associative (multiplication)

   (c) Commutative (addition)

8. (a) $5 - 5z + 7 + z = 5 + 7 - 5z + z = 12 + (-5 + 1)z = 12 + (-4)z = 12 - 4z$

   (b) $12x - (6 - 3x) = 12x - 6 + 3x = 12x + 3x - 6 = (12 + 3)x - 6 = 15x - 6$

   (c) $5 - 4(x + 6) + \dfrac{15x}{3} = 5 - 4x - 24 + \dfrac{15}{3}x = 5 - 4x - 24 + 5x = 5x - 4x + 5 - 24 =$

   $(5 - 4)x - 19 = 1x - 19 = x - 19$

9. (a) Let x be the number of hours. Then, the first person can mow $\dfrac{4}{3} \cdot x$ acres in x hours, and the second person

   can mow $\dfrac{1}{4} \cdot x$ acres in x hours. Thus, $\dfrac{4}{3}x + \dfrac{1}{4}x = \dfrac{16}{12}x + \dfrac{3}{12}x = \left(\dfrac{16}{12} + \dfrac{3}{12}\right) = \dfrac{19}{12}x.$

   (b) Let $x = 8$. Then, $\dfrac{19}{12} \cdot 8 = \dfrac{19 \cdot 8}{12} = \dfrac{152}{12} = \dfrac{38 \cdot 4}{3 \cdot 4} = \dfrac{38}{3} = 12\dfrac{2}{3}$ acres.

10. (a) Because $39 \div 3 = 13$, each ticket costs \$13.

    Then, let $c = \text{cost}$ and x be the number of tickets to obtain $c = 13x$.

    (b) Let $x = 17$. Thus, $13 \cdot 17 = \$221$.

11. Find $7\dfrac{4}{5} \div 3$ to find the length of three equal parts.

    Because $7\dfrac{4}{5} = \dfrac{39}{5}, \dfrac{39}{5} \div 3 = \dfrac{39}{5} \cdot \dfrac{1}{3} = \dfrac{39}{15} = \dfrac{13 \cdot 3}{5 \cdot 3} = \dfrac{13}{5} = 2\dfrac{3}{5}$ feet.

12. Subtract the withdrawals from and add the deposits to the initial balance.

    Thus, $892 - 57 + 150 - 345 = \$640$.

Chapter 1 Extended and Discovery Exercises

1. $2 + 2 - 2 - 2 = 4 - 4 = 0; \; 3 \cdot 3 + 3 \div 3 = 9 + 1 = 10; \; 4 \div 4 + 4 - 4 = 1 + 0 = 1;$

   $6 \cdot 6 + 6 - 6 = 36 + 0 = 36; \; 7 \cdot 7 + 7 + 7 = 49 + 14 = 63$ *Answers may vary.*

2.

16	2	3	13
5	11	10	8
9	7	6	12
4	14	15	1

Critical Thinking Solutions for Chapter 1

Section 1.1

- Because you can not find a fraction of a population, this is an example natural or whole number use.

- Because a prime number has as it's only factors itself and 1, the tree diagram will consist of a single dot.

Section 1.2

- Fractions are needed when baking a cake from scratch, because the measurements of cake ingredients are in fractions.

Section 1.3

- A gigabyte is $2^{30} = 1,073,741,824$ bytes, which is more than 1 billion bytes.

Section 1.4

- $-\pi + \pi = 0$

Section 1.5

- Change the problem to an addition problem. Then, if you are adding a negative number, you move left on the number line, and if adding a positive number you move right on the number line.

Section 1.6

- The estimate for 1995 would generally be more accurate because you are making an estimate based on known numbers.

Section 1.7

- Subtract 200 from 5283 to obtain 5083 and then add 2. The result is 5085.

Section 1.8

- Draw rectangles x by y and $2x$ by y. Their combined areas equal $3xy$.

Chapter 2: Linear Equations and Inequalities

2.1: Introduction to Equations

Concepts

1. equal

3. solution set

5. solutions

7. $b + c$

9. 1

The Addition Property of Equality

11. 22

13. $x + 5 = 0 \Rightarrow x + 5 - 5 = 0 - 5 \Rightarrow x + 0 = -5 \Rightarrow x = -5$; To check you answer, substitute -5 for x in the original equation, $-5 + 5 = 0$. This statement is true. Thus, the solution $x = -5$ is correct.

15. $x - 7 = 1 \Rightarrow x - 7 + 7 = 1 + 7 \Rightarrow x + 0 = 8 \Rightarrow x = 8$

17. $9 = y - 8 \Rightarrow 9 + 8 = y - 8 + 8 \Rightarrow 17 = y + 0 \Rightarrow 17 = y \Rightarrow y = 17$

19. $\dfrac{1}{2} = z - \dfrac{3}{2} \Rightarrow \dfrac{1}{2} + \dfrac{3}{2} = z - \dfrac{3}{2} + \dfrac{3}{2} \Rightarrow \dfrac{4}{2} = z + 0 \Rightarrow 2 = z \Rightarrow z = 2$

21. $t - 0.8 = 4.2 \Rightarrow t - 0.8 + 0.8 = 4.2 + 0.8 \Rightarrow t + 0 = 5 \Rightarrow t = 5$

23. $25 + x = 10 \Rightarrow 25 - 25 + x = 10 - 25 \Rightarrow 0 + x = -15 \Rightarrow x = -15$

25. $1989 = 26 + y \Rightarrow 1989 + (-26) = 26 + (-26) + y \Rightarrow 1963 = 0 + y \Rightarrow 1963 = y \Rightarrow y = 1963$

The Multiplication Property of Equality

27. 5

29. $5x = 15 \Rightarrow \dfrac{5x}{5} = \dfrac{15}{5} \Rightarrow x = 3$

31. $-7x = 0 \Rightarrow \dfrac{-7x}{-7} = \dfrac{0}{-7} \Rightarrow x = 0$

33. $\dfrac{1}{2}x = \dfrac{3}{2} \Rightarrow \dfrac{2}{1} \cdot \dfrac{1}{2}x = \dfrac{3}{2} \cdot \dfrac{2}{1} \Rightarrow x = 3$

35. $\dfrac{1}{2} = \dfrac{2}{5}z \Rightarrow \dfrac{5}{2} \cdot \dfrac{1}{2} = \dfrac{5}{2} \cdot \dfrac{2}{5}z \Rightarrow \dfrac{5}{4} = z \Rightarrow z = \dfrac{5}{4}$

37. $25 = 5z \Rightarrow \dfrac{25}{5} = \dfrac{5z}{5} \Rightarrow 5 = z \Rightarrow z = 5$

39. $0.5t = 3.5 \Rightarrow \dfrac{0.5t}{0.5} = \dfrac{3.5}{0.5} \Rightarrow t = 7$

41. $\dfrac{3}{8} = \dfrac{1}{4}y \Rightarrow \dfrac{3}{8} \cdot \dfrac{4}{1} = \dfrac{4}{1} \cdot \dfrac{1}{4}y \Rightarrow \dfrac{3}{2} = y \Rightarrow y = \dfrac{3}{2}$

Applications

43. (a) See Figure 43.

   (b) Let R represent total rainfall and let x represent the number of hours past noon. Start with 3 inches of rain and then add $\dfrac{1}{2}$, or 0.5, inches per hour after noon, $3 + 0.5x = R$, or equivalently $R = 0.5x + 3$.

   (c) At 3 pm, $x = 3$. Substituting x with 3 in the formula, $R = 0.5 \cdot 3 + 3 \Rightarrow R = 4.5$ inches. This answer agrees with the table from part (a).

   (d) At 2:15 pm, $x = 2.25$. Substituting x with 2.25 in the formula, $R = 0.5 \cdot 2.25 + 3 \Rightarrow R = 4.125$ inches.

Hours (x)	0	1	2	3	4	5	6
Rainfall (R)	3	3.5	4	4.5	5	5.5	6

   Figure 43

45. (a) Let L be the length of the football fields and x be the number of fields. Because each field x contains 300 feet, $L = 300x$.

   (b) Substitute L with 870. Then $870 = 300x$.

   (c) $870 = 300x \Rightarrow \dfrac{870}{300} = \dfrac{300x}{300} \Rightarrow x = \dfrac{870}{300} \Rightarrow x = 2.9$

47. Let x represent the total number of cubic miles that have melted and let y represent the number of years. Because the glaciers are melting at a rate of 24 cubic miles per year, $x = 24y$. Substitute x with 420. Then, $420 = 24y \Rightarrow \dfrac{420}{24} = \dfrac{24y}{24} \Rightarrow y = \dfrac{420}{24} \Rightarrow y = 17.5$. Thus, it takes 17.5 years for 420 cubic miles of the glacier to melt.

49. Let x represent the cost of the car to obtain the equation $0.07x = 1750$. Then the solution is $\dfrac{0.07x}{0.07} = \dfrac{1750}{0.07} \Rightarrow x = \dfrac{1750}{0.07} \Rightarrow x = 25{,}000$. Thus, the cost of the car is \$25,000.

2.2: Linear Equations

Concepts

1. $ax + b = 0$

3. addition, multiplication

5. LCD

7. Infinitely many

Identifying Linear Equations

9. $3x - 7$ is a linear equation. $a = 3$ and $b = -7$.

11. $\dfrac{1}{2}x = 0$ is a linear equation. $a = \dfrac{1}{2}$ and $b = 0$.

13. $4x^2 - 6 = 11$ is not a linear equation because in cannot be written in the form $ax + b = 0$. It has a non-zero term containing x^2.

15. $1.1x = 0.9$ is a linear equation. $1.1x = 0.9 \Rightarrow 1.1x - 0.9 = 0.9 - 0.9 \Rightarrow 1.1x - 0.9 = 0$.

$a = 1.1$ and $b = -0.9$.

17. $2(x - 3) = 0$ is a linear equation. Use the distributive property to obtain $2x - 6 = 0$. $a = 2$ and $b = -6$.

19. $6x - x^2 = 0$ is not a linear equation because in cannot be written in the form $ax + b = 0$. It has a non-zero term containing x^2.

21. For $x = 0$, substitute 0 for x and solve: $-3(0) + 7 = 0 + 7 = 7$.

For $x = 1$, substitute 1 for x and solve: $-3(1) + 7 = -3 + 7 = 4$.

For $x = 2$, substitute 2 for x and solve: $-3(2) + 7 = -6 + 7 = 1$.

For $x = 3$, substitute 3 for x and solve: $-3(3) + 7 = -9 + 7 = -2$.

For $x = 4$, substitute 4 for x and solve: $-3(4) + 7 = -12 + 7 = -5$.

See Figure 21. From the table, we see that the equation $-3x + 7 = 1$ is true when $x = 2$. Therefore, the solution to the equation $-3x + 7 = 1$ is $x = 2$.

x	0	1	2	3	4
$-3x + 7$	7	4	1	-2	-5

x	-2	-1	0	1	2
$4 - 2x$	8	6	4	2	0

Figure 21   Figure 23

23. For $x = -2$, substitute -2 for x and solve: $4 - 2(-2) = 4 + 4 = 8$.

For $x = -1$, substitute -1 for x and solve: $4 - 2(-1) = 4 + 2 = 6$.

For $x = 0$, substitute 0 for x and solve: $4 - 2(0) = 4 + 0 = 4$.

For $x = 1$, substitute 1 for x and solve: $4 - 2(1) = 4 - 2 = 2$.

For $x = 2$, substitute 2 for x and solve: $4 - 2(2) = 4 - 4 = 0$.

See Figure 23. From the table, we see that the equation $4 - 2x = 6$ is true when $x = -1$. Therefore, the solution to the equation $4 - 2x = 6$ is $x = -1$.

Solving Linear Equations

25. $11x = 3 \Rightarrow \dfrac{11x}{11} = \dfrac{3}{11} \Rightarrow x = \dfrac{3}{11}$

27. $x - 18 = 5 \Rightarrow x - 18 + 18 = 5 + 18 \Rightarrow x = 23$

29. $2x - 1 = 13 \Rightarrow 2x - 1 + 1 = 13 + 1 \Rightarrow 2x = 14 \Rightarrow \dfrac{2x}{2} = \dfrac{14}{2} \Rightarrow x = 7$

31. $5x + 5 = -6 \Rightarrow 5x + 5 - 5 = -6 - 5 \Rightarrow 5x = -11 \Rightarrow \dfrac{5x}{5} = \dfrac{-11}{5} \Rightarrow x = -\dfrac{11}{5}$

33. $3z + 2 = z - 5 \Rightarrow 3z + 2 - 2 = z - 5 - 2 \Rightarrow 3z = z - 7 \Rightarrow 3z - z = z - z - 7 \Rightarrow 2z = -7 \Rightarrow$

$\dfrac{2z}{2} = \dfrac{-7}{2} \Rightarrow z = -\dfrac{7}{2}$

35. $12y - 6 = 33 - y \Rightarrow 12y - 6 + 6 = 33 + 6 - y \Rightarrow 12y = 39 - y \Rightarrow 12y + y = 39 - y + y \Rightarrow$

$13y = 39 \Rightarrow \dfrac{13y}{13} = \dfrac{39}{13} \Rightarrow y = 3$

37. $4(x - 1) = 5 \Rightarrow 4x - 4 = 5 \Rightarrow 4x - 4 + 4 = 5 + 4 \Rightarrow 4x = 9 \Rightarrow \dfrac{4x}{4} = \dfrac{9}{4} \Rightarrow x = \dfrac{9}{4}$

39. $1 - (3x + 1) = 5 - x \Rightarrow 1 - 3x - 1 = 5 - x \Rightarrow -3x = 5 - x \Rightarrow -3x + x = 5 - x + x \Rightarrow$
$-2x = 5 \Rightarrow \dfrac{-2x}{-2} = \dfrac{5}{-2} \Rightarrow x = -\dfrac{5}{2}$

41. $5t - 6 + 2(t + 1) = 0 \Rightarrow 5t - 6 + 2t + 2 = 0 \Rightarrow 7t - 4 = 0 \Rightarrow 7t - 4 + 4 = 0 + 4 \Rightarrow$
$7t = 4 \Rightarrow \dfrac{7t}{7} = \dfrac{4}{7} \Rightarrow t = \dfrac{4}{7}$

43. $3(4z - 1) - 2(z + 2) = 2(z + 1) \Rightarrow 12z - 3 - 2z - 4 = 2z + 2 \Rightarrow 10z - 7 = 2z + 2 \Rightarrow$
$10z - 7 - 2 = 2z + 2 - 2 \Rightarrow 10z - 9 = 2z \Rightarrow 10z - 9 + 9 = 2z + 9 \Rightarrow 10z = 2z + 9 \Rightarrow$
$10z - 2z = 2z - 2z + 9 \Rightarrow 8z = 9 \Rightarrow \dfrac{8z}{8} = \dfrac{9}{8} \Rightarrow z = \dfrac{9}{8}$

45. $7.3x - 1.7 = 5.6 \Rightarrow 7.3x - 1.7 + 1.7 = 5.6 + 1.7 \Rightarrow 7.3x = 7.3 \Rightarrow \dfrac{7.3x}{7.3} = \dfrac{7.3}{7.3} \Rightarrow x = 1$

47. $-9.5x - 0.05 = 10.5x + 1.05 \Rightarrow -9.5x - 10.5x - 0.05 = 10.5x - 10.5x + 1.05 \Rightarrow$
$-20x - 0.05 = 1.05 \Rightarrow -20x - 0.05 + 0.05 = 1.05 + 0.05 \Rightarrow -20x = 1.1 \Rightarrow \dfrac{-20x}{-20} = \dfrac{1.1}{-20} \Rightarrow$
$x = -0.055$

49. $\dfrac{1}{2}x - \dfrac{3}{2} = \dfrac{5}{2} \Rightarrow \dfrac{1}{2}x - \dfrac{3}{2} + \dfrac{3}{2} = \dfrac{5}{2} + \dfrac{3}{2} \Rightarrow \dfrac{1}{2}x = 4 \Rightarrow 2 \cdot \dfrac{1}{2}x = 4 \cdot 2 \Rightarrow x = 8$

51. $-\dfrac{3}{8}x + \dfrac{1}{4} = \dfrac{1}{2}x + \dfrac{1}{8} \Rightarrow -\dfrac{3}{8}x - \dfrac{1}{2}x + \dfrac{1}{4} = \dfrac{1}{2}x - \dfrac{1}{2}x + \dfrac{1}{8} \Rightarrow -\dfrac{7}{8}x + \dfrac{1}{4} = \dfrac{1}{8} \Rightarrow$
$-\dfrac{7}{8}x + \dfrac{1}{4} - \dfrac{1}{4} = \dfrac{1}{8} - \dfrac{1}{4} \Rightarrow -\dfrac{7}{8}x = -\dfrac{1}{8} \Rightarrow \left(-\dfrac{8}{7}\right)\left(-\dfrac{7}{8}\right)x = \left(-\dfrac{1}{8}\right)\left(-\dfrac{8}{7}\right) \Rightarrow x = \dfrac{8}{56} \Rightarrow x = \dfrac{1}{7}$

53. $4y - 2(y + 1) = 0 \Rightarrow 47 - 2y - 2 = 0 \Rightarrow 2y - 2 = 0 \Rightarrow 2y - 2 + 2 = 0 + 2 \Rightarrow 2y = 2 \Rightarrow$
$\dfrac{2y}{2} = \dfrac{2}{2} \Rightarrow y = 1$

55. $5x = 5x + 1 \Rightarrow 5x - 5x = 5x - 5x + 1 \Rightarrow 0 = 1$

    Because the equation $0 = 1$ is always false, there are zero solutions.

57. $8x = 0 \Rightarrow \dfrac{8x}{8} = \dfrac{0}{8} \Rightarrow x = 0$ Thus, there is only one solution.

59. $4(x + 2) - 2(2x + 3) = 10 \Rightarrow 4x + 8 - 4x - 6 = 10 \Rightarrow 8 - 6 = 10 \Rightarrow 2 = 10$

    Because the equation $2 = 10$ is always false, there are zero solutions.

61. $4x = 5(x + 3) - x \Rightarrow 4x = 5x + 15 - x \Rightarrow 4x = 4x + 15 \Rightarrow 43x - 4x = 4x - 4x + 15 \Rightarrow 0 = 15$

    Because the equation $0 = 15$ is always false, there are zero solutions.

63. $2x - (x + 5) = x - 5 \Rightarrow 2x - x - 5 = x - 5 \Rightarrow x - 5 = x - 5 \Rightarrow x - x - 5 = x - x - 5 \Rightarrow$
$-5 = -5$ Since the equation $-5 = -5$ is always true, there are infinitely many solutions.

Applications

65. (a) See Figure 65.

    (b) Let D represent the distance from home and x represent the number of hours. Then $D = 4 + 8x$.

    (c) Substitute 3 for x. Then, $D = 4 + 8(3) = 28$ miles. This agrees with the value found in the table.

    (d) Using the formula $D = 4 + 8x$, substitute 22 for D. Then, $22 = 4 + 8x$. Then, solving for x:

    $22 - 4 = 4 - 4 + 8x \Rightarrow 18 = 8x \Rightarrow \dfrac{18}{8} = \dfrac{8x}{8} \Rightarrow \dfrac{9}{4} = x \Rightarrow x = 2.25$ miles. Thus, the bicyclist is

    22 miles from home after 2 hours and 15 minutes.

Hours (x)	0	1	2	3	4
Distance (D)	4	12	20	28	36

Figure 65

x	3	3.5	4	4.5	5
$4x - 3$	9	11	13	15	17

Figure 1

67. Using the formula, substitute 815 for N and solve for x. $815 = 40x - 79{,}065 \Rightarrow$

$815 + 79{,}065 = 40x - 79{,}065 + 79{,}065 \Rightarrow 79{,}880 = 40x \Rightarrow \dfrac{79{,}880}{40} = \dfrac{40x}{40} \Rightarrow 1997 = x \Rightarrow x = 1997$

69. Using the formula, substitute 908 for N and solve for x. $908 = 70x - 138{,}532 \Rightarrow$

$908 + 138{,}532 = 70x - 138{,}532 + 138{,}532 \Rightarrow 139{,}440 = 70x \Rightarrow \dfrac{139{,}440}{70} = \dfrac{70x}{70} \Rightarrow 1992 = x \Rightarrow$

$x = 1992$

Checking Basic Concepts for Sections 2.1 & 2.2

1. For $x = 3$, substitute 3 for x and solve: $4(3) - 3 = 12 - 3 = 9$

   For $x = 3.5$, substitute 3.5 for x and solve: $4(3.5) - 3 = 14 - 3 = 11$

   For $x = 4$, substitute 4 for x and solve: $4(4) - 3 = 16 - 3 = 13$

   For $x = 4.5$, substitute 4.5 for x and solve: $4(4.5) - 3 = 18 - 3 = 15$

   For $x = 5$, substitute 5 for x and solve: $4(5) - 3 = 20 - 3 = 17$

   See Figure 1. To solve $4x - 3 = 13$, the table tells us that when $x = 4$, $4x - 3 = 13$.

2. (a) $x - 12 = 6 \Rightarrow x - 12 + 12 = 6 + 12 \Rightarrow x = 18$ To check the answer, substitute 18 for x in the original

   equation $x - 12 = 6$. $18 - 12 = 6 \Rightarrow 6 = 6$. Since this is true $x = 18$ is correct.

   (b) $\dfrac{3}{4}z = \dfrac{1}{8} \Rightarrow \dfrac{4}{3} \cdot \dfrac{3}{4}z = \dfrac{1}{8} \cdot \dfrac{4}{3} \Rightarrow z = \dfrac{4}{24} \Rightarrow z = \dfrac{1}{6}$

   (c) $0.6t + 0.4 = 2 \Rightarrow 0.6t + 0.4 - 0.4 = 2 - 0.4 \Rightarrow 0.6t = 1.6 \Rightarrow \dfrac{0.6t}{0.6} = \dfrac{1.6}{0.6} \Rightarrow t = 2.\overline{6}$

   (d) $5 - 2(x - 2) = 3(4 - x) \Rightarrow 5 - 2x + 4 = 12 - 3x \Rightarrow 9 - 2x = 12 - 3x \Rightarrow$

   $9 - 2x + 3x = 12 - 3x + 3x \Rightarrow 9 + x = 12 \Rightarrow 9 - 9 + x = 12 - 9 \Rightarrow x = 3$

3. (a) $x - 5 = 6x \Rightarrow x - x - 5 = 6x - x \Rightarrow -5 = 5x \Rightarrow \dfrac{-5}{5} = \dfrac{5x}{5} \Rightarrow -1 = x$. Thus, the equation has 1 solution.

   (b) $-2(x - 5) = 10 - 2x \Rightarrow -2x + 10 = 10 - 2x \Rightarrow -2x + 2x + 10 = 10 - 2x + 2x \Rightarrow 10 = 10$

   Since $10 = 10$ is always true, the equation has infinitely many solutions.

   (c) $-(x - 1) = -x - 1 \Rightarrow -x + 1 = -x - 1 \Rightarrow -x + x + 1 = -x + x - 1 \Rightarrow 1 = -1$

   Since this is never true, the equation has zero solutions.

4. (a) Let D represent distance from home and x represent hours driven. Note that the driver is initially 300 miles

   from home and that each hour driven the driver gets closer to home by 75 miles. Thus, the formula is

   $D = 300 - 75x.$

   (b) Since the distance from home, when the drive is home, is 0, use the formula and set D equal to 0.

   Thus, $0 = 300 - 75x.$

   (c) $0 = 300 - 75x \Rightarrow 0 + 75x = 300 - 75x + 75x \Rightarrow 75x = 300 \Rightarrow \dfrac{75x}{75} = \dfrac{300}{75} \Rightarrow x = 4$ hours.

2.3: Introduction to Problem Solving

Concepts

1. Check your solution

3. $\dfrac{x}{100}$

5. 50

7. $\dfrac{P_2 - P_1}{P_1} \times 100$

Number Problems

9. Let x represent the number. $2 + x = 12 \Rightarrow 2 - 2 + x = 12 - 2 \Rightarrow x = 10$

11. $\dfrac{x}{5} = x - 24 \Rightarrow \dfrac{x}{5} \cdot 5 = 5(x - 24) \Rightarrow x = 5x - 120 \Rightarrow x - 5x = 5x - 5x - 120 \Rightarrow -4x = -120 \Rightarrow$

    $\dfrac{-4x}{-4} = \dfrac{-120}{-4} \Rightarrow x = 30$

13. $\dfrac{x + 5}{2} = 7 \Rightarrow \dfrac{x + 2}{2} \cdot 2 = 7 \cdot 2 \Rightarrow x + 5 = 14 \Rightarrow x + 5 - 5 = 14 - 5 \Rightarrow x = 9$

15. $\dfrac{x}{2} = 17 \Rightarrow \dfrac{x}{2} \cdot 2 = 17 \cdot 2 \Rightarrow x = 34$

17. Let the smallest natural number be represented by x. $x + (x + 1) + (x + 2) = 96 \Rightarrow 3x + 3 = 96 \Rightarrow$

    $3x + 3 - 3 = 96 - 3 \Rightarrow 3x = 93 \Rightarrow \dfrac{3x}{3} = \dfrac{93}{3} \Rightarrow x = 31$ Thus, the numbers are 31, 32 and 33.

19. $3x = 102 \Rightarrow \dfrac{3x}{3} = \dfrac{102}{3} \Rightarrow x = 34$

21. $5x = 2x + 24 \Rightarrow 5x - 2x = 2x - 2x + 24 \Rightarrow 3x = 24 \Rightarrow \dfrac{3x}{3} = \dfrac{24}{3} \Rightarrow x = 8$

23. $\dfrac{6x}{7} = 18 \Rightarrow \dfrac{6x}{7} \cdot 7 = 18 \cdot 7 \Rightarrow 6x = 126 \Rightarrow \dfrac{6x}{6} = \dfrac{126}{6} \Rightarrow x = 21$

25. $4(x + 5) = 64 \Rightarrow 4x + 20 = 64 \Rightarrow 4x + 20 - 20 = 64 - 20 \Rightarrow 4x = 44 \Rightarrow \dfrac{4x}{4} = \dfrac{44}{4} \Rightarrow x = 11$

Percent Problems

27. $37\% = \dfrac{37}{100}$

    $37\% = 37 \times 0.01 = 0.37$

29. $148\% = \dfrac{148}{100} = \dfrac{37 \cdot 4}{25 \cdot 4} = \dfrac{37}{25}$

    $148\% = 148 \times 0.01 = 1.48$

31. $6.9\% = \dfrac{6.9}{100} = \dfrac{6.9}{100} \cdot \dfrac{10}{10} = \dfrac{69}{1000}$

    $6.9\% = 6.9 \times 0.01 = 0.069$

33. $0.05\% = \dfrac{0.05}{100} = \dfrac{0.05}{100} \cdot \dfrac{100}{100} = \dfrac{5}{10,000} = \dfrac{1 \cdot 5}{2000 \cdot 5} = \dfrac{1}{2000}$

    $0.05\% = 0.05 \times 0.01 = 0.0005$

35. $0.45 = 0.45 \times 100 = 45\%$

37. $1.8 = 1.8 \times 100 = 180\%$

39. $\dfrac{2}{5} = 0.4 = 0.4 \times 100 = 40\%$

41. $\dfrac{3}{4} = 0.75 = 0.75 \times 100 = 75\%$

43. $\dfrac{5}{6} = 0.83\overline{3} = 0.83\overline{3} \times 100 = 83.\overline{3}\%$

45. Let P_2 represent voters in 2000 and let P_1 represent voters in 1980. Then, the percent change in the number of

    voters is $\dfrac{P_2 - P_1}{P_1} = \dfrac{105.4 - 86.5}{86.5} = \dfrac{18.9}{86.5} \approx .218$ or about 21.8%.

47. Calculate the value of 4% of 950, then add the value to 950. Thus, 4% of $950 = .04(950) = 38$.

    Then, $950 + 38 = \$988$ per credit.

49. Let x represent the number of returns in 1998. Then, $\dfrac{125 - x}{x} = 0.0162 \Rightarrow \dfrac{125 - x}{x} \cdot x = 0.0162 \cdot x \Rightarrow$

    $125 - x = 0.0162x \Rightarrow 125 - x + x = 0.0162x + x \Rightarrow 125 = 1.0162x \Rightarrow \dfrac{125}{1.0162} = \dfrac{1.0162x}{1.0162} \Rightarrow$

    $123 \approx x \Rightarrow x \approx 123$ Thus, about 123 million returns were processed in 1998.

51. Let x represent the number of AIDS deaths in 1995. Then, $0.345x = 17{,}047 \Rightarrow \dfrac{0.345x}{0.345} = \dfrac{17{,}047}{0.345} \Rightarrow$

    $x \approx 49{,}412$ Thus, there were about 49,412 AIDS deaths in 1995.

53. To calculate the total area of Wisconsin, let x represent the unknown number and note that 13.6 is 38% of the

    unknown number. Then, $0.38x = 13.6 \Rightarrow \dfrac{0.38x}{0.38} = \dfrac{13.6}{0.38} \Rightarrow x \approx 35.8$. Thus, the total area of Wisconsin is

    about 35.8 million acres.

Distance Problems

55. $d = rt \Rightarrow d = 4 \cdot 2 \Rightarrow d = 8$ miles

57. $d = rt \Rightarrow 1000 = r \cdot 50 \Rightarrow \dfrac{1000}{50} = \dfrac{r \cdot 50}{50} \Rightarrow 20 = r \Rightarrow r = 20$ feet/second

59. $d = rt \Rightarrow 200 = 40t \Rightarrow \dfrac{200}{40} = \dfrac{40t}{40} \Rightarrow 5 = t \Rightarrow t = 5$ hours

61. Given that the distance traveled (d) is 255 and that the time spent traveling (t) is 4.25 hours, calculate the speed

    of the car (r). Then, $d = rt \Rightarrow 255 = r \cdot 4.25 \Rightarrow \dfrac{255}{4.25} = \dfrac{r \cdot 4.25}{4.25} \Rightarrow 60 = r \Rightarrow r = 60$ miles/hour.

63. Let the slower runner be standing still. Then, the faster runner will be traveling at $0 + 2$ mph. Then, this

    problem is equivalent to solving how long it takes the faster runner to travel $\dfrac{3}{4}$ of a mile. Using the $d = rt$

    formula: $\dfrac{3}{4} = 2t \Rightarrow \dfrac{3}{4} \cdot \dfrac{1}{2} = \dfrac{2}{1} \cdot \dfrac{1}{2}t \Rightarrow \dfrac{3}{8} = t \Rightarrow t = \dfrac{3}{8}$. So, in $\dfrac{3}{8}$ hour the faster runner will be $\dfrac{3}{4}$ mile

    ahead of the slower runner.

65. Let x represent the amount of time spent running 5 mph. Since the total time spent running was 1.1 hours, let $1.1 - x$ represent the amount of time running at 8 mph. Using the $d = rt$ formula, the distance run will equal the sum of $5x$ and $8(1.1 - x)$. Thus, $7 = 5x + 8(1.1 - x) \Rightarrow 7 = 5x + 8.8 - 8x \Rightarrow 7 = 7.8 - 3x \Rightarrow 3x + 7 = 8.8 - 3x + 3x \Rightarrow 3x + 7 = 8.8 \Rightarrow 3x + 7 - 7 = 8.8 - 7 \Rightarrow 3x = 1.8 \Rightarrow x = \dfrac{1.8}{3} = 0.6$.

    Therefore, the athlete ran at 5 mph for 0.6 hour and ran at 8 mph for $(1.1 - 0.6) = 0.5$ hour.

67. Since the plane is already 300 miles west of Chicago, it will have to fly $2175 - 300 = 1875$ miles to be 2175 miles west of Chicago. The plane is traveling at 500 mph. Then,

    $1875 = 500t \Rightarrow \dfrac{1875}{500} = \dfrac{500t}{500} \Rightarrow 3.75 = t \Rightarrow t = 3.75$. Therefore, it will take the plane 3.75 hours to be

    2175 miles west of Chicago.

Other Types of Problems

69. Let x represent the amount of water that should be added. Note that there is no salt in pure water and that we will add the amount of pure water to the 3% salt solution to obtain a 1.2% solution. Therefore, set up the equation so that the amount of salt on both sides of the equation is equal. Thus,

    $x(0.00) + 20(0.03) = (x + 20)(0.012) \Rightarrow 0.00x + 0.6 = 0.012x + 0.24 \Rightarrow$

    $0.6 - 0.24 = 0.012x + 0.24 - 0.24 \Rightarrow 0.36 = 0.012x \Rightarrow \dfrac{0.36}{0.012} = \dfrac{0.012x}{0.012} \Rightarrow 30 = x \Rightarrow x = 30$.

    Therefore, 30 ounces of water should be added.

71. Let x represent the amount of the loan at 6% and let $x + 1000$ represent the amount of the loan at 5%. The total interest for one year is $215 and this is the sum of the interest paid on the two loans. Therefore:

    $0.06x + 0.05(x + 1000) = 215 \Rightarrow 0.06x + 0.05x + 50 = 215 \Rightarrow 0.11x + 50 - 50 = 215 - 50 \Rightarrow$

    $0.11x = 165 \Rightarrow \dfrac{0.11x}{0.11} = \dfrac{165}{0.11} \Rightarrow x = 1500$. Therefore, the amount of the loan at 6% interest is $1500 and

    the amount of the loan at 5% interest is $1500 + 1000 = \$2500$.

73. Let x represent the amount of 70% antifreeze. Then, the 45% antifreeze mixture is the sum of the 70% mixture and the 30% mixture. Therefore: $0.7x + 10(0.3) = (x + 10)(0.45) \Rightarrow 0.7x + 3 = 0.45x + 4.5 \Rightarrow$

    $0.7x + 3 - 3 = 0.45x + 4.5 - 3 \Rightarrow 0.7x = 0.45x + 1.5 \Rightarrow 0.7x - 0.45x = 0.45x - 0.45x + 1.5 \Rightarrow$

    $0.25x = 1.5 \Rightarrow \dfrac{0.25x}{0.25} = \dfrac{1.5}{0.25} \Rightarrow x = 6$. Therefore, 6 gallons of 70% antifreeze should be mixed with 10

    gallons of 30% antifreeze to obtain the 45% mixture.

2.4: Formulas

Concepts

1. formula

3. $\dfrac{1}{2}bh$

5. 360

7. $2\pi r$

9. lwh

Formulas from Geometry

11. $A = lw$. Thus, $A = 6 \cdot 3 = 18 \text{ ft}^2$.

13. $A = \dfrac{1}{2}bh$. Thus, $A = \dfrac{1}{2} \cdot 6 \cdot 3 = 9 \text{ in}^2$.

15. $A = \pi r^2$. Thus, $A = \pi 4^2 \approx 50.3 \text{ ft}^2$.

17. $A = \dfrac{1}{2}(a + b)h$. Thus, $A = \dfrac{1}{2}(5 + 6)2 = \dfrac{1}{2}(11)2 = 11 \text{ ft}^2$.

19. $A = lw$. Thus, $A = 13 \cdot 7 = 91 \text{ in}^2$.

21. $A = \dfrac{1}{2}bh$. Thus, $A = \dfrac{1}{2} \cdot 12 \cdot 6 = 36 \text{ in}^2$.

23. $C = 2\pi r$. Because the circle has a diameter of 8 inches, the radius is $= \dfrac{8}{2} = 4$ inches. Thus,

   $C = 2\pi r = 2\pi 4 = 8\pi \approx 25.1$ inches.

25. The total area of the lot is the sum of the area of the square and the area of the triangle. The area of the square

   is $lw = 52 \cdot 52 = 2704 \text{ ft}^2$. The area of the triangle is $\dfrac{1}{2}bh = \dfrac{1}{2} \cdot 73 \cdot 52 = 1898 \text{ ft}^2$. Thus, the area of the

   lot is $1898 + 2704 = 4602 \text{ ft}^2$.

27. The sum of the angles of a triangle is $180°$. Let the unknown angle be represented by x. Then,

   $x + 75 + 40 = 180 \Rightarrow x + 75 + 40 - 75 - 40 = 180 - 75 - 40 \Rightarrow x = 65$. Thus, the third angle is $65°$.

29. The sum of the angles of a triangle is $180°$. Let the unknown angle be represented by x. Then,

   $x + 23 + 76 = 180 \Rightarrow x + 23 + 76 - 23 - 76 = 180 - 23 - 76 \Rightarrow x = 81$. Thus, the third angle is $81°$.

31. Because the sum of the angles of a triangle is 180, $x + 2x + 3x = 180 \Rightarrow 6x = 180 \Rightarrow \dfrac{6x}{6} = \dfrac{180}{6} \Rightarrow$

   $x = 30$. Thus, the value of x is $30°$.

33. Let x represent the largest angle. Then, $x + \dfrac{1}{3}x + \dfrac{1}{3}x = 180 \Rightarrow \dfrac{5}{3}x = 180 \Rightarrow \dfrac{3}{5} \cdot \dfrac{5}{3}x = \dfrac{180}{1} \cdot \dfrac{3}{5} \Rightarrow$

   $x = \dfrac{540}{5} \Rightarrow x = 108$. Thus, the largest angle has a measure of $108°$ and the two small angles each have

   measure $\dfrac{1}{3} \cdot \dfrac{108}{1} = \dfrac{108}{3} = 36°$.

35. $C = 2\pi r$. Since the diameter of the circle is 12 inches, the radius is $\dfrac{12}{2} = 6$ inches. Then,

   $C = 2\pi 6 = 12\pi \approx 37.7$ inches. Then, $A = \pi r^2 = \pi 6^2 = 36\pi \approx 113.1 \text{ in}^2$.

37. $C = 2\pi r$. Then, set C equal to 2π and solve for r. $2\pi = 2\pi r \Rightarrow \dfrac{2\pi}{2\pi} = \dfrac{2\pi r}{2\pi} \Rightarrow 1 = r \Rightarrow r = 1$ inch. Then,

   $A = \pi r^2$. Because $r = 1$, substitute 1 for r and solve for A. $A = \pi(1)^2 = \pi$. Thus, the area is equal to π,

   which is approximately equal to 3.1 in^2.

39. $V = lwh$. Thus, $V = 22 \cdot 12 \cdot 10 = 2640$ in³. Surface area equals $2lw + 2lh + 2wh$.

Thus, $S = 2 \cdot 22 \cdot 12 + 2 \cdot 22 \cdot 10 + 2 \cdot 12 \cdot 10 = 528 + 440 + 240 = 1208$ in².

41. Convert yards to feet. Then, $\dfrac{2}{3}$ yard $= \dfrac{2}{3} \cdot 3 = 2$ feet. Then, $V = lwh = 2 \cdot \dfrac{2}{3} \cdot \dfrac{3}{2} = 2$ ft³. Surface area

equals $2lw + 2lh + 2wh$. Thus, $S = 2 \cdot 2 \cdot \dfrac{2}{3} + 2 \cdot 2 \cdot \dfrac{3}{2} + 2 \cdot \dfrac{2}{3} \cdot \dfrac{3}{2} = \dfrac{8}{3} + 6 + 2 = 8\dfrac{8}{3} = 10\dfrac{2}{3}$ ft².

43. $V = \pi r^2 h$. Thus, $V = \pi 2^2 \cdot 5 = \pi \cdot 4 \cdot 5 = 20\pi$ in³.

45. Convert feet to inches to obtain $h = 2$ feet $= 2 \cdot 12 = 24$ inches. Then, $V = \pi r^2 h$. Thus, $V = \pi 5^2 \cdot 24 =$

$\pi \cdot 25 \cdot 24 = 600\pi$ in³.

47. The volume formula for a cylindrical container is given by $V = \pi r^2 h$. Because the diameter of the barrel is

$1\dfrac{3}{4} = \dfrac{7}{4}$ feet, the radius is $\left(\dfrac{1}{2}\right)\left(\dfrac{7}{4}\right) = \dfrac{7}{8}$ feet. Thus, $V = \pi r^2 h = \pi\left(\dfrac{7}{8}\right)^2(3) = \pi\left(\dfrac{49}{64}\right)(3) = \pi\left(\dfrac{147}{64}\right) =$

$\dfrac{147}{64}\pi \approx 7.2$ ft³.

Solving for a Variable

49. The formula is given as $A = lw$. To solve for W, proceed as follows: $A = lw \Rightarrow \dfrac{A}{l} = \dfrac{lw}{l} \Rightarrow w = \dfrac{A}{l}$.

51. The formula is given as $V = \pi r^2 h$. To solve for h, proceed as follows: $V = \pi r^2 h \Rightarrow \dfrac{V}{\pi r^2} = \dfrac{\pi r^2 h}{\pi r^2} \Rightarrow$

$h = \dfrac{V}{\pi r^2}$.

53. The formula is given as $\dfrac{1}{2}(a + b)h = A$. To solve for a, proceed as follows: $A = \dfrac{1}{2}(a + b)h \Rightarrow$

$2A = \dfrac{1}{2}(2)(a + b)h \Rightarrow 2A = (a + b)h \Rightarrow \dfrac{2A}{h} = \dfrac{(a + b)h}{h} \Rightarrow \dfrac{2A}{h} = a + b \Rightarrow \dfrac{2A}{h} - b = a + b - b \Rightarrow$

$a = \dfrac{2A}{h} - b$.

55. The formula is given as $V = lwh$. To solve for W, proceed as follows: $V = lwh \Rightarrow \dfrac{V}{lh} = \dfrac{lwh}{lh} \Rightarrow w = \dfrac{V}{lh}$.

57. $s = \dfrac{a + b + c}{2} \Rightarrow 2s = \dfrac{a + b + c}{2} \cdot 2 \Rightarrow 2s = a + b + c \Rightarrow 2s - a - c = a + b + c - a - c \Rightarrow$

$2s - a - c = b \Rightarrow b = 2s - a - c$

59. $\dfrac{a}{b} - \dfrac{c}{b} = 1 \Rightarrow b\left(\dfrac{a}{b} - \dfrac{c}{b}\right) = 1(b) \Rightarrow a - c = b \Rightarrow b = a - c$

61. $ab = cd + ad \Rightarrow ab - ad = cd + ad - ad \Rightarrow ab - ad = cd \Rightarrow a(b - d) = cd \Rightarrow$

$\dfrac{a(b - d)}{(b - d)} = \dfrac{cd}{(b - d)} \Rightarrow a = \dfrac{cd}{b - d}$

63. Because the perimeter equals the lengths of the four sides, $P = 2w + 2l$. Thus, $P = 2w + 2l \Rightarrow$

$40 = 2(5) + 2l \Rightarrow 40 = 10 + 2l \Rightarrow 40 - 10 = 10 + 2l - 10 \Rightarrow 2l = 30 \Rightarrow \dfrac{2l}{2} = \dfrac{30}{2} \Rightarrow l = 15$

Thus, the length of the rectangle is 15 inches.

Other Formulas and Applications

65. The formula for GPA is given by $\dfrac{4a + 3b + 2c + d}{a + b + c + d + f}$.

$\dfrac{4(30) + 3(45) + 2(12) + 1(4)}{30 + 45 + 12 + 4 + 4} = \dfrac{120 + 135 + 24 + 4}{95} = \dfrac{283}{95} \approx 2.98$. Thus, the GPA is 2.98.

67. The formula for GPA is given by $\dfrac{4a + 3b + 2c + d}{a + b + c + d + f}$.

$\dfrac{4(0) + 3(60) + 2(80) + 1(10)}{0 + 60 + 80 + 10 + 6} = \dfrac{0 + 180 + 160 + 10}{156} = \dfrac{350}{156} \approx 2.24$. Thus, the GPA is 2.24.

69. To convert Celsius to Fahrenheit temperature, the formula given is $\dfrac{9}{5}C + 32 = F$.

$\dfrac{9}{5}(25) + 32 = F \Rightarrow \dfrac{225}{5} + \dfrac{160}{5} = F \Rightarrow \dfrac{385}{5} = F \Rightarrow F = 77°F.$

71. To convert Celsius to Fahrenheit temperature, the formula given is $\dfrac{9}{5}C + 32 = F$.

$\dfrac{9}{5}(-40) + 32 = F \Rightarrow \dfrac{-360}{5} + \dfrac{160}{5} = F \Rightarrow \dfrac{-200}{5} = F \Rightarrow F = -40°F.$

73. To convert Fahrenheit to Celsius temperature, the formula given is $C = \dfrac{5}{9}(F - 32)$.

$C = \dfrac{5}{9}(23 - 32) \Rightarrow C = \dfrac{5}{9}(-9) \Rightarrow C = \dfrac{-45}{9} \Rightarrow C = -5°C.$

75. To convert Fahrenheit to Celsius temperature, the formula given is $C = \dfrac{5}{9}(F - 32)$.

$C = \dfrac{5}{9}(-4 - 32) \Rightarrow C = \dfrac{5}{9}(-36) \Rightarrow C = \dfrac{-180}{9} \Rightarrow C = -20°C.$

77. The formula given for calculating the delay between seeing lightning and hearing the thunder is $D = \dfrac{x}{5}$ where

D represents the distance form the lightning and x represents the delay. Therefore, $D = \dfrac{x}{5} \Rightarrow D = \dfrac{12}{5} \Rightarrow$

$D = 2\dfrac{2}{5} = 2.4$ miles.

Checking Basic Concepts for Sections 2.3 & 2.4

1. (a) $3x = 36 \Rightarrow \dfrac{3x}{3} = \dfrac{36}{3} \Rightarrow x = 12$

   (b) $35 - x = 43 \Rightarrow 35 - 35 - x = 43 - 35 \Rightarrow -x = 8 \Rightarrow -1(x) = 8(-1) \Rightarrow x = -8$

2. $x + (x + 1) + (x + 2) = -93 \Rightarrow 3x + 3 = -93 \Rightarrow 3x + 3 - 3 = -93 - 3 \Rightarrow 3x = -96 \Rightarrow$

   $\dfrac{3x}{3} = \dfrac{-96}{3} \Rightarrow x = -32$. The three consecutive integers are $-32, -31, -30$.

3. $9.5\% = 0.095$

4. $\dfrac{5}{4} = 1\dfrac{1}{4} = 1.25 = 125\%$

5. Convert 8% to the decimal 0.08 and let x represent the unknown rate. Therefore, $x - 0.08x = 3850$. Thus,

   $x - 0.08x = 3850 \Rightarrow 0.92x = 3850 \Rightarrow \dfrac{0.92x}{0.92} = \dfrac{3850}{0.92} \Rightarrow x \approx 4285$. Thus, the rate in 1998 was about 4185.

6. Use the formula $D = rt$, where D is distance, r is the speed and t is the time. Thus, $390 = 60t \Rightarrow$

   $\dfrac{390}{60} = \dfrac{60t}{60} \Rightarrow 6.5 = t$. Thus, the travel time is 6.5 hours.

7. Let x represent the amount of the loan at 7% and $x + 2000$ represent the amount of the loan at 6%. Thus,

   $0.07x + 0.06(x + 2000) = 510 \Rightarrow 0.07x + 0.06x + 120 = 510 \Rightarrow 0.13x + 120 - 120 = 510 - 120 \Rightarrow$

   $0.13x = 390 \Rightarrow \dfrac{0.13x}{0.13} = \dfrac{390}{0.13} \Rightarrow x = 3000$. Thus, the loan at 7% was $3000 and the loan at 6% was $5000.

8. The area of a triangle is given by $A = \dfrac{1}{2}bh$. Thus, $A = \dfrac{1}{2}bh \Rightarrow 36 = \dfrac{1}{2}(6)h \Rightarrow 36 = 3h \Rightarrow \dfrac{36}{3} = \dfrac{3h}{3} \Rightarrow$

   $12 = h$. Thus, the height of the triangle is 12 inches.

9. The area of a circle is given by $A = \pi r^2$. Thus, $A = \pi r^2 \Rightarrow A = \pi(3)^2 \Rightarrow A = 9\pi \approx 28.3 \text{ ft}^2$.

   The circumference of a circle is given by $C = 2\pi r$. Thus, $C = 2\pi r \Rightarrow C = 2\pi 3 \Rightarrow C = 6\pi \approx 18.8$ feet.

10. Notice that the angle denoted by $3x$ is a right angle, that is, it is an angle measuring 90°. Thus,

    $3x = 90 \Rightarrow \dfrac{3x}{3} = \dfrac{90}{3} \Rightarrow x = 30$. Thus, the value of x is 30°.

11. $A = \pi r^2 + \pi r l \Rightarrow A - \pi r^2 = \pi r^2 - \pi r^2 + \pi r l \Rightarrow A - \pi r^2 = \pi r l \Rightarrow \dfrac{A - \pi r^2}{\pi r} = \dfrac{\pi r l}{\pi r} \Rightarrow l = \dfrac{A - \pi r^2}{\pi r}$

2.5: Linear Inequalities

Concepts

1. equals sign; $<$; $\le$; $>$; $\ge$

3. one

5. number line

7. $>$

9. $>$

Solutions and Number Line Graphs

11.

13.

15.

17.

19. $x < 0$

21. $x \le 3$

23. $x \ge 10$

25. Substitute x with 4 in order to test the inequality. Thus, $x + 5 > 5 \Rightarrow 4 + 5 > 5 \Rightarrow 9 > 5$. Because this inequality statement is true, $x = 4$ is a solution.

27. First, isolate x on one side of the statement. Thus, $5x \geq 25 \Rightarrow \dfrac{5x}{5} \geq \dfrac{25}{5} \Rightarrow x \geq 5$. Then substitute x with 5 in order to test the inequality. Thus, $x \geq 5 \Rightarrow 5 \geq 5$. Because this inequality statement is true, $x = 5$ is a solution.

29. First, isolate y on one side of the statement. Thus, $4y - 3 \leq 5 \Rightarrow 4y - 3 + 3 \leq 5 + 3 \Rightarrow 4y \leq 8 \Rightarrow$ $\dfrac{4y}{4} \leq \dfrac{8}{4} \Rightarrow y \leq 2$. Then substitute y with -3 in order to test the inequality. Thus, $y \leq 2 \Rightarrow -3 \leq 2$. Because this inequality statement is true, $y = -3$ is a solution.

31. First, isolate z on one side of the statement. Thus, $5(z + 1) < 3z - 7 \Rightarrow 5z + 5 < 3z - 7 \Rightarrow$ $5z - 3z + 5 < 3z - 3z - 7 \Rightarrow 2z + 5 < -7 \Rightarrow 2z + 5 - 5 < -7 - 5 \Rightarrow 2z < -12 \Rightarrow \dfrac{2z}{2} < \dfrac{-12}{2} \Rightarrow$ $z \leq -6$. Then substitute z with -7 in order to test the inequality. Thus, $z < -6 \Rightarrow -7 < -6$. Because this inequality statement is true, $z = -7$ is a solution.

33. First, isolate t on one side of the statement. Thus, $\dfrac{3}{2}t - \dfrac{1}{2} \geq 1 - t \Rightarrow \dfrac{3}{2}t + t - \dfrac{1}{2} \geq 1 - t + t \Rightarrow$ $\dfrac{5}{2}t - \dfrac{1}{2} \geq 1 \Rightarrow \dfrac{5}{2}t - \dfrac{1}{2} + \dfrac{1}{2} \geq 1 + \dfrac{1}{2} \Rightarrow \dfrac{5}{2}t \geq \dfrac{3}{2} \Rightarrow \dfrac{2}{5} \cdot \dfrac{5}{2}t \geq \dfrac{3}{2} \cdot \dfrac{2}{5} \Rightarrow t \geq \dfrac{3}{5}$. Then substitute t with -2 in order to test the inequality. Thus, $t \geq \dfrac{3}{5} \Rightarrow -2 \geq \dfrac{3}{5}$. Because this inequality statement is not true, $t = -2$ is not a solution.

Tables and Linear Inequalities

35. $x > -2$

37. $x < 1$

39. To complete the table, insert the x value into $-2x + 6$ whenever there is a missing value in the table. Thus,
$-2x + 6 \Rightarrow -2(2) + 6 \Rightarrow -4 + 6 = 2; -2x + 6 \Rightarrow -2(3) + 6 \Rightarrow -6 + 6 = 0;$
$-2x + 6 \Rightarrow -2(4) + 6 \Rightarrow -8 + 6 = -2$. Thus, the missing values in the table are 2, 0 and -2. See Figure 39.
From the table, we see that $-2x + 6 \leq 0$ whenever $x \geq 3$. Thus, the solution to the inequality is $x \geq 3$.

x	1	2	3	4	5
$-2x + 6$	4	2	0	-2	-4

Figure 39

x	-3	-2	-1	0	1
$5 - x$	8	7	6	5	4
$x + 7$	4	5	6	7	8

Figure 41

41. To complete the table, insert the x value into $5 - x$ and $x + 7$ whenever there is a missing value in the table.
$5 - x \Rightarrow 5 - (-2) = 7; 5 - x \Rightarrow 5 - (-1) = 6; 5 - x \Rightarrow 5 - (0) = 5.$
Thus, the missing values in the table that correspond to $5 - x$ are 7, 6 and 5.
$x + 7 \Rightarrow (-2) + 7 = 5; x + 7 \Rightarrow (-1) + 7 = 6; x + 7 \Rightarrow (0) + 7 = 7.$
Thus, the missing values in the table that correspond to $x + 7$ are 5, 6 and 7. See Figure 41.
From the table, we see that $5 - x > x + 7$ whenever $x < -1$. Thus, the solution to the inequality is $x < -1$.

Solving Linear Inequalities

43. $x - 3 > 0 \Rightarrow x - 3 + 3 > 0 + 3 \Rightarrow x > 3$. See Figure 43.

Figure 43   Figure 45

45. $3 - y \leq 5 \Rightarrow 3 - 3 - y \leq 5 - 3 \Rightarrow -y \leq 2 \Rightarrow -1(-y) \geq 2(-1) \Rightarrow y \geq -2$. See Figure 45.

47. $12 < 4 + z \Rightarrow 12 - 4 < 4 - 4 + z \Rightarrow 8 < z \Rightarrow z > 8$. See Figure 47.

Figure 47   Figure 49

49. $5 - 2t \geq 10 - t \Rightarrow 5 - 2t + t \geq 10 - t + t \Rightarrow 5 - t \geq 10 \Rightarrow 5 - 5 - t \geq 10 - 5 \Rightarrow -t \geq 5 \Rightarrow$

$-1(-t) \leq 5(-1) \Rightarrow t \leq -5$. See Figure 49.

51. $2x < 10 \Rightarrow \dfrac{2x}{2} < \dfrac{10}{2} \Rightarrow x < 5$. See Figure 51.

Figure 51   Figure 53

53. $-\dfrac{1}{2}t \geq 1 \Rightarrow \dfrac{-\frac{1}{2}t}{-\frac{1}{2}} \leq \dfrac{1}{-\frac{1}{2}} \Rightarrow t \leq -2$. See Figure 53.

55. $\dfrac{3}{4} > -5y \Rightarrow -5y < \dfrac{3}{4} \Rightarrow \dfrac{-5y}{-5} < \dfrac{\frac{3}{4}}{-5} \Rightarrow y < \dfrac{3}{4} \cdot \left(-\dfrac{1}{5}\right) \Rightarrow y > -\dfrac{3}{20}$. See Figure 55.

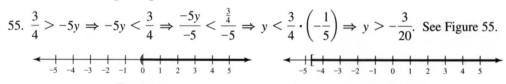

Figure 55   Figure 57

57. $-\dfrac{2}{3} \leq \dfrac{1}{7}z \Rightarrow \dfrac{1}{7}z \geq -\dfrac{2}{3} \Rightarrow \dfrac{7}{1}\left(\dfrac{1}{7}z\right) \geq -\dfrac{2}{3}\left(\dfrac{7}{1}\right) \Rightarrow z \geq -\dfrac{14}{3}$. See Figure 57.

59. $3x + 1 < 22 \Rightarrow 3x + 1 - 1 < 22 - 1 \Rightarrow 3x < 21 \Rightarrow \dfrac{3x}{3} < \dfrac{21}{3} \Rightarrow x < 7 \Rightarrow \{x \mid x < 7\}$

61. $5 - \dfrac{3}{4}x \geq 6 \Rightarrow 5 - 5 - \dfrac{3}{4}x \geq 6 - 5 \Rightarrow -\dfrac{3}{4}x \geq 1 \Rightarrow -\dfrac{4}{3}\left(-\dfrac{3}{4}x\right) \leq 1\left(-\dfrac{4}{3}\right) \Rightarrow x \leq -\dfrac{4}{3} \Rightarrow \left\{x \mid x \leq -\dfrac{4}{3}\right\}$

63. $45 > 6 - 2x \Rightarrow 6 - 2x < 45 \Rightarrow 6 - 6 - 2x < 45 - 6 \Rightarrow -2x < 39 \Rightarrow \dfrac{-2x}{-2} > \dfrac{39}{-2} \Rightarrow x > -\dfrac{39}{2} \Rightarrow$

$\left\{x \mid x > -\dfrac{39}{2}\right\}$

65. $5x - 2 \leq 3x + 1 \Rightarrow 5x - 3x - 2 \leq 3x - 3x + 1 \Rightarrow 2x - 2 \leq 1 \Rightarrow 2x - 2 + 2 \leq 1 + 2 \Rightarrow 2x \leq 3 \Rightarrow$

$\dfrac{2x}{2} \leq \dfrac{3}{2} \Rightarrow x \leq \dfrac{3}{2} \Rightarrow \left\{x \mid x \leq \dfrac{3}{2}\right\}$

67. $-x + 24 < x + 23 \Rightarrow -x - x + 24 < x - x + 23 \Rightarrow -2x + 24 < 23 \Rightarrow -2x + 24 - 24 < 23 - 24 \Rightarrow$

$-2x < -1 \Rightarrow \dfrac{-2x}{-2} > \dfrac{-1}{-2} \Rightarrow x > \dfrac{1}{2} \Rightarrow \left\{x \mid x > \dfrac{1}{2}\right\}$

69. $-(x + 1) \geq 3(x - 2) \Rightarrow -x - 1 \geq 3x - 6 \Rightarrow -x - 3x - 1 \geq 3x - 3x - 6 \Rightarrow -4x - 1 \geq -6 \Rightarrow$

$-4x - 1 + 1 \geq -6 + 1 \Rightarrow -4x \geq -5 \Rightarrow \dfrac{-4x}{-4} \leq \dfrac{-5}{-4} \Rightarrow x \leq \dfrac{5}{4} \Rightarrow \left\{ x \,\middle|\, x \leq \dfrac{5}{4} \right\}$

71. $3(2x - 1) > -(5 - 3x) \Rightarrow 6x + 3 > -5 + 3x \Rightarrow 6x - 3x + 3 > -5 + 3x - 3x \Rightarrow 3x + 3 > -5 \Rightarrow$

$3x + 3 - 3 > -5 - 3 \Rightarrow 3x > -8 \Rightarrow \dfrac{3x}{3} > \dfrac{-8}{3} \Rightarrow x > -\dfrac{8}{3} \Rightarrow \left\{ x \,\middle|\, x > -\dfrac{8}{3} \right\}$

73. $-(7x + 5) + 1 \geq 3x - 1 \Rightarrow -7x - 5 + 1 \geq 3x - 1 \Rightarrow -7x - 4 \geq 3x - 1 \Rightarrow$

$-7x - 3x - 4 \geq 3x - 3x - 1 \Rightarrow -10x - 4 \geq -1 \Rightarrow -10x - 4 + 4 \geq -1 + 4 \Rightarrow -10x \geq 3 \Rightarrow$

$\dfrac{-10x}{-10} \leq \dfrac{3}{-10} \Rightarrow x \leq -\dfrac{3}{10} \Rightarrow \left\{ x \,\middle|\, x \leq -\dfrac{3}{10} \right\}$

75. $1.6x + 0.4 \leq 0.4x \Rightarrow 1.6x - 0.4x + 0.4 \leq 0.4x - 0.4x \Rightarrow 1.2x + 0.4 \leq 0 \Rightarrow$

$1.2x + 0.4 - 0.4 \leq 0 - 0.4 \Rightarrow 1.2x \leq -0.4 \Rightarrow \dfrac{1.2x}{1.2} \leq \dfrac{-0.4}{1.2} \Rightarrow x \leq -\dfrac{1}{3} \Rightarrow \left\{ x \,\middle|\, x \leq -\dfrac{1}{3} \right\}$

77. $0.8x - 0.5 < x + 1 - 0.5x \Rightarrow 0.8x - 0.5 < 0.5x + 1 \Rightarrow 0.8x - 0.5x - 0.5 < 0.5x - 0.5x + 1 \Rightarrow$

$0.3x - 0.5 < 1 \Rightarrow 0.3x - 0.5 + 0.5 < 1 + 0.5 \Rightarrow 0.3x < 1.5 \Rightarrow \dfrac{0.3x}{0.3} < \dfrac{1.5}{0.3} \Rightarrow x < 5 \Rightarrow \{x \,|\, x < 5\}$

79. $-\dfrac{1}{2}\left(\dfrac{2}{3}x + 4\right) \geq x \Rightarrow -\dfrac{1}{3}x - 2 \geq x \Rightarrow -\dfrac{1}{3}x - x - 2 \geq x - x \Rightarrow -\dfrac{4}{3}x - 2 \geq 0 \Rightarrow$

$-\dfrac{4}{3}x - 2 + 2 \geq 0 + 2 \Rightarrow -\dfrac{4}{3}x \geq 2 \Rightarrow -\dfrac{3}{4}\left(-\dfrac{4}{3}x\right) \leq 2\left(-\dfrac{3}{4}\right) \Rightarrow x \leq -\dfrac{3}{2} \Rightarrow \left\{ x \,\middle|\, x \leq -\dfrac{3}{2} \right\}$

81. $\dfrac{3}{7}x + \dfrac{2}{7} > -\dfrac{1}{7}x - \dfrac{5}{14} \Rightarrow \dfrac{3}{7}x - \dfrac{1}{7}x + \dfrac{2}{7} > -\dfrac{1}{7}x + \dfrac{1}{7}x - \dfrac{5}{14} \Rightarrow \dfrac{4}{7}x + \dfrac{2}{7} > -\dfrac{5}{14} \Rightarrow$

$\dfrac{4}{7}x + \dfrac{2}{7} - \dfrac{2}{7} > -\dfrac{5}{14} - \dfrac{2}{7} \Rightarrow \dfrac{4}{7}x > -\dfrac{5}{14} - \dfrac{4}{14} \Rightarrow \dfrac{4}{7}x > -\dfrac{9}{14} \Rightarrow \dfrac{7}{4}\left(\dfrac{4}{7}x\right) > -\dfrac{9}{14}\left(\dfrac{7}{4}\right) \Rightarrow x > -\dfrac{63}{56} \Rightarrow$

$x > -\dfrac{9}{8} \Rightarrow \left\{ x \,\middle|\, x > -\dfrac{9}{8} \right\}$

83. $\dfrac{x}{3} + \dfrac{5x}{6} \leq \dfrac{2}{3} \Rightarrow \dfrac{2x}{6} + \dfrac{5x}{6} \leq \dfrac{2}{3} \Rightarrow \dfrac{7x}{6} \leq \dfrac{2}{3} \Rightarrow 6\left(\dfrac{7x}{6}\right) \leq \dfrac{2}{3}(6) \Rightarrow 7x \leq 4 \Rightarrow \dfrac{7x}{7} \leq \dfrac{4}{7} \Rightarrow x \leq \dfrac{4}{7} \Rightarrow$

$\left\{ x \,\middle|\, x \leq \dfrac{4}{7} \right\}$

85. $\dfrac{6x}{7} < \dfrac{1}{3}x + 1 \Rightarrow \dfrac{6x}{7} - \dfrac{1}{3}x < \dfrac{1}{3}x - \dfrac{1}{3}x + 1 \Rightarrow \dfrac{6x}{7} - \dfrac{x}{3} < 1 \Rightarrow \dfrac{18x}{21} - \dfrac{7x}{21} < 1 \Rightarrow \dfrac{11x}{21} < 1 \Rightarrow$

$21\left(\dfrac{11x}{21}\right) < 1(21) \Rightarrow 11x < 21 \Rightarrow \dfrac{11x}{11} < \dfrac{21}{11} \Rightarrow x < \dfrac{21}{11} \Rightarrow \left\{ x \,\middle|\, x < \dfrac{21}{11} \right\}$

Translating Inequalities

87. $x > 60$

89. $x \geq 21$

91. $x > 40,000$

93. $x \leq 70$

Applications

95. $2(x + 5) + 2x < 50 \Rightarrow 2x + 10 + 2x < 50 \Rightarrow 4x + 10 < 50 \Rightarrow 4x + 10 - 10 < 50 - 10 \Rightarrow$

    $4x < 40 \Rightarrow \dfrac{4x}{4} < \dfrac{40}{4} \Rightarrow x < 10$ feet.

97. The area of a triangle is $\dfrac{1}{2}bh$. Substitute 12 for h and solve. $\dfrac{1}{2}bh < 120 \Rightarrow \dfrac{1}{2}b(12) < 120 \Rightarrow$

    $6b < 120 \Rightarrow \dfrac{6b}{6} < \dfrac{120}{6} \Rightarrow b < 20$. Thus, the base of the triangle must be less than 20 inches.

99. Let x represent the unknown test score. Then, $\dfrac{74 + x}{2} \geq 80 \Rightarrow 2\left(\dfrac{74 + x}{2}\right) \geq 80(2) \Rightarrow 74 + x \geq 160 \Rightarrow$

    $74 - 74 + x \geq 160 - 74 \Rightarrow x \geq 86$. Thus, the student needs a score of 86 or more to maintain an average of

    at least 80.

101. Let x represent the number of hours. We see that there is a \$2.00 cost for the first half hour and \$1.25 cost for

    each hour after that. Therefore, $2 + 1.25x \leq 8 \Rightarrow 2 - 2 + 1.25x \leq 8 - 2 \Rightarrow 1.25x \leq 6 \Rightarrow$

    $\dfrac{1.25x}{1.25} \leq \dfrac{6}{1.25} \Rightarrow x \leq 4.8$. This result would indicate that the student can park for as long as 4.8 hours for

    \$8.00. However, because a partial hour of parking is charged as a full hour, the longest amount of time that

    the student could park for \$8.00 is 4.5 hours.

103. Let x represent the number of days. Then, $25x + 0.20(90)x \leq 200 \Rightarrow 25x + 18x \leq 200 \Rightarrow 43x \leq 200 \Rightarrow$

    $\dfrac{43x}{43} \leq \dfrac{200}{43} \Rightarrow x \leq 4.65$. Because the car can not be rented for a partial day, the person can rent the car for 4 days.

105. (a) $C = 1.5x + 2000$

    (b) $R = 12x$

    (c) $P = 12x - (1.5x + 2000) \Rightarrow P = 10.5x - 2000$

    (d) To yield a positive profit, revenue must be greater than cost. Then, $12x > 1.5x + 2000 \Rightarrow$

    $12x - 1.5x > 1.5x - 1.5x + 2000 \Rightarrow 10.5x > 2000 \Rightarrow \dfrac{10.5x}{10.5} > \dfrac{2000}{10.5} \Rightarrow x > 190.476$. Thus, 191

    or more compact discs must be sold to yield a profit.

107. (a) Set the distances equal and then solve for x. Then, $\dfrac{1}{6}x = \dfrac{1}{8}x + 2 \Rightarrow 4x = 3x + 48 \Rightarrow x = 48$.

    Thus, at 48 minutes the athletes are the same distance from the parking lot.

    (b) $\dfrac{1}{6}x > \dfrac{1}{8}x + 2 \Rightarrow 4x > 3x + 48 \Rightarrow x > 48$. Thus, after more than 48 minutes, the first athlete is

    farther from the parking lot than the second athlete.

109. Because $T = 80 - 29x$, set an inequality statement with T equal to 7.5 and solve. Then,

    $80 - 29x < 7.5 \Rightarrow 80 - 80 - 29x < 7.5 - 80 \Rightarrow -29x < -72.5 \Rightarrow \dfrac{-29x}{-29} > \dfrac{-72.5}{-29} \Rightarrow x > 2.5$.

    Thus, at altitudes more than 2.5 miles, the air temperature is less than 7.5°F.

111. $0.1(x - 1970) + 13.1 \geq 15.5 \Rightarrow 0.1x - 197 + 13.1 \geq 15.5 \Rightarrow 0.1x - 183.9 \geq 15.5 \Rightarrow$

    $0.1x - 183.9 + 183.9 \geq 15.5 + 183.9 \Rightarrow 0.1x \geq 199.4 \Rightarrow \dfrac{0.1x}{0.1} \geq \dfrac{199.4}{0.1} \Rightarrow x \geq 1994$. Thus, in

    year 1994 and later, a 65-year-old man could expect to live an additional 15.5 years or more.

Checking Basic Concepts for Section 2.5

1.

2. $x < 1$

3. When $x = -2$, then $5 - 2(-2) = 5 + 4 = 9$; When $x = -1$, then $5 - 2(-1) = 5 + 2 = 7$; When $x = 0$, then $5 - 2(0) = 5 - 0 = 5$; When $x = 1$, then $5 - 2(1) = 5 - 2 = 3$. Therefore, the numbers that complete the table are 9, 7, 5 and 3. See Figure 3.

x	-2	-1	0	1	2
$5 - 2x$	9	7	5	3	1

Figure 3

From the table, we see that $5 - 2x \le 7$ whenever $x \ge -1$. Thus, the solution to the inequality is $x \ge -1$.

4. (a) $x + 5 > 8 \Rightarrow x + 5 - 5 > 8 - 5 \Rightarrow x > 3 \Rightarrow \{x \mid x > 3\}$

   (b) $-\dfrac{5}{7}x \le 25 \Rightarrow -\dfrac{7}{5}\left(-\dfrac{5}{7}x\right) \ge 25\left(-\dfrac{7}{5}\right) \Rightarrow x \ge -\dfrac{175}{5} \Rightarrow x \ge -35 \Rightarrow \{x \mid x \ge -35\}$

   (c) $3x \ge -2(1 - 2x) + 3 \Rightarrow 3x \ge -2 + 4x + 3 \Rightarrow 3x \ge 1 + 4x \Rightarrow 3x - 4x \ge 1 + 4x - 4x \Rightarrow$
   $-x \ge 1 \Rightarrow -1(-x) \le -1(1) \Rightarrow x \le -1 \Rightarrow \{x \mid x \le -1\}$

5. Let l represent length and w represent width. Then, $l = 2w + 5$. Therefore, $2(2w + 5) + 2w > 88 \Rightarrow$
   $4w + 10 + 2w > 88 \Rightarrow 6w + 10 > 88 \Rightarrow 6w + 10 - 10 > 88 - 10 \Rightarrow 6w > 78 \Rightarrow$
   $\dfrac{6w}{6} > \dfrac{78}{6} \Rightarrow w > 13$. Thus, the possible widths must be more than 13 inches.

Chapter 2 Review Exercises

Section 2.1

1. $x + 9 = 3 \Rightarrow x + 9 - 9 = 3 - 9 \Rightarrow x = -6$

2. $x - 4 = -2 \Rightarrow x - 4 + 4 = -2 + 4 \Rightarrow x = 2$

3. $x - \dfrac{3}{4} = \dfrac{3}{2} \Rightarrow x - \dfrac{3}{4} + \dfrac{3}{4} = \dfrac{3}{2} + \dfrac{3}{4} \Rightarrow x = \dfrac{6}{4} + \dfrac{3}{4} \Rightarrow x = \dfrac{9}{4}$

4. $x + 0.5 = 0 \Rightarrow x + 0.5 - 0.5 = 0 - 0.5 \Rightarrow x = -0.5 \Rightarrow x = -\dfrac{1}{2}$

5. $4x = 12 \Rightarrow \dfrac{4x}{4} = \dfrac{12}{4} \Rightarrow x = 3$

6. $3x = -7 \Rightarrow \dfrac{3x}{3} = \dfrac{-7}{3} \Rightarrow x = -\dfrac{7}{3}$

7. $-0.5x = 1.25 \Rightarrow \dfrac{-0.5x}{-0.5} = \dfrac{1.25}{-0.5} \Rightarrow x = -2.5$

8. $-\dfrac{1}{3}x = \dfrac{7}{6} \Rightarrow -\dfrac{3}{1}\left(-\dfrac{1}{3}x\right) = \dfrac{7}{6}\left(-\dfrac{3}{1}\right) \Rightarrow x = -\dfrac{21}{6} \Rightarrow x = -\dfrac{7}{2}$

Section 2.2

9. The equation $5x - 3 = 0$ is linear; $a = 5, b = -3$

10. The equation $-4x + 3 = 2$ is linear.

$-4x + 3 = 2 \Rightarrow -4x + 3 - 2 = 2 - 2 \Rightarrow -4x + 1 = 0;\ a = -4, b = 1$

11. The equation $0.55x = 0.05$ is linear.

$0.55x = 0.05 \Rightarrow 0.55x - 0.05 = 0.05 - 0.05 \Rightarrow 0.55x - 0.05 = 0;\ a = 0.55, b = -0.05$

12. The equation $\dfrac{3}{8}x^2 - x = \dfrac{1}{4}$ is not a linear equation because it cannot be written in the form $ax + b = 0$.

13. $4x - 5 = 3 \Rightarrow 4x - 5 + 5 = 3 + 5 \Rightarrow 4x = 8 \Rightarrow \dfrac{4x}{4} = \dfrac{8}{4} \Rightarrow x = 2$. To check the solution, substitute

    2 for x in the original equation: $4x - 5 = 3 \Rightarrow 4(2) - 5 = 3 \Rightarrow 8 - 5 = 3$. Because this statement is true,

    the solution checks.

14. $7 - \dfrac{1}{2}x = -4 \Rightarrow 7 - 7 - \dfrac{1}{2}x = -4 - 7 \Rightarrow -\dfrac{1}{2}x = -11 \Rightarrow -\dfrac{2}{1}\left(-\dfrac{1}{2}x\right) = -\dfrac{11}{1}\left(-\dfrac{2}{1}\right) \Rightarrow x = 22$. To check

    the solution, substitute 22 for x in the original equation: $7 - \dfrac{1}{2}x = -4 \Rightarrow 7 - \dfrac{1}{2}(22) = -4 \Rightarrow 7 - 11 = -4$.

    Because this statement is true, the solution checks.

15. $5(x - 3) = 12 \Rightarrow 5x - 15 = 12 \Rightarrow 5x - 15 + 15 = 12 + 15 \Rightarrow 5x = 27 \Rightarrow \dfrac{5x}{5} = \dfrac{27}{5} \Rightarrow x = \dfrac{27}{5}$. To

    check the solution, substitute $\dfrac{27}{5}$ for x in the original equation: $5\left(\dfrac{27}{5} - 3\right) = 12 \Rightarrow 5\left(\dfrac{27}{5} - \dfrac{15}{5}\right) = 12 \Rightarrow$

    $5\left(\dfrac{12}{5}\right) = 12 \Rightarrow \dfrac{60}{5} = 12$. Because this statement is true, the solution checks.

16. $1 - (x - 3) = 6 + 2x \Rightarrow 1 - x + 3 = 6 + 2x \Rightarrow 4 - x = 6 + 2x \Rightarrow 4 - x + x = 6 + 2x + x \Rightarrow$

    $4 = 6 + 3x \Rightarrow 4 - 6 = 6 - 6 + 3x \Rightarrow -2 = 3x \Rightarrow \dfrac{-2}{3} = \dfrac{3x}{3} \Rightarrow -\dfrac{2}{3} = x \Rightarrow x = -\dfrac{2}{3}$. To check the

    solution, substitute $-\dfrac{2}{3}$ for x in the original equation: $1 - \left(-\dfrac{2}{3} - 3\right) = 6 + 2\left(-\dfrac{2}{3}\right) \Rightarrow$

    $1 + \dfrac{2}{3} + 3 = 6 - \dfrac{4}{3} \Rightarrow 4\dfrac{2}{3} = 4\dfrac{2}{3}$. Because this statement is true, the solution checks.

17. $3.4x - 4 = 5 - 0.6x \Rightarrow 3.4x - 4 + 4 = 5 + 4 - 0.6x \Rightarrow 3.4x = 9 - 0.6x \Rightarrow$

    $3.4x + 0.6x = 9 - 0.6x + 0.6x \Rightarrow 4x = 9 \Rightarrow \dfrac{4x}{4} = \dfrac{9}{4} \Rightarrow x = \dfrac{9}{4}$. To check the solution, substitute $\dfrac{9}{4}$ for x

    in the original equation: $3.4\left(\dfrac{9}{4}\right) - 4 = 5 - 0.6\left(\dfrac{9}{4}\right) \Rightarrow 3.4(2.25) - 4 = 5 - 0.6(2.25) \Rightarrow$

    $7.65 - 4 = 5 - 1.35 \Rightarrow 3.65 = 3.65$. Because this statement is true, the solution checks.

18. $-\dfrac{1}{3}(3 - 6x) = -(x + 2) + 1 \Rightarrow -1 + 2x = -x - 2 + 1 \Rightarrow 2x - 1 = -x - 1 \Rightarrow$

    $2x - 1 + 1 = -x - 1 + 1 \Rightarrow 2x = -x \Rightarrow 2x + x = -x + x \Rightarrow 3x = 0 \Rightarrow \dfrac{3x}{3} = \dfrac{0}{3} \Rightarrow x = 0$. To check

    the solution, substitute 0 for x in the original equation: $-\dfrac{1}{3}(3 - 6(0)) = -(0 + 2) + 1 \Rightarrow$

    $-\dfrac{1}{3}(3) = -2 + 1 \Rightarrow -1 = -1$. Because this statement is true, the solution checks.

19. $\frac{2}{3}x - \frac{1}{6} = \frac{5}{12} \Rightarrow \frac{2}{3}x - \frac{1}{6} + \frac{1}{6} = \frac{5}{12} + \frac{1}{6} \Rightarrow \frac{2}{3}x = \frac{5}{12} + \frac{2}{12} \Rightarrow \frac{2}{3}x = \frac{7}{12} \Rightarrow \frac{3}{2}\left(\frac{2}{3}x\right) = \frac{7}{12}\left(\frac{3}{2}\right) \Rightarrow$

$x = \frac{21}{24} \Rightarrow x = \frac{7}{8}$. To check the solution, substitute $\frac{7}{8}$ for x in the original equation: $\frac{2}{3}\left(\frac{7}{8}\right) - \frac{1}{6} = \frac{5}{12} \Rightarrow$

$\frac{14}{24} - \frac{4}{24} = \frac{10}{24} \Rightarrow \frac{10}{24} = \frac{10}{24}$. Because this statement is true, the solution checks.

20. $2y - 3(2 - y) = 5 + y \Rightarrow 2y - 6 + 3y = 5 + y \Rightarrow 5y - 6 = 5 + y \Rightarrow 5y - y - 6 = 5 + y - y \Rightarrow$

$4y - 6 = 5 \Rightarrow 4y - 6 + 6 = 5 + 6 \Rightarrow 4y = 11 \Rightarrow \frac{4y}{4} = \frac{11}{4} \Rightarrow y = \frac{11}{4}$. To check the solution,

substitute $\frac{11}{4}$ for y in the original equation: $2\left(\frac{11}{4}\right) - 3\left(2 - \frac{11}{4}\right) = 5 + \frac{11}{4} \Rightarrow \frac{22}{4} - 6 + \frac{33}{4} = \frac{20}{4} + \frac{11}{4} \Rightarrow$

$\frac{22}{4} - \frac{24}{4} + \frac{33}{4} = \frac{20}{4} + \frac{11}{4} \Rightarrow \frac{31}{4} = \frac{31}{4}$. Because this statement is true, the solution checks.

21. First, solve for x: $4(3x - 2) = 2(6x + 5) \Rightarrow 12x - 8 = 12x + 10 \Rightarrow$

$12x - 12x - 8 = 12x - 12x + 10 \Rightarrow -8 = 10$. Because this statement is not true, the equation has zero solutions.

22. First, solve for x: $5(3x - 1) = 15x - 5 \Rightarrow 15x - 5 = 15x - 3$. Because this statement is true for any value

of x, the equation has infinitely many solutions.

23. First, solve for x: $8x = 5x + 3x \Rightarrow 8x = 8x$. Because this statement is true for any value of x, the equation

has infinitely many solutions.

24. First solve for x: $9x - 2 = 8x - 2 \Rightarrow 9x - 8x - 2 = 8x - 8x - 2 \Rightarrow x - 2 = -2 \Rightarrow$

$x - 2 + 2 = -2 + 2 \Rightarrow x = 0$. Thus, there is one solution to the equation.

25. When $x = 1.0$, then $-2(1.0) + 3 = -2 + 3 = 1$; When $x = 1.5$, then $-2(1.5) + 3 = -3 + 3 = 0$;

When $x = 2.0$, then $-2(2.0) + 3 = -4 + 3 = -1$; When $x = 2.5$, then $-2(2.5) + 3 = -5 + 3 = -2$;

Thus, the missing values in the table are $1, 0, -1$ and -2. See Figure 25. From the table we see that when

$x = 1.5$, the value of $-2x + 3$ is 0.

x	0.5	1.0	1.5	2.0	2.5
$-2x + 3$	2	1	0	-1	-2

Figure 25

x	-2	-1	0	1	2
$-(x + 1) + 3$	4	3	2	1	0

Figure 26

26. When $x = -2$, then $-(-2 + 1) + 3 = 2 - 1 + 3 = 4$; When $x = -1$, then $-(-1 + 1) + 3 = 1 - 1 + 3 = 3$;

When $x = 0$, then $-(0 + 1) + 3 = 0 - 1 + 3 = 2$; When $x = 1$, then $-(1 + 1) + 3 = -2 + 3 = 1$;

Thus, the missing values in the table are $4, 3, 2$ and 1. See Figure 26. From the table we see that when $x = 0$,

the value of $-(x + 1) + 3$ is 2.

Section 2.3

27. $6x = 72 \Rightarrow \frac{6x}{6} = \frac{72}{6} \Rightarrow x = 12$

28. $x + 18 = -23 \Rightarrow x + 18 - 18 = -23 - 18 \Rightarrow x = -41$

29. $2x - 5 = x + 4 \Rightarrow 2x - 5 + 5 = x + 4 + 5 \Rightarrow 2x = x + 9 \Rightarrow 2x - x = x - x + 9 \Rightarrow x = 9$

30. $x + 4 = 3x \Rightarrow x - 3x + 4 = 3x - 3x \Rightarrow -2x + 4 = 0 \Rightarrow -2x + 4 - 4 = 0 - 4 \Rightarrow -2x = -4 \Rightarrow$

$\dfrac{-2x}{-2} = \dfrac{-4}{-2} \Rightarrow x = 2$

31. $x + (x + 1) + (x + 2) + (x + 3) = 70 \Rightarrow 4x + 6 = 70 \Rightarrow 4x + 6 - 6 = 70 - 6 \Rightarrow 4x = 64 \Rightarrow$

$\dfrac{4x}{4} = \dfrac{64}{4} \Rightarrow x = 16.$ The numbers are 16, 17, 18 and 19.

32. $x + (x + 1) + (x + 2) = -153 \Rightarrow 3x + 3 = -153 \Rightarrow 3x + 3 - 3 = -153 - 3 \Rightarrow 3x = -156 \Rightarrow$

$\dfrac{3x}{3} = \dfrac{-156}{3} \Rightarrow x = -52.$ The numbers are $-52, -51$ and -50.

33. $85\% = \dfrac{85}{100} = \dfrac{17}{20};\ 85\% = 0.85$

34. $5.6\% = \dfrac{56}{1000} = \dfrac{7}{125};\ 5.6\% = 0.056$

35. $0.03\% = \dfrac{.03}{100} = \dfrac{3}{10,000};\ 0.03\% = 0.0003$

36. $342\% = \dfrac{342}{100} = \dfrac{171}{50};\ 342\% = 3.42$

37. $0.89 = 89\%$

38. $0.005 = 0.5\%$

39. $2.3 = 230\%$

40. $1 = 100\%$

Section 2.4

41. $d = rt \Rightarrow d = 8(3) \Rightarrow d = 24$ miles.

42. $d = rt \Rightarrow d = 70(55) \Rightarrow d = 3850$ feet.

43. $d = rt \Rightarrow 500 = r(20) \Rightarrow \dfrac{500}{20} = r\dfrac{20}{20} \Rightarrow \dfrac{500}{20} = r \Rightarrow r = 25$ yd/sec.

44. $d = rt \Rightarrow 125 = 15t \Rightarrow \dfrac{125}{15} = \dfrac{15t}{15} \Rightarrow \dfrac{125}{15} = t \Rightarrow t = \dfrac{25}{3}$ hours.

45. The area of a triangle is given as $\dfrac{1}{2}$(base)(height). Thus, $A = \dfrac{1}{2}(b)(h) = \dfrac{1}{2}(5)(3) = 7.5$ m^2.

46. The area of a circle is given as πr^2 where r represents radius. Thus, $A = \pi r^2 = \pi(6^2) = 36\pi \approx 113.1$ ft^2.

47. The area of a rectangle is given as length (l) times width (w). Thus, $A = lw = (36)(24) = 864$ in^2 or 6 ft^2.

48. $A = \dfrac{1}{2}bh$, where A represents area, b represents the length of the base and h represents the height. Thus,

$A = \dfrac{1}{2}bh = \dfrac{1}{2}(13)(7) = \dfrac{1}{2}(91) = 45\dfrac{1}{2} = 45.5$ in^2.

49. The circumference of a circle is given as $2\pi r$, where r represents radius. Thus, $r = \dfrac{1}{2}$(diameter) $= \dfrac{1}{2}(18) = 9.$

$C = 2\pi r = 2\pi(9) = 18\pi \approx 56.5$ feet.

50. $A = \pi r^2$, where A represents area and r represents radius. Thus, $A = \pi r^2 = \pi(5^2) = 25\pi \approx 78.5$ in^2.

51. The angles in a triangle must add up to $180°$. Let x represent the unknown angle. Thus,

$90 + 40 + x = 180 \Rightarrow 130 + x = 180 \Rightarrow 130 - 130 + x = 180 - 130 \Rightarrow x = 50°$.

52. The angles in a triangle must add up to $180°$. Thus, $x + 3x + 4x = 180 \Rightarrow 8x = 180 \Rightarrow \dfrac{8x}{8} = \dfrac{180}{8} \Rightarrow$
$x = 22.5°$.

53. $V = \pi r^2 h = \pi(5^2)(25) = \pi(25)(25) = 625\pi \approx 1963.5 \text{ in}^3$.

54. First, convert height (h) and base (b) to inches. $h = 5 \text{ feet} = 5(12) = 60 \text{ inches}$ and
$b = 3 \text{ feet} = 3(12) = 36 \text{ inches}$. Then, $A = \dfrac{1}{2}(a + b)h = \dfrac{1}{2}(36 + 18)60 = \dfrac{1}{2}(54)60 = (27)60 = 1620 \text{ in}^2$.

Or, convert the base in inches to feet. $b = 18 \text{ inches} = \dfrac{18}{12} = 1.5 \text{ feet}$. Then,

$A = \dfrac{1}{2}(a + b)h = \dfrac{1}{2}(3 + 1.5)5 = \dfrac{1}{2}(4.5)5 = (2.25)5 = 11.25 \text{ ft}^2$.

55. $a = x + y \Rightarrow a - y = x + y - y \Rightarrow a - y = x \Rightarrow x = a - y$

56. $P = 2x + 2y \Rightarrow P - 2y = 2x + 2y - 2y \Rightarrow P - 2y = 2x \Rightarrow \dfrac{P - 2y}{2} = \dfrac{2x}{2} \Rightarrow \dfrac{P - 2y}{2} = x \Rightarrow$
$x = \dfrac{P - 2y}{2}$

57. $z = 2xy \Rightarrow \dfrac{z}{2x} = \dfrac{2xy}{2x} \Rightarrow \dfrac{z}{2x} = y \Rightarrow y = \dfrac{z}{2x}$

58. $S = \dfrac{a + b + c}{3} \Rightarrow 3S = \dfrac{a + b + c}{3} \cdot 3 \Rightarrow 3S = a + b + c \Rightarrow 3S - a - c = a + b + c - a - c \Rightarrow$
$3S - a - c = b \Rightarrow b = 3S - a - c$

59. $T = \dfrac{a}{3} + \dfrac{b}{4} \Rightarrow \dfrac{12T}{12} = \dfrac{4a}{12} + \dfrac{3b}{12} \Rightarrow 12\left(\dfrac{12T}{12}\right) = 12\left(\dfrac{4a}{12}\right) + 12\left(\dfrac{3b}{12}\right) \Rightarrow 12T = 4a + 3b \Rightarrow$

$12T - 4a = 4a - 4a + 3b \Rightarrow 12T - 4a = 3b \Rightarrow \dfrac{12T - 4a}{3} = \dfrac{3b}{3} \Rightarrow \dfrac{12T - 4a}{3} = b \Rightarrow b = \dfrac{12T - 4a}{3}$

60. $cd = ab + bc \Rightarrow cd - bc = ab + bc - bc \Rightarrow cd - bc = ab \Rightarrow c(d - b) = ab \Rightarrow$
$\dfrac{c(d - b)}{(d - b)} = \dfrac{ab}{(d - b)} \Rightarrow c = \dfrac{ab}{d - b}$

Section 2.5

61.

62.

63.

64.

65. $x < 3$

66. $x \geq -1$

67. Substitute -3 for x and check for accuracy: $2x + 1 \leq 5 \Rightarrow 2(-3) + 1 \leq 5 \Rightarrow -6 + 1 \leq 5 \Rightarrow -5 \leq 5$.
Because this statement is true, $x = -3$ is a solution to the inequality.

68. Substitute 4 for x and check for accuracy: $5 - \dfrac{1}{2}(x) \geq -1 \Rightarrow 5 - \dfrac{1}{2}(4) \geq -1 \Rightarrow 5 - 2 \geq -1 \Rightarrow 3 \geq -1$.

    Because this statement is true, $x = 4$ is a solution to the inequality.

69. Substitute -2 for x and check for accuracy: $1 - (x + 3) \geq x \Rightarrow 1 - (-2 + 3) \geq -2 \Rightarrow 1 - 1 \geq -2 \Rightarrow$

    $0 \geq -2$. Because this statement is true, $x = -2$ is a solution to the inequality.

70. Substitute -1 for x and check for accuracy: $4(x + 1) < -(5 - x) \Rightarrow 4(-1 + 1) < -(5 - (-1)) \Rightarrow$

    $4(0) < -(6) \Rightarrow 0 < -6$. Because this statement is not true, $x = -1$ is not a solution to the inequality.

71. When $x = 1$, then $5 - x = 5 - 1 = 4$; When $x = 2$, then $5 - x = 5 - 2 = 3$;

    When $x = 3$, then $5 - x = 5 - 3 = 2$; When $x = 4$, then $5 - x = 5 - 4 = 1$;

    Thus, the missing values in the table are 4, 3, 2 and 1. See Figure 71. From the table we see that

    $5 - x > 3$, when $x < 2$.

x	0	1	2	3	4
$5 - x$	5	4	3	2	1

Figure 71

x	1	1.5	2	2.5	3
$2x - 5$	-3	-2	-1	0	1

Figure 72

72. When $x = 1.5$, then $2x - 5 = 2(1.5) - 5 = 3 - 5 = -2$;

    When $x = 2$, then $2x - 5 = 2(2) - 5 = 4 - 5 = -1$;

    When $x = 2.5$, then $2x - 5 = 2(2.5) - 5 = 5 - 5 = 0$;

    When $x = 3$, then $2x - 5 = 2(3) - 5 = 6 - 5 = 1$;

    Thus, the missing values in the table are $-2, -1, 0$ and 1. See Figure 72. From the table we see that

    $2x - 5 \leq 0$ when $x \leq 2.5$.

73. $x - 3 > 0 \Rightarrow x - 3 + 3 > 0 + 3 \Rightarrow x > 3 \Rightarrow \{x \,|\, x > 3\}$

74. $-2x \leq 10 \Rightarrow \dfrac{-2x}{-2} \geq \dfrac{10}{-2} \Rightarrow x \geq -5 \Rightarrow \{x \,|\, x \geq -5\}$

75. $5 - 2x \geq 7 \Rightarrow 5 - 5 - 2x \geq 7 - 5 \Rightarrow -2x \geq 2 \Rightarrow \dfrac{-2x}{-2} \leq \dfrac{2}{-2} \Rightarrow x \leq -1 \Rightarrow \{x \,|\, x \leq -1\}$

76. $3(x - 1) < 20 \Rightarrow 3x - 3 < 20 \Rightarrow 3x - 3 + 3 < 20 + 3 \Rightarrow 3x < 23 \Rightarrow \dfrac{3x}{3} < \dfrac{23}{3} \Rightarrow x < \dfrac{23}{3} \Rightarrow$

    $\left\{x \,\middle|\, x < \dfrac{23}{3}\right\}$

77. $5x \leq 3 - (4x + 2) \Rightarrow 5x \leq 3 - 4x - 2 \Rightarrow 5x + 4x \leq 3 - 4x + 4x - 2 \Rightarrow 9x \leq 1 \Rightarrow \dfrac{9x}{9} \leq \dfrac{1}{9} \Rightarrow$

    $x \leq \dfrac{1}{9} \Rightarrow \left\{x \,\middle|\, x \leq \dfrac{1}{9}\right\}$

78. $3x - 2(4 - x) \geq x + 1 \Rightarrow 3x - 8 + 2x \geq x + 1 \Rightarrow 5x - 8 \geq x + 1 \Rightarrow 5x - 8 + 8 \geq x + 1 + 8 \Rightarrow 5x \geq x + 9 \Rightarrow$

    $5x - x \geq x - x + 9 \Rightarrow 4x \geq 9 \Rightarrow \dfrac{4x}{4} \geq \dfrac{9}{4} \Rightarrow x \geq \dfrac{9}{4} \Rightarrow \left\{x \,\middle|\, x \geq \dfrac{9}{4}\right\}$

79. $x < 50$

80. $x \leq 45{,}000$

81. $x \geq 16$

82. $x < 1995$

Applications

83. (a) See Figure 83.

(b) $R = 2 + \dfrac{3}{4}x$

(c) At 5 PM, $x = 5$; $R = 2 + \dfrac{3}{4}(5) = 2 + \dfrac{15}{4} = \dfrac{23}{4} = 5\dfrac{3}{4}$ inches. This value does agree with the table.

(d) At 3:45 PM, $x = 3.75$; $R = 2 + \dfrac{3}{4}\left(3\dfrac{3}{4}\right) = 2 + \dfrac{3}{4}\left(\dfrac{15}{4}\right) = 2 + \dfrac{45}{16} = \dfrac{32}{16} + \dfrac{45}{16} = \dfrac{77}{16} = 4\dfrac{13}{16}$ inches.

Time	12:00	1:00	2:00	3:00	4:00	5:00
Rainfall (R)	2	2.75	3.5	4.25	5	5.75

Figure 83

Hours (x)	1	2	3	4	5
Distance (D)	40	30	20	10	0

Figure 85

84. Let x represent the cost of the laptop. $0.05x = 106.25 \Rightarrow \dfrac{0.05x}{0.05} = \dfrac{106.25}{0.05} \Rightarrow x = 2125$. Thus, the cost of the laptop is \$2125.

85. (a) See Figure 85.

(b) $D = 50 - 10x$

(c) $D = 50 - 10x = 50 - 10(3) = 50 - 30 = 20$ miles. This value does agree with the table.

(d) $D \geq 20$. Thus, $50 - 10x \geq 20 \Rightarrow 50 - 50 - 10x \geq 20 - 50 \Rightarrow -10x \geq -30 \Rightarrow \dfrac{-10x}{-10} \leq \dfrac{-30}{-10} \Rightarrow$

$x \leq 3$. Thus, the bicyclist was at least 20 miles from home when he had traveled for 3 or fewer hours, or from noon to 3 PM.

86. $N = \dfrac{1}{15}x - 130.4$. Substitute 2.8 for N and solve for x: $2.8 = \dfrac{1}{15}x - 130.4 \Rightarrow$

$2.8 + 130.4 = \dfrac{1}{15}x - 130.4 + 130.4 \Rightarrow 133.2 = \dfrac{1}{15}x \Rightarrow 133.2\left(\dfrac{15}{1}\right) = \dfrac{15}{1}\left(\dfrac{1}{15}x\right) \Rightarrow 1998 = x \Rightarrow$

$x = 1998$. Thus, in the year 1998, the number reached 2.8 million.

87. First, subtract the smaller number from the larger to obtain the difference between the:

419,401 − 230,500 = 188,901. Then, determine what percentage 188,901 is of 230,500. Do this by dividing

the smaller number by the larger: $\dfrac{188,901}{230,500} \approx 0.82$. Thus, there was about an 82% change in master's degrees

received between 1971 and 1997.

88. Use the distance (d) = rate (r) × time (t) formula. Determine how long it takes the faster car to be 2 miles

ahead of the slower car, let ($r + 12$) be the rate of the faster car and r be the rate of the slower car. Thus,

$d = rt \Rightarrow 2 = (r + 12 - r)t \Rightarrow 2 = 12t \Rightarrow \dfrac{2}{12} = \dfrac{12t}{12} \Rightarrow \dfrac{1}{6} = t \Rightarrow t = \dfrac{1}{6}$ hour, or 10 minutes.

89. Let x represent the amount of water. The amount of salt on one side of the equation must equal the amount of

salt on the other side. Thus, $100(0.03) + x(0.00) = (100 + x)(0.02) \Rightarrow 3 + 0 = 2 + 0.02x \Rightarrow$

$3 - 2 = 2 - 2 + 0.02x \Rightarrow 1 = 0.02x \Rightarrow \dfrac{1}{0.02} = \dfrac{0.02x}{0.02} \Rightarrow 50 = x \Rightarrow x = 50$. Thus, 50 ml of water must

be added.

90. Let x represent the higher interest rate. Then, $800(x) + 500(x - 0.02) = 55 \Rightarrow 800x + 500x - 10 = 55 \Rightarrow$

    $1300x - 10 + 10 = 55 + 10 \Rightarrow 1300x = 65 \Rightarrow \dfrac{1300x}{1300} = \dfrac{65}{1300} \Rightarrow x = 0.05$. Thus, the interest rate on the

    $800 loan is 5% and the interest rate on the $500 loan is 3%.

91. Perimeter $(P) = 2 \times$ width $(w) =$ length (l). Then, $w = l - 10 \Rightarrow 2(l - 10) + 2l = 112 \Rightarrow$

    $2l - 20 + 2l = 112 \Rightarrow 2l - 20 + 20 + 2l = 112 + 20 \Rightarrow 4l = 132 \Rightarrow \dfrac{4l}{4} = \dfrac{132}{4} \Rightarrow l = 33$. Because

    the length is 33, the width is $(l - 10) = 23$. Thus, the dimensions are 33 by 23 inches.

92. Area (A) of a triangle is $\dfrac{1}{2} \times$ base $(b) \times$ height (h). Thus, $A = \dfrac{1}{2}bh \Rightarrow \dfrac{1}{2}bh \le 100 \Rightarrow \dfrac{1}{2}b(8) \le 100 \Rightarrow$

    $4b \le 100 \Rightarrow \dfrac{4b}{4} \le \dfrac{100}{4} \Rightarrow b \le 25$. Therefore, the base must be 25 inches or less.

93. Let x represent the unknown test score. Then, $\dfrac{75 + 91 + x}{3} = 80 \Rightarrow \dfrac{166 + x}{3} = 80 \Rightarrow$

    $3\left(\dfrac{166 + x}{3}\right) = 3(80) \Rightarrow 166 + x = 240 \Rightarrow 166 - 166 + x = 240 - 166 \Rightarrow x = 74$. Thus, the student

    must score 74 or more.

94. Let x represent the unknown number of hours. Then, $2.25 + 1.25x = 9 \Rightarrow$

    $2.25 - 2.25 + 1.25x = 9 - 2.25 \Rightarrow 1.25x = 6.75 \Rightarrow \dfrac{1.25x}{1.25} = \dfrac{6.75}{1.25} \Rightarrow x = 5.4$. Because each partial hour

    is charged as a full hour, the person can park for 6 hours.

95. (a) $C = 150{,}000 + 85x$

    (b) $R = 225x$

    (c) $P = 225x - (150{,}000 + 85x) \Rightarrow P = 140x - 150{,}000$

    (d) $140x - 150{,}000 < 0 \Rightarrow 140x - 150{,}000 + 150{,}000 < 0 + 150{,}000 \Rightarrow 140x < 150{,}000 \Rightarrow$

    $\dfrac{140x}{140} < \dfrac{150{,}000}{140} \Rightarrow x < 1071.43$. Therefore, if 1071 or fewer DVD players are sold, there will be a loss.

Chapter 2 Test

1. $9 = 3 - x \Rightarrow 9 - 3 = 3 - 3 - x \Rightarrow 6 = -x \Rightarrow 6(-1) = (-x)(-1) \Rightarrow -6 = x \Rightarrow x = -6$

   To check the solution: $9 - 3 - (-6) \Rightarrow 9 = 9$. The solution checks.

2. $4x - 3 = 7 \Rightarrow 4x - 3 + 3 = 7 + 3 \Rightarrow 4x = 10 \Rightarrow \dfrac{4x}{4} = \dfrac{10}{4} \Rightarrow x = \dfrac{5}{2}$

   To check the solution: $4\left(\dfrac{5}{2}\right) - 3 = 7 \Rightarrow \dfrac{20}{2} - \dfrac{6}{2} = 7 \Rightarrow \dfrac{14}{2} = 7 \Rightarrow 7 = 7$. The solution checks.

3. $4x - (2 - x) = -3(2x + 6) \Rightarrow 4x - 2 + x = -6x - 18 \Rightarrow 5x - 2 = -6x - 18 \Rightarrow$

$5x - 2 + 2 = -6x - 18 + 2 \Rightarrow 5x = -6x - 16 \Rightarrow 5x + 6x = -6x + 6x - 16 \Rightarrow 11x = -16 \Rightarrow$

$\dfrac{11x}{11} = \dfrac{-16}{11} \Rightarrow x = -\dfrac{16}{11}$. To check the solution: $4\left(-\dfrac{16}{11}\right) - \left(2 - \left(-\dfrac{16}{11}\right)\right) = -3\left(2\left(-\dfrac{16}{11}\right) + 6\right) \Rightarrow$

$-\dfrac{64}{11} - 2 - \dfrac{16}{11} = -6\left(-\dfrac{16}{11}\right) - 18 \Rightarrow -\dfrac{64}{11} - \dfrac{22}{11} - \dfrac{16}{11} = \dfrac{96}{11} - \dfrac{198}{11} \Rightarrow -\dfrac{102}{11} = -\dfrac{102}{11}$. The solution checks.

4. $\dfrac{1}{12}x - \dfrac{2}{3} = \dfrac{1}{2}\left(\dfrac{3}{4} - \dfrac{1}{3}x\right) \Rightarrow \dfrac{1}{12}x - \dfrac{2}{3} = \dfrac{3}{8} - \dfrac{1}{6}x \Rightarrow \dfrac{1}{12}x + \dfrac{1}{6}x - \dfrac{2}{3} = \dfrac{3}{8} - \dfrac{1}{6}x + \dfrac{1}{6}x \Rightarrow$

$\dfrac{3}{12}x - \dfrac{2}{3} + \dfrac{2}{3} = \dfrac{3}{8} + \dfrac{2}{3} \Rightarrow \dfrac{3}{12}x = \dfrac{9}{24} + \dfrac{16}{24} \Rightarrow \dfrac{3}{12}x = \dfrac{25}{24} \Rightarrow \dfrac{12}{3}\left(\dfrac{3}{12}x\right) = \dfrac{12}{3}\left(\dfrac{25}{24}\right) \Rightarrow x = \dfrac{300}{72} = \dfrac{25}{6}$.

To check the solution: $\dfrac{1}{12}\left(\dfrac{25}{6}\right) - \dfrac{2}{3} = \dfrac{1}{2}\left(\dfrac{3}{4} - \dfrac{1}{3}\left(\dfrac{25}{6}\right)\right) \Rightarrow \dfrac{25}{72} - \dfrac{48}{72} = \dfrac{1}{2}\left(\dfrac{27}{36} - \dfrac{50}{36}\right) \Rightarrow$

$-\dfrac{23}{72} = \dfrac{1}{2}\left(-\dfrac{23}{36}\right) \Rightarrow -\dfrac{23}{72} = -\dfrac{23}{72}$. The solution checks.

5. First, solve for x: $6(2x - 1) = -4(3 - 3x) \Rightarrow 12x - 6 = -12 + 12x \Rightarrow$

$12x - 12x - 6 = -12 + 12x - 12x \Rightarrow -6 = -12$. Because this statement is not true, there are no solutions.

6. When $x = 1$, then $6 - 2x = 6 - 2(1) = 4$; When $x = 2$, then $6 - 2x = 6 - 2(2) = 2$;

When $x = 3$, then $6 - 2x = 6 - 2(3) = 0$; When $x = 4$, then $6 - 2x = 6 - 2(4) = -2$;

Thus, the missing values in the table are 4, 2, 0 and -2. See Figure 6. From the table we see that

$6 - 2x = 0$, when $x = 3$.

x	0	1	2	3	4
$6 - 2x$	6	4	2	0	-2

Figure 6

7. $x + (-7) = 6 \Rightarrow x - 7 = 6 \Rightarrow x - 7 + 7 = 6 + 7 \Rightarrow x = 13$

8. $2x + 6 = x - 7 \Rightarrow 2x - x + 6 = x - x - 7 \Rightarrow x + 6 = -7 \Rightarrow x + 6 - 6 = -7 - 6 \Rightarrow x = -13$

9. $x + (x + 1) + (x + 2) = 336 \Rightarrow 3x + 3 = 336 \Rightarrow 3x + 3 - 3 = 336 - 3 \Rightarrow 3x = 333 \Rightarrow$

$\dfrac{3x}{3} = \dfrac{333}{3} \Rightarrow x = 111$. Thus, the three numbers are 111, 112 and 113.

10. $5.6\% = 0.056;\ 5.6\% = \dfrac{56}{1000} = \dfrac{14}{250} = \dfrac{7}{125}$

11. $0.345 = 34.5\%$

12. Let x represent the unknown number. To find 7.5% of \$500, multiply 500 by 0.075. Then, $500(0.075) = x \Rightarrow$

$37.5 = x \Rightarrow x = 37.5$. Thus, 7.5% of \$500 is \$37.50.

13. $\dfrac{5280}{5} = \dfrac{5280}{5} \div \dfrac{5}{5} = 1056$ ft/sec.

14. Area $(A) = \dfrac{1}{2} \times$ base $(b) \times$ height (h). Thus, $A = \dfrac{1}{2}bh = \dfrac{1}{2}(5)(3) = 7.5$ in^2.

15. Circumference of a circle is given as $C = 2\pi r$. Then, $C = 2\pi r = 2\pi\left(\dfrac{30}{2}\right) = 2\pi(15) = 30\pi \approx 94.2$ inches.

    Area of a circle is given as $A = \pi r^2$. Then, $A = \pi r^2 = \pi(15)^2 = 225\pi \approx 706.9$ in^2.

16. The angles in a triangle must add up to 180°.

    Then, $x + 2x + 3x = 180 \Rightarrow 6x = 180 \Rightarrow \dfrac{6x}{6} = \dfrac{180}{6} \Rightarrow x = 30$. Thus, the angles are 30°, 60° and 90°.

17. $z = y - 3xy \Rightarrow z - y = y - y - 3xy \Rightarrow z - y = -3xy \Rightarrow \dfrac{z - y}{-3y} = \dfrac{-3xy}{-3y} \Rightarrow \dfrac{z - y}{-3y} = x \Rightarrow x = \dfrac{y - z}{3y}$

18. $3(6 - 5x) < 20 - x \Rightarrow 18 - 15x < 20 - x \Rightarrow 18 - 18 - 15x < 20 - 18 - x \Rightarrow -15x < 2 - x \Rightarrow$

    $-15x + x < 2 - x + x \Rightarrow -14x < 2 \Rightarrow \dfrac{-14x}{-14} > \dfrac{2}{-14} \Rightarrow x > -\dfrac{1}{7} \Rightarrow \left\{x \,\middle|\, x > -\dfrac{1}{7}\right\}$

19. (a) $S = 5 + 2x$, where x represents hours past noon.

    (b) $x = 8$. Thus, $S = 5 + 2(8) = 21$ inches.

    (c) $x = 6.25$. Thus, $S = 5 + 2(6.25) = 17.5$ inches.

20. The amount of acid on the left side of the equation must equal the amount of acid on the right side of the equation. Let x represent the unknown amount of water. Then, $1000(0.45) + x(0) = (1000 + x)(0.15) \Rightarrow$

    $450 = 150 + 0.15x \Rightarrow 450 - 150 = 150 - 150 + 0.15x \Rightarrow 300 = 0.15x \Rightarrow \dfrac{300}{0.15} = \dfrac{0.15x}{0.15} \Rightarrow$

    $2000 = x \Rightarrow x = 2000$. Thus, 2000 ml. of water must be added.

21. Subtract the lesser amount from the larger amount and then calculate the percentage difference as compared to

    the smaller amount. Then, $32 - 8 = 24$; $\dfrac{24}{8} = 3 = 300\%$. Therefore, there was a 300% increase in premiums

    from 1998 to 2003.

Chapter 2 Extended and Discovery Exercises

1. For the first hour, the distance traveled was $d = rt$ such that $d = (50)(1) = 50$ miles. For the second hour, the

    distance traveled was $d = rt$ such that $d = (70)(1) = 70$ miles. Thus, for the two hours $r = \dfrac{d}{t}$ such that

    $r = \dfrac{70 + 50}{1 + 1} = \dfrac{120}{2} = 60$. Thus, the average speed of the car was 60 mph.

2. Uphill, $d = \dfrac{d}{r}$ such that $t = \dfrac{1}{5} = \dfrac{1}{5}$ of an hour. Downhill, $t = \dfrac{d}{r}$ such that $t = \dfrac{1}{10} = \dfrac{1}{10}$ of an hour. Thus, the

    average speed $r = \dfrac{d}{t}$ is $r = \dfrac{1 + 1}{\frac{1}{5} + \frac{1}{10}} = \dfrac{2}{\frac{3}{10}} = \dfrac{20}{3} = 6.\overline{6}$ mph.

3. For the first two miles, $t = \dfrac{d}{r}$ such that $t = \dfrac{2}{8} = \dfrac{1}{4}$ of an hour. For the third mile, $t = \dfrac{d}{t}$ such that $t = \dfrac{1}{10} = \dfrac{1}{10}$

    of an hour. Thus, the average speed of the athlete is $r = \dfrac{d}{t} = \dfrac{3}{\frac{1}{4} + \frac{1}{10}} = \dfrac{3}{\frac{5}{20} + \frac{2}{20}} = \dfrac{3}{\frac{7}{20}} = \dfrac{60}{7} \approx 8.6$ mph.

4. Choose a distance of 400 miles as the distance between the two cities (the distance is arbitrary because any distance gives the same average speed). Then, the pilot flew at 200 mph for 1 hour and at 100 mph for 2 hours. Then, $r = \dfrac{d}{t} = \dfrac{400}{1+2} = \dfrac{400}{3} = 133.\overline{3}$. Thus, the average speed is $133.\overline{3}$ mph.

5. The lighter coin can be found in two weighings as follows: Place two coins on each pan of the balance and set three coins off to the side. Case 1: The pans balance and the lighter coin is one of the three coins that were set off to the side. Case 2: The pans do not balance and the lighter coin is one of the two coins on the higher pan. To find the lighter coin in Case 1, work only with the three remaining coins. Place one coin on each side of the balance and set one coin off to the side. If the pans do not balance, the lighter coin is the one on the higher pan. To find the lighter coin in Case 2, work with only the two coins from the higher pan. Place one coin on each side of the balance. The lighter coin is on the higher pan.

6. (a) Surface area $(A) = 4\pi r^2 = 4\pi(3960)^2 \approx 197{,}060{,}797$ mi^2.

    (b) $.71(197{,}060{,}797) \approx 139{,}913{,}166$ mi^2.

    (c) $\dfrac{680{,}000}{139{,}913{,}166} \approx 0.00486$ miles. To convert 0.00486 miles to feet: $0.00486(5280) \approx 25.7$ feet.

    (d) They would be flooded.

    (e) Divide the volume of the Antarctic ice cap by the surface area of the oceans: $\dfrac{6{,}300{,}000}{139{,}913{,}166} \approx 0.045$ miles.

    To convert 0.0045 miles to feet: $0.045(5280) \approx 237.7$ feet.

Critical Thinking Solutions for Chapter 2

Section 2.1

•   If an error is made, the resulting equation may not be equivalent to the given equation.

Section 2.2

•   Solve for x: $bx - 2 = dx + 7 \Rightarrow bx - 2 + 2 = dx + 7 + 2 \Rightarrow bx = dx + 9 \Rightarrow$
    $bx - dx = dx - dx + 9 \Rightarrow bx - dx = 9 \Rightarrow x(b - d) = 9 \Rightarrow \dfrac{x(b-d)}{b-d} = \dfrac{9}{b-d} \Rightarrow x = \dfrac{9}{b-d}$. Thus, if $b = d$, then $x = \dfrac{9}{0}$. Because dividing by 0 is not allowed, there are no solutions. If $b \neq d$, then there is one solution.

Section 2.3

•   Let x represent the lower salary. Then, $x + 2x$ equals the increased salary amount. Thus, because $x + 2x = 3x$, the lower salary increased by a factor of 3.

Section 2.4

- $C = 2\pi r = \pi 2r = \pi d; \; A = \pi r^2 = \pi\left(\dfrac{1}{2}d\right)^2 = \dfrac{1}{4}\pi d^2$

- Yes. Multiply one expression by 1 in the form $\dfrac{-1}{-1}$ to transform it to the other.

Section 2.5

- $-5 - 3x > -2x + 7 \Rightarrow -5 - 3x + 3x > -2x + 3x + 7 \Rightarrow -5 > x + 7 \Rightarrow -5 - 7 > x + 7 - 7 \Rightarrow$
  $-12 > x \Rightarrow x < -12$

Chapter 3: Graphing Equations

3.1: Introduction to Graphing

Concepts

1. xy plane

3. 4

5. III

7. scatterplot

Cartesian Coordinate Plane

9. $(-2, -2), (-2, 2), (0, 0), (2, 2)$

11. $(-1, 0), (0, -3), (0, 2), (2, 0)$

13. (a) Quadrant I

    (b) Quadrant III

15. (a) None, because the point is on the axis.

    (b) Quadrant I

17. (a) Quadrant II

    (b) Quadrant IV

19. See Figure 19.

21. See Figure 21.

Figure 19

Figure 21

Figure 23

23. See Figure 23.

25. See Figure 25.

Figure 25

27. See Figure 27.

29. See Figure 29.

Figure 27

Figure 29

Figure 31

31. See Figure 31.

33. See Figure 33.

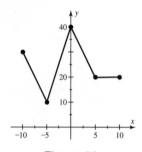

Figure 33

35. (1940, 182), (1960, 484), (1980, 632), (2000, 430); In 1940, there were 182 billion cigarettes consumed in the U.S. *Answers may vary slightly.*

Graphing Real Data

37. (a) See Figure 37.

   (b) Federal income tax receipts increased.

39. (a) See Figure 39.

   (b) The number of welfare beneficiaries increased and then decreased.

Figure 37

Figure 39

Figure 41

41. (a) See Figure 41.

   (b) The number of farms decreased.

3.2: Linear Equations in Two Variables

Concepts

1. two

3. linear

5. graph

Solutions to Equations

7. Substitute 5 for x and 6 for y: $y = x + 1 \Rightarrow 6 = 5 + 1 \Rightarrow 6 = 6$. This is a true statement, so the ordered pair (5, 6) is a solution.

9. Substitute 2 for x and 13 for y: $y = 4x + 7 \Rightarrow 13 = 4(2) + 7 \Rightarrow 13 = 8 + 7 \Rightarrow 13 = 15$. This is not a true statement, so the ordered pair (2, 13) is not a solution.

11. Substitute -2 for x and 3 for y: $4x - y = -13 \Rightarrow 4(-2) - 3 = -13 \Rightarrow -8 - 3 = -13 \Rightarrow -11 = -13$. This is not a true statement, so the ordered pair $(-2, 3)$ is not a solution.

13. Substitute $\frac{1}{2}$ for x and 2 for y: $y - 6x = -1 \Rightarrow 2 - 6\left(\frac{1}{2}\right) = -1 \Rightarrow 2 - 3 = -1 \Rightarrow - = -1$. This is a true statement, so the ordered pair $\left(\frac{1}{2}, 2\right)$ is a solution.

15. Substitute 100 for x and 100 for y: $0.31x - 0.42y = -9 \Rightarrow 0.31(100) - 0.42(100) = -9 \Rightarrow 31 - 42 = -9 \Rightarrow -11 = -9$. This is not a true statement, so the ordered pair (100, 100) is not a solution.

17. When $x = -1$: $y = 4x \Rightarrow y = 4(-1) \Rightarrow y = -4$; when $x = 0$: $y = 4x \Rightarrow y = 4(0) \Rightarrow y = 0$; when $x = 1$: $y = 4x \Rightarrow y = 4(1) \Rightarrow y = 4$; when $x = 2$: $y = 4x \Rightarrow y = 4(2) \Rightarrow y = 8$. Thus, the missing values in the table are $-4, 0, 4$ and 8. See Figure 17.

x	-2	-1	0	1	2
y	-8	-4	0	4	8

Figure 17

x	-8	-4	0	4	8
y	-4	0	4	8	12

Figure 19

x	6	3	0	-3	-9
y	-2	0	2	4	8

Figure 21

19. When $y = 0$: $y = x + 4 \Rightarrow 0 = x + 4 \Rightarrow 0 - 4 = x + 4 - 4 \Rightarrow -4 = x \Rightarrow x = -4$;

    when $y = 4$: $y = x + 4 \Rightarrow 4 = x + 4 \Rightarrow 4 - 4 = x + 4 - 4 \Rightarrow 0 = x \Rightarrow x = 0$;

    when $y = 8$: $y = x + 4 \Rightarrow 8 = x + 4 \Rightarrow 8 - 4 = x + 4 - 4 \Rightarrow 4 = x \Rightarrow x = 4$;

    when $y = 12$: $y = x + 4 \Rightarrow 12 = x + 4 \Rightarrow 12 - 4 = x + 4 - 4 \Rightarrow 8 = x \Rightarrow x = 8$.

    Thus, the missing values in the table are $-4, 0, 4$ and 8. See Figure 19.

21. When $y = -2$: $3y + 2x = 6 \Rightarrow 3(-2) + 2x = 6 \Rightarrow -6 + 2x = 6 \Rightarrow -6 + 6 + 2x = 6 + 6 \Rightarrow$

    $2x = 12 \Rightarrow \frac{2x}{2} = \frac{12}{2} \Rightarrow x = 6$; when $y = 0$: $3y + 2x = 6 \Rightarrow 3(0) + 2x = 6 \Rightarrow 2x = 6 \Rightarrow \frac{2x}{2} = \frac{6}{2} \Rightarrow$

    $x = 3$; when $y = 2$: $3y + 2x = 6 \Rightarrow 3(2) + 2x = 6 \Rightarrow 6 + 2x = 6 \Rightarrow 6 - 6 + 2x = 6 - 6 \Rightarrow$

    $2x = 0 \Rightarrow \frac{2x}{2} = \frac{0}{2} \Rightarrow x = 0$; when $y = 4$: $3y + 2x = 6 \Rightarrow 3(4) + 2x = 6 \Rightarrow 12 + 2x = 6 \Rightarrow$

    $12 - 12 + 2x = 6 - 12 \Rightarrow 2x = -6 \Rightarrow \frac{2x}{2} = \frac{-6}{2} \Rightarrow x = -3$; when $y = 8$: $3y + 2x = 6 \Rightarrow$

    $3(8) + 2x = 6 \Rightarrow 24 + 2x = 6 \Rightarrow 24 - 24 + 2x = 6 - 24 \Rightarrow 2x = -18 \Rightarrow \frac{2x}{2} = \frac{-18}{2} \Rightarrow x = -9$.

    Thus, the missing values in the table are $6, 3, 0, -3$ and -9. See Figure 21.

23. See Figure 23.

25. See Figure 25.

x	-3	0	3	6
y	-9	0	9	18

Figure 23

x	-8	-4	0	4
y	-2	0	2	4

Figure 25

x	8	6	4	2
y	-2	0	2	4

Figure 27

27. See Figure 27.

29. See Figure 29.

x	$-\frac{1}{2}$	$-\frac{1}{4}$	0	$\frac{1}{4}$
y	-2	-1	0	1

Figure 29

Graphing Equations

31. See Figure 31.

33. See Figure 33.

Figure 31

Figure 33

Figure 35

35. See Figure 35.

37. See Figure 37.

39. See Figure 39.

Figure 37

Figure 39

Figure 41

41. See Figure 41.

43. See Figure 43.

45. See Figure 45.

Figure 43

Figure 45

Figure 47

47. See Figure 47.

49. See Figure 49.

51. See Figure 51.

Figure 49

Figure 51

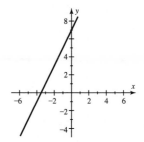

Figure 53

53. See Figure 53.

55. See Figure 55.

57. See Figure 57.

Figure 55

Figure 57

Figure 59

Applications

59. (a) See Figure 59.

   (b) Set $A = 100$ and solve for t: $A = 2.7t \Rightarrow 100 = 2.7t \Rightarrow \dfrac{100}{2.7} = \dfrac{2.7t}{2.7} \Rightarrow t \approx 37$. Therefore, about 37 days.

61. (a) For year 1996, set $t = 1996$ and solve for P: $P = 5.5t - 10{,}911 = 5.5(1996) - 10{,}911 = 10{,}978 - 10{,}911 = 67$. Therefore, in year 1996 it was 67%.

   For year 2000, set $t = 2000$ and solve for P: $P = 5.5t - 10{,}911 = 5.5(2000) - 10{,}911 = 11{,}000 - 10{,}911 = 89$. Therefore, in year 2000 it was 89%.

   (b) See Figure 61.

   (c) P was 83.5% in year 1999.

Figure 61

Checking Basic Concepts for Sections 3.1 & 3.2

1. $(-2,2)$, II; $(-1,-2)$, III; $(1,3)$, I; $(3,0)$, none.

2. See Figure 2.

Figure 2

x	-2	-1	0	1	2
y	5	3	1	-1	-3

Figure 3

3. When $x = -1$: $Y = -2x + 1 = -2(-1) + 1 = 2 + 1 = 3$;

   when $x = 0$: $Y = -2x + 1 = -2(0) + 1 = 1$;

   when $x = 1$: $Y = -2x + 1 = -2(1) + 1 = -2 + 1 = -1$;

   when $x = 2$: $Y = -2x + 1 = -2(2) + 1 = -4 + 1 = -3$.

   Thus, the missing values in the table are $3, 1, -1, -3$. See Figure 3.

4. (a) $Y = 3 - x = 3 - (-2) = 3 + 2 = 5$

   (b) $Y = \dfrac{4 + x}{3} = \dfrac{4 + 8}{3} = \dfrac{12}{3} = 4$

   (c) $2x - 3y = 6 \Rightarrow 2(0) - 3y = 6 \Rightarrow -3y = 6 \Rightarrow \dfrac{-3y}{-3} = \dfrac{6}{-3} \Rightarrow y = -2$

5. (a) See Figure 5a.

    (b) See Figure 5b.

Figure 5a

Figure 5b

Figure 7

6. (1800,1), (1955, 3), (2000, 6); in 2000, the world population was 6 billion.

7. (a) Set $t = 1995$ and solve for A: $A = 0.115t - 228 = 0.115(1995) - 228 = 229.425 - 228 = 1.425$

    Set $t = 2001$ and solve for A: $A = 0.115t - 228 = 0.115(2001) - 228 = 230.115 - 228 = 2.115$

    In 1995, receipts were \$1.425 trillion; in 2001, receipts were \$2.115 trillion.

    (b) See Figure 7.

    (c) 1996

3.3: More Graphing of Lines

Concepts

1. Two

3. x-intercept

5. y-intercept

7. horizontal; 3

9. vertical; 3

Finding Intercepts

11. Because the graph crosses the x-axis at $x = 3$, $x = 3$ is the x-intercept.

     Because the graph crosses the y-axis at $y = -2$, $y = -2$ is the y-intercept.

13. Because the graph crosses the x-axis at $x = 0$, $x = 0$ is the x-intercept.

     Because the graph crosses the y-axis at $y = 0$, $y = 0$ is the y-intercept.

15. Because the graph crosses the x-axis at $x = -2$ and at $x = 2$, $x = -2$ and $x = 2$ are the x-intercepts.

     Because the graph crosses the y- axis at $y = 4$, $y = 4$ is the y-intercept.

17. Because the graph touches the x-axis at $x = 1$, $x = 1$ is the x-intercept.

     Because the graph crosses the y-axis at $y = 1$, $y = 1$ is the y-intercept.

19. When $x = -2$: $y = x + 2 = -2 + 2 = 0$; when $x = -1$: $y = x + 2 = -1 + 2 = 1$;

when $x = 0$: $y = x + 2 = 0 + 2 = 2$; when $x = 1$: $y = x + 2 = 1 + 2 = 3$;

when $x = 2$: $y = x + 2 = 2 + 2 = 4$. Therefore, the missing values in the table are 0, 1, 2, 3 and 4.

See Figure 19. The x-intercept is at $x = -2$, because at $x = -2$ the value of y is 0.

The y-intercept is at $y = 2$, because at $y = 2$ the value of x is 0.

x	-2	-1	0	1	2
y	0	1	2	3	4

x	-4	-2	0	2	4
y	-6	-4	-2	0	2

Figure 19   Figure 21

21. When $x = -4$: $-x + y = -2 \Rightarrow -(-4) + y = -2 \Rightarrow 4 + y = -2 \Rightarrow 4 - 4 + y = -2 - 4 \Rightarrow y = -6$;

when $x = -2$: $-x + y = -2 \Rightarrow -(-2) + y = -2 \Rightarrow 2 + y = -2 \Rightarrow 2 - 2 + y = -2 - 2 \Rightarrow y = -4$;

when $x = 0$: $-x + y = -2 \Rightarrow -(0) + y = -2 \Rightarrow y = -2$;

when $x = 2$: $-x + y = -2 \Rightarrow -(2) + y = -2 \Rightarrow -2 + y = -2 \Rightarrow -2 + 2 + y = -2 + 2 \Rightarrow y = 0$;

when $x = 4$: $-x + y = -2 \Rightarrow -(4) + y = -2 \Rightarrow -4 + y = -2 \Rightarrow -4 + 4 + y = -2 + 4 \Rightarrow y = 2$.

Therefore, the missing values in the table are $-6, -4, -2, 0$ and 2. See Figure 21.

The x-intercept is at $x = 2$, because at $x = 2$ the value of y is 0.

The y-intercept is at $y = -2$, because at $y = -2$ the value of x is 0.

23. To find the x-intercept, set $y = 0$ and solve for x: $-2x + 3y = -6 \Rightarrow -2x + 3(0) = -6 \Rightarrow$

$-2x = -6 \Rightarrow \dfrac{-2x}{-2} = \dfrac{-6}{-2} \Rightarrow x = 3$. Therefore, the x-intercept is at $x = 3$.

To find the y-intercept, set $x = 0$ and solve for y: $-2x + 3y = -6 \Rightarrow -2(0) + 3y = -6 \Rightarrow$

$3y = -6 \Rightarrow \dfrac{3y}{3} = \dfrac{-6}{3} \Rightarrow y = -2$. Therefore, the y-intercept is at $y = -2$. See Figure 23.

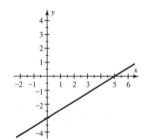

Figure 23   Figure 25

25. To find the x-intercept, set $y = 0$ and solve for x: $3x - 5y = 15 \Rightarrow 3x - 5(0) = 15 \Rightarrow$

$3x = 15 \Rightarrow \dfrac{3x}{3} = \dfrac{15}{3} \Rightarrow x = 5$. Therefore, the x-intercept is at $x = 5$.

To find the y-intercept, set $x = 0$ and solve for y: $3x - 5y = 15 \Rightarrow 3(0) - 5y = 15 \Rightarrow$

$-5y = 15 \Rightarrow \dfrac{-5y}{-5} = \dfrac{15}{-5} \Rightarrow y = -3$. Therefore, the y-intercept is at $y = -3$. See Figure 25.

27. To find the *x*-intercept, set $y = 0$ and solve for *x*: $x - 3y = 6 \Rightarrow x - 3(0) = 6 \Rightarrow x = 6$.

Therefore, the *x*-intercept is at $x = 6$.

To find the *y*-intercept, set $x = 0$ and solve for *y*: $x - 3y = 6 \Rightarrow 0 - 3y = 6 \Rightarrow$

$-3y = 6 \Rightarrow \dfrac{-3y}{-3} = \dfrac{6}{-3} \Rightarrow y = -2$. Therefore, the *y*-intercept is at $y = -2$. See Figure 27.

29. To find the *x*-intercept, set $y = 0$ and solve for *x*: $6x - y = -6 \Rightarrow 6x - 0 = -6 \Rightarrow$

$6x = -6 \Rightarrow \dfrac{6x}{6} = \dfrac{-6}{6} \Rightarrow x = -1$. Therefore, the *x*-intercept is at $x = -1$.

To find the *y*-intercept, set $x = 0$ and solve for *y*: $6x - y = -6 \Rightarrow 6(0) - y = -6 \Rightarrow -y = -6 \Rightarrow$

$-1(-y) = -1(-6) \Rightarrow y = 6$. Therefore, the *y*-intercept is at $y = 6$. See Figure 29.

Figure 27

Figure 29

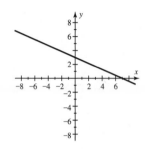
Figure 31

31. To find the *x*-intercept, set $y = 0$ and solve for *x*: $3x + 7y = 21 \Rightarrow 3x + 7(0) = 21 \Rightarrow$

$3x = 21 \Rightarrow \dfrac{3x}{3} = \dfrac{21}{3} \Rightarrow x = 7$. Therefore, the *x*-intercept is at $x = 7$.

To find the *y*-intercept, set $x = 0$ and solve for *y*: $3x + 7y = 21 \Rightarrow 3(0) + 7y = 21 \Rightarrow$

$7y = 21 \Rightarrow \dfrac{7y}{7} = \dfrac{21}{7} \Rightarrow y = 3$. Therefore, the *y*-intercept is at $y = 3$. See Figure 31.

33. To find the *x*-intercept, set $y = 0$ and solve for *x*: $40y - 30x = -120 \Rightarrow 40(0) - 30x = -120 \Rightarrow$

$-30x = -120 \Rightarrow \dfrac{-30x}{-30} = \dfrac{-120}{-30} \Rightarrow x = 4$. Therefore, the *x*-intercept is at $x = 4$.

To find the *y*-intercept, set $x = 0$ and solve for *y*: $40y - 30x = -120 \Rightarrow 40y - 30(0) = -120 \Rightarrow$

$40y = -120 \Rightarrow \dfrac{40y}{40} = \dfrac{-120}{40} \Rightarrow y = -3$. Therefore, the *y*-intercept is at $y = -3$. See Figure 33.

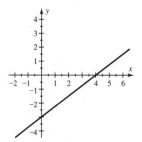
Figure 33

35. To find the x-intercept, set $y = 0$ and solve for x: $\frac{1}{2}x - y = 2 \Rightarrow \frac{1}{2}x - 0 = 2 \Rightarrow$

    $\frac{1}{2}x = 2 \Rightarrow 2\left(\frac{1}{2}x\right) = 2(2) \Rightarrow x = 4$. Therefore, the x-intercept is at $x = 4$.

    To find the y-intercept, set $x = 0$ and solve for y: $\frac{1}{2}x - y = 2 \Rightarrow \frac{1}{2}(0) - y = 2 \Rightarrow$

    $-y = 2 \Rightarrow -1(-y) = 2(-1) \Rightarrow y = -2$. Therefore, the y-intercept is at $y = -2$. See Figure 35.

37. To find the x-intercept, set $y = 0$ and solve for x: $-\frac{x}{4} + \frac{y}{3} = 1 \Rightarrow -\frac{x}{4} + \frac{0}{3} = 1 \Rightarrow$

    $-\frac{x}{4} = 1 \Rightarrow -4\left(-\frac{x}{4}\right) = 1(-4) \Rightarrow x = -4$. Therefore, the x-intercept is at $x = -4$.

    To find the y-intercept, set $x = 0$ and solve for y: $-\frac{x}{4} + \frac{y}{3} = 1 \Rightarrow -\frac{0}{4} + \frac{y}{3} = 1 \Rightarrow$

    $\frac{y}{3} = 1 \Rightarrow 3\left(\frac{y}{3}\right) = 3(1) \Rightarrow y = 3$. Therefore, the y-intercept is at $y = 3$. See Figure 37.

Figure 35

Figure 37

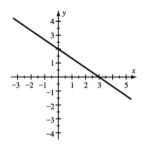

Figure 39

39. To find the x-intercept, set $y = 0$ and solve for x: $\frac{x}{3} + \frac{y}{2} = 1 \Rightarrow \frac{x}{3} + \frac{0}{2} = 1 \Rightarrow$

    $\frac{x}{3} = 1 \Rightarrow 3\left(\frac{x}{3}\right) = 1(3) \Rightarrow x = 3$. Therefore, the x-intercept is at $x = 3$.

    To find the y-intercept, set $x = 0$ and solve for y: $\frac{x}{3} + \frac{y}{2} = 1 \Rightarrow \frac{0}{3} + \frac{y}{2} = 1 \Rightarrow$

    $\frac{y}{2} = 1 \Rightarrow 2\left(\frac{y}{2}\right) = 2(1) \Rightarrow y = 2$. Therefore, the y-intercept is at $y = 2$. See Figure 39.

41. To find the x-intercept, set $y = 0$ and solve for x: $0.6y - 1.5x = 3 \Rightarrow 0.6(0) - 1.5x = 3 \Rightarrow -1.5x = 3 \Rightarrow$

    $\frac{-1.5x}{-1.5} = \frac{3}{-1.5} \Rightarrow x = -2$. Therefore, the x-intercept is at $x = -2$.

    To find the y-intercept, set $x = 0$ and solve for y: $0.6y - 1.5x = 3 \Rightarrow 0.6y - 1.5(0) = 3 \Rightarrow 0.6y = 3 \Rightarrow$

    $\frac{0.6y}{0.6} = \frac{3}{0.6} \Rightarrow y = 5$. Therefore, the y-intercept is at $y = 5$. See Figure 41.

Figure 41

Horizontal and Vertical Lines

43. (a) See Figure 43a.

    (b) See Figure 43b.

Figure 43a

Figure 43b

45. (a) See Figure 45a.

    (b) See Figure 45b.

Figure 45a

Figure 45b

47. (a) See Figure 47a.

    (b) See Figure 47b.

Figure 47a

Figure 47b

49. (a) See Figure 49a.

(b) See Figure 49b.

Figure 49a   Figure 49b

51. $y = 4$

53. $x = -1$

55. $y = -6$

57. $x = 5$

59. Because $y = 1$ for every x-value, the graph is a horizontal line. The equation for the line is $y = 1$.

61. Because $x = -6$ for every y-value, the graph is a vertical line. The equation for the line is $x = -6$.

63. A horizontal line that passes through $(1, 2)$ has a y-value of 2 for every x-value. Therefore, the equation for the horizontal line is $y = 2$.

A vertical line that passes through $(1, 2)$ has an x-value of 1 for every y-value. Therefore, the equation for the vertical line is $x = 1$.

65. A horizontal line that passes through $(20, -45)$ has a y-value of -45 for every x-value. Therefore, the equation for the horizontal line is $y = -45$.

A vertical line that passes through $(20, -45)$ has an x-value of 20 for every y-value. Therefore, the equation for the vertical line is $x = 20$.

67. A horizontal line that passes through $(0, 5)$ has a y-value of 5 for every x-value. Therefore, the equation for the horizontal line is $y = 5$.

A vertical line that passes through $(0, 5)$ has an x-value of 0 for every y-value. Therefore, the equation for the vertical line is $x = 0$.

69. A vertical line that passes through $(-1, 6)$ has an x-value of -1 for every y-value. Therefore, the equation for the vertical line is $x = -1$.

71. A horizontal line that passes through $\left(\dfrac{3}{4}, -\dfrac{5}{6}\right)$ has a y-value of $-\dfrac{5}{6}$ for every x-value. Therefore, the equation for the horizontal line is $y = -\dfrac{5}{6}$.

73. Because $y = \dfrac{1}{2}$ is the equation of a horizontal line, a line perpendicular to $y = \dfrac{1}{2}$ is a vertical line. Therefore, the equation of the vertical line passing through $(4, -9)$ is $x = 4$.

75. Because $x = 4$ is the equation of a vertical line, a line parallel to $x = 4$ is also a vertical line. Therefore, the equation of the vertical line passing through $\left(-\dfrac{2}{3}, \dfrac{1}{2}\right)$ is $x = -\dfrac{2}{3}$.

Applications

77. (a) *y*-intercept, 200; *x*-intercept, 4.

    (b) The driver was initially 200 mi from home; the driver arrived home after 4 hr.

79. (a) *y*-intercept, 2000; *x*-intercept, 4.

    (b) The pool initially contained 2000 gal ; the pool was empty after 4 hr.

81. (a) To find the *v*-intercept, set $t = 0$ and solve for *v*: $v = 128 - 32t = 128 - 32(0) = 128$.

    To find the *t*-intercept, set $v = 0$ and solve for *t*: $v = 128 - 32t \Rightarrow 0 = 128 - 32t \Rightarrow$

    $0 + 32t = 128 - 32t + 32t \Rightarrow 32t = 128 \Rightarrow \dfrac{32t}{32} = \dfrac{128}{32} \Rightarrow t = 4$. See figure 81.

    (b) The initial velocity was 128 ft/sec; the velocity after 4 seconds was 0.

Figure 81

3.4: Slope and Rates of Change

Concepts

1. horizontal

3. rise; run

5. vertical

7. Because the graph of the line falls as it goes from left to right, the slope is negative.

9. Because the graph of the line neither falls or rises as it goes from left to right, the slope is zero.

11. Because the graph of the line falls as it goes from left to right, the slope is negative.

Finding Slopes of Lines

13. Because the graph is a horizontal line, the slope is 0. Thus, the rise always equals 0.

15. A point on the graph is $(0, -2)$ and another point is $(2, 0)$. Let $x_1 = 0, x_2 = 2, y_1 = -2$ and $y_2 = 0$. Then:

    $m \text{ (slope)} = \dfrac{y_2 - y_1}{x_2 - x_1} = \dfrac{0 - (-2)}{2 - 0} = \dfrac{2}{2} = 1$. Thus, the slope is 1; the graph rises 1 unit for each unit of run.

17. A point on the graph is $(-1, -1)$ and another point is $(0, 1)$. Let $x_1 = -1$, $x_2 = 0$, $y_1 = -1$ and $y_2 = 1$. Then:

$$m \text{ (slope)} = \frac{y_2 - y_1}{x_2 - x_1} = \frac{1 - (-1)}{0 - (-1)} = \frac{2}{1} = 2.$$ Thus, the slope is 2; the graph rises 2 units for each unit of run.

19. Because the run always equals 0, the slope is undefined.

21. A point on the graph is $(0, -2)$ and another point is $(2, -1)$. Let $x_1 = 0$, $x_2 = 2$, $y_1 = -2$ and $y_2 = -1$. Then:

$$m \text{ (slope)} = \frac{y_2 - y_1}{x_2 - x_1} = \frac{-1 - (-2)}{2 - 0} = \frac{1}{2}.$$ Thus, the slope is $\frac{1}{2}$; the graph rises 1 unit for each 2 units of run.

23. A point on the graph is $(0, 4)$ and another point is $(4, 0)$. Let $x_1 = 0$, $x_2 = 4$, $y_1 = 4$ and $y_2 = 0$. Then:

$$m \text{ (slope)} = \frac{y_2 - y_1}{x_2 - x_1} = \frac{0 - 4}{4 - 0} = \frac{-4}{4} = -1.$$ Thus, the slope is -1; the graph falls 1 unit for each unit of run.

25. $m = \dfrac{y_2 - y_1}{x_2 - x_1} = \dfrac{4 - 2}{2 - 1} = \dfrac{2}{1} = 2.$ Thus, the slope of the line is 2. See Figure 25.

27. $m = \dfrac{y_2 - y_1}{x_2 - x_1} = \dfrac{5 - 3}{-2 - 1} = \dfrac{2}{-3} = -\dfrac{2}{3}.$ Thus, the slope of the line is $-\dfrac{2}{3}$. See Figure 27.

          Figure 25   Figure 27

29. $m = \dfrac{y_2 - y_1}{x_2 - x_1} = \dfrac{-7 - (-2)}{-3 - 4} = \dfrac{-5}{-7} = \dfrac{5}{7}.$ Thus, the slope of the line is $\dfrac{5}{7}$.

31. $m = \dfrac{y_2 - y_1}{x_2 - x_1} = \dfrac{-2 - 4}{4 - (-3)} = \dfrac{-6}{7} = -\dfrac{6}{7}.$ Thus, the slope of the line is $-\dfrac{6}{7}$.

33. $m = \dfrac{y_2 - y_1}{x_2 - x_1} = \dfrac{5 - 5}{2 - (-3)} = \dfrac{0}{5} = 0.$ Thus, the slope of the line is 0.

35. $m = \dfrac{y_2 - y_1}{x_2 - x_1} = \dfrac{-4 - 6}{-1 - (-1)} = \dfrac{-10}{0}.$ Because the denominator is 0, the slope is undefined.

37. $m = \dfrac{y_2 - y_1}{x_2 - x_1} = \dfrac{18 - 5}{2000 - 1980} = \dfrac{13}{20}.$ Thus, the slope of the line is $\dfrac{13}{20}$.

39. $m = \dfrac{y_2 - y_1}{x_2 - x_1} = \dfrac{10.6 - 6.1}{2000 - 1950} = \dfrac{4.5}{50} = \dfrac{9}{100}.$ Thus, the slope of the line is $\dfrac{9}{100}$.

41. $m = \dfrac{y_2 - y_1}{x_2 - x_1} = \dfrac{\frac{3}{7} - \left(-\frac{2}{7}\right)}{-\frac{2}{3} - \frac{1}{3}} = \dfrac{\frac{5}{7}}{-\frac{3}{3}} = -\dfrac{5}{7}.$ Thus, the slope of the line is $-\dfrac{5}{7}$.

43. $m = \dfrac{y_2 - y_1}{x_2 - x_1} = \dfrac{64 - (-34)}{14 - 12} = \dfrac{98}{2} = 49.$ Thus, the slope of the line is 49.

45. See Figure 45.

47. See Figure 47.

Figure 45

Figure 47

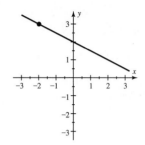
Figure 49

49. See Figure 49.

51. See Figure 51.

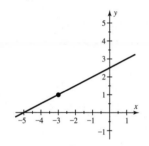
Figure 51

53. Because the *y*-value increases by 2 when the *x*-value increases by 1, the slope is 2. Because $y = 0$ when $x = 1$, the *x*-intercept is at $x = 1$. Because $x = 0$ when $y = -2$, the *y*-intercept is at $y = -2$.

55. Because the *y*-value decreases by 9 when the *x*-value increases by 1, the slope is -9. Because $y = 0$ when $x = -1$, the *x*-intercept is at $x = -1$. Because $x = 0$ when $y = -9$, the *y*-intercept is at $y = -9$.

57. Because the slope is 2, the *y*-value increases by 2 when the *x*-value increases by 1. Thus, when $x = 1, y = -4 + 2 = -2$; when $x = 2, y = -2 + 2 = 0$; when $x = 3, y = 0 + 2 = 2$. See Figure 57.

59. Because the slope is -3, the *y*-value decreases by 3 when the *x*-value increases by 1. Thus, when $x = 2, y = 4 - 3 = 1$; when $x = 3, y = 1 - 3 = -2$; when $x = 4, y = -2 - 3 = -5$; See Figure 59.

x	0	1	2	3
y	−4	−2	0	2

Figure 57

x	1	2	3	4
y	4	1	−2	−5

Figure 59

x	−4	−2	0	2
y	0	3	6	9

Figure 61

61. Because the slope is $\dfrac{3}{2}$, the *y*-value increases by $\dfrac{3}{2}$ when the *x*-value increases by 1 and the *y*-value increases by $2\left(\dfrac{3}{2}\right) = 3$ when the *x*-value increases by 2. Thus, when $x = -2, y = 0 + 3 = 3$; when $x = 0, y = 3 + 3 = 6$; when $x = 2, y = 6 + 3 = 9$. See Figure 61.

63. (a) See Figure 63.

(b) A point on the graph is $(0, -1)$ and another point is $\left(\dfrac{1}{2}, 0\right)$. Thus: $m = \dfrac{y_2 - y_1}{x_2 - x_1} = \dfrac{0 - (-1)}{\frac{1}{2} - 0} = \dfrac{1}{\frac{1}{2}} = 2.$

Therefore, the slope of the line is 2.

65. (a) See Figure 65.

(b) A point on the graph is $(1, -1)$ and another point is $(0, 2)$. Thus: $m = \dfrac{y_2 - y_1}{x_2 - x_1} = \dfrac{2 - (-1)}{0 - 1} = \dfrac{3}{-1} = -3.$

Therefore, the slope of the line is -3.

Figure 63

Figure 65

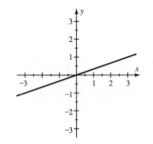

Figure 67

67. (a) See Figure 67.

(b) A point on the graph is $(0, 0)$ and another point is $(3, 1)$. Thus: $m = \dfrac{y_2 - y_1}{x_2 - x_1} = \dfrac{1 - 0}{3 - 0} = \dfrac{1}{3}.$

Therefore, the slope of the line is $\dfrac{1}{3}$.

69. (a) See Figure 69.

(b) Because the line is horizontal, the rise is always 0 and therefore the slope is 0.

Figure 69

Slope as a Rate of Change

71. Because zero gumballs cost zero cents, the graph must pass through $(0, 0)$. c

73. The average cost of a new car has increased over the past 30 years. b

75. (a) When $0 \le x \le 3$, the y-value increases by 1000 when x increases by 1. Therefore, $m_1 = 1000$.

When $3 \le x \le 5$, the y-value decreases by 1000 when x increases by 1. Therefore, $m_2 = -1000$.

(b) $m_1 = 1000$: Water is being added to the pool at a rate of 1000 gallons per hour.

$m_2 = -1000$: Water is being removed from the pool at a rate of 1000 gallons per hour.

(c) Initially the pool contained 2000 gallons of water. Over the first 3 hours, water was pumped into the pool at a rate of 1000 gallons per hour. For the next 2 hours, water was pumped out of the pool at a rate of 1000 gallons per hour.

77. (a) When $0 \le x \le 2$, the y-value increases by 50 when x increases by 1. Therefore, $m_1 = 50$.

When $2 \le x \le 3$, the y-value remains constant when x increases. Therefore, $m_2 = 0$.

When $3 \le x \le 4$, the y-value decreases by 50 when x increases by 1. Therefore, $m_3 = -50$.

(b) $m_1 = 50$: The car is moving away from home at a rate of 50 mph.

$m_2 = 0$: The car is not moving.

$m_3 = -50$: The car is moving toward home at a rate of 50 mph.

(c) Initially the car is at home. Over the first 2 hours, the car travels away from home at a rate of 50 mph.

Then the car is parked for 1 hour. Finally, the car travels toward home at a rate of 50 mph.

79. See Figure 79.

Figure 79

Figure 81

81. See Figure 81.

Applications

83. (a) $m = \dfrac{y_2 - y_1}{x_2 - x_1} = \dfrac{70 - 50}{2000 - 1990} = \dfrac{20}{10} = 2$. Thus, the slope of the line is 2.

(b) The birth rate increased on average by 2000 children per year.

85. (a) A point on the line is (40, 100) and another point is (0, 0). Thus: $m = \dfrac{y_2 - y_1}{x_2 - x_1} = \dfrac{100 - 0}{40 - 0} = \dfrac{100}{40} = 2.5$.

Thus, the slope of the line is 2.5.

(b) The revenue is $2.50 per screwdriver.

87. (a) Substitute 50 for G and solve for O: $O = \dfrac{1}{50}G = \dfrac{1}{50}(50) = 1$. Thus, 1 gallon of oil should be added to

50 gallons of gasoline. Then substitute 100 for G and solve for O: $O = \dfrac{1}{50}G = \dfrac{1}{50}(100) = 2$. Thus,

2 gallons of oil should be added to 100 gallons of gasoline.

(b) When G increases by 1, O increases by $\dfrac{1}{50}$. Thus, the slope of the graph is $\dfrac{1}{50}$.

(c) Oil should be added at a rate of 1 gallon of oil per 50 gallons of gasoline.

89. (a) See Figure 89.

(b) $m_1 = \dfrac{y_2 - y_1}{x_2 - x_1} = \dfrac{100 - 0}{5 - 0} = \dfrac{100}{5} = 20$; $m_2 = \dfrac{y_2 - y_1}{x_2 - x_1} = \dfrac{250 - 100}{10 - 5} = \dfrac{150}{5} = 30$;

$m_3 = \dfrac{y_2 - y_1}{x_2 - x_1} = \dfrac{450 - 250}{15 - 10} = \dfrac{200}{5} = 40$.

(c) $m_1 = 20$: Each mile between 0 and 5 miles is worth \$20/mile.

$m_2 = 30$: Each mile between 5 and 10 miles is worth \$30/mile.

$m_3 = 40$: Each mile between 10 and 15 miles is worth \$40/mile.

Figure 89

91. (a) $m = \dfrac{y_2 - y_1}{x_2 - x_1} = \dfrac{42,000 - 18,000}{2000 - 1980} = \dfrac{24,000}{20} = 1200$. Thus, the slope of the line is 1200.

(b) Median family income increased on average by \$1200/year over this period of time.

(c) $42,000 + 5(1200) = \$48,000$

Checking Basic Concepts for Sections 3.3 & 3.4

1. The line crosses the *x*-axis at $x = -2$; therefore, the *x*-intercept is -2.

   The line crosses the *y*-axis at $y = 3$; therefore, the *y*-intercept is 3.

2. $2x - y = 2 \Rightarrow 2x - y + y = 2 + y \Rightarrow 2x - 2 = 2 - 2 + y \Rightarrow y = 2x - 2$. Therefore:

   When $x = -1$: $y = 2(-1) - 2 \Rightarrow y = -2 - 2 \Rightarrow y = -4$; When $x = 0$: $y = 2x - 2 = 2(0) - 2 = -2$;

   When $x = 1$: $y = 2x - 2 = 2(1) - 2 = 0$; When $x = 2$: $y = 2x - 2 = 2(2) - 2 = 2$.

   Therefore, the missing values in the table are $-4, -2, 0$, and 1. See Figure 2.

   When $y = 0$, $x = 1$. Therefore the *x*-intercept is $x = 1$.

   When $x = 0$, $y = -2$. Therefore, the *y*-intercept is $y = -2$.

x	-2	-1	0	1	2
y	-6	-4	-2	0	2

Figure 2

3. (a) To find the *x*-intercept, set $y = 0$ and solve for *x*: $x - 2y = 6 \Rightarrow x - 2(0) = 6 \Rightarrow x = 6$. Therefore, the

    x-intercept is $x = 6$.

    To find the *y*-intercept, set $x = 0$ and solve for *y*: $x - 2y = 6 \Rightarrow 0 - 2(y) = 6 \Rightarrow -2y = 6 \Rightarrow$

    $\dfrac{-2y}{-2} = \dfrac{6}{-2} \Rightarrow y = -3$. Therefore, the *y*-intercept is $y = -3$. See Figure 3a.

    (b) $y = 2$ is the graph of a horizontal line. Therefore, the line does not cross the *x*-axis and does not have an

    x-intercept. The line crosses the *y*-axis at $y = 2$, and therefore it's *y*-intercept is at $y = 2$. See Figure 3b.

    (c) $x = -1$ is the graph of a vertical line. Therefore, the line crosses the *x*-axis at $x = -1$ and therefore it's

    x-intercept is at $x = -1$. The line does not cross the *y*-axis, and therefore does not have a *y*-intercept.

    See Figure 3c.

Figure 3a

Figure 3b

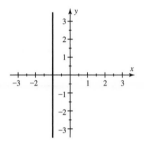

Figure 3c

4. A horizontal line passing through $(-2, 4)$ has the equation $y = 4$.

    A vertical line passing through $(-2, 4)$ has the equation $x = -2$.

5. (a) $\dfrac{6 - 3}{2 - (-2)} = \dfrac{3}{4}$ Therefore, the slope of the line is $\dfrac{3}{4}$.

    (b) $\dfrac{3 - 3}{0 - (-5)} = \dfrac{0}{5} = 0$ Therefore, the slope of the line is 0.

    (c) $\dfrac{8 - 5}{1 - 1} = \dfrac{3}{0}$ Therefore, the slope of the line is undefined.

6. A point on the line is $(2, 1)$ and another point is $(0, 2)$. Thus, $\dfrac{2 - 1}{0 - 2} = \dfrac{1}{-2} = -\dfrac{1}{2}$.

    Therefore, the slope of the line is $-\dfrac{1}{2}$.

7. See Figure 7.

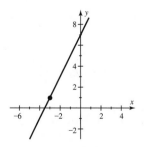

Figure 7

8. (a) $\dfrac{5-5}{1-0} = \dfrac{0}{1} = 0$. Thus $m_1 = 0$. $\dfrac{7-5}{2-1} = \dfrac{2}{1} = 2$. Thus $m_2 = 2$. $\dfrac{5-7}{5-2} = \dfrac{-2}{3} = -\dfrac{2}{3}$. Thus $m_3 = -\dfrac{2}{3}$.

(b) $m_1 = 0$: before the rain, the depth of water in the pond does not change.

$m_2 = 2$: while it rains, the depth of water in the pond increases by 2 feet for every hour of rain.

$m_3 = -\dfrac{2}{3}$: after it stops raining, the depth of water in the pond decreases by $-\dfrac{2}{3}$ feet per hour until it reaches its original depth.

(c) Initially the pond had a depth of 5 feet. For the first hour, there was no change in the depth of the pond. For the next hour, the depth of the pond increased at a rate of 2 feet per hour to a depth of 7 feet. Finally, the depth of the pond decreased for 3 hours at a rate of $\dfrac{2}{3}$ foot per hour until it was 5 feet deep.

9. (a) $\dfrac{22,300 - 18,100}{600 - 450} = \dfrac{4200}{150} = 28$. Therefore, the slope of the line is 28.

(b) For counties between 450 and 600 mi^2, the population increases at a rate of 28 people/mi^2.

(c) No. We do not know whether this trend continues.

3.5: Slope-Intercept Form

Concepts

1. $y = mx + b$

3. y-intercept

5. origin

7. f

9. a

11. e

Slope-Intercept Form

13. The graph of the line shows the y-intercept at -1. For every x-increase of 1, the y-value increases by 1, so the slope is 1. Therefore: $y = mx + b \Rightarrow y = x - 1$.

15. The graph of the line shows the y-intercept at 1. For every x-increase of 1, the y-value decreases by 2, so the slope is -2. Therefore: $y = mx + b \Rightarrow y = -2x + 1$.

17. The graph of the line shows the y-intercept at -2. For every x-increase of 2, the y-value increases by 1, so the slope is $\dfrac{1}{2}$. Therefore: $y = mx + b \Rightarrow y = \dfrac{1}{2}x - 2$.

19. The graph of the line shows the y-intercept at 0. For every x-increase of 1, the y-value decreases by 2, so the slope is -2. Therefore: $y = mx + b = -2x + 0 \Rightarrow y = -2x$.

21. The graph of the line shows the y-intercept at 2. For every x-increase of 4, the y-value increases by 3, so the slope is $\dfrac{3}{4}$. Therefore: $y = mx + b \Rightarrow y = \dfrac{3}{4}x + 2$.

23. See Figure 23. The slope-intercept form is $y = mx + b$, so with $m = 1$ and $b = 2$, $y = x + 2$.

25. See Figure 25. The slope-intercept form is $y = mx + b$, so with $m = 2$ and $b = -1$, $y = 2x - 1$.

Figure 23

Figure 25

Figure 27

27. See Figure 27. The slope-intercept form is $y = mx + b$, so with $m = -\dfrac{1}{2}$ and $b = -2$, $y = -\dfrac{1}{2}x - 2$.

29. See Figure 29. $y = mx + b = \dfrac{1}{3}x + 0 \Rightarrow y = \dfrac{1}{3}x$.

Figure 29

Figure 31

31. See Figure 31. $y = mx + b \Rightarrow y = -2x + 1$.

33. (a) To write the equation in slope-intercept form, solve for y:

$$x + y = 4 \Rightarrow x - x + y = 4 - x \Rightarrow y = 4 - x \Rightarrow y = -x + 4$$

(b) Because the slope-intercept form is $y = mx + b$, the slope is -1 and the y-intercept is 4.

35. (a) To write the equation in slope-intercept form, solve for y:

$$2x + y = 4 \Rightarrow 2x - 2x + y = 4 - 2x \Rightarrow y = 4 - 2x \Rightarrow y = -2x + 4$$

(b) Because the slope-intercept form is $y = mx + b$, the slope is -2 and the y-intercept is 4.

37. (a) To write the equation in slope-intercept form, solve for y: $x - 2y = -4 \Rightarrow x - x - 2y = -4 - x \Rightarrow$

$$-2y = -4 - x \Rightarrow -2y = -x - 4 \Rightarrow \frac{-2y}{-2} = \frac{-x - 4}{-2} \Rightarrow y = \frac{-x}{-2} - \frac{4}{-2} \Rightarrow y = \frac{1}{2}x + 2$$

(b) Because the slope-intercept form is $y = mx + b$, the slope is $\dfrac{1}{2}$ and the y-intercept is 2.

39. (a) To write the equation in slope-intercept form, solve for y: $2x - 3y = 6 \Rightarrow 2x - 2x - 3y = 6 - 2x \Rightarrow$

$$-3y = 6 - 2x \Rightarrow -3y = -2x + 6 \Rightarrow \frac{-3y}{-3} = \frac{-2x + 6}{-3} \Rightarrow y = \frac{-2x}{-3} + \frac{6}{-3} \Rightarrow y = \frac{2}{3}x - 2$$

(b) Because the slope-intercept form is $y = mx + b$, the slope is $\dfrac{2}{3}$ and the y-intercept is -2.

41. (a) To write the equation in slope-intercept form, solve for y: $x = 4y - 6 \Rightarrow x - 4y = 4y - 4y - 6 \Rightarrow$

$x - 4y = -6 \Rightarrow x - x - 4 = -6 - x \Rightarrow -4y = -x - 6 \Rightarrow \dfrac{-4y}{-4} = \dfrac{-x}{-4} - \dfrac{6}{-4} \Rightarrow y = \dfrac{1}{4}x + \dfrac{3}{2}$

(b) Because the slope-intercept form is $y = mx + b$, the slope is $\dfrac{1}{4}$ and the y-intercept is $\dfrac{3}{2}$.

43. (a) To write the equation in slope-intercept form, solve for y: $\dfrac{1}{2}x + \dfrac{3}{2}y = 1 \Rightarrow \dfrac{1}{2}x - \dfrac{1}{2}x + \dfrac{3}{2}y = 1 - \dfrac{1}{2}x \Rightarrow$

$\dfrac{3}{2}y = -\dfrac{1}{2}x + 1 \Rightarrow \dfrac{2}{3}\left(\dfrac{3}{2}y\right) = \dfrac{2}{3}\left(-\dfrac{1}{2}x + 1\right) \Rightarrow y = -\dfrac{1}{3}x + \dfrac{2}{3}$

(b) Because the slope-intercept form is $y = mx + b$, the slope is $-\dfrac{1}{3}$ and the y-intercept is $\dfrac{2}{3}$.

45. See Figure 45.

47. See Figure 47.

Figure 45

Figure 47

Figure 49

49. See Figure 49.

51. See Figure 51.

53. See Figure 53.

Figure 51

Figure 53

Figure 55

55. See Figure 55.

\7. For every increase in x of 1, the y-value increases by 2. Therefore, the slope $m = 2$. When $x = 0, y = 2$.

Therefore the y-intercept $b = 2$. Therefore: $y = mx + b \Rightarrow y = 2x + 2$.

59. For every increase in x of 2, the y-value increases by 2. Therefore, the slope $m = 1$. When $x = 0, y = -2$.

Therefore the y-intercept $b = -2$. Therefore: $y = mx + b \Rightarrow y = x - 2$.

Parallel and Perpendicular Lines

61. $y = \dfrac{4}{7}x + 3$

63. Because the line parallel to $y = 3x + 1$ has slope $3, m = 3$.

Because when $x = 0, y = 0$, the y-intercept $b = 0$. Therefore: $y = 3x$.

65. Solve $2x + 4y = 5$ for y: $2x + 4y = 5 \Rightarrow 2x - 2x + 4y = 5 - 2x \Rightarrow 4y = -2x + 5 \Rightarrow$

$\dfrac{4y}{4} = \dfrac{-2x}{4} + \dfrac{5}{4} \Rightarrow y = -\dfrac{1}{2}x + \dfrac{5}{4}$.

Because the line parallel to $2x + 4y = 5$ has slope $-\dfrac{1}{2}$, $m = -\dfrac{1}{2}$. Then, to find the y-intercept b, replace x with

1 and y with 2: $y = -\dfrac{1}{2}x + b \Rightarrow 2 = -\dfrac{1}{2}(1) + b \Rightarrow 2 = -\dfrac{1}{2} + b \Rightarrow 2 + \dfrac{1}{2} = -\dfrac{1}{2} + \dfrac{1}{2} + b \Rightarrow \dfrac{5}{2} = b$.

Therefore, $y = -\dfrac{1}{2}x + \dfrac{5}{2}$.

67. Because the line $y = -\dfrac{1}{2}x - 3$ has slope $-\dfrac{1}{2}$, the line perpendicular to it has slope 2, the negative reciprocal of

$-\dfrac{1}{2}$. Because when $x = 0, y = -4$, the y-intercept $b = -4$. Therefore, $y = mx + b \Rightarrow y = 2x - 4$.

69. Solve $x = -\dfrac{1}{3}y$ for y: $x = -\dfrac{1}{3}y \Rightarrow -3(x) = -3\left(-\dfrac{1}{3}y\right) \Rightarrow -3x = y \Rightarrow y = -3x$.

Because the line $y = -3x$ has slope -3, the line perpendicular to it has slope $\dfrac{1}{3}$, the negative reciprocal of -3.

Then, to find the y-intercept b, replace y with 0 and x with -1: $0 = \dfrac{1}{3}(-1) + b \Rightarrow 0 = -\dfrac{1}{3} + b \Rightarrow$

$0 + \dfrac{1}{3} = -\dfrac{1}{3} + \dfrac{1}{3} + b \Rightarrow \dfrac{1}{3} = b$. Therefore, $y = \dfrac{1}{3}x + \dfrac{1}{3}$.

Applications

71. (a) When $y = 0, x = 25$. Therefore, $25.

(b) It costs $0.25x$ for each additional mile x. Therefore, 25 cents.

(c) When $x = 0, y = 25$. Therefore the y-intercept is 25. This represents the fixed cost of renting a car.

(d) The slope is 0.25. This represents the cost per mile of renting the car.

73. (a) Because $b = 3.95$ and $m = 0.07$, $y = 0.07x + 3.95$. Set $x = 50$ and solve for y:

$y = 0.07(50) + 3.95 = 3.5 + 3.95 = 7.45$. Therefore, the charge is $7.45.

(b) $C = 0.07x + 3.95$

(c) Set $C = 8.65$ and solve for x: $8.65 = 0.07x + 3.95 \Rightarrow 8.65 - 3.95 = 0.07x \Rightarrow 4.7 = 0.07x \Rightarrow$

$\dfrac{4.7}{0.07} = \dfrac{0.07x}{0.07} \Rightarrow x \approx 67$ min.

75. (a) Because the y-value increases by $0.35 for every increase of 1 in the x-value, the slope $m = 0.35$. Because

the fixed cost of $164.30 represents the y-value when $x = 0, b = 164.3$.

(b) The fixed cost of owning the car.

3.6: Point-Slope Form

Concepts

1. One

3. $y = mx + b$

5. Yes; every nonvertical line has one slope and one y-intercept.

Point-Slope Form

7. Substitute -3 for x and 3 for y: $y - 1 = -\dfrac{2}{3}x \Rightarrow 3 - 1 = -\dfrac{2}{3}(-3) \Rightarrow 2 = \dfrac{6}{3} \Rightarrow 2 = 2$. Because this is a

    true statement, the point $(-3, 3)$ lies on the line.

9. Substitute 1 for x and 4 for y: $y - 3 = -(x - 1) \Rightarrow 4 - 3 = -(1 - 1) \Rightarrow 1 = 0$. Because this is not a true

    statement, the point $(1, 4)$ does not lie on the line.

11. Substitute 0 for x and 4 for y: $y = \dfrac{1}{2}(x + 4) + 2 \Rightarrow 4 = \dfrac{1}{2}(0 + 4) + 2 \Rightarrow 4 = \dfrac{1}{2}(4) + 2 \Rightarrow$

    $4 = 2 + 2 \Rightarrow 4 = 4$. Because this is a true statement, the point $(0, 4)$ lies on the line.

13. The points $(1, 2)$ and $(-3, -1)$ are on the line. First, determine the slope: $m = \dfrac{y_2 - y_1}{x_2 - x_1} = \dfrac{-1 - 2}{-3 - 1} = \dfrac{-3}{-4} = \dfrac{3}{4}$.

    Then substitute the x and y values of the point $(1, 2)$ into the point-slope form: $y - y_1 = m(x - x_1) \Rightarrow$

    $y - 2 = m(x - 1)$. Then, substitute the value of the slope for m: $y - 2 = \dfrac{3}{4}(x - 1)$.

15. The points $(3, -1)$ and $(-1, 1)$ are on the line. First, determine the slope:

    $m = \dfrac{y_2 - y_1}{x_2 - x_1} = \dfrac{1 - (-1)}{-1 - 3} = \dfrac{1 + 1}{-4} = \dfrac{2}{-4} = -\dfrac{1}{2}$.

    Then substitute the x and y values of the point $(3, -1)$ and the value of the slope into the point-slope form:

    $y - y_1 = m(x - x_1) \Rightarrow y - (-1) = -\dfrac{1}{2}(x - 3) \Rightarrow y + 1 = -\dfrac{1}{2}(x - 3)$.

17. $y - y_1 = m(x - x_1) \Rightarrow y - (-2) = -3(x - 1) \Rightarrow y + 2 = -3(x - 1)$

19. $y - y_1 = m(x - x_1) \Rightarrow y - 30 = 1.5(x - 2000)$

21. First, determine the slope: $m = \dfrac{y_2 - y_1}{x_2 - x_1} = \dfrac{-3 - 4}{-1 - 2} = \dfrac{-7}{-3} = \dfrac{7}{3}$. Then, insert the values of the first point and

    the value of the slope into the point-slope form: $y - y_1 = m(x - x_1) \Rightarrow y - 4 = \dfrac{7}{3}(x - 2)$.

23. First determine the slope: $m = \dfrac{y_2 - y_1}{x_2 - x_1} = \dfrac{-3 - 0}{0 - 5} = \dfrac{-3}{-5} = \dfrac{3}{5}$. Then, insert the values of the first point and

    the value of the slope into the point-slope form: $y - y_1 = m(x - x_1) \Rightarrow y - 0 = \dfrac{3}{5}(x - 5) \Rightarrow y = \dfrac{3}{5}(x - 5)$.

25. First determine the slope: $m = \dfrac{y_2 - y_1}{x_2 - x_1} = \dfrac{65 - 15}{2000 - 1990} = \dfrac{50}{10} = 5$. Then, insert the values of the first point

    and the value of the slope into the point-slope form: $y - y_1 = m(x - x_1) \Rightarrow y - 15 = 5(x - 1990)$.

27. To convert to slope-intercept form, use the distributive property of multiplication and solve for y:

    $y - 4 = 3(x - 2) \Rightarrow y - 4 = 3x - 6 \Rightarrow y - 4 + 4 = 3x - 6 + 4 \Rightarrow y = 3x - 2$.

29. To convert to slope-intercept form, use the distributive property of multiplication and solve for y:

$$y + 2 = \frac{1}{3}(x + 6) \Rightarrow y + 2 = \frac{1}{3}x + 2 \Rightarrow y + 2 - 2 = \frac{1}{3}x + 2 - 2 \Rightarrow y = \frac{1}{3}x.$$

31. Use the distributive property of multiplication and solve for y: $y = -2(x - 2) + 5 \Rightarrow y = -2x + 4 + 5 \Rightarrow$

$y = -2x + 9.$

33. $y = -16(x + 1.5) + 5 \Rightarrow y = -16x - 24 + 5 \Rightarrow y = -16x - 19$

$y = -15(x - 1) + 100 \Rightarrow y = -15x + 15 + 100 \Rightarrow y = -15x + 115$

35. First, find the point-slope form for the line:.

Then, to find the slope-intercept form, use the distributive property of multiplication, then solve for y:

$$y + 3 = -2x + 8 \Rightarrow y + 3 - 3 = -2x + 8 - 3 \Rightarrow y = -2x + 5.$$

37. First, find the slope of the line: $m = \dfrac{y_2 - y_1}{x_2 - x_1} = \dfrac{-1 - (-2)}{2 - 3} = \dfrac{-1 + 2}{-1} = \dfrac{1}{-1} = -1$. Then, find the point-slope

form for the line by inserting the values of the point $(3, -2)$ and the value of the slope into the point-slope form:

$y - y_1 = m(x - x_1) \Rightarrow y - (-2) = -1(x - 3) \Rightarrow y + 2 = -1(x - 3)$. Then, use the distributive property of

multiplication and solve for y: $y + 2 = -x + 3 \Rightarrow y + 2 - 2 = -x + 3 - 2 \Rightarrow y = -x + 1.$

39. The points $(3, 0)$ and $\left(0, \dfrac{1}{3}\right)$ are on the line. First find the slope of the line:

$m = \dfrac{y_2 - y_1}{x_2 - x_1} = \dfrac{\frac{1}{3} - 0}{0 - 3} = \dfrac{\frac{1}{3}}{-3} = \dfrac{1}{3}\left(-\dfrac{1}{3}\right) = -\dfrac{1}{9}$. Then, insert the values of the point $(3, 0)$ and the value of the

slope into the point-slope form: $y - y_1 = m(x - x_1) \Rightarrow y - 0 = -\dfrac{1}{9}(x - 3).$

Then, use the distributive property of multiplication and solve for y: $y = -\dfrac{1}{9}x + \dfrac{1}{3}.$

41. The line parallel to $y = 2x - 1$ has slope 2. Insert the values of the point $(2, -3)$ and the value of the slope

into the point-slope form: $y - y_1 = m(x - x_1) \Rightarrow y - (-3) = 2(x - 2) \Rightarrow y + 3 = 2(x - 2)$. Then,

convert to slope-intercept form: $y + 3 = 2x - 4 \Rightarrow y + 3 - 3 = 2x - 4 - 3 \Rightarrow y = 2x - 7.$

43. The line perpendicular to $y = -\dfrac{1}{2}x + 3$ has slope 2. Insert the values of the point $(6, -3)$ and the value of the

slope into the point-slope form: $y - y_1 = m(x - x_1) \Rightarrow y - (-3) = 2(x - 6) \Rightarrow y + 3 = 2(x - 6)$. Then,

convert to slope-intercept form: $y + 3 = 2x - 12 \Rightarrow y + 3 - 3 = 2x - 12 - 3 \Rightarrow y = 2x - 15.$

45. As x increases by 1, y decreases by 2. Thus, the slope is -2. Insert the values of the point $(1, -3)$ and the value of

the slope into the point slope form: $y - y_1 = m(x - x_1) \Rightarrow y - (-3) = -2(x - 1) \Rightarrow y + 3 = -2(x - 1)$.

Then, convert to slope-intercept form: $y + 3 = -2x + 2 \Rightarrow y + 3 - 3 = -2x + 2 - 3 \Rightarrow y = -2x - 1.$

47. As x increases by 2, y increases by 1. Thus, the slope is $\dfrac{1}{2}$. Insert the values of the point $(-1, -3)$ and the value of

the slope into the point slope form: $y - y_1 = m(x - x_1) \Rightarrow y - (-3) = \dfrac{1}{2}(x - (-1)) \Rightarrow y + 3 = \dfrac{1}{2}(x + 1)$.

Then, convert to slope-intercept form: $y + 3 = \dfrac{1}{2}x + \dfrac{1}{2} \Rightarrow y + 3 - 3 = \dfrac{1}{2}x + \dfrac{1}{2} - 3 \Rightarrow y = \dfrac{1}{2}x - \dfrac{5}{2}.$

Graphical Interpretation

49. (a) As x increases, the y-value decreases. Because y represents the distance from home, the person is traveling toward home.

   (b) After 1 hour, the person is 250 miles from home; after 4 hours, the person is 100 miles from home.

   (c) Because in 3 hours the person travels 150 miles, the driver is traveling at 50 mph.

   (d) First, find the slope: $m = \dfrac{y_2 - y_1}{x_2 - x_1} = \dfrac{100 - 250}{4 - 1} = \dfrac{-150}{3} = -50$. Then, $y = -50x + b$. Because when $x = 0, y = 300$, the y-intercept b is 300. Then, $y = -50x + 300$. The car is traveling toward home at 50 mph.

51. (a) Because y increases as x increases, water is entering the tank. After 4 minutes, 300 gallons.

   (b) When $x = 0, y = 100$. therefore, the y-intercept is 100. This means that the tank held 100 gallons of water initially.

   (c) First, find the slope: $m = \dfrac{y_2 - y_1}{x_2 - x_1} = \dfrac{200 - 100}{2 - 0} = \dfrac{100}{2} = 50$.

   Then: $y = mx + b \Rightarrow y = 50x + 100$; the amount of water is increasing at a rate of 50 gal/min.

   (d) The tank will be full after 8 minutes.

53. (a) Find the slope: $m = \dfrac{y_2 - y_1}{x_2 - x_1} = \dfrac{15 - 40}{6 - 1} = \dfrac{-25}{5} = -5°\text{F/hr}$.

   (b) One point of the graph of the line is $(1, 40)$ and another point is $(2, 35)$. First, find the point-slope form of the line: $y - y_1 = m(x - x_1) \Rightarrow y - 40 = -5(x - 1)$. Then convert to slope-intercept form: $T = -5x + 5 + 40 \Rightarrow T = -5x + 45$. The temperature is decreasing at a rate of 5°F per hour.

   (c) To find the x-intercept, use the slope-intercept form of the line and set $T = 0$: $T = -5x + 45 \Rightarrow 0 = -5x + 45 \Rightarrow 5x = 45 \Rightarrow x = 9$. Therefore, at 9 A.M. the temperature was 0°F.

   (d) See Figure 53.

   (e) At 4 A.M., the temperature was 25°F.

Figure 53

Applications

55. (a) First, substitute 1988 for x: $y = 64(x - 1998) + 628 = 64(1998 - 1998) + 628 = 64(0) + 628 = 628$.

    Thus, in 1998 the were 628,000 inmates.

    Then, substitute 2000 for x: $y = 64(x - 1998) + 628 = 64(2000 - 1998) + 628 = 64(12) + 628 =$

    $768 - 628 = 1396$. Thus, in 2000 the were 1,396,000 inmates.

   (b) One point on the graph of the line is (1998, 628) and another point is (2000, 1396), Thus:

    $m = \dfrac{y_2 - y_1}{x_2 - x_1} = \dfrac{1396 - 628}{2000 - 1988} = \dfrac{768}{12} = 64$. Therefore, the number of inmates increased on average by

    64,000/yr.

57. (a) In 1984, tuition and fees were \$1225; in 1987, tuition and fees were \$1621.

   (b) First, find the slope: $m = \dfrac{y_2 - y_1}{x_2 - x_1} = \dfrac{1621 - 1225}{1987 - 1984} = \dfrac{396}{3} = 132$. Then, substitute the value of the first

    point and the value of the slope into the point-slope form: $y - y_1 = m(x - x_1) \Rightarrow$

    $y - 1225 = 132(x - 1984)$; tuition and fees increased on average by \$132/yr.

   (c) Substitute 1990 for x: $y - 1225 = 132(1990 - 1984) \Rightarrow y - 1225 = 132(6) \Rightarrow y - 1225 = 792 \Rightarrow$

    $y - 1225 + 1225 = 792 + 1225 \Rightarrow y = 2017$. Thus, in 1990, tuition and fees would be about \$2017.

59. (a) The slope-intercept form is $y = mx + b$. Solve for b by setting y equal to 22, m equal to 3.1, and x equal to 1996:

    $22 = 3.1(1996) + b \Rightarrow 22 = 6187.6 + b \Rightarrow 22 - 6187.6 = 6187.6 - 6187.6 + b \Rightarrow -6165.6 = b$.

    Therefore, $y = 3.1x - 6165.6$.

   (b) Substitute 2003 for x: $y = 3.1(2003) - 6165.6 = 6209.3 - 6165.6 \Rightarrow y = 43.7$ million.

Checking Basic Concepts for Sections 3.5 & 3.6

1. For every x-value increase of 1, the y-value decreases by 3. Therefore, the slope is -3. When $x = 0, y = 1$.

   Thus, the y-intercept is 1. Therefore: $y = mx + b \Rightarrow y = -3x + 1$.

2. To convert to slope-intercept form, solve for y: $4x - 5y = 20 \Rightarrow 4x - 4x - 5y = 20 - 4x \Rightarrow$

   $-5y = -4x + 20 \Rightarrow \dfrac{-5y}{-5} = \dfrac{-4x}{-5} + \dfrac{20}{-5} \Rightarrow y = \dfrac{4}{5}x - 4$. Therefore, the slope is $\dfrac{4}{5}$ and the y-intercept is -4.

3. See Figure 3.

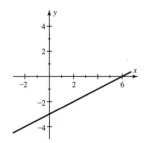

Figure 3

4. (a) The slope m is 3 and the y-intercept b is -2. Therefore: $y = mx + b \Rightarrow y = 3x - 2$.

   (b) The slope of the line $y = \dfrac{2}{3}x$ is $\dfrac{2}{3}$. Therefore, the slope of the line perpendicular to $y = \dfrac{2}{3}x$ has slope $-\dfrac{3}{2}$.

   Because for every 2 units of increase in run the rise decreases by 3, the y-intercept b exists when $x = 0$.

   Thus, $b = 0$. Then: $y = mx + b \Rightarrow y = -\dfrac{3}{2}x + 0 \Rightarrow y = -\dfrac{3}{2}x$.

   (c) First, find the slope: $m = \dfrac{y_2 - y_1}{x_2 - x_1} = \dfrac{3 - (-4)}{-2 - 1} = \dfrac{3 + 4}{-2 - 1} = \dfrac{7}{-3} = -\dfrac{7}{3}$. Then insert the values of the

   point $(1, -4)$ and the value of the slope into the point-slope form: $y - y_1 = m(x - x_1) \Rightarrow$

   $y - (-4) = -\dfrac{7}{3}(x - 1) \Rightarrow y + 4 = -\dfrac{7}{3}(x - 1)$. Then, convert to slope-intercept form:

   $y + 4 = -\dfrac{7}{3}x + \dfrac{7}{3} \Rightarrow y + 4 - 4 = -\dfrac{7}{3}x + \dfrac{7}{3} - 4 \Rightarrow y = -\dfrac{7}{3}x + \dfrac{7}{3} - \dfrac{12}{3} \Rightarrow y = -\dfrac{7}{3}x - \dfrac{5}{3}$.

5. First, use the points $(0, 3)$ and $(1, 5)$ to find the slope: $m = \dfrac{y_2 - y_1}{x_2 - x_1} = \dfrac{5 - 3}{1 - 0} = \dfrac{2}{1} = 2$.

   When $x = 0$, $y = 3$. Thus, the y-intercept b is 3. Therefore: $y = mx + b \Rightarrow y = 2x + 3$.

6. (a) First, find the slope: $m = \dfrac{y_2 - y_1}{x_2 - x_1} = \dfrac{12 - 36}{3 - 1} = \dfrac{-24}{2} = -12$. Then, insert the values for the point $(1, 36)$

   and the value of the slope into the point-slope form: $y - y_1 = m(x - x_1) \Rightarrow y - 36 = -12(x - 1)$. Then

   convert to slope-intercept form: $y - 36 = -12x + 12 \Rightarrow y - 36 + 36 = -12x + 12 + 36 \Rightarrow$

   $y = -12x + 48$.

   (b) Because the slope is -12, the bicyclist gets 12 miles closer to home every hour ridden. Therefore the

   bicyclist is traveling at 12 mph.

   (c) The y-value will equal 0 when the rider reaches home Therefore, substitute 0 for y in the slope-intercept

   form and solve for x: $y = -12x + 48 \Rightarrow 0 = -12x + 48 \Rightarrow 0 - 48 = -12x + 48 - 48 \Rightarrow$

   $-48 = -12x \Rightarrow \dfrac{-48}{-12} = \dfrac{-12x}{-12} \Rightarrow 4 = x \Rightarrow x = 4$. Therefore, the rider will arrive home at 4 pm.

   (d) At noon, $x = 0$. Substitute 0 for x in the slope-intercept form and solve for y: $y = -12x + 48 \Rightarrow$

   $y = -12(0) + 48 \Rightarrow y = 48$. Therefore, at noon the rider was 48 miles from home.

7. (a) At noon, $t = 0$. Substitute 0 for t in the equation and solve for s: $s = 2t + 5 = 2(0) + 5 \Rightarrow s = 5$.

   Therefore, 5 inches of snow fell by noon.

   (b) Because the slope equals 2, the snow fell at a rate of 2 inches per hour in the afternoon.

   (c) The y-intercept is 5. This represents the total inches of snow that fell before noon.

   (d) The slope is 2. This represents that the rate of snowfall was 2 inches per hour.

3.7: Introduction to Modeling

Concepts

1. abstraction

3. linear

5. approximate

7. f

9. a

11. e

Modeling Linear Data

13. For the linear equation $y = 2x + 2$, the y-intercept is 2 and the slope is 2. The ordered pairs in the table are modeled exactly by the linear equation.

15. For the linear equation $y = -4x$, the y-intercept is 0 and the slope is -4. The ordered pairs in the table are not modeled exactly by the linear equation.

17. For the linear equation $y = 1.4x - 4$, the y-intercept is -4 and the slope is 1.4. The ordered pairs in the table are not modeled exactly by the linear equation.

19. Because the line goes through the points on the graph, the linear model is exact. To find the equation of the line, first find the slope: $m = \dfrac{y_2 - y_1}{x_2 - x_1} = \dfrac{6 - 4}{4 - 3} = \dfrac{2}{1} = 2$. Then to find the y-intercept b, insert the values of the point $(4, 6)$ and the value of the slope into the slope-intercept form and solve for b: $y = mx + b \Rightarrow$ $6 = 2(4) + b \Rightarrow 6 = 8 + b \Rightarrow 6 - 8 = 8 - 8 + b \Rightarrow -2 = b \Rightarrow b = -2$. Thus, the equation of the line is $y = 2x - 2$.

21. Because the line does not go through all the points on the graph, the linear model is approximate. To find the equation of the line, first find the slope: $m = \dfrac{y_2 - y_1}{x_2 - x_1} = \dfrac{6 - 4}{2 - 1} = \dfrac{2}{1} = 2$. Then to find the y-intercept b, insert the values of the point $(2, 6)$ and the value of the slope into the slope-intercept form and solve for b: $y = mx + b \Rightarrow 6 = 2(2) + b \Rightarrow 6 = 4 + b \Rightarrow 6 - 4 = 4 - 4 + b \Rightarrow 2 = b \Rightarrow b = 2$. Thus, the equation of the line is $y = 2x + 2$.

23. Because the line does not go through all the points on the graph, the linear model is approximate. The equation of the line is $y = 2$ because the slope is 0 and because the y-intercept is at $y = 2$.

25. The initial value is 40, so the y-intercept b is 40. The rate of increase is 5 per minute, so the slope is 5. Thus: $y = mx + b \Rightarrow y = 5x + 40$.

27. The initial value is -5, so the y-intercept b is -5. The rate of decrease is 20 per day, so the slope is -20. Thus: $y = mx + b \Rightarrow y = -20x - 5$.

29. The initial value is 8, so the y-intercept b is 8. Because y remains constant, the slope is 0. Thus: $y = mx + b \Rightarrow y = 0(x) + 8 \Rightarrow y = 8$.

31. (a) See Figure 31a. A line could pass through all five points.

    (b) See Figure 31b.

    (c) Because y decreases by 2 for every increase in x, the slope m is -2. Because when $x = 0$, $y = 4$, the y-intercept b is 4. Thus: $y = mx + b \Rightarrow y = -2x + 4$.

Figure 31a

Figure 31b

33. (a) See Figure 33a. A line could not pass through all five points.

    (b) See Figure 33b.

    (c) To find the equation of the line, first find the slope: $m = \dfrac{y_2 - y_1}{x_2 - x_1} = \dfrac{0 - 4}{0 - (-2)} = \dfrac{-4}{2} = -2$.

    Then, the line passes through the origin, so the y-intercept b is 0. Thus: $y = mx + b \Rightarrow y = -2x + 0 \Rightarrow y = -2x$.

Figure 33a

Figure 33b

35. (a) See Figure 35a. A line could pass through all five points.

    (b) See Figure 35b.

    (c) To find the equation of the line, first find the slope: $m = \dfrac{y_2 - y_1}{x_2 - x_1} = \dfrac{-2 - 0}{0 - (-4)} = \dfrac{-2}{4} = -\dfrac{1}{2}$.

    Then, when $x = 0$, $y = -2$, the y-intercept b is -2. Thus: $y = mx + b \Rightarrow y = -\dfrac{1}{2}x - 2$.

Figure 35a

Figure 35b

37. (a) See Figure 37a. A line could not pass through all five points.

    (b) See Figure 37b.

    (c) To find the equation of the line, first find the slope: $m = \dfrac{y_2 - y_1}{x_2 - x_1} = \dfrac{0 - (-1)}{3 - 0} = \dfrac{1}{3}$.

      Then, when $x = 0$, $y = -1$, the y-intercept b is -1. Thus: $y = mx + b \Rightarrow y = \dfrac{1}{3}x - 1$.

                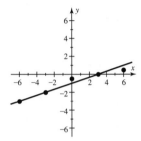

Figure 37a   Figure 37b

Applications

39. The initial value is 200, so the g-intercept b is 200. The barrel is being filled at a rate of 5 gallons per minute, so the slope m is 5. Thus: $g = mt + b \Rightarrow g = 5t + 200$, where g represents gallons of water and t represents time in minutes.

41. The initial value is 5, so the d-intercept b is 5. The athlete is jogging at 6 miles per hour, so the slope m is 6. Thus: $d = mt + b \Rightarrow d = 6t + 5$, where d represents distance in miles and t represents time in hours.

43. The initial value is 200, so the p-intercept b is 200. The worker is being paid \$8 per hour, so the slope m is 8. Thus: $p = mt + b \Rightarrow p = 8t + 200$, where p represents total pay in dollars and t represents time in hours.

45. The initial value is 5, so the r-intercept b is 5. The carpenter is shingling roofs at a rate of 1 per day, so the slope m is 1. Thus: $r = mt + b \Rightarrow r = t + 5$, where r represents total number of roofs shingled and t represents time in days.

47. (a) A point on the graph of the volume of the glacier is (1912, 5) and another point is (2002, 1). Because there is assumed to be a constant melt rate, to find the yearly rate find the slope of the line connecting the two points: $m = \dfrac{y_2 - y_1}{x_2 - x_1} = \dfrac{1 - 5}{2002 - 1912} = \dfrac{-4}{90} = -\dfrac{2}{45}$ acres per year.

    (b) The slope m is $-\dfrac{2}{45}$. The initial value b is 5. Thus: $A = mt + b \Rightarrow A = -\dfrac{2}{45}t + 5$, where A represents acres of glacier and t represents time in years.

49. (a) First, use the first and last date points to determine slope: $m = \dfrac{y_2 - y_1}{x_2 - x_1} = \dfrac{145 - 113}{2000 - 1997} = \dfrac{32}{3}$. Then,

insert the values of the first point into the point-slope form: $y - y_1 = m(x - x_1) \Rightarrow$

$y - 113 = \dfrac{32}{3}(x - 1997)$. Then, convert to slope-intercept form: $y - 113 = \dfrac{32}{3}x - \dfrac{63{,}904}{3} \Rightarrow$

$y - 113 + 113 = \dfrac{32}{3}x - \dfrac{63{,}904}{3} + 113 \Rightarrow y = \dfrac{32}{3}x - \dfrac{63{,}904}{3} + \dfrac{339}{3} \Rightarrow y = \dfrac{32}{3}x - \dfrac{63{,}565}{3} \Rightarrow$

$y = \dfrac{32}{3}x - 21{,}188$ (approx.).

(b) Set $x = 2003$ and solve for y: $y = \dfrac{32}{3}(2003) - 21{,}188 = \dfrac{64{,}096}{3} - \dfrac{63{,}565}{3} = \dfrac{531}{3} \approx 177$. Thus, the

prison population in 2003 is about 177,000.

51. (a) See Figure 51a.

(b) See Figure 51b.

(c) $m = \dfrac{y_2 - y_1}{x_2 - x_1} = \dfrac{120 - 60}{6 - 3} = \dfrac{60}{3} = 20$. For every gallon of gasoline, the car travels 20 miles.

(d) Because when $x = 0$, $y = 0$, the y-intercept b is 0. Thus, $y = 20x$.

(e) $y = 20x = 20(7) = 140$ miles.

Figure 51a

Figure 51b

Checking Basic Concepts for Section 3.7

1. The ordered pairs in the table indicate that the y-intercept is 10 and the slope is -5. Thus, the line

   $y = -5x + 10$ models exactly the ordered pairs.

2. Because the line does not pass through each point on the graph, the linear model is approximate. For each

   increase in run of 1, the value of the rise increases by 1, so the slope m is 1. When $x = 0$, $y = -1$, so the

   y-intercept b is -1. Thus: $y = mx + b \Rightarrow y = x - 1$.

3. (a) The initial value b is 50 and the slope m is 10. Thus: $y = 10x + 50$.

   (b) The initial value b is 200 and the slope m is -2. Thus: $y = -2x + 200$.

4. (a) See Figure 4a. A line could pass through all four points.

    (b) See Figure 4b.

    (c) The *y*-intercept b is 1 and the slope m is $\dfrac{1-2}{0-(-2)} = \dfrac{-1}{2} = -\dfrac{1}{2}$. Thus: $y = -\dfrac{1}{2}x + 1$.

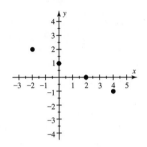

Figure 4a   Figure 4b

5. (a) The slope *m* is 0.05 and the *y*-intercept is 0. Thus, $T = 0.05x$.

    (b) First substitute 1975 for *x* and solve for *T*: $T = 0.05(1975) = 98.75$. Thus, a point on the graph is (1975, 98.75). Then, substitute 1959 for *x* and solve for *T*: $T = 0.05(1959) = 97.95$. Thus, a second point on the graph is (1959, 97.95). Then, subtract 97.95 from 98.75 to obtain the temperature increase: $98.75 - 97.95 = 0.8°F$.

Chapter 3 Review Exercises

Section 3.1

1. $(-2, 0)$: none; $(-1, 2)$: Quadrant II; $(0, 0)$: none; $(1, -2)$: Quadrant IV; $(1, 3)$: Quadrant I

2. See Figure 2.

3. See Figure 3.

Figure 2   Figure 3   Figure 4

4. See Figure 4.

Section 3.2

5. Substitute 6 for *x* and 3 for *y*: $y = x - 3 \Rightarrow 3 = 6 - 3 \Rightarrow 3 = 3$. Because this is a true statement, the ordered pair (6, 3) is a solution.

6. Substitute -2 for x and 1 for y: $y = 5 - 2x \Rightarrow 1 = 5 - 2(-2) \Rightarrow 1 = 5 + 4 \Rightarrow 1 = 9$. Because this is not a true statement, the ordered pair $(-2, 1)$ is not a solution.

7. Substitute -1 for x and 6 for y: $3x - y = 3 \Rightarrow 3(-1) - 6 = 3 \Rightarrow -3 - 6 = 3 \Rightarrow -9 = 3$. Because this is not a true statement, the ordered pair $(-1, 6)$ is not a solution.

8. Substitute -4 for x and -3 for y: $\frac{1}{2}x + 2y = -8 \Rightarrow \frac{1}{2}(-4) + 2(-3) = -8 \Rightarrow -2 - 6 = -8 \Rightarrow -8 = -8$.

   Because this is a true statement, the ordered pair $(-4, -3)$ is a solution.

9. For $x = -2$: $y = -3x = -3(-2) \Rightarrow y = 6$; for $x = -1$: $y = -3x = -3(-1) \Rightarrow y = 3$;

   for $x = 0$: $y = -3x = -3(0) \Rightarrow y = 0$; for $x = 1$: $y = -3x = -3(1) \Rightarrow y = -3$;

   for $x = 2$: $y = -3x = -3(2) \Rightarrow y = -6$. Therefore, the missing values in the table are $6, 3, 0, -3$, and -6.

   See Figure 9.

10. For $y = -3$: $2x + y = 5 \Rightarrow 2x + (-3) = 5 \Rightarrow 2x - 3 = 5 \Rightarrow 2x + 3 - 3 = 5 + 3 \Rightarrow 2x = 8 \Rightarrow$

    $\frac{2x}{2} = \frac{8}{2} \Rightarrow x = 4$; for $y = -1$: $2x + y = 5 \Rightarrow 2x + (-1) = 5 \Rightarrow 2x - 1 = 5 \Rightarrow 2x - 1 + 1 = 5 + 1 \Rightarrow$

    $2x = 6 \Rightarrow \frac{2x}{2} = \frac{6}{2} \Rightarrow x = 3$; for $y = 0$: $2x + y = 5 \Rightarrow 2x + 0 = 5 \Rightarrow 2x = 5 \Rightarrow \frac{2x}{2} = \frac{5}{2} \Rightarrow x = 2.5$;

    for $y = 1$: $2x + y = 5 \Rightarrow 2x + 1 = 5 \Rightarrow 2x + 1 - 1 = 5 - 1 \Rightarrow 2x = 4 \Rightarrow \frac{2x}{2} = \frac{4}{2} \Rightarrow x = 2$;

    for $y = 3$: $2x + y = 5 \Rightarrow 2x + 3 = 5 \Rightarrow 2x + 3 - 3 = 5 - 3 \Rightarrow 2x = 2 \Rightarrow \frac{2x}{2} = \frac{2}{2} \Rightarrow x = 1$.

    Therefore, the missing values in the tables are $4, 3, 2.5, 2$, and 1. See Figure 10.

x	-2	-1	0	1	2
y	6	3	0	-3	-6

Figure 9

x	4	3	2.5	2	1
y	-3	-1	0	1	3

Figure 10

x	-2	0	2	4
y	-4	2	8	14

Figure 11

11. See Figure 11.

12. See Figure 12.

13. See Figure 13.

x	1	2	3	4
y	6	5	4	3

Figure 12

x	-0.5	0	0.5	1
y	-1	0	1	2

Figure 13

x	-1	-3	-5	-7
y	1	2	3	4

Figure 14

14. See Figure 14.

15. See Figure 15.

16. See Figure 16.

Figure 15

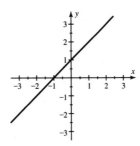

Figure 16

17. See Figure 17.

18. See Figure 18.

Figure 17

Figure 18

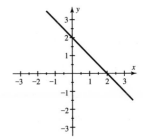

Figure 19

19. See Figure 19.

20. See Figure 20.

21. See Figure 21.

Figure 20

Figure 21

Figure 22

22. See Figure 22.

Section 3.3

23. The line crosses the x-axis at $x = 3$, therefore the x-intercept is 3. The line crosses the y-axis at $y = -2$, therefore the y-intercept is -2.

24. The graph crosses the x-axis at $x = -2$ and $x = 2$. Therefore, the x-intercepts are $2, -2$. The graph crosses the y-axis at $y = -4$, therefore, the y-intercept is -4.

25. For $x = -2$: $y = 2 - x = 2 - (-2) \Rightarrow y = 4$; for $x = -1$: $y = 2 - x = 2 - (-1) = 2 + 1 \Rightarrow y = 3$;

for $x = 0$: $y = 2 - x = 2 - 0 \Rightarrow y = 2$; for $x = 1$: $y = 2 - x = 2 - 1 \Rightarrow y = 1$;

for $x = 2$: $y = 2 - x = 2 - 2 \Rightarrow y = 0$. Therefore, the missing values in the table are 4, 3, 2, 2 ,1 ,0.

See Figure 25. When $y = 0$, $x = 2$. Therefore the x-intercept is 2. When $x = 0$, $y = 2$. Therefore, the

y-intercept is 2.

x	-2	-1	0	1	2
y	4	3	2	1	0

Figure 25

x	-4	-2	0	2	4
y	-4	-3	-2	-1	0

Figure 26

26 For $x = -4$: $x - 2y = 4 \Rightarrow -4 - 2y = 4 \Rightarrow -4 + 4 - 2y = 4 + 4 \Rightarrow -2y = 8 \Rightarrow \dfrac{-2y}{-2} = \dfrac{8}{-2} \Rightarrow$

$y = -4$; for $x = -2$: $x - 2y = 4 \Rightarrow -2 - 2y = 4 \Rightarrow -2 + 2 - 2y = 4 + 2 \Rightarrow -2y = 6 \Rightarrow$

$\dfrac{-2y}{-2} = \dfrac{6}{-2} \Rightarrow y = -3$; for $x = 0$: $x - 2y = 4 \Rightarrow 0 - 2y = 4 \Rightarrow -2y = 4 \Rightarrow \dfrac{-2y}{-2} = \dfrac{4}{-2} \Rightarrow y = -2$;

for $x = 2$: $x - 2y = 4 \Rightarrow 2 - 2y = 4 \Rightarrow 2 - 2 - 2y = 4 - 2 \Rightarrow -2y = 2 \Rightarrow \dfrac{-2y}{-2} = \dfrac{2}{-2} \Rightarrow y = -1$;

for $x = 4$: $x - 2y = 4 \Rightarrow 4 - 2y = 4 \Rightarrow 4 - 4 - 2y = 4 - 4 \Rightarrow -2y = 0 \Rightarrow \dfrac{-2y}{-2} = \dfrac{0}{-2} \Rightarrow y = 0$.

Therefore, the missing values in the table are $-4, -3, -2, -1, 0$. See Figure 26. When $y = 0$, $x = 4$.

Therefore, the x-intercept is 4. When $x = 0$, $y = -2$. Therefore, the y-intercept is -2.

27 To find the x-intercept, set $y = 0$: $2x - 3y = 6 \Rightarrow 2x - 3(0) = 6 \Rightarrow 2x = 6 \Rightarrow \dfrac{2x}{2} = \dfrac{6}{2} \Rightarrow x = 3$.

Therefore, the x-intercept is 3.

To find the y-intercept, set $x = 0$: $2x - 3y = 6 \Rightarrow 2(0) - 3y = 6 \Rightarrow -3y = 6 \Rightarrow \dfrac{-3y}{-3} = \dfrac{6}{-3} \Rightarrow y = -2$.

Therefore, the y-intercept is -2. See Figure 27.

28. Set $y = 0$ and solve for x: $5x - y = 5 \Rightarrow 5x - 0 = 5 \Rightarrow 5x = 5 \Rightarrow \dfrac{5x}{5} = \dfrac{5}{5} \Rightarrow x = 1$. Therefore, the

x-intercept is 1. Then set $x = 0$ and solve for y: $5x - y = 5 \Rightarrow 5(0) - y = 5 \Rightarrow -y = 5 \Rightarrow$

$-1(-y) = -1(5) \Rightarrow y = -5$. Therefore, the y-intercept is -5. See Figure 28.

Figure 27

Figure 28

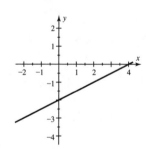

Figure 29

29. Set $y = 0$ and solve for x: $0.1x - 0.2y = 0.4 \Rightarrow 0.1x - 0.2(0) = 0.4 \Rightarrow 0.1x = 0.4 \Rightarrow \dfrac{0.1x}{0.1} = \dfrac{0.4}{0.1} \Rightarrow$

$x = 4$. Therefore the x-intercept is 4. Then set $x = 0$ and solve for y: $0.1x - 0.2y = 0.4 \Rightarrow$

$0.1(0) - 0.2y = 0.4 \Rightarrow -0.2y = 0.4 \Rightarrow \dfrac{-0.2y}{-0.2} = \dfrac{0.4}{-0.2} \Rightarrow y = -2$. Therefore, the y-intercept is -2.

See Figure 29.

30. Set $y = 0$ and solve for x: $\dfrac{x}{2} + \dfrac{y}{3} = 1 \Rightarrow \dfrac{x}{2} + \dfrac{0}{3} = 1 \Rightarrow \dfrac{x}{2} = 1 \Rightarrow 2\left(\dfrac{x}{2}\right) = 2(1) \Rightarrow x = 2.$

Therefore the x-intercept is 2. Then set $x = 0$ and solve for y: $\dfrac{x}{2} + \dfrac{y}{3} = 1 \Rightarrow \dfrac{0}{2} + \dfrac{y}{3} = 1 \Rightarrow \dfrac{y}{3} = 1 \Rightarrow$

$3\left(\dfrac{y}{3}\right) = 3(1) \Rightarrow y = 3.$ Therefore, the y-intercept is 3. See Figure 30.

31. (a) See Figure 31a.

    (b) See Figure 31b.

Figure 30

Figure 31a

Figure 31b

32. $x = -1; y = 1$

33. Because the y-value is constant, the slope $m = 0$. Because when $x = 0, y = 1$, the y-intercept $b = 1$.

    Thus: $y = mx + b \Rightarrow y = 0x + 1 \Rightarrow y = 1.$

34. Because the x-value is a constant 3, the graph is a vertical line with slope m undefined. Thus, $x = 3.$

35. horizontal line: $y = 3$; vertical line: $x = -2$

36. (a) When $x = 0, y = 90$. Therefore, the y-intercept is 90. When $y = 0, x = 3$. Therefore, the x-intercept is 3.

    (b) The driver is initially 90 miles from home; the driver arrives home after 3 hours.

Section 3.4

37. $m = \dfrac{y_2 - y_1}{x_2 - x_1} = \dfrac{7 - 3}{4 - 2} = \dfrac{4}{2} = 2.$

38. $m = \dfrac{y_2 - y_1}{x_2 - x_1} = \dfrac{-1 - 1}{2 - (-3)} = \dfrac{-2}{2 + 3} = \dfrac{-2}{5} = -\dfrac{2}{5}.$

39. $m = \dfrac{y_2 - y_1}{x_2 - x_1} = \dfrac{1 - 1}{5 - 2} = \dfrac{0}{3} = 0.$

40. $m = \dfrac{y_2 - y_1}{x_2 - x_1} = \dfrac{10 - 6}{-5 - (-5)} = \dfrac{4}{-5 + 5} = \dfrac{4}{0}.$ Thus, undefined.

41. The points $(1, 3)$ and $(0, 0)$ are on the graph. Insert these two points into the slope formula:

$m = \dfrac{y_2 - y_1}{x_2 - x_1} = \dfrac{0 - 3}{0 - 1} = \dfrac{-3}{-1} = 3.$

42. The points $(-2, 3)$ and $(0, 2)$ are on the graph. Insert these two points into the slope formula:

$$m = \frac{y_2 - y_1}{x_2 - x_1} = \frac{2 - 3}{0 - (-2)} = \frac{-1}{0 + 2} = \frac{-1}{2} = -\frac{1}{2}.$$

43. (a) See Figure 43.

    (b) The slope is -2 and the y-intercept is 0.

44. (a) See Figure 44.

    (b) The slope is 1 and the y-intercept is -1.

Figure 43

Figure 44

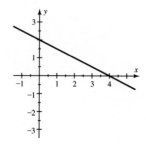

Figure 45

45. (a) See Figure 45.

    (b) Solve for y:

$$x + 2y = 4 \Rightarrow x - x + 2y = 4 - x \Rightarrow 2y = -x + 4 \Rightarrow \frac{1}{2}(2y) = \frac{1}{2}(-x + 4) \Rightarrow y = -\frac{1}{2}x + 2.$$

Therefore, the slope is $-\dfrac{1}{2}$ and the y-intercept is 2.

46. (a) See Figure 46.

    (b) Solve for y:

$$2x - 3y = -6 \Rightarrow 2x - 2x - 3y = -6 - 2x \Rightarrow -3y = -2x - 6 \Rightarrow -\frac{1}{3}(-3y) = -\frac{1}{3}(-2x - 6) \Rightarrow$$

$y = \dfrac{2}{3}x + 2$. Therefore, the slope is $\dfrac{2}{3}$ and the y-intercept is 2.

47. See Figure 47.

Figure 46

Figure 47

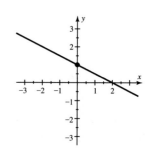

Figure 48

48. See Figure 48.

49. See Figure 49.

Figure 49

Figure 50

Figure 52

50. See Figure 50.

51. For every increase of 1 in the run, the rise increases by 2. Thus, the slope is 2. When $y = 0$, $x = 1$. Thus, the x-intercept is 1. When $x = 0$, $y = -2$. Thus, the y-intercept is -2.

52. Because the slope is $\frac{1}{2}$, for every increase of 1 in the run, the rise increases by $\frac{1}{2}$. Thus, when

$$x = 1, y = 1 + \frac{1}{2} = \frac{3}{2}. \text{ When } x = 2, y = \frac{3}{2} + \frac{1}{2} = \frac{4}{2} = 2. \text{ When } x = 3, y = 2 + \frac{1}{2} = \frac{4}{2} + \frac{1}{2} = \frac{5}{2}.$$

See Figure 52.

Section 3.5

53. For every increase of 1 in the run, the rise increases by 1. Therefore, the slope m is 1. When $x = 0$, $y = 1$. Therefore, the y-intercept is 1. Thus, $y = mx + b \Rightarrow y = 1x + 1 \Rightarrow y = x + 1$.

54. For every increase of 1 in the run, the rise decreases by 2. Therefore, the slope m is -2. When $x = 0$, $y = 2$. Therefore, the y-intercept is 2. Thus, $y = mx + b \Rightarrow y = -2x + 2$.

55. See Figure 55. $y = mx + b \Rightarrow y = 2x - 2$

Figure 55

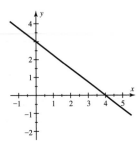

Figure 56

56. See Figure 56. $y = mx + b \Rightarrow y = -\frac{3}{4}x + 3$

57. (a) Solve for y: $x + y = 3 \Rightarrow x - x + y = 3 - x \Rightarrow y = -x + 3$.

(b) The slope is -1 and the y-intercept is 3.

58. (a) Solve for y: $-3x + 2y = -6 \Rightarrow -3x + 3x + 2y = -6 + 3x \Rightarrow 2y = 3x - 6 \Rightarrow$

$$\frac{1}{2}(2y) = \frac{1}{2}(3x - 6) \Rightarrow y = \frac{3}{2}x - 3.$$

(b) The slope is $\frac{3}{2}$ and the y-intercept is -3.

59. (a) Solve for y: $20x - 10y = 200 \Rightarrow 20x - 20x - 10y = 200 - 20x \Rightarrow -10y = -20x + 200 \Rightarrow$

$$-\frac{1}{10}(-10y) = -\frac{1}{10}(-20x + 200) \Rightarrow y = 2x - 20.$$

(b) The slope is 2 and the y-intercept is -20.

60. (a) Solve for y: $5x - 6y = 30 \Rightarrow 5x - 5x - 6y = 30 - 5x \Rightarrow -6y = -5x + 30 \Rightarrow$

$$-\frac{1}{6}(-6y) = -\frac{1}{6}(-5x + 30) \Rightarrow y = \frac{5}{6}x - 5.$$

(b) The slope is $\frac{5}{6}$ and the y-intercept is -5.

61. See Figure 61.

62. See Figure 62.

Figure 61   Figure 62   Figure 63

63. See Figure 63.

64. See Figure 64.

65. See Figure 65.

Figure 64   Figure 65   Figure 66

66. See Figure 66.

67. See Figure 67.

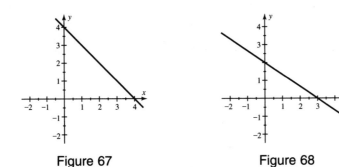

Figure 67   Figure 68

68. See Figure 68.

69. When the run increases by 1, the rise increases by 5. Thus, the slope m is 5. When $x = 0$, $y = -5$. Therefore, the y-intercept b is -5. Thus, $y = mx + b \Rightarrow y = 5x - 5$.

70. When the run increases by 1, the rise decreases by 2. Thus, the slope m is -2. When $x = 0$, $y = -5$. Therefore, the y-intercept b is 0. Thus, $y = mx + b \Rightarrow y = -2x + 0 \Rightarrow y = -2x$.

71. $y = mx + b \Rightarrow y = -\dfrac{5}{6}x + 2$.

72. The line parallel to $y = -2x + 1$ has slope -2. Insert the values of the point $(1, -1)$ and the value of the slope into the slope-intercept form and solve for b: $y = mx + b \Rightarrow -1 = -2(1) + b \Rightarrow -1 = -2 + b \Rightarrow$ $-1 + 2 = -2 + 2 + b \Rightarrow 1 = b \Rightarrow b = 1$. Thus, the equation of the line is $y = -2x + 1$.

73. The line perpendicular to $y = -\dfrac{3}{2}x$ has slope $\dfrac{2}{3}$, the negative reciprocal of $-\dfrac{3}{2}$. Insert the values of the point $(3, 0)$ and the value of the slope into the slope-intercept form and solve for b: $y = mx + b \Rightarrow$ $0 = \dfrac{2}{3}(3) + b \Rightarrow 0 = 2 + b \Rightarrow 0 - 2 = 2 - 2 + b \Rightarrow -2 = b \Rightarrow b = -2$. Thus, $y = \dfrac{2}{3}x - 2$.

74. The line perpendicular to $y = 5x - 3$ has slope $-\dfrac{1}{5}$, the negative reciprocal of 5. Insert the values of the point $(0, -2)$ and the value of the slope into the slope-intercept form and solve for b: $y = mx + b \Rightarrow$ $-2 = -\dfrac{1}{5}(0) + b \Rightarrow -2 = 0 + b \Rightarrow -2 = b \Rightarrow b = -2$. Thus, $y = -\dfrac{1}{5}x - 2$.

Section 3.6

75. Substitute -3 for x and 1 for y: $y - 1 = 2(x + 3) \Rightarrow \ - 1 - \ = 2(-3 + 3) \Rightarrow 0 = 2(0) \Rightarrow 0 = 0$. Because this is a true statement, the point $(-3, 1)$ lies on the line.

76. Substitute 3 for x and -8 for y: $y = -3(x - 1) + 2 \Rightarrow -8 = -3(3 - 1) + 2 \Rightarrow -8 = -3(2) + 2 \Rightarrow$ $-8 = -6 + 2 \Rightarrow -8 = -4$. Because this is not a true statement, the point $(3, -8)$ is not on the line.

77. Substitute the values of the point $(1, 2)$ and the value of the slope into the slope-intercept form and solve for b: $y = mx + b \Rightarrow 2 = 5(1) + b \Rightarrow 2 = 5 + b \Rightarrow 2 - 5 = 5 - 5 + b \Rightarrow -3 = b \Rightarrow b = -3$. Thus, $y = mx + b \Rightarrow y = 5x - 3$.

78. $y = mx + b \Rightarrow -5 = 20(3) + b \Rightarrow -5 = 60 + b \Rightarrow -5 - 60 = 60 - 60 + b \Rightarrow -65 = b \Rightarrow b = -65.$

   Thus, $y = mx + b \Rightarrow y = 20x - 65.$

79. Find the slope: $m = \dfrac{y_2 - y_1}{x_2 - x_1} = \dfrac{-1 - 1}{1 - (-2)} = \dfrac{-2}{1 + 2} = \dfrac{-2}{3} = -\dfrac{2}{3}.$ Then, insert the values of the point $(-2, 1)$

   and the value of the slope into the point-slope form: $y - y_1 = m(x - x_1) \Rightarrow y - 1 = -\dfrac{2}{3}(x - (-2)) \Rightarrow$

   $y - 1 = -\dfrac{2}{3}(x + 2).$ Then, convert to slope-intercept form: $y - 1 = -\dfrac{2}{3}x - \dfrac{4}{3} \Rightarrow$

   $y - 1 + 1 = -\dfrac{2}{3}x - \dfrac{4}{3} + 1 \Rightarrow y = -\dfrac{2}{3}x - \dfrac{4}{3} + \dfrac{3}{3} \Rightarrow y = -\dfrac{2}{3}x - \dfrac{1}{3}.$

80. Find the slope: $m = \dfrac{y_2 - y_1}{x_2 - x_1} = \dfrac{30 - (-30)}{40 - 20} = \dfrac{60}{20} = 3.$ Then, insert the values of the point $(20, -30)$

   and the value of the slope into the point-slope form: $y - y_1 = m(x - x_1) \Rightarrow y - (-30) = 3(x - 20) \Rightarrow$

   $y + 30 = 3(x - 20).$ Then, convert to slope-intercept form: $y + 30 = 3(x - 20) \Rightarrow$

   $y + 30 - 30 = 3(x - 20) - 30 \Rightarrow y = 3x - 60 - 30 \Rightarrow y = 3x - 90.$

81. One point on the line is $(3, 0)$ and another point is $(0, -4).$ Find the slope: $m = \dfrac{y_2 - y_1}{x_2 - x_1} = \dfrac{-4 - 0}{0 - 3} = \dfrac{-4}{-3} = \dfrac{4}{3}.$

   Then, insert the values of the point $(3, 0)$ and the value of the slope into the point-slope form:

   $y - y_1 = m(x - x_1) \Rightarrow y - 0 = \dfrac{4}{3}(x - 3).$ Then, convert to slope-intercept form: $y = \dfrac{4}{3}x - 4.$

82. One point on the line is $\left(\dfrac{1}{2}, 0\right)$ and another point is $(0, -1).$ Find the slope: $m = \dfrac{-1 - 0}{0 - \frac{1}{2}} = \dfrac{-1}{-\frac{1}{2}} = -2(-1) = 2.$

   The y-intercept b is $-1.$ Thus, $y = mx + b \Rightarrow y = 2x - 1.$

83. The line parallel to $y = 2x$ has slope 2. Insert the values of the point $(5, 7)$ and the value of the slope into the

   point-slope form: $y - y_1 = m(x - x_1) \Rightarrow y - 7 = 2(x - 5).$ Then, convert to slope-intercept form:

   $y - 7 = 2x - 10 \Rightarrow y - 7 + 7 = 2x - 10 + 7 \Rightarrow y = 2x - 10 + 7 \Rightarrow y = 2x - 3.$

84. First, find the slope by converting to slope-intercept form: $y - 4 = \dfrac{3}{2}(x + 1) \Rightarrow y - 4 = \dfrac{3}{2}x + \dfrac{3}{2} \Rightarrow$

   $y - 4 + 4 = \dfrac{3}{2}x + \dfrac{3}{2} + 4 \Rightarrow y = \dfrac{3}{2}x + \dfrac{3}{2} + \dfrac{8}{2} \Rightarrow y = \dfrac{3}{2}x + \dfrac{11}{2}.$ The line perpendicular to $y = \dfrac{3}{2}x + \dfrac{11}{2}$

   slope $-\dfrac{2}{3},$ the negative reciprocal of $\dfrac{3}{2}.$ Insert the values of the point $(-1, 0)$ and the value of the slope into the

   point-slope form: $y - y_1 = m(x - x_1) \Rightarrow y - 0 = -\dfrac{2}{3}(x - (-1)) \Rightarrow y - 0 = -\dfrac{2}{3}(x + 1).$ Then, convert to

   slope-intercept form: $y = -\dfrac{2}{3}x - \dfrac{2}{3}.$

Section 3.7

85. Because a straight line would not pass through all the points, no.

86. Because the line does not pass through all the points, the linear model is approximate. When the runs increase

   by 1, the rise decreases by 1. Therefore, the slope is $-1.$ When $x = 0, y = 5.$ Thus the y-intercept is 5.

   Therefore: $y = mx + b \Rightarrow y = -1x + 5 \Rightarrow y = -x + 5.$

87. Because the initial value is 40, $b = 40$. Because y decreases at a rate of 2 pounds per minute, the slope is -2. Therefore: $y = mx + b \Rightarrow y = -2x + 40$.

88. Because the initial value is 200, $b = 200$. Because the rate of increase is 20 gallons per hour, the slope is 20. Therefore: $y = mx + b \Rightarrow y = 20x + 200$.

89. Because the initial value is 50, $b = 50$. Because y remains constant, the slope is 0. Therefore: $y = 50$.

90. Because the initial value is -20, $b = -20$. Because the rise is 5 feet per second, the slope is 5. Therefore:

    $y = 5x - 20$.

91. (a) See Figure 91a. The line could pass through all five points.

    (b) See Figure 91b

    (c) The initial value is 10, and the slope is -4. Thus, $y = -4 + 10$.

Figure 91a

Figure 91b

92. (a) See Figure 92a. The line could not pass through all five points.

    (b) See Figure 92b.

    (c) $\dfrac{3 - 1}{0 - (-4)} = \dfrac{2}{4} = \dfrac{1}{2}$, so the slope is $\dfrac{1}{2}$. The y-intercept is 3, so $y = \dfrac{1}{2}x + 3$.

Figure 92a

Figure 92b

Figure 93

Applications

93. (a) See Figure 93.

    (b) The number of divorces remained unchanged from 1950 to 1960, increased significantly between 1960 and 1980, and then remined unchanged from 1980 to 1990.

94. (a) $G = 100t$

    (b) See Figure 94.

    (c) When $y = 5, x = 50$. Therefore, 50 days.

95. (a) See Figure 95.

    (b) v-intercept, 160; t-intercept, 5; the initial velocity was 160 ft/sec. and the velocity after 5 seconds was 0.

Figure 94

Figure 95

Figure 97

96. (a) $m_1 = 0$; $m_2 = -1500$; $m_3 = 500$

    (b) $m_1 = 0$: The population remained unchanged. $m_2 = -1500$: The population decreased at a rate of 1500 insects per week. $m_3 = 500$: The population increased at a rate of 500 insects per week.

    (c) For the first week the population did not change from the initial value of 4000. Over the next two weeks the population decreased at a rate of 1500 insects per week until it reached 1000. Finally, the population increased at a rate of 500 per week fro two weeks, reaching 2000.

97. See Figure 97.

98. (a) $\dfrac{17,000 - 19,100}{1997 - 1985} = \dfrac{-2100}{12} = -175$

    (b) The number of nursing homes decreased on average at a rate of 175/yr.

99. (a) $\dfrac{70 - 60}{2010 - 1990} = \dfrac{10}{20} = \dfrac{1}{2} = 0.5$

    (b) School enrollment is increasing on average at a rate of 0.5 million students/yr.

    (c) $70 + 0.5(20) = 70 + 10 = 80$ million students.

100. (a) Because the initial value is 35, $35.

     (b) Because the slope is 0.2, each additional mile costs 20¢.

     (c) 35; the fixed cost of renting the car.

     (d) The slope is 0.2; the cost of each mile driven.

101. (a) The person is driving toward home; the slope is negative.

     (b) After 1 hour the car is 200 miles from home, after 3 hours the car is 100 miles from home.

     (c) The initial value is 250, so the y-intercept b is 250. For each increase of 1 in run, the rise decreases by 50, so the slope is -50. Thus, $y = -50x + 250$. The car is moving toward home at 50 mph.

     (d) When time $= 2$, the distance from home is 150. Because the initial value was 250, the person has traveled 100 miles.

         Then: $y = -50x + 250 = -50(2) + 250 = -100 + 250 = 150$, so $250 - 150 = 100$.

102. (a) Substitute 1990 for x: $D = 1.59(1990 - 1990) + 77.4 = 1.59(0) + 77.4 = 0 + 77.4 = 77.4 \Rightarrow$

$D = 77,400$. Then, substitute 1998 for x: $D = 1.59(1998 - 1990) + 77.4 = 1.59(8) + 77.4 =$

$12.72 + 77.4 \ = 90.12 \Rightarrow D = 90,120$.

(b) $\dfrac{90.12 - 77.4}{1998 - 1990} = \dfrac{12.72}{8} = 1.59$; deaths from pneumonia increased at a rate of 1590 per year.

103. (a) See Figure 103.

(b) Find the slope: $\dfrac{600 - 400}{1980 - 1970} = \dfrac{200}{10} = 20$. Then, insert the values of the point $(1970, 400)$ and the value

of the slope into the point-slope form: $y - y_1 = m(x - x_1) \Rightarrow y - 400 = 20(x - 1970)$. Then, convert

to slope-intercept form: $y - 400 = 20x - 39,400 \Rightarrow y - 400 + 400 = 20x - 39,400 + 400 \Rightarrow$

$y = 20x - 39,000$; the number of icebergs increased at a rate of 20 per year.

(c) Because you could draw a straight line through all the points on the graph, yes.

Figure 103

Figure 104a

Figure 104b

104. (a) See Figure 104a.

(b) See Figure 104b.

(c) $\dfrac{200 - 40}{10 - 2} = \dfrac{160}{8} = 20$; The mileage is 20 miles per gallon.

(d) $y = 20x$; it is not an exact model.

(e) $y = 20(9) = 180$; about 180 miles.

Chapter 3 Test

1. $(-2, -2)$: Quadrant III; $(-2, 1)$: Quadrant II; $(0, -2)$: none; $(1, 0)$: none; $(2, 3)$: Quadrant I;

   $(3, -1)$: Quadrant IV; $(3, 1)$: Quadrant I.

2. See Figure 2.

Figure 2

Figure 4

Figure 5

3.   For $x = -2$: $y = 2x - 4 = 2(-2) - 4 = -4 - 4 \Rightarrow y = -8$.

For $x = -1$: $y = 2x - 4 = 2(-1) - 4 = -2 - 4 \Rightarrow y = -6$.

For $x = 0$: $y = 2x - 4 = 2(0) - 4 \Rightarrow y = -4$.

For $x = 1$: $y = 2x - 4 = 2(1) - 4 = 2 - 4 \Rightarrow y = -2$.

For $x = 2$: $y = 2x - 4 = 2(2) - 4 = 4 - 4 \Rightarrow y = 0$. See Figure 3.

The x-intercept is 2 and the y-intercept is -4.

x	-2	-1	0	1	2
y	-8	-6	-4	-2	0

Figure 3

4.   See Figure 4.

5.   See Figure 5.

6.   See Figure 6.

7.   See Figure 7.

Figure 6

Figure 7

Figure 8

8.   See Figure 8.

9.   For every increase of 1 in the run, the rise decreases by 1, so the slope is -1. When $x = 0$, $y = 2$, so the y-intercept is 2. Therefore, the equation of the line is $y = -x + 2$.

10. Solve for y: $-4x + 2y = 1 \Rightarrow -4x + 4x + 2y = 1 + 4x \Rightarrow 2y = 4x + 1 \Rightarrow \dfrac{2y}{2} = \dfrac{4x}{2} + \dfrac{1}{2} \Rightarrow$

$y = 2x + \dfrac{1}{2}$. The slope is 2 and the y-intercept is $\dfrac{1}{2}$.

11. $y = -\dfrac{4}{3}x - 5$

12. The line parallel to $y = 3x - 1$ has slope 3. Insert the values of the point $(2, -5)$ and the value of the slope into the point-slope form: $y - y_1 = m(x - x_1) \Rightarrow y - (-5) = 3(x - 2) \Rightarrow y + 5 = 3(x - 2)$. Then, convert to slope-intercept form: $y + 5 = 3x - 6 \Rightarrow y + 5 - 5 = 3x - 6 - 5 \Rightarrow y = 3x - 11$.

13. The line perpendicular to $y = \dfrac{1}{3}x$ has slope -3, the negative reciprocal to $\dfrac{1}{3}$. Insert the values of the point $(1, 2)$ and the value of the slope into the point-slope form: $y - y_1 = m(x - x_1) \Rightarrow y - 2 = -3(x - 1)$. Then, convert to slope-intercept form: $y - 2 = -3x + 3 \Rightarrow y - 2 + 2 = -3x + 3 + 2 \Rightarrow y = -3x + 5$.

14. Find the slope: $\dfrac{-1 - 2}{2 - (-4)} = \dfrac{-3}{6} = -\dfrac{1}{2}$. Then, insert the values of the point $(-4, 2)$ and the value of the slope into the point-slope form: $y - 2 = -\dfrac{1}{2}(x - (-4)) \Rightarrow y - 2 = -\dfrac{1}{2}(x + 4)$. Then, convert to slope-intercept form: $y - 2 = -\dfrac{1}{2}x - 2 \Rightarrow y - 2 + 2 = -\dfrac{1}{2}x - 2 + 2 \Rightarrow y = -\dfrac{1}{2}x$.

15. The linear model is approximate, because it does not go through all the points exactly. For every increase of 1 in the run, the rise is 1, so the slope is 1. Insert the values of the point $(3, 2)$ and the value of the slope into the point-slope form: $y - 2 = 1(x - 3)$. Then, convert to slope-intercept form: $y - 2 = x - 3 \Rightarrow y - 2 + 2 = x - 3 + 2 \Rightarrow y = x - 1$.

16. (a) $m_1 = 2$; $m_2 = -9$; $m_3 = 2$; $m_4 = 5$

    (b) $m_1 = 2$: The population increased at a rate of 2000 fish per year. $m_2 = -9$: The population decreased at a rate of 9000 fish per year. $m_3 = 2$: The population increased at a rate of 2000 fish per year. $m_4 = 5$: The population increased at a rate of 5000 fish per year.

    (c) For the first year the population increased from an initial value of 8000 to 10,000 at a rate of 2000 fish per year. During the second year the population dropped dramatically to 1000 at a rate of 9000 fish per year. Over the third year the population grew to 3000 at a rate of 2000 fish per year. Finally, over the fourth year, the population grew at a rate of 5000 fish per year to reach 8000.

17. See Figure 17.

Figure 17

18. (a) $\dfrac{60 - 47}{1998 - 1988} = \dfrac{13}{10} = 1.3$

    (b) Delinquency cases increased at a rate of 1.3 cases per 1000 youths per year, on average.

    (c) $2004 - 1998 = 6$. Because the slope is 1.3, $6 \cdot 1.3 = 7.8$. Thus, $60 + 7.8 = 67.8$ cases per 1000 youths.

19. $n = 100x + 2000$

Chapter 3 Extended and Discovery Exercises

1. (a) See Figure 1.

   (b) Find the slope: $\dfrac{281 - 179}{2000 - 1960} = \dfrac{102}{40} = 2.55$. Then, insert the values of the point $(1960, 179)$ and the

   value of the slope into the point-slope form: $P - 179 = 2.55(x - 1960) \Rightarrow$

   $P - 179 + 179 = 2.55(x - 1960) + 179 \Rightarrow P = 2.55(x - 1960) + 179$. *Answers may vary.*

   (c) Substitute 2005 for x in the equation and solve for P: $P = 2.55(2005 - 1960) + 179 \Rightarrow$

   $P = 2.55(45) + 179 \Rightarrow P \approx 294$ million.

Figure 1

Figure 3

Figure 2

2. (a) See Figure 2.

   (b) Insert the values of the points $(1995, 20.7)$ and $(1981, 12.1)$ into the slope formula:

   $\dfrac{20.7 - 12.1}{1995 - 1981} = \dfrac{8.6}{14} = 0.62$. Then insert the values of the point $(1981, 12.1)$ and the value of the slope into

   the point-slope form: $P - 12.1 = 0.62(x - 1981) \Rightarrow P - 12.1 + 12.1 = 0.62(x - 1981) + 12.1 \Rightarrow$

   $P = 0.62(x - 1981) + 12.1$.

   (c) Substitute 2000 for x and solve for P: $P = 0.62(2000 - 1981) + 12.1 \Rightarrow P = 0.62(19) + 12.1 \Rightarrow$

   $P \approx 23.9$ percent.

Creating Geometric Shapes

3. (a) The slope of the line connecting the points $(0, 0)$ and $(2, 3)$ is $\dfrac{3}{2}$, and the y-intercept is 0. Therefore the

   equation of the line is $y = \dfrac{3}{2}x$. The slope of the line connection the points $(2, 3)$ and $(3, 6)$ is 3. Therefore

   the point-slope form is: $y - 3 = 3(x - 2)$. The slope-intercept form is thus: $y - 3 + 3 = 3x - 6 + 3 \Rightarrow$

   $y = 3x - 3$. The slope of the line connecting the points $(3, 6)$ and $(0, 0)$ is 2. The y-intercept is 0.

   Therefore the equation of the line is: $y = 2x$.

   (b) See Figure 3. A triangle is formed by the line segments connecting the three points.

4. (a) $y = -x + 1$

   (b) See Figure 4. A parallelogram is formed.

| Figure 4 | Figure 5 | Figure 6 |

5. (a) $y = \frac{1}{2}x$; $y = \frac{1}{2}x + 3$; $y = -2x$; $y = -2x + 10$

   (b) See Figure 5. A rectangle is formed.

6. (a) $(1, 5)$

   (b) $x = 1$; $x = 4$; $y = 2$; $y = 5$

   (c) See Figure 6. A square is formed.

Chapters 1-3 Cumulative Review Exercises

1. Composite; $40 = 2 \times 2 \times 2 \times 5$

2. Prime

3. $5x - 4y \Rightarrow 5(3) - 4(2) = 15 - 8 = 7$

4. $y = \dfrac{10}{4 + 1} = \dfrac{10}{5} = 2$

5. $n + 10$

6. $n^2 - 2$

7. Factors of 32 are: $32 \times 1, 16 \times 2, 8 \times 4$. Factors of 24 are $24 \times 1, 12 \times 2, 8 \times 3, 6 \times 4$.

   Thus, the greatest common factor is 8.

8. $\dfrac{32}{40} = \dfrac{8 \cdot 4}{8 \cdot 5} = \dfrac{4}{5}$

9. $\dfrac{1}{4} \cdot \dfrac{2}{5} = \dfrac{2}{20} = \dfrac{1}{10}$

10. $\dfrac{3}{7}$

11. $\dfrac{4}{3} \cdot \dfrac{21}{24} = \dfrac{84}{72} = \dfrac{12 \cdot 7}{12 \cdot 6} = \dfrac{7}{6}$

12. $\dfrac{3}{4} \div \dfrac{9}{8} = \dfrac{3}{4} \cdot \dfrac{8}{9} = \dfrac{24}{36} = \dfrac{12 \cdot 2}{12 \cdot 3} = \dfrac{2}{3}$

13. $\dfrac{3}{4} \div \dfrac{9}{8} = \dfrac{3}{4} \cdot \dfrac{8}{9} = \dfrac{24}{36} = \dfrac{12 \cdot 2}{12 \cdot 3} = \dfrac{2}{3}$

14. $\dfrac{7}{10} - \dfrac{2}{15} = \dfrac{7 \cdot 3}{10 \cdot 3} - \dfrac{2 \cdot 2}{15 \cdot 2} = \dfrac{21}{30} - \dfrac{4}{30} = \dfrac{21 - 4}{30} = \dfrac{17}{30}$

15. 4^3

16. $2^4 = 2 \times 2 \times 2 \times 2 = 16$

17. $20 - 2 \cdot 3 = 20 - (2 \cdot 3) = 20 - 6 = 14$

18. $14 - 5 - 2 = (14 - 5) - 2 = 9 - 2 = 7$

19. $\dfrac{1 + 4}{1 + 2} = \dfrac{5}{3}$

20. $-3^2 = -(3^2) = -(9) = -9$

21. $10 \div 2 \cdot 5 = (10 \div 2) \cdot 5 = (5) \cdot 5 = 25$

22. $10 - 2^3 = 10 - (2 \times 2 \times 2) = 10 - 8 = 2$

23. Rational

24. Irrational, because $\sqrt{3}$ cannot be expressed as a fraction.

25.

26. $|3 - 5| = |-2| = 2$

27. $-3.1, -\dfrac{1}{2}, \sqrt{2}, 3, \pi$

28. $2^2 - (-4);\ 2^2 - (-4) = 2^2 + 4 = 4 + 4 = 8$

29. $-10 - (-4) = -10 + 4 = -6$

30. $-5 \cdot (-3) = 15$

31. $-12 \div \left(-\dfrac{2}{3}\right) = -\dfrac{12}{1} \cdot \left(-\dfrac{3}{2}\right) = \dfrac{36}{2} = 18$

32. $-\dfrac{2x}{5y} \div \left(\dfrac{x}{10y}\right) = -\dfrac{2x}{5y} \cdot \dfrac{10y}{x} = -\dfrac{20xy}{5xy} = -\dfrac{20}{5} \cdot \dfrac{xy}{xy} = -4 \cdot 1 = -4$

33. Commutative and associative properties.

34. $11 + 22 + 8 + 9 = (11 + 22) + (8 + 9) = 33 + 17 = 50$

35. $3 + 4x - 2 + 3x = 3 - 2 + 4x + 3x = 1 + 7x = 7x + 1$

36. $2(x - 1) - (x + 2) = 2x - 2 - x - 2 = 2x - x - 2 - 2 = x - 4$

37. $x + 5 = 2 \Rightarrow x + 5 - 5 = 2 - 5 \Rightarrow x = -3$. To check the solution, replace x with -3 in the original

equation: $x + 5 = 2 \Rightarrow -3 + 5 = 2 \Rightarrow 2 = 2$. The solution checks.

38. $\frac{1}{3}z = 7 \Rightarrow 3\left(\frac{1}{3}z\right) = 3(7) \Rightarrow z = 21$. Replace z with 21 in the original equation:

   $\frac{1}{3}z = 7 \Rightarrow \frac{1}{3}(21) = 7 \Rightarrow \frac{21}{3} = 7 \Rightarrow 7 = 7$. The solution checks.

39. $3t - 5 = 1 \Rightarrow 3t - 5 + 5 = 1 + 5 \Rightarrow 3t = 6 \Rightarrow \frac{3t}{3} = \frac{6}{3} \Rightarrow t = 2$. Replace t with 2 in the original

   equation: $3t - 5 = 1 \Rightarrow 3(2) - 5 = 1 \Rightarrow 6 - 5 = 1 \Rightarrow 1 = 1$. The solution checks.

40. $\frac{1}{2}(x - 2) = 3 - (x + 4) \Rightarrow \frac{1}{2}x - 1 = 3 - x - 4 \Rightarrow \frac{1}{2}x + x - 1 = 3 - x + x - 4 \Rightarrow$

   $\frac{3}{2}x - 1 = 3 - 4 \Rightarrow \frac{3}{2}x - 1 + 1 = 3 - 4 + 1 \Rightarrow \frac{3}{2}x = 0 \Rightarrow \frac{2}{3}\left(\frac{3}{2}x\right) = 0\left(\frac{2}{3}\right) \Rightarrow x = 0$. Replace x with

   0 in the original equation: $\frac{1}{2}(x - 2) = 3 - (x + 4) \Rightarrow \frac{1}{2}(0 - 2) = 3 - (0 + 4) \Rightarrow \frac{1}{2}(-2) = 3 - 4 \Rightarrow$

   $-1 = -1$. The solution checks.

41. When $x = -2$: $6 - 2x = 6 - 2(-2) = 6 - (-4) = 6 + 4 = 10$;

   when $x = -1$: $6 - 2x = 6 - 2(-1) = 6 - (-2) = 6 + 2 = 8$;

   when $x = 0$: $6 - 2x = 6 - 2(0) = 6 - 0 = 6$; when $x = 1$: $6 - 2x = 6 - 2(1) = 6 - 2 = 4$;

   when $x = 2$: $6 - 2x = 6 - 2(2) = 6 - 4 = 2$; thus, the missing values in the table are 10, 8, 6, 4, and 2.

   See Figure 41. From the table, $6 - 2x = 4$, when $x = 1$.

x	-2	-1	0	1	2
y	10	8	6	4	2

   Figure 41

42. $2n + 2 = n - 5 \Rightarrow 2n - n + 2 = n - n - 5 \Rightarrow n + 2 = -5 \Rightarrow n + 2 - 2 = -5 - 2 \Rightarrow n = -7$

43. Let n represent the lowest integer. Then: $n + (n + 1) + (n + 2) + (n + 3) = -98 \Rightarrow$

   $n + n + 1 + n + 2 + n + 3 = -98 \Rightarrow 4n + 6 = -98 \Rightarrow 4n + 6 - 6 = -98 - 6 \Rightarrow$

   $4n = -104 \Rightarrow \frac{4n}{4} = -\frac{104}{4} \Rightarrow n = -26$. Thus, the four integers are $-26, -25, -24$ and -23.

44. $9.8\% = \frac{9.8}{100} = \frac{9.8 \cdot 5}{100 \cdot 5} = \frac{49}{500}$; $9.8\% = \frac{9.8}{100} = 0.098$

45. $0.234 = 23.4\%$

46. $d = rt \Rightarrow 80 = 10t \Rightarrow \frac{80}{10} = \frac{10t}{10} \Rightarrow 8 = t \Rightarrow t = 8$ hours.

47. Area of a rectangle is width multiplied by length, $A = lw$. Replace w with 18 and l with 40 and solve for A:

   $A = lw \Rightarrow 18 \cdot 40 = 720 \text{ ft}^2$.

48. Area of a triangle is $\frac{1}{2}$ times base times height, $A = \frac{1}{2}bh$. Replace b with 8 and h with 5 and solve for A:

$$A = \frac{1}{2}bh \Rightarrow A = \frac{1}{2}(8)(5) = \frac{1}{2}(40) = 20 \text{ ft}^2.$$

49. Area of a circle is π times radius squared. Because the diameter is 4, the radius is $\frac{4}{2} = 2$. Thus:

$$A = \pi(2)^2 = \pi(4) = 4\pi \approx 12.6 \text{ ft}^2.$$

50. Because the angles of a triangle add up to 180, $23 + 95 + x = 180$. Thus:

$$23 + 95 + x = 180 \Rightarrow 118 + x = 180 \Rightarrow 118 - 118 + x = 180 - 118 \quad x = 62°.$$

51. $A = \frac{1}{2}bh \Rightarrow 2A = 2\left(\frac{1}{2}bh\right) \Rightarrow 2A = bh \Rightarrow \frac{2A}{h} = \frac{bh}{h} \Rightarrow \frac{2A}{h} = b \Rightarrow b = \frac{2A}{h}$

52. $P = 2w + 2l \Rightarrow P - 2w = 2w - 2w + 2l \Rightarrow P - 2w = 2l \Rightarrow \frac{P - 2w}{2} = \frac{2l}{2} \Rightarrow \frac{P - 2w}{2} = l \Rightarrow$

$$l = \frac{P - 2w}{2}$$

53. $x < 2$

54.

55. Replace x with 2: $3x - 2(1 + x) \geq 0 \Rightarrow 3(2) - 2(1 + 2) \geq 0 \Rightarrow 6 - 2(3) \geq 0 \Rightarrow 6 - 6 \geq 0 \Rightarrow 0 \geq 0$.

Because this is a true statement, 2 is a solution.

56. When $x = 0$: $2x - 3 = 2(0) - 3 = 0 - 3 = -3$; when $x = 1$: $2x - 3 = 2(1) - 3 = 2 - 3 = -1$;

when $x = 2$: $2x - 3 = 2(2) - 3 = 4 - 3 = 1$; when $x = 3$: $2x - 3 = 2(3) - 3 = 6 - 3 = 3$;

when $x = 4$: $2x - 3 = 2(4) - 3 = 8 - 3 = 5$; thus, the missing values in the table are $-3, -1, 1, 3$ and 5.

See Figure 56. From the table, $2x - 3 \leq 1$, when $x \leq 2$.

x	0	1	2	3	4
$2x - 3$	-3	-1	1	3	5

Figure 56

57. $3 - 6x < 3 \Rightarrow 3 - 3 - 6x < 3 - 3 \Rightarrow -6x < 0 \Rightarrow \frac{-6x}{-6} > \frac{0}{-6} \Rightarrow x > 0;\ \{x \mid x > 0\}$

58. $2x \leq 1 - (2x - 1) \Rightarrow 2x \leq 1 - 2x + 1 \Rightarrow 2x + 2x \leq 1 - 2x + 2x + 1 \Rightarrow 4x \leq 2 \Rightarrow \frac{4x}{4} \leq \frac{2}{4} \Rightarrow$

$$x \leq \frac{1}{2};\ \left\{x \mid x \leq \frac{1}{2}\right\}$$

59. $(-2, -3)$: Quadrant III; $(0, 3)$: none; $(2, -2)$: Quadrant IV; $(2, 1)$: Quadrant I

60. See Figures 60a and 60b.

Figure 60a

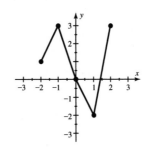

Figure 60b

x	−2	−1	0	1	2
y	3	2.5	2	1.5	1

Figure 62

61. Replace x with 5 and y with −1: $x − 3y = 8 \Rightarrow 5 − 3(−1) = 8 \Rightarrow 5 + 3 = 8 \Rightarrow 8 = 8$. Because this is a true statement, $(5, −1)$ is a solution.

62. Solve the equation for y: $x + 2y = 4 \Rightarrow x − x + 2y = 4 − x \Rightarrow 2y = 4 − x \Rightarrow \dfrac{2y}{2} = \dfrac{4}{2} − \dfrac{x}{2} \Rightarrow$

$y = 2 − \dfrac{x}{2}$. Then, when $x = −2$: $y = 2 − \dfrac{x}{2} \Rightarrow y = 2 − \dfrac{−2}{2} = 2 − (−1) = 2 + 1 = 3$;

when $x = −1$: $y = 2 − \dfrac{x}{2} \Rightarrow y = 2 − \left(\dfrac{−1}{2}\right) = 2 + \dfrac{1}{2} = \dfrac{5}{2} = 2.5$;

when $x = 0$: $y = 2 − \dfrac{x}{2} \Rightarrow y = 2 − \dfrac{0}{2} = 2 − 0 = 2$; when $x = 1$: $y = 2 − \dfrac{x}{2} \Rightarrow y = 2 − \dfrac{1}{2} = \dfrac{3}{2} = 1.5$;

when $x = 2$: $y = 2 − \dfrac{x}{2} \Rightarrow y = 2 − \dfrac{2}{2} = 2 − 1 = 1$. Thus, the missing values in the table are

3, 2.5, 2, 1.5, and 1. See Figure 62.

63. See Figure 63.

64. See Figure 64.

Figure 63

Figure 64

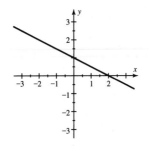

Figure 65

65. See Figure 65.

66. See Figure 66.

67. See Figure 67.

Figure 66

Figure 67

Figure 68

68. See Figure 68.

69. See Figure 69.

Figure 69

Figure 70

70. See Figure 70.

71. The x-intercept is $\dfrac{3}{2}$ and the y-intercept is -3. When the run increases by 1, the rise increases by 2, so the slope is 2. Thus, the equation of the line is $y = 2x - 3$.

72. The x-intercept is 2 and the y-intercept is 1. When the run increases by 2, the rise decreases by 1, so the slope is $-\dfrac{1}{2}$. Thus, the equation of the line is $y = -\dfrac{1}{2}x + 1$.

73. To find the x-intercept, set $y = 0$ and solve for x: $-4x + 5y = 40 \Rightarrow -4x + 5(0) = 40 \Rightarrow -4x + 0 = 40 \Rightarrow$

    $-4x = 40 \Rightarrow \dfrac{-4x}{-4} = \dfrac{40}{-4} \Rightarrow x = -10$. Thus, the x-intercept is -10.

    To find the y-intercept, set $x = 0$ and solve for y: $-4x + 5y = 40 \Rightarrow -4(0) + 5y = 40 \Rightarrow 0 + 5y = 40 \Rightarrow$

    $5y = 40 \Rightarrow \dfrac{5y}{5} = \dfrac{40}{5} \Rightarrow y = 8$. Thus, the y-intercept is 8.

74. $x = \dfrac{3}{2}$; $y = -2$

75. See Figure 75.

76. See Figure 76.

Figure 75   Figure 76   Figure 78

77. When x increases by 1, y increases by 3; therefore the slope is 3. When $x = 0$, $y = -3$; therefore the y-intercept is -3. Thus, the slope-intercept form of the line is $y = 3x - 3$.

78. Solve for y: $3x - 5y = 15 \Rightarrow 3x - 3x - 5y = 15 - 3x \Rightarrow -5y = -3x + 15 \Rightarrow$
$\dfrac{-5y}{-5} = \dfrac{-3x}{-5} + \dfrac{15}{-5} \Rightarrow y = \dfrac{3}{5}x - 3$. See Figure 78.

79. The line parallel to $y = -\dfrac{1}{3}x - 5$ has slope $-\dfrac{1}{3}$. Insert the values of the point $(-3, 8)$ and the value of the slope into the point-slope form: $y - 8 = -\dfrac{1}{3}(x - (-3)) \Rightarrow y - 8 = -\dfrac{1}{3}(x + 3)$. Then, convert to slope-intercept form: $y - 8 + 8 = -\dfrac{1}{3}x - 1 + 8 \Rightarrow y = -\dfrac{1}{3}x + 7$.

80. First, solve for y: $3x - 2y = 6 \Rightarrow 3x - 3x - 2y = 6 - 3x \Rightarrow -2y = -3x + 6 \Rightarrow \dfrac{-2y}{-2} = \dfrac{-3x}{-2} + \dfrac{6}{-2} \Rightarrow$
$y = \dfrac{3}{2}x - 3$. The line perpendicular to $y = \dfrac{3}{2}x - 3$ has slope $-\dfrac{2}{3}$, the negative reciprocal of $\dfrac{3}{2}$. Insert the values of the point $(0, -3)$ and the value of the point-slope form:
$y - (-3) = -\dfrac{2}{3}(x - 0) \Rightarrow y + 3 + (-3) = -\dfrac{2}{3}x - 3 \Rightarrow y = -\dfrac{2}{3}x - 3$.

81. First, find the slope: $\dfrac{-3 - 3}{2 - (-1)} = \dfrac{-6}{2 + 1} = \dfrac{-6}{3} = -2$. Then, insert the values of the point $(-1, 3)$ and the value of the slope into the point-slope form: $y - 3 = -2(x - (-1)) \Rightarrow y - 3 = -2(x + 1) \Rightarrow$
$y - 3 = -2x - 2 \Rightarrow y - 3 + 3 = -2x - 2 + 3 \Rightarrow y = -2x + 1$.

82. One point on the line is $(-2, 0)$ and another point is $\left(0, \dfrac{1}{2}\right)$. Find the slope: $\dfrac{\frac{1}{2} - 0}{0 - (-2)} = \dfrac{\frac{1}{2}}{2} = \dfrac{1}{2} \cdot \dfrac{1}{2} = \dfrac{1}{4}$.
The y-intercept is $\dfrac{1}{2}$. Thus, $y = \dfrac{1}{4}x + \dfrac{1}{2}$.

83. The linear model is approximate because it does not pass exactly through all the points. When the run increases by 2, the rise increases by 1. Thus, the slope is $\dfrac{1}{2}$. The y-intercept is 1. Thus, $y = \dfrac{1}{2}x + 1$.

84. $y = 5x + 100$

85. $I = 5000x + 20{,}000$

86. (a) See Figure 86a. A line could pass though all four points.

(b) See Figure 86b.

(c) The y-intercept is 5 and the slope is -2. Thus, $y = -2x + 5$.

Figure 86a

Figure 86b

87. (a) Let x represent the number of minutes. Then, $50x + 30x = 80x$.

(b) $80x = 20{,}000 \Rightarrow \dfrac{80x}{80} = \dfrac{20{,}000}{80} \Rightarrow x = 250$ minutes.

88. $C = 8x$

89. 9 out of 10, or $\dfrac{9}{10}$, of the portion of mail consisting of first-class mail and periodicals were first class mail.

Thus, $\dfrac{9}{10} \cdot \dfrac{11}{20} = \dfrac{99}{200}$ represents the fraction of all mail that was first-class mail.

90. Add the distances: $\dfrac{5}{2} + \dfrac{19}{4} + \dfrac{13}{4} = \dfrac{10}{4} + \dfrac{19}{4} + \dfrac{13}{4} = \dfrac{42}{4} = 10\dfrac{1}{2}$ miles.

91. Let x represent the cost of the car. Then, $0.06x = 330 \Rightarrow \dfrac{0.06x}{0.06} = \dfrac{330}{0.06} \Rightarrow x = \$5500$.

92. (a) The slope of the line of the equation $I = 807.4x - 1{,}587{,}300$ is 807.4. Thus, the yearly average increase is \$807.40.

(b) Set I equal to 19,400 and solve for x: $19{,}400 = 807.4x - 1{,}587{,}300 \Rightarrow$

$19{,}400 + 1{,}587{,}300 = 807.4x - 1{,}587{,}300 + 1{,}587{,}300 \Rightarrow 1{,}603{,}700 = 807.4x \Rightarrow$

$\dfrac{1{,}603{,}700}{807.4} = \dfrac{807.4x}{807.4} \Rightarrow 1990 = x \Rightarrow x = 1990$.

93. $127 - 112 = 15$. Divide 15 by 112 to find the percentage increase: $\dfrac{15}{112} \approx 0.134 \approx 13.4\%$.

94. Let x represent the amount of money invested at 3%. Then, $2x$ represent the amount of money invested at 4%.

Thus, $0.03x + 0.04(2x) = 110 \Rightarrow 0.03x + 0.08x = 110 \Rightarrow 0.11x = 110 \Rightarrow \dfrac{0.11x}{0.11} = \dfrac{110}{0.11} \Rightarrow x = 1000$.

Thus, \$1000 is invested at 3% and \$2000 is invested at 4%.

95. Let x represent the length. Then, $x - 5$ represent the width. Thus: $2x + 2(x - 5) > 4550 \Rightarrow$

$2x + 2x - 10 > 4550 \Rightarrow 4x - 10 + 10 > 4550 + 10 \Rightarrow 4x > 4560 \Rightarrow \dfrac{4x}{4} > \dfrac{4560}{4} \Rightarrow x > 1140.$

Because x represents the length, and the width is 5 inches less that the length, the values possible for the width

are $w > 1135$ inches.

96. (a) $C = 0.25x + 200$

(b) $R = 10x$

(c) $P = R - C \Rightarrow P = 10x - (0.25x + 200) \Rightarrow P = 10x - 0.25x - 200 \Rightarrow P = 9.75x - 200$

(d) $9.75x - 200 > 0 \Rightarrow 9.75x - 200 + 200 > 0 + 200 \Rightarrow 9.75x > 200 \Rightarrow \dfrac{9.75x}{9.75} > \dfrac{200}{9.75} \Rightarrow$

$x > 20.5.$ Thus, 21 CDs must be sold to yield a profit.

97. (a) $m_1 = 1.5$; $m_2 = 1$; $m_3 = 0$

(b) $m_1 = 1.5$: The fish grew 1.5 inches for each additional pound of food. $m_2 = 1$: The fish grew 1 inch for

each additional pound of food. $m_3 = 0$: The fish stopped growing.

98. (a) $\dfrac{27.2 - 22.4}{2000 - 1970} = \dfrac{4.8}{30} = 0.16$

(b) Participation increased at a rate of 0.16 million students/year.

(c) 2005 is 5 additional years beyond 2000. Since the slope is 0.16, $5 \cdot 0.16 = 0.80$ additional students.

Because the number in 2000 was 27.2, $27.2 + 0.80 = 28$ million.

99. (a) Replace x with 200: $C = 0.3(200) + 25 = 60 + 25 = \$85.$

(b) Because the initial value is 25, it costs \$25 to rent the car but not drive it.

(c) Because the slope is 0.3, it costs 30¢ to drive the car 1 additional mile.

100. (a) Selling 20 hats generates \$240 in revenue; selling 50 hats generates \$600 in revenue.

(b) The slope is $\dfrac{600 - 240}{50 - 20} = 12.$ The initial value when $x = 0$ is 0. Thus, the equation of the line is

$y = 12x$; the hats cost \$12 each.

Critical Thinking Solutions for Chapter 3

Section 3.1

• *Answers may vary.*

Section 3.3

• $y = 0$; the x-axis has y-intercept 0.

• $x = 0$; the y-axis has x-intercept 0.

Section 3.4

- See Figure 4. The slope of the two segments are 10 and −5, which are the two speeds of the runner. The second slope is negative because the distance between the runner and home is decreasing.

Figure 4

Section 3.6

- A positive slope indicates that water is entering the pool. A negative slope indicates water is leaving the pool.

Chapter 4: Systems of Linear Equations in Two Variables

4.1: Solving Systems of Linear Equations Graphically and Numerically

Concepts

1. ordered

3. The intersection is the solution $\Rightarrow (11, 9)$.

5. table

Solving Systems of Equations

7. Graph the system $y = 2, y = 2x$. See Figure 7. The intersection $x = 1$ is the solution.

9. Graph the system $y = 2, y = 4 - x \Rightarrow y = -x + 4$. See Figure 9. The intersection $x = 2$ is the solution.

Figure 7   Figure 9   Figure 11

11. Graph the system $y = 2, y = -\dfrac{1}{2}x + 1$. See Figure 11. The intersection $x = -2$ is the solution.

13. Graph the system $y = 2, y = 2x + y = 6 \Rightarrow y = -2x + 6$. See Figure 13. The intersection $x = 2$ is the

    solution.

Figure 13

15. For the system $x + y = 2$ and $x - y = 0$, $(1, 1)$ is the solution because $(1) + (1) = 2$ and $(1) - (1) = 0$.

17. For the system $2x + 3y = -5$ and $4x - 5y = 23$, $(2, -3)$ is the solution because $2(2) + 3(-3) = 4 + -9 = -5$

    and $4(2) - 5(-3) = 8 - (-15) = 8 + 15 = 23$.

19. For the system $-5x + 5y = -10$ and $4x + 9y = 8$, $(2, 0)$ is the solution because $-5(2) + 5(0) = -10 + 0 =$

    -10 and $4(2) + 9(0) = 8 + 0 = 8$.

21. The intersection and solution is $(2, 1)$, $y = 1$ and $2 + 1 = 3$.

23. The intersection and solution is $(3, 2)$, $3 + 2 = 5$ and $3 - 2 = 1$.

25. The intersection and solution is $(-1, 1)$, $-(-1) + 2(1) = 1 + 2 = 3$ and $2(-1) + 3(1) = -2 + 3 = 1$.

27. Since $y = 4$ for both equations when $x = 2$, the solution is $(2, 4)$.

29. Since $y = 1$ for both equations when $x = 3$, the solution is $(3, 1)$.

31. See Figure 31. Since $Y_1 = Y_2 = 3$ when $x = 1$, the solution is $(1, 3)$.

x	0	1	2	3
$y = x + 2$	2	3	4	5
$y = 4 - x$	4	3	2	1

Figure 31

33. (a) Graph the system. See Figure 33a. The intersection and solution is $(-1, 1)$.

    (b) See Figure 33b. Since $y = 1$ for both equations, when $x = -1$ the solution is $(-1, 1)$.

Figure 33a

x	-2	-1	0	1
$y = 2x + 3$	-1	1	3	5
$y = 1$	1	1	1	1

Figure 33b

35. (a) Graph the system. See Figure 35a. The intersection and solution is $(3, 1)$.

    (b) See Figure 35b. Since $y = 1$ for both equations, when $x = 3$ the solution is $(3, 1)$.

Figure 35a

x	2	3	4	5
$y = 4 - x$	2	1	0	-1
$y = x - 2$	0	1	2	3

Figure 35b

37. (a) Graph the system. See Figure 37a. The intersection and solution is $(1, 3)$.

    (b) See Figure 37b. Since $y = 3$ for both equations, when $x = 1$ the solution is $(1, 3)$.

Figure 37a

x	-1	0	1	2
$y = 3x$	-3	0	3	6
$y = x + 2$	1	2	3	4

Figure 37b

39. Graph the system. See Figure 39. The intersection and solution is $(-1, -2)$.

41. Graph the system. See Figure 41. The intersection and solution is $(1, -1)$.

Figure 39

Figure 41

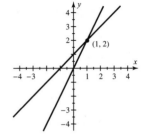
Figure 43

43. Graph the system. See Figure 43. The intersection and solution is $(1, 2)$.

45. Graph the system. See Figure 45. The intersection and solution is $(3, 2)$.

47. Graph the system. See Figure 47. The intersection and solution is $(3, 1)$.

Figure 45

Figure 47

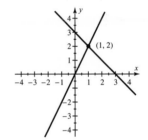
Figure 49

49. Graph the system. See Figure 49. The intersection and solution is $(1, 2)$.

Applications

51. (a) x = miles, c = cost, then $c = 0.5x + 50$.

   (b) Graph $c = 0.5x + 50$ and $c = 80$. See Figure 51b. The intersection and solution $(60, 80) \Rightarrow 60$ miles.

   (c) See Figure 51c. Since $c = 80$ for both equations when $x = 60$, the solution is $(60, 80) \Rightarrow 60$ miles.

Figure 51b

x	40	50	60	70
$C = 0.5x + 50$	70	75	80	85

Figure 51c

Figure 53

53. (a) x = % rock music, y = % country music, then $x + y = 35$ and $x = 2.5y$.

   (b) Graph $x + y = 35$ and $x = 2.5y$. See Figure 53. The intersection and solution is $(25, 10)$.

55. (a) Let x = length, y = width, then $2x + 2y = 28$ and $x = y + 4$ or $x - y = 4$.

(b) Graph $2x + 2y = 28$ and $x - y = 4$. See Figure 55. The intersection and solution is $(9, 5) \Rightarrow$ 9 in $\times$ 5 in.

Figure 55

4.2: Solving Systems of Linear Equations by Substitution

Concepts

1. substitution

3. Because $1 = 1$ is true, it has infinitely many solutions.

5. consistent

7. independent

Solving System of Equations

9. Substituting $y = 2x$ into the first equation yields the following: $x + (2x) = 9 \Rightarrow 3x = 9 \Rightarrow x = 3$
    and so $y = 2(3) \Rightarrow y = 6$. The solution is $(3, 6)$.

11. Substituting $x = 2y$ into the first equation yields the following: $(2y) + 2y = 4 \Rightarrow 4y = 4 \Rightarrow y = 1$
    and so $x = 2(1) \Rightarrow x = 2$. The solution is $(2, 1)$.

13. Substituting $y = x + 1$ into the first equation yields the following: $2x + (x + 1) = -2 \Rightarrow 3x + 1 = -2 \Rightarrow$
    $3x = -3 \Rightarrow x = -1$ and so $y = -1 + 1 \Rightarrow y = 0$. The solution is $(-1, 0)$.

15. Substituting $x = y + 3$ into the first equation yields the following: $(y + 3) + 3y = 3 \Rightarrow 4y + 3 = 3 \Rightarrow$
    $4y = 0 \Rightarrow y = 0$ and so $x = 0 + 3 \Rightarrow x = 3$. The solution is $(3, 0)$.

17. Substituting $y = 2x - 1$ into the first equation yields the following: $-3x + 2(2x - 1) = \dfrac{3}{2} \Rightarrow$

    $3x + 4x - 2 = \dfrac{3}{2} \Rightarrow 7x - 2 = \dfrac{3}{2} \Rightarrow 7x = \dfrac{7}{2} \Rightarrow x = \dfrac{1}{2}$ and so $y = 2\left(\dfrac{1}{2}\right) - 1 \Rightarrow y = 0$.

    The solution is $\left(\dfrac{1}{2}, 0\right)$.

19. Substituting $x = 2 - \dfrac{1}{2}y$ into the first equation yields the following: $2\left(2 - \dfrac{1}{2}y\right) - 3y = -12 \Rightarrow$

    $4 - y - 3y = -12 \Rightarrow 4 - 4y = -12 \Rightarrow 4y = -16 \Rightarrow y = 4$ and so $x = 2 - \dfrac{1}{2}(4) \Rightarrow x = 2 - 2 \Rightarrow$

    $x = 0$. The solution is $(0, 4)$.

21. Note that $3x - y = 1 \Rightarrow -y = -3x + 1 \Rightarrow y = 3x - 1$, substituting $y = 3x - 1$ into the first equation yields

    the following: $2x - 3(3x - 1) = -4 \Rightarrow 2x - 9x + 3 = -4 \Rightarrow -7x + 3 = -4 \Rightarrow -7x = -7 \Rightarrow x = 1$ and

    so $y = 3(1) - 1 \Rightarrow y = 2$. The solution is $(1, 2)$.

23. Note that $x - 5y = 26 \Rightarrow x = 5y + 26$, substituting $x = 5y + 26$ into the second equation yields the

    following: $2(5y + 26) + 6y = -12 \Rightarrow 10y + 52 + 6y = -12 \Rightarrow 16y + 52 = -12 \Rightarrow 16y = -64 \Rightarrow$

    $y = -4$ and so $x = 5(-4) + 26 \Rightarrow x = 6$. The solution is $(6, -4)$.

25. Note that $y - 3z = 13 \Rightarrow y = 3z + 13$, substituting $y = 3z + 13$ into the first equation yields the following:

    $\dfrac{1}{2}(3z + 13) - z = 5 \Rightarrow \dfrac{3}{2}z + \dfrac{13}{2} - z = 5 \Rightarrow \dfrac{1}{2}z + \dfrac{13}{2} = 5 \Rightarrow \dfrac{1}{2}z = -\dfrac{3}{2} \Rightarrow z = -3$ and so

    $y = 3(-3) + 13 \Rightarrow y = -9 + 13 \Rightarrow y = 4$. The solution is $(4, -3)$.

27. Note that $r + 60t = -29 \Rightarrow r = -60t - 29$, substituting $r = -60t - 29$ into the first equation yields the

    following: $10(-60t - 29) - 20t = 20 \Rightarrow -600t - 290 - 20t = 20 \Rightarrow -620t - 290 = 20 \Rightarrow$

    $-620t = 310 \Rightarrow t = -\dfrac{1}{2}$ and so $r = -60\left(-\dfrac{1}{2}\right) - 29 \Rightarrow r = 30 - 29 \Rightarrow r = 1$. The solution is $\left(1, -\dfrac{1}{2}\right)$.

29. Note that $3x + 2y = 9 \Rightarrow 3x = -2y + 9 \Rightarrow x = -\dfrac{2}{3}y + 3$, substituting $x = -\dfrac{2}{3}y + 3$ into the second

    equation yields the following: $2\left(-\dfrac{2}{3}y + 3\right) - 3y = -7 \Rightarrow \dfrac{4}{3}y + 6 - 3y = -7 \Rightarrow -\dfrac{13}{3}y + 6 = -7 \Rightarrow$

    $-\dfrac{13}{3}y = -13 \Rightarrow y = 3$ and so $x = -\dfrac{2}{3}(3) + 3 \Rightarrow x = -2 + 3 \Rightarrow x = 1$. The solution is $(1, 3)$.

31. Note that $2a - 3b = 6 \Rightarrow 2a = 3b + 6 \Rightarrow a = \dfrac{3}{2}b + 3$, substituting $a = \dfrac{3}{2}b + 3$ into the first equation

    yields the following: $-5\left(\dfrac{3}{2}b + 3\right) - 3b = 6 \Rightarrow -\dfrac{15}{2}b - 15 - 3b = 6 \Rightarrow -\dfrac{21}{2}b - 15 = 6 \Rightarrow$

    $-\dfrac{21}{2}b = 21 \Rightarrow b = -2$ and so $a = \dfrac{3}{2}(-2) + 3 \Rightarrow a = -3 + 3 \Rightarrow a = 0$. The solution is $(0, -2)$.

33. Note that $2x - \dfrac{1}{2}y = 3 \Rightarrow -\dfrac{1}{2}y = -2x + 3 \Rightarrow y = 4x - 6$, substituting $y = 4x - 6$ into the first

    equation yields the following: $-\dfrac{1}{2}x + 3(4x - 6) = 5 \Rightarrow -\dfrac{1}{2}x + 12x - 18 = 5 \Rightarrow \dfrac{23}{2}x - 18 = 5 \Rightarrow$

    $\dfrac{23}{2}x = 23 \Rightarrow x = 2$ and so $y = 4(2) - 6 \Rightarrow y = 8 - 6 \Rightarrow y = 2$. The solution is $(2, 2)$.

35. Note that $-8a + 2b = 34 \Rightarrow 2b = 8a + 34 \Rightarrow b = 4a + 17$, substituting $y = 4a + 17$ into the first equation

    yields the following: $3a + 5(4a + 17) = 16 \Rightarrow 3a + 20a + 85 = 16 \Rightarrow 23a = -69 \Rightarrow a = -3$ and so

    $b = 4(-3) + 17 \Rightarrow b = -12 + 17 \Rightarrow b = 5$. The solution is $(-3, 5)$.

37. The lines intersect at one point, so there is one solution $\Rightarrow$ the system is consistent and the equations independent.

39. The lines coincide, so the are infinitely many solutions $\Rightarrow$ the system is consistent and the equations are dependent.

41. The lines are parallel, so there are zero solutions $\Rightarrow$ the system is inconsistent.

43. Note that $x + y = 4 \Rightarrow y = -x + 4$, substituting $y = -x + 4$ into the second equation yields the following:

    $x + (-x + 4) = 2 \Rightarrow 4 = 2$, which is false $\Rightarrow$ there are no solutions.

    Graph the system. See Figure 43. The lines are parallel $\Rightarrow$ there are no solutions. The system is inconsistent.

45. Note that $x - 2y = 0 \Rightarrow x = 2y$, substituting $x = 2y$ into the first equation yields the following:

    $2(2y) - y = 3 \Rightarrow 3y = 3 \Rightarrow y = 1$ and so $x = 2(1) \Rightarrow x = 2$. The solution is $(2, 1)$.

    Graph the system. See Figure 45. The lines intersect at the solution $(2, 1)$. The system has one solution $\Rightarrow$ the system is consistent and the equations are independent.

Figure 43   Figure 45   Figure 47

47. Note that $x - y = 1 \Rightarrow x = y + 1$, substituting $x = y + 1$ into the second equation yields the following:

    $2(y + 1) - 2y = 2 \Rightarrow 2y + 2 - 2y = 2 \Rightarrow 2 = 2$, which is true $\Rightarrow$ infinitely many solutions.

    Graph the system. See Figure 47. The lines coincide $\Rightarrow$ infinitely many solutions.The system has infinitely many solutions $\Rightarrow$ the system is consistent and the equations dependent.

49. Substituting $x + 2y$ into the first equation yields the following: $(2y) - 2y = 4 \Rightarrow 0 = 4$ which is false $\Rightarrow$ no solution. Graph the system. See Figure 49. The lines are parallel $\Rightarrow$ no solutions. The system has no solutions $\Rightarrow$ the system is inconsistent.

Figure 49   Figure 71

51. Note that $x + y = 7 \Rightarrow y = -x + 7$, substituting $y = -x + 7$ into the first equation yields the following:

    $x + (-x + 7) = 9 \Rightarrow 7 = 9$, which is false $\Rightarrow$ no solutions.

53. Note that $x - y = 4 \Rightarrow x = y + 4$, substituting $x = y + 4$ into the second equation yields the following:

    $2(y + 4) - 2y = 8 \Rightarrow 2y + 8 - 2y = 8 \Rightarrow 8 = 8$, which is true $\Rightarrow$ infinitely many solutions.

55. Note that $x + y = 4 \Rightarrow y = -x + 4$, substituting $y = -x + 4$ into the second equation yields the following:

    $x - (-x + 4) = 2 \Rightarrow 2x = 6 \Rightarrow x = 3$ and so $y = -(3) + 4 \Rightarrow y = 1$. The solution is $(3, 1)$.

57. Note that $-x + y = -7 \Rightarrow y = x - 7$, substituting $y = x - 7$ into the first equation yields the following:

    $x - (x - 7) = 7 \Rightarrow 7 = 7$, which is true $\Rightarrow$ infinitely many solutions.

59. Note that $u - 2v = 5 \Rightarrow u = 2v + 5$, substituting $u = 2v + 5$ into the second equation yields the following:

    $2(2v + 5) - 4v = -2 \Rightarrow 4v + 10 - 4v = -2 \Rightarrow 10 = -2$, which is false $\Rightarrow$ no solutions.

61. Note that $r - 3t = -5 \Rightarrow r = 3t - 5$, substituting $r = 3t - 5$ into the first equation yields the following:

    $2(3t - 5) + 3t = 1 \Rightarrow 6t - 10 + 3t = 1 \Rightarrow 9t - 10 = 1 \Rightarrow 9t = 11 \Rightarrow t = \dfrac{11}{9}$ and so

    $r = 3\left(\dfrac{11}{9}\right) - 5 \Rightarrow r = \dfrac{11}{3} - 5 \Rightarrow r = -\dfrac{4}{3}$. The solution is $\left(-\dfrac{4}{3}, \dfrac{11}{9}\right)$.

63. Substituting $y = 5x$ into the second equation yields the following: $5x = -3x \Rightarrow 8x = 0 \Rightarrow x = 0$, and so

    $y = 5(0) \Rightarrow y = 0$. The solution is $(0, 0)$.

65. Note that $5a = 4 - b \Rightarrow a = \dfrac{4}{5} - \dfrac{1}{5}b$, substituting $a = \dfrac{4}{5} - \dfrac{1}{5}b$ into the second equation yields the

    following: $5\left(\dfrac{4}{5} - \dfrac{1}{5}b\right) = 3 - b \Rightarrow 4 - b = 3 - b \Rightarrow 4 = 3$, which is false $\Rightarrow$ no solutions.

67. Note that $2x + 4y = 0 \Rightarrow 2x = -4y \Rightarrow x = -2y$, substituting $x = -2y$ into the second equation yields the

    following: $3(-2y) + 6y = 5 \Rightarrow -6y + 6y = 5 \Rightarrow 0 = 5$, which is false $\Rightarrow$ no solutions.

Applications

69. (a) $2L + 2W = 72$ and $L = W + 10$

    (b) Substituting $L = W + 10$ into the first equation yields the following: $2(W + 10) + 2W = 72 \Rightarrow$

    $2W = 20 + 2W = 72 \Rightarrow 4W = 52 \Rightarrow W = 13$ and so $L = 13 + 10 \Rightarrow L = 23$. The solution is

    $(23, 13)$. Checking: $2(23) + 2(13) = 46 + 26 = 72$, yes. $23 = 13 + 10$, yes.

71. (a) $x + y = 90$ and $x = \dfrac{1}{2}y$

    (b) Substituting $x = \dfrac{1}{2}y$ into the first equation yields the following: $\dfrac{1}{2}y + y = 90 \Rightarrow \dfrac{3}{2}y = 90 \Rightarrow y = 60$

    and so $x = \dfrac{1}{2}(60) \Rightarrow x = 30$. The solution is $(30, 60)$.

    (c) Graph the system. See Figure 71. The lines intersect at the solution $(30, 60)$.

73. (a) $x - y = 1.68$ and $y = 0.98x$

    (b) Substituting $y = 0.98x$ into the first equation yields the following: $x - 0.98x = 1.68 \Rightarrow$

    $0.02x = 1.68 \Rightarrow x = 84$ and so $84 - y = 1.68 \Rightarrow y = 82.32$. The solution is $(84, 82.32)$.

75. Let L = length and W = width, then let $L = W + 44$ and $2L + 2W = 288$, substituting $L = W + 44$ into the

    second equation yields the following: $2(W + 44) + 2W = 288 \Rightarrow 2W + 88 + 2W = 288 \Rightarrow$

    $4W = 200 \Rightarrow W = 50$ and so $L = 50 + 44 \Rightarrow L = 94$. The solution is $(94, 50)$ or 94 ft $\times$ 50 ft.

77. Let x = larger number and y = smaller number, then $x + y = 70$ and $x = 3y + 2$, substituting $x = 3y + 2$ into the first equation yields the following: $(3y + 2) + y = 70 \Rightarrow 4y + 2 = 70 \Rightarrow 4y = 68 \Rightarrow y = 17$ and so $x = 3(17) + 2 \Rightarrow x = 51 + 2 \Rightarrow x = 53$. The numbers are 17 and 53.

79. Let x = liters of 20% solution and y = liters of 50% solution, then $x + y = 10$ and $0.2x + 0.5y = 0.4(10) \Rightarrow 0.2x + 0.5y = 4$. Note that $x + y = 10 \Rightarrow y = -x + 10$, substituting $y = -x + 10$ into the second equation yields the following: $0.2x + 0.5(-x + 10) = 4 \Rightarrow 0.2x - 0.5x + 5 = 4 \Rightarrow -0.3x = -1 \Rightarrow x = 3.33$ and so $3.33 + y = 10 \Rightarrow y = 6.67$. The amounts are: 3.33% liters of 20 % solution and 6.67 liters of 50% solution.

81. Let x = speed of tugboat and y = speed of current, then $15x - 15y = 120$ and $10x + 10y = 120$. Note that $10x + 10y = 120 \Rightarrow 10y = -10x + 120 \Rightarrow y = -x + 12$, substituting $y = -x + 12$ into the first equation yields the following: $15x - 15(-x + 12) = 120 \Rightarrow 15x + 15x - 180 = 120 \Rightarrow 30x = 300 \Rightarrow x = 10$ and so $y = -10 + 2 \Rightarrow y = 2$. The tugboat speed is 10 mph and the current's speed is 2 mph.

83. Let x = mi^2 of Lake Superior and y = mi^2 of Lake Michigan, then $x + y = 54{,}000$ and $x = y + 10{,}000$, substituting $x = y + 10{,}000$ into the first equation yields the following: $(y + 10{,}000) + y = 54{,}000 \Rightarrow 2y + 10{,}000 = 54{,}000 \Rightarrow 2y = 44{,}000 \Rightarrow y = 22{,}000$ and so $x = 22{,}000 + 10{,}000 \Rightarrow x = 32{,}000$. So Lake Superior has 32,000 mi^2 and Lake Michigan has 22,000 mi^2.

Checking Basic Concepts for Sections 4.1 & 4.2

1. (a) Graph the system $y = 2$ and $y = 1 - \dfrac{1}{2}x$. See Figure 1a. The intersection and solution is $(-2, 2) \Rightarrow x = -2$.

   (b) Graph the system $y = 2$ and $2x - 3y = 6$. See Figure 1b. The intersection and solution is $(6, 2) \Rightarrow x = 6$.

Figure 1a

Figure 1b

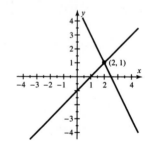

Figure 3

2. $(4, 2)$ is the solution because $2(4) - 5(2) = 8 - 10 = -2$ and $3(4) + 2(2) = 12 + 4 = 16$.

3. Graph the system. See Figure 3. The intersection and solution is $(2, 1)$.

   Checking: $2 - 1 = 1$ (yes) and $2(2) + 1 = 5$ (yes).

4. (a) Substituting $y = 2 - x$ into the first equation yields the following: $x + (2 - x) = -1 \Rightarrow 2 = -1$ which is false $\Rightarrow$ no solution.

   (b) Note that $-x + y = -2 \Rightarrow y = x - 2$, substituting $y = x - 2$ into the first equation yields the following: $4x - (x - 2) = 5 \Rightarrow 3x + 2 = 5 \Rightarrow 3x = 3 \Rightarrow x = 1$ and so $y = 1 - 2 \Rightarrow y = -1$. The solution is $(1, -1)$, one solution.

   (c) Note that $x + 2y = 3 \Rightarrow x = -2y + 3$, substituting $x = -2y + 3$ into the second equation yields the following: $-(-2y + 3) - 2y = -3 \Rightarrow 2y - 3 - 2y = -3 \Rightarrow -3 = -3$, which is true $\Rightarrow$ infinitely many solutions.

5. (a) $x + y = 300, 50x + 60y = 17,000$

   (b) Note that $x + y = 300 \Rightarrow y = -x + 300$, substituting $y = -x + 300$ into the second equation yields the following: $50x + 60(-x + 300) = 17,000 \Rightarrow 50x - 60x + 18,000 = 17,000 \Rightarrow -10x = -1000 \Rightarrow x = 100$ and so $y = -100 + 300 \Rightarrow y = 200$. The solution is $(100, 200)$. Checking the answer $100 + 200 = 300$ (yes) and $50(100) + 60(200) = 5000 + 12,000 = 17,000$ (true).

4.3: Solving Systems of Linear Equations by Elimination

Concepts

1. Substitution; elimination

3. $=$

5. Add the equation to eliminate the y variable.

Using Elimination

7. Adding the two equations will eliminate the variable y.

   $x + y = 2$
   $\underline{x - y = 0}$
   $2x = 2$ Thus, $x = 1$. And so $1 + y = 2 \Rightarrow y = 1$. The solution is $(1, 1)$.
   The result is supported by the graph's intersection point of $(1, 1)$.

9. Adding the two equations will eliminate the variable y.

   $2x + 3y = -1$
   $\underline{2x - 3y = -7}$
   $4x = -8$ Thus, $x = -2$. And so $2(-2) + 3y = -1 \Rightarrow -4 + 3y = -1 \Rightarrow 3y = 3 \Rightarrow y = 1$.
   The solution is $(-2, 1)$. The result is supported by the graph's intersection point of $(-2, 1)$.

11. Multiplying the first equation by -1 and adding the two equations will eliminate both variables.

   $-x - y = -3$
   $\underline{x + y = -1}$
   $0 = -4$ This is false $\Rightarrow$ no solution. This result is supported by the graph's parallel lines which has no solution.

13. Multiplying the second equation by -2 and adding the two equations will eliminate both variables.

$$2x + 2y = 6$$
$$-2x - 2y = -6$$

$0 = 0$ Which is true $\Rightarrow$ there are infinitely many solutions. This result is supported by the graph having two lines that coincide.

15. Adding the two equations will eliminate the variable y.

$$2x + y = 7$$
$$x - y = 5$$

$2x = 12$ Thus, $x = 6$. And so $6 + y = 7 \Rightarrow y = 1$. The solution is $(6, 1)$.

17. Adding the two equations will eliminate the variable x.

$$-x + y = 5$$
$$x + y = 3$$

$2y = 8$ Thus, $y = 4$. And so $x + 4 = 3 \Rightarrow x = -1$. The solution is $(-1, 4)$.

19. Adding the two equations will eliminate the variable y.

$$2x + y = 8$$
$$3x - y = 2$$

$5x = 10$ Thus, $x = 2$. And so $2(2) + y = 8 \Rightarrow 4 + y = 8 \Rightarrow y = 4$. The solution is $(2, 4)$.

21. Adding the two equations will eliminate the variable x.

$$-2x + y = -3$$
$$2x - 4y = 0$$

$-3y = -3$ Thus, $y = 1$. And so $-2x + 1 = -3 \Rightarrow -2x = -4 \Rightarrow x = 2$. The solution is $(2, 1)$.

23. Multiplying the second equation by -1 and adding the two equations will eliminate the variable a.

$$a + 6b = 2$$
$$-a - 3b = 1$$

$3b = 3$ Thus, $b = 1$. And so $a + 6(1) = 2 \Rightarrow a = -4$. The solution is $(-4, 1)$.

25. Multiplying the second equation by -1 and adding the two equations will eliminate the variable t.

$$3r - t = 7$$
$$-2r + t = -2$$

$r = 5$ And so, $-2(5) + t = -2 \Rightarrow t = 8$. The solution is $(5, 8)$.

27. Multiplying the second equation by -2 and adding the two equations will eliminate the variable v.

$$3u + 2v = -16$$
$$-4u - 2v = 18$$

$-u = 2$ Thus $u = -2$. And so $3(-2) + 2v = -16 \Rightarrow -6 + 2v = -16 \Rightarrow 2v = -10 \Rightarrow v = -5$.
The solution is $(-2, -5)$.

29. Multiplying the first equation by -2 and adding the two equations will eliminate the variable x.

$$-4x - 14y = -12$$
$$4x - 3y = -22$$

$-17y = -34$ Thus $y = 2$. And so $4x - 3(2) = -22 \Rightarrow 4x - 6 = -22 \Rightarrow 4x = -16 \Rightarrow x = -4$.
The solution is $(-4, 2)$.

31. Multiplying the second equation by -5 and adding the two equations will eliminate the variable x.

$$5x - 3y = 4$$
$$-5x - 20y = -50$$
$$\overline{}$$
$$-23y = -46 \quad \text{Thus } y = 2. \text{ And so } 5x - 3(2) = 4 \Rightarrow 5x - 6 = 4 \Rightarrow 5x = 10 \Rightarrow x = 2.$$

The solution is $(2, 2)$.

33. Adding the two equations will eliminate the variable y.

$$\frac{1}{2}x - y = 3$$
$$\frac{3}{2}x + y = 5$$
$$\overline{}$$
$$2x = 8 \quad \text{Thus, } x = 4. \text{ And so } \frac{1}{2}(4) - y = 3 \Rightarrow 2 - y = 3 \Rightarrow -y = 1 \Rightarrow y = -1.$$

The solution is $(4, -1)$.

35. Multiplying the first equation by 2 and adding the two equations will eliminate the variable x.

$$-10x - 20y = -44$$
$$10x + 15y = 35$$
$$\overline{}$$
$$-5y = -9 \quad \text{Thus } y = \frac{9}{5}. \text{ And so } 10x + 15\left(\frac{9}{5}\right) = 35 \Rightarrow 10x + 27 = 35 \Rightarrow 10x = 8 \Rightarrow x = \frac{4}{5}.$$

The solution is $\left(\dfrac{4}{5}, \dfrac{9}{5}\right)$.

37. Since $y = 2$, when $x = 3$ for both equations $\Rightarrow$ the solution is $(3, 2)$.

39. Since $y = 1$, when $x = 0$ for both equations $\Rightarrow$ the solution is $(0, 1)$.

Using More Than One Method

41. (a) Adding the two equations will eliminate the variable y.

$$2x + y = 5$$
$$x - y = 1$$
$$\overline{}$$
$$3x = 6 \quad \text{Thus, } x = 2. \text{ And so } 2 - y = 1 \Rightarrow y = 1. \text{ The solution is } (2, 1).$$

(b) Graph the system. See Figure 41b. The intersection and solution is $(2, 1)$.

(c) See Figure 41c. Since $y = 1$ when $x = 2$ for both equations the solution is $(2, 1)$.

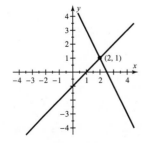

Figure 41b

x	0	1	2	3
$y = 5 - 2x$	5	3	1	-1
$y = x - 1$	-1	0	1	2

Figure 41c

43. (a) Multiplying the second equation by -1 and adding the two equations will eliminate the variable y.

$$2x + y = 5$$
$$-x - y = -1$$

$x = 4$ And so $-4 - y = -1 \Rightarrow -y = 3 \Rightarrow y = -3$. The solution is $(4, -3)$.

(b) Graph the system. See Figure 43b. The intersection and solution is $(4, -3)$.

(c) See Figure 43c. Since $y = -3$ when $x = 4$ for both equations the solution is $(4, -3)$.

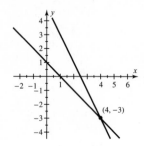

Figure 43b

x	2	3	4	5
$y = 5 - 2x$	1	-1	-3	-5
$y = 1 - x$	-1	-2	-3	-4

Figure 43c

45. (a) Multiplying the second equation by 3 and adding the two equations will eliminate the variable x.

$$6x + 3y = 6$$
$$-6x + 6y = -6$$

$9y = 0$ Thus, $y = 0$. And so $6x + 3(0) = 6 \Rightarrow 6x = 6 \Rightarrow x = 1$. The solution is $(1, 0)$.

(b) Graph the system. See Figure 45b. The intersection and solution is $(1, 0)$.

(c) See Figure 45c. Since $y = 0$ when $x = 1$ for both equations the solution is $(1, 0)$.

Figure 45b

x	-1	0	1	2
$y = 2 - 2x$	4	2	0	-1
$y = x - 1$	-2	-1	0	1

Figure 45c

Figure 47

Elimination and Other Types of Systems

47. Multiplying the second equation by 2 and adding the two equations will eliminate both variables.

$$2x - 2y = 4$$
$$-2x + 2y = -4$$

$0 = 0$ This is always true $\Rightarrow$ infinitely many solutions. See Figure 47.

49. Adding the two equations will eliminate the variable y.

$$x - y = 0$$
$$x + y = 0$$

$2x = 0$ Thus, $x = 0$. And so $0 - y = 0 \Rightarrow -y = 0 \Rightarrow y = 0$. The solution is $(0, 0) \Rightarrow$ one solution.

See Figure 49.

51. Multiplying the first equation by −1 and adding the two equations will eliminate both variables.

$$-x + y = -4$$
$$\underline{x - y = 1}$$

$0 = -3$ This is never true $\Rightarrow$ zero solutions. See Figure 51.

Figure 49   Figure 51   Figure 53

53. Multiplying the first equation by −1 and adding the two equations will eliminate the variable y.

$$-x + y = -5$$
$$\underline{2x - y = 4}$$

$x = -1$ And so $-(-1) + y = -5 \Rightarrow 1 + y = -5 \Rightarrow y = -6$. The solution is $(-1, -6) \Rightarrow$ one

solution. See Figure 53.

55. Multiplying the first equation by 3, the second by −2 and adding the two equations will eliminate both

variables.

$$12x - 24y = 72$$
$$\underline{-12x - 24y = 72}$$

$0 = 0$ This is always true $\Rightarrow$ infinitely many solutions. See Figure 55.

Figure 55

Applications

57. Let x = skin cancer in men and let y = skin cancer in women. Then $x + y = 56,400$ and $x = y + 7000$. Note

that $x = y + 7000 \Rightarrow x - y = 7000$. Adding the two equations will eliminate the variable y.

$$x + y = 56,400$$
$$\underline{x - y = 7000}$$

$2x = 63,400$ Thus $x = 31,700$. And so $31,700 - y = 7000 \Rightarrow -y = -24,700 \Rightarrow y = 24,700$.

Therefore men: 31,700; Women: 24,700.

59. Let x = minutes on a stationary bike and let y = minutes on a stair climber. Then $x + y = 30$ and

$9x + 11.5y = 300$. Multiplying the first equation by -9 and adding the two equations will eliminate the

variable x.

$$-9x - 9y = -270$$
$$9x + 11.5y = 300$$

$2.5y = 30$ Thus $y = 12$. And so $x + 12 = 30 \Rightarrow x = 18$. Therefore bicycle: 18 minutes;

stairclimber: 12 minutes.

61. Let x = speed of riverboat and let y = speed of the current. Then $8x + 8y = 64$ and $16x - 16y = 64$.

Multiplying the first equation by 2 and adding the two equations will eliminate the variable y.

$$16x + 16y = 128$$
$$16x - 16y = 64$$

$32x = 192$ Thus $x = 6$. And so $8(6) + 8y = 64 \Rightarrow 48 + 8y = 64 \Rightarrow 8y = 16 \Rightarrow y = 2$.

Therefore current: 2 mph; boat: 6 mph.

63. Let x = amount of money invested at 3% and let y = amount of money invested at 5%. Then $x + y = 5000$

and $0.03x - 0.05y = 210$. Multiplying the second equation by -20 and adding the two equations will eliminate

the variable y.

$$x + y = 5000$$
$$-0.6x - y = 4200$$

$0.4x = 800$ Thus $x = 2000$. And so $2000 + y = 5000 \Rightarrow y = 3000$.

Therefore $2000 invested at 3%; $3000 invested at 5%.

65. Let x = one of two integers and let y = the other of two integers. Then $x + y = -17$ and $x - y = 69$. Adding

the two equations will eliminate the variable y.

$$x + y = -17$$
$$x - y = 69$$

$2x = 52$ Thus $x = 26$. And so $26 + y = -17 \Rightarrow y = -43$. Therefore the numbers are -43 and 26.

67. (a) The graphs intersection is 20×40 in.

(b) Note that $l = 2w \Rightarrow -2w + l = 0$, using this and $2w + 2l = 120$ and adding the two equations will

eliminate the variable w.

$$-2w + l = 0$$
$$2w + 2l = 120$$

$3l = 120$ Thus $l = 40$. And so $2w + 2(40) = 120 \Rightarrow 2w + 80 = 120 \Rightarrow 2w = 40 \Rightarrow w = 20$.

Therefore $l = 40$ and $w = 20$ so 20×40 in.

4.4: Systems of Linear Inequalities

Concepts

1.   All points below and including the line $y = k$.

3. All points above and including the line $y = x$.

5. dashed

7. $Ax + By = C$

Solutions to Linear Inequalities

9. Yes, $3 > 2$ is true.

11. No, $0 \geq 2$ is false.

13. No, $4 \geq 5$ is false.

15. Yes, $0 < 3 - 1 \Rightarrow 0 < 2$ is true.

17. Yes, $-2 + 6 \leq 4 \Rightarrow 4 \leq 4$ is true.

19. No, $2(-1) + (-1) \geq -1 \Rightarrow -2 + (-1) \geq -1 \Rightarrow -3 \geq -1$ is false.

21. ***Answers may vary.*** $(3, 1)$, because $3 > 2$ is true. Shade side of the line with point $(3, 1)$. See Figure 21.

Figure 21   Figure 23   Figure 43

23. ***Answers may vary.*** $(-2, -1)$, because $\frac{1}{2}(-2) + (-1) \leq 0 \Rightarrow -2 \leq 0$ is true. Shade side of the line with point $(-2, -1)$. See Figure 23.

25. Yes, because $3 - 1 < 3 \Rightarrow 2 < 3$ is true and $3 + 1 > 3 \Rightarrow 4 > 3$ is true.

27. No, because $3(-2) - 2(3) \geq 1 \Rightarrow -6 - 6 \geq 1 \Rightarrow -12 \geq 1$ is false.

29. Yes, because $4 - 2(-2) \geq 8 \Rightarrow 4 + 4 \geq 8 \Rightarrow 8 \geq 8$ is true and $-2(4) - 5(-2) > 0 \Rightarrow -8 + 10 > 0 \Rightarrow 2 > 0$ is true.

31. The region containing $(1, 2)$, because $1 \leq 2$ is true and $1 + 2 \geq 2 \Rightarrow 3 \geq 2$ is true.

33. The region containing $(1, 0)$, because $1 + 0 \leq 3 \Rightarrow 1 \leq 3$ is true and $0 \leq 2(1) \Rightarrow 0 \leq 2$ is true.

35. $x > 1$

37. $y \geq 2$

39. $y < x$

41. $-x + y \leq 1$

43. See Figure 43.

45. See Figure 45.

47. See Figure 47.

Figure 45

Figure 47

Figure 49

49. See Figure 49.

51. See Figure 51.

53. See Figure 53.

Figure 51

Figure 53

Figure 55

55. See Figure 55.

57. See Figure 57.

59. See Figure 59.

Figure 57

Figure 59

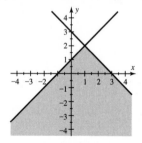

Figure 61

61. See Figure 61.

63. See Figure 63.

65. See Figure 65.

Figure 63

Figure 65

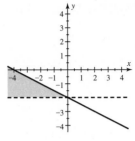

Figure 67

67. See Figure 67.

69. See Figure 69.

71. See Figure 71.

Figure 69

Figure 71

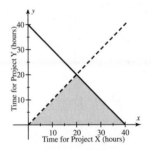

Figure 73

Applications

73. Graph the system, $x > y$ and $x + y \leq 40$. See Figure 73.

75. (a) $R = 220 - 20 \Rightarrow R = 200$ bpm for a 20 year old person and $R = 220 - 70 \Rightarrow R = 150$ bpm for a 70 year old person.

　　(b) See Figure 75.

　　(c) The shaded region represents possible heart rates for ages 20 to 70.

Figure 75

77. 150 to 200 lbs.

Checking Basic Concepts for Sections 4.3 & 4.4

1. Multiplying the second equation by -2 and adding the two equations will eliminate the variable x.

    $2x + 3y = 5$
    $-2x + 14y = 12$

    $\overline{}$

    $17y = 17$ Thus $y = 1$. And so $x - 7(1) = -6 \Rightarrow x = 1$. The solution is $(1, 1)$.

2. (a) Multiplying the first equation by -1 and adding the two equations will eliminate the variable x.

    $-x - y = 1$
    $x - 2y = 2$

    $\overline{}$

    $-3y = 3$ Thus $y = -1$. And so $x - 2(-1) = 2 \Rightarrow x + 2 = 2 \Rightarrow x = 0$. The solution is $(0, -1)$.

    There is one solution.

    (b) Adding the two equations will eliminate both variables.

    $5x - 6y = 4$
    $-5x + 6y = 1$

    $\overline{}$

    $0 = 5$ This is false, therefore there are no solutions.

    (c) Multiplying the first equation by -2 and adding the two equations will eliminate both variables.

    $-2x + 6y = 0$
    $2x - 6y = 0$

    $\overline{}$

    $0 = 0$ This is true, therefore there are infinitely many solutions.

3. Substituting $y = 2x$ into the first equation yields the following: $-2x + (2x) = 0 \Rightarrow 0 = 0$. This is true $\Rightarrow$ infinitely many solutions. Graph the system. See Figure 3a. Line coincides $\Rightarrow$ infinitely many solutions. Numerically: See Figure 3b. Since for all values of x both equations produce the same solutions $\Rightarrow$ infinitely many solutions.

Figure 3a

x	0	1	2	3
$y = 2x$	0	2	4	6
$y = 2x$	0	2	4	6

Figure 3b

4. (a) See Figure 4a.

    (b) See Figure 4b.

Figure 4a

Figure 4b

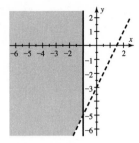

Figure 5

5. See Figure 5.

6. (a) $x + y = 11$

    $x = y + 5$ or $x - y = 5$.

    (b) Substituting $x = y + 5$ into the first equation yields the following: $(y + 5) + y = 11 \Rightarrow$

    $2y + 5 = 11 \Rightarrow 2y = 6 \Rightarrow y = 3$. And so $x + 3 = 11 \Rightarrow x = 8$. The solution is $(8, 3)$ or New York

    has a population of 8 million people and Chicago has a population of 3 million people.

Chapter 4 Review Exercises

Section 4.1

1. Graph the system $y = 3$ and $y = 2x - 3$. See Figure 1. The intersection and solution is $(3, 3) \Rightarrow x = 3$.

Figure 1

Figure 2

2. Graph the system $y = 3$ and $y = \dfrac{3}{2}x$. See Figure 2. The intersection and solution is $(2, 3) \Rightarrow x = 2$.

3. $(1, 2)$, because $1 + 2(2) = 5 \Rightarrow 1 + 4 = 5$ is true and $1 - (2) = -1$ is true.

4. $(5, 2)$, because $2(5) - 2 = 8 \Rightarrow 10 - 2 = 8$ is true and $5 + 3(2) = 11 \Rightarrow 5 + 6 = 11$ is true.

5. $(4, 3)$, because $\dfrac{1}{2}(4) = 3 - 1 \Rightarrow 2 = 2$ is true and $2(4) = 3(3) - 1 \Rightarrow 8 = 9 - 1$ is true.

6. $(2, -4)$, because $5(2) - 2(-4) = 18 \Rightarrow 10 + 8 = 18$ is true and $-4 = -2(2)$ is true.

7. The intersection and solution is $(2, 2)$. Checking: $2 = 2$ is true and $-2(2) + 2 = -2 \Rightarrow -4 + 2 = -2$ is true.

8. The intersection and solution is $(1, 2)$. Checking: $1 + 2 = 3$ is true and $2 = 2(1)$ is true.

9. Since when $x = 2$, $y = 6$ for both equations $\Rightarrow$ the solution is $(2, 6)$.

10. Since when $x = 1$, $y = 1$ for both equations $\Rightarrow$ the solution is $(1, 1)$.

11. Graph the system. See Figure 11. The intersection and solution is $(4, -3)$.

12. Graph the system. See Figure 12. The intersection and solution is $(1, 2)$.

Figure 11

Figure 12

Figure 13

13. Graph the system. See Figure 13. The intersection and solution is $(1, 1)$.

14. Graph the system. See Figure 14. The intersection and solution is $(1, 2)$.

15. Graph the system. See Figure 15. The intersection and solution is $(1, 1)$.

Figure 14

Figure 15

Figure 16

16. Graph the system. See Figure 16. The intersection and solution is $(-2, -1)$.

Section 4.2

17. Substituting $y = 3x$ into the first equation yields the following: $x + (3x) = 8 \Rightarrow 4x = 8 \Rightarrow x = 2$, and so $y = 3(2) \Rightarrow y = 6$. The solution is $(2, 6)$.

18. Substituting $y = -5x$ into the first equation yields the following: $x - 2(-5x) = 22 \Rightarrow x + 10x = 22 \Rightarrow 11x = 22 \Rightarrow x = 2$, and so $y = -5(2) \Rightarrow y = -10$. The solution is $(2, -10)$.

19. Note that $2x + y = 5 \Rightarrow y = -2x + 5$. Substituting $y = -2x + 5$ into the second equation yields the following: $-3x + (-2x + 5) = 0 \Rightarrow -5x + 5 = 0 \Rightarrow -5x = -5 \Rightarrow x = 1$, and so $y = -2(1) + 5 \Rightarrow y = 3$. The solution is $(1, 3)$.

20. Note that $x - y = -5 \Rightarrow x = y - 5$. Substituting $x = y - 5$ into the first equation yields the following: $3(y - 5) - y = 5 \Rightarrow 3y - 15 - y = 5 \Rightarrow 2y = 20 \Rightarrow y = 10$, and so $x = 10 - 5 \Rightarrow x = 5$. The solution is $(5, 10)$.

21. Note that $x + 3y = 1 \Rightarrow x = -3y + 1$. Substituting $x = -3y + 1$ into the second equation yields the following: $-2(-3y + 1) + 2y = 6 \Rightarrow 6y - 2 + 2y = 6 \Rightarrow 8y - 2 = 6 \Rightarrow 8y = 8 \Rightarrow y = 1$, and so $x = -3(1) + 1 \Rightarrow x = -2$. The solution is $(-2, 1)$.

22. Note that $2x - y = -4 \Rightarrow -y = -2x - 4 \Rightarrow y = 2x + 4$. Substituting $y = 2x + 4$ into the first equation yields the following: $3x - 2(2x + 4) = -4 \Rightarrow 3x - 4x - 8 = -4 \Rightarrow -x - 8 = -4 \Rightarrow -x = 4 \Rightarrow x = -4$, and so $y = 2(-4) + 4 \Rightarrow y = -8 + 4 \Rightarrow y = -4$. The solution is $(-4, -4)$.

23. (a) Parallel lines so zero solutions.

    (b) No solutions so inconsistent.

24. (a) An intersection so one solution.

    (b) One solution is consistent and dependent.

25. (a) Coinciding lines so infinitely many solutions.

    (b) Infinitely many solutions is consistent and dependent.

26. (a) parallel lines so no solutions.

    (b) No solutions is inconsistent.

27. Substituting $y = -x$ into the first equation yields the following: $x + (-x) = 2 \Rightarrow 0 = 2$. This is not true $\Rightarrow$ no solutions. See Figure 27. The lines are parallel so no solutions.

28. Substituting $x + y = -2 \Rightarrow y = -x - 2$ into the second equation yields the following: $x + (-x - 2) = 3 \Rightarrow -2 = 3$. This is not true $\Rightarrow$ no solutions. See Figure 28. The lines are parallel so no solutions.

Figure 27

Figure 28

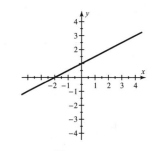
Figure 29

29. Note that $x - 2y = -2 \Rightarrow x = 2y - 2$. Substituting $x = 2y - 2$ into the first equation yields the following: $-(2y - 2) + 2y = 2 \Rightarrow -2y + 2 + 2y = 2 \Rightarrow 2 = 2$. This is true $\Rightarrow$ infinitely many solutions. See Figure 29. The lines coincide, so there are infinitely many solutions.

30. Note that $-x - y = -2 \Rightarrow -y = x - 2 \Rightarrow y = -x + 2$. Substituting $y = -x + 2$ into the second equation yields the following: $2x - (-x + 2) = 1 \Rightarrow 2x + x - 2 = 1 \Rightarrow 3x = 3 \Rightarrow x = 1$, and so $y = -1 + 2 \Rightarrow y = 1$. The solution is $(1, 1)$. See Figure 30. The lines intersect at the solution $(1, 1)$.

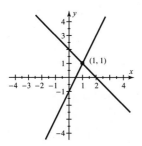
Figure 30

Section 4.3

31. The lines intersect at the solution $(2, 1)$. Adding the two equations will eliminate the variable y.

$$x + y = 3$$
$$\underline{x - y = 1}$$
$$2x = 4 \quad \text{Thus } x = 2. \text{ And so } 2 + y = 3 \Rightarrow y = 1. \text{ The solution is } (2, 1).$$

32. The lines intersect at the solution $(-1, 2)$. Multiplying the second equation by -2 and adding the two equations will eliminate the variable x.

$$2x + 3y = 4$$
$$\underline{-2x + 4y = 10}$$
$$7y = 14 \quad \text{Thus } y = 2. \text{ And so } 2x + 3(2) = 4 \Rightarrow 2x + 6 = 4 \Rightarrow 2x = -2 \Rightarrow x = -1. \text{ The solution is } (-1, 2).$$

33. Adding the two equations will eliminate the variable y.

$$x + y = 10$$
$$\underline{x - y = 12}$$
$$2x = 22 \quad \text{Thus } x = 11. \text{ And so } 11 + y = 10 \Rightarrow y = -1. \text{ The solution is } (11, -1).$$

34. Adding the two equations will eliminate the variable y.

$$2x - y = 2$$
$$\underline{3x + y = 3}$$
$$5x = 5 \quad \text{Thus } x = 1. \text{ And so } 2(1) - y = 2 \Rightarrow 2 - y = 2 \Rightarrow -y = 0 \Rightarrow y = 0. \text{ The solution is } (1, 0).$$

35. Multiplying the second equation by 2 and adding the two equations will eliminate the variable x.

$$-2x + 2y = -1$$
$$\underline{2x - 6y = -6}$$
$$-4y = -7 \quad \text{Thus } y = \frac{7}{4}. \text{ And so } -2x + 2\left(\frac{7}{4}\right) = -1 \Rightarrow -2x + \frac{14}{4} = -1 \Rightarrow -2x = -\frac{18}{4} \Rightarrow x = \frac{9}{4}.$$

The solution is $\left(\frac{9}{4}, \frac{7}{4}\right)$.

36. Multiplying the first equation by -1 and adding the two equations will eliminate the variable x.

$$-2x + 5y = 0$$
$$\underline{2x + 4y = 9}$$
$$9y = 9 \quad \text{Thus } y = 1. \text{ And so } 2x + 4(1) = 9 \Rightarrow 2x + 4 = 9 \Rightarrow 2x = 5 \Rightarrow x = \frac{5}{2}.$$

The solution is $\left(\frac{5}{2}, 1\right)$.

37. Multiplying the first equation by 2 and adding the two equations will eliminate the variable b.

$$4a + 2b = 6$$
$$\underline{-3a - 2b = -1}$$
$$a = 5 \quad \text{And so } 4(5) + 2b = 6 \Rightarrow 20 + 2b = 6 \Rightarrow 2b = -14 \Rightarrow b = -7. \text{ The solution is } (5, -7).$$

38. Multiplying the first equation by -3 and adding the two equations will eliminate the variable a.

$$-3a + 9b = -6$$
$$\underline{3a + b = 26}$$
$$10b = 20 \quad \text{Thus } b = 2. \text{ And so } 3a + 2 = 26 \Rightarrow 3a = 24 \Rightarrow a = 8. \text{ The solution is } (8, 2).$$

39. Multiplying the first equation by 2, the second equation by 5 and adding the two equations will eliminate the variable r.

$$10r + 6t = -2$$
$$-10r - 25t = -55$$

$-19t = -57$ Thus $t = 3$. And so $10r + 6(3) = -2 \Rightarrow 10r + 18 = -2 \Rightarrow 10r = -20 \Rightarrow r = -2$.

The solution is $(-2, 3)$.

40. Multiplying the first equation by 7, the second equation by 2 and adding the two equations will eliminate the variable t.

$$35r + 14t = 35$$
$$6r - 14t = 6$$

$41r = 41$ Thus $r = 1$. And so $6(1) - 14t = 6 \Rightarrow 6 - 14t = 6 \Rightarrow -14t = 0 \Rightarrow t = 0$.

The solution is $(1, 0)$.

41. (a) Adding the two equations will eliminate the variable y.

$$3x + y = 6$$
$$x - y = -2$$

$4x = 4$ Thus $x = 1$. And so $1 - y = -2 \Rightarrow -y = -3 \Rightarrow y = 3$. The solution is $(1, 3)$.

(b) See Figure 41b. The intersection and solution is $(1, 3)$.

(c) See Figure 41c. Since when $x = 1$, $y = 3$ for both equations the solution is $(1, 3)$.

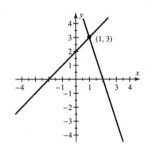

Figure 41b

x	-1	0	1	2
$y = 6 - 3x$	9	6	3	0
$y = x + 2$	1	2	3	4

Figure 41c

42. (a) Multiplying the second equation by 2 and adding the two equations will eliminate the variable x.

$$2x + y = 3$$
$$-2x + 4y = -8$$

$5y = -5$ Thus $y = -1$. And so $2x - 1 = 3 \Rightarrow 2x = 4 \Rightarrow x = 2$. The solution is $(2, -1)$.

(b) See Figure 42b. The intersection and solution is $(2, -1)$.

(c) See Figure 42c. Since when $x = 2$, $y = -1$ for both equations the solution is $(2, -1)$.

Figure 42b

x	-2	0	2	4
$y = 3 - 2x$	7	3	-1	-5
$y = (x - 4)/2$	-3	-2	-1	0

Figure 42c

43. Adding the two equations will eliminate both variables.

$$x - y = 5$$
$$-x + y = -5$$

$0 = 0$ Since this is true, there are infinitely many solutions.

44. Multiplying the second equation by 3 and adding the two equations will eliminate both variables.

$$3x - 3y = 0$$
$$-3x + 3y = 0$$

$0 = 0$ Since this is true, there are infinitely many solutions.

45. Adding the two equations will eliminate both variables.

$$-2x + y = 3$$
$$2x - y = 3$$

$0 = 6$ Since this is false, there are zero solutions.

46. Adding the two equations will eliminate the variable y.

$$-2x + y = 2$$
$$3x - y = 3$$

$x = 5$ And so $3(5) - y = 3 \Rightarrow 15 - y = 3 \Rightarrow -y = -12 \Rightarrow y = 12$. The solution is $(5, 12)$,

therefore there is one solution.

Section 4.4

47. Yes, because $-3 \le 2$ is true.

48. No, because $-1 > -1$ is false.

49. No, because $1 + 2 < -2$ is false.

50. Yes, because $2(1) - 3(-4) \ge 2 \Rightarrow 2 + 12 \ge 2$ is true.

51. Point $(1, -2)$ is a solution because $-2 \le -1$ is true. See Figure 51.

Figure 51

Figure 52

52. Point $(1, 1)$ is a solution because $2(1) + 1 > 1$ is true. See Figure 52.

53. Yes, because $1 - 2(-2) > 3 \Rightarrow 1 + 4 > 3$ is true and $2(1) + (-2) < 3 \Rightarrow 0 < 3$ is true.

54. No, because $4 - (-3) \ge 1 \Rightarrow 4 + 3 \ge 1$ is true but $4(4) + 3(-3) \le 4 \Rightarrow 16 - 9 \le 4$ is false.

55. The region containing $(2, -2)$, because $-2 < 1$ is true and $2(2) + (-2) \ge -1 \Rightarrow 4 - 2 \ge -1$ is true.

56. The region containing $(1, 3)$, because $3 \geq 1$ is true and $1 + 3 \geq 2$ is true.

57. $y > 1$

58. $y \leq 2x + 1$

59. See Figure 59.

60. See Figure 60.

Figure 59

Figure 60

Figure 61

61. See Figure 61.

62. See Figure 62.

63. See Figure 63.

Figure 62

Figure 63

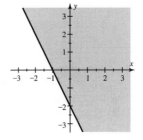

Figure 64

64. See Figure 64.

65. See Figure 65.

66. See Figure 66.

Figure 65

Figure 66

Figure 67

67. See Figure 67.

68. See Figure 68.

69. See Figure 69.

Figure 68

Figure 69

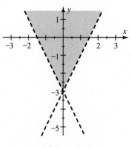
Figure 70

70. See Figure 70.

Applications

71. Let x = number of motor vehicle deaths in 1912 and let y = number of motor vehicle deaths in 1999. Then $13.3x = y$ and $y = x + 38,130$. Substituting $13.3x = y$ into the second equation yields the following: $13.3x = x + 38,130 \Rightarrow 12.3x = 38,130 \Rightarrow x = 3100$, and so $y = 3100 + 38,130 \Rightarrow y = 41,230$. Therefore 3100 deaths in 1912 and 41,230 deaths in 1999.

72. Let x = lung cancer cases in men and let y = lung cancer cases in women. Then $x + y = 185,000$ and $x = y + 20,000$. Substituting $x = y + 20,000$ into the first equation yields the following: $(y + 20,000) + y = 185,000 \Rightarrow 2y = 165,000 \Rightarrow y = 82,500$, and so $x = 82,500 + 20,000 \Rightarrow x = 102,500$. Therefore men will have 102,500 cases of lung cancer reported and women will have 82,500 cases of lung cancer reported.

73. (a) $c = 0.2x + 40$

    (b) See Figure 73b. The intersection and solution is $(250, 90)$ or 250 miles.

    (c) See Figure 73c. Since when $x = 250$, $c = 90$ for both equations, the solution is $(250, 90) \Rightarrow 250$ miles.

Figure 73b

x	150	200	250	300
$C = 0.2x + 40$	70	80	90	100

Figure 73c

74. Let x = gardens width and let y = gardens length. Then $2x + 2y = 88$ and $y = x + 4$. Substituting $y = x + 4$ into the first equation yields the following: $2x + 2(x + 4) = 88 \Rightarrow 2x + 2x + 8 = 88 \Rightarrow 4x + 8 = 88 \Rightarrow 4x = 80 \Rightarrow x = 20$, and so $y = 20 + 4 \Rightarrow y = 24$. The solution is $(20, 24)$. The dimensions of the garden are 20×24 feet.

75. (a) $2x + y = 180$ and $2x = y + 40$

(b) Note that $2x + y = 180 \Rightarrow y = -2x + 180$. Substituting $y = -2x + 180$ into the second equation yields the following: $2x = (-2x + 180) + 40 \Rightarrow 2x = -2x + 220 \Rightarrow 4x = 220 \Rightarrow x = 55$, and so $y = -2(55) + 180 \Rightarrow y = -110 + 180 \Rightarrow y = 70$. The solution is $(55, 70)$ or two angles at $55°$ and one at $70°$.

(c) Note that $2x = y + 40 \Rightarrow 2x - y = 40$. Adding the two equations will eliminate the variable y.

$2x + y = 180$
$\underline{2x - y = 40}$
$\qquad 4x = 220$ Thus $x = 55$. And so $2(55) = y + 40 \Rightarrow 110 = y + 40 \Rightarrow y = 70$. The solution is $(55, 70)$ or two angles at $55°$ and one angle at $70°$.

76. Let $x =$ smaller angle and let $y =$ larger angle. Then $x + y = 180$ and $x = y - 30$. Substituting $x = y - 30$ into the first equation yields the following: $(y - 30) + y = 180 \Rightarrow 2y = 210 \Rightarrow y = 105$, and so $x = 105 - 30 \Rightarrow x = 75$. The angles are $75°$ and $105°$.

77. (a) Let $x =$ number of $80 rooms and let $y =$ number of $120 rooms. Then $x + y = 10$ and $80x + 120y = 920$.

(b) Multiplying the first equation by -80 and adding the two equations will eliminate the variable x.

$-80x - 80y = -800$
$\underline{80x + 120y = 920}$
$\qquad 40y = 120$ Thus $y = 3$. And so $x + 3 = 10 \Rightarrow x = 7$. The solution is $(7, 3)$ or 7 $80 rooms and 3 $120 rooms.

78. Let $x =$ pounds of $2 candy and let $y =$ pounds of $3 candy. Then $x + y = 18$ and $2x + 3y = 47$.

Multiplying the first equation by -2 and adding the two equations will eliminate the variable x.

$-2x - 2y = -36$
$\underline{2x + 3y = 47}$
$\qquad y = 11$ And so $x + 11 = 18 \Rightarrow x = 7$. The solution is $(7, 11)$ or 7 pounds of $2 candy and 11 pounds of $3 candy.

79. Let $x =$ minutes on the stationary bike and let $y =$ minutes on the stair climber. Then $x + y = 60$ and $9x + 11y = 590$. Multiplying the first equation by -9 and adding the two equations will eliminate the variable x.

$-9x - 9y = -540$
$\underline{9x + 11y = 590}$
$\qquad 2y = 50$ Thus $y = 25$. And so $x + 25 = 60 \Rightarrow x = 35$. The solution is $(35, 25)$ or 35 minutes on the bike and 25 minutes on the stair climber.

80. Let $x =$ speed of the boat and let $y =$ speed of the current. Then $10x + 10y = 140$ and $14x - 14y = 140$.

Multiplying the first equation by 7, the second by 5 and adding the two equations will eliminate the variable y.

$70x + 70y = 980$
$\underline{70x - 70y = 700}$
$\qquad 140x = 1680$ Thus $x = 12$. And so $10(12) + 10y = 140 \Rightarrow 120 + 10y = 140 \Rightarrow 10y = 20 \Rightarrow y = 2$. The solution is $(12, 2)$. The current is 2 mph.

81. (a) The intersection and solution is approximately 16×24 feet.

(b) Using the system $2L + 2W = 80$ and $L = \dfrac{3}{2}W$ and substituting $L = \dfrac{3}{2}W$ into the first equation yields the

   following: $2\left(\dfrac{3}{2}W\right) + 2W = 80 \Rightarrow 3W + 2W = 80 \Rightarrow 5W = 80 \Rightarrow W = 16$, and so $L = \dfrac{3}{2}(16) \Rightarrow$

   $L = 24$. The dimensions are 16×24 feet.

82. Let x = number of wheels made and let y = number of trailers made. Then $x + y \le 30$ and $x \ge 2y$. Graph
    this system and shade. See Figure 82.

Figure 82

Figure 83

Figure 4

83. (a) $T = 150 - 0.7(20) \Rightarrow T = 150 - 14 \Rightarrow T = 136$ bpm for a 20 year old person and

   $T = 150 - 0.7(60) \Rightarrow T = 150 - 42 \Rightarrow T = 108$ bpm for a 60 year old person.

(b) See Figure 83.

(c) The shaded region represents target heart rates above 70% of the maximum heart rate for ages 20 to 60.

Chapter 4 Test

1. $(1, 2)$, because $3(1) + 2(2) = 7 \Rightarrow 3 + 4 = 7 \Rightarrow$ is true and $2(1) - 2 = 0$ is true.

2. The intersection and solution is $(-2, -1)$. Checking: $-2 + 4(-1) = -6 \Rightarrow -2 + (-4) = -6$ is true and
   $2(-2) + (-1) = -5 \Rightarrow -4 + (-1) = -5$.

3. Since when $x = -1, y = -2$ for both equations, the solution is $(-1, -2)$.

4. See Figure 4. The intersection and solution is $(-2, 3)$.

5. Substituting $y = 3x$ into the first equation yields the following: $3x + 2(3x) = 9 \Rightarrow 3x + 6x = 9 \Rightarrow$
   $9x = 9 \Rightarrow x = 1$, and so $y = 3(1) \Rightarrow y = 3$. The solution is $(1, 3)$.

6. (a) Multiplying the first equation by -3 and adding the two equations will eliminate the variable x.
   $$-3x - 9y = -15$$
   $$\underline{3x - 2y = 4}$$
   $$-11y = -11$$ Thus $y = 1$. And so $3x - 2(1) = 4 \Rightarrow 3x - 2 = 4 \Rightarrow 3x = 6 \Rightarrow x = 2$.
   The solution is $(2, 1) \Rightarrow$ one solution $\Rightarrow$ consistent.

(b) Multiplying the first equation by 2 and adding the two equations will eliminate both variables.
   $$-2x + y = 24$$
   $$\underline{2x - y = -4}$$
   $$0 = 20$$ This is false $\Rightarrow$ no solutions $\Rightarrow$ inconsistent.

7. Adding the two equations will eliminate the variable y.

$$x + 2y = 5$$
$$3x - 2y = -17$$

$$4x = -12$$ Thus $x = -3$. And so $-3 + 2y = 5 \Rightarrow 2y = 8 \Rightarrow y = 4$. The solution is $(-3, 4)$.

8. Multiplying the second equation by 2 and adding the two equations will eliminate both variables.

$$2x - 2y = 3$$
$$-2x + 2y = 10$$

$$0 = 13$$ This is false $\Rightarrow$ no solutions.

9. $y \leq -\dfrac{1}{2}x$

10. See Figure 10.

Figure 10

Figure 11

11. See Figure 11.

12. See Figure 12.

Figure 12

Figure 13

13. See Figure 13.

14. Let x = taxes collected in 1998 and let y = taxes collected in 1999. Then $x + y = 3.7$ and $y = x + 0.1$. Substituting $y = x + 0.1$ into the first equation yields the following: $x + (x + 0.1) = 3.7 \Rightarrow$ $2x + 0.1 = 3.7 \Rightarrow 2x = 3.6 \Rightarrow x = 1.8$, and so $y = 1.8 + 0.1 \Rightarrow y = 1.9$. The solution is $(1.8, 1.9)$ or $1.8 trillion collected in 1998 and $1.9 trillion collected in 1999.

15. Let x = hrs jogged at 6 mph and let y = hrs jogged at 9 mph. Then $x + y = 1$ and $6x + 9y = 7$. Multiplying the first equation by -6 and adding the two equations will eliminate the variable x.

$$-6x - 6y = -6$$
$$6x + 9y = 7$$

$$3y = 1$$ Thus $y = \dfrac{1}{3}$. And so $x + \dfrac{1}{3} = 1 \Rightarrow x = \dfrac{2}{3}$. The solution is $\left(\dfrac{2}{3}, \dfrac{1}{3}\right)$ or $\dfrac{2}{3}$ hour at 6 miles per

hour and $\dfrac{1}{3}$ hour at 9 miles per hour.

Chapter 4 Extended and Discovery Exercises

1. The forest has higher precipitation for higher temperatures than grasslands $\Rightarrow 7P - 5T \geq -70$.

2. The deserts have less precipitation for high temperatures than grasslands $\Rightarrow 35P - 3T \leq 140$.

3. The grassland is lower precipitation for higher temperatures than forests and higher than desert
    $\Rightarrow 7P - 5T \leq -70$ and $35P - 3T \geq 140$.

4. From the graph, grasslands would be the type of plant growth, and $7(14) - 5(50) \leq -70 \Rightarrow$
    $98 - 250 \leq -70$ is true and $35(14) - 3(50) \geq 140 \Rightarrow 490 - 150 \geq 140$ is true $\Rightarrow$ yes.

5. -0.5; average the x-values -1 and 0 because the solution y-value 0 is half way between their corresponding y-values -1 and 1.

6. 0.5; average the x-values 0 and 1 because the solution y-value 5 is half way between their corresponding y-values 3 and 7.

7. 1.5; average the x-values 1 and 2 because the solution y-value 3.75 is half way between their corresponding y-values 3.5 and 4.

8. $\dfrac{1}{3}$; because 0 is one-third of the way between the y-values -1 and 2, you must choose a value one-third of the way between the corresponding x-values 0 and 1.

Critical Thinking Solutions for Chapter 4

Section 4.1

-   Parallel lines have no intersection, therefore there are no solutions.

Section 4.2

-   Since it helps downstream and hurts upstream the current would be half the difference $\Rightarrow \dfrac{16 - 10}{2} = 3$ mph.

Section 4.4

-   No, $(2, -2)$ is not a true solution for both equations, it does not satisfy $x + 2y < -2$ because $2 + 2(-2) < -2 \Rightarrow -2 < -2$ which is false.

-   This region represents heavier weights and shorter heights. These ordered pairs correspond to people who weigh more than recommended.

Chapter 5: Polynomials and Exponents

5.1: Rules for Exponents

Concepts

1. $b = $ base; $n = $ exponent

3. $\dfrac{1}{2} \cdot \dfrac{1}{2} \cdot \dfrac{1}{2} = \left(\dfrac{1}{2}\right)^3$

5. a^{m+n}

7. $a^n b^n$

Properties of Exponents

9. $8^2 = 8 \cdot 8 = 64$

11. $(-2)^3 = (-2) \cdot (-2) \cdot (-2) = -8$

13. $-2^3 = -(2 \cdot 2 \cdot 2) = -8$

15. $6^0 = 1$

17. $2 \cdot 4^2 = 2 \cdot (4 \cdot 4) = 2 \cdot 16 = 32$

19. $1 + 5^2 = 1 + (5 \cdot 5) = 1 + 25 = 26$

21. $\dfrac{4^2}{2} = \dfrac{(4 \cdot 4)}{2} = \dfrac{16}{2} = 8$

23. $4 \cdot \dfrac{1}{2^3} = 4 \cdot \dfrac{1}{(2 \cdot 2 \cdot 2)} = 4 \cdot \dfrac{1}{8} = \dfrac{4}{8} = \dfrac{1}{2}$

25. $4^2 \cdot 4^6 = 4^{2+6} = 4^8 = 65{,}536$

27. $2^3 \cdot 2^2 = 2^{3+2} = 2^5 = 32$

29. $x^3 \cdot x^6 = x^{3+6} = x^9$

31. $z^0 z^4 = z^{0+4} = z^4$

33. $x^2 x^2 x^2 = x^{2+2+2} = x^6$

35. $4x^2 \cdot 5x^5 = 20x^{2+5} = 20x^7$

37. $3(-xy^3)(x^2 y) = 3(-x^{1+2} y^{3+1}) = 3(-x^3 y^4) = -3x^3 y^4$

39. $(2^3)^2 = 2^{2 \cdot 3} = 2^6 = 64$

41. $(n^3)^4 = n^{3 \cdot 4} = n^{12}$

43. $x(x^3)^2 = x(x^{3 \cdot 2}) = x(x^6) = x^{1+6} = x^7$

45. $(-7b)^2 = (-7) \cdot (-7) \cdot (b \cdot b) = 49b^2$

47. $(ab)^3 = (a \cdot a \cdot a)(b \cdot b \cdot b) = a^3 b^3$

49. $(2x^2)^2 = (2 \cdot 2)(x^{2 \cdot 2}) = 4x^4$

51. $(-4b^2)^3 = (-4) \cdot (-4) \cdot (-4)(b^{2 \cdot 3}) = -64b^6$

53. $(x^2 y^3)^7 = (x^{2 \cdot 7} y^{3 \cdot 7}) = x^{14} y^{21}$

55. $(y^3)^2(x^4y)^3 = (y^{3\cdot2})(x^{4\cdot3}y^{1\cdot3}) = (y^6)(x^{12}y^3) = x^{12}y^{6+3} = x^{12}y^9$

57. $\left(\dfrac{2}{3}\right)^3 = \dfrac{(2\cdot2\cdot2)}{(3\cdot3\cdot3)} = \dfrac{8}{27}$

59. $\left(\dfrac{a}{b}\right)^5 = \dfrac{(a\cdot a\cdot a\cdot a\cdot a)}{(b\cdot b\cdot b\cdot b\cdot b)} = \dfrac{a^5}{b^5}$

61. $\left(\dfrac{2x}{5}\right)^3 = \dfrac{(2\cdot2\cdot2)(x^{1\cdot3})}{(5\cdot5\cdot5)} = \dfrac{8x^3}{125}$

63. $\left(\dfrac{3x^2}{5y^4}\right)^3 = \dfrac{(3\cdot3\cdot3)(x^{2\cdot3})}{(5\cdot5\cdot5)(y^{4\cdot3})} = \dfrac{27x^6}{125y^{12}}$

65. $(a+b)^2(a+b)^3 = (a+b)^{2+3} = (a+b)^5$

67. $6(x^4y^6)^0 = 6(x^{4\cdot0}y^{6\cdot0}) = 6(x^0y^0) = 6\cdot1\cdot1 = 6$

69. $a(a^2+2b^2) = a^{1+2}+2ab^2 = a^3+2ab^2$

71. $(r+t)(rt) = (r^{1+1}t)+(rt^{1+1}) = r^2t+rt^2$

Applications

73. $2x^2\cdot5x^2 = 10x^{2+2} = 10x^4$ square units

75. $x\cdot2x\cdot4x = 8x^{1+1+1} = 8x^3$

77. $\pi(3x^2)^2 = \pi(3\cdot3)(x^{2\cdot2}) = \pi(9x^4) = 9\pi x^4$

79. $1000(1+0.05)^3 = 1000(1.05)^3 = 1000(1.05\cdot1.05\cdot1.05) = 1000(1.157625) \approx \$1157.63$

81. See Figure 81.

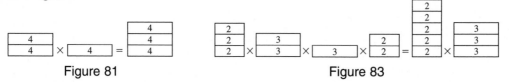

Figure 81   Figure 83

83. See Figure 83.

5.2: Addition and Subtraction of Polynomials

Concepts

1. monomial

3. polynomial

5. binomial

7. 2 terms; degree $= 3$

9. like

11. opposite

Properties of Polynomials

13. Because $x^2 \Rightarrow$ the degree is 2; the coefficient is 3.

15. Because $ab = a^1b^1$ and $1 + 1 = 2 \Rightarrow$ the degree is 2; $-ab = -1ab \Rightarrow$ the coefficient is -1.

17. Because $rt = r^1t^1$ and $1 + 1 = 2 \Rightarrow$ the degree is 2; the coefficient is -5.

19. Because there are no variables the degree is 0; the coefficient is -6.

21. Yes it is polynomial; 1 term $-x$; one variable x; $x^1 \Rightarrow$ degree is 1.

23. Yes it is polynomial; 3 terms $4x^2$, $-5x$, and 9; one variable x; $x^2 \Rightarrow$ degree is 2.

25. Not a polynomial because it has a variable in the denominator.

27. Yes it is polynomial; 2 terms $3x^2y$ and $-xy^3$; two variables x and y; $xy^3 = x^1y^3$ and $1 + 3 = 4 \Rightarrow$ degree is 4.

29. Yes, $5x + (-4x) = (5 - 4)x = 1x = x$.

31. Yes, $x^3 + (-6x^3) = [1 + (-6)]x^3 = -5x^3$.

33. No, x and y are not like terms.

35. Yes $\Rightarrow ab + ba = (1 + 1)ab = 2ab$.

37. Yes $\Rightarrow 7xy^2 + (-3xy^2) = (7 - 3)xy^2 = 4xy^2$.

Addition of Polynomials

39. $(3x + 5) + (-4x + 4) = 3x + (-4x) + 5 + 4 = (3 - 4)x + (5 + 4) = -x + 9$

41. $(3x^2 + 4x + 1) + (x^2 + 4x - 6) = 3x^2 + x^2 + 4x + 4x + 1 + (-6) = (3 + 1)x^2 + (4 + 4)x + (1 - 6) =$
    $4x^2 + 8x - 5$

43. $(a^3 - 6) + (4a^3 + 7) = 4a^3 + a^3 + 7 + (-6) = (4 + 1)a^3 + (7 - 6) = 5a^3 + 1$

45. $(y^3 + 3y^2 - 5) + (3y^3 + 4y - 4) = 3y^3 + y^3 + 3y^2 + 4y + (-5) + (-4) =$
    $(3 + 1)y^3 + 3y^2 + 4y + (-5 - 4) = 4y^3 + 3y^2 + 4y - 9$

47. $(-xy + 5) + (5xy - 4) = 5xy + (-xy) + 5 + (-4) = (5 - 1)xy + (5 - 4) = 4xy + 1$

49. $(a^3b^2 + a^2b^3) + (a^2b^3 - a^3b^2) = a^3b^2 + (-a^3b^2) + a^2b^3 + a^2b^3 = (1 - 1)a^3b^2 + (1 + 1)a^2b^3 =$
    $0a^3b^2 + 2a^2b^3 = 2a^2b^3$

51. $\quad 4x^2 - 2x + 1$
    $\quad \underline{+\ 5x + 3x - 7}$
    $\quad\ 9x^2 +\ x - 6$

53. $\quad -x^2 +\ x + 0$
    $\quad \underline{+\ 2x^2 - 8x - 1}$
    $\quad\ x^2 - 7x - 1$

Subtraction of Polynomials

55. $-5x^2$

57. $-3a^2 + a - 4$

59. $2t^2 + 3t - 4$

61. $3x^3 + x - 5$

63. $-9xy + x^2$

65. $(3x + 1) - (-x + 3) = (3x + 1) + (x - 3) = (3 + 1)x + (1 - 3) = 4x - 2$

67. $(-x^2 + 6x + 8) - (2x^2 + x - 2) = (-x^2 + 6x + 8) + (2x^2 - x + 2) =$

    $(-1 - 2)x^2 + (6 - 1)x + (8 + 2) = -3x^2 + 5x + 10$

69. $(a^2 - 2a) - (4a^2 + 3a) = (a^2 - 2a) + (-4a^2 - 3a) = (1 - 4)a^2 + (-2 - 3)a = -3a^2 - 5a$

71. $(z^3 - 2z^2 - z) - (4z^2 + 5z + 1) = (z^3 - 2z^2 - z) + (-4z^2 - 5z - 1) =$

    $z^3 + (-2 - 4)z^2 + (-1 - 5)z - 1 = z^3 - 6z^2 - 6z - 1$

73. $(4xy + x^2y^2) - (xy - x^2y^2) = (4xy + x^2y^2) + (-xy + x^2y^2) = (4 - 1)xy + (1 + 1)x^2y^2 = 3xy + 2x^2y^2$

75. $(ab^2) - (ab^2 + a^3b) = (ab^2) + (-ab^2 - a^3b) = (1 - 1)ab^2 - a^3b = 0ab^2 - a^3b = -a^3b$

77. $(x^2 + 2x - 3) - (2x^2 + 7x + 1) = x^2 \ + 2x - 3$

$$\underline{+ \ (-2x^2) - 7x - 1}$$
$$-x^2 - 5x - 4$$

79. $(3x^3 - 2x) - (5x^3 + 4x + 2) = 3x^3 \ - 2x + 0$

$$\underline{+ \ (-5x^3) - 4x - 2}$$
$$-2x^3 - 6x - 2$$

Applications

81. $x = 3$ in., $x^3 = 3^3 = 27$ in^3

83. (a) Let $t = 0$, then $1.6t^2 - 28t + 200 = 1.6(0^2) - 28(0) + 200 = 0 - 0 + 200 = 200$ bpm.

    (b) Let $t = 5$, then $1.6t^2 - 28t + 200 = 1.6(5^2) - 28(5) + 200 = 1.6(25) - 28(5) + 200 =$

    $40 - 140 + 200 = 100$ bpm.

    (c) It decreases quickly at first and then more slowly.

85. $z^2 + z^2 = (1 + 1)z^2$; Let $z = 10$ in., then $2(10^2) = 2(100) = 200$ in^2

87. $2x \cdot x + x \cdot x = 2x^2 + x^2$ or $3x^2$; Let $x = 6$ feet, then $3x^2 = 3(6^2) = 3(36) = 108$ ft^2

89. $\pi x^2 + \pi y^2$; Let $x = 2$ feet and $y = 3$ feet, then $\pi x^2 + \pi y^2 = \pi(2^2) + \pi(3^2) = \pi(4) + \pi(9) = 13\pi$ ft^2

91. (a) Slope $m = \dfrac{P_2 - P_1}{t_2 - t_1}$, so $m_1 = \dfrac{5 - 4}{1987 - 1974} = \dfrac{1}{13} \Rightarrow m_1 = 0.077$; $m_2 = \dfrac{6 - 5}{1999 - 1987} = \dfrac{1}{12} \Rightarrow$

    $m_2 = 0.083$; $m_3 = \dfrac{7 - 6}{2012 - 1999} = \dfrac{1}{13} \Rightarrow m_3 = 0.077$. A line is a reasonable estimate, it is not exact.

    (b) Substituting different years for t shows that the polynomial gives a reasonable estimate. Example:

    $0.077(1987) - 148 = 4.999$ million, close to the five million estimate of 1987.

Checking Basic Concepts for Sections 5.1 & 5.2

1. (a) $-5^2 = -(5 \cdot 5) = -25$

   (b) $3^2 - 2^3 = (3 \cdot 3) - (2 \cdot 2 \cdot 2) = 9 - 8 = 1$

2. (a) $10^3 \cdot 10^5 = 10^{3+5} = 10^8$

   (b) $(3x^2)(-4x^5) = -12x^{2+5} = -12x^7$

   (c) $(a^3b)^2 = a^{3\cdot2}b^{1\cdot2} = a^6b^2$

   (d) $\left(\dfrac{x}{z^3}\right)^4 = \dfrac{x^{1\cdot4}}{z^{3\cdot4}} = \dfrac{x^4}{z^{12}}$

3. 3 terms $5x^3y, -2x^2y$, and 5; 2 variables x and y; $x^3y = x^3y^1, 3 + 1 = 4 \Rightarrow$ the degree is 4.

4. (a) Let length $= 2W$, width $= W$, and height $= H$, then $2W \cdot W \cdot H = 2W^2H$.

   (b) Let $W = 12$ and $H = 10$, then $2W^2H = 2(12^2)(10) = 2(144)(10) = 2880 \text{ in}^3$.

5. (a) $(2a^2 + 3a - 1) + (a^2 - 3a + 7) = 2a^2 + a^2 + 3a + (-3a) + (-1) + 7 =$

      $(2 + 1)a^2 + (3 - 3)a + (-1 + 7) = 3a^2 + 0a + 6 = 3a^2 + 6$

   (b) $(4z^3 + 5z) - (2z^3 - 2z + 8) = (4z^3 + 5z) + (-2z^3 + 2z - 8) = (4 - 2)z^3 + (5 + 2)z - 8 =$

      $2z^3 + 7z - 8$

   (c) $(x^2 + 2xy + y^2) - (x^2 - 2xy + y^2) = (x^2 + 2xy + y^2) + (-x^2 + 2xy - y^2) =$

      $(1 - 1)x^2 + (2 + 2)xy + (1 - 1)y^2 = 0x^2 + 4xy + 0y^2 = 4xy$

6. Let $x = -2$, then $5x^2 - 7x = 5(-2)^2 - 7(-2) = 5(4) - 7(-2) = 20 - (-14) = 20 + 14 = 34$.

5.3: Multiplication of Polynomials

Concepts

1. The product rule

3. $x^2 - 7$; *Answers may vary.*

5. term; term

Multiplication of Monomials

7. $x^2 \cdot x^5 = x^{2+5} = x^7$

9. $-3a \cdot 4a = (-3)(4)aa = -12a^{1+1} = -12a^2$

11. $4x^3 \cdot 5x^2 = (4)(5)x^3x^2 = 20x^{3+2} = 20x^5$

13. $xy^2 \cdot 4xy = (1)(4)xxy^2y = 4x^{1+1}y^{2+1} = 4x^2y^3$

15. $(-3xy^2)(4x^2y) = (-3)(4)xx^2y^2y = -12x^{1+2}y^{2+1} = -12x^3y^3$

Multiplication of Monomials and Polynomials

17. $3(x + 4) = 3 \cdot x + 3 \cdot 4 = 3x + 12$

19. $-5(9x + 1) = -5 \cdot 9x + (-5 \cdot 1) = -45x - 5$

21. $(4 - z)z = 4 \cdot z + (-z \cdot z) = 4z - z^2$

23. $-y(5 + 3y) = -y \cdot 5 + (-y \cdot 3y) = -5y - 3y^2$

25. $3x(5x^2 - 4) = 3x \cdot 5x^2 + 3x \cdot (-4) = (3)(5)xx^2 - 12x = 15x^{1+2} - 12x = 15x^3 - 12x$

27. $(6x - 6)x^2 = 6x \cdot x^2 + (-6) \cdot x^2 = 6x^{1+2} - 6x^2 = 6x^3 - 6x^2$

29. $-8(4t^2 + t + 1) = -8 \cdot 4t^2 + (-8)(t) + (-8)(1) = -32t^2 - 8t - 8$

31. $4m(-2m^2 + 7m - 6) = 4m \cdot (-2m^2) + (4m)(7m) + (4m)(-6) = (4)(-2)mm^2 + (4)(7)mm - 24m =$
    $-8m^{1+2} + 28m^{1+1} - 24m = -8m^3 + 28m^2 - 24m$

33. $n^2(-5n^2 + n - 2) = (n^2)(-5n^2) + (n^2)(n) + (n^2)(-2) = -5n^{2+2} + n^{2+1} - 2n^2 = -5n^4 + n^3 - 2n^2$

35. $xy(x + y) = xy \cdot x + xy \cdot y = x^{1+1}y + xy^{1+1} = x^2y + xy^2$

37. $x^2(x^2y - xy^2) = x^2 \cdot x^2y + (x^2)(-xy^2) = x^{2+2}y - x^{2+1}y^2 = x^4y - x^3y^2$

39. $-ab(a^3 - 2b^3) = -ab \cdot a^3 + (-ab)(-2b^3) = -a^{1+3}b + 2ab^{3+1} = -a^4b + 2ab^4$

Multiplication of Polynomials

41. (a) Area $= x^2 + 3x$. See Figure 41.

   (b) $x(x + 3) = x \cdot x + x \cdot 3 = x^{1+1} + 3x = x^2 + 3x$

43. (a) Area $= x^2 + 2x + 2x + 4 = x^2 + 4x + 4$. See Figure 43.

   (b) $(x + 2)(x + 2) = x \cdot x + x \cdot 2 + 2 \cdot x + 2 \cdot 2 = x^{1+1} + 2x + 2x + 4 = x^2 + 4x + 4$

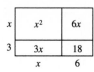

Figure 41   Figure 43   Figure 45

45. (a) Area $= x^2 + 3x + 6x + 18 = x^2 + 9x + 18$. See Figure 45.

   (b) $(x + 3)(x + 6) = x \cdot x + x \cdot 6 + 3 \cdot x + 3 \cdot 6 = x^{1+1} + 6x + 3x + 18 = x^2 + 9x + 18$

47. $(x + 3)(x + 5) = x \cdot x + x \cdot 5 + 3 \cdot x + 3 \cdot 5 = x^{1+1} + 5x + 3x + 15 = x^2 + 8x + 15$

49. $(x - 8)(x - 9) = x \cdot x + (x)(-9) + (-8)(x) + (-8)(-9) = x^{1+1} + (-9x) + (-8x) + 72 = x^2 - 17x + 72$

51. $(3z - 2)(2z - 5) = 3z \cdot 2z + (3z)(-5) + (-2)(2z) + (-2)(-5) = 6z^{1+1} + (-15z) + (-4z) + 10 =$
    $6z^2 - 19z + 10$

53. $(8b - 1)(8b + 1) = 8b \cdot 8b + 8b \cdot 1 + (-1)(8b) + (-1)(1) = 64b^{1+1} + 8b - 8b - 1 = 64b^2 - 1$

55. $(10y + 7)(y - 1) = 10y \cdot y + (10y)(-1) + 7 \cdot y + (7)(-1) = 10y^{1+1} - 10y + 7y - 7 = 10y^2 - 3y - 7$

57. $(5 - 3a)(1 - 2a) = 5 \cdot 1 + (5)(-2a) + (-3a)(1) + (-3a)(-2a) = 5 + (-10a) + (-3a) + 6a^{1+1} =$
    $5 - 13a + 6a^2$

59. $(1 - 3x)(1 + 3x) = 1 \cdot 1 + 1 \cdot 3x + (-3x)(1) + (-3x)(3x) = 1 + 3x - 3x - 9x^{1+1} = 1 - 9x^2$

61. $(x - 1)(x^2 + 1) = x \cdot x^2 + x \cdot 1 + (-1)(x^2) + (-1)(1) = x^{1+2} + x - x^2 - 1 = x^3 - x^2 + x - 1$

63. $(x^2 + 4)(4x - 3) = x^2 \cdot 4x + (x^2)(-3) + 4 \cdot 4x + (4)(-3) = 4x^{2+1} - 3x^2 + 16x - 12 =$
    $4x^3 - 3x^2 + 16x - 12$

65. $(2n + 1)(n^2 + 3) = 2n \cdot n^2 + 2n \cdot 3 + 1 \cdot n^2 + 1 \cdot 3 = 2n^{1+2} + 6n + n^2 + 3 = 2n^3 + n^2 + 6n + 3$

67. $(m + 1)(m^2 + 3m + 1) = m \cdot m^2 + m \cdot 3m + m \cdot 1 + 1 \cdot m^2 + 1 \cdot 3m + 1 \cdot 1 =$

    $m^{1+2} + 3m^{1+1} + m + m^2 + 3m + 1 = m^3 + 3m^2 + m + m^2 + 3m + 1 = m^3 + 4m^2 + 4m + 1$

69. $(3x - 2)(2x^2 - x + 4) = 3x \cdot 2x^2 + (3x)(-x) + 3x \cdot 4 + (-2)(2x^2) + (-2)(-x) + (-2)(4) =$

    $6x^{1+2} - 3x^{1+1} + 12x - 4x^2 + 2x - 8 = 6x^3 - 3x^2 + 12x - 4x^2 + 2x - 8 = 6x^3 - 7x^2 + 14x - 8$

71. $(x + 1)(x^2 - x + 1) = x \cdot x^2 + (x)(-x) + x \cdot 1 + 1 \cdot x^2 + (1)(-x) + 1 \cdot 1 =$

    $x^{1+2} - x^{1+1} + x + x^2 - x + 1 = x^3 - x^2 + x + x^2 - x + 1 = x^3 + 1$

73. $(4b^2 + 3b + 7)(b^2 + 3) = 4b^2 \cdot b^2 + 4b^2 \cdot 3 + 3b \cdot b^2 + 3b \cdot 3 + 7 \cdot b^2 + 7 \cdot 3 =$

    $4b^{2+2} + 12b^2 + 3b^{1+2} + 9b + 7b^2 + 21 = 4b^4 + 12b^2 + 3b^3 + 9b + 7b^2 + 21 =$

    $4b^4 + 3b^3 + 19b^2 + 9b + 21$

Applications

75. (a) Let $h = $ height, $ht^2 = $ length, and $h - 4 = $ width, then $(h - 4)(h + 2) =$

    $h \cdot h + h \cdot 2 + (-4)(h) + (-4)(2) = h^{1+1} + 2h - 4h - 8 = h^2 - 2h - 8 \Rightarrow (h)(h^2 - 2h - 8) =$

    $h \cdot h^2 + (h)(-2h) + (h)(-8) = h^{1+2} - 2h^{1+1} - 8h = h^3 - 2h^2 - 8h.$

   (b) $h^3 - 2h^2 - 8h = 25^3 - 2(25)^2 - 8(25) = 15{,}625 - 2(625) - 200 = 15{,}625 - 1250 - 200 =$

    $14{,}175$ in^3

77. $(x + 1)(x + 1) = x \cdot x + x \cdot 1 + 1 \cdot x + 1 \cdot 1 = x^{1+1} + x + x + 1 = x^2 + 2x + 1 \Rightarrow 1$ side $=$

    $x^2 + 2x + 1.$ A cube has all sides the same $\Rightarrow 6$ sides $= (6)(x^2 + 2x + 1) = 6 \cdot x^2 + 6 \cdot 2x^2 + 6 \cdot 1 =$

    $6x^2 + 12x + 6.$

79. (a) $t(64 - 16t) = t \cdot 64 + (t)(-16t) = 64t - 16t^{1+1} = 64t - 16t^2$

   (b) $64 - 16t^2 = 64(2) - 16(2)^2 = 128 - 16(4) = 128 - 64 = 64;$

    $t(64 - 16t) = 2(64 - 16(2)) = 2(64 - 32) = 2(32) = 64$

   (c) Yes; yes.

81. (a) $x(50 - x) = x \cdot 50 + (x)(-x) = 50x - x^{1+1} = 50x - x^2$

   (b) $50x - x^2 = 50(25) - (25^2) = 1250 - 625 = 625$

5.4: Special Products

Concepts

1. $(a + b)(a - b) = (a)^2 - (b)^2 = a^2 - b^2$

3. $(a + b)^2 = (a)^2 + 2(a)(b) + (b)^2 = a^2 + 2ab + b^2$

5. No, let $x = 1$, $y = 1$, then $(1 + 1)^2 = 2^2 = 4$ and $1^2 + 1^2 = 1 + 1 = 2$, *Answers may vary.*

7. No, let $z = 1$, then $(1 + 5)^3 = 6^3 = 216$ and $1^3 + 5^3 = 1 + 125 = 126$, *Answers may vary.*

Product of a Sum and Difference

9. $(x + 1)(x - 1) = (x)^2 - (1)^2 = x^2 - 1$

11. $(4x - 1)(4x + 1) = (4x)^2 - (1)^2 = 16x^2 - 1$

13. $(1 + 2a)(1 - 2a) = (1)^2 - (2a)^2 = 1 - 4a^2$

15. $(2x + 3y)(2x - 3y) = (2x)^2 - (3y)^2 = 4x^2 - 9y^2$

17. $(ab - 5)(ab + 5) = (ab)^2 - (5)^2 = a^2b^2 - 25$

19. $(ab + 4)(ab - 4) = (ab)^2 - (4)^2 = a^2b^2 - 16$

21. $(a^2 - b^2)(a^2 + b^2) = (a^2)^2 - (b^2)^2 = a^4 - b^4$

23. $(x^3 - y^3)(x^3 + y^3) = (x^3)^2 - (y^3)^2 = x^6 - y^6$

25. $101 \cdot 99 = (100 + 1)(100 - 1) = (100)^2 - (1)^2 = 10,000 - 1 = 9999$

27. $23 \cdot 17 = (20 + 3)(20 - 3) = (20)^2 - (3)^2 = 400 - 9 = 391$

29. $90 \cdot 110 = (100 - 10)(100 + 10) = (100)^2 - (10)^2 = 10,000 - 100 = 9900$

Squaring Binomials

31. $(x + 1)^2 = (x)^2 + 2(x)(1) + (1)^2 = x^2 + 2x + 1$

33. $(a - 2)^2 = (a)^2 - 2(a)(2) + (2)^2 = a^2 - 4a + 4$

35. $(2x + 3)^2 = (2x)^2 + 2(2x)(3) + (3)^2 = 4x^2 + 12x + 9$

37. $(3b + 5)^2 = (3b)^2 + 2(3b)(5) + (5)^2 = 9b^2 + 30b + 25$

39. $\left(\dfrac{3}{4}a - 4\right)^2 = \left(\dfrac{3}{4}a\right)^2 - 2\left(\dfrac{3}{4}a\right)(4) + (4)^2 = \dfrac{9}{16}a^2 - 6a + 16$

41. $(1 - b)^2 = (1)^2 - 2(1)(b) + (b)^2 = 1 - 2b + b^2$

43. $(5 + y^3)^2 = (5)^2 + 2(5)(y^3) + (y^3)^2 = 25 + 10y^3 + y^6$

45. $(a^2 + b)^2 = (a^2)^2 + 2(a^2)(b) + (b)^2 = a^4 + 2a^2b + b^2$

Cubing Binomials

47. $(a + 1)^3 = (a + 1)(a + 1)^2 = (a + 1)(a^2 + 2a + 1) =$

    $a \cdot a^2 + a \cdot 2a + a \cdot 1 + 1 \cdot a^2 + 1 \cdot 2a + 1 \cdot 1 = a^3 + 2a^2 + a + a^2 + 2a + 1 = a^3 + 3a^2 + 3a + 1$

49. $(x - 2)^3 = (x - 2)(x - 2)^2 = (x - 2)(x^2 - 4x + 4) =$

    $x \cdot x^2 + x \cdot (-4x) + x \cdot 4 + (-2) \cdot x^2 + (-2)(-4x) + (-2)4 =$

    $x^3 + (-4x^2) + 4x + (-2x^2) + 8x + (-8) = x^3 - 6x^2 + 12x - 8$

51. $(2x + 1)^3 = (2x + 1)(2x + 1)^2 = (2x + 1)(4x^2 + 4x + 1) =$

    $2x \cdot 4x^2 + 2x \cdot 4x + 2x \cdot 1 + 1 \cdot 4x^2 + 1 \cdot 4x + 1 \cdot 1 =$

    $8x^3 + 8x^2 + 2x + 4x^2 + 4x + 1 = 8x^3 + 12x^2 + 6x + 1$

53. $(6u - 1)^3 = (6u - 1)(6u - 1)^2 = (6u - 1)(36u^2 - 12u + 1) =$

    $6u \cdot 36u^2 + 6u \cdot (-12u) + 6u \cdot 1 + (-1) \cdot 36u^2 + (-1) \cdot (-12u) + (-1) \cdot 1 =$

    $216u^3 + (-72u^2) + 6u + (-36u^2) + 12u + (-1) = 216u^3 - 108u^2 + 18u - 1$

55. $t(t + 2)^3 = t(t + 2)(t + 2)^2 = t(t + 2)(t^2 + 4t + 4) = (t^2 + 2t)(t^2 + 4t + 4) =$

$t^2 \cdot t^2 + t^2 \cdot 4t + t^2 \cdot 4 + 2t \cdot t^2 + 2t \cdot 4t + 2t \cdot 4 =$

$t^4 + 4t^3 + 4t^2 + 2t^3 + 8t^2 + 8t = t^4 + 6t^3 + 12t^2 + 8t$

Multiplication of Polynomials

57. $4(5x + 9) = 4 \cdot 5x + 4 \cdot 9 = 20x + 36$

59. $(x - 5)(x + 7) = x \cdot x + x \cdot 7 + (-5)(x) + (-5)(7) = x^2 + 2x - 35$

61. $(3x - 5)^2 = (3x)^2 - 2(3x)(5) + (5x)^2 = 9x^2 - 30x + 25$

63. $(5x + 3)(5x + 4) = 5x \cdot 5x + 5x \cdot 4 + 3 \cdot 5x + 3 \cdot 4 = 25x^2 + 35x + 12$

65. $(4b - 5)(4b + 5) = (4b)^2 - (5)^2 = 16b^2 - 25$

67. $-5x(4x^2 - 7x + 2) = (-5x)(4x^2) + (-5x)(-7x) + (-5x)(2) = -20x^3 + 35x^2 - 10x$

69. $(4 - a)^3 = (4 - a)(4 - a)^2 = (4 - a)(16 - 8a + a^2) =$

$4 \cdot 16 + (4)(-8a) + 4 \cdot a^2 + (-a)(16) + (-a)(-8a) + (-a)(a^2) = 64 - 48a + 12a^2 - a^3$

Applications

71. (a) $(x + 2)(x + 2) = (x)^2 + 2(x)(2) + (2)^2 = x^2 + 4x + 4$

(b) $x \cdot x + 2 \cdot x + x \cdot 2 + 2 \cdot 2 = x^2 + 2x + 2x + 4 = x^2 + 4x + 4$

73. (a) $(2x + 3)(2x + 3) = (2x)^2 + 2(2x)(3) + (3)^2 = 4x^2 + 12x + 9$

(b) $2x \cdot 2x + 3 \cdot 2x + 2x \cdot 3 + 3 \cdot 3 = 4x^2 + 6x + 6x + 9 = 4x^2 + 12x + 9$

75 (a) $6(x + 5)^2 = 6(x^2 + 10x + 25) = 6x^2 + 60x + 150$

(b) $(x + 5)^3 = (x + 5)(x + 5)^2 = (x + 5)(x^2 + 10x + 25) =$

$x \cdot x^2 + x \cdot 10x + x \cdot 25 + 5 \cdot x^2 + 5 \cdot 10x + 5 \cdot 25 = x^3 + 15x^2 + 75x + 125$

77. (a) $(1 + x)^2 = (1)^2 + 2(1)(x) + (x)^2 = 1 + 2x + x^2$

(b) $1 + 2x + x^2 = 1 + 2(0.10) + (0.10)^2 = 1 + 0.20 + 0.01 = 1.21;$ the money increases by 1.21 times in

2 years if the interest rate is 10%.

79. (a) $(1 - x)^2 = (1)^2 - 2(1)(x) + (x)^2 = 1 - 2x + x^2$

(b) $1 - 2x + x^2 = 1 - 2(0.50) + (0.50)^2 = 1 - 1 + 0.25 = 0.25;$ if the chance of rain on each day is

50%, then there is a 25% chance of no rain on either day.

81. (a) $(z + 16)^2 - (z)^2 = (z^2 + 32z + 256) - (z^2) = 32z + 256$

(b) $32z + 256 = 32(60) + 256 = 1920 + 256 = 2176;$ the area of an 8 foot wide sidewalk around a

60×60 pool is 2176 ft^2.

Checking Basic Concepts for Sections 5.3 & 5.4

1. (a) $(-3xy^4)(5x^2y) = (-3)(5)xx^2y^4y = -15x^3y^5$

   (b) $-x(6 - 4x) = (-x)(6) + (-x)(-4x) = -6x + 4x^2$

   (c) $3ab(a^2 - 2ab + b^2)3ab \cdot a^2 + (3ab)(-2ab) + 3ab \cdot b^2 = 3a^3b - 6a^2b^2 + 3ab^3$

2. (a) $(x + 3)(4x - 3) = x \cdot 4x + (x)(-3) + 3 \cdot 4x + (3)(-3) = 4x^2 + 9x - 9$

   (b) $(x^2 - 1)(2x^2 + 2) = x^2 \cdot 2x^2 + x^2 \cdot 2 + (-1)(2x^2) + (-1)(2) = 2x^4 - 2$

   (c) $(x + y)(x^2 - xy + y^2) = x \cdot x^2 + (x)(-xy) + x \cdot y^2 + y \cdot x^2 + (y)(-xy) + y \cdot y^2 = x^3 + y^3$

3. (a) $(5x + 2)(5x - 2) = (5x)^2 - (2)^2 = 25x^2 - 4$

   (b) $(x + 3)^2 = (x)^2 + 2(x)(3) - (3)^2 = x^2 + 6x + 9$

   (c) $(2 - 7x)^2 = (2)^2 - 2(2)(7x) + (7x)^2 = 4 - 28x + 49x^2$

   (d) $(t + 2)^3 = (t + 2)(t + 2)^2 = (t + 2)(t^2 + 4t + 4) = t \cdot t^2 + t \cdot 4t + t \cdot 4 + 2 \cdot t^2 + 2 \cdot 4t + 2 \cdot 4 =$
   $t^3 + 6t^2 + 12t + 8$

4. (a) $4\pi(a + 7)^2 = 4\pi(a^2 + 14a + 49) = 4\pi(a^2) + 4\pi(14a) + 4\pi(49) = 4\pi a^2 + 56\pi a + 196\pi$

   (b) $4\pi a^2 + 56\pi a + 196\pi = 4\pi(8)^2 + 56\pi(8) + 196\pi = 256\pi + 448\pi + 196\pi = 900\pi$

5. (a) $(m + 5)^2 = (m)^2 + 2(5)(m) + (5)^2 = m^2 + 10m + 25$

   (b) $m \cdot m + m \cdot 5 + 5 \cdot m + 5 \cdot 5 = m^2 + 5m + 5m + 25 = m^2 + 10m + 25$

5.5: Integer Exponents and the Quotient Rule

Concepts

1. $a^{-n} = \dfrac{1}{a^n}$

3. $\dfrac{1}{a^{-n}} = \dfrac{a^n}{1} = a^n$

5. $\dfrac{a^m}{a^n} = a^{m-n}$

7. $\left(\dfrac{a}{b}\right)^{-n} = \left(\dfrac{b}{a}\right)^n$

9. $1 \le |b| < 10$

Negative Exponents

11. $4^{-1} = \dfrac{1}{4^1} = \dfrac{1}{4}$

13. $\left(\dfrac{1}{3}\right)^{-2} = \left(\dfrac{3}{1}\right)^2 = \dfrac{3^2}{1^2} = \dfrac{3 \cdot 3}{1 \cdot 1} = \dfrac{9}{1} = 9$

15. $2^3 \cdot 2^{-2} = 2^{3+(-2)} = 2^1 = 2$

17. $10^4 \cdot 10^{-2} = 10^{4+(-2)} = 10^2 = 10 \cdot 10 = 100$

19. $3^{-2} \cdot 3^{-1} \cdot 3^{-1} = 3^{-2+(-1)+(-1)} = 3^{-4} = \dfrac{1}{3^4} = \dfrac{1}{3 \cdot 3 \cdot 3 \cdot 3} = \dfrac{1}{81}$

21. $(2^3)^{-1} = 2^{(3)(-1)} = 2^{-3} = \dfrac{1}{2^3} = \dfrac{1}{2 \cdot 2 \cdot 2} = \dfrac{1}{8}$

23. $(3^2 4^3)^{-1} = 3^{(2)(-1)} 4^{(3)(-1)} = 3^{-2} 4^{-3} = \dfrac{1}{3^2 4^3} = \dfrac{1}{(3 \cdot 3)(4 \cdot 4 \cdot 4)} = \dfrac{1}{9 \cdot 64} = \dfrac{1}{576}$

25. $\dfrac{4^5}{4^2} = 4^{5-2} = 4^3 = 4 \cdot 4 \cdot 4 = 64$

27. $\dfrac{1^9}{1^7} = 1^{9-7} = 1^2 = 1 \cdot 1 = 1$

29. $\dfrac{1}{4^{-3}} = 4^3 = 4 \cdot 4 \cdot 4 = 64$

31. $\dfrac{5^{-2}}{5^{-4}} = 5^{-2-(-4)} = 5^2 = 5 \cdot 5 = 25$

33. $\left(\dfrac{2}{7}\right)^{-2} = \left(\dfrac{7}{2}\right)^2 = \dfrac{7^2}{2^2} = \dfrac{7 \cdot 7}{2 \cdot 2} = \dfrac{49}{4}$

35. $x^{-1} = \dfrac{1}{x}$

37. $a^{-4} = \dfrac{1}{a^4}$

39. $x^{-2} \cdot x^{-1} \cdot x = x^{-2+(-1)+1} = x^{-2} = \dfrac{1}{x^2}$

41. $a^{-5} \cdot a^{-2} \cdot a^{-1} = a^{-5+(-2)+(-1)} = a^{-8} = \dfrac{1}{a^8}$

43. $x^2 y^{-3} x^{-5} y^6 = x^{2+(-5)} y^{-3+6} = x^{-3} y^3 = \dfrac{y^3}{x^3}$

45. $(xy)^{-3} = x^{-3} y^{-3} = \dfrac{1}{x^3 y^3}$

47. $(2t)^{-4} = 2^{-4} t^{-4} = \dfrac{1}{2^4 t^4} = \dfrac{1}{16 t^4}$

49. $(x+1)^{-7} = \dfrac{1}{(x+1)^7}$

51. $(a^{-2})^{-4} = a^{(-2)(-4)} = a^8$

53. $(rt^3)^{-2} = r^{-2} t^{(3)(-2)} = r^{-2} t^{-6} = \dfrac{1}{r^2 t^6}$

55. $(ab)^2 (a^2)^{-3} = (a^2 b^2)(a^{(2)(-3)}) = (a^2 b^2)(a^{-6}) = a^{2+(-6)} b^2 = a^{-4} b^2 = \dfrac{b^2}{a^4}$

57. $\dfrac{x^4}{x^2} = x^{4-2} = x^2$

59. $\dfrac{a^{10}}{a^{-3}} = a^{10-(-3)} = a^{13}$

61. $\dfrac{4z}{2z^4} = \dfrac{4}{2} \cdot \dfrac{z}{z^4} = 2z^{1-4} = 2z^{-3} = \dfrac{2}{z^3}$

63. $\dfrac{-4xy^5}{6x^3 y^2} = \dfrac{-4}{6} \cdot \dfrac{xy^5}{x^3 y^2} = \dfrac{-2}{3} x^{1-3} y^{5-2} = \dfrac{-2}{3} x^{-2} y^3 = -\dfrac{2y^3}{3x^2}$

65. $\dfrac{x^{-4}}{x^{-1}} = x^{-4-(-1)} = x^{-3} = \dfrac{1}{x^3}$

67. $\dfrac{10b^{-4}}{5b^{-5}} = \dfrac{10}{5} \cdot \dfrac{b^{-4}}{b^{-5}} = 2b^{-4-(-5)} = 2b$

69. $\left(\dfrac{a}{b}\right)^3 = \dfrac{a^3}{b^3}$

71. $\dfrac{1}{y^{-5}} = y^5$

73. $\dfrac{4}{2t^{-3}} = \dfrac{4}{2} \cdot \dfrac{1}{t^{-3}} = 2 \cdot t^3 = 2t^3$

75. $\dfrac{1}{(xy)^{-2}} = \dfrac{1}{x^{-2}y^{-2}} = x^2y^2$

77. $\dfrac{1}{(a^2b)^{-3}} = \dfrac{1}{a^{(2)(-3)}b^{-3}} = \dfrac{1}{a^{-6}b^{-3}} = a^6b^3$

79. $\left(\dfrac{a}{b}\right)^{-2} = \left(\dfrac{b}{a}\right)^2 = \dfrac{b^2}{a^2}$

81. $\left(\dfrac{u}{4v}\right)^{-1} = \left(\dfrac{4v}{u}\right)^1 = \dfrac{4v}{u}$

Scientific Notation

83. Thousand

85. Billion

87. Hundredth

89. Move the decimal point three places to the right, $2 \times 10^3 = 2000$.

91. Move the decimal point four places to the right, $4.5 \times 10^4 = 45,000$.

93. Move the decimal point three places to the left, $8 \times 10^{-3} = 0.008$.

95. Move the decimal point four places to the left, $4.56 \times 10^{-4} = 0.000456$.

97. Move the decimal point seven places to the right, $3.9 \times 10^7 = 39,000,000$.

99. Move the decimal point five places to the right, $-5 \times 10^5 = -500,000$.

101. Move the decimal point three places to the left, $2000 = 2 \times 10^3$.

103. Move the decimal point two places to the left, $567 = 5.67 \times 10^2$.

105. Move the decimal point seven places to the left, $12,000,000 = 1.2 \times 10^7$.

107. Move the decimal point three places to the right, $0.004 = 4 \times 10^{-3}$.

109. Move the decimal point four places to the right, $0.000895 = 8.95 \times 10^{-4}$.

111. Move the decimal point two places to the right, $-0.05 = -5 \times 10^{-2}$.

113. $(5 \times 10^3)(3 \times 10^2) = (5 \cdot 3) \times (10^3 \cdot 10^2) = 15 \times 10^{3+2} = 15 \times 10^5 = 1.5 \times 10^6;$

Move the decimal point six places to the right, $1.5 \times 10^6 = 1,500,000$.

115. $(-3 \times 10^{-3})(5 \times 10^2) = (-3 \cdot 5) \times (10^{-3} \cdot 10^2) = -15 \times 10^{-3+2} = -15 \times 10^{-1} = -1.5 \times 10^0 = -1.5$

117. $\dfrac{4 \times 10^5}{2 \times 10^2} = \dfrac{4}{2} \cdot \dfrac{10^5}{10^2} = 2 \times 10^{5-2} = 2 \times 10^3;$

Move the decimal point three places to the right, $2 \times 10^3 = 2000$.

119. $\dfrac{8 \times 10^{-6}}{4 \times 10^{-3}} = \dfrac{8}{4} \cdot \dfrac{10^{-6}}{10^{-3}} = 2 \times 10^{-6-(-3)} = 2 \times 10^{-3};$

Move the decimal point two places to the left, $2 \times 10^{-3} = 0.002.$

Applications

121. (a) $(1.86 \times 10^5)(3.15 \times 10^7) = (1.86 \cdot 3.15) \times (10^5 \cdot 10^7) \approx 5.859 \times 10^{5+7} \approx 5.859 \times 10^{12}$ miles.

   (b) $(5.859 \times 10^{12})(4.27) = (5.859 \cdot 4.27) \times (10^{12}) \approx 25 \times 10^{12} \approx 2.5 \times 10^{13}$ miles.

123. $\dfrac{10^5 \cdot \pi \text{ (light years)}}{1} \div \dfrac{2 \times 10^8 \text{ (years)}}{1} \cdot \dfrac{5.859 \times 10^{12}}{1} \approx 9.2 \times 10^9$ miles.

125. (a) Move the decimal point 12 places to the left, $9,963,000,000,000 = 9.963 \times 10^{12}.$

   (b) $\dfrac{9.963 \times 10^{12}}{2.81 \times 10^8} = \dfrac{9.963}{2.81} \cdot \dfrac{10^{12}}{10^8} \approx 3.5456 \times 10^{12-8} \approx 3.5456 \times 10^4 \approx \$35,456$

5.6: Division of Polynomials

Concepts

1. $\dfrac{a+b}{d} = \dfrac{a}{d} + \dfrac{b}{d}$

3. $\dfrac{5x^2 + 2x}{2x} = \dfrac{5x^2}{2x} + \dfrac{2x}{2x} = \dfrac{5x}{2} + 1 \neq 5x^2 + 1;$ No

5. $9 \cdot 4 + 1 = 37$

Division by a Monomial

7. $\dfrac{6x^2}{3x} = \dfrac{6}{3} \cdot \dfrac{x^2}{x} = 2x^{2-1} = 2x;$ Checking: $3x \cdot 2x = (3 \cdot 2)(x \cdot x) = 6x^2$

9. $\dfrac{z^4 + z^3}{z} = \dfrac{z^4}{z} + \dfrac{z^3}{z} = z^{4-1} + x^{3-1} = z^3 + z^2;$ Checking: $(z)(z^3 + z^2) = (z^3)(z) + (z^2)(z) = z^4 + z^3$

11. $\dfrac{a^5 - 6a^3}{2a^3} = \dfrac{a^5}{2a^3} - \dfrac{6a^3}{2a^3} = \dfrac{1}{2}a^{5-3} - 3a^{3-3} = \dfrac{a^2}{2} - 3a^0 = \dfrac{a^2}{2} - 3$

   Checking: $(2a^3)\left(\dfrac{a^2}{2} - 3\right) = (2a^3)\left(\dfrac{a^2}{2}\right) - (2a^3)(3) = \dfrac{2a^{3+2}}{2} - 6a^3 = a^5 - 6a^3$

13. $\dfrac{4x - 7x^4}{x^2} = \dfrac{4x}{x^2} - \dfrac{7x^4}{x^2} = 4x^{1-2} - 7x^{4-2} = 4x^{-1} - 7x^2 = \dfrac{4}{x} - 7x^2$

15. $\dfrac{9x^4 - 3x + 6}{3x} = \dfrac{9x^4}{3x} - \dfrac{3x}{3x} + \dfrac{6}{3x} = 3x^{4-1} - 1 + \dfrac{2}{x} = 3x^3 - 1 + \dfrac{2}{x}$

17. $\dfrac{12y^4 - 3y^2 + 6y}{3y^2} = \dfrac{12y^4}{3y^2} - \dfrac{3y^2}{3y^2} + \dfrac{6y}{3y^2} = 4y^{4-2} - 1 + 2y^{1-2} = 4y^2 - 1 + 2y^{-1} = 4y^2 - 1 + \dfrac{2}{y}$

19. $\dfrac{15m^4 - 10m^3 + 20m^2}{5m^2} = \dfrac{15m^4}{5m^2} - \dfrac{10m^3}{5m^2} + \dfrac{20m^2}{5m^2} = 3m^{4-2} - 2m^{3-2} + 4m^{2-2} = 3m^2 - 2m + 4$

21.

$$
\begin{array}{r}
2x + 1 \\
x - 2\overline{)2x^2 - 3x + 1} \\
\underline{2x^2 - 4x} \\
x + 1 \\
\underline{x - 2} \\
3
\end{array}
$$

The solution is: $2x + 1 + \dfrac{3}{x - 2}$

Checking:

$(x - 2)(2x + 1) + 3 = x \cdot 2x + x \cdot 1 + (-2)(2x) + (-2)(1) + 3 = 2x^2 + x - 4x - 2 + 3 = 2x^2 - 3x + 1$

23.

$$
\begin{array}{r}
x + 1 \\
x + 1\overline{)x^2 + 2x + 1} \\
\underline{x^2 + x} \\
x + 1 \\
\underline{x + 1} \\
0
\end{array}
$$

The solution is: $x + 1$

Checking: $(x + 1)(x + 1) = (x)^2 + (2)(x)(1) + (1)^2 = x^2 + 2x + 1$

25.

$$
\begin{array}{r}
x^2 + 1 \\
x - 1\overline{)x^3 - x^2 + x - 2} \\
\underline{x^3 - x^2} \\
x - 2 \\
\underline{x - 1} \\
-1
\end{array}
$$

The solution is: $x^2 + 1 + \dfrac{-1}{x - 1}$

Checking: $(x - 1)(x^2 + 1) + (-1) = x \cdot x^2 + x \cdot 1 + (-1)(x^2) + (-1)(1) + (-1) =$

$x^3 + x - x^2 - 1 - 1 = x^3 - x^2 + x - 2$

27.

$$
\begin{array}{r}
x^2 - x + 2 \\
4x + 1\overline{)4x^3 - 3x^2 + 7x + 3} \\
\underline{4x^3 + x^2} \\
-4x^2 + 7x \\
\underline{-4x^2 - x} \\
8x + 3 \\
\underline{8x + 2} \\
1
\end{array}
$$

The solution is: $x^2 - x + 2 + \dfrac{1}{4x + 1}$

29.

$$
x - 2\overline{)x^3 - x + 2} \Rightarrow
$$

$$
\begin{array}{r}
x^2 + 2x + 3 \\
x - 2\overline{)x^3 - 0x^2 - x + 2} \\
\underline{x^3 - 2x^2} \\
2x^2 - x \\
\underline{2x^2 - 4x} \\
3x + 2 \\
\underline{3x - 6} \\
8
\end{array}
$$

The solution is: $x^2 + 2x + 3 + \dfrac{8}{x - 2}$

31.

$$x - 1 \overline{) 3x^3 + 2} \Rightarrow$$

$$
\begin{array}{r}
3x^2 + 3x + 3 \\
x - 1 \overline{) 3x^3 - 0x^2 + 0x + 2} \\
\underline{3x^3 - 3x^2} \\
3x^2 + 0x \\
\underline{3x^2 - 3x} \\
3x + 2 \\
\underline{3x - 3} \\
5
\end{array}
$$

The solution is: $3x^2 + 3x + 3 + \dfrac{5}{x - 1}$

33.

$$x^2 + 1 \overline{) x^3 + 3x^2 + 1} \Rightarrow$$

$$
\begin{array}{r}
x + 3 \\
x^2 + 1 \overline{) x^3 + 3x^2 + 0x + 1} \\
\underline{x^3 + 0x^2 + x} \\
3x^2 - x + 1 \\
\underline{3x^2 + 0x + 3} \\
-x - 2
\end{array}
$$

The solution is: $x + 3 + \dfrac{-x - 2}{x^2 + 1}$

35.

$$x^2 - x + 1 \overline{) x^3 + 1} \Rightarrow$$

$$
\begin{array}{r}
x + 1 \\
x^2 - x + 1 \overline{) x^3 + 0x^2 + 0x + 1} \\
\underline{x^3 - x^2 + x} \\
x^2 - x + 1 \\
\underline{x^2 - x + 1} \\
0
\end{array}
$$

The solution is: $x + 1$

37.

$$x + 2 \overline{) x^3 + 8} \Rightarrow$$

$$
\begin{array}{r}
x^2 - 2x + 4 \\
x + 2 \overline{) x^3 + 0x^2 + 0x + 8} \\
\underline{x^3 + 2x^2} \\
-2x^2 + 0x \\
\underline{-2x^2 - 4x} \\
4x + 8 \\
\underline{4x + 8} \\
0
\end{array}
$$

The solution is: $x^2 - 2x + 4$

Applications

39. $2x \cdot L = 8x^2 \Rightarrow L = \dfrac{8x^2}{2x} \Rightarrow L = 4x^{2-1} \Rightarrow L = 4x$

41. $2x^2 \cdot H = 2x^2 + 4x^2 \Rightarrow H = \dfrac{2x^3 + 4x^2}{2x^2} \Rightarrow H = \dfrac{2x^3}{2x^2} + \dfrac{4x^2}{2x^2} = x^{3-2} + 2x^{2-2} = x + 2.$ See Figure 41.

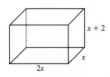

Figure 41

Checking Basic Concepts for Sections 5.5 & 5.6

1. (a) $9^{-2} = \dfrac{1}{9^2} = \dfrac{1}{9 \cdot 9} = \dfrac{1}{81}$

    (b) $\dfrac{3x^{-3}}{6x^4} = \dfrac{1}{2}x^{-3-4} = \dfrac{1}{2}x^{-7} = \dfrac{1}{2x^7}$

    (c) $(4ab^{-4})^{-2} = 4^{-2}a^{-2}b^8 = \dfrac{b^8}{16a^2}$

2. (a) $\dfrac{1}{z^{-5}} = z^5$

    (b) $\dfrac{x^{-3}}{y^{-6}} = \dfrac{y^6}{x^3}$

    (c) $\left(\dfrac{3}{x^2}\right)^{-3} = \left(\dfrac{x^2}{3}\right)^3 = \dfrac{x^{2 \cdot 3}}{3^3} = \dfrac{x^6}{27}$

3. (a) Move the decimal point four places to the left: $45{,}000 = 4.5 \times 10^4$.

    (b) Move the decimal point four places to the right: $0.000234 = 2.34 \times 10^{-4}$.

    (c) Move the decimal point two places to the right: $0.01 = 1 \times 10^{-2}$.

4. (a) Move the decimal point four places to the right: $4.71 \times 10^4 = 47{,}100$.

    (b) Move the decimal point three places to the left: $6 \times 10^{-3} = 0.006$.

5. $\dfrac{25a^4 - 15a^3}{5a^3} = \dfrac{25a^4}{5a^3} - \dfrac{15a^3}{5a^3} = 5a^{4-3} - 3a^{3-3} = 5a - 3$

6.
    $$\begin{array}{r} 3x + 2 \\ x - 1 \overline{)\ 3x^2 - x - 4} \\ \underline{3x^2 - 3x } \\ 2x - 4 \\ \underline{2x - 2} \\ -2 \end{array}$$
    The quotient is: $3x + 2$; The remainder is: -2

7. (a) Move the decimal point seven places to the left: $93{,}000{,}000 = 9.3 \times 10^7$.

    (b) $\dfrac{9.3 \times 10^7}{1.86 \times 10^5} = \dfrac{9.3}{1.86} \cdot \dfrac{10^7}{10^5} \approx 5 \times 10^{7-5} \approx 5 \times 10^2 \approx 500$ seconds. (About 8 minutes 20 seconds)

Chapter 5 Review Exercises

Section 5.1

1. $5^3 = 5 \cdot 5 \cdot 5 = 125$

2. $-3^4 = -(3 \cdot 3 \cdot 3 \cdot 3) = -81$

3. $4(-2)^0 = 4(1) = 4$

4. $3 + 3^2 - 3^0 = 3 + (3 \cdot 3) - 1 = 3 + 9 - 1 = 11$

5. $\dfrac{-5^2}{5} = \dfrac{-(5 \cdot 5)}{5} = \dfrac{-25}{5} = -5$

6. $\left(\dfrac{-5}{5}\right)^2 = \dfrac{(-5)(-5)}{(5)(5)} = \dfrac{25}{25} = 1$

7. $6^2 \cdot 6^3 = 6^{2+3} = 6^5$

8. $10^5 \cdot 10^7 = 10^{5+7} = 10^{12}$

9. $z^4 \cdot z^5 = z^{4+5} = z^9$

10. $y^2 \cdot y \cdot y^3 = y^{2+1+3} = y^6$

11. $5x^2 \cdot 6x^7 = 5 \cdot 6 \cdot x^{2+7} = 30x^9$

12. $(ab^3)(a^3b) = a^{1+3}b^{3+1} = a^4b^4$

13. $(2^5)^2 = 2^{5 \cdot 2} = 2^{10}$

14. $(m^4)^5 = m^{4 \cdot 5} = m^{20}$

15. $(ab)^3 = a^3b^3$

16. $(x^2y^3)^4 = x^{2 \cdot 4}y^{3 \cdot 4} = x^8y^{12}$

17. $(xy)^3(x^2y^4)^2 = (x^3y^3)(x^{2 \cdot 2}y^{4 \cdot 2}) = (x^3y^3)(x^4y^8) = x^{3+4}y^{3+8} = x^7y^{11}$

18. $(a^2b^9)^0 = 1$

19. $(r - t)^4(r - t)^5 = (r - t)^{4+5} = (r - t)^9$

20. $(a + b)^2(a + b)^4 = (a + b)^{2+4} = (a + b)^6$

Section 5.2

21. degree is 7; coefficient is 6

22. degree is 5; coefficient is -1

23. Yes, it is a polynomial; 1 term: $8y$; 1 variable: y; y^1 so it is a 1st degree polynomial.

24. Yes, it is a polynomial; 4 terms: $8x^3, -3x^2, x$ and -5; 1 variable: x; x^3 so it is a 3rd degree polynomial.

25. Yes, it is a polynomial; 3 terms: $a^2, 2ab$ and b^2; 2 variable: a and b; a^2 so it is a 2nd degree polynomial.

26. No, it is not a polynomial, because there are variables in the denominator.

27. $$\begin{array}{r} 3x^2 + 4x + 8 \\ + 2x^2 - 5x - 5 \\ \hline 5x^2 - x + 3 \end{array}$$

28. $-6x^2 + 3x + 7$

29. $(4x - 3) + (-x + 7) = 4x + (-x) + (-3) + 7 = 3x + 4$

30. $(3x^2 - 1) - (5x^2 + 12) = (3x^2 - 1) + (-5x^2 - 12) = 3x^2 + (-5x^2) + (-1) + (-12) = -2x^2 - 13$

31. $(x^2 + 5x + 6) - (3x^2 - 4x + 1) = (x^2 + 5x + 6) + (-3x^2 + 4x - 1) =$
    $x^2 + (-3x^2) + 5x + 4x + 6 + (-1) = -2x^2 + 9x + 5$

32. $(a^3 + 4a^2) + (a^3 - 5a^2 + 7a) = a^3 + a^3 + 4a^2 + (-5a^2) + 7a = 2a^3 - a^2 + 7a$

33. $(xy + y^2) + (4y^2 - 4xy) = y^2 + 4y^2 + xy + (-4xy) = 5y^2 - 3xy$

34. $(7x^2 + 2xy + y^2) - (7x^2 - 2xy + y^2) = (7x^2 + 2xy + y^2) + (7x^2 + 2xy - y^2) =$
    $7x^2 + (-7x^2) + 2xy + 2xy + y^2 + (-y^2) = 4xy$

Section 5.3

35. $-x^2 \cdot x^3 = -x^{2+3} = -x^5$

36. $-(r^2t^3)(rt) = -(r^{2+1}t^{3+1}) = -r^3t^4$

37. $-3(2t - 5) = (-3)(2t) + (-3)(-5) = -6t + 15$

38. $2y(1 - 6y) = 2y \cdot 1 + 2y(-6y) = 2y - 12y^2$

39. $6x^3(3x^2 + 5x) = 6x^3 \cdot 3x^2 + 6x^3 \cdot 5x = 18x^{3+2} + 30x^{3+1} = 18x^5 + 30x^4$

40. $-x(x^2 - 2x + 9) = (-x)(x^2) + (-x)(-2x) + (-x)(9) = -x^{1+2} + 2x^{1+1} - 9x = -x^3 + 2x^2 - 9x$

41. $-ab(a^2 - 2ab + b^2) = -ab \cdot a^2 + (-ab)(-2ab) + (-ab)(b^2) = -a^3b + 2a^2b^2 - ab^3$

42. $(a - 2)(a + 5) = a \cdot a + a \cdot 5 + (-2)(a) + (-2)(5) = a^2 + 5a - 2a - 10 = a^2 + 3a - 10$

43. $(8x - 3)(x + 2) = 8x \cdot x + 8x \cdot 2 + (-3)(x) + (-3)(2) = 8x^2 + 16x - 3x - 6 = 8x^2 + 13x - 6$

44. $(2x - 1)(1 - x) = 2x \cdot 1 + (2x)(-x) + (-1)(1) + (-1)(-x) = 2x - 2x^2 - 1 + x = -2x^2 + 3x - 1$

45. $(y^2 + 1)(2y + 1) = y^2 \cdot 2y + y^2 \cdot 1 + 1 \cdot 2y + 1 \cdot 1 = 2y^3 + y^2 + 2y + 1$

46. $(y^2 - 1)(2y^2 + 1) = y^2 \cdot 2y^2 + y^2 \cdot 1 + (-1)(2y^2) + (-1)(1) = 2y^4 + y^2 - 2y^2 - 1 = 2y^4 - y^2 - 1$

47. $(z + 1)(z^2 - z + 1) = z \cdot z^2 + (z)(-z) + z \cdot 1 + 1 \cdot z^2 + (1)(-z) + 1 \cdot 1 = z^3 - z^2 + z + z^2 - z + 1 = z^3 + 1$

48. $(4z - 3)(z^2 - 3z + 1) = 4z \cdot z^2 + (4z)(-3z) + 4z \cdot 1 + (-3)(z^2) + (-3)(-3z) + (-3)(1) = 4z^3 - 12z^2 + 4z - 3z^2 + 9z - 3 = 4z^3 - 15z^2 + 13z - 3$

49. (a) $z^2 + z$; See Figure 49.

    (b) $z(z + 1) = z \cdot z + z \cdot 1 = z^2 + 1$

50. (a) $2x^2 + 4x$; See Figure 50.

    (b) $2x(x + 2) = 2x \cdot x + 2x \cdot 2 = 2x^2 + 4x$

Figure 49

Figure 50

Section 5.4

51. $(z + 2)(z - 2) = (z)^2 - (2)^2 = z^2 - 4$

52. $(5z - 9)(5z + 9) = (5z)^2 - (9)^2 = 25z^2 - 81$

53. $(1 - 3y)(1 + 3y) = (1)^2 - (3y)^2 = 1 - 9y^2$

54. $(5x + 4y)(5x - 4y) = (5x)^2 - (4y)^2 = 25x^2 - 16y^2$

55. $(rt + 1)(rt - 1) = (rt)^2 - (1)^2 = r^2t^2 - 1$

56. $(2m^2 - n^2)(2m^2 + n^2) = (2m^2)^2 - (n^2)^2 = 4m^4 - n^4$

57. $(x + 1)^2 = (x)^2 + (2)(x)(1) + (1)^2 = x^2 + 2x + 1$

58. $(4x + 3)^2 = (4x)^2 + (2)(4x)(3) + (3)^2 = 16x^2 + 24x + 9$

59. $(y - 3)^2 = (y)^2 - (2)(y)(3) + (3)^2 = y^2 - 6y + 9$

60. $(2y - 5)^2 = (2y)^2 - (2)(2y)(5) + (5)^2 = 4y^2 - 20y + 25$

61. $(4 + a)^2 = (4)^2 + (2)(4)(a) + (a)^2 = 16 + 8a + a^2$

62. $(4 - a)^2 = (4)^2 - (2)(4)(a) + (a)^2 = 16 - 8a + a^2$

63. $(x^2 + y^2)^2 = (x^2)^2 + (2)(x^2)(y^2) + (y^2)^2 = x^4 + 2x^2y^2 + y^4$

64. $(xy - 2)^2 = (xy)^2 - (2)(xy)(2) + (2)^2 = x^2y^2 - 4xy + 4$

65. $(z + 5)^3 = (z + 5)(z + 5)^2 = (z + 5)(z^2 + 10z + 25) =$

$z \cdot z^2 + z \cdot 10z + z \cdot 25 + 5 \cdot z^2 + 5 \cdot 10z + 5 \cdot 25 = z^3 + 10z^2 + 25z + 5z^2 + 50z + 125 =$

$z^3 + 15z^2 + 75z + 125$

66. $(2z - 1)^3 = (2z - 1)(2z - 1)^2 = (2z - 1)(4z^2 - 4z + 1) =$

$2z \cdot 4z^2 + (2z)(-4z) + 2z \cdot 1 + (-1)(4z^2) + (-1)(-4z) + (-1)(1) = 8z^3 - 8z^2 + 2z - 4z^2 + 4z - 1 =$

$8z^3 - 12z^2 + 6z - 1$

Section 5.5

67. $9^{-1} = \dfrac{1}{9}$

68. $3^{-2} = \dfrac{1}{3^2} = \dfrac{1}{3 \cdot 3} = \dfrac{1}{9}$

69. $4^3 \cdot 4^{-2} = 4^{3+(-2)} = 4^1 = 4$

70. $10^{-6} \cdot 10^3 = 10^{-6+3} = 10^{-3} = \dfrac{1}{10^3} = \dfrac{1}{10 \cdot 10 \cdot 10} = \dfrac{1}{1000}$

71. $\dfrac{1}{6^{-2}} = 6^2 = 36$

72. $\dfrac{5^7}{5^9} = 5^{7-9} = 5^{-2} = \dfrac{1}{5^2} = \dfrac{1}{5 \cdot 5} = \dfrac{1}{25}$

73. $z^{-2} = \dfrac{1}{z^2}$

74. $y^{-4} = \dfrac{1}{y^4}$

75. $a^{-4} \cdot a^2 = a^{-4+2} = a^{-2} = \dfrac{1}{a^2}$

76. $x^2 \cdot x^{-5} \cdot x = x^{2+(-5)+1} = x^{-2} = \dfrac{1}{x^2}$

77. $(2t)^{-2} = 2^{-2}t^{-2} = \dfrac{1}{2^2 t^2} = \dfrac{1}{4t^2}$

78. $(ab^2)^{-3} = a^{-3}b^{(2)(-3)} = a^{-3}b^{-6} = \dfrac{1}{a^3 b^6}$

79. $(xy)^{-2}(x^{-2}y)^{-1} = (x^{-2}y^{-2})(x^{(-2)(-1)}y^{-1}) = x^{-2+2}y^{-2+(-1)} = y^{-3} = \dfrac{1}{y^3}$

80. $\dfrac{x^6}{x^2} = x^{6-2} = x^4$

81. $\dfrac{4x}{2x^4} = 2x^{1-4} = 2x^{-3} = \dfrac{2}{x^3}$

82. $\dfrac{20x^5y^3}{30xy^6} = \dfrac{2}{3}x^{5-1}y^{3-6} = \dfrac{2}{3}x^4y^{-3} = \dfrac{2x^4}{3y^3}$

83. $\left(\dfrac{a}{b}\right)^5 = \dfrac{a^5}{b^5}$

84. $\dfrac{4}{t^{-4}} = 4t^4$

85. $\left(\dfrac{x}{3}\right)^{-3} = \left(\dfrac{3}{x}\right)^3 = \dfrac{3^3}{x^3} = \dfrac{27}{x^3}$

86. $\dfrac{2}{(ab)^{-1}} = 2ab$

87. $\left(\dfrac{x}{y}\right)^{-2} = \left(\dfrac{y}{x}\right)^2 = \dfrac{y^2}{x^2}$

88. $\left(\dfrac{3u}{2v}\right)^{-1} = \left(\dfrac{2v}{3u}\right)^1 = \dfrac{2v}{3u}$

89. Move the decimal point two places to the right, $6 \times 10^2 = 600$.

90. Move the decimal point four places to the right, $5.24 \times 10^4 = 52{,}400$.

91. Move the decimal point three places to the left, $3.7 \times 10^{-3} = 0.0037$.

92. Move the decimal point two places to the left, $6.234 \times 10^{-2} = 0.06234$.

93. Move the decimal point four places to the left, $10{,}000 = 1 \times 10^4$.

94. Move the decimal point seven places to the left, $56{,}100{,}000 = 5.61 \times 10^7$.

95. Move the decimal point five places to the right, $0.000054 = 5.4 \times 10^{-5}$.

96. Move the decimal point three places to the right, $0.001 = 1 \times 10^{-3}$.

97. $(4 \times 10^2)(6 \times 10^4) = (4 \cdot 6) \times (10^2 \cdot 10^4) = 24 \times 10^6 = 2.4 \times 10^7$;

    Move the decimal point seven places to the right, $2.4 \times 10^7 = 24{,}000{,}000$.

98. $\left(\dfrac{8 \times 10^3}{4 \times 10^4}\right) = \dfrac{8}{4} \times \dfrac{10^3}{10^4} = 2 \times 10^{3-4} = 2 \times 10^{-1}$;

    Move the decimal point one place to the left, $2 \times 10^{-1} = 0.2$.

Section 5.6

99. $\dfrac{5x^2 + 3x}{3x} = \dfrac{5x^2}{3x} + \dfrac{3x}{3x} = \dfrac{5}{3}x^{2-1} + 1 = \dfrac{5}{3}x + 1$; Checking: $3x\left(\dfrac{5}{3}x + 1\right) = 3x \cdot \dfrac{5}{3}x + 3x \cdot 1 = 5x^2 + 3x$

100. $\dfrac{6b^4 - 4b^2 + 2}{2b^2} = \dfrac{6b^4}{2b^2} - \dfrac{4b^2}{2b^2} + \dfrac{2}{2b^2} = 3b^{4-2} - 2b^{2-2} + \dfrac{1}{b^2} = 3b^2 - 2 + \dfrac{1}{b^2}$;

    Checking: $(2b^2)\left(3b^2 - 2 + \dfrac{1}{b^2}\right) = 2b^2 \cdot 3b^2 + (2b^2)(-2) + 2b^2 \cdot \dfrac{1}{b^2} = 6b^4 - 4b^2 + 2$

101.

$$\begin{array}{r} 3x + 2 \\ x - 1 \overline{)3x^2 - x + 2} \\ \underline{3x^2 - 3x} \\ 2x + 2 \\ \underline{2x - 2} \\ 4 \end{array}$$

The solution is: $3x + 2 + \dfrac{4}{x - 1}$

Checking: $(x - 1)(3x + 2) + 4 = x \cdot 3x + x \cdot 2 + (-1)(3x) + (-1)(2) + 4 =$
$3x^2 + 2x - 3x - 2 + 4 = 3x^2 - x + 2$

102.

$$\begin{array}{r} 3x - 4 \\ 3x + 2 \overline{)9x^2 - 6x - 2} \\ \underline{9x^2 + 6x} \\ -12x - 2 \\ \underline{-12x - 8} \\ 6 \end{array}$$

The solution is: $3x - 4 + \dfrac{6}{3x + 2}$

Checking: $(3x + 2)(3x - 4) + 6 = 3x \cdot 3x + (3x)(-4) + 2 \cdot 3x + (2)(-4) + 6 =$
$9x^2 - 12x + 6x - 8 + 6 = 9x^2 - 6x - 2$

103.

$$\begin{array}{r} x^2 - 3x - 1 \\ 4x + 1 \overline{)4x^3 - 11x^2 - 7x - 1} \\ \underline{4x^3 + x^2} \\ -12x^2 - 7x \\ \underline{-12x^2 - 3x} \\ -4x - 1 \\ \underline{-4x - 1} \\ 0 \end{array}$$

The solution is: $x^2 - 3x - 1$

Checking: $(4x + 1)(x^2 - 3x - 1) = 4x \cdot x^2 + (4x)(-3x) + (4x)(-1) + 1 \cdot x^2 + (1)(-3x) + (1)(-1) =$
$4x^3 - 12x^2 - 4x + x^2 - 3x - 1 = 4x^3 - 11x^2 - 7x - 1$

104.

$$\begin{array}{r} x^2 \\ 2x - 1 \overline{)2x^3 - x^2 - 1} \\ \underline{2x^3 - x^2} \\ 0 - 1 \\ -1 \end{array}$$

The solution is: $x^2 + \dfrac{-1}{2x - 1}$

Checking: $(x^2)(2x - 1) + (-1) = x^2 \cdot 2x + (x^2)(-1) + (-1) = 2x^3 - x^2 - 1$

105.

$$\begin{array}{r} x - 1 \\ x^2 + 1 \overline{)x^3 - x^2 - x + 1} \\ \underline{x^3 + 0x^2 + x} \\ -x^2 - 2x \\ \underline{-x^2 + 0x - 1} \\ -2x + 2 \end{array}$$

The solution is: $x - 1 + \dfrac{-2x + 2}{x^2 + 1}$

Checking: $(x - 1)(x^2 + 1) + (-2x + 2) = x \cdot x^2 + x \cdot 1 + (-1)(x^2) + (-1)(1) + (-2x + 2) =$
$x^3 + x - x^2 - 1 - 2x + 2 = x^3 - x^2 - x + 1$

106.

$$x^2 + x + 1\overline{)x^4 + 3x^3 + 8x^2 + 7x + 5}$$

      The solution is: $x^2 + 2x + 5$

$$
\begin{array}{r}
x^2 + 2x + 5 \\
x^4 + x^3 + x^2 \\
\hline
2x^3 + 7x^2 + 7x \\
2x^3 + 2x^2 + 2x \\
\hline
5x^2 + 5x + 5 \\
5x^2 + 5x + 5 \\
\hline
0
\end{array}
$$

Checking: $(x^2 + x + 1)(x^2 + 2x + 5) =$

$x^2 \cdot x^2 + x^2 \cdot 2x + x^2 \cdot 5 + x \cdot x^2 + x \cdot 2x + x \cdot 5 + 1 \cdot x^2 + 1 \cdot 2x + 1 \cdot 5 =$

$x^4 + 2x^3 + 5x^2 + x^3 + 2x^2 + 5x + x^2 + 2x + 5 = x^4 + 3x^3 + 8x^2 + 7x + 5$

Applications

107. (a) $t^2 + 60 \Rightarrow 0^2 + 60 = 60 \, \text{bpm}$

     (b) $t^2 + 60 \Rightarrow 10^2 + 60 = 100 + 60 = 160 \, \text{bpm}$

     (c) It increases.

108. $L \times W = 2xy = 1 \text{ rectangle} \Rightarrow 3 \text{ rectangles} = 3 \cdot 2xy = 6xy; \text{ for } x = 3 \text{ ft}, y = 4 \text{ ft}, 6xy = 6(3)(4) =$

     $72 \, \text{ft}^2$

109. $5 \cdot 3z = 15z, 5 \cdot 2z = 10z, 2z \cdot (3z + 2z) = 6z^2 + 4z^2 \Rightarrow 15z + 10z + 6z^2 + 4z^2 = 10z^2 + 25z; \text{ for }$

     $z = 6 \text{ in} \Rightarrow 10z^2 + 25z = 10(6)^2 + 25(6) = 10(36) + 150 = 360 + 150 = 510 \, \text{in}^2$

110. $(x^2 y)(x^2 y) = x^{2+2} y^{1+1} = x^4 y^2$

111. $P(1 + 0.06)^3 = P(1.06)^3 = P(1.191016); \text{ let } P = \$700 \Rightarrow \$700(1.191016) = \$833.71.$

112. (a) $(2x)(x + 5) = 2x \cdot x + 2x \cdot 5 = 2x^2 + 10x$

     (b) $(x + 2)(x + 5) = x \cdot x + x \cdot 5 + 2 \cdot x + 2 \cdot 5 = x^2 + 5x + 2x + 10 = x^2 + 7x + 10$

     (c) $(2x)(x + 2) = 2x \cdot x + 2x \cdot 2 = 2x^2 + 4x$

     (d) 3 sides $= (2x^2 + 10x) + (x^2 + 7x + 10) + (2x^2 + 4x) = 5x^2 + 21x + 10$

       6 sides $= 2(5x^2 + 21x + 10) = 10x^2 + 42x + 20$

113. $\dfrac{4}{3}\pi(x + 2)^3 = \dfrac{4}{3}\pi(x + 2)(x + 2)^2 = \dfrac{4}{3}\pi(x + 2)(x^2 + 4x + 4) =$

$\dfrac{4}{3}\pi(x \cdot x^2 + x \cdot 4x + x \cdot 4 + 2 \cdot x^2 + 2 \cdot 4x + 2 \cdot 4) = \dfrac{4}{3}\pi(x^3 + 4x^2 + 4x + 2x^2 + 8x + 8) =$

$\dfrac{4}{3}\pi(x^3 + 6x^2 + 12x + 8) = \dfrac{4}{3}\pi \cdot x^3 + \dfrac{4}{3}\pi \cdot 6x^2 + \dfrac{4}{3}\pi \cdot 12x + \dfrac{4}{3}\pi \cdot 8 = \dfrac{4}{3}\pi x^3 + 8\pi x^2 + 16\pi x + \dfrac{32}{3}\pi$

114. (a) $t(96 - 16t) = 96t - 16t^2$

     (b) $t = 2 \Rightarrow 96t - 16t^2 = 96(2) = 16(2)^2 = 192 - 16(4) = 192 - 64 = 128, \text{ after 2 seconds the ball is}$

       128 feet high.

115. (a) If $P = 2L + 2W$ then $1200 = 2L + 2W \Rightarrow 1200 - 2L = 2W \Rightarrow 600 - L = W$. Now $A = L \cdot W$ so

$A = L \cdot (600 - L) \Rightarrow A = 600L - L^2$.

(b) $L = 50 \Rightarrow 600L - L^2 = 600(50) - (50)^2 = 30,000 - 2500 = 27,500$. A rectangular building with a

perimeter of 1200 ft and a side of length 50 ft has an area of 27,500 ft^2.

116. (a) $(x + 5)(x + 5) = (x)^2 + 2(x)(5) + (5)^2 = x^2 + 10x + 25$

(b) $x \cdot x + 5 \cdot x + x \cdot 5 + 5 \cdot 5 = x^2 + 5x + 5x + 25 = x^2 + 10x + 25$

117. (a) $(x + 4)(x + 4) - (x - 4)(x - 4) = x^2 + 8x + 16 - (x^2 - 8x + 16) = 16x$

(b) $x = 100 \Rightarrow 16x = 16(100) = 1600$

118. $P = 6(1.014)^x \Rightarrow P = 6(1.014)^5 \Rightarrow P = 6(1.07199) \Rightarrow P \approx 6.43$ billion.

119. 2.19 trillion $= 2.19 \times 10^{12}$, 249 million $= 2.49 \times 10^8$

$$\frac{2.19 \times 10^{12}}{2.49 \times 10^8} = \frac{2.19}{2.49} \times \frac{10^{12}}{10^8} = 0.8795 \times 10^{12-8} = 0.8795 \times 10^4 = 8.795 \times 10^3 \approx \$8,795/\text{person}.$$

120. 211 million $= 2.11 \times 10^8$;

$(2.21)(2.11 \times 10^8) = (2.21)(2.11) \times 10^8 = 4.6631 \times 10^8 \approx 466,310,000$ gal. or 4.6631×10^8 gal.

Chapter 5 Test

1. Yes, it is a polynomial; 3 terms $5x^2, -3xy, -7y^3$; 2 variables x and y; $y^3 \Rightarrow$ 3rd degree.

2. $x^3 - 4x + 8$

3. $(-3x + 4) + (7x + 2) = (-3x) + (7x) + 4 + 2 = 4x + 6$

4. $(5x^2 - x + 3) - (4x^2 - 2x + 10) = (5x^2 - x + 3) + (-4x^2 + 2x - 10) =$

$5x^2 + (-4x^2) + (-x) + 2x + 3 + (-10) = x^2 + x - 7$

5. $(a^3 + 5ab) + (3a^3 - 3ab) = a^3 + 3a^3 + 5ab + (-3ab) = 4a^3 + 2ab$

6. (a) $-4^2 + 10 = -(4 \cdot 4) + 10 = -16 + 10 = -6$

(b) $8^{-2} = \dfrac{1}{8^2} = \dfrac{1}{8 \cdot 8} = \dfrac{1}{64}$

(c) $\dfrac{1}{2^{-3}} = 2^3 = 2 \cdot 2 \cdot 2 = 8$

7. $x^7 \cdot x^{-3} = x^{7+(-3)} = x^4$

8. $(a^{-1}b^2)^{-3} = a^{(-1)(-3)}b^{(2)(-3)} = a^3b^{-6} = \dfrac{a^3}{b^6}$

9. $ab(a^2 - b^2) = ab \cdot a^2 + ab(-b^2) = a^3b - ab^3$

10. $\left(\dfrac{3a^2}{2b^{-3}}\right)^{-2} = \dfrac{3^{-2}a^{(2)(-2)}}{2^{-2}b^{(-3)(-2)}} = \dfrac{2^2}{3^2a^4b^6} = \dfrac{4}{9a^4b^6}$

11. $\dfrac{12xy^4}{6x^2y} = 2x^{1-2}y^{4-1} = 2x^{-1}y^3 = \dfrac{2y^3}{x}$

12. $3x^2(4x^3 - 6x + 1) = 3x^2 \cdot 4x^3 + (3x^2)(-6x) + 3x^2 \cdot 1 = 12x^5 - 18x^3 + 3x^2$

13. $(z - 3)(2z + 4) = z \cdot 2z + z \cdot 4 + (-3)(2z) + (-3)(4) = 2z^2 + 4z - 6z - 12 = 2z^2 - 2z - 12$

14. $(7y^2 - 3)(7y^2 + 3) = (7y^2)^2 - (3)^2 = 49y^4 - 9$

15. $(3x - 2)^2 = (3x)^2 - (2)(3x)(2) + (2)^2 = 9x^2 - 12x + 4$

16. $(m + 3)^3 = (m + 3)(m + 3)^2 = (m + 3)(m^2 + 6m + 9) =$

    $m \cdot m^2 + m \cdot 6m + m \cdot 9 + 3 \cdot m^2 + 3 \cdot 6m + 3 \cdot 9 = m^3 + 6m^2 + 9m + 3m^2 + 18m + 27 =$

    $m^3 + 9m^2 + 27m + 27$

17. Move the decimal point three places to the left, $6.1 \times 10^{-3} = 0.0061$.

18. Move the decimal point three places to the left, $5410 = 5.41 \times 10^3$.

19. $\dfrac{9x^3 - 6x^2 + 3x}{3x^2} = \dfrac{9x^3}{3x^2} - \dfrac{6x^2}{3x^2} + \dfrac{3x}{3x^2} = 3x^{3-2} - 2x^{2-2} + \dfrac{1}{x} = 3x - 2 + \dfrac{1}{x}$

20.
$$
\begin{array}{r}
x^2 - x + 1 \\
x + 2 \overline{)\, x^3 + x^2 - x + 1} \\
\underline{x^3 + 2x^2} \\
-x^2 - x \\
\underline{-x^2 - 2x} \\
x + 1 \\
\underline{x + 2} \\
-1
\end{array}
$$
   The solution is: $x^2 - x + 1 + \dfrac{-1}{x + 2}$

21. (a) $20t$

    (b) $2t + 2000$

    (c) $(20t) - (2t + 2000) = 20t - 2t - 2000 = 18t - 2000$; profit from selling t tickets.

22. $(3x)(2x) + (3x)(2x) = 6x^2 + 6x^2 = 12x^2$; For $x = 10$ feet $\Rightarrow 12x^2 = 12(10)^2 = 12(100) = 1200 \text{ ft}^2$

23. $(3x)(x + 3)(x + 6) = (3x)(x \cdot x + x \cdot 6 + 3 \cdot x + 3 \cdot 6) = (3x)(x^2 + 9x + 18) =$

    $3x \cdot x^2 + 3x \cdot 9x + 3x \cdot 18 = 3x^3 + 27x^2 + 54x$

24. (a) $t(88 - 16t) = t \cdot 88 - t \cdot 16t = 88t - 16t^2$

    (b) $t = 3 \Rightarrow 88t - 16t^2 = 88(3) - 16(3)^2 = 264 - 16(9) = 264 - 144 = 120$

       After 3 seconds the ball is 120 feet high.

Chapter 5 Extended and Discovery Exercises

1. Conjecture: Make the power of the 10's the same and you can add or subtract the lead numbers and multiply by that power of 10. $(4 \times 10^3) + (3 \times 10^3) = (4 + 3) \times 10^3 = 7 \times 10^3$; Answer checks.

2. Conjecture: Make the power of the 10's the same and you can add or subtract the lead numbers and multiply by that power of 10. $(5 \times 10^{-2}) - (2 \times 10^{-2}) = (5 - 2) \times 10^{-2} = 3 \times 10^{-2}$; Answer checks.

3. Conjecture: Make the power of the 10's the same and you can add or subtract the lead numbers and multiply by that power of 10. $(1.2 \times 10^4) - (3 \times 10^3) = (12 \times 10^3) - (3 \times 10^3) = (12 - 3) \times 10^3 = 9 \times 10^3$; Answer checks.

4. Conjecture: Make the power of the 10's the same and you can add or subtract the lead numbers and multiply by that power of 10. $(2 \times 10^2) + (6 \times 10^1) = (2 \times 10^2) + (0.6 \times 10^2) = (2 + 0.6) \times 10^2 = 2.6 \times 10^2$; Answer checks.

5. Conjecture: Make the power of the 10's the same and you can add or subtract the lead numbers and multiply by that power of 10. $(2 \times 10^{-1}) + (4 \times 10^{-2}) = (2 \times 10^{-1}) + (0.4 \times 10^{-1}) = (2 + 0.4) \times 10^{-1} = 2.4 \times 10^{-1}$; Answer checks.

6. Conjecture: Make the power of the 10's the same and you can add or subtract the lead numbers and multiply by that power of 10. $(2 \times 10^{-3}) - (5 \times 10^{-2}) = (0.2 \times 10^{-2}) - (5 \times 10^{-2}) = (0.2 - 5) \times 10^{-2} = -4.8 \times 10^{-2}$; Answer checks.

7. (a) The length of the box is $30 - 2x$, the width is $20 - 2x$, and the height is x. If $V = L \times W \times H$ then,
$V = (30 - 2x)(20 - 2x)(x) = (600 - 60x - 40x + 4x^2)(x) = (4x^2 - 100x + 600)(x) = 4x^3 - 100x^2 + 600x$

   (b) Let $x = 4$, then $4(4)^3 - 100(4)^2 + 600(4) = 4(64) - 100(16) - 600(4) = 256 - 1600 + 2400 = 1056$ in^3

8. (a) The length and width would be $25 - 2x$ and the height would be x. Therefore the base is equal to $(25 - 2x)^2 = 625 - 100x + 4x^2$ and the four sides are each $(25 - 2x)(x) = 25x - 2x^2 \cdot$ 4 sides $= 100x - 8x^2$. Adding $625 - 100x + 4x^2 + 100x - 8x^2 = 625 - 4x^2$.

   (b) Let $x = 3$, then $625 - 4(3)^2 = 625 - 4(9) = 625 - 36 = 589$ in^2.

9. See Figure 9a & 9b. No, not equal for all values of x; $3x(4 - 5x) = 12x - 15x^2$

Figure 9a

Figure 9b

Figure 10a

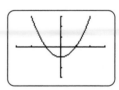
Figure 10b

10. See Figure 10a & 10b. No, not equal for all values of x; $(x - 1)^2 = x^2 - 2x + 1$

11. See Figure 11a & 11b. Yes, equal for all values of x.

Figure 11a

Figure 11b

Figure 12a

Figure 12b

12. See Figure 12a & 12b. No, not equal for all values of x; $(x - 2)^3 = (x - 2)^2(x - 2) = (x^2 - 4x + 4)(x - 2) = x^3 - 4x^2 + 4x - 2x^2 + 8x - 8 = x^3 - 6x^2 + 12x - 8$

Critical Thinking Solutions for Chapter 5

Section 5.2

•   Volume of a cube is side cubed $\Rightarrow L^3$, then multiply by 6 of them $\Rightarrow 6L^3$.

•   The result is zero.

Section 5.4

•   Let $x = 2$ and $y = 3$, then $(x + y)^3 = (2 + 3)^3 = 5^3 = 125$ and $x^3 + y^3 = 2^3 + 3^3 = 8 + 27 = 35$, $125 \neq 35$ therefore $(x + y)^3 \neq x^3 + y^3$

Section 5.6

• $P = m + n$ or degree of dividend = degree of divisor + degree of quotient

Chapter 6: Factoring Polynomials and Solving Equations

6.1: Introduction to Factoring

Concepts

1. factoring

3. greatest common factor (GCF)

5. Factors of $2x^2$ are 1, 2, $2x$, x^2 and $2x^2$; factors of $4x$ are 1, 2, 4, $2x$ and $4x$. Therefore, common factors are 1, 2, x and $2x$.

Common Factors

7. $2x = 2 \cdot x$ and $4 = 2 \cdot 2 \Rightarrow 2(x + 2)$. See Figure 7.

Figure 7   Figure 9

9. $z^2 = z \cdot z$ and $4z = 4 \cdot z \Rightarrow z(z + 4)$. See Figure 9.

11. $6x - 18x^2$; because $6x = 2 \cdot 3 \cdot x$ and $18x^2 = 3 \cdot 3 \cdot 2 \cdot x \cdot x$, common factors are $2 \cdot 3 \cdot x \Rightarrow$ GCF $= 6x$ and $\Rightarrow 6x(1 - 3x)$.

13. $8y^3 - 12y^2$; because $8y^3 = 2 \cdot 2 \cdot 2 \cdot y \cdot y \cdot y$ and $12y^2 = 2 \cdot 2 \cdot 3 \cdot y \cdot y$, common factors are $2 \cdot 2 \cdot y \cdot y \Rightarrow$ GCF $= 4y^2$ and $\Rightarrow 4y^2(2y - 3)$.

15. $6z^3 + 3z^2 + 9z$; because $6z^3 = 2 \cdot 3 \cdot z \cdot z \cdot z$ and $3z^2 = 3 \cdot z \cdot z$ and $9z = 3 \cdot 3 \cdot z$, common factors are $3 \cdot z \Rightarrow$ GCF $= 3z$ and $\Rightarrow 3z(2z^2 + z + 3)$.

17. $x^4 - 5x^3 - 4x^2$; because $x^4 = x \cdot x \cdot x \cdot x$ and $5x^3 = 5 \cdot x \cdot x \cdot x$ and $4x^2 = 2 \cdot 2 \cdot x \cdot x$, common factors are $x \cdot x \Rightarrow$ GCF $= x^2$ and $\Rightarrow x^2(x^2 - 5x - 4)$.

19. $5y^5 + 10y^4 - 15y^3 + 10y^2$; because $5y^5 = 5 \cdot y \cdot y \cdot y \cdot y \cdot y$ and $10y^4 = 2 \cdot 5 \cdot y \cdot y \cdot y \cdot y$ and $15y^3 = 3 \cdot 5 \cdot y \cdot y \cdot y$ and $10y^2 = 2 \cdot 5 \cdot y \cdot y$, common factors are $5 \cdot y \cdot y \Rightarrow$ GCF $= 5y^2$ and $\Rightarrow 5y^2(y^3 + 2y^2 - 3y + 2)$.

21. $xy + xz$; because $xy = x \cdot y$ and $xz = x \cdot z$, common factors are $x \Rightarrow$ GCF $= x$ and $\Rightarrow x(y + z)$.

23. $ab^2 - a^2b$; because $ab^2 = a \cdot b \cdot b$ and $a^2b = a \cdot a \cdot b$, common factors are $a \cdot b \Rightarrow$ GCF $= ab$ and $\Rightarrow ab(b - a)$.

25. $5x^2y^4 + 10x^3y^3$; because $5x^2y^4 = 5 \cdot x \cdot x \cdot y \cdot y \cdot y \cdot y$ and $10x^3y^3 = 2 \cdot 5 \cdot x \cdot x \cdot x \cdot y \cdot y \cdot y$, common factors are $5 \cdot x \cdot x \cdot y \cdot y \cdot y \Rightarrow$ GCF $= 5x^2y^3$ and $\Rightarrow 5x^2y^3(y + 2x)$.

27. $a^2b + ab^2 + ab$; because $a^2b = a \cdot a \cdot b$ and $ab^2 = a \cdot b \cdot b$ and $ab = a \cdot b$, common factors $= a \cdot b \Rightarrow$ GCF $= ab$ and $\Rightarrow ab(a + b + 1)$.

Factoring by Grouping

29. $x(x + 1) - 2(x + 1)$ has common binomial $(x + 1) \Rightarrow (x - 2)(x + 1)$

31. $(z + 5)z + (z + 5)4$ has common binomial $(z + 5) \Rightarrow (z + 4)(z + 5)$

33. $y^2(y + 7) - 4y(y + 7) \Rightarrow (y^2 - 4y)(y + 7) \Rightarrow y(y - 4)(y + 7)$

35. $4x^3(x - 5) + (x - 5)$ has common binomial $(x - 5) \Rightarrow (4x^3 + 1)(x - 5)$

37. $x^3 + 2x^2 + 3x + 6$ by associative property $= (x^3 + 2x^2) + (3x + 6) \Rightarrow$

    common factors $= x^2(x + 2) + 3(x + 2) \Rightarrow (x^2 + 3)(x + 2)$

39. $2y^3 + y^2 + 2y + 1$ by associative property $= (2y^3 + y^2) + (2y + 1) \Rightarrow$

    common factors $= y^2(2y + 1) + (2y + 1) \Rightarrow (y^2 + 1)(2y + 1)$

41. $2z^3 - 6z^2 + 5z - 15$ by associative property $= (2z^3 - 6z^2) + (5z - 15) \Rightarrow$

    common factors $= 2z^2(z - 3) + 5(z - 3) \Rightarrow (2z^2 + 5)(z - 3)$

43. $4t^3 - 20t^2 + 3t - 15$ by associative property $= (4t^3 - 20t^2) + (3t - 15) \Rightarrow$

    common factors $= 4t^2(t - 5) + 3(t - 5) \Rightarrow (4t^2 + 3)(t - 5)$

45. $9r^3 + 6r^2 - 6r - 4$ by associative property $= (9r^3 + 6r^2) - (6r - 4) \Rightarrow$

    common factors $= 3r^2(3r + 2) - 2(3r + 2) \Rightarrow (3r^2 - 2)(3r + 2)$

47. $7x^3 + 21x^2 - 2x - 6$ by associative property $= (7x^3 + 21x^2) - (2x - 6) \Rightarrow$

    common factors $= 7x^2(x + 3) - 2(x + 3) \Rightarrow (7x^2 - 2)(x + 3)$

49. $2y^3 - 7y^2 - 4y + 14$ by associative property $= (2y^3 - 7y^2) - (4y + 14) \Rightarrow$

    common factors $= y^2(2y - 7) - 2(2y - 7) \Rightarrow (y^2 - 2)(2y - 7)$

51. $z^3 - 4z^2 - 7z + 28$ by associative property $= (z^3 - 4z^2) - (7z + 28) \Rightarrow$

    common factors $= z^2(z - 4) - 7(z - 4) \Rightarrow (z^2 - 7)(z - 4)$

53. $2x^4 - 3x^3 + 4x - 6$ by associative property $= (2x^4 - 3x^3) + (4x - 6) \Rightarrow$

    common factors $= x^3(2x - 3) + 2(2x - 3) \Rightarrow (x^3 + 2)(2x - 3)$

55. $ax + bx + ay + by$ by associative property $= (ax + bx) + (ay + by) \Rightarrow$

    common factors $= x(a + b) + y(a + b) \Rightarrow (x + y)(a + b)$

Applications

57. (a) $80t = 2 \cdot 2 \cdot 2 \cdot 2 \cdot 5 \cdot t$ and $16t^2 = 2 \cdot 2 \cdot 2 \cdot 2 \cdot t \cdot t$, common factors are $2 \cdot 2 \cdot 2 \cdot 2 \cdot t \Rightarrow$

    GCF $= 2 \cdot 2 \cdot 2 \cdot 2 \cdot t = 16t$.

    (b) $80t - 16t^2 = 16t(5 - t)$

59. (a) $x = 3, 4x^3 - 60x^2 + 200x \Rightarrow 4(3)^3 - 60(3)^2 + 200(3) = 108 - 540 + 600 = 168 \Rightarrow V = 168$ in^3.

    (b) $4x^3 = 2 \cdot 2 \cdot x \cdot x \cdot x$ and $60x^2 = 2 \cdot 2 \cdot 3 \cdot 5 \cdot x \cdot x$ and $200x = 2 \cdot 2 \cdot 2 \cdot 5 \cdot 5 \cdot x$, common factors are

    $2 \cdot 2 \cdot x \Rightarrow$ GCF $= 4x \Rightarrow 4x(x^2 - 15x + 50)$.

6.2: Factoring Trinomials I $(x^2 + bx + c)$

Concepts

1. F: multiply the first term; O: multiply the outside term; I: multiply the inside term; L: multiply the last term

3. $x^2 + bx + c$, so c is the third term $\Rightarrow$ $mn = c$ and b is the second term $\Rightarrow$ $m + n = b$.

5. Product of 12 by factors: 1, 12; 2, 6; and 3, 4.

7. Factors of 28 are 1, 28; 2, 14; 4, 7 and only $4 + 7 = 11 \Rightarrow 4, 7$.

9. Factors of 30 are 1, 30; 2, 15; 3, 10; 5, 6 and only $3 + 10 = 13 \Rightarrow 3, 10$.

11. Factors of -50 are $-1, 50$; $1, -50$; $-2, 25$; $2, -25$; $-5, 10$; $5, -10$ and only $-5 + 10 = 5 \Rightarrow -5, 10$.

13. Factors of 28 are 1, 28; $-1, -28$; 2, 14; $-2, -14$; 4, 7; $-4, -7$ and only $(-4) + (-7) = -11 \Rightarrow -4, -7$.

Factoring Trinomials

15. Factors of 2 with sum of 3 are 1 and 2 $\Rightarrow x^2 + 3x + 2 = (x + 1)(x + 2)$.

17. Factors of 4 with sum of 4 are 2 and 2 $\Rightarrow y^2 + 4y + 4 = (y + 2)(y + 2)$.

19. Factors of 9 with sum of 6 are 3 and 3 $\Rightarrow z^2 + 6z + 9 = (z + 3)(z + 3)$.

21. Factors of 15 with sum of 8 are 3 and 5 $\Rightarrow x^2 + 8x + 15 = (x + 3)(x + 5)$.

23. Factors of 36 with sum of 13 are 4 and 9 $\Rightarrow m^2 + 13m + 36 = (m + 4)(m + 9)$.

25. Factors of 100 with sum of 20 are 10 and 10 $\Rightarrow n^2 + 20n + 100 = (n + 10)(n + 10)$.

27. Factors of 5 with sum of -6 are -1 and $-5 \Rightarrow x^2 - 6x + 5 = (x - 1)(x - 5)$.

29. Factors of 12 with sum of -7 are -3 and $-4 \Rightarrow y^2 - 7y + 12 = (y - 3)(y - 4)$.

31. Factors of 40 with sum of -13 are -5 and $-8 \Rightarrow z^2 - 13z + 40 = (z - 5)(z - 8)$.

33. Factors of 63 with sum of -16 are -7 and $-9 \Rightarrow a^2 - 16a + 63 = (a - 7)(a - 9)$.

35. Factors of 125 with sum of -30 are -5 and $-25 \Rightarrow b^2 - 30b + 125 = (b - 5)(b - 25)$.

37. Factors of -90 with sum of 13 are -5 and $18 \Rightarrow x^2 + 13x - 90 = (x - 5)(x + 18)$.

39. Factors of -45 with sum of 4 are -5 and $9 \Rightarrow m^2 + 4m - 45 = (m - 5)(m + 9)$.

41. Factors of -200 with sum of 10 are -10 and $20 \Rightarrow n^2 + 10n - 200 = (n - 10)(n + 20)$.

43. Factors of -23 with sum of 22 are -1 and $23 \Rightarrow x^2 + 22x - 23 = (x - 1)(x + 23)$.

45. Factors of -32 with sum of 4 are -4 and $8 \Rightarrow a^2 + 4a - 32 = (a - 4)(a + 8)$.

47. Factors of -20 with sum of -1 are 4 and $-5 \Rightarrow b^2 - b - 20 \Rightarrow (b + 4)(b - 5)$.

49. Factors of -72 with sum of -1 are 8 and $-9 \Rightarrow x^2 - x - 72 \Rightarrow (x + 8)(x - 9)$.

51. Factors of -34 with sum of -15 are 2 and $-17 \Rightarrow y^2 - 15y - 34 \Rightarrow (y + 2)(y - 17)$.

53. Factors of -66 with sum of -5 are 6 and $-11 \Rightarrow z^2 - 5z - 66 \Rightarrow (z + 6)(z - 11)$.

55. $5 + 6x + x^2$ in standard form $x^2 + 6x + 5$ and factors of 5 with a sum of $6 = 1, 5 \Rightarrow (x + 5)(x + 1)$.

57. $3 - 4x + x^2$ in standard form is $x^2 - 4x + 3$ and factors of 3 with a sum of $-4 = -1, -3 \Rightarrow (x - 1)(x - 3)$.

59. Using the hint, the answer will be in the form of $(m - x)(n + x)$ we need to find m and n. Factors of 12 with a difference of 4 are 6 and 2 $\Rightarrow 12 + 4x - x^2 = (6 - x)(2 + x)$.

61. Factors of 32 with a difference of 4 are 8 and 4 $\Rightarrow 32 - 4x - x^2 = (8 + x)(4 - x)$.

Geometry

63. $x^2 + 2x + 1 \Rightarrow (x + 1)(x + 1) \Rightarrow L \cdot W = x^2 + 2x + 1 \Rightarrow L = x + 1$. See Figure 63.

Figure 63   Figure 65

65. $x^2 + 3x + 2 = (x + 2)(x + 1) = L \cdot W \Rightarrow L = x + 2$ or $x + 1$. See Figure 65.

67. $6x^2 + 12x + 6$ divided by 6 (for 6 surfaces) $= x^2 + 2x + 1 = (x + 1)(x + 1) \Rightarrow$ each side is $x + 1$.

69. Add the four regions: $x^2 + 2x + 6x + 12 = x^2 + 8x + 12 = (x + 2)(x + 6)$.

Checking Basic Concepts for Sections 6.1 & 6.2

1. $8x^3 = 2 \cdot 2 \cdot 2 \cdot x \cdot x \cdot x$ and $12x^2 = 2 \cdot 2 \cdot 3 \cdot x \cdot x$ and $24x = 2 \cdot 2 \cdot 2 \cdot 3 \cdot x \Rightarrow$ GCF $= 2 \cdot 2 \cdot x = 4x$.

2. GCF of $12z^3$ and $18z^2$ is $6z^2 \Rightarrow 6z^2(2z - 3)$.

3. (a) $6y(y - 2) + 5(y - 2) = (6y + 5)(y - 2)$

    (b) $(2x^3 + x^2) + (10x + 5) = x^2(2x + 1) + 5(2x + 1) = (x^2 + 5)(2x + 1)$

4. (a) Factors of 8 with a sum of 6 are 2 and 4 $\Rightarrow (x + 2)(x + 4)$.

    (b) Factors of -42 with a sum of -1 are -7 and 6 $\Rightarrow (x - 7)(x + 6)$.

5. $x^2 + 5x + 5x + 25 \Rightarrow x^2 + 10x + 25 \Rightarrow (x + 5)(x + 5)$

6.3: Factoring Trinomials II ($ax^2 + bx + c$)

Concepts

1. ac; b

3. By $ax^2 + bx + c$, if $a > 0, b > 0$ and $c > 0$ then: $+$; $+$

5. By $ax^2 + bx + c$, if $a > 0, b < 0$ and $c > 0$ then: $-$; $-$

7. If $(4x + a)(b + 2) = 4x^2 + 11x + 6$, then by FOIL: $4x \cdot b = 4x^2 \Rightarrow b = x$ and $a \cdot 2 = 6 \Rightarrow a = 3 \Rightarrow 3; x$.

9. If $(2x - a)(b + 3) = 4x^2 + 4x - 3$, then by FOIL: $2x \cdot b = 4x^2 \Rightarrow b = 2x$ and $-a \cdot 3 = -3 \Rightarrow$
    $a = 1 \Rightarrow 1; 2x$.

Factoring Trinomials

11. Using factoring by grouping: For $2x^2 + 7x + 3, m \cdot n = a \cdot c = 2 \cdot 3 = 6$ and $m + n = b = 7 \Rightarrow$
    $m = 6, n = 1 \Rightarrow 2x^2 + 6x + x + 3 \Rightarrow 2x(x + 3) + (x + 3) \Rightarrow (2x + 1)(x + 3)$.

13. Using factoring by grouping: For $3x^2 + 4x + 1$, $m \cdot n = a \cdot c = 3 \cdot 1 = 3$ and $m + n = b = 4 \Rightarrow$
    $m = 3, n = 1 \Rightarrow 3x^2 + 3x + x + 1 \Rightarrow 3x(x + 1) + (x + 1) \Rightarrow (3x + 1)(x + 1)$.

15. Using factoring by grouping: For $6x^2 + 11x + 3$, $m \cdot n = a \cdot c = 6 \cdot 3 = 18$ and $m + n = b = 11 \Rightarrow$
    $m = 9, n = 2 \Rightarrow 6x^2 + 9x + 2x + 3 \Rightarrow 3x(2x + 3) + (2x + 3) \Rightarrow (3x + 1)(2x + 3)$.

17. Using factoring by grouping: For $5x^2 - 11x + 2$, $m \cdot n = a \cdot c = 5 \cdot 2 = 10$ and $m + n = b = -11 \Rightarrow$
    $m = -10, n = -1 \Rightarrow 5x^2 - 10x - x + 2 \Rightarrow 5x(x - 2) - (x - 2) \Rightarrow (5x - 1)(x - 2)$.

19. Using factoring by grouping: For $2y^2 - 7y + 5$, $m \cdot n = a \cdot c = 2 \cdot 5 = 10$ and $m + n = b = -7 \Rightarrow$
    $m = -5, n = -2 \Rightarrow 2y^2 - 5y - 2y + 5 \Rightarrow y(2y - 5) - (2y - 5) \Rightarrow (y - 1)(2y - 5)$.

21. Using factoring by grouping: For $7z^2 - 37z + 10$, $m \cdot n = a \cdot c = 7 \cdot 10 = 70$ and $m + n = b = -37 \Rightarrow$
    $m = -35, n = -2 \Rightarrow 7z^2 - 35z - 2z + 10 \Rightarrow 7z(z - 5) - 2(z - 5) \Rightarrow (7z - 2)(z - 5)$.

23. Using factoring by grouping: For $3t^2 - 7t - 6$, $m \cdot n = a \cdot c = 3 \cdot (-6) = -18$ and $m + n = b = -7 \Rightarrow$
    $m = -9, n = 2 \Rightarrow 3t^2 - 9t + 2t - 6 \Rightarrow 3t(t - 3) + 2(t - 3) \Rightarrow (3t + 2)(t - 3)$.

25. Using factoring by grouping: For $15r^2 + r - 6$, $m \cdot n = a \cdot c = 15 \cdot (-6) = -90$ and $m + n = b = 1 \Rightarrow$
    $m = 10, n = -9 \Rightarrow 15r^2 + 10r - 9r - 6 \Rightarrow 5r(3r + 2) - 3(3r + 2) \Rightarrow (5r - 3)(3r + 2)$.

27. Using factoring by grouping:

    For $24m^2 - 23m - 12$, $m \cdot n = a \cdot c = 24 \cdot (-12) = -288$ and $m + n = b = -23 \Rightarrow$
    $m = -32, n = 9 \Rightarrow 24m^2 - 32m + 9m - 12 \Rightarrow 8m(3m - 4) + 3(3m - 4) \Rightarrow (8m + 3)(3m - 4)$.

29. Using factoring by grouping: For $25x^2 + 5x - 2$, $m \cdot n = a \cdot c = 25 \cdot (-2) = -50$ and $m + n = b = 5 \Rightarrow$
    $m = 10, n = -5 \Rightarrow 25x^2 + 10x - 5x - 2 \Rightarrow 5x(5x + 2) - (5x + 2) \Rightarrow (5x - 1)(5x + 2)$.

31. Using factoring by grouping: For $6x^2 + 11x - 2$, $m \cdot n = a \cdot c = 6 \cdot (-2) = -12$ and $m + n = b = 11 \Rightarrow$
    $m = 12, n = -1 \Rightarrow 6x^2 + 12x - x - 2 \Rightarrow 6x(x + 2) - (x + 2) \Rightarrow (6x - 1)(x + 2)$.

33. Using factoring by grouping: For $21n^2 + 4n - 1$, $m \cdot n = a \cdot c = 21 \cdot (-1) = -21$ and $m + n = b = 4 \Rightarrow$
    $m = 7, n = -3 \Rightarrow 21n^2 + 7n - 3n - 1 \Rightarrow 7n(3n + 1) - (3n + 1) \Rightarrow (7n - 1)(3n + 1)$.

35. Using factoring by grouping: For $14y^2 + 23y + 3$, $m \cdot n = a \cdot c = 14 \cdot 3 = 42$ and $m + n = b = 23 \Rightarrow$
    $m = 21, n = 2 \Rightarrow 14y^2 + 21y + 2y + 3 \Rightarrow 7y(2y + 3) + (2y + 3) \Rightarrow (7y + 1)(2y + 3)$.

37. Using factoring by grouping: For $28z^2 - 25z + 3$, $m \cdot n = a \cdot c = 28 \cdot 3 = 84$ and $m + n = b = -25 \Rightarrow$
    $m = -21, n = -4 \Rightarrow 28z^2 - 21z - 4z + 3 \Rightarrow 7z(4z - 3) - (4z - 3) \Rightarrow (7z - 1)(4z - 3)$.

39. Using factoring by grouping: For $30x^2 - 29x + 6$, $m \cdot n = a \cdot c = 30 \cdot 6 = 180$ and $m + n = b = -29 \Rightarrow$
    $m = -20, n = -9 \Rightarrow 30x^2 - 20x - 9x + 6 \Rightarrow 10x(3x - 2) - 3(3x - 2) \Rightarrow (10x - 3)(3x - 2)$.

41. Using factoring by grouping: For $18t^2 + 23t - 6$, $m \cdot n = a \cdot c = 18 \cdot (-6) = -108$ and $m + n = b = 23 \Rightarrow$
    $m = 27, n = -4 \Rightarrow 18t^2 + 27t - 4t - 6 \Rightarrow 9t(2t + 3) - 2(2t + 3) \Rightarrow (9t - 2)(2t + 3)$.

43. Put $2 + 15x + 7x^2$ in standard form $7x^2 + 15x + 2$, $m \cdot n = a \cdot c = 7 \cdot 2 = 14$ and $m + n = b = 15 \Rightarrow$
    $m = 14, n = 1 \Rightarrow 7x^2 + 14x + x + 2 \Rightarrow 7x(x + 2) + (x + 2) \Rightarrow (7x + 1)(x + 2)$.

45. Put $2 - 5x + 2x^2$ in standard form $2x^2 - 5x + 2$, $m \cdot n = a \cdot c = 2 \cdot 2 = 4$ and $m + n = b = -5 \Rightarrow$
    $m = -4, n = -1 \Rightarrow 2x^2 - 4x - x + 2 \Rightarrow 2x(x - 2) - (x - 2) \Rightarrow (2x - 1)(x - 2)$.

47. Put $3 - 2x - 8x^2$ in standard form $-8x^2 - 2x + 3 = -(8x^2 + 2x - 3)$, $m \cdot n = a \cdot c = 8 \cdot (-3) = -24$

   and $m + n = b = 2 \Rightarrow m = 6, n = -4 \Rightarrow -(8x^2 + 6x - 4x - 3) \Rightarrow -[2x(4x + 3) - (4x + 3)] \Rightarrow$

   $-(2x - 1)(4x + 3)$.

49. $-2x^2 - 7x + 15 = -(2x^2 + 7x - 15)$, $m \cdot n = a \cdot c = 2 \cdot (-15) = -30$ and $m + n = b = 7 \Rightarrow$

   $m = 10, n = -3 \Rightarrow -(2x^2 + 10x - 3x - 15) \Rightarrow -[2x(x + 5) - 3(x + 5)] \Rightarrow -(2x - 3)(x + 5)$.

51. $-5x^2 + 14x + 3 = -(5x^2 - 14x - 3)$, $m \cdot n = a \cdot c = 5 \cdot (-3) = -15$ and $m + n = b = -14 \Rightarrow$

   $m = -15, n = 1 \Rightarrow -(5x^2 - 15x + x - 3) \Rightarrow -[5x(x - 3) + (x - 3)] \Rightarrow -(5x + 1)(x - 3)$.

53. $6x^2 + 7x + 2$, $m \cdot n = a \cdot c = 6 \cdot 2 = 12$ and $m + n = b = 7 \Rightarrow m = 4, n = 3 \Rightarrow$

   $(6x^2 + 4x + 3x + 2) \Rightarrow 2x(3x + 2) + (3x + 2) \Rightarrow (2x + 1)(3x + 2)$. See Figure 53.

Figure 53

55. $(2x^2 + 6x + x + 3) \Rightarrow 2x(x + 3) + (x + 3) \Rightarrow (2x + 1)(x + 3)$.

6.4: Special Types of Factoring

Concepts

1. $a^2 - b^2 = (a - b)(a + b)$

3. $36x^2 - 49y^2 = (6x)^2 - (7y)^2 \Rightarrow a = 6x$ and $b = 7y$.

5. $a^2 - 2ab + b^2 = (a - b)^2$

7. $a^2 - 2ab + b^2 = (a - b)^2 \Rightarrow 4r^2 = (2r)^2$ and $25t^2 = (5t)^2$ and so by $2ab = 2(2r)(5t) = 20rt$.

9. $a^3 - b^3 = (a - b)(a^2 + ab + b^2)$

11. $y^3 - 8 = (y - 2)(y + 2y + 4) \Rightarrow\ -\ ;\ +$

Factoring the Difference of Two Squares

13. $x^2 - 1 = (x)^2 - (1)^2 \Rightarrow (x - 1)(x + 1)$

15. $z^2 - 100 = (z)^2 - (10)^2 \Rightarrow (z - 10)(z + 10)$

17. $4y^2 - 1 = (2y)^2 - (1)^2 \Rightarrow (2y - 1)(2y + 1)$

19. $36z^2 - 25 = (6z)^2 - (5)^2 \Rightarrow (6z - 5)(6z + 5)$

21. $9 - x^2 = (3) - (x)^2 \Rightarrow (3 - x)(3 + x)$

23. $1 - 9y^2 = (1) - (3y)^2 \Rightarrow (1 - 3y)(1 + 3y)$

25. $4a^2 - 9b^2 = (2a)^2 - (3b)^2 \Rightarrow (2a - 3b)(2a + 3b)$

27. $36m^2 - 25n^2 = (6m)^2 - (5n)^2 \Rightarrow (6m - 5n)(6m + 5n)$

29. $81r^2 - 49t^2 = (9r)^2 - (7t)^2 \Rightarrow (9r - 7t)(9r + 7t)$

Factoring Perfect Square Trinomials

31. $x^2 + 8x + 16$ is a perfect square trinomial, $a^2 = x^2$ so $a = x$, $b^2 = 4^2$ so $b = 4$, $2ab = 8x$, the middle term $\Rightarrow$

$(a + b)^2 \Rightarrow (x + 4)^2$.

33. $z^2 + 12z + 25$ is not a perfect square trinomial because $a^2 = z^2$ so $a = z$, $b^2 = 5^2$ so $b = 5$, $2ab = 10z \neq 12z$,

the middle term and also, FOIL does not work, therefore: Not possible.

35. $x^2 - 6x + 9$ is a perfect square trinomial, $a^2 = x^2$ so $a = x$, $b^2 = (\pm 3)^2$ so $b = \pm 3$, using $b = -3$,

$2ab = -6x$, the middle term $\Rightarrow (a + b)^2 \Rightarrow (x - 3)^2$.

37. $9y^2 + 6y + 1$ is a perfect square trinomial,

$a^2 = (3y)^2$ so $a = 3y$, $b^2 = 1^2$ so $b = 1$, $2ab = 6y$, the middle term $\Rightarrow (a + b)^2 \Rightarrow (3y + 1)^2$.

39. $4z^2 - 4z + 1$ is a perfect square trinomial, $a^2 = (2z)^2$ so $a = 2z$, $b^2 = (\pm 1)^2$ so $b = \pm 1$,

using $b = -1$, $2ab = -4z$, the middle term $\Rightarrow (a + b)^2 \Rightarrow (2z - 1)^2$.

41. $9t^2 + 16t + 4$ is not a perfect square trinomial because $a^2 = (3t)^2$ so $a = 3t$, $b^2 = (\pm 1)^2$ so $b = \pm 1$,

$2ab = \pm 6t \neq 16t$, the middle term and also, FOIL does not work, therefore: Not possible.

43. $9x^2 + 30x + 25$ is a perfect square trinomial, $a^2 = (3x)^2$ so $a = 3x$, $b^2 = (5)^2$ so $b = 5$,

$2ab = 30x$, the middle term $\Rightarrow (a + b)^2 \Rightarrow (3x + 5)^2$.

45. $4a^2 - 36a + 81$ is a perfect square trinomial, $a^2 = (2a)^2$ so $a = 2a$, $b^2 = (\pm 9)^2$ so $b = \pm 9$, using $b = -9$,

$2ab = -36a$, the middle term $\Rightarrow (a + b)^2 \Rightarrow (2a - 9)^2$.

47. $x^2 + 2xy + y^2$ is a perfect square trinomial, $a^2 = x^2$ so $a = x$, $b^2 = \sqrt{y^2}$ so $b = y$,

$2ab = 2xy$, the middle term $\Rightarrow (a + b)^2 \Rightarrow (x + y)^2$.

49. $r^2 - 10rt + 25t^2$ is a perfect square trinomial, $a^2 = r^2$ so $a = r$, $b^2 = (\pm 5t)^2$ so $b = \pm 5t$, using $b = -5t$,

$2ab = -10rt$, the middle term $\Rightarrow (a + b)^2 \Rightarrow (r - 5t)^2$.

51. $4y^2 - 10yz + 9z^2$ is not a perfect square trinomial because $a^2 = (2y)^2$ so $a = 2y$, $b^2 = (\pm 3z)^2$ so $b = \pm 3z$,

$2ab = \pm 6z \neq -10yz$, the middle term and also, FOIL does not work, therefore: Not possible.

Factoring Sums and Differences of Two Cubes

53. Using the sum of cubes for $z^3 + 1$, $a^3 = z^3$ so $a = z$, $b^3 = 1^3$ so $b = 1 \Rightarrow$

$(a + b)(a^2 - ab + b^2) \Rightarrow (z + 1)(z^2 - z + 1)$.

55. Using the sum of cubes for $x^3 + 64$, $a^3 = x^3$ so $a = x$, $b^3 = 4^3$ so $b = 4 \Rightarrow$

$(a + b)(a^2 - ab + b^2) \Rightarrow (x + 4)(x^2 - 4x + 16)$.

57. Using the difference of cubes for $y^3 - 8$, $a^3 = y^3$ so $a = y$, $b^3 = 2^3$ so $b = 2 \Rightarrow$

$(a - b)(a^2 + ab + b^2) \Rightarrow (y - 2)(y^2 + 2y + 4)$.

59. Using the difference of cubes for $n^3 - 1$, $a^3 = n^3$ so $a = n$, $b^3 = 1^3$ so $b = 1 \Rightarrow$

$(a - b)(a^2 + ab + b^2) \Rightarrow (n - 1)(n^2 + n + 1)$.

61. Using the sum of cubes for $8x^3 + 1$, $a^3 = (2x)^3$ so $a = 2x$, $b^3 = 1^3$ so $b = 1 \Rightarrow$

$(a + b)(a^2 - ab + b^2) \Rightarrow (2x + 1)(4x^2 - 2x + 1)$.

63. Using the differences of cubes for $m^3 - 64n^3$, $a^3 = m^3$ so $a = m$, $b^3 = (4n)^3$ so $b = 4n$ $\Rightarrow$

    $(a - b)(a^2 + ab + b^2)$ $\Rightarrow$ $(m - 4n)(m^2 + 4mn + 16n^2)$.

65. Using the sum of cubes for $16a^3 + 2b^3 = 2(8a^3 + b^3)$, $a^3 = (2a)^3$ so $a = 2a$, $b^3 = b^3$ so $b = b$ $\Rightarrow$

    $(a + b)(a^2 - ab + b^2)$ $\Rightarrow$ $2(2a + b)(4a^2 - 2ab + b^2)$.

67. Using the sum of cubes for $8x^3 + 125y^3$, $a^3 = (2x)^3$ so $a = 2x$, $b^3 = (5y)^3$ so $b = 5y$ $\Rightarrow$

    $(a + b)(a^2 - ab + b^2)$ $\Rightarrow$ $(2x + 5y)(4x^2 - 10xy + 25y^2)$.

69. Using the differences of cubes for $500r^3 - 32t^3 = 4(125r^3 - 8t^3)$,

    $a^3 = (5r)^3$ so $a = 5r$, $b^3 = (2t)^3$ so $b = 2t$ $\Rightarrow$ $(a - b)(a^2 + ab + b^2)$ $\Rightarrow$ $4(5r - 2t)(25r^2 + 10rt + 4t^2)$.

71. $9x^4 - 3x^3 = 3x^3(3x - 1)$

73. $4y^2 - 9$ (difference of squares) $\Rightarrow$ $(2y + 3)(2y - 3)$

75. $25z^2 - 80z + 64$ (perfect trinomial square), $a^2 = (5z)^2$ so $a = 5z$, $b^2 = (\pm 8)^2$ so $b = \pm 8$, using $b = -8$,

    $2ab = -80z$ the middle term $\Rightarrow$ $(a + b)^2$ $\Rightarrow$ $(5z - 8)^2$.

77. $2x^2 - 15x + 7$ (factor by grouping), $m \cdot n = 14$, $m + n = -15$ $\Rightarrow$ $m = -14$, $n = -1$ $\Rightarrow$

    $2x^2 - 14x - x + 7$ $\Rightarrow$ $2x(x - 7) - (x - 7)$ $\Rightarrow$ $(2x - 1)(x - 7)$.

79. $2n^2 + 21n + 27$ (factor by grouping), $m \cdot n = 54$, $m + n = 21$ $\Rightarrow$ $m = 18$, $n = 3$ $\Rightarrow$

    $2n^2 + 18n + 3n + 27$ $\Rightarrow$ $2n(n + 9) + 3(n + 9)$ $\Rightarrow$ $(2n + 3)(n + 9)$.

81. $8x^3 - 27$ (difference of cubes), $a^3 = (2x)^3$ so $a = 2x$, $b^3 = 3^3$ so $b = 3$ $\Rightarrow$ $(2x - 3)(4x^2 + 6x + 9)$.

83. $x^3 + 2x^2 - 5x - 10$ (factor by grouping) $\Rightarrow$ $x^2(x + 2) - 5(x + 2)$ $\Rightarrow$ $(x^2 - 5)(x + 2)$.

85. $a^2 + 18ab + 81b^2$ (perfect trinomial square), $a^2 = a^2$ so $a = a$, $b^2 = (9b)^2$ so $b = 9b$,

    $2ab = 18ab$ the middle term $\Rightarrow$ $(a + 9b)^2$.

87. Sides must be the same $\Rightarrow$ perfect trinomial, $4x^2 + 12x + 9$, $a^2 = (2x)^2$ so $a = 2x$, $b^2 = 3^2$ so $b = 3$,

    $2ab = 12x$ the middle term $\Rightarrow$ $(2x + 3)^2$. See Figure 87.

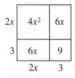

Figure 87

Checking Basic Concepts for Sections 6.3 & 6.4

1. (a) $2x^2 - 5x - 12$ (factor by grouping), $m \cdot n = -24$, $m + n = -5$ $\Rightarrow$ $m = -8$, $n = 3$ $\Rightarrow$

    $2x^2 - 8x + 3x - 12$ $\Rightarrow$ $2x(x - 4) + 3(x - 4)$ $\Rightarrow$ $(2x + 3)(x - 4)$.

    (b) $6x^2 + 17x - 14$ (factor by grouping), $m \cdot n = -84$, $m + n = 17$ $\Rightarrow$ $m = 21$, $n = -4$ $\Rightarrow$

    $6x^2 + 21x - 4x - 14$ $\Rightarrow$ $3x(2x + 7) - 2(2x + 7)$ $\Rightarrow$ $(3x - 2)(2x + 7)$.

2. $3x^2 + 2x + 9x + 6$ $\Rightarrow$ $x(3x + 2) + 3(3x + 2)$ $\Rightarrow$ $(x + 3)(3x + 2)$

3. (a) $z^2 - 64$ (difference of squares), $a^2 = z^2$ so $a = z$, $b^2 = 8^2$ so $b = 8$ $\Rightarrow$ $(z + 8)(z - 8)$.

(b) $9r^2 - 4t^2$ (difference of squares), $a^2 = (3r)^2$ so $a = 3r$, $b^2 = (2t)^2$ so $b = 2t \Rightarrow (3r + 2t)(3r - 2t)$.

(c) $x^2 + 12x + 36$ (FOIL in reverse) $\Rightarrow (x + 6)(x + 6) \Rightarrow (x + 6)^2$.

(d) $9a^2 - 12ab + 4b^2$ (perfect trinomial square), $a^2 = (3a)^2$ so $a = 3a$, $b^2 = (\pm 2b)^2$ so $b = \pm 2b$,

using $b = -2b$, $2ab = -12ab$ the second term $\Rightarrow (3a - 2b)^2$.

4. (a) $m^3 - 27$ (difference of cubes), $a^3 = m^3$ so $a = m$, $b^3 = 3^3$ so $b = 3 \Rightarrow (m - 3)(m^2 + 3m + 9)$.

(b) $125n^3 + 27$ (sum of cubes), $a^3 = (5n)^3$ so $a = 5n$, $b^3 = 3^3$ so $b = 3 \Rightarrow (5n + 3)(25n^2 - 15n + 9)$.

6.5: Solving Equations by Factoring I (Quadratics)

Concepts

1. 0, 0

3. $2x = 0$, $x + 6 = 0$

5. Apply the zero-product property by setting $x + 5 = 0$ and $x - 4 = 0$.

7. $ax^2 + bx + c = 0$ with $a \neq 0$.

Zero-Product Property

9. $x = 0$ or $y = 0$.

11. $2x = 0$ or $x + 8 = 0$, so $x = -8, 0$.

13. $y - 1 = 0$ or $y - 2 = 0$, so $y = 1, 2$.

15. $2z - 1 = 0$ or $4z - 3 = 0$, then $2z - 1 = 0 \Rightarrow 2z = 1 \Rightarrow z = \dfrac{1}{2}$ or $4z - 3 = 0 \Rightarrow 4z = 3 \Rightarrow$

$z = \dfrac{3}{4}$, so $z = \dfrac{1}{2}, \dfrac{3}{4}$.

17. $1 - 3n = 0$ or $3 - 7n = 0$, then $1 - 3n = 0 \Rightarrow -3n = -1 \Rightarrow n = \dfrac{-1}{-3} = \dfrac{1}{3}$ or $3 - 7n = 0 \Rightarrow$

$-7n = -3 \Rightarrow n = \dfrac{-3}{-7} = \dfrac{3}{7}$, so $n = \dfrac{1}{3}, \dfrac{3}{7}$.

19. $x = 0$ or $x - 5 = 0$ or $x - 8 = 0$, then $x - 5 = 0 \Rightarrow x = 5$ or $x - 8 = 0 \Rightarrow x = 8$, so $x = 0, 5, 8$.

Solving Quadratic Equations

21. $x^2 - x = 0 \Rightarrow x(x - 1) = 0$, then $x = 0$ or $x - 1 = 0 \Rightarrow x = 1$, so $x = 0, 1$.

23. $z^2 - 5z = 0 \Rightarrow z(z - 5) = 0$, then $z = 0$ or $z - 5 = 0 \Rightarrow z = 5$, so $z = 0, 5$.

25. $10y^2 + 15y = 0 \Rightarrow 5y(2y + 3) = 0$, then $5y = 0 \Rightarrow y = 0$ or $2y + 3 = 0 \Rightarrow 2y = -3 \Rightarrow$

$y = \dfrac{-3}{2}$, so $y = 0, \dfrac{-3}{2}$.

27. $x^2 - 1 = 0 \Rightarrow (x + 1)(x - 1)$ then $x + 1 = 0 \Rightarrow x = -1$ or $x - 1 = 0 \Rightarrow x = 1$ so $x = -1, 1$.

29. $4n^2 - 1 = 0 \Rightarrow (2n + 1)(2n - 1) = 0$, then $2n + 1 = 0 \Rightarrow 2n = -1 \Rightarrow n = \dfrac{-1}{2}$ or $2n - 1 = 0 \Rightarrow$

$2n = 1 \Rightarrow n = \dfrac{1}{2}$, so $n = -\dfrac{1}{2}, \dfrac{1}{2}$.

31. $z^2 + 3z + 2 = 0 \Rightarrow (z + 2)(z + 1) = 0$, then $z + 2 = 0 \Rightarrow z = -2$ or $z + 1 = 0 \Rightarrow z = -1$, so $z = -2, -1$.

33. $x^2 - 12x + 35 = 0 \Rightarrow (x - 7)(x - 5) = 0$, then $x - 7 = 0 \Rightarrow x = 7$ or $x - 5 = 0 \Rightarrow x = 5$, so $x = 5, 7$.

35. $2b^2 + 3b - 2 = 0 \Rightarrow (2b - 1)(b + 2) = 0$, then $2b - 1 = 0 \Rightarrow 2b = 1 \Rightarrow$

$b = \dfrac{1}{2}$ or $b + 2 = 0 \Rightarrow b = -2$, so $b = -2, \dfrac{1}{2}$.

37. $6y^2 + 19y + 10 = 0$, (factor by grouping), $m \cdot n = 60$, $m + n = 19 \Rightarrow m = 15, n = 4 \Rightarrow$

$6y^2 + 15y + 4y + 10 = 0 \Rightarrow 3y(2y + 5) + 2(2y + 5) = 0 \Rightarrow (3y + 2)(2y + 5) = 0$, then $3y + 2 = 0 \Rightarrow$

$3y = -2 \Rightarrow y = \dfrac{-2}{3}$ or $2y + 5 = 0 \Rightarrow 2y = -5 \Rightarrow y = \dfrac{-5}{2}$, so $y = -\dfrac{5}{2}, -\dfrac{2}{3}$.

39. $x^2 = 25 \Rightarrow x^2 - 25 = 0 \Rightarrow (x + 5)(x - 5) = 0$, then $x + 5 = 0 \Rightarrow x = -5$ or $x - 5 = 0 \Rightarrow$

$x = 5$, so $x = -5, 5$.

41. $t^2 = 5t \Rightarrow t^2 - 5t = 0 \Rightarrow t(t - 5) = 0$, then $t = 0$ or $t - 5 = 0 \Rightarrow t = 5$, so $x = 0, 5$.

43. $3m^2 = -9m \Rightarrow 3m^2 + 9m = 0 \Rightarrow 3m(m + 3) = 0$, then $3m = 0 \Rightarrow m = 0$ or $m + 3 = 0 \Rightarrow$

$m = -3$, so $m = -3, 0$.

45. $x^2 = 5x + 6 \Rightarrow x^2 - 5x - 6 = 0 \Rightarrow (x + 1)(x - 6) = 0$, then $x + 1 = 0 \Rightarrow x = -1$ or $x - 6 = 0 \Rightarrow$

$x = 6$, so $x = -1, 6$.

47. $12z^2 + 11z = 15 \Rightarrow 12z^2 + 11z - 15 = 0$, (factor by grouping), $m \cdot n = -180$, $m + n = 11 \Rightarrow$

$m = 20, n = -9 \Rightarrow 12z^2 + 20z - 9z - 15 = 0 \Rightarrow 4z(3z + 5) - 3(3z + 5) = 0 \Rightarrow (4z - 3)(3z + 5) = 0$,

then $4z - 3 = 0 \Rightarrow 4z = 3 \Rightarrow z = \dfrac{3}{4}$ or $3z + 5 = 0 \Rightarrow 3z = -5 \Rightarrow z = \dfrac{-5}{3}$, so $z = -\dfrac{5}{3}, \dfrac{3}{4}$.

49. $t(t + 1) = 2 \Rightarrow t^2 + t = 2 \Rightarrow t^2 + t - 2 = 0 \Rightarrow (t + 2)(t - 1) = 0$, then $t + 2 = 0 \Rightarrow$

$t = -2$ or $t - 1 = 0 \Rightarrow t = 1$, so $t = -2, 1$.

51. $x(2x + 5) = 3 \Rightarrow 2x^2 + 5x = 3 \Rightarrow 2x^2 + 5x - 3 = 0 \Rightarrow (2x - 1)(x + 3) = 0$, then $2x - 1 = 0 \Rightarrow$

$2x = 1 \Rightarrow x = \dfrac{1}{2}$ or $x + 3 = 0 \Rightarrow x = -3$, so $x = -3, \dfrac{1}{2}$.

Geometry

53. Both sides are the same so $x^2 = 144 \Rightarrow x^2 - 144 = 0 \Rightarrow (x + 12)(x - 12) = 0$, then $x + 12 = 0 \Rightarrow$

$x = -12$ or $x - 12 = 0 \Rightarrow x = 12$, so $x = -12, 12$, but length is not negative so $x = 12$ feet.

55. Area of circle πr^2 − circumference of circle $2\pi r = 8\pi \Rightarrow r^2\pi - 2r\pi = 8\pi \Rightarrow r^2 - 2r = 8 \Rightarrow$

$r^2 - 2r - 8 = 0 \Rightarrow (r - 4)(r + 2) = 0$, then $r - 4 = 0 \Rightarrow r = 4$ or $r + 2 = 0 \Rightarrow r = -2$, so $r = -2, 4$,

but radius cannot be -2 inches long so $r = 4$ inches.

57. Using pythagorean theorem $a^2 + b^2 = c^2$, $(x - 1)^2 + x^2 = (x + 1)^2 \Rightarrow x^2 - 2x + 1 + x^2 = x^2 + 2x + 1 \Rightarrow$

$2x^2 - 2x + 1 = x^2 + 2x + 1 \Rightarrow x^2 - 4x = 0 \Rightarrow x(x - 4) = 0$, then $x = 0$ or $x - 4 = 0 \Rightarrow$

$x = 4$, so $x = 0, 4$, but length cannot be 0 so $x = 4$.

Applications

59. (a) Height is zero at ground, $0 = 96t - 16t^2 \Rightarrow 0 = 16t(6 - t) = 0$, then $16t = 0 \Rightarrow t = 0$ or $6 - t = 0 \Rightarrow$ $-t = -6 \Rightarrow t = 6$, so $t = 0, 6$, but $t = 0$ is when it was first hit, so after it was hit, it took 6 seconds to hit the ground.

(b) 3 seconds. See figure 59.

Time (t)	0	1	2	3	4	5	6
Height (h)	0	80	128	144	128	80	0

Figure 59

61. (a) For $x = 30, D = \dfrac{1}{11}(30)^2 \Rightarrow D = \dfrac{1}{11}(900) \Rightarrow d = 81.8$ feet.

For $x = 60, D = \dfrac{1}{11}(60)^2 \Rightarrow D = \dfrac{1}{11}(3600) \Rightarrow d = 327.3$ feet.

When the speed doubles, the braking distance quadruples.

(b) $33 = \dfrac{1}{11}x^2 \Rightarrow 363 = x^2 \Rightarrow x \approx 19$ mph.

(c) See Figure 61. About 19 miles per hour: yes.

Figure 61

Figure 63

63. (a) 1930, $x = 30 \Rightarrow W = \dfrac{19}{3125}(30)^2 + \dfrac{11}{2} \Rightarrow W = \dfrac{19}{3125}(900) + \dfrac{11}{2} \Rightarrow$

$W = 10.972$ million ≈ 11 million.

2000, $x = 100 \Rightarrow W = \dfrac{19}{3125}(100)^2 + \dfrac{11}{2} \Rightarrow W = \dfrac{19}{3125}(10,000) + \dfrac{11}{2} \Rightarrow$

$W = 66.3$ million ≈ 66 million.

(b) See Figure 63. About 1981.

65. Width $= x$, Length $= x + 10$, $x(x + 10) = 2000 \Rightarrow x^2 + 10x = 2000 \Rightarrow x^2 + 10x - 2000 = 0 \Rightarrow$ $(x + 50)(x - 40) = 0$, then $x + 50 = 0 \Rightarrow x = -50$ or $x - 40 = 0 \Rightarrow x = 40$, so $x = -50, 40$, but we can not have -50 pixels, so $x = 40 \Rightarrow$ width 40 and length $40 + 10 = 50 \Rightarrow 40 \times 50$ pixels.

6.6: Solving Equations by Factoring II (Higher Degrees)

Concepts

1. GCF

3. $(z^2 + 1)(z^2 + 2)$

5. Subtract x from both sides.

Factoring Polynomials

7. $5x^2 - 5x - 30 \Rightarrow 5(x^2 - x - 6) \Rightarrow 5(x + 2)(x - 3)$

9. $-4y^2 - 32y - 48 \Rightarrow -4(y^2 + 8y + 12) \Rightarrow -4(y + 6)(y + 2)$

11. $-20z^2 - 110z - 50 \Rightarrow -10(2z^2 + 11z + 5) \Rightarrow -10(2z + 1)(z + 5)$

13. $60 - 64t - 28t^2 \Rightarrow -4(7t^2 + 16t - 15) \Rightarrow -4(7t - 5)(t + 3)$

15. $r^3 - r \Rightarrow r(r^2 - 1) \Rightarrow r(r + 1)(r - 1)$

17. $3x^3 + 3x^2 - 18x \Rightarrow 3x(x^2 + x - 6) \Rightarrow 3x(x + 3)(x - 2)$

19. $72z^3 + 12z^2 - 24z \Rightarrow 12z(6z^2 + z - 2) \Rightarrow 12z(3z + 2)(2z - 1)$

21. $x^4 - 4x^2 \Rightarrow x^2(x^2 - 4) \Rightarrow x^2(x + 2)(x - 2)$

23. $t^4 + t^3 - 2t^2 \Rightarrow t^2(t^2 + t - 2) \Rightarrow t^2(t + 2)(t - 1)$

25. $x^4 - 5x^2 + 6 \Rightarrow (x^2 - 2)(x^2 - 3)$

27. $2x^4 + 7x^2 + 3 \Rightarrow (2x^2 + 1)(x^2 + 3)$

29. $y^4 + 6y^2 + 9 \Rightarrow (y^2 + 3)(y^2 + 3) \Rightarrow (y^2 + 3)^2$

31. $x^4 - 9 \Rightarrow (x^2 + 3)(x^2 - 3)$

33. $x^4 - 81 \Rightarrow (x^2 + 9)(x^2 - 9) \Rightarrow (x^2 + 9)(x + 3)(x - 3)$

35. $z^5 + 2z^4 + z^3 \Rightarrow z^3(z^2 + 2z + 1) \Rightarrow z^3(z + 1)(z + 1) \Rightarrow z^3(z + 1)^2$

37. $2x^2 + xy - y^2 \Rightarrow (2x - y)(x + y)$

39. $a^4 - 2a^2b^2 + b^4 \Rightarrow (a^2 - b^2)(a^2 - b^2) \Rightarrow (a + b)(a - b)(a + b)(a - b) \Rightarrow (a + b)^2(a - b)^2$

41. $x^3 - xy^2 \Rightarrow x(x^2 - y^2) \Rightarrow x(x + y)(x - y)$

43. $4x^3 + 4x^2y + xy^2 \Rightarrow x(4x^2 + 4xy + y^2) \Rightarrow x(2x + y)(2x + y) \Rightarrow x(2x + y)^2$

Solving Equations

45. (a) $x^3 - 4x \Rightarrow x(x^2 - 4) \Rightarrow x(x + 2)(x - 2)$

    (b) $x(x + 2)(x - 2) = 0$, then $x = 0$ or $x + 2 = 0$ or $x - 2 = 0 \Rightarrow x = -2, 0, 2$.

47. (a) $2y^3 - 6y^2 - 36y \Rightarrow 2y(y^2 - 3y - 18) \Rightarrow 2y(y - 6)(y + 3)$

    (b) $2y(y - 6)(y + 3) = 0$, then $2y = 0$ or $y - 6 = 0$ or $y + 3 = 0 \Rightarrow y = -3, 0, 6$.

49. $3x^2 + 33x + 72 = 0 \Rightarrow 3(x^2 + 11x + 24) = 0 \Rightarrow 3(x + 8)(x + 3) = 0$, then $x + 8 = 0$ or $x + 3 = 0 \Rightarrow x = -8, -3$.

51. $25x^2 = 50x + 75 \Rightarrow 25x^2 - 50x - 75 = 0 \Rightarrow 25(x^2 - 2x - 3) = 0 \Rightarrow 25(x - 3)(x + 1) = 0$, then $x - 3 = 0$ or $x + 1 = 0 \Rightarrow x = -1, 3$.

53. $y^3 - 3y^2 - 4y = 0 \Rightarrow y(y^2 - 3y - 4) = 0 \Rightarrow y(y - 4)(y + 1) = 0$, then $y = 0$ or $y - 4 = 0$ or $y + 1 = 0 \Rightarrow y = -1, 0, 4$.

55. $3z^3 + 6z^2 = 72z \Rightarrow 3z^3 + 6z^2 - 72z = 0 \Rightarrow 3z(z^2 + 2z - 24) = 0 \Rightarrow 3z(z + 6)(z - 4) = 0$, then $3z = 0$ or $z + 6 = 0$ or $z - 4 = 0 \Rightarrow z = -6, 0, 4$.

57. $x^4 - 36x^2 = 0 \Rightarrow x^2(x^2 - 36) = 0 \Rightarrow x^2(x + 6)(x - 6) = 0$, then $x^2 = 0$ or $x + 6 = 0$ or $x - 6 = 0 \Rightarrow x = -6, 0, 6$.

59. $r^4 + 6r^3 = 7r^2 \Rightarrow r^4 + 6r^3 - 7r^2 = 0 \Rightarrow r^2(r^2 + 6r - 7) = 0 \Rightarrow r^2(r + 7)(r - 1) = 0$, then $r^2 = 0$ or

$r + 7 = 0$ or $r - 1 = 0 \Rightarrow r = -7, 0, 1.$

61. $x^4 - 13x^2 + 36 = 0 \Rightarrow (x^2 - 9)(x^2 - 4) = 0 \Rightarrow (x + 3)(x - 3)(x + 2)(x - 2) = 0$, then $x + 3 = 0$ or

$x - 3 = 0$ or $x + 2 = 0$ or $x - 2 = 0 \Rightarrow x = -3, -2, 2, 3.$

63. $x^4 + 1 = 2x^2 \Rightarrow x^4 - 2x^2 + 1 = 0 \Rightarrow (x^2 - 1)(x^2 - 1) = 0 \Rightarrow (x + 1)(x - 1)(x + 1)(x - 1) = 0$, then

$x + 1 = 0$ or $x - 1 = 0 \Rightarrow x = -1, 1.$

65. $a^4 = 81 \Rightarrow a^4 - 81 = 0 \Rightarrow (a^2 + 9)(a^2 - 9) = 0 \Rightarrow (a^2 + 9)(a + 3)(a - 3) = 0$, then $a^2 + 9 = 0$ or

$a + 3 = 0$ or $a - 3 = 0$, but $a^2 + 9 = 0$ does not produce real solutions so $x = -3, 3.$

67. $x^3 - 2x^2 - x + 2 = 0 \Rightarrow x^2(x - 2) - (x - 2) = 0 \Rightarrow (x^2 - 1)(x - 2) = 0 \Rightarrow$

$(x + 1)(x - 1)(x - 2) = 0$, then $x + 1 = 0$ or $x - 1 = 0$ or $x - 2 = 0 \Rightarrow x = -1, 1, 2.$

69. $x^3 - 5x^2 + x - 5 = 0 \Rightarrow x^2(x - 5) + (x - 5) = 0 \Rightarrow (x^2 + 1)(x - 5) = 0 \Rightarrow$ then $x^2 + 1 = 0$ or

$x - 5 = 0$ but $x^2 + 1 = 0$ does not produce real solutions so $x = 5.$

Applications

71. (a) $x < 7.5$ because the width is 15 inches.

   (b) Area of rectangle with 4 cut out pieces $15 \times 20 = 300$. Area of cut out piece $x^2 \cdot 4$ pieces $= 4x^2 \Rightarrow$

   surface area $300 - 4x^2.$

   (c) $300 - 4x^2 = 275 \Rightarrow 0 = 4x^2 - 25 \Rightarrow (2x + 5)(2x - 5) = 0$, then $2x + 5 = 0$ or $2x - 5 = 0$, but

   $2x + 5 = 0$ produces a negative length which we can not have so $2x - 5 = 0 \Rightarrow 2x = 5 \Rightarrow$

   $x = \dfrac{5}{2} \Rightarrow x = 2.5$ inches.

73. $1990 = 30 \Rightarrow 0.0013(30)^3 - 0.085(30)^2 + 1.6(30) + 12 = 35.1 - 76.5 + 48 + 12 = 18.6$ trillion ft^3

75. Factoring is very difficult.

Checking Basic Concepts for Sections 6.5 & 6.6

1. (a) $4y^2 - 6y = 0 \Rightarrow 2y(2y - 3) = 0$, then $2y = 0$ or $2y - 3 = 0 \Rightarrow y = 0, \dfrac{3}{2}$

   (b) $5z^2 + 2z = 3 \Rightarrow 5z^2 + 2z - 3 = 0 \Rightarrow (5z - 3)(z + 1) = 0$, then $5z - 3 = 0 \Rightarrow 5z = 3 \Rightarrow z = \dfrac{3}{5}$ or

   $z + 1 = 0$, so $z = -1, \dfrac{3}{5}$

2. $x^2 + 2x - 3 = 0 \Rightarrow (x + 3)(x - 1) = 0$, then $x + 3 = 0$ or $x - 1 = 0$, so $x = -3, 1$

3. $88t - 16t^2 = 0 \Rightarrow -8t(2t - 11) = 0$, then $-8t = 0$ or $2t - 11 = 0 \Rightarrow 2t = 11 \Rightarrow t = \dfrac{11}{2}$, so $t = 0, \dfrac{11}{2}$;

   $t = 0$ is when the ball was hit so the golf ball will hit the ground 5.5 seconds after it is hit.

4. (a) $x^4 - 8x^2 + 16 \Rightarrow (x^2 - 4)(x^2 - 4) \Rightarrow (x + 2)(x - 2)(x + 2)(x - 2) \Rightarrow (x + 2)^2(x - 2)^2$

   (b) $2y^3 + 17y^2 - 30y \Rightarrow y(2y^2 + 17y - 30) \Rightarrow y(2y - 3)(y + 10)$

   (c) $x^4 - 16y^4 \Rightarrow (x^2 + 4y^2)(x^2 - 4y^2) \Rightarrow (x^2 + 4y^2)(x + 2y)(x - 2y)$

5. $t^4 + t^3 = 12t^2 \Rightarrow t^4 + t^3 - 12t^2 = 0 \Rightarrow t^2(t^2 + t - 12) = 0 \Rightarrow t^2(t + 4)(t - 3) = 0$, then $t^2 = 0$ or

   $t + 4 = 0$ or $t - 3 = 0 \Rightarrow t = -4, 0, 3$.

Chapter 6 Review Exercises

Section 6.1

1. Factors of $8z^3 = 2 \cdot 2 \cdot 2 \cdot z \cdot z \cdot z \Rightarrow$ factors of $4z^2 = 2 \cdot 2 \cdot z \cdot z \Rightarrow$ GCF $= 2 \cdot 2 \cdot z \cdot z = 4z^2$;

   $4z^2(2z - 1)$

2. Factors of $6x^4 = 2 \cdot 3 \cdot x \cdot x \cdot x \cdot x \Rightarrow$ factors of $3x^3 = 3 \cdot x \cdot x \cdot x \Rightarrow$ factors of $12x^2 = 2 \cdot 2 \cdot 3 \cdot x \cdot x \Rightarrow$

   GCF $= 3 \cdot x \cdot x = 3x^2$; $3x^2(2x^2 + x - 4)$.

3. Factors of $9xy = 3 \cdot 3 \cdot x \cdot y \Rightarrow$ factors of $15yz^2 = 3 \cdot 5 \cdot y \cdot z \cdot z \Rightarrow$ GCF $= 3 \cdot y = 3y$; $3y(3x + 5z^2)$.

4. Factors of $a^2b^3 = a \cdot a \cdot b \cdot b \cdot b \Rightarrow$ factors of $a^3b^2 = a \cdot a \cdot a \cdot b \cdot b \Rightarrow$ GCF $= a \cdot a \cdot b \cdot b = a^2b^2$;

   $a^2b^2(b + a)$.

5. $x(x + 2) - 3(x + 2) \Rightarrow (x - 3)(x + 2)$

6. $y^2(x - 5) + 3y(x - 5) \Rightarrow (y^2 + 3y)(x - 5) \Rightarrow y(y + 3)(x - 5)$

7. $z^3 - 2z^2 + 5z - 10 \Rightarrow z^2(z - 2) + 5(z - 2) \Rightarrow (z^2 + 5)(z - 2)$

8. $t^3 + t^2 + 8t + 8 \Rightarrow t^2(t + 1) + 8(t + 1) \Rightarrow (t^2 + 8)(t + 1)$

9. $x^3 - 3x^2 + 6x - 18 \Rightarrow x^2(x - 3) + 6(x - 3) \Rightarrow (x^2 + 6)(x - 3)$

10. $ax + bx - ay - by \Rightarrow x(a + b) - y(a + b) \Rightarrow (x - y)(a + b)$

Section 6.2

11. $4, 5$

12. $-3, 7$

13. $-9, -4$

14. $-25, 4$

15. Product -12, sum -1 is $-4, 3 \Rightarrow (x - 4)(x + 3)$.

16. Product 24, sum 10 is $4, 6 \Rightarrow (x + 4)(x + 6)$.

17. Product -16, sum 6 is $-2, 8 \Rightarrow (x - 2)(x + 8)$.

18. Product -42, sum -1 is $-7, 6 \Rightarrow (x - 7)(x + 6)$.

19. Product -3, sum 2 is $-1, 3 \Rightarrow (x - 1)(x + 3)$.

20. Product 120, sum 22 is $10, 12 \Rightarrow (x + 10)(x + 12)$.

21. Product 10, sum -7 is $-5, -2 \Rightarrow (2 - x)(5 - x)$.

22. Product 24, sum 2 is $6, -4 \Rightarrow (6 - x)(4 + x)$.

Section 6.3

23. Using FOIL: $9x^2 + 3x - 2 = (3x + 2)(3x - 1)$.

24. Using FOIL: $2x^2 + 3x - 5 = (2x + 5)(x - 1)$.

25. Using FOIL: $3x^2 + 14x + 15 = (3x + 5)(x + 3)$.

26. Using FOIL: $35x^2 - 2x - 1 = (5x - 1)(7x + 1)$.

27. Using FOIL: $24x^2 - 7x - 5 = (8x - 5)(3x + 1)$.

28. Using FOIL: $4x^2 + 33x - 27 = (x + 9)(4x - 3)$.

29. Using FOIL: $12 - 5x - 2x^2 = (3 - 2x)(4 + x)$.

30. Using FOIL: $1 + 3x - 10x^2 = (1 + 5x)(1 - 2x)$.

Section 6.4

31. Difference of squares, $x^2 - 4 = (x + 2)(x - 2)$.

32. Difference of squares, $9z^2 - 64 = (3z + 8)(3z - 8)$.

33. Difference of squares, $36 - y^2 = (6 + y)(6 - y)$.

34. Difference of squares, $100a^2 - 81b^2 = (10a + 9b)(10a - 9b)$.

35. Perfect trinomial, $a^2 = x^2$ so $a = x$, $b^2 = 7^2$ so $b = 7$, then $2ab = 2 \cdot 7 \cdot x = 14x$ the middle term $\Rightarrow$
    $(x + 7)^2$.

36. Perfect trinomial, $a^2 = x^2$ so $a = x$, $b^2 = (\pm 5)^2$ so $b = \pm 5$, using $b = -5$, then $2ab = 2 \cdot (-5)x =$
    $-10x$ the middle term $\Rightarrow (x - 5)^2$.

37. Perfect trinomial, $a^2 = (2x)^2$ so $a = 2x$, $b^2 = (\pm 3)^2$ so $b = \pm 3$, using $b = -3$, then $2ab = 2 \cdot (-3)2x =$
    $-12x$ the middle term $\Rightarrow (2x - 3)^2$.

38. Perfect trinomial, $a^2 = 3x^2$ so $a = 3x$, $b^2 = 8^2$ so $b = 8$, then $2ab = 2 \cdot 8 \cdot 3x = 48x$ the middle term $\Rightarrow$
    $(3x + 8)^2$.

39. Difference of cubes, $8t^3 - 1$, $a^3 = (2t)^3$ so $a = 2t$, $b^3 = 1^3$ so $b = 1 \Rightarrow (2t - 1)(4t^2 + 2t + 1)$.

40. Sum of cubes, $27r^3 + 8t^3$, $a^3 = (3r)^3$ so $a = 3r$, $b^3 = (2t)^3$ so $b = 2t \Rightarrow (3r + 2t)(9r^2 - 6rt + 4t^2)$.

Section 6.5

41. $m = 0$ or $n = 0$

42. $y = 0$

43. $(4x - 3)(x + 9) = 0$, then $4x - 3 = 0 \Rightarrow 4x = 3 \Rightarrow x = \dfrac{3}{4}$ or $x + 9 = 0 \Rightarrow x = -9$, so $x = -9, \dfrac{3}{4}$.

44. $(1 - 4x)(6 + 5x) = 0$, then $1 - 4x = 0 \Rightarrow -4x = -1 \Rightarrow x = \dfrac{-1}{-4} \Rightarrow x = \dfrac{1}{4}$ or $6 + 5x = 0 \Rightarrow 5x = -6 \Rightarrow$
    $x = \dfrac{-6}{5}$, so $x = -\dfrac{6}{5}, \dfrac{1}{4}$.

45. $z(z - 1)(z - 2) = 0$, then $z = 0$ or $z - 1 = 0 \Rightarrow z = 1$ or $z - 2 = 0 \Rightarrow z = 2$, so $z = 0, 1, 2$.

46. $z^2 - 7z = 0 \Rightarrow z(z - 7) = 0$, then $z = 0$ or $z - 7 = 0 \Rightarrow z = 7$, so $z = 0, 7$.

47. $y^2 - 64 = 0$, difference of squares $(y + 8)(y - 8) = 0$, then $y + 8 = 0 \Rightarrow y = -8$ or $y - 8 = 0 \Rightarrow$
    $y = 8$, so $y = -8, 8$.

48. $y^2 + 9y + 14 = 0 \Rightarrow (y + 2)(y + 7) = 0$, then $y + 2 = 0 \Rightarrow y = -2$ or $y + 7 = 0 \Rightarrow$

$y = -7$, so $y = -2, -7$.

49. $x^2 = x + 6 \Rightarrow x^2 - x - 6 = 0 \Rightarrow (x - 3)(x + 2) = 0$, then $x - 3 = 0 \Rightarrow x = 3$ or $x + 2 = 0 \Rightarrow$

$x = -2$, so $x = -2, 3$.

50. $10x^2 + 11x = 6 \Rightarrow 10x^2 + 11x - 6 = 0 \Rightarrow (2x + 3)(5x - 2) = 0$, then $2x + 3 = 0 \Rightarrow 2x = -3 \Rightarrow$

$x = \dfrac{-3}{2}$ or $5x - 2 = 0 \Rightarrow 5x = 2 \Rightarrow x = \dfrac{2}{5}$, so $x = -\dfrac{3}{2}, \dfrac{2}{5}$.

51. $t(t - 14) = 72 \Rightarrow t^2 - 14t = 72 \Rightarrow t^2 - 14t - 72 = 0 \Rightarrow (t - 18)(t + 4) = 0$, then $t - 18 = 0 \Rightarrow$

$t = 18$ or $t + 4 = 0 \Rightarrow t = -4$, so $t = -4, 18$.

52. $t(2t - 1) = 10 \Rightarrow 2t^2 - t = 10 \Rightarrow 2t^2 - t - 10 = 0 \Rightarrow (2t - 5)(t + 2) = 0$, then $2t - 5 = 0 \Rightarrow$

$2t = 5 \Rightarrow t = \dfrac{5}{2}$ or $t + 2 = 0 \Rightarrow t = -2$, so $t = -2, \dfrac{5}{2}$.

Section 6.6

53. $5x^2 - 15x - 50 \Rightarrow 5(x^2 - 3x - 10) \Rightarrow 5(x - 5)(x + 2)$

54. $-3x^2 - 6x + 45 \Rightarrow -3(x^2 + 2x - 15) \Rightarrow -3(x + 5)(x - 3)$

55. $y^3 - 4y \Rightarrow y(y^2 - 4) \Rightarrow y(y + 2)(y - 2)$

56. $3y^3 + 6y^2 - 9y \Rightarrow 3y(y^2 + 2y - 3) \Rightarrow 3y(y + 3)(y - 1)$

57. $2z^4 + 14z^3 + 20z^2 \Rightarrow 2z^2(z^2 + 7z + 10) \Rightarrow 2z^2(z + 2)(z + 5)$

58. $8z^4 - 32z^2 \Rightarrow 8z^2(z^2 - 4) \Rightarrow 8z^2(z + 2)(z - 2)$

59. $x^4 - 6x^2 + 9 \Rightarrow (x^2 - 3)(x^2 - 3) \Rightarrow (x^2 - 3)^2$

60. $2x^4 - 15x^2 - 27 \Rightarrow (2x^2 + 3)(x^2 - 9) \Rightarrow (2x^2 + 3)(x + 3)(x - 3)$

61. $a^2 + 10ab + 25b^2 \Rightarrow (a + 5b)(a + 5b) \Rightarrow (a + 5b)^2$

62. $x^3 - xy^2 \Rightarrow x(x^2 - y^2) \Rightarrow x(x + y)(x - y)$

63. $16x^2 - 72x - 40 = 0 \Rightarrow 8(2x^2 - 9x - 5) = 0 \Rightarrow 8(2x + 1)(x - 5) = 0$, then $2x + 1 = 0 \Rightarrow 2x = -1 \Rightarrow$

$x = -\dfrac{1}{2}$ or $x - 5 = 0 \Rightarrow x = 5$, so $x = -\dfrac{1}{2}, 5$.

64. $2x^3 - 11x^2 - 15x = 0 \Rightarrow x(2x^2 - 11x + 15) = 0 \Rightarrow x(2x - 5)(x - 3) = 0$, then $x = 0$ or $2x - 5 = 0 \Rightarrow$

$2x = 5 \Rightarrow x = \dfrac{5}{2}$ or $x - 3 = 0 \Rightarrow x = 3$, so $x = 0, \dfrac{5}{2}, 3$.

65. $t^3 - 25t = 0 \Rightarrow t(t^2 - 25) = 0 \Rightarrow t(t + 5)(t - 5) = 0$, then $t = 0$ or $t + 5 = 0 \Rightarrow$

$t = -5$ or $t - 5 = 0 \Rightarrow t = 5$, so $t = -5, 0, 5$.

66. $t^4 - 7t^3 + 12t^2 = 0 \Rightarrow t^2(t^2 - 7t + 12) = 0 \Rightarrow t^2(t - 3)(t - 4) = 0$, then $t^2 = 0$ or $t - 3 = 0 \Rightarrow$

$t = 3$ or $t - 4 = 0 \Rightarrow t = 4$, so $t = 0, 3, 4$.

67. $z^4 + 16 = 8z^2 \Rightarrow z^4 - 8z^2 + 16 = 0 \Rightarrow (z^2 - 4)(z^2 - 4) = 0 \Rightarrow (z + 2)(z - 2)(z + 2)(z - 2) = 0$, then

$z + 2 = 0 \Rightarrow z = -2$ or $z - 2 = 0 \Rightarrow z = 2$, so $z = -2, 2$.

68. $z^4 - 256 = 0 \Rightarrow (z^2 + 16)(z^2 - 16) = 0 \Rightarrow (z^2 + 16)(z + 4)(z - 4) = 0$, then $z^2 + 16 = 0$ which

produces no real solutions, or $z + 4 = 0 \Rightarrow z = -4$ or $z - 4 = 0 \Rightarrow z = 4$, so $z = -4, 4$.

69. $y^3 = -64 \Rightarrow y^3 + 64 = 0 \Rightarrow (y + 4)(y^2 - 4y + 16) = 0$, then $y + 4 = 0 \Rightarrow$

$y = -4$ or $y^2 - 4y + 16 = 0$ which produces no real solutions, so $y = -4$.

70. $y^3 - y^2 - y + 1 = 0 \Rightarrow y^2(y - 1) - 1(y - 1) = 0 \Rightarrow (y^2 - 1)(y - 1) = 0 \Rightarrow$

$(y + 1)(y - 1)(y - 1) = 0$, then $y + 1 = 0 \Rightarrow y = -1$ or $y - 1 = 0 \Rightarrow y = 1$, so $y = -1, 1$.

Applications

71. The sides of a square are equal so the trinomial must be a perfect trinomial, $a^2 = (3x)^2$ so $a = 3x$, $b^2 = 7^2$ so

$b = 7$, then $2ab = 2 \cdot 3x \cdot 7 = 42x$ the middle term, so $(3x + 7)^2$, so each side is $3x + 7$. See Figure 71.

Figure 71   Figure 72

72. $x^2 + 6x + 5 = 0 \Rightarrow (x + 5)(x + 1) = 0$ so the sides are $(x + 5)$ by $(x + 1)$. See Figure 72.

73. A cube has six sides, so $(6x^2 + 12x + 6) \div 6 = x^2 + 2x + 1$, the area of each side $\Rightarrow (x + 1)(x + 1) \Rightarrow$

each side is $(x + 1)$.

74. $x^2 + 3x + x + 3 = x^2 + 4x + 3 \Rightarrow (x + 3)(x + 1)$

75. $2x^2 + 3x + 12x + 18 = 2x^2 + 15x + 18 \Rightarrow (2x + 3)(x + 6)$

76. (area) $\pi r^2 = 2r\pi$ (circumference) $\Rightarrow r^2 = 2r \Rightarrow r = 2$

77. $x(x + 7) = 120 \Rightarrow x^2 + 7x - 120 = 0 \Rightarrow (x + 15)(x - 8) = 0$, $x = -15$ (not possible), 8, so rectangle

8×15.

78. $100 = -16t^2 + 80t + 4 \Rightarrow 16t^2 - 80t + 96 = 0 \Rightarrow 16(t^2 - 5t + 6) = 0 \Rightarrow 16(t - 2)(t - 3) = 0$, so

$x = 2, 3$ so at 2 seconds and 3 seconds.

79. (a) $D = \dfrac{1}{9}(45)^2 + \dfrac{11}{3}(45) \Rightarrow D = \dfrac{1}{9}(2025) + \dfrac{11}{3}(45) \Rightarrow D = 225 + 165 \Rightarrow D = 390$ feet.

(b) $80 = \dfrac{1}{9}x^2 + \dfrac{11}{3}x \Rightarrow \dfrac{1}{9}x^2 + \dfrac{11}{3}x - 80 = 0 \Rightarrow$ multiply by 9 $\Rightarrow x^2 + 33x - 720 = 0 \Rightarrow$

$(x + 48)(x - 15) = 0$, so $D = -48$ (not possible) or 15mph.

(c) See Figure 79. 15mph, yes.

80. (a) $R = 100(200 - 100) \Rightarrow R = 100(100) \Rightarrow R = \$10,000$

(b) $7500 = p(200 - p) \Rightarrow 7500 = 200p - p^2 \Rightarrow p^2 - 200p + 7500 = 0 \Rightarrow (p - 50)(p - 150) = 0 \Rightarrow$

$p = 50, 150 \Rightarrow \$50$ or $\$150$.

(c) See Figure 80. $50 or $150, yes.

Figure 79   Figure 80

81. (a) $x = 20$ for 1970, $N = 0.68(20)^2 + 3.8(20) + 24 \Rightarrow N = 272 + 76 + 24 \Rightarrow N = 372$ million.

(b) See Figure 81. 1975.

        Figure 81

82. $x(x + 30) = 4000 \Rightarrow x^2 + 30x - 4000 = 0 \Rightarrow (x + 80)(x - 50) = 0$, so $x = -80$ (not possible) or 50, so 50 $\times$ 80 pixels.

83. (a) Bottom $(50 - 2x)(40 - 2x) = 2000 - 80x - 100x + 4x^2 = 2000 - 180 + 4x^2$;

    2 sides $x(50 - 2x) = 50x - 2x^2(2) = 100x - 4x^2$; 2 sides $x(40 - 2x) = 40x - 2x^2(2) = 80x - 4x^2$.

    Add all sides $2000 - 180x + 4x^2 + 100x - 4x^2 + 80x - 4x^2 = 2000 - 4x^2$.

(b) $1900 = 2000 - 4x^2 \Rightarrow -100 = -4x^2 \Rightarrow 25 = x^2 \Rightarrow x = 5$ inches.

Chapter 6 Test

1. $4x^2y = 2 \cdot 2 \cdot x \cdot x \cdot y$; $20xy^2 = 2 \cdot 2 \cdot 5 \cdot x \cdot y \cdot y$; $12xy = 2 \cdot 2 \cdot 3 \cdot x \cdot y \Rightarrow$
    GCF $= 2 \cdot 2 \cdot x \cdot y = 4xy \Rightarrow 4x^2y - 20xy^2 + 12xy = 4xy(x - 5y + 3)$

2. $9a^3b^2 = 3 \cdot 3 \cdot a \cdot a \cdot a \cdot b \cdot b$; $3a^2b^2 = 3 \cdot a \cdot a \cdot b \cdot b \Rightarrow$ GCF $= 3 \cdot a \cdot a \cdot b \cdot b = 3a^2b^2 \Rightarrow$
    $9a^3b^2 + 3a^2b^2 = 3a^2b^2(3a + 1)$

3. $ay + by + az + bx \Rightarrow y(a + b) + z(a + b) \Rightarrow (y + z)(a + b)$

4. $3x^3 + x^2 - 15x - 5 \Rightarrow x^2(3x + 1) - 5(3x + 1) \Rightarrow (x^2 - 5)(3x + 1)$

5. $y^2 + 4y - 12 = (y + 6)(y - 2)$

6. $4x^2 + 20x + 25 = (2x + 5)(2x + 5) = (2x + 5)^2$

7. $4z^2 - 19z + 12 = (4z - 3)(z - 4)$

8. $21 - 17t + 2t^2 = 2t^2 - 17t + 21 = (2t - 3)(t - 7)$

9. $x^2 - 16 = 0 \Rightarrow (x + 4)(x - 4) = 0$, then $x + 4 = 0$ or $x - 4 = 0$, so $x = -4, 4$.

10. $y^2 = y + 20 \Rightarrow y^2 - y - 20 = 0 \Rightarrow (y - 5)(y + 4) = 0$, then $y - 5 = 0$ or $y + 4 = 0$, so $y = -4, 5$.

11. $9z^2 + 16 = 24z \Rightarrow 9z^2 - 24z + 16 = 0$ is a perfect trinomial $a^2 = (3z)^2$ so $a = 3z$, $b^2 = \pm 4^2$ so $b = \pm 4$,
    using $b = -4$, $2ab = 2 \cdot 3z \cdot -4 = -24z$ the middle term $\Rightarrow (3z - 4)^2$, then $3z - 4 = 0 \Rightarrow$
    $3z = 4 \Rightarrow z = \dfrac{4}{3}$.

12. $x(x - 5) = 66 \Rightarrow x^2 - 5x - 66 = 0 \Rightarrow (x - 11)(x + 6) = 0$, then $x - 11 = 0$ or $x + 6 = 0$, so $x = -6, 11$

13. $6x^3 + 3x^2 - 3x \Rightarrow 3x(2x^2 + x - 1) \Rightarrow 3x(2x - 1)(x + 1)$

14. $2z^4 - 12z^2 - 54 \Rightarrow 2(z^4 - 6z - 27) \Rightarrow 2(z^2 - 9)(z^2 + 3) \Rightarrow 2(z + 3)(z - 3)(z^2 + 3)$

15. $y^3 = 9y \Rightarrow y^3 - 9y = 0 \Rightarrow y(y^2 - 9) = 0 \Rightarrow y(y + 3)(y - 3) = 0$, then $y = 0$ or $y + 3 = 0$ or $y - 3 = 0$,
    so $y = -3, 0, 3$.

16. $x^4 - 5x^2 + 4 = 0 \Rightarrow (x^2 - 4)(x^2 - 1) = 0 \Rightarrow (x + 2)(x - 2)(x + 1)(x - 1) = 0$, then $x + 2 = 0$ or

   $x - 2 = 0$ or $x + 1 = 0$ or $x - 1 = 0$, so $x = -2, -1, 1, 2$.

17. In a square the sides must be equal so $9x^2 + 30x + 25$ must be a perfect trinomial $\Rightarrow a^2 = (3x)^2$ so $a = 3x$,

   $b^2 = 5^2$ so $b = 5$, $2ab = 2(3x)5 = 30x$ the middle term $\Rightarrow (3x + 5)^2 \Rightarrow$ each side is $3x + 5$.

18. $x^2 + 3x + 2x + 6 = x^2 + 5x + 6 = (x + 2)(x + 3)$

19. (a) $D = \dfrac{1}{11}(55)^2 = \dfrac{1}{11}(3025) = 275$ ft.

   (b) $99 = \dfrac{1}{11}x^2 \Rightarrow \dfrac{1}{11}x^2 - 99 = 0 \Rightarrow x^2 - 1089 = 0 \Rightarrow (x + 33)(x - 33) = 0$, then $x + 33 = 0$ or

      $x - 33 = 0$, so $x = -33$ (not possible) or 33, so 33 mph.

20. $36 = -16t^2 + 48t + 4 \Rightarrow 16t^2 - 48t + 32 = 0 \Rightarrow 16(t^2 - 3t + 2) = 0 \Rightarrow 16(t - 2)(t - 1) = 0$, then

   $t - 2 = 0$ or $t - 1 = 0$, so $t = 1, 2$ so 1 sec. or 2 sec.

Chapter 6 Extended and Discovery Exercises

1. $x^2 - 5 = (x + \sqrt{5})(x - \sqrt{5})$

2. $y^2 - 7 = (x + \sqrt{7})(x - \sqrt{7})$

3. $3z^2 - 25 = (\sqrt{3}z + 5)(\sqrt{3}z - 5)$

4. $7t^2 - 11 = (\sqrt{7}t + \sqrt{11})(\sqrt{7}t - \sqrt{11})$

5. $x - 4 = (\sqrt{x} + 2)(\sqrt{x} - 2)$

6. $x - 7 = (\sqrt{x} + \sqrt{7})(\sqrt{x} - \sqrt{7})$

7. $x^2 - 3 = 0 \Rightarrow (x + \sqrt{3})(x - \sqrt{3}) = 0$, then $x + \sqrt{3} = 0 \Rightarrow x = -\sqrt{3}$ or $x - \sqrt{3} = 0 \Rightarrow x = \sqrt{3}$,

   so $x = -\sqrt{3}, \sqrt{3}$.

8. $y^2 - 7 = 0 \Rightarrow (y + \sqrt{7})(y - \sqrt{7}) = 0$, then $y + \sqrt{7} = 0 \Rightarrow y = -\sqrt{7}$ or $y - \sqrt{7} = 0 \Rightarrow y = \sqrt{7}$,

   so $x = -\sqrt{7}, \sqrt{7}$.

9. $3x^2 - 25 = 0 \Rightarrow (\sqrt{3}x + 5)(\sqrt{3}x - 5) = 0$, then $\sqrt{3}x + 5 = 0 \Rightarrow \sqrt{3}x = -5 \Rightarrow x = \dfrac{-5}{\sqrt{3}}$ or

   $\sqrt{3}x - 5 = 0 \Rightarrow \sqrt{3}x = 5 \Rightarrow x = \dfrac{5}{\sqrt{3}}$, so $x = \dfrac{-5}{\sqrt{3}}, \dfrac{5}{\sqrt{3}}$.

10. $3x^2 - 11 = 0 \Rightarrow (\sqrt{7}x + \sqrt{11})(\sqrt{7}x - \sqrt{11}) = 0$, then $\sqrt{7}x + \sqrt{11} = 0 \Rightarrow \sqrt{7}x = -\sqrt{11} \Rightarrow$

   $x = \dfrac{-\sqrt{11}}{\sqrt{7}}$ or $\sqrt{7}x - \sqrt{11} = 0 \Rightarrow \sqrt{7}x = \sqrt{11} \Rightarrow x = \dfrac{\sqrt{11}}{\sqrt{7}}$, so $x = \dfrac{-\sqrt{11}}{\sqrt{7}}, \dfrac{\sqrt{11}}{\sqrt{7}}$.

11. $x^4 - 9 = 0 \Rightarrow (x^2 + 3)(x^2 - 3) = 0 \Rightarrow (x^2 + 3)(x + \sqrt{3})(x - \sqrt{3}) = 0$, then $x^2 + 3 = 0 \Rightarrow x^2 = -3$,

   which has no real solutions, or $x + \sqrt{3} = 0 \Rightarrow x = -\sqrt{3}$ or $x - \sqrt{3} = 0 \Rightarrow x = \sqrt{3}$, so $x = -\sqrt{3}, \sqrt{3}$.

12. $x^4 - 25 = 0 \Rightarrow (x^2 + 5)(x^2 - 5) = 0 \Rightarrow (x^2 + 5)(x + \sqrt{5})(x - \sqrt{5}) = 0$, then $x^2 + 5 = 0 \Rightarrow x^2 = -5$,

   which has no real solutions, or $x + \sqrt{5} = 0 \Rightarrow x = -\sqrt{5}$ or $x - \sqrt{5} = 0 \Rightarrow x = \sqrt{5}$, so $x = -\sqrt{5}, \sqrt{5}$.

Chapters 1-6 Cumulative Review Exercises

1. $144 = 2 \times 2 \times 2 \times 2 \times 3 \times 3$

2. $-2(-2) + 3(4) = 4 + 12 = 16$

3. $2n + 5$

4. $-\dfrac{5}{8}$

5. $\dfrac{3}{5} \cdot \dfrac{15}{21} = \dfrac{45}{105} = \dfrac{3}{7}$

6. $\dfrac{1}{2} \div \dfrac{5}{4} = \dfrac{1}{2} \cdot \dfrac{4}{5} = \dfrac{4}{10} = \dfrac{2}{5}$

7. $\dfrac{5}{8} + \dfrac{1}{8} = \dfrac{6}{8} = \dfrac{3}{4}$

8. $\dfrac{4}{5} - \dfrac{1}{10} = \dfrac{8}{10} - \dfrac{1}{10} = \dfrac{7}{10}$

9. $26 - 3 \cdot 6 \div 2 = 26 - 18 \div 2 = 26 - 9 = 17$

10. $-2^2 + \dfrac{3 + 2}{8 + 2} = -(2^2) + \dfrac{5}{10} = -4 + \dfrac{1}{2} = -\dfrac{8}{2} + \dfrac{1}{2} = -\dfrac{7}{2}$

11.

12. $\dfrac{4x}{9y} \div \dfrac{6x}{3y} = \dfrac{4x}{9y} \cdot \dfrac{3y}{6x} = \dfrac{12xy}{54xy} = \dfrac{2}{9}$

13. $-2 + 7x + 4 - 5x = 2x + 2$

14. $-4(4 - y) + (5 - 3y) = -16 + 4y + 5 - 3y = y - 11$

15. $4t - 7 = 25 \Rightarrow 4t = 32 \Rightarrow t = \dfrac{32}{4}$, so $t = 8$.

16. See Figure 16. $2x + 3 = 5$ when $x = 1$.

x	-2	-1	0	1	2
$2x + 3$	-1	1	3	5	7

Figure 16

17. $3n - 5 = n - 7$; $3n - 5 = n - 7 \Rightarrow 3n - n = -7 + 5 \Rightarrow 2n = -2 \Rightarrow n = -1$

18. $\dfrac{5.7}{100} = \dfrac{57}{1000}$; 0.057

19. $0.123 = 12.3\%$

20. For $r = 60$, $d = 150$, $d = rt \Rightarrow 150 = 60t \Rightarrow \dfrac{150}{60} = t \Rightarrow t = \dfrac{5}{2} \Rightarrow t = 2.5$ hrs.

21. $d = 5 \Rightarrow r = \dfrac{5}{2}$, $A = \pi r^2 \Rightarrow A = \pi\left(\dfrac{5}{2}\right)^2 \Rightarrow A = \pi\dfrac{25}{4}$, so $A = \dfrac{25}{4}\pi$ ft^2

22. $P = 2W + 2L \Rightarrow P - 2L = 2W \Rightarrow \dfrac{P - 2L}{2} = W \Rightarrow W = \dfrac{P - 2L}{2}$

23.

24. $5 - 3z < -1 \Rightarrow -3z < -6 \Rightarrow z > 2 \Rightarrow \{z \,|\, z > 2\}$

25. See Figure 25.

26. See Figure 26.

x-intercept: $0 = 3x - 2 \Rightarrow 2 = 3x \Rightarrow x = \dfrac{2}{3}$; y-intercept: $y = 3(0) - 2 \Rightarrow y = 0 - 2 \Rightarrow y = -2$

Figure 25

Figure 26

Figure 27

27. See Figure 27.

x-intercept: $2x - 3(0) = 6 \Rightarrow 2x = 6 \Rightarrow x = 3$; y-intercept: $2(0) - 3y = 6 \Rightarrow -3y = 6 \Rightarrow y = -2$.

28. See Figure 28. x-intercept: $x = 1$; y-intercept: None.

29. See Figure 29. x-intercept: None; y-intercept: $y = -2$.

Figure 28

Figure 29

Figure 31

30. x-intercept: $x = -1 \Rightarrow (-1, 0)$; y-intercept: $y = -2 \Rightarrow (0, -2)$; $m = \dfrac{-2 - 0}{0 - (-1)} = \dfrac{-2}{1} = -2$;

$y = mx + b \Rightarrow y = -2x - 2$.

31. See Figure 31. Using $y = mx + b \Rightarrow y = 3x + 5$.

32. Using $(-2, -5)$ and $(-1, -3)$, $m = \dfrac{-5 - (-3)}{-2 - (-1)} = \dfrac{-2}{-1} = 2$, the y-intercept is $(0, -1)$ or $b = -1$, so $y = 2x - 1$.

33. Parallel lines have equal slopes $\Rightarrow m = -\dfrac{2}{3}$, now using $(2, -1)$ and $y - y_1 = m(x - x_1) \Rightarrow$

$y - (-1) = -\dfrac{2}{3}(x - 2) \Rightarrow y + 1 = -\dfrac{2}{3}x + \dfrac{4}{3} \Rightarrow y = -\dfrac{2}{3}x + \dfrac{1}{3}$.

34. $2x - 3y = -6 \Rightarrow -2y = -2x - 6 \Rightarrow y = \dfrac{2}{3}x + 2$, since perpendicular lines have a negative reciprocal

slope, $m = -\dfrac{3}{2}$, now using $(1, 2)$ and $y - y_1 = m(x - x_1) \Rightarrow y - 2 = -\dfrac{3}{2}(x - 1) \Rightarrow$

$y - 2 = -\dfrac{3}{2}x + \dfrac{3}{2} \Rightarrow y = -\dfrac{3}{2}x + \dfrac{7}{2}$.

35. $m = \dfrac{5 - 1}{1 - (-2)} = \dfrac{4}{3}$, using $(-2, 1)$ and $y - y_1 = m(x - x_1) \Rightarrow y - 1 = \dfrac{4}{3}[x - (-2)] \Rightarrow$

    $y - 1 = \dfrac{4}{3}x + \dfrac{8}{3} \Rightarrow y = \dfrac{4}{3}x + \dfrac{11}{3}.$

36. $N = 200x + 2000$

37. Using $(2, -4)$ for $4x + y = 2 \Rightarrow 4(2) + (-4) = 2 \Rightarrow 8 - 4 = 2$, No;

    Using $(2, -4)$ for $x - 4y = 9 \Rightarrow 2 - 4(-4) = 9 \Rightarrow 2 + 16 = 9$, No;

    Using $(1, -2)$ for $4x + y = 2 \Rightarrow 4(1) + (-2) = 2 \Rightarrow 4 - 2 = 2$, Yes;

    Using $(1, -2)$ for $x - 4y = 9 \Rightarrow 1 - 4(-2) = 9 \Rightarrow 1 + 8 = 9$, Yes; $(1, -2)$ is true for both equations,

    therefore a solution to the system of equations.

38. $(1, 2)$; $x + y = 3 \Rightarrow 1 + 2 = 3$, Yes; $-2x + y = 0 \Rightarrow -2(1) + 2 = 0 \Rightarrow -2 + 2 = 0$, Yes

39. When $x = 1$ both solutions are 2, therefore $(1, 2)$ is a solution to both equations.

40. Using substitution $y = -1$ into $2x + y = 1 \Rightarrow 2x + (-1) = 1 \Rightarrow 2x = 2 \Rightarrow x = 1 \Rightarrow (1, -1).$

41. Using substitution $5x + y = -5 \Rightarrow y = -5x - 5$, substituting into $-x + 2y = 12 \Rightarrow$

    $-x + 2(-5x - 5) = 12 \Rightarrow -x - 10x - 10 = 12 \Rightarrow -11x = 22 \Rightarrow x = -2$ and $y = -5(-2) - 5 \Rightarrow$

    $y = 10 - 5 \Rightarrow y = 5 \Rightarrow (-2, 5).$

42. Using substitution $2r + t = -4 \Rightarrow t = -2r - 4$, substituting into $-3r - t = 2 \Rightarrow$

    $-3r - (-2r - 4) = 2 \Rightarrow -r + 4 = 2 \Rightarrow -r = -2 \Rightarrow r = 2$ and $t = -2(2) - 4 \Rightarrow$

    $t = -4 - 4 \Rightarrow t = -8 \Rightarrow (2, -8).$

43. (a) One solution, the intersection of the lines.

    (b) Consistent, independent.

44. (a) Zero solutions, no intersection of the lines.

    (b) Inconsistent

45. $2x - y = 5$
      $\underline{-2x + y = -5}$
      $\quad\quad 0 = 0$, if $0 = 0$ then infinitely many solutions.

46. $(4x - 6y = 12)3 = \quad 12x - 18y = 36$
      $\underline{(-6x + 9y = 18)2 = -12x + 18y = 36}$
      $\quad\quad\quad\quad\quad 0 = 72$, if $0 = 72$ then no solutions.

47. $-2x + y = 0$
      $\underline{\; - x - y = -3}$
      $\quad\quad -3x = -3 \Rightarrow x = 1$, then $1 + y = 3 \Rightarrow y = 2 \Rightarrow (1, 2).$

48. See Figure 48. $(0, 0)$; answers may vary.

49. See Figure 49. $x \le 2$

50. See Figure 50. $2x + 3y \geq 6 \Rightarrow 3y \geq -2x + 6 \Rightarrow y \geq -\dfrac{2}{3}x + 2$

Figure 48

Figure 49

Figure 50

51. See Figure 51.

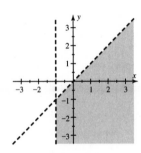

Figure 51

52. See figure 52. $2x - y \leq 4 \Rightarrow -y \leq -2x + 4 \Rightarrow y \geq 2x - 4$ and $x + 2y \geq 2 \Rightarrow 2y \geq -x + 2 \Rightarrow$

$y \geq -\dfrac{1}{2}x + 1.$

Figure 52

53. $(5x^2 - 3) + (-x^2 + 4) \Rightarrow 5x^2 - 3 - x^2 + 4 \Rightarrow 4x^2 + 1$

54. $(2xy + x^2) - (2x^2 - 5xy) \Rightarrow 2xy + x^2 - 2x^2 + 5xy \Rightarrow -x^2 + 7xy$

55. $-2^4 = -(2^4) = -16$

56. $(xy)^0 = 1$

57. $3z^2 \cdot 5z^6 = 3 \cdot 5 \cdot z^2 \cdot z^6 = 15z^8$

58. $(a^2b^4)(ab^2) = a^2 \cdot a \cdot b^4 \cdot b^2 = a^3b^6$

59. $(ab)^3 = a^3b^3$

60. $(xy)^4(x^3y^{-4}) = x^4 \cdot y^4 \cdot x^6 \cdot y^{-8} = x^{10}y^{-4} = \dfrac{x^{10}}{y^4}$

61. $7x^3(-2x^2 + 3x) = -14x^5 + 21x^4$

62. $(a - b)(a^2 + ab + b^2) = a^3 + a^2b + ab^2 - a^2b - ab^2 - b^3 = a^3 - b^3$

63. By FOIL, $(7x - 2)(3x + 5) = 21x^2 + 35x - 6x - 10 = 21x^2 + 29x - 10$.

64. By FOIL, $(2y^2 - 3)(5y^2 + 2) = 10y^4 + 4y^2 - 15y^2 - 6 = 10y^4 - 11y^2 - 6$.

65. By FOIL, $(2rt + 3)(2rt - 3) = 4r^2t^2 - 6rt + 6rt - 9 = 4r^2t^2 - 9$.

66. By FOIL, $(2t + 5)^2 = (2t + 5)(2t + 5) = 4t^2 + 10t + 10t + 25 = 4t^2 + 20t + 25$.

67. By FOIL, $(x - 7)^2 = (x - 7)(x - 7) = x^2 - 7x - 7x + 49 = x^2 - 14x + 49$.

68. By FOIL, $(x^2 - y^2)^2 = (x^2 - y^2)(x^2 - y^2) = x^4 - x^2y^2 - x^2y^2 + y^4 = x^4 - 2x^2y^2 + y^4$.

69. $2^{-4} \cdot 2^5 = 2^1 = 2$

70. $\dfrac{1}{3^{-2}} = \dfrac{3^2}{1} = 9$

71. $a^{-4} \cdot a^2 = a^{-2} = \dfrac{1}{a^2}$

72. $(2t^3)^{-2} = 2^{-2} \cdot t^{-6} = \dfrac{1}{2^2} \cdot \dfrac{1}{t^6} = \dfrac{1}{4t^6}$

73. $(xy)^{-3}(x^{-1}y^2)^{-1} = x^{-3}y^{-3} \cdot x^1 \cdot y^{-2} = x^{-2} \cdot y^{-5} = \dfrac{1}{x^2y^5}$

74. $\dfrac{4x^2}{2x^4} = \dfrac{4}{2} \cdot \dfrac{x^2}{x^4} = \dfrac{2}{1} \cdot \dfrac{1}{x^2} = \dfrac{2}{x^2}$

75. $\left(\dfrac{2x}{y^{-2}}\right)^5 = \dfrac{2^5x^5}{y^{-10}} = \dfrac{32x^5}{y^{-10}} = 32x^5y^{10}$

76. $8.3 \times 10^4 = 83{,}000$

77. $6.23 \times 10^{-3} = 0.00623$

78. $543{,}000 = 5.43 \times 10^5$

79. $0.00123 = 1.23 \times 10^{-3}$

80. $\dfrac{6x^3 + 12x^2}{3x} = \dfrac{6x^3}{3x} + \dfrac{12x^2}{3x} = 2x^2 + 4x$

81.

$$
\begin{array}{r}
2x + 1 + \frac{4}{x-1} \\
x - 1 \overline{\smash{\big)}\ 2x^2 - x + 3} \\
\underline{2x^2 - 2x} \\
x + 3 \\
\underline{x - 1} \\
4
\end{array}
$$

82.
$$\begin{array}{r} 3x + \frac{-4x + 1}{x^2 + 1} \\ x^2 + 1\overline{)3x^3 - x + 1} \\ \underline{3x^3 + 3x} \\ -4x + 1 \end{array}$$

83. $20z^3 = 2 \cdot 2 \cdot 5 \cdot z \cdot z \cdot z$ and $15z^2 = 3 \cdot 5 \cdot z \cdot z \Rightarrow$ GCF $= 5 \cdot z \cdot z = 5z^2$; $20z^3 - 15z^2 = 5z^2(4z - 3)$

84. $12x^2y = 2 \cdot 2 \cdot 3 \cdot x \cdot x \cdot y$ and $15xy^2 = 3 \cdot 5 \cdot x \cdot y \cdot y \Rightarrow$ GCF $= 3 \cdot x \cdot y = 3xy$;

$12x^2y + 15xy^2 = 3xy(4x + 5y)$

85. $2y^2(x + 2) - 5(x + 2) = (2y^2 - 5)(x + 2)$

86. $t^3 + 6t^2 + t + 6 = (t^3 + 6t^2) + (t + 6) = t^2(t + 6) + (t + 6) = (t^2 + 1)(t + 6)$

87. FOIL, $x^2 + 3x - 28 = (x - 4)(x + 7)$

88. FOIL, $6y^2 + y - 12 = (2y + 3)(3y - 4)$

89. FOIL, $6 + 13x - 5x^2 = (3 - x)(2 + 5x)$

90. Difference of squares, $9z^2 - 4 = (3z + 2)(3z - 2)$

91. Difference of squares, $25x^2 - 4y^2 = (5x + 2y)(5x - 2y)$

92. FOIL, $t^2 + 16t + 64 = (t + 8)(t + 8) = (t + 8)^2$

93. FOIL, $64x^2 - 16x + 1 = (8x - 1)(8x - 1) = (8x - 1)^2$

94. Difference of cubes, $27t^3 - 8 = (3t - 2)(9t^2 + 6t + 4)$

95. $-4x^2 + 4x + 24 = -4(x^2 - x - 6) \Rightarrow$ FOIL, $-4(x - 3)(x + 2)$

96. $x^3 - 16x = x(x^2 - 16) \Rightarrow$ Difference of squares, $x(x - 4)(x + 4)$

97. $x^3 + 2x^2 - 99x = x(x^2 + 2x - 99) \Rightarrow$ FOIL, $x(x + 11)(x - 9)$

98. FOIL, $x^4 - 12x^2 + 27 = (x^2 - 3)(x^2 - 9) = (x^2 - 3)(x + 3)(x - 3)$

99. FOIL, $a^2 + 6ab + 9b^2 = (a + 3b)(a + 3b) = (a + 3b)^2$

100. $x^3y - x^2y^2 = x^2y(x - y)$

101. $(2x - 7)(x + 5) = 0 \Rightarrow 2x - 7 = 0 \Rightarrow 2x = 7 \Rightarrow x = \frac{7}{2}$ or $x + 5 = 0 \Rightarrow x = -5$, so $x = -5, \frac{7}{2}$

102. $2x^2 - 4x = 0 \Rightarrow 2x(x - 2) = 0$, then $2x = 0 \Rightarrow x = 0$ or $x - 2 = 0 \Rightarrow x = 2$, so $x = 0, 2$

103. $y^2 + 5y - 14 = 0 \Rightarrow (y + 7)(y - 2) = 0$, then $y + 7 = 0 \Rightarrow y = -7$ or $y - 2 = 0 \Rightarrow y = 2$,

so $y = -7, 2$.

104. $y^4 = 25y^2 \Rightarrow y^4 - 25y^2 = 0 \Rightarrow y^2(y^2 - 25) = 0 \Rightarrow y^2(y + 5)(y - 5) = 0$, then $y^2 = 0 \Rightarrow y = 0$ or

$y + 5 = 0 \Rightarrow y = -5$ or $y - 5 = 0 \Rightarrow y = 5$, so $y = -5, 0, 5$.

105. $8z^2 + 8z - 16 = 0 \Rightarrow 8(z^2 + z - 2) = 0 \Rightarrow 8(z + 2)(z - 1) = 0$, then $z + 2 = 0 \Rightarrow z = -2$ or

$z - 1 = 0 \Rightarrow z = 1$, so $z = -2, 1$.

106. $4z^3 = 49z \Rightarrow 4z^3 - 49z = 0 \Rightarrow z(4z^2 - 49) = 0 \Rightarrow z(2z + 7)(2z - 7) = 0$, then $z = 0$ or

$2z + 7 = 0 \Rightarrow 2z = -7 \Rightarrow z = \dfrac{-7}{2}$ or $2z - 7 = 0 \Rightarrow 2z = 7 \Rightarrow z = \dfrac{7}{2}$, so $z = \dfrac{-7}{2}, 0, \dfrac{7}{2}$.

107. $x^4 - 18x^2 + 81 = 0 \Rightarrow (x^2 - 9)(x^2 - 9) = 0 \Rightarrow (x + 3)(x - 3)(x + 3)(x - 3) = 0$, then

$x + 3 = 0 \Rightarrow x = -3$ or $x - 3 = 0 \Rightarrow x = 3$, so $x = -3, 3$.

Applications

108. (a) $10x + 8x = 18x$

(b) $18x = 900 \Rightarrow x = 50$ min.

109. $1\dfrac{3}{4} + 2\dfrac{1}{2} + 2\dfrac{2}{3} = 1\dfrac{9}{12} + 2\dfrac{6}{12} + 2\dfrac{8}{12} = 5\dfrac{23}{12} = 6\dfrac{11}{12}$ miles.

110. $0.07(C) = 1470 \Rightarrow C = \$21,000$

111. Let x represent the minutes cross country skiing and $60 - x$ represent minutes running.

$12(x) + 9(60 - x) = 615 \Rightarrow 12x + 540 - 9x = 615 \Rightarrow 3x = 75 \Rightarrow x = 25$, so 25 minutes skiing and

35 minutes running.

112. (a) $m = \dfrac{y_2 - y_1}{x_2 - x_1}$, so $m = \dfrac{858 - 376}{2000 - 1980} = \dfrac{482}{20} = 24.1$

(b) Participating in Head Start increased by 24.1 thousand children per year on average.

(c) $24.1(10) + 858 = 241 + 858 = 1099$ thousand or 1.099 million.

113. (a) $C = 0.25x + 20$

(b) $100 = 0.25x + 20 \Rightarrow 80 = 0.25x \Rightarrow x = 320$ or 320 miles.

114. (a) $x =$ one angle $\Rightarrow x + x + y = 180 \Rightarrow 2x + y = 180$ and $2x = y + 20 \Rightarrow 2x - y = 20$

(b) Using elimination,

$2x + y = 180$
$\underline{2x - y = 20}$
$\quad\quad 4x = 200 \Rightarrow x = 50 \Rightarrow 50, 50, 80$ degrees.

115. See Figure 115.

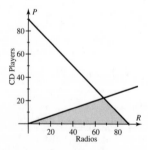

Figure 115

116. (a) $G = -0.036(5)^2 + 0.76(5) + 18.7 = -0.036(25) + 3.80 + 18.7 = -0.900 + 3.80 + 18.7 = 21.6 \Rightarrow$

    $G = 21.6$ trillion ft^3 was the natural gas consumption in 1995.

    (b) $22.7 = -0.036x^2 + 0.76x + 18.7 \Rightarrow 0 = -0.036x^2 + 0.76x + 4 \Rightarrow 0 = -36x^2 + 760x + 4000 \Rightarrow$

    $0 = -4(9x^2 - 190x + 1000)$ (factor by grouping)

    $\Rightarrow m \cdot n = 9000, m + n = -190 \Rightarrow m = -90$ and $n = -100 \Rightarrow 9x^2 - 90x - 100x + 1000 = 0 \Rightarrow$

    $9x(x - 10) - 100(x - 10) = 0 \Rightarrow (9x - 100)(x - 10) = 0$, then

    $9x - 100 = 0 \Rightarrow 9x = 100 \Rightarrow x = \dfrac{100}{9} \Rightarrow x = 11\dfrac{1}{9}$ or $x - 10 = 0 \Rightarrow x = 10$, so $x = 10, 11\dfrac{1}{9}$

    Thus, $x = 10 \Rightarrow 2000$ and $x = 11\dfrac{1}{9} \Rightarrow > 2001$, therefore 2000.

117. $3(3x)(2y) = 18xy; \ 18(2)(3) = 108$ yds^2.

118. $V = s^3 \Rightarrow V = (2xy^2)^3 \Rightarrow V = 2^3 \cdot x^3 \cdot (y^2)^3 \Rightarrow V = 8x^3y^6$

119. (a) $(x + 2)(x + 2) = x^2 + 4x + 4$

    (b) $2(x) + x \cdot x + 2 \cdot 2 + 2 \cdot x = 2x + x^2 + 4 + 2x = x^2 + 4x + 4$

120. $x^2 + 12x + 36 = (x + 6)(x + 6) = (x + 6)^2 \Rightarrow$ each side is $x + 6$

121. (a) $0 = 64t - 16t^2 \Rightarrow -16t(t - 4) = 0$, then $-16t = 0 \Rightarrow t = 0$ (when hit) or $t - 4 = 0 \Rightarrow t = 4$ sec.

    (b) $48 = 64t - 16t^2 \Rightarrow 16t^2 - 64t + 48 = 0 \Rightarrow 16(t^2 - 4t + 3) = 0 \Rightarrow 16(t - 3)(t - 1) = 0$, then

    $t - 3 = 0 \Rightarrow t = 3$ or $t - 1 = 0 \Rightarrow t = 1$, so at 1 and 3 sec.

Critical Thinking Solutions for Chapter 6

Section 6.2

- A cube has 6 sides so $(6x^2 + 24x + 24) \div 6 = x^2 + 4x + 4$, the area of each side. Factoring gives

  $(x + 2)(x + 2)$, so each side is $(x + 2)$.

Section 6.3

- $x^2 + x + 5$, No factors of 5 add up to equal 1, can not factor.

  $x^2 - 2x + 6$, No factors of 6 add up to equal -2, can not factor.

  $2x^2 + 3x + 2$, Using grouping, $m \cdot n = 4$ and $m + n = 3$, No factors of 4 add up to equal 3, can not factor.

  Conjecture: Not all polynomials are factorable.

Section 6.4

- Yes, $x^2 - 5 = (x - \sqrt{5})(x + \sqrt{5})$, because $a^2 = x^2$, so $a = x$ and $b^2 = 5$, so $b = \sqrt{5}$.

Section 6.5

- No, the zero-product property does not work for 1. We solve instead for zero, $x(2x + 1) = 1 \Rightarrow$

  $2x^2 + x - 1 = 0 \Rightarrow (2x - 1)(x + 1) = 0;\ 2x - 1 = 0 \Rightarrow x = \dfrac{1}{2}$ and $x + 1 = 0 \Rightarrow x = -1.$

  The solutions are $\dfrac{1}{2}$ and $-1.$

Section 6.6

- The area of the metal square is 100 in^2 and the area of the four cutout squares is $4x^2$, so the surface area is

  $100 - 4x^2$. The sum of the areas of the four sides and the bottom is $4x(10 - 2x) + (10 - 2x)^2 = 100 - 4x^2.$

Chapter 7: Rational Expressions

7.1: Introduction to Rational Expressions

Concepts

1. $\dfrac{P}{Q}$; polynomials

3. the denominator is zero

5. $\dfrac{a}{b}$

7. $-1, \dfrac{x-a}{a-x} = \dfrac{1(x-a)}{a-x} = \dfrac{-1(-x+a)}{a-x} = \dfrac{-1(a-x)}{a-x} = -1$

Evaluating Rational Expressions

9. $x = -7, \dfrac{3}{x} = \dfrac{3}{-7} = -\dfrac{3}{7}$

11. $x = -4, -\dfrac{x}{x-5} = -\dfrac{-4}{-4-5} = \dfrac{-(-4)}{-9} = \dfrac{4}{-9} = -\dfrac{4}{9}$

13. $y = -2, \dfrac{y+1}{y^2} = \dfrac{-2+1}{(-2)^2} = \dfrac{-1}{4} = -\dfrac{1}{4}$

15. $z = -2, \dfrac{7z}{z^2-4} = \dfrac{7(-2)-1}{(-2)^2-4} = \dfrac{-14}{4-4} = \dfrac{-14}{0} = $ undefined

17. $t = -2, \dfrac{5}{3t+6} = \dfrac{5}{3(-2)+6} = \dfrac{5}{-6+6} = \dfrac{5}{0} = $ undefined

19. $x = 0, -\dfrac{6-x}{x-6} = -\dfrac{6-0}{0-6} = -\dfrac{6}{-6} = \dfrac{-(6)}{-6} = \dfrac{-6}{-6} = 1$

21. $x = -2, \dfrac{x}{x+1} = \dfrac{-2}{-2+1} = \dfrac{-2}{-1} = 2;\ x = -1, \dfrac{x}{x+1} = \dfrac{-1}{-1+1} = \dfrac{-1}{0} = $ undefined;

$x = 0, \dfrac{x}{x+1} = \dfrac{0}{0+1} = \dfrac{0}{1} = 0;\ x = 1, \dfrac{x}{x+1} = \dfrac{1}{1+1} = \dfrac{1}{2};\ x = 2, \dfrac{x}{x+1} = \dfrac{2}{2+1} = \dfrac{2}{3}.$ See Figure 21.

x	-2	-1	0	1	2
$\frac{x}{x+1}$	2	—	0	$\frac{1}{2}$	$\frac{2}{3}$

Figure 21

x	-2	-1	0	1	2
$\frac{3x}{2x^2+1}$	$-\frac{2}{3}$	-1	0	1	$\frac{2}{3}$

Figure 23

23. $x = -2, \dfrac{3x}{2x^2+1} = \dfrac{3(-2)}{2(-2)^2+1} = \dfrac{-6}{2(4)+1} = \dfrac{-6}{8+1} = \dfrac{-6}{9} = \dfrac{-2}{3} = -\dfrac{2}{3};$

$x = -1, \dfrac{3x}{2x^2+1} = \dfrac{3(-1)}{2(-1)^2+1} = \dfrac{-3}{2(1)+1} = \dfrac{-3}{2+1} = \dfrac{-3}{3} = -1;$

$x = 0, \dfrac{3x}{2x^2+1} = \dfrac{3(0)}{2(0)^2+1} = \dfrac{0}{2(0)+1} = \dfrac{0}{0+1} = \dfrac{0}{1} = 0;$

$x = 1, \dfrac{3x}{2x^2+1} = \dfrac{3(1)}{2(1)^2+1} = \dfrac{3}{2(1)+1} = \dfrac{3}{2+1} = \dfrac{3}{3} = 1;$

$x = 2, \dfrac{3x}{2x^2+1} = \dfrac{3(2)}{2(2)^2+1} = \dfrac{6}{2(4)+1} = \dfrac{6}{8+1} = \dfrac{6}{9} = \dfrac{2}{3}.$ See Figure 23.

25. A rational expression is undefined when the denominator = 0. $x = 0$

27. A rational expression is undefined when the denominator = 0. $z - 3 = 0 \Rightarrow z = 3$

29. A rational expression is undefined when the denominator = 0. $5y + 4 = 0 \Rightarrow 5y = -4 \Rightarrow y = \dfrac{-4}{5}$

31. A rational expression is undefined when the denominator = 0. $t^2 + 1 = 0 \Rightarrow t^2 = -1$ which is impossible, so none.

33. A rational expression is undefined when the denominator = 0. $x^2 - 25 = 0 \Rightarrow x^2 = 25 \Rightarrow x = -5, 5$

35. A rational expression is undefined when the denominator = 0. $x^2 + 5x + 6 = 0 \Rightarrow (x + 3)(x + 2) = 0 \Rightarrow$
    $x + 3 = 0 \Rightarrow x = -3$ or $x + 2 = 0 \Rightarrow x = -2$, so $x = -3, -2$

37. A rational expression is undefined when the denominator = 0. $2z^2 - 7z + 5 = 0 \Rightarrow (2z - 5)(z - 1) = 0 \Rightarrow$
    $2z - 5 = 0 \Rightarrow 2z = 5 \Rightarrow z = \dfrac{5}{2}$ or $z - 1 = 0 \Rightarrow z = 1$, so $z = 1, \dfrac{5}{2}$

Simplifying Rational Expressions

39. $\dfrac{12}{18} = \dfrac{2}{3} \cdot \dfrac{6}{6} = \dfrac{2}{3} \cdot 1 = \dfrac{2}{3}$

41. $\dfrac{24}{48} = \dfrac{1}{2} \cdot \dfrac{24}{24} = \dfrac{1}{2} \cdot 1 = \dfrac{1}{2}$

43. $-\dfrac{6}{15} = -\dfrac{2}{5} \cdot \dfrac{3}{3} = -\dfrac{2}{5} \cdot 1 = -\dfrac{2}{5}$

45. $-\dfrac{25}{75} = -\dfrac{1}{3} \cdot \dfrac{25}{25} = -\dfrac{1}{3} \cdot 1 = -\dfrac{1}{3}$

47. $\dfrac{5x^4}{10x^6} = \dfrac{1}{2}x^{4-6} = \dfrac{1}{2}x^{-2} = \dfrac{1}{2x^2}$

49. $\dfrac{8xy^3}{6x^2y^2} = \dfrac{4}{3}x^{1-2}y^{3-2} = \dfrac{4}{3}x^{-1}y = \dfrac{4y}{3x}$

51. $\dfrac{x + 4}{2x + 8} = \dfrac{x + 4}{2(x + 4)} = \dfrac{1}{2} \cdot \dfrac{x + 4}{x + 4} = \dfrac{1}{2} \cdot 1 = \dfrac{1}{2}$

53. $\dfrac{3z - 9}{5z - 15} = \dfrac{3(z - 3)}{5(z - 3)} = \dfrac{3}{5} \cdot \dfrac{z - 3}{z - 3} = \dfrac{3}{5} \cdot 1 = \dfrac{3}{5}$

55. $\dfrac{(x + 1)(x - 1)}{(x + 6)(x - 1)} = \dfrac{x + 1}{x + 6} \cdot \dfrac{x - 1}{x - 1} = \dfrac{x + 1}{x + 6} \cdot 1 = \dfrac{x + 1}{x + 6}$

57. $\dfrac{(5y + 3)(2y - 1)}{(2y - 1)(y + 2)} = \dfrac{(5y + 3)(2y - 1)}{(y + 2)(2y - 1)} = \dfrac{5y + 3}{y + 2} \cdot \dfrac{2y - 1}{2y - 1} = \dfrac{5y + 3}{y + 2} \cdot 1 = \dfrac{5y + 3}{y + 2}$

59. $\dfrac{x - 7}{7 - x} = \dfrac{x - 7}{-1(-7 + x)} = \dfrac{x - 7}{-1(x - 7)} = -1$

61. $\dfrac{a - b}{b - a} = \dfrac{a - b}{-1(-b + a)} = \dfrac{a - b}{-1(a - b)} = -1$

63. $\dfrac{(3x + 5)(x - 1)}{(3x - 5)(1 - x)} = \dfrac{3x + 5}{3x - 5} \cdot \dfrac{(x - 1)}{-1(-1 + x)} = \dfrac{3x + 5}{3x - 5} \cdot \dfrac{x - 1}{-1(x - 1)} = \dfrac{3x + 5}{3x - 5} \cdot -1 = -\dfrac{3x + 5}{3x - 5}$

65. $\dfrac{n^2 - n}{n^2 - 5n} = \dfrac{n(n-1)}{n(n-5)} = \dfrac{n}{n} \cdot \dfrac{n-1}{n-5} = 1 \cdot \dfrac{n-1}{n-5} = \dfrac{n-1}{n-5}$

67. $\dfrac{x^2 - 3x}{6x - 18} = \dfrac{x(x-3)}{6(x-3)} = \dfrac{x}{6} \cdot \dfrac{x-3}{x-3} = \dfrac{x}{6} \cdot 1 = \dfrac{x}{6}$

69. $\dfrac{z^2 - 3z + 2}{z^2 - 4z + 3} = \dfrac{(z-2)(z-1)}{(z-3)(z-1)} = \dfrac{z-2}{z-3} \cdot \dfrac{z-1}{z-1} = \dfrac{z-2}{z-3} \cdot 1 = \dfrac{z-2}{z-3}$

71. $\dfrac{2x^2 + 7x - 4}{6x^2 + x - 2} = \dfrac{(x+4)(2x-1)}{(3x+2)(2x-1)} = \dfrac{x+4}{3x+2} \cdot \dfrac{2x-1}{2x-1} = \dfrac{x+4}{3x+2} \cdot 1 = \dfrac{x+4}{3x+2}$

73. $\dfrac{x-3}{3x^2 - 11x + 6} = \dfrac{x-3}{(x-3)(3x-2)} = \dfrac{x-3}{x-3} \cdot \dfrac{1}{3x-2} = 1 \cdot \dfrac{1}{3x-2} = \dfrac{1}{3x-2}$

75. $-\dfrac{a-9}{9-a} = \dfrac{-(a-9)}{9-a} = \dfrac{-a+9}{9-a} = \dfrac{9-a}{9-a} = 1$

77. $\dfrac{-2x-1}{4x+2} = \dfrac{-2x-1}{2(2x+1)} = \dfrac{-1(2x+1)}{2(2x+1)} = -\dfrac{1}{2} \cdot \dfrac{2x+1}{2x+1} = -\dfrac{1}{2} \cdot 1 = -\dfrac{1}{2}$

Applications

79. (a) For $x = 3$, $T = \dfrac{1}{5-x} \Rightarrow T = \dfrac{1}{5-3} = \dfrac{1}{2}$; When traffic arrives at an average rate of 3 vehicles/min., the average wait is one-half minute.

(b) For $x = 2$, $T = \dfrac{1}{5-x} \Rightarrow T = \dfrac{1}{5-2} = \dfrac{1}{3}$;

For $x = 4$, $T = \dfrac{1}{5-x} \Rightarrow T = \dfrac{1}{5-4} = \dfrac{1}{1} = 1$;

For $x = 4.5$, $T = \dfrac{1}{5-x} \Rightarrow T = \dfrac{1}{5-4.5} = \dfrac{1}{0.5} = 2$;

For $x = 4.9$, $T = \dfrac{1}{5-x} \Rightarrow T = \dfrac{1}{5-4.9} = \dfrac{1}{0.1} = 10$;

For $x = 4.99$, $T = \dfrac{1}{5-x} \Rightarrow T = \dfrac{1}{5-4.99} = \dfrac{1}{0.01} = 100$; See Figure 79.

As x nears 5 vehicles/min., a small increase in x increases the wait dramatically.

x	2	4	4.5	4.9	4.99
T	$\frac{1}{3}$	1	2	10	100

Figure 79

81. $\dfrac{1}{2}$

83. (a) $\dfrac{3}{n}$

(b) $\dfrac{n-3}{n}$; $n = 100$, $\dfrac{n-3}{n} = \dfrac{100-3}{100} = \dfrac{97}{100}$; There is a 97% chance that a winning ball will not be drawn.

85. (a) $\dfrac{360}{60} = 6$ hours

(b) $\dfrac{m}{60}$

87. (a) $T = \dfrac{1}{5 - x}, 5 - x = 0 \Rightarrow -x = -5 \Rightarrow x = 5$

    (b) As the average arrival rate nears 5 cars/min., a small increase in x increases the waiting time dramatically.

7.2: Multiplication and Division of Rational Expressions

Concepts

1. $\dfrac{AC}{BD}$

3. $\dfrac{(x + 7)(x + 2)}{(x + 1)(x + 2)} = \dfrac{x + 7}{x + 1} \cdot \dfrac{x + 2}{x + 2} = \dfrac{x + 7}{x + 1} \cdot 1 = \dfrac{x + 7}{x + 1}$

5. No, it equals $1 + \dfrac{2}{x}$.

Review of Fractions

7. $\dfrac{1}{2} \cdot \dfrac{4}{5} = \dfrac{4}{10} = \dfrac{2}{5}$

9. $\dfrac{3}{7} \cdot 4 = \dfrac{3}{7} \cdot \dfrac{4}{1} = \dfrac{12}{7}$

11. $\dfrac{1}{3} \cdot \dfrac{2}{3} \cdot \dfrac{9}{11} = \dfrac{2}{9} \cdot \dfrac{9}{11} = \dfrac{18}{99} = \dfrac{2}{11}$

13. $\dfrac{2}{3} \div \dfrac{1}{6} = \dfrac{2}{3} \cdot \dfrac{6}{1} = \dfrac{12}{3} = 4$

15. $\dfrac{8}{9} \div \dfrac{5}{3} = \dfrac{8}{9} \cdot \dfrac{3}{5} = \dfrac{24}{45} = \dfrac{8}{15}$

17. $8 \div \dfrac{4}{5} = \dfrac{8}{1} \cdot \dfrac{5}{4} = \dfrac{40}{4} = 10$

Multiplying Rational Expressions

19. $\dfrac{x + 5}{x + 5} = 1$

21. $\dfrac{(z + 1)(z + 2)}{(z + 4)(z + 2)} = \dfrac{z + 1}{z + 4} \cdot \dfrac{z + 2}{z + 2} = \dfrac{z + 1}{z + 4} \cdot 1 = \dfrac{z + 1}{z + 4}$

23. $\dfrac{8y(y + 7)}{12y(y + 7)} = \dfrac{8}{12} \cdot \dfrac{y}{y} \cdot \dfrac{y + 7}{y + 7} = \dfrac{8}{12} \cdot 1 \cdot 1 = \dfrac{8}{12} = \dfrac{2}{3}$

25. $\dfrac{x(x + 2)(x + 3)}{x(x - 2)(x + 3)} = \dfrac{x}{x} \cdot \dfrac{x + 2}{x - 2} \cdot \dfrac{y + 3}{y + 3} = 1 \cdot \dfrac{x + 2}{x - 2} \cdot 1 = \dfrac{x + 2}{x - 2}$

27. $\dfrac{8}{x} \cdot \dfrac{x + 1}{x} = \dfrac{8(x + 1)}{x^2}$

29. $\dfrac{8 + x}{x} \cdot \dfrac{x - 3}{x + 8} = \dfrac{8 + x}{8 + x} \cdot \dfrac{x - 3}{x} = 1 \cdot \dfrac{x - 3}{x} = \dfrac{x - 3}{x}$

31. $\dfrac{z+3}{z+4} \cdot \dfrac{z+4}{z-7} = \dfrac{z+4}{z+4} \cdot \dfrac{z+3}{z-7} = 1 \cdot \dfrac{z+3}{z-7} = \dfrac{z+3}{z-7}$

33. $\dfrac{5x+1}{3x+2} \cdot \dfrac{3x+2}{5x+1} = \dfrac{5x+1}{5x+1} \cdot \dfrac{3x+2}{3x+2} = 1 \cdot 1 = 1$

35. $\dfrac{(t+1)^2}{t+2} \cdot \dfrac{(t+2)^2}{t+1} = \dfrac{(t-1)(t+1)}{t+2} \cdot \dfrac{(t+2)(t+2)}{t+1} = \dfrac{t+1}{t+1} \cdot \dfrac{t+1}{1} \cdot \dfrac{t+2}{t+2} \cdot \dfrac{t+2}{1} =$

$1 \cdot (t+1) \cdot 1 \cdot (t+2) = (t+1)(t+2)$

37. $\dfrac{x^2}{x^2+4} \cdot \dfrac{x+4}{x} = \dfrac{x^2}{x} \cdot \dfrac{x+4}{x^2+4} = \dfrac{x}{x} \cdot \dfrac{x(x+4)}{x^2+4} = 1 \cdot \dfrac{x(x+4)}{x^2+4} = \dfrac{x(x+4)}{x^2+4}$

39. $\dfrac{(z^2-1)}{(z^2-4)} \cdot \dfrac{z-2}{z+1} = \dfrac{(z-1)(z+1)}{(z-2)(z+2)} \cdot \dfrac{z-2}{z+1} = \dfrac{z-1}{z+2} \cdot \dfrac{z+1}{z+1} \cdot \dfrac{z-2}{z-2} = \dfrac{z-1}{z+2} \cdot 1 \cdot 1 = \dfrac{z-1}{z+2}$

41. $\dfrac{y^2-2y}{y^2-1} \cdot \dfrac{y+1}{y-2} = \dfrac{y(y-2)}{(y-1)(y+1)} \cdot \dfrac{y+1}{y-2} = \dfrac{y}{y-1} \cdot \dfrac{y+1}{y+1} \cdot \dfrac{y-2}{y-2} = \dfrac{y}{y-1} \cdot 1 \cdot 1 = \dfrac{y}{y-1}$

43. $\dfrac{2x^2-x-3}{3x^2-8x-3} \cdot \dfrac{3x+1}{2x-3} = \dfrac{(2x-3)(x+1)}{(3x+1)(x-3)} \cdot \dfrac{3x+1}{2x-3} = \dfrac{2x-3}{2x-3} \cdot \dfrac{3x+1}{3x+1} \cdot \dfrac{x+1}{x-1} = 1 \cdot 1 \cdot \dfrac{x+1}{x-3} = \dfrac{x+1}{x-3}$

45. $\dfrac{(x-3)^3}{x^2-2x+1} \cdot \dfrac{x-1}{(x-3)^2} = \dfrac{(x-3)(x-3)^2}{(x-1)(x-1)} \cdot \dfrac{x-1}{(x-3)^2} = \dfrac{x-3}{x-1} \cdot \dfrac{(x-3)^2}{(x-3)^2} \cdot \dfrac{x-1}{x-1} = \dfrac{x-3}{x-1} \cdot 1 \cdot 1 = \dfrac{x-3}{x-1}$

47. $\dfrac{2}{x} \div \dfrac{2x+3}{x} = \dfrac{2}{x} \cdot \dfrac{x}{2x+3} = \dfrac{x}{x} \cdot \dfrac{2}{2x+3} = 1 \cdot \dfrac{2}{2x+3} = \dfrac{2}{2x+3}$

49. $\dfrac{x-2}{3x} \div \dfrac{2-x}{6x} = \dfrac{x-2}{3x} \cdot \dfrac{6x}{2-x} = \dfrac{x-2}{-1(-2+x)} \cdot \dfrac{6x}{3x} = \dfrac{x-2}{-1(-2+x)} \cdot 2 = -1 \cdot 2 = -2$

51. $\dfrac{z+2}{z+1} \div \dfrac{z+2}{z-1} = \dfrac{z+2}{z+1} \cdot \dfrac{z-1}{z+2} = \dfrac{z+2}{z+2} \cdot \dfrac{z-1}{z+1} = 1 \cdot \dfrac{z-1}{z+1} = \dfrac{z-1}{z+1}$

53. $\dfrac{3y+4}{2y+1} \div \dfrac{3y+4}{y+2} = \dfrac{3y+4}{2y+1} \cdot \dfrac{y+2}{3y+4} = \dfrac{3y+4}{3y+4} \cdot \dfrac{y+2}{2y+1} = 1 \cdot \dfrac{y+2}{2y+1} = \dfrac{y+2}{2y+1}$

55. $\dfrac{t^2-1}{t^2+1} \div \dfrac{t+1}{4} = \dfrac{t^2-1}{t^2+1} \cdot \dfrac{4}{t+1} = \dfrac{(t+1)(t-1)}{t^2+1} \cdot \dfrac{4}{t+1} = \dfrac{t+1}{t+1} \cdot \dfrac{4(t-1)}{t^2+1} = 1 \cdot \dfrac{4(t-1)}{t^2+1} = \dfrac{4(t-1)}{t^2+1}$

57. $\dfrac{y^2-9}{y^2-25} \div \dfrac{y+3}{y+5} = \dfrac{y^2-9}{y^2-25} \cdot \dfrac{y+5}{y+3} = \dfrac{(y-3)(y+3)}{(y-5)(y+5)} \cdot \dfrac{y+5}{y+3} = \dfrac{y-3}{y-5} \cdot \dfrac{y+3}{y+3} \cdot \dfrac{y+5}{y+5} =$

$\dfrac{y-3}{y-5} \cdot 1 \cdot 1 = \dfrac{y-3}{y-5}$

59. $\dfrac{2x^2-4x}{2x-1} \div \dfrac{x-2}{2x-1} = \dfrac{2x^2-4x}{2x-1} \cdot \dfrac{2x-1}{x-2} = \dfrac{2x(x-2)}{x-2} \cdot \dfrac{2x-1}{2x-1} = 2x \cdot 1 \cdot 1 = 2x$

61. $\dfrac{2z^2-5z-3}{z^2+z-20} \div \dfrac{z-3}{z-4} = \dfrac{(2z+1)(z-3)}{(z+5)(z-4)} \cdot \dfrac{z-4}{z-3} = \dfrac{2z+1}{z+5} \cdot \dfrac{z-3}{z-4} \cdot \dfrac{z-4}{z-4} = \dfrac{2z+1}{z+5} \cdot 1 \cdot 1 = \dfrac{2z+1}{z+5}$

63. $\dfrac{t^2-1}{t^2+5t-6} \div (t+1) = \dfrac{(t+1)(t-1)}{(t-1)(t+6)} \cdot \dfrac{1}{(t+1)} = \dfrac{t+1}{t+1} \cdot \dfrac{t-1}{t-1} \cdot \dfrac{1}{t+6} = 1 \cdot 1 \cdot \dfrac{1}{t+6} = \dfrac{1}{t+6}$

65. $\dfrac{a-b}{a+b} \div \dfrac{a-b}{2a+3b} = \dfrac{a-b}{a+b} \cdot \dfrac{2a+3b}{a-b} = \dfrac{a-b}{a-b} \cdot \dfrac{2a+3b}{a+b} = 1 \cdot \dfrac{2a+3b}{a+b} = \dfrac{2a+3b}{a+b}$

67. $\dfrac{x-y}{x^2+2xy+y^2} \div \dfrac{1}{(x+y)^2} = \dfrac{x-y}{(x+y)^2} \cdot \dfrac{(x+y)^2}{1} = \dfrac{x-y}{1} \cdot \dfrac{(x+y)^2}{(x+y)^2} = x-y \cdot 1 = x-y$

Applications

69. (a) $\dfrac{1}{n} \cdot \dfrac{n}{n+1} = \dfrac{n}{n} \cdot \dfrac{1}{n+1} = 1 \cdot \dfrac{1}{n+1} = \dfrac{1}{n+1}$

    (b) $\dfrac{1}{n+1} \Rightarrow \dfrac{1}{99+1} = \dfrac{1}{100}$

Checking Basic Concepts for Sections 7.1 & 7.2

1. For $x = -1$, $\dfrac{3}{x^2-1} = \dfrac{3}{(-1)^2-1} = \dfrac{3}{1-1} = \dfrac{3}{0} =$ undefined. For $x = 3$, $\dfrac{3}{x^2-1} = \dfrac{3}{(3)^2-1} = \dfrac{3}{9-1} = \dfrac{3}{8}$

2. (a) $\dfrac{6x^3y^2}{15x^2y^3} = \dfrac{2}{5}xy^{-1} = \dfrac{2x}{5y}$

   (b) $\dfrac{5x-15}{x-3} = \dfrac{5(x-3)}{x-3} = \dfrac{5}{1} \cdot \dfrac{x-3}{x-3} = 5 \cdot 1 = 5$

   (c) $\dfrac{x^2-x-6}{x^2+x-12} = \dfrac{(x+2)(x-3)}{(x+4)(x-3)} = \dfrac{x+2}{x+4} \cdot \dfrac{x-3}{x-3} = \dfrac{x+2}{x+4} \cdot 1 = \dfrac{x+2}{x+4}$

3. (a) $\dfrac{4}{3x} \cdot \dfrac{2x}{6} = \dfrac{8x}{18x} = \dfrac{8}{18} \cdot \dfrac{x}{x} = \dfrac{8}{18} \cdot 1 = \dfrac{8}{18} = \dfrac{4}{9}$

   (b) $\dfrac{2x+4}{x^2-1} \cdot \dfrac{x+1}{x+2} = \dfrac{2(x+2)}{(x-1)(x+1)} \cdot \dfrac{x+1}{x+2} = \dfrac{2}{x-1} \cdot \dfrac{x+2}{x+2} \cdot \dfrac{x+1}{x+1} = \dfrac{2}{x-1} \cdot 1 \cdot 1 = \dfrac{2}{x-1}$

4. (a) $\dfrac{7}{3z^2} \div \dfrac{14}{5z^3} = \dfrac{7}{3z^2} \cdot \dfrac{5z^3}{14} = \dfrac{35z^3}{42z^2} = \dfrac{35z}{42} \cdot \dfrac{z^2}{z^2} = \dfrac{35z}{42} \cdot 1 = \dfrac{35z}{42} = \dfrac{5z}{6}$

   (b) $\dfrac{x^2+x}{x-3} \div \dfrac{x}{x-3} = \dfrac{x(x-1)}{x-3} \cdot \dfrac{x-3}{x} = \dfrac{x}{x} \cdot \dfrac{x-3}{x-3} \cdot \dfrac{x+1}{1} = 1 \cdot 1 \cdot x+1 = x+1$

5. (a) For $x = 0.5$, $T = \dfrac{1}{2-x} \Rightarrow T = \dfrac{1}{2-0.5} = \dfrac{1}{1.5} = \dfrac{2}{3}$;

   For $x = 1$, $T = \dfrac{1}{2-x} \Rightarrow T = \dfrac{1}{2-1} = \dfrac{1}{1} = 1$;

   For $x = 1.5$, $T = \dfrac{1}{2-x} \Rightarrow T = \dfrac{1}{2-1.5} = \dfrac{1}{0.5} = 2$;

   For $x = 1.9$, $T = \dfrac{1}{2-x} \Rightarrow T = \dfrac{1}{2-1.9} = \dfrac{1}{0.1} = 10$; See Figure 5.

   (b) As x nears 2 customers/min., a small increase in x increases the wait dramatically.

x	0.5	1.0	1.5	1.9
T	$\frac{2}{3}$	1	2	10

Figure 5

7.3: Addition and Subtraction with Like Denominators

Concepts

1. add, numerators; denominators

3. $\dfrac{A + B}{C}$

5. $5 - (x + 1) = 5 - x - 1 = 4 - x$

7. $3x - (2x - 5) = 3x - 2x + 5 = x + 5$

Addition and Subtraction of Fractions

9. $\dfrac{1}{2} + \dfrac{1}{2} = \dfrac{1 + 1}{2} = \dfrac{2}{2} = 1$

11. $\dfrac{4}{5} + \dfrac{2}{5} = \dfrac{4 + 2}{5} = \dfrac{6}{5}$

13. $\dfrac{1}{6} + \dfrac{5}{6} = \dfrac{1 + 1}{6} = \dfrac{6}{6} = 1$

15. $\dfrac{4}{7} - \dfrac{1}{7} = \dfrac{4 - 1}{7} = \dfrac{3}{7}$

17. $\dfrac{7}{8} - \dfrac{3}{8} = \dfrac{7 - 3}{8} = \dfrac{4}{8} = \dfrac{1}{2}$

19. $\dfrac{11}{12} - \dfrac{5}{12} = \dfrac{11 - 5}{12} = \dfrac{6}{12} = \dfrac{1}{2}$

21. $\dfrac{7}{15} + \dfrac{4}{15} - \dfrac{1}{15} = \dfrac{7 + 4 - 1}{15} = \dfrac{11 - 1}{15} = \dfrac{10}{15} = \dfrac{2}{3}$

Addition and Subtraction of Rational Expressions

23. $\dfrac{2}{x} + \dfrac{1}{x} = \dfrac{2 + 1}{x} = \dfrac{3}{x}$

25. $\dfrac{7 + 2x}{4x} - \dfrac{7}{4x} = \dfrac{(7 + 2x) - 7}{4x} = \dfrac{2x}{4x} = \dfrac{1}{2} \cdot \dfrac{x}{x} = \dfrac{1}{2} \cdot 1 = \dfrac{1}{2}$

27. $\dfrac{x + 3}{y - 3} + \dfrac{27 - 12}{y - 3} = \dfrac{(y + 3) + (2y - 12)}{y - 3} = \dfrac{3y - 9}{y - 3} = \dfrac{3(y - 3)}{y - 3} = 3 \cdot \dfrac{y - 3}{y - 3} = 3 \cdot 1 = 3$

29. $\dfrac{5z}{4z + 3} - \dfrac{z}{4z + 3} = \dfrac{5z - z}{4z + 3} = \dfrac{4z}{4z + 3}$

31. $\dfrac{t + 5}{t + 6} + \dfrac{t + 7}{t + 6} = \dfrac{(t + 5) + (t + 7)}{t + 6} = \dfrac{2t + 12}{t + 6} = \dfrac{2(t + 6)}{t + 6} = 2 \cdot \dfrac{t + 6}{t + 6} = 2 \cdot 1 = 2$

33. $\dfrac{5x}{2x + 3} - \dfrac{3x - 3}{2x + 3} = \dfrac{5x - (3x - 3)}{2x + 3} = \dfrac{2x + 3}{2x + 3} = 1$

35. $\dfrac{x^2 + 4x - 1}{4x + 2} - \dfrac{x^2 - 4x - 5}{4x + 2} = \dfrac{(x^2 + 4x - 1) - (x^2 - 4x - 5)}{4x + 2} = \dfrac{8x + 4}{4x + 2} = \dfrac{2(4x + 2)}{4x + 2} = 2 \cdot \dfrac{4x + 2}{4x + 2} =$
    $2 \cdot 1 = 2$

37. $\dfrac{3y}{5} + \dfrac{2y - 5}{5} = \dfrac{3y + (2y - 5)}{5} = \dfrac{5y - 5}{5} = \dfrac{5(y - 1)}{5} = \dfrac{5}{5} \cdot (y - 1) = 1 \cdot (y - 1) = y - 1$

39. $\dfrac{x + y}{4} + \dfrac{x - y}{4} = \dfrac{(x + y) + (x - y)}{4} = \dfrac{2x}{4} = \dfrac{1x}{2} = \dfrac{x}{2}$

41. $\dfrac{z^2 + 4}{z - 2} - \dfrac{4z}{z - 2} = \dfrac{(z^2 + 4) - 4z}{z - 2} = \dfrac{z^2 - 4z + 4}{z - 2} = \dfrac{(z - 2)(z - 2)}{z - 2} = \dfrac{z - 2}{z - 2} \cdot \dfrac{z - 2}{1} = 1 \cdot z - 2 = z - 2$

43. $\dfrac{2x^2 - 5x}{2x + 1} - \dfrac{3}{2x + 1} = \dfrac{(2x^2 - 5x) - 3}{2x + 1} = \dfrac{2x^2 - 5x - 3}{2x + 1} = \dfrac{(2x + 1)(x - 3)}{2x + 1} = \dfrac{2x + 1}{2x + 1} \cdot \dfrac{x - 3}{1} =$

$1 \cdot x - 3 = x - 3$

45. $\dfrac{3n}{2n^2 - n + 5} + \dfrac{4n}{2n^2 - n + 5} = \dfrac{3n + 4n}{2n^2 - n + 5} = \dfrac{7n}{2n^2 - n + 5}$

47. $\dfrac{1}{x + 3} + \dfrac{2}{x + 3} + \dfrac{3}{x + 3} = \dfrac{1 + 2 + 3}{x + 3} = \dfrac{6}{x + 3}$

49. $\dfrac{x}{x + y} + \dfrac{y}{x + y} = \dfrac{x + y}{x + y} = 1$

51. $\dfrac{a^2}{a + b} - \dfrac{b^2}{a + b} = \dfrac{a^2 - b^2}{a + b} = \dfrac{(a + b)(a - b)}{a + b} = \dfrac{a + b}{a + b} \cdot \dfrac{a - b}{1} = 1 \cdot a - b = a - b$

53. $\dfrac{4x^2}{2x + 3y} - \dfrac{9y^2}{2x + 3y} = \dfrac{4x^2 - 9y^2}{2x + 3y} = \dfrac{(2x + 3y)(2x - 3y)}{2x + 3y} = \dfrac{2x + 3y}{2x + 3y} \cdot \dfrac{2x - 3y}{1} = 1 \cdot 2x - 3y = 2x - 3y$

Applications

55. (a) $\dfrac{6}{n + 1} + \dfrac{5}{n + 1} + \dfrac{3}{n + 1} = \dfrac{6 + 5 + 3}{n + 1} = \dfrac{14}{n + 1}$

(b) For $n = 99$, $\dfrac{14}{n + 1} \Rightarrow \dfrac{14}{99 + 1} = \dfrac{14}{100} = \dfrac{7}{50}$; there are 7 chances in 50 that a defective battery is chosen.

7.4: Addition and Subtraction with Unlike Denominators

Concepts

1. Examples include 36 and 54. *Answers may vary.*

3. $\dfrac{3}{3}$

5. Factoring 4 and 6 completely yields: 2^2 and $2 \cdot 3$, a list of factors is $2^2 \cdot 3 = 12$.

7. Factoring 4 and 6 completely yields: 2^2 and $2 \cdot 3$, a list of factors is $2^2 \cdot 3 = 12$.

9. 2 and 3 are both prime $\Rightarrow$ a list of factors is $2 \cdot 3 = 6$.

11. Factoring 10 and 15 completely yields: $2 \cdot 5$ and $3 \cdot 5$, a list of factors is $2 \cdot 3 \cdot 5 = 30$.

13. Factoring 24 and 36 completely yields: $2^3 \cdot 3$ and $2^2 \cdot 3^2$, a list of factors is $2^3 \cdot 3^2 = 72$.

15. Factoring $4x$ and $6x$ completely yields: $2^2 \cdot x$ and $2 \cdot 3 \cdot x$, a list of factors is $2^2 \cdot 3 \cdot x = 12x$.

17. Factoring $5x$ and $10x^2$ completely yields: $5 \cdot x$ and $2 \cdot 5 \cdot x^2$, a list of factors is $2 \cdot 5 \cdot x^2 = 10x^2$.

19. Both x and $x + 1$ are prime $\Rightarrow$ a list of factors is $x(x + 1)$.

21. Both $2x + 1$ and $x + 3$ are prime $\Rightarrow$ a list of factors is $(2x + 1)(x + 3)$.

23. Factoring $4x^2$ and $9x^3$ completely yields: $2^2 \cdot x^2$ and $3^2 \cdot x^3$, a list of factors is $3^2 \cdot 2^2 \cdot x^3 = 36x^3$.

25. Factoring $x^2 - x$ and $x^2 + x$ completely yields: $x(x - 1)$ and $x(x + 1)$, a list of factors is $x(x - 1)(x + 1)$.

27. Both $(x + 1)^2$ and $x + 1$ are factored completely $\Rightarrow$ a list of factors is $(x + 1)^2$.

29. Both $(2x - 1)^3$ and $(2x - 1)(x + 3)$ are factored completely $\Rightarrow$ a list of factors is $(2x - 1)^3(x + 3)$.

31. Factoring $4x^2 - 1$ and $2x + 1$ completely yields: $(2x + 1)(2x - 1)$ and $(2x + 1)$, a list of factors is

$(2x + 1)(2x - 1)$.

33. Factoring $x^2 - 1$ and $x + 1$ completely yields: $(x + 1)(x - 1)$ and $(x + 1)$, a list of factors is $(x + 1)(x - 1)$.

35. Both $x^2 + 4$ and $4x$ are factored completely $\Rightarrow$ a list of factors is $4x(x^2 + 4)$.

37. Factoring $2x^2 + 7x + 6$ and $x^2 + 5x + 6$ completely yields: $(2x + 3)(x + 2)$ and $(x + 2)(x + 3)$, a list of

factors is $(2x + 3)(x + 2)(x + 3)$.

Addition and Subtraction of Rational Expressions

39. $\dfrac{1}{3}, D = 9 \Rightarrow \dfrac{1}{3} \cdot \dfrac{3}{3} = \dfrac{3}{9}$

41. $\dfrac{5}{7}, D = 21 \Rightarrow \dfrac{5}{7} \cdot \dfrac{3}{3} = \dfrac{15}{21}$

43. $\dfrac{1}{4x}, D = 8x^3 \Rightarrow \dfrac{1}{4x} \cdot \dfrac{2x^2}{2x^2} = \dfrac{2x^2}{8x^3}$

45. $\dfrac{1}{x + 2}, D = x^2 - 4 \Rightarrow \dfrac{1}{x + 2} \cdot \dfrac{x - 2}{x - 2} = \dfrac{x - 2}{x^2 - 4}$

47. $\dfrac{1}{x + 1}, D = x^2 + x \Rightarrow \dfrac{1}{x + 1} \cdot \dfrac{x}{x} = \dfrac{x}{x^2 + x}$

49. $\dfrac{2x}{x + 1}, D = x^2 + 2x + 1 \Rightarrow \dfrac{2x}{x + 1} \cdot \dfrac{x + 1}{x + 1} = \dfrac{2x^2 + 2x}{x^2 + 2x + 1}$

51. $\dfrac{4}{5} + \dfrac{1}{2} = \dfrac{8}{10} + \dfrac{5}{10} = \dfrac{13}{10}$

53. $\dfrac{5}{9} - \dfrac{1}{3} = \dfrac{5}{9} - \dfrac{3}{9} = \dfrac{2}{9}$

55. $\dfrac{1}{3x} + \dfrac{3}{4x} = \dfrac{4}{12x} + \dfrac{9}{12x} = \dfrac{13}{12x}$

57. $\dfrac{5}{z^2} - \dfrac{7}{z^3} = \dfrac{5z}{z^3} - \dfrac{7}{z^3} = \dfrac{5z - 7}{z^3}$

59. $\dfrac{1}{x} - \dfrac{1}{y} = \dfrac{y}{xy} - \dfrac{x}{xy} = \dfrac{y - x}{xy}$

61. $\dfrac{a}{b} + \dfrac{b}{a} = \dfrac{a^2}{ab} + \dfrac{b^2}{ab} = \dfrac{a^2 + b^2}{ab}$

63. $\dfrac{1}{2x + 4} + \dfrac{3}{x + 2} = \dfrac{1}{2(x + 2)} + \dfrac{3}{x + 2} \cdot \dfrac{2}{2} = \dfrac{1}{2(x + 2)} + \dfrac{6}{2(x + 2)} = \dfrac{7}{2(x + 2)}$

65. $\dfrac{2}{t - 2} - \dfrac{1}{t} = \dfrac{2}{t - 2} \cdot \dfrac{t}{t} - \dfrac{1}{t} \cdot \dfrac{t - 2}{t - 2} = \dfrac{2t}{t(t - 2)} - \dfrac{t - 2}{t(t - 2)} = \dfrac{t + 2}{t(t - 2)}$

67. $\dfrac{5}{n - 1} + \dfrac{n}{n + 1} = \dfrac{5}{n - 1} \cdot \dfrac{n + 1}{n + 1} + \dfrac{n}{n + 1} \cdot \dfrac{n - 1}{n - 1} = \dfrac{5n + 5}{(n - 1)(n + 1)} + \dfrac{n^2 - n}{(n - 1)(n + 1)} = \dfrac{n^2 + 4n + 5}{(n - 1)(n + 1)}$

69. $\dfrac{3}{x - 3} + \dfrac{6}{3 - x} = \dfrac{3}{x - 3} + \dfrac{6}{-(x - 3)} = \dfrac{3}{x - 3} - \dfrac{6}{x - 3} = -\dfrac{3}{x - 3}$

71. $\dfrac{1}{5k - 1} + \dfrac{1}{1 - 5k} = \dfrac{1}{5k - 1} + \dfrac{1}{-(5k - 1)} = \dfrac{1}{5k - 1} - \dfrac{1}{5k - 1} = 0$

73. $\dfrac{2x}{(x-1)^2} + \dfrac{4}{x-1} = \dfrac{2x}{(x-1)^2} + \dfrac{4}{x-1} \cdot \dfrac{x-1}{x-1} = \dfrac{2x}{(x-1)^2} + \dfrac{4x-4}{(x-1)^2} = \dfrac{6x-4}{(x-1)^2}$

75. $\dfrac{2y}{y(2y-1)} + \dfrac{1}{2y-1} = \dfrac{2y}{y(2y-1)} + \dfrac{1}{2y-1} \cdot \dfrac{y}{y} = \dfrac{2y}{y(2y-1)} + \dfrac{y}{y(2y-1)} = \dfrac{3y}{y(2y-1)} = \dfrac{3}{2y-1} \cdot \dfrac{y}{y} =$

$\dfrac{3}{2y-1} \cdot 1 = \dfrac{3}{2y-1}$

77. $\dfrac{1}{x+2} - \dfrac{1}{x^2+2x} = \dfrac{1}{x+2} \cdot \dfrac{x}{x} - \dfrac{1}{x(x+2)} = \dfrac{x}{x(x+2)} - \dfrac{1}{x(x+2)} = \dfrac{x-1}{x(x+2)}$

79. $\dfrac{x}{x^2+4x+4} + \dfrac{1}{x+2} = \dfrac{x}{(x+2)^2} + \dfrac{1}{x+2} \cdot \dfrac{x+2}{x+2} = \dfrac{x}{(x+2)^2} + \dfrac{x+2}{(x+2)^2} = \dfrac{2x+2}{(x+2)^2}$

81. $\dfrac{x}{(x+1)(x+2)} - \dfrac{1}{(x+2)(x+3)} = \dfrac{x}{(x+1)(x+2)} \cdot \dfrac{x+3}{x+3} - \dfrac{1}{(x+2)(x+3)} \cdot \dfrac{x+1}{x+1} =$

$\dfrac{x^2+3x}{(x+1)(x+2)(x+3)} - \dfrac{x+1}{(x+1)(x+2)(x+3)} = \dfrac{x^2+2x-1}{(x+1)(x+2)(x+3)}$

83. $\dfrac{1}{a+b} - \dfrac{1}{a-b} = \dfrac{1}{a+b} \cdot \dfrac{a-b}{a-b} - \dfrac{1}{a-b} \cdot \dfrac{a+b}{a+b} = \dfrac{a-b}{(a+b)(a-b)} - \dfrac{a+b}{(a+b)(a-b)} = -\dfrac{2b}{(a+b)(a-b)}$

85. $\dfrac{r}{r-t} + \dfrac{t}{t-r} - 1 = \dfrac{r}{r-t} + \dfrac{t}{-(r-t)} - 1 = \dfrac{r}{r-t} - \dfrac{t}{r-t} - 1 = \dfrac{r-t}{r-r} - 1 = 1 - 1 = 0$

87. $\dfrac{1}{2a} + \dfrac{1}{3a} + \dfrac{1}{4a} = \dfrac{1}{2a} \cdot \dfrac{6}{6} + \dfrac{1}{3a} \cdot \dfrac{4}{4} + \dfrac{1}{4a} \cdot \dfrac{3}{3} = \dfrac{6}{12a} + \dfrac{4}{12a} + \dfrac{3}{12a} = \dfrac{13}{12a}$

89. $\dfrac{2}{x-y} + \dfrac{3}{y-x} + \dfrac{1}{x-y} = \dfrac{2}{x-y} + \dfrac{3}{-(x-y)} + \dfrac{1}{x-y} = \dfrac{2}{x-y} - \dfrac{3}{x-y} + \dfrac{1}{x-y} = \dfrac{0}{x-y} = 0$

91. $\dfrac{3}{x-3} - \dfrac{3}{x^2-3x} - \dfrac{6}{x(x-3)} = \dfrac{3}{x-3} \cdot \dfrac{x}{x} - \dfrac{3}{x(x-3)} + \dfrac{6}{x(x-3)} = \dfrac{3x}{x(x-3)} - \dfrac{3}{x(x-3)} - \dfrac{6}{x(x-3)} =$

$\dfrac{3x-9}{x(x-3)} = \dfrac{3(x-3)}{x(x-3)} = \dfrac{3}{x} \cdot \dfrac{x-3}{x-3} = \dfrac{3}{x} \cdot 1 = \dfrac{3}{x}$

Applications

93. $R = 120, S = 200; \dfrac{1}{R} + \dfrac{1}{S} \Rightarrow \dfrac{1}{120} + \dfrac{1}{200} = \dfrac{1}{120} \cdot \dfrac{5}{5} + \dfrac{1}{200} \cdot \dfrac{3}{3} = \dfrac{5}{600} + \dfrac{3}{600} = \dfrac{8}{600} = \dfrac{1}{75}$ and

$\dfrac{S+R}{RS} \Rightarrow \dfrac{120+200}{120(200)} = \dfrac{320}{24,000} = \dfrac{1}{75}.$ Yes, they are the same.

95. $\dfrac{1}{F} - \dfrac{1}{D} \Rightarrow F, D = F \cdot D = FD \Rightarrow \dfrac{1}{F} \cdot \dfrac{D}{D} - \dfrac{1}{D} \cdot \dfrac{F}{F} = \dfrac{D}{FD} - \dfrac{F}{FD} = \dfrac{D-F}{FD}$

Checking Basic Concepts for Sections 7.3 & 7.4

1. (a) $\dfrac{x}{x+2} + \dfrac{2}{x+2} = \dfrac{x+2}{x+2} = 1$

(b) $\dfrac{2}{3x} - \dfrac{x}{3x} = \dfrac{2-x}{3x}$

(c) $\dfrac{z^2+z}{z+2} + \dfrac{z}{z+2} = \dfrac{z^2+2z}{z+2} = \dfrac{z(z+2)}{z+2} = \dfrac{z}{1} \cdot \dfrac{z+2}{z+2} = \dfrac{z}{1} \cdot 1 = z$

2. (a) Factoring $3x$ and $5x$ completely yields: $3 \cdot x$ and $5 \cdot x$, a list of factors is $3 \cdot 5 \cdot x = 15x$.

   (b) Factoring $4x$ and $x^2 + x$ completely yields:

   $2^2 \cdot x$ and $x(x + 1)$, a list of factors is $2^2 \cdot x \cdot (x + 1) = 4x(x + 1)$.

   (c) Both $x + 1$ and $x - 1$ are factored completely, a list of factors is $(x + 1)(x - 1)$.

3. (a) $\dfrac{1}{x + 1} + \dfrac{5}{x} = \dfrac{1}{x + 1} \cdot \dfrac{x}{x} + \dfrac{5}{x} \cdot \dfrac{x + 1}{x + 1} = \dfrac{x}{x(x + 1)} + \dfrac{5x + 5}{x(x + 1)} = \dfrac{6x + 5}{x(x + 1)}$

   (b) $\dfrac{5}{x - 3} + \dfrac{1}{3 - x} = \dfrac{5}{x - 3} + \dfrac{1}{-(x - 3)} = \dfrac{5}{x - 3} - \dfrac{1}{x - 3} = \dfrac{4}{x - 3}$

   (c) $\dfrac{-4}{4x + 2} - \dfrac{x + 2}{2x + 1} = \dfrac{-4}{2(2x + 1)} - \dfrac{x + 2}{2x + 1} = \dfrac{-4}{2(2x + 1)} - \dfrac{x + 2}{2x + 1} \cdot \dfrac{2}{2} = \dfrac{-4}{2(2x + 1)} - \dfrac{2x + 4}{2(2x + 1)} =$

   $\dfrac{-2x - 8}{2(2x + 1)} = \dfrac{-2(x + 4)}{2(2x + 1)} = -\dfrac{x + 4}{2x + 1}$

4. $\dfrac{a}{a - b} - \dfrac{b}{a + b} = \dfrac{a}{a - b} \cdot \dfrac{a + b}{a + b} - \dfrac{b}{a + b} \cdot \dfrac{a - b}{a - b} = \dfrac{a^2 + ab}{(a - b)(a + b)} - \dfrac{ab - b^2}{(a - b)(a + b)} = \dfrac{a^2 + b^2}{(a - b)(a + b)}$

7.5: Complex Fractions

Concepts

1. $\dfrac{\frac{1}{2}}{\frac{3}{4}} = \dfrac{1}{2} \cdot \dfrac{4}{3} = \dfrac{4}{6} = \dfrac{2}{3}$

3. fraction

5. Division

7. $\dfrac{\frac{a}{b}}{\frac{c}{d}}$

Simplifying Complex Fractions

9. For $\dfrac{\frac{x}{5} - \frac{1}{6}}{\frac{2}{15} - 3x}$, the denominators 5, 6 and 15 have prime factorization of 5, $2 \cdot 3$ and $3 \cdot 5$, therefore $2 \cdot 3 \cdot 5 = 30$.

11. For $\dfrac{\frac{2}{x + 1} - x}{\frac{2}{x - 1} - x}$, the denominators $x + 1$ and $x - 1$ are prime, therefore $(x + 1)(x - 1)$.

13. For $\dfrac{\frac{1}{2x - 1} - \frac{1}{2x + 1}}{\frac{x + 1}{x}}$, the denominators $2x - 1$, $2x + 1$ and x are prime, therefore $x(2x - 1)(2x + 1)$.

15. $\dfrac{\frac{2}{3}}{\frac{5}{6}} = \dfrac{2}{3} \div \dfrac{5}{6} = \dfrac{2}{3} \cdot \dfrac{6}{5} = \dfrac{12}{15} = \dfrac{4}{5}$

17. $\dfrac{\frac{r}{t}}{\frac{2r}{t}} = \dfrac{r}{t} \div \dfrac{2r}{t} = \dfrac{r}{t} \cdot \dfrac{t}{2r} = \dfrac{t}{t} \cdot \dfrac{1}{2} \cdot \dfrac{r}{r} = 1 \cdot \dfrac{1}{2} \cdot 1 = \dfrac{1}{2}$

19. $\dfrac{\frac{6}{x}}{\frac{2}{y}} = \dfrac{6}{x} \div \dfrac{2}{y} = \dfrac{6}{x} \cdot \dfrac{y}{2} = \dfrac{6y}{2x} = \dfrac{3y}{x}$

21. $\dfrac{\frac{6}{m-2}}{\frac{2}{m-2}} = \dfrac{6}{m-2} \div \dfrac{2}{m-2} = \dfrac{6}{m-2} \cdot \dfrac{m-2}{2} = \dfrac{m-2}{m-2} \cdot \dfrac{6}{2} = 1 \cdot 3 = 3$

23. $\dfrac{\frac{p+1}{p}}{\frac{p+2}{p}} = \dfrac{p+1}{p} \div \dfrac{p+2}{p} = \dfrac{p+1}{p} \cdot \dfrac{p}{p+2} = \dfrac{p}{p} \cdot \dfrac{p+1}{p+2} = 1 \cdot \dfrac{p+1}{p+2} = \dfrac{p+1}{p+2}$

25. $\dfrac{\frac{5}{z^2-1}}{\frac{z}{z^2-1}} = \dfrac{5}{z^2-1} \div \dfrac{z}{z^2-1} = \dfrac{5}{z^2-1} \cdot \dfrac{z^2-1}{z} = \dfrac{z^2-1}{z^2-1} \cdot \dfrac{5}{z} = 1 \cdot \dfrac{5}{z} = \dfrac{5}{z}$

27. $\dfrac{\frac{y}{y^2-9}}{\frac{1}{y+3}} = \dfrac{y}{y^2-9} \div \dfrac{1}{y+3} = \dfrac{y}{y^2-9} \cdot \dfrac{y+3}{1} = \dfrac{y}{(y+3)(y-3)} \cdot \dfrac{y+3}{1} = \dfrac{y}{y-3} \cdot \dfrac{y+3}{y+3} =$

$\dfrac{y}{y-3} \cdot 1 = \dfrac{y}{y-3}$

29. $\dfrac{\frac{3}{x+1}}{\frac{4}{x+1} - \frac{1}{x+1}} = \dfrac{\frac{3}{x+1}}{\frac{3}{x+1}} = \dfrac{3}{x+1} \div \dfrac{3}{x+1} = \dfrac{3}{x+1} \cdot \dfrac{x+1}{3} = \dfrac{x+1}{x+1} \cdot \dfrac{3}{3} = 1 \cdot 1 = 1$

31. $\dfrac{\frac{1}{m^2n} + \frac{1}{mn^2}}{\frac{1}{m^2n} - \frac{1}{mn^2}} = \dfrac{\frac{1}{m^2n} + \frac{1}{mn^2}}{\frac{1}{m^2n} - \frac{1}{mn^2}} \cdot \dfrac{m^2n^2}{m^2n^2} = \dfrac{\frac{m^2n^2}{m^2n} + \frac{m^2n^2}{mn^2}}{\frac{m^2n^2}{m^2n} - \frac{m^2n^2}{mn^2}} = \dfrac{\left(\frac{m^2}{m^2} \cdot \frac{n}{n} \cdot n\right) + \left(m \cdot \frac{m}{m} \cdot \frac{n^2}{n^2}\right)}{\left(\frac{m^2}{m^2} \cdot \frac{n}{n} \cdot n\right) - \left(m \cdot \frac{m}{m} \cdot \frac{n^2}{n^2}\right)} = \dfrac{(1 \cdot 1 \cdot n) + (m \cdot 1 \cdot 1)}{(1 \cdot 1 \cdot n) - (m \cdot 1 \cdot 1)} = \dfrac{n+m}{n-m}$

33. $\dfrac{\frac{1}{2x} + \frac{1}{y}}{\frac{1}{y} - \frac{1}{2x}} = \dfrac{\frac{1}{2x} + \frac{1}{y}}{\frac{1}{y} - \frac{1}{2x}} \cdot \dfrac{2xy}{2xy} = \dfrac{\frac{2xy}{2x} + \frac{2xy}{y}}{\frac{2xy}{y} - \frac{2xy}{2x}} = \dfrac{\frac{2x}{2x} \cdot y + 2x \cdot \frac{y}{y}}{2x \cdot \frac{y}{y} - \frac{2x}{2x} \cdot y} = \dfrac{1 \cdot y + 2x \cdot 1}{2x \cdot 1 - 1 \cdot y} = \dfrac{2x+y}{2x-y}$

35. $\dfrac{\frac{1}{ab} + \frac{1}{a}}{\frac{1}{ab} - \frac{1}{b}} = \dfrac{\frac{1}{ab} + \frac{b}{ab}}{\frac{1}{ab} - \frac{a}{ab}} = \dfrac{\frac{1+b}{ab}}{\frac{1-a}{ab}} = \dfrac{1+b}{ab} \div \dfrac{1-a}{ab} = \dfrac{1+b}{ab} \cdot \dfrac{ab}{1-a} = \dfrac{ab}{ab} \cdot \dfrac{1+b}{1-a} = 1 \cdot \dfrac{1+b}{1-a} = \dfrac{1+b}{1-a}$

37. $\dfrac{\frac{2}{q} - \frac{1}{q+1}}{\frac{1}{q+1}} = \dfrac{\frac{2}{q} - \frac{1}{q+1}}{\frac{1}{q+1}} \cdot \dfrac{q(q+1)}{q(q+1)} = \dfrac{\frac{2q(q+1)}{q} - \frac{q(q+1)}{q+1}}{\frac{q(q+1)}{q+1}} = \dfrac{\frac{q}{q} \cdot 2(q+1) - q \cdot \frac{q+1}{q+1}}{q \cdot \frac{q+1}{q+1}} = \dfrac{2q+2-q}{q} = \dfrac{q+2}{q}$

39. $\dfrac{\frac{1}{x+1} + \frac{1}{x+2}}{\frac{1}{x+1} - \frac{1}{x+2}} = \dfrac{\frac{1}{x+1} + \frac{1}{x+2}}{\frac{1}{x+1} - \frac{1}{x+2}} \cdot \dfrac{(x+1)(x+2)}{(x+1)(x+2)} = \dfrac{\frac{(x+1)(x+2)}{x+1} + \frac{(x+1)(x+2)}{x+2}}{\frac{(x+1)(x+2)}{x+1} - \frac{(x+1)(x+2)}{x+2}} =$

$\dfrac{\frac{x+1}{x+1} \cdot x + 2 + \frac{x+2}{x+2} \cdot x + 1}{\frac{x+1}{x+1} \cdot x + 2 - \frac{x+2}{x+2} \cdot (x+1)} = \dfrac{1 \cdot x + 2 + 1 \cdot x + 1}{1 \cdot x + 2 - 1 \cdot (x+1)} = \dfrac{x+2+x+1}{x+2-x-1} = \dfrac{2x+3}{1} = 2x+3$

41. $\dfrac{\frac{1}{2x-1} - \frac{1}{2x+1}}{\frac{x+1}{x}} = \dfrac{\frac{2x+1}{(2x-1)(2x+1)} - \frac{2x-1}{(2x-1)(2x+1)}}{\frac{x+1}{x}} = \dfrac{\frac{2}{(2x-1)(2x+1)}}{\frac{x+1}{x}} =$

$\dfrac{2}{(2x-1)(2x+1)} \div \dfrac{x+1}{x} = \dfrac{2}{(2x-1)(2x+1)} \cdot \dfrac{x}{x+1} = \dfrac{2x}{(x+1)(2x-1)(2x+1)}$

43. $\dfrac{\frac{1}{ab^2} - \frac{1}{a^2b}}{\frac{1}{b} - \frac{1}{a}} = \dfrac{\frac{a}{a^2b^2} - \frac{b}{a^2b^2}}{\frac{a}{ab} - \frac{b}{ab}} = \dfrac{\frac{a-b}{a^2b^2}}{\frac{a-b}{ab}} = \dfrac{a-b}{a^2b^2} \div \dfrac{a-b}{ab} = \dfrac{a-b}{a^2b^2} \cdot \dfrac{ab}{a-b} = \dfrac{a-b}{a-b} \cdot \dfrac{ab}{a^2b^2} = 1 \cdot \dfrac{1}{ab} = \dfrac{1}{ab}$

45. $\dfrac{1}{a^{-1} + b^{-1}} = \dfrac{1}{\frac{1}{a} + \frac{1}{b}} = \dfrac{1}{\frac{1}{a} \cdot \frac{b}{b} + \frac{1}{b} \cdot \frac{a}{a}} = \dfrac{1}{\frac{b}{ab} + \frac{a}{ab}} = \dfrac{1}{\frac{a+b}{ab}} = 1 \div \dfrac{a+b}{ab} = 1 \cdot \dfrac{ab}{a+b} = \dfrac{ab}{a+b}$

Applications

47. $\dfrac{P\left(1 + \frac{r}{26}\right)^{52} - P}{\frac{r}{26}}$

49. $R = \dfrac{1}{\frac{1}{T} + \frac{1}{S}} = \dfrac{1}{\frac{1}{T} + \frac{1}{S}} \cdot \dfrac{ST}{ST} = \dfrac{ST}{\frac{ST}{T} + \frac{ST}{S}} = \dfrac{ST}{S \cdot \frac{T}{T} + \frac{S}{S} \cdot T} = \dfrac{ST}{S \cdot 1 + 1 \cdot T} = \dfrac{ST}{S + T}$

7.6: Rational Equations and Formulas

Concepts

1. rational

3. $ad = bc$; b; d

5. $12x$

Solving Rational Equations

7. $\dfrac{x}{2} = \dfrac{3}{4} \Rightarrow x \cdot 4 = 2 \cdot 3 \Rightarrow 4x = 6 \Rightarrow \dfrac{4x}{4} = \dfrac{6}{4} \Rightarrow x = \dfrac{6}{4} \Rightarrow x = \dfrac{3}{2}$

    Check: $\dfrac{\frac{3}{2}}{2} = \dfrac{3}{4} \Rightarrow \dfrac{3}{2} \div \dfrac{2}{1} = \dfrac{3}{2} \cdot \dfrac{1}{2} = \dfrac{3}{4}$

9. $\dfrac{3}{z} = \dfrac{6}{5} \Rightarrow 3 \cdot 5 = z \cdot 6 \Rightarrow 15 = 6z \Rightarrow \dfrac{15}{6} = \dfrac{6z}{6} \Rightarrow z = \dfrac{15}{6} \Rightarrow z = \dfrac{5}{2}$

    Check: $\dfrac{3}{\frac{5}{2}} = \dfrac{6}{5} \Rightarrow \dfrac{3}{1} \div \dfrac{5}{2} = \dfrac{3}{1} \cdot \dfrac{2}{5} = \dfrac{6}{5}$

11. $\dfrac{12}{7} = \dfrac{2}{t} \Rightarrow 12 \cdot t = 7 \cdot 2 \Rightarrow 12t = 14 \Rightarrow \dfrac{12t}{12} = \dfrac{14}{12} \Rightarrow t = \dfrac{14}{12} \Rightarrow t = \dfrac{7}{6}$

    Check: $\dfrac{12}{7} = \dfrac{2}{\frac{7}{6}} \Rightarrow \dfrac{2}{1} \div \dfrac{7}{6} = \dfrac{2}{1} \cdot \dfrac{6}{7} = \dfrac{12}{7}$

13. $\dfrac{3y}{4} = \dfrac{7y}{2} \Rightarrow 3y \cdot 2 = 4 \cdot 7y \Rightarrow 6y = 28y \Rightarrow 34y = 0 \Rightarrow \dfrac{34y}{34} = \dfrac{0}{34} \Rightarrow y = 0$

    Check: $\dfrac{3(0)}{4} = \dfrac{7(0)}{2} \Rightarrow \dfrac{0}{4} = \dfrac{0}{2} \Rightarrow 0 = 0$

15. $\dfrac{2}{3} = \dfrac{1}{2x + 1} \Rightarrow 2(2x + 1) = 3 \cdot 1 \Rightarrow 4x + 2 = 3 \Rightarrow 4x = 1 \Rightarrow \dfrac{4x}{4} = \dfrac{1}{4} \Rightarrow x = \dfrac{1}{4}$

    Check: $\dfrac{2}{3} = \dfrac{1}{2(\frac{1}{4}) + 1} \Rightarrow \dfrac{1}{\frac{2}{4} + 1} = \dfrac{1}{\frac{6}{4}} = \dfrac{1}{1} \div \dfrac{6}{4} = \dfrac{1}{1} \cdot \dfrac{4}{6} = \dfrac{4}{6} = \dfrac{2}{3}$

17. $\dfrac{5}{2x} = \dfrac{8}{x + 2} \Rightarrow 5(x + 2) = 2x \cdot 8 \Rightarrow 5x + 10 = 16x \Rightarrow -11x = -10 \Rightarrow \dfrac{-11x}{-11} = \dfrac{-10}{-11} \Rightarrow x = \dfrac{10}{11}$

    Check: $\dfrac{5}{2(\frac{10}{11})} = \dfrac{8}{\frac{10}{11} + 2} \Rightarrow \dfrac{5}{\frac{20}{11}} = \dfrac{8}{\frac{32}{11}} \Rightarrow \dfrac{5}{1} \div \dfrac{20}{11} = \dfrac{8}{1} \div \dfrac{32}{11} \Rightarrow \dfrac{5}{1} \cdot \dfrac{11}{20} = \dfrac{8}{1} \cdot \dfrac{11}{32} \Rightarrow \dfrac{55}{20} = \dfrac{88}{32} \Rightarrow \dfrac{11}{4} = \dfrac{11}{4}$

19. $\dfrac{1}{z - 1} = \dfrac{z}{z + 1} \Rightarrow 1 \cdot (z + 1) = (z - 1) \cdot 2 \Rightarrow z + 1 = 2z - 2 \Rightarrow 3 = z \Rightarrow z = 3$

    Check: $\dfrac{1}{3 - 1} = \dfrac{2}{3 + 1} \Rightarrow \dfrac{1}{2} = \dfrac{2}{4} \Rightarrow \dfrac{1}{2} = \dfrac{1}{2}$

21. $\dfrac{3}{n+5} = \dfrac{2}{n-5} \Rightarrow 3 \cdot (n-5) = (n+5) \cdot 2 \Rightarrow 3n - 15 = 2n + 10 \Rightarrow n = 25$

Check: $\dfrac{3}{25+5} = \dfrac{2}{25-5} \Rightarrow \dfrac{3}{30} = \dfrac{2}{20} \Rightarrow \dfrac{1}{10} = \dfrac{1}{10}$

23. $\dfrac{m}{m-1} = \dfrac{5}{4} \Rightarrow m \cdot 4 = (m-1) \cdot 5 \Rightarrow 4m = 5m - 5 \Rightarrow -m = -5 \Rightarrow \dfrac{-m}{-1} = \dfrac{-5}{-1} \Rightarrow m = 5$

Check: $\dfrac{5}{5-1} = \dfrac{5}{4} \Rightarrow \dfrac{5}{4} = \dfrac{5}{4}$

25. $\dfrac{5x}{5-x} = \dfrac{1}{3} \Rightarrow 5x \cdot 3 = (5-x) \cdot 1 \Rightarrow 15x = 5 - x \Rightarrow 16x = 5 \Rightarrow \dfrac{16x}{16} = \dfrac{5}{16} \Rightarrow x = \dfrac{5}{16}$

Check: $\dfrac{5(\frac{5}{16})}{2 - \frac{5}{16}} = \dfrac{1}{3} \Rightarrow \dfrac{\frac{25}{16}}{\frac{75}{16}} = \dfrac{25}{16} \div \dfrac{75}{16} = \dfrac{25}{16} \cdot \dfrac{16}{75} = \dfrac{16}{16} \cdot \dfrac{25}{75} = 1 \cdot \dfrac{1}{3} = \dfrac{1}{3}$

27. $\dfrac{6}{5-2x} = \dfrac{2}{1} \Rightarrow 6 \cdot 1 = (5 - 2x) \cdot 2 \Rightarrow 6 = 10 - 4x \Rightarrow -4 = -4x \Rightarrow \dfrac{-4}{-4} = \dfrac{-4x}{-4} \Rightarrow 1 = x \Rightarrow x = 1$

Check: $\dfrac{6}{5 - 2(1)} = 2 \Rightarrow \dfrac{6}{5-2} = \dfrac{6}{3} \Rightarrow 2 = 2$

29. $\dfrac{1}{1-x} = \dfrac{3}{1+x} \Rightarrow 1 \cdot (1+x) = (1-x) \cdot 3 \Rightarrow 1 + x = 3 - 3x \Rightarrow 4x = 2 \Rightarrow \dfrac{4x}{4} = \dfrac{2}{4} \Rightarrow x = \dfrac{1}{2}$

Check: $\dfrac{1}{1-\frac{1}{2}} = \dfrac{3}{1+\frac{1}{2}} \Rightarrow \dfrac{1}{\frac{1}{2}} = \dfrac{3}{\frac{3}{2}} \Rightarrow \dfrac{1}{1} \div \dfrac{1}{2} = \dfrac{3}{1} \div \dfrac{3}{2} \Rightarrow \dfrac{1}{1} \cdot \dfrac{3}{1} = \dfrac{3}{1} \cdot \dfrac{2}{3} \Rightarrow 2 = \dfrac{6}{3} \Rightarrow 2 = 2$

31. $\dfrac{1}{z+2} = \dfrac{-z}{1} \Rightarrow 1 \cdot 1 = -z(z+2) \Rightarrow 1 = -z^2 - 2z \Rightarrow z^2 + 2z + 1 = 0 \Rightarrow (z+1)^2 = 0 \Rightarrow z = -1$

Check: $\dfrac{1}{-1+2} = \dfrac{-(-1)}{1} \Rightarrow \dfrac{1}{1} = \dfrac{1}{1} \Rightarrow 1 = 1$

33. $\dfrac{-1}{2x+5} = \dfrac{x}{3} \Rightarrow -1 \cdot 3 = (2x+5) \cdot x \Rightarrow -3 = 2x^2 + 5x \Rightarrow 0 = 2x^2 + 5x + 3 \Rightarrow$

$0 = (2x+3)(x+1) \Rightarrow 0 = 2x + 3 \Rightarrow -\dfrac{3}{2} = \dfrac{2}{2}x \Rightarrow -\dfrac{3}{2} = x, 0 = x + 1 \Rightarrow -1 = x \Rightarrow x = -\dfrac{3}{2}, -1$

Check: $\dfrac{-1}{2(\frac{-3}{2}) + 5} = \dfrac{\frac{-3}{2}}{3} \Rightarrow \dfrac{-1}{\frac{4}{2}} = \dfrac{\frac{-3}{2}}{3} \Rightarrow \dfrac{-1}{1} \div \dfrac{4}{2} = \dfrac{-3}{2} \div \dfrac{3}{1} \Rightarrow \dfrac{-1}{1} \cdot \dfrac{2}{4} = \dfrac{-3}{2} \cdot \dfrac{1}{3} \Rightarrow \dfrac{-2}{4} = \dfrac{-3}{6} \Rightarrow$

$\dfrac{-1}{2} = \dfrac{-1}{2(-1)+5} = \dfrac{-1}{3} \Rightarrow \dfrac{-1}{-2+5} \Rightarrow \dfrac{-1}{3}$

35. $\dfrac{x}{2} + \dfrac{x}{4} = 3 \Rightarrow \dfrac{x(4)}{2} + \dfrac{x(4)}{4} = 3(4) \Rightarrow \dfrac{4x}{2} + \dfrac{4x}{4} = 12 \Rightarrow 2x + x = 12 \Rightarrow 3x = 12 \Rightarrow \dfrac{3x}{3} = \dfrac{12}{3} \Rightarrow x = 4$

Check: $\dfrac{4}{2} + \dfrac{4}{4} = 3 \Rightarrow 2 + 1 = 3 \Rightarrow 3 = 3$

37. $\dfrac{3x}{4} - \dfrac{x}{2} = 1 \Rightarrow \dfrac{3x(4)}{4} - \dfrac{x(4)}{2} = 1(4) \Rightarrow \dfrac{12x}{4} - \dfrac{4x}{2} = 4 \Rightarrow 3x - 2x = 4 \Rightarrow x = 4$

Check: $\dfrac{3(4)}{4} - \dfrac{4}{2} = 1 \Rightarrow \dfrac{12}{4} - \dfrac{4}{2} = 1 \Rightarrow 3 - 2 = 1 = 1$

39. $\dfrac{4}{t+1} + \dfrac{1}{t+1} = -1 \Rightarrow \dfrac{5}{t+1} = -1 \Rightarrow (t+1) \cdot \dfrac{5}{t+1} = -1 \cdot (t+1) \Rightarrow 5 = -t - 1 \Rightarrow 6 = -t \Rightarrow$

$\dfrac{6}{-1} = \dfrac{-t}{-1} \Rightarrow t = -6$

Check: $\dfrac{4}{t+1} + \dfrac{1}{t+1} = -1 \Rightarrow \dfrac{5}{t+1} = -1 \Rightarrow \dfrac{5}{-6+1} = -1 \Rightarrow \dfrac{5}{-5} = -1 \Rightarrow -1 = -1$

41. $\dfrac{1}{x} + \dfrac{2}{x} = \dfrac{1}{2} \Rightarrow \dfrac{3}{x} = \dfrac{1}{2} \Rightarrow x \cdot \dfrac{3}{x} = \dfrac{1}{2} \cdot x \Rightarrow 3 = \dfrac{1}{2}x \Rightarrow 3 \cdot 2 = \dfrac{1}{2}x \cdot 2 \Rightarrow 6 = x \Rightarrow x = 6$

Check: $\dfrac{1}{6} + \dfrac{2}{6} = \dfrac{1}{2} \Rightarrow \dfrac{3}{6} = \dfrac{1}{2} \Rightarrow \dfrac{1}{2} = \dfrac{1}{2}$

43. $\dfrac{5}{4z} - \dfrac{2}{3z} = 1 \Rightarrow \dfrac{5(12z)}{4z} - \dfrac{2(12z)}{3z} = 1(12z) \Rightarrow \dfrac{60z}{4z} - \dfrac{24z}{3z} = 12z \Rightarrow 15 - 8 = 12z \Rightarrow \dfrac{7}{12} = \dfrac{12z}{12} \Rightarrow$

$\dfrac{7}{12} = z \Rightarrow z = \dfrac{7}{12}$ Check: $\dfrac{5}{4\left(\frac{7}{12}\right)} - \dfrac{2}{3\left(\frac{7}{12}\right)} = 1 \Rightarrow \dfrac{5}{\frac{7}{3}} - \dfrac{2}{\frac{7}{4}} = 1 \Rightarrow \dfrac{5}{1} \div \dfrac{7}{3} - \dfrac{2}{1} \div \dfrac{7}{4} = 1 \Rightarrow$

$\dfrac{5}{1} \cdot \dfrac{3}{7} - \dfrac{2}{1} \cdot \dfrac{4}{7} = 1 \Rightarrow \dfrac{15}{7} - \dfrac{8}{7} = 1 \Rightarrow \dfrac{7}{7} = 1 \Rightarrow 1 = 1$

45. $\dfrac{4}{y-1} + \dfrac{1}{y} = \dfrac{6}{5} \Rightarrow \dfrac{4(5)(y)(y-1)}{y-1} + \dfrac{1(5)(y)(y-1)}{y} = \dfrac{6(5)(y)(y-1)}{5} \Rightarrow$

$\dfrac{20y(y-1)}{y-1} + \dfrac{5y(y-1)}{y} = \dfrac{6y^2 - 6y(5)}{5} \Rightarrow 20y + 5y - 5 = 6y^2 - 6y \Rightarrow 25y - 5 = 6y^2 - 6y \Rightarrow$

$6y^2 - 31y + 5 = 0 \Rightarrow (6y - 1)(y - 5) = 0 \Rightarrow 6y - 1 = 0 \Rightarrow 6y = 1 \Rightarrow y = \dfrac{1}{6}, y - 5 = 0 \Rightarrow$

$y = 5 \Rightarrow y = \dfrac{1}{6}, 5$

Check: $\dfrac{4}{y-1} + \dfrac{1}{y} = \dfrac{6}{5} \Rightarrow \dfrac{4}{\frac{1}{6}-1} + \dfrac{1}{\frac{1}{6}} = \dfrac{6}{5} \Rightarrow \dfrac{4}{-\frac{5}{6}} + \dfrac{1}{\frac{1}{6}} = \dfrac{6}{5} \Rightarrow \dfrac{4}{1} \cdot -\dfrac{6}{5} + \dfrac{1}{1} \cdot \dfrac{6}{1} = \dfrac{6}{5} \Rightarrow -\dfrac{24}{5} + \dfrac{6}{1} = \dfrac{6}{5} \Rightarrow$

$-\dfrac{24}{5} + \dfrac{30}{5} = \dfrac{6}{5} \Rightarrow \dfrac{6}{5} = \dfrac{6}{5}, \dfrac{4}{5-1} + \dfrac{1}{5} = \dfrac{6}{5} \Rightarrow \dfrac{4}{4} + \dfrac{1}{5} = \dfrac{6}{5} \Rightarrow \dfrac{20}{20} + \dfrac{4}{20} = \dfrac{24}{20} \Rightarrow \dfrac{24}{20} = \dfrac{24}{20} \Rightarrow \dfrac{6}{5} = \dfrac{6}{5}$

47. $\dfrac{1}{2x} - \dfrac{1}{x+3} = 0 \Rightarrow \dfrac{1(2x)(x+3)}{2x} - \dfrac{2(2x)(x+3)}{x+3} = 0(2x)(x+3) \Rightarrow \dfrac{x+3(2x)}{2x} - \dfrac{2x(x+3)}{x+3} = 0 \Rightarrow$

$x + 3 - 2x = 0 \Rightarrow -x + 3 = 0 \Rightarrow -x = -3 \Rightarrow x = 3$

Check: $\dfrac{1}{2(3)} - \dfrac{1}{3+3} = 0 \Rightarrow \dfrac{1}{6} - \dfrac{1}{6} = 0 \Rightarrow 0 = 0$

49. $\dfrac{1}{x-2} + \dfrac{1}{x+2} = \dfrac{6}{x^2-4} \Rightarrow \dfrac{1(x-2)(x+2)}{x-2} + \dfrac{1(x-1)(x+2)}{x+2} = \dfrac{6(x-2)(x+2)}{(x-2)(x+2)} \Rightarrow$

$\dfrac{x+2(x-2)}{x-2} + \dfrac{x-2(x+2)}{x+2} = \dfrac{6(x-2)(x+2)}{(x-2)(x+2)} \Rightarrow x + 2 + x - 2 = 6 \Rightarrow 2x = 6 \Rightarrow x = \dfrac{6}{2} \Rightarrow x = 3$

Check: $\dfrac{1}{3-2} + \dfrac{1}{3+2} = \dfrac{6}{(3)^2-4} \Rightarrow \dfrac{1}{1} + \dfrac{1}{5} = \dfrac{6}{5} \Rightarrow \dfrac{5}{5} + \dfrac{1}{5} = \dfrac{6}{5} \Rightarrow \dfrac{6}{5} = \dfrac{6}{5}$

51. $\dfrac{1}{p+1} + \dfrac{1}{p+2} = \dfrac{1}{p^2+3p+2} \Rightarrow \dfrac{1}{p+1} \cdot \dfrac{p+2}{p+2} + \dfrac{1}{p+2} \cdot \dfrac{p+1}{p+1} = \dfrac{1}{(p+1)(p+2)} \Rightarrow$

$\dfrac{p+2}{(p+1)(p+2)} + \dfrac{p+1}{(p+1)(p+2)} = \dfrac{1}{(p+1)(p+2)} \Rightarrow 2p+3 = 1 \Rightarrow 2p = -2 \Rightarrow$

$p = -1$, but $p = -1$ makes $\dfrac{1}{p+1} = \dfrac{1}{0}$ which is undefined $\Rightarrow$ no solution

53. $\dfrac{1}{x-2} + \dfrac{3}{2x-4} = \dfrac{6}{3x-6} \Rightarrow \dfrac{1}{x-2} + \dfrac{3}{2(x-2)} = \dfrac{6}{3(x-2)} \Rightarrow$

$\dfrac{1}{x-2} \cdot \dfrac{6}{6} + \dfrac{3}{2(x-2)} \cdot \dfrac{3}{3} = \dfrac{6}{3(x-2)} \cdot \dfrac{2}{2} \Rightarrow \dfrac{6}{6(x-2)} + \dfrac{9}{6(x-2)} = \dfrac{12}{6(x-2)} \Rightarrow 6+9 = 12 \Rightarrow$

$15 = 12$, which is false $\Rightarrow$ no solution

55. $\dfrac{1}{r^2-r-2} + \dfrac{2}{r^2-2r} = \dfrac{1}{r^2+r} \Rightarrow \dfrac{1(r)(r-2)(r+1)}{(r-2)(r+1)} + \dfrac{2(r)(r-2)(r+1)}{r(r-2)} = \dfrac{1(r)(r-2)(r+1)}{r(r+1)} \Rightarrow$

$\dfrac{r(r-2)(r+1)}{(r-2)(r+1)} + \dfrac{2r+2(r)(r-2)}{r(r-2)} = \dfrac{r-2(r)(r+1)}{r(r+1)} \Rightarrow r+2r+2 = r-2 \Rightarrow 3r+2 = r-2 \Rightarrow$

$3r = r-4 \Rightarrow 2r = -4 \Rightarrow r = \dfrac{-4}{2} \Rightarrow r = -2$

Check: $\dfrac{1}{(-2)^2-(-2)-2} + \dfrac{2}{(-2)^2-2(-2)} = \dfrac{1}{(-2)^2+(-2)} \Rightarrow \dfrac{1}{4} + \dfrac{2}{8} = \dfrac{1}{2} \Rightarrow \dfrac{1}{4} + \dfrac{1}{4} = \dfrac{1}{2} \Rightarrow \dfrac{2}{4} = \dfrac{1}{2} \Rightarrow$

$\dfrac{1}{2} = \dfrac{1}{2}$

Graphical and Numerical Solutions

57. (a) $-3, 1$; $y_1 = \dfrac{3}{x}$, $y_2 = x+2$. See Figure 57a.

(b) See Figure 57b. $-3, 1$

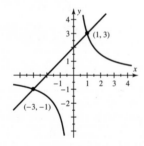

Figure 57a

x	-3	-1	1	3
y = 3/x	-1	-3	3	1
y = x + 2	-1	1	3	5

Figure 57b

59. (a) -1; $y_1 = \dfrac{3x}{2}$, $y_2 = \dfrac{1}{2}x - 1$. See Figure 59a.

(b) See Figure 59b. -1

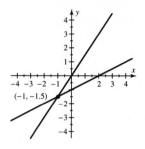

Figure 59a

x	-2	-1	1	2
$y = 3x/2$	-3	-1.5	1.5	3
$y = x/2 - 1$	-2	-1.5	-0.5	0

Figure 59b

61. (a) 2; $y_1 = \dfrac{3}{x-1}$, $y_2 = 3$. See Figure 61a.

    (b) See Figure 61b. 2

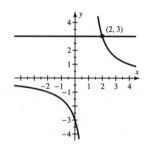

Figure 61a

x	-2	0	2	4
$y = 3/(x-1)$	-1	-3	3	1
$y = 3$	3	3	3	3

Figure 61b

63. (a) $-2, 2$; $y_1 = \dfrac{4}{x^2}$, $y_2 = 1$. See Figure 63a.

    (b) See Figure 63b. $-2, 2$

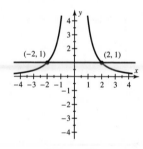

Figure 63a

x	-2	-1	1	2
$y = 4/x^2$	1	4	4	1
$y = 1$	1	1	1	1

Figure 63b

Solving an Equation for a Variable

65. $m = \dfrac{F}{a}$ for $a \Rightarrow a \cdot m = \dfrac{F}{a} \cdot a \Rightarrow am = F \Rightarrow \dfrac{am}{m} = \dfrac{F}{m} \Rightarrow a = \dfrac{F}{m}$

67. $I = \dfrac{V}{R+r}$ for $r \Rightarrow I(R+r) = \dfrac{V}{R+r} \cdot R + r \Rightarrow I(R+r) = V \Rightarrow \dfrac{I(R+r)}{I} = \dfrac{V}{I} \Rightarrow R+r = \dfrac{V}{I} \Rightarrow$

    $r = \dfrac{V}{I} - R$

69. $h = \dfrac{2A}{b}$ for $b \Rightarrow b \cdot h = \dfrac{2A}{b} \cdot b \Rightarrow bh = 2A \Rightarrow \dfrac{bh}{h} = \dfrac{2A}{h} \Rightarrow b = \dfrac{2A}{h}$

71. $\dfrac{3}{k} = \dfrac{z}{z+5}$ for $z \Rightarrow 3(z+5) = kz \Rightarrow 3z + 15 = kz \Rightarrow 15 = kz - 3z \Rightarrow 15 = z(k-3) \Rightarrow z = \dfrac{15}{k-3}$

73. $T = \dfrac{ab}{a+b}$ for $b \Rightarrow T(a+b) = ab \cdot 1 \Rightarrow aT + bT = ab \Rightarrow aT = ab - bT \Rightarrow aT = b(a-T) \Rightarrow$

   $b = \dfrac{aT}{a-T}$

75. $\dfrac{3}{k} = \dfrac{1}{x} - \dfrac{2}{y}$ for $x \Rightarrow \dfrac{3}{k} \cdot \dfrac{xy}{xy} = \dfrac{1}{x} \cdot \dfrac{ky}{ky} - \dfrac{2}{y} \cdot \dfrac{xk}{xk} \Rightarrow \dfrac{3xy}{kxy} = \dfrac{ky}{kxy} - \dfrac{2xk}{kxy} \Rightarrow 3xy = ky - 2xk \Rightarrow$

   $3xy + 2xk = ky \Rightarrow x(3y + 2k) = ky \Rightarrow x = \dfrac{ky}{3y + 2k}$

Applications

77. $\dfrac{1}{10-x} = 1 \Rightarrow 10 - x \cdot \dfrac{1}{10-x} = 1(10-x) \Rightarrow 1 = 10 - x \Rightarrow x = 9$ cars/minute.

79. $\dfrac{t}{4} + \dfrac{t}{3} = 1 \Rightarrow \dfrac{t(12)}{4} + \dfrac{t(12)}{3} = 12 \Rightarrow \dfrac{12t}{4} + \dfrac{12t}{3} = 12 \Rightarrow 3t + 4t = 12 \Rightarrow 7t = 12 \Rightarrow t = \dfrac{12}{7} \Rightarrow$

   $t = 1.7$ hr

81. $\dfrac{d}{8} + \dfrac{d}{4} = 1 \Rightarrow \dfrac{(8)d}{8} + \dfrac{(8)d}{4} = 8 \Rightarrow \dfrac{8d}{8} + \dfrac{8d}{4} = 8 \Rightarrow d + 2d = 8 \Rightarrow 3d = 8 \Rightarrow d = \dfrac{8}{3} \Rightarrow d \approx 2.7$ days

83. Let x represent the speed of the teammate. Then $x + 2$ represents the speed of the winner. The finishing time

   for the teammate is $\dfrac{6}{x}$ and the finishing time for the winner is $\dfrac{6}{x+2}$. Since the winner's time is 2 minutes, or

   $\dfrac{1}{30}$ hour, faster than the teammate's time, the needed equation is $\dfrac{6}{x} - \dfrac{6}{x+2} = \dfrac{1}{30}$. Multiply each term by the

   LCD, $30x(x+2)$. $\dfrac{6}{x} - \dfrac{6}{x+2} = \dfrac{1}{30} \Rightarrow 30x(x+2) \cdot \dfrac{6}{x} - 30x(x+2) \cdot \dfrac{6}{x+2} = 30x(x+2) \cdot \dfrac{1}{30} \Rightarrow$

   $180x + 360 - 180x = x^2 + 2x \Rightarrow x^2 + 2x - 360 = 0 \Rightarrow (x + 20)(x - 18) = 0 \Rightarrow x = -20$ or 18

   Since x must be positive, the teammate's speed is 18 mph and the winner's speed is $18 + 2 = 20$ mph.

85. (a) $m = -0.05, B = \dfrac{30}{0.3 + (-0.05)} \Rightarrow B = \dfrac{30}{0.25} \Rightarrow B = 120$, the breaking distance is 120 feet when the

   slope of the road is -0.05.

   (b) $B = 150, 150 = \dfrac{30}{0.3 + m} \Rightarrow 0.3 + m(150) = 30 \Rightarrow 0.3 + m = \dfrac{30}{150} \Rightarrow 0.3 + m = .2 \Rightarrow m = -0.1$

87. $\dfrac{36}{x-3} = \dfrac{54}{x+3} \Rightarrow 36x + 108 = 54x - 162 \Rightarrow 270 = 18x \Rightarrow 15 = x \Rightarrow x = 15$ mph

89. $\dfrac{450}{x-50} = \dfrac{750}{x+50} \Rightarrow 450x + 22{,}500 = 750x - 37{,}500 \Rightarrow 60{,}000 = 300x \Rightarrow 200 = x \Rightarrow x = 200$ mph

91. Let $x = $ walking in mph and $x + 5 = $ running in mph, then $x \cdot (t + 1) = 10$ and $(x+5)t = 10$, so

   $t + 1 = \dfrac{10}{x} \Rightarrow t = \dfrac{10}{x} - 1$ and $t = \dfrac{10}{x+5}$.

   Now, $\dfrac{10}{x} - 1 = \dfrac{10}{x+5} \Rightarrow \dfrac{10}{x} \cdot \dfrac{x+5}{x+5} - \dfrac{1}{1} \cdot \dfrac{x(x+5)}{x(x+5)} = \dfrac{10}{x+5} \cdot \dfrac{x}{x} \Rightarrow 10(x+5) - x(x+5) = 10x \Rightarrow$

   $10x + 50 - x^2 - 5x = 10x \Rightarrow x^2 + 5x - 50 = 0 \Rightarrow (x + 10)(x - 5) = 0$, so $x = -10, 5$ but -10 cannot

   be the rate so $x = 5$. So 10 mph running and 5 mph walking.

93. $\dfrac{2+n}{8-n} = 1 \Rightarrow 2 + n = 8 - n \Rightarrow 2n = 6 \Rightarrow n = 3$

95. $\dfrac{4+6n}{4-4n} = -\dfrac{49}{31} \Rightarrow 124 + 186n = -196 + 196n \Rightarrow 320 = 10n \Rightarrow 32 = n \Rightarrow n = 32$

Checking Basic Concepts for Sections 7.5 & 7.6

1. (a) $\dfrac{\frac{x}{3}}{\frac{2x}{5}} = \dfrac{x}{3} \div \dfrac{2x}{5} = \dfrac{x}{3} \cdot \dfrac{5}{2x} = \dfrac{5x}{6x} = \dfrac{5}{6} \cdot \dfrac{x}{x} = \dfrac{5}{6} \cdot 1 = \dfrac{5}{6}$

   (b) $\dfrac{\frac{2}{2x} - \frac{1}{3x}}{6x} = \dfrac{\frac{6}{6x} - \frac{2}{6x}}{6x} = \dfrac{\frac{4}{6x}}{6x} = \dfrac{4}{6x} \div \dfrac{6x}{1} = \dfrac{4}{6x} \cdot \dfrac{1}{6x} = \dfrac{4}{36x^2} = \dfrac{1}{9x^2}$

   (c) $\dfrac{\frac{1}{a} - \frac{1}{b}}{\frac{1}{a} + \frac{1}{b}} = \dfrac{\frac{b}{ab} - \frac{a}{ab}}{\frac{b}{ab} + \frac{a}{ab}} = \dfrac{\frac{b-a}{ab}}{\frac{b+a}{ab}} = \dfrac{b-a}{ab} \div \dfrac{b+a}{ab} = \dfrac{b-a}{ab} \cdot \dfrac{ab}{b+a} = \dfrac{ab}{ab} \cdot \dfrac{b-a}{b+a} = 1 \cdot \dfrac{b-a}{b+a} = \dfrac{b-a}{b+a}$

   (d) $\dfrac{\frac{1}{r^2} - \frac{1}{t^2}}{\frac{2}{r} - \frac{2}{t}} = \dfrac{\frac{t^2}{r^2t^2} - \frac{r^2}{r^2t^2}}{\frac{2t}{rt} - \frac{2r}{rt}} = \dfrac{\frac{t^2 - r^2}{r^2t^2}}{\frac{2t - 2r}{rt}} = \dfrac{t^2 - r^2}{r^2t^2} \div \dfrac{2t - 2r}{rt} = \dfrac{t^2 - r^2}{r^2t^2} \cdot \dfrac{rt}{2t - 2r} = \dfrac{rt}{r^2t^2} \cdot \dfrac{t^2 - r^2}{2t - 2r} =$

   $\dfrac{1}{2rt} \cdot \dfrac{(t+r)(t-r)}{t-r} = \dfrac{t+r}{2rt} = \dfrac{r+t}{2rt}$

2. (a) $\dfrac{1}{2x} = \dfrac{3}{x+1} \Rightarrow 6x = x + 1 \Rightarrow 5x = 1 \Rightarrow x = \dfrac{1}{5}$

   Check: $\dfrac{1}{2(\frac{1}{5})} = \dfrac{3}{(\frac{1}{5}) + 1} \Rightarrow \dfrac{1}{\frac{2}{5}} = \dfrac{3}{\frac{6}{5}} \Rightarrow \dfrac{1}{1} \cdot \dfrac{5}{2} = \dfrac{3}{1} \cdot \dfrac{5}{6} \Rightarrow \dfrac{5}{2} = \dfrac{15}{6} \Rightarrow \dfrac{5}{2} = \dfrac{5}{2}$

   (b) $\dfrac{x}{2x + 3} = \dfrac{4}{5} \Rightarrow 5x = 8x + 12 \Rightarrow -3x = 12 \Rightarrow x = \dfrac{12}{-3} \Rightarrow x = -4$

   Check: $\dfrac{-4}{2(-4) + 3} = \dfrac{4}{5} \Rightarrow \dfrac{-4}{-5} = \dfrac{4}{5} \Rightarrow \dfrac{4}{5} = \dfrac{4}{5}$

3. (a) $\dfrac{1}{2x} + \dfrac{3}{2x} = 1 \Rightarrow \dfrac{4}{2x} = 1 \Rightarrow 2x = 4 \Rightarrow x = \dfrac{4}{2} \Rightarrow x = 2$

   Check: $\dfrac{1}{2(2)} + \dfrac{3}{2(2)} = 1 \Rightarrow \dfrac{1}{4} + \dfrac{3}{4} = 1 \Rightarrow \dfrac{4}{4} = 1 \Rightarrow 1 = 1$

   (b) $\dfrac{3}{x+1} - \dfrac{2}{x} = -2 \Rightarrow \dfrac{3}{x+1} \cdot \dfrac{x}{x} - \dfrac{2}{x} \cdot \dfrac{x+1}{x+1} = \dfrac{-2}{1} \cdot \dfrac{x(x+1)}{x(x+1)} \Rightarrow 3x - 2x - 2 = -2x^2 - 2x \Rightarrow$

   $x - 2 = -2x^2 - 2x \Rightarrow 2x^2 + 3x - 2 = 0 \Rightarrow (2x - 1)(x + 2) = 0, \text{ so } x = \dfrac{1}{2}, -2$

   Check: $\dfrac{3}{\frac{1}{2} + 1} - \dfrac{2}{\frac{1}{2}} = -2 \Rightarrow \dfrac{3}{1\frac{1}{2}} - \dfrac{2}{\frac{1}{2}} = -2 \Rightarrow \dfrac{6}{3} - \dfrac{12}{3} = -2 \Rightarrow \dfrac{-6}{3} = -2 \Rightarrow -2 = -2$

   Check: $\dfrac{3}{-2 + 1} - \dfrac{2}{-2} = -2 \Rightarrow \dfrac{3}{-1} - \dfrac{2}{-2} = -2 \Rightarrow -3 - (-1) = -2 \Rightarrow -2 = -2$

4. (a) $\dfrac{ax}{2} - 3y = b \text{ for } x \Rightarrow \dfrac{ax}{2} = b + 3y \Rightarrow ax = 2(b + 3y) \Rightarrow x = \dfrac{2(b + 3y)}{a}$

   (b) $\dfrac{1}{2m - 1} = \dfrac{k}{m} \text{ for } m \Rightarrow m \cdot 1 = k(2m - 1) \Rightarrow m = 2km - k \Rightarrow m - 2km = -k \Rightarrow$

   $m(1 - 2k) = -k \Rightarrow m = \dfrac{-k}{1 - 2k} \Rightarrow m = \dfrac{-k}{-(2k - 1)} \Rightarrow m = \dfrac{k}{2k - 1}$

5. (a) $m = 0.1, D = \dfrac{120}{0.3 + 0.1} \Rightarrow D = \dfrac{120}{0.4} \Rightarrow D = 300;$ when the slope of the hill is 0.1, the braking

distance is 300 ft.

(b) $D = 200, \ 200 = \dfrac{120}{0.3 + m} \Rightarrow 200(0.3 + m) = 120 \Rightarrow 0.3 + m = \dfrac{120}{200} \Rightarrow 0.3 + m = 0.6 \Rightarrow$

$m = 0.3;$ the braking distance is 200 ft. when the slope of the road is 0.3.

7.7: Proportions and Variation

Concepts

1. A statement that two ratios are equal.

3. It doubles

5. constant

7. Directly; doubling the number being fed doubles the bill.

Proportions

9. $\dfrac{x}{24} = \dfrac{5}{8} \Rightarrow 120 = 8x \Rightarrow \dfrac{120}{8} = x \Rightarrow x = 15$

11. $\dfrac{14}{x} = \dfrac{2}{3} \Rightarrow 42 = 2x \Rightarrow \dfrac{42}{2} = x \Rightarrow x = 21$

13. $\dfrac{3}{16} = \dfrac{h}{256} \Rightarrow 768 = 16h \Rightarrow \dfrac{768}{16} = h \Rightarrow h = 48$

15. $\dfrac{3}{4} = \dfrac{2x}{7} \Rightarrow 21 = 8x \Rightarrow \dfrac{21}{8} = x \Rightarrow x = \dfrac{21}{8}$

17. (a) $\dfrac{5}{8} = \dfrac{9}{x}$

(b) $\dfrac{5}{8} = \dfrac{9}{x} \Rightarrow 72 = 5x \Rightarrow \dfrac{72}{5} = x \Rightarrow x = \dfrac{72}{5}$

19. (a) $\dfrac{4}{8} = \dfrac{10}{x}$

(b) $\dfrac{4}{8} = \dfrac{10}{x} \Rightarrow 4x = 80 \Rightarrow x = \dfrac{80}{4} \Rightarrow x = 20$

21. (a) $\dfrac{98}{7} = \dfrac{x}{11}$

(b) $\dfrac{98}{7} = \dfrac{x}{11} \Rightarrow 1078 = 7x \Rightarrow \dfrac{1078}{7} = x \Rightarrow x = \$154$

23. (a) $\dfrac{3}{180} = \dfrac{7}{x}$

(b) $\dfrac{3}{180} = \dfrac{7}{x} \Rightarrow 3x = 1260 \Rightarrow x = \dfrac{1260}{3} \Rightarrow x = 420 \text{ min.}$

Variation

25. (a) $k = \dfrac{y}{x}, y = 6, x = 3 \Rightarrow k = \dfrac{4}{2} = 2$

    (b) $y = kx, k = 2, x = 6 \Rightarrow y = (2)(6) = 12$

27. (a) $k = \dfrac{y}{x}, y = 3, x = 2 \Rightarrow k = \dfrac{3}{2}$

    (b) $y = kx, k = \dfrac{3}{2}, x = 6 \Rightarrow y = \left(\dfrac{3}{2}\right)(6) = 9$

29. (a) $k = \dfrac{y}{x}, y = -60, x = 8 \Rightarrow k = \dfrac{-60}{8} = -\dfrac{15}{2}$

    (b) $y = kx, k = -\dfrac{15}{2}, x = 6 \Rightarrow y = \left(-\dfrac{15}{2}\right)(6) = -45$

31. (a) $k = yx, y = 6, x = 4 \Rightarrow k = 6 \cdot 4 = 24$

    (b) $y = \dfrac{k}{x}, k = 24, x = 8 \Rightarrow y = \dfrac{24}{8} = 3$

33. (a) $k = yx, y = 80\ x = \dfrac{1}{2} \Rightarrow k = 80 \cdot \dfrac{1}{2} = \dfrac{80}{2} = 40$

    (b) $y = \dfrac{k}{x}, k = 40, x = 8 \Rightarrow y = \dfrac{40}{8} = 5$

35. (a) $k = yx, y = 20, x = 20 \Rightarrow k = 20 \cdot 20 = 400$

    (b) $y = \dfrac{k}{x}, k = 400, x = 8 \Rightarrow y = \dfrac{400}{8} = 50$

37. (a) Direct, because as x increases, y increases and $k = \dfrac{y}{x} \Rightarrow k = \dfrac{3}{2} = \dfrac{4.5}{3} = \dfrac{6}{4}$, etc.

    (b) $k = \dfrac{y}{x} \Rightarrow k = \dfrac{3}{2} \Rightarrow y = kx \Rightarrow y = \dfrac{3}{2}x$

    (c) See Figure 37.

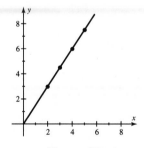

Figure 37

39. (a) Neither, because as x increases, y decreases, but $k = xy \Rightarrow 10(12) \neq 30(5)$

    (b) NA

    (c) NA

41. (a) Neither, because as x increases, y increases, but $k = \dfrac{y}{x} \Rightarrow \dfrac{10}{4} \neq \dfrac{40}{20}$

    (b) NA

    (c) NA

43. Direct, $k = \dfrac{y}{x} \Rightarrow k = \dfrac{6}{3} \Rightarrow k = 2$

45. Neither

47. Inverse, $k = xy \Rightarrow k = 4 \cdot 2 \Rightarrow k = 8$

Applications

49. $\dfrac{85}{750} = \dfrac{x}{420} \Rightarrow 750x = 35{,}700 \Rightarrow x = \dfrac{35{,}700}{750} \Rightarrow x = 47.6$ minutes

51. $\dfrac{8}{1} = \dfrac{13}{x} \Rightarrow 8x = 13 \Rightarrow x = \dfrac{13}{8} \Rightarrow x = 1.625$ inches

53. (a) Direct, the ratios $\dfrac{R}{W}$ always equal 0.012

 (b) $\dfrac{R}{W} = 0.012 \Rightarrow R = 0.012W$. See Figure 53.

 (c) $W = 3200, R = 0.012(3200) \Rightarrow R = 38.4$ pounds.

Figure 53

Figure 55

55. (a) Direct, the ratios $\dfrac{G}{A}$ always equal 27.

 (b) $\dfrac{G}{A} = 27 \Rightarrow G = 27A$. See Figure 55.

 (c) For each square inch in the cross-sectional area of the hose, the flow increases by 27 gal/min.

57. (a) $k = FL \Rightarrow k = 120 \cdot 10 \Rightarrow k = 1200 \Rightarrow F = \dfrac{k}{L} \Rightarrow F = \dfrac{1200}{L}$

 (b) $L = 15 \Rightarrow F = \dfrac{1200}{15} \Rightarrow F = 80$ pounds

59. (a) Direct

 (b) $k = \dfrac{y}{x} \Rightarrow k - \dfrac{-145}{5} \Rightarrow k = -29 \Rightarrow y = kx \Rightarrow y = -29x$

 (c) Negative, for each 1-mile increase in altitude the temperature decreases by 29°F.

 (d) $y = kx, k = -29, x = 2.5, y = -29 \cdot 2.5 \Rightarrow y = -72.5 \Rightarrow 72.5$°F decrease

61. $\dfrac{30}{3} = \dfrac{18}{x} \Rightarrow 30x = 54 \Rightarrow x = \dfrac{54}{30} \Rightarrow x = 1.8$ ohms

Checking Basic Concepts for Section 7.7

1. (a) $\dfrac{x}{9} = \dfrac{2}{5} \Rightarrow 5x = 18 \Rightarrow x = \dfrac{18}{5}$

   (b) $\dfrac{4}{3} \cdot \dfrac{5}{b} \Rightarrow 4b = 15 \Rightarrow b = \dfrac{15}{4}$

2. (a) $\dfrac{4}{6} = \dfrac{8}{x} \Rightarrow 4x = 48 \Rightarrow x = \dfrac{48}{4} \Rightarrow x = 12$

   (b) $\dfrac{2}{148} = \dfrac{5}{x} \Rightarrow 2x = 740 \Rightarrow x = \dfrac{740}{2} \Rightarrow x = 370$ minutes

3. $k = xy, x = 15, y = 4 \Rightarrow k = 15 \cdot 4 \Rightarrow k = 60;\ y = \dfrac{k}{x}, k = 60, x = 10 \Rightarrow y = \dfrac{60}{10} \Rightarrow y = 6$

4. (a) Directly, the ratios $\dfrac{y}{x}$ always equal $\dfrac{3}{2}, \dfrac{3}{2};\ \dfrac{x}{y} = \dfrac{3}{2}, \dfrac{6}{4} = \dfrac{3}{2}, \dfrac{9}{6} = \dfrac{3}{2}, \dfrac{12}{8} = \dfrac{3}{2}$

   (b) Inverse, the products xy always equal 24, 24; $xy = 24, 2 \cdot 12 = 24, 4 \cdot 6 = 24, 6 \cdot 4 = 24, 8 \cdot 3 = 24$

5. $\dfrac{272}{17} = \dfrac{x}{10} \Rightarrow 2720 = 17x \Rightarrow \dfrac{2720}{17} = x \Rightarrow x = 160 \Rightarrow x = \$160$

Chapter 7 Review Exercises

Section 7.1

1. $x = -2, \dfrac{3}{x-3} = \dfrac{3}{-2-3} = \dfrac{3}{-5} = -\dfrac{3}{5}$

2. $x = 3, \dfrac{4x}{5 - x^2} = \dfrac{4(3)}{5 - (3)^2} = \dfrac{12}{5 - 9} = \dfrac{12}{-4} = -3$

3. $x = 7, \dfrac{-x}{7 - x} = \dfrac{-(7)}{7 - (7)} = \dfrac{-7}{0} =$ undefined

4. $x = 2, \dfrac{4x}{x^2 - 3x + 2} = \dfrac{4(2)}{(2)^2 - 3(2) + 2} = \dfrac{8}{4 - 6 + 2} = \dfrac{8}{0} =$ undefined

5. $x = -2, \dfrac{3x}{x-1} = \dfrac{3(-2)}{-2-1} = \dfrac{-6}{-3} = 2;\ x = -1, \dfrac{3x}{x-1} = \dfrac{3(-1)}{-1-1} = \dfrac{-3}{-2} = \dfrac{3}{2};$

   $x = 0, \dfrac{3x}{x-1} = \dfrac{3(0)}{0-1} = \dfrac{0}{-1} = 0;\ x = 1, \dfrac{3x}{x-1} = \dfrac{3(1)}{1-1} = \dfrac{3}{0} =$ undefined;

   $x = 2, \dfrac{3x}{x-1} = \dfrac{3(2)}{2-1} = \dfrac{6}{1} = 6.$ See Figure 5.

x	-2	-1	0	1	2
$\frac{3x}{x-1}$	2	$\frac{3}{2}$	0	—	6

   Figure 5

6. $\dfrac{8}{x^2 - 4} \Rightarrow x^2 - 4 \neq 0 \Rightarrow (x - 2)(x + 2) \neq 0 \Rightarrow x - 2 = 0 \Rightarrow x \neq 2 \text{ or } x + 2 = 0 \Rightarrow x \neq 0$

   Therefore $x = 2, -2$ make the expression undefined.

7. $\dfrac{25x^3 y^4}{15x^5 y} = \dfrac{5}{3} x^{3-5} y^{4-1} = \dfrac{5}{3} x^{-2} y^3 = \dfrac{5y^3}{3x^2}$

8. $\dfrac{x^2 - 36}{x + 6} = \dfrac{(x + 6)(x - 6)}{x + 6} = \dfrac{x + 6}{x + 6} \cdot \dfrac{x - 6}{1} = 1 \cdot x - 6 = x - 6$

9. $\dfrac{x - 9}{9 - x} = \dfrac{x - 9}{-1(-9 + x)} = \dfrac{x - 9}{-1(x - 9)} = -1$

10. $\dfrac{x^2 - 5x}{5x} = \dfrac{x(x - 5)}{x(5)} = \dfrac{x}{x} \cdot \dfrac{x - 5}{5} = 1 \cdot \dfrac{x - 5}{5} = \dfrac{x - 5}{5}$

11. $\dfrac{2x^2 + 5x - 3}{2x + x - 1} = \dfrac{(x + 3)(2x - 1)}{(x + 1)(2x - 1)} = \dfrac{x + 3}{x + 1} \cdot \dfrac{2x - 1}{2x - 1} = \dfrac{x + 3}{x + 1} \cdot 1 = \dfrac{x + 3}{x + 1}$

12. $\dfrac{3x^2 + 10x - 8}{3x + x - 2} = \dfrac{(x + 4)(3x - 2)}{(x + 1)(3x - 2)} = \dfrac{x + 4}{x + 1} \cdot \dfrac{3x - 2}{3x - 2} = \dfrac{x + 4}{x + 1} \cdot 1 = \dfrac{x + 4}{x + 1}$

Section 7.2

13. $\dfrac{x - 3}{x + 1} \cdot \dfrac{2x + 2}{x - 3} = \dfrac{x - 3}{x + 1} \cdot \dfrac{2(x + 1)}{x - 3} = \dfrac{x - 3}{x - 3} \cdot \dfrac{x + 1}{x + 1} \cdot 2 = 1 \cdot 1 \cdot 2 = 2$

14. $\dfrac{2x + 5}{(x + 5)(x - 1)} \cdot \dfrac{x - 1}{2x + 5} = \dfrac{2x + 5}{2x + 5} \cdot \dfrac{x - 1}{x - 1} \cdot \dfrac{1}{x + 5} = 1 \cdot 1 \cdot \dfrac{1}{x + 5} = \dfrac{1}{x + 5}$

15. $\dfrac{(z + 3)^2}{(z + 3)(z - 4)} = \dfrac{z + 3}{z + 3} \cdot \dfrac{z + 3}{z - 4} = 1 \cdot \dfrac{z + 3}{z - 4} = \dfrac{z + 3}{z - 4}$

16. $\dfrac{x^2}{x^2 - 4} \cdot \dfrac{x + 2}{x} = \dfrac{x(x)}{(x - 2)(x + 2)} \cdot \dfrac{x + 2}{x} = \dfrac{x}{x} \cdot \dfrac{x + 2}{x + 2} \cdot \dfrac{x}{x - 2} = 1 \cdot 1 \cdot \dfrac{x}{x - 2} = \dfrac{x}{x - 2}$

17. $\dfrac{x + 1}{2x} \div \dfrac{3x + 3}{5x} = \dfrac{x + 1}{2x} \cdot \dfrac{5x}{3(x + 1)} = \dfrac{5}{6} \cdot \dfrac{x + 1}{x + 1} \cdot \dfrac{x}{x} = \dfrac{5}{6} \cdot 1 \cdot 1 = \dfrac{5}{6}$

18. $\dfrac{4}{x^3} \div \dfrac{x + 1}{2x^2} = \dfrac{4}{x^3} \cdot \dfrac{2x^2}{x + 1} = \dfrac{8}{x} \cdot \dfrac{x^2}{x^2} \cdot \dfrac{1}{x + 1} = \dfrac{8}{x} \cdot 1 \cdot \dfrac{1}{x + 1} = \dfrac{8}{x(x + 1)}$

19. $\dfrac{x - 5}{x + 2} \div \dfrac{2x - 10}{x + 2} = \dfrac{x - 5}{x + 2} \cdot \dfrac{x + 2}{2(x - 5)} = \dfrac{1}{2} \cdot \dfrac{x - 5}{x - 5} \cdot \dfrac{x + 2}{x + 2} = \dfrac{1}{2} \cdot 1 \cdot 1 = \dfrac{1}{2}$

20. $\dfrac{x^2 - 6x + 5}{x^2 - 25} \div \dfrac{x - 1}{x + 5} = \dfrac{(x - 1)(x - 5)}{(x - 5)(x + 5)} \cdot \dfrac{x + 5}{x - 1} = \dfrac{x - 1}{x - 1} \cdot \dfrac{x + 5}{x + 5} \cdot \dfrac{x - 5}{x - 5} = 1 \cdot 1 \cdot 1 = 1$

21. $\dfrac{x^2 - y^2}{x + y} \div \dfrac{x - y}{x + y} = \dfrac{(x - y)(x + y)}{x + y} \cdot \dfrac{x + y}{x - y} = \dfrac{x - y}{x - y} \cdot \dfrac{x + y}{x + y} \cdot x + y = 1 \cdot 1 \cdot x + y = x + y$

22. $\dfrac{a^3 - b^3}{a + b} \div \dfrac{a - b}{2a + 2b} = \dfrac{(a - b)(a^2 + ab + b^2)}{a + b} \cdot \dfrac{2(a + b)}{a - b} = \dfrac{a - b}{a - b} \cdot \dfrac{a + b}{a + b} \cdot \dfrac{2(a^2 + ab + b^2)}{1} =$

$1 \cdot 1 \cdot 2(a^2 + ab + b^2) = 2(a^2 + ab + b^2)$

Section 7.3

23. $\dfrac{2}{x + 10} + \dfrac{8}{x + 10} = \dfrac{2 + 8}{x + 10} = \dfrac{10}{x + 10}$

24. $\dfrac{9}{x - 1} - \dfrac{8}{x - 1} = \dfrac{9 - 8}{x - 1} = \dfrac{1}{x - 1}$

25. $\dfrac{x + 2y}{2x} + \dfrac{x - 2y}{2x} = \dfrac{(x + 2y) + (x - 2y)}{2x} = \dfrac{2x}{2x} = 1$

26. $\dfrac{x}{x+3} + \dfrac{3}{x+3} = \dfrac{x+3}{x+3} = 1$

27. $\dfrac{x}{x^2-1} - \dfrac{1}{x^2-1} = \dfrac{x-1}{x^2-1} = \dfrac{x-1}{(x-1)(x+1)} = \dfrac{x-1}{x-1}\cdot\dfrac{1}{x+1} = 1\cdot\dfrac{1}{x+1} = \dfrac{1}{x+1}$

28. $\dfrac{2x}{x^2-25} + \dfrac{10}{x^2-25} = \dfrac{2x+10}{x^2-25} = \dfrac{2(x+5)}{(x-5)(x+5)} = \dfrac{2}{x-5}\cdot\dfrac{x+5}{x+5} = \dfrac{2}{x-5}\cdot 1 = \dfrac{2}{x-5}$

Section 7.4

29. $2x = 3\cdot x$ and $5x = 5\cdot x \Rightarrow 3\cdot 5\cdot x = 15x$

30. $5x^2 = 5\cdot x^2$ and $10x = 2\cdot 5\cdot x \Rightarrow 2\cdot 5\cdot x^2 = 10x^2$

31. x and $x-5$ are both prime $\Rightarrow x(x-5)$

32. $10x^2 = 2\cdot 5\cdot x^2$ and $x^2 - x = x(x-1) \Rightarrow 2\cdot 5\cdot x^2\cdot(x-1) = 10x^2(x-1)$

33. $x^2 - 1 = (x+1)(x-1)$ and $(x+1)^2$ is prime $\Rightarrow (x+1)^2(x-1)$

34. $x^2 - 4x = x(x-4)$ and $x^2 - 16 = (x+4)(x-4) \Rightarrow x(x-4)(x+4)$

35. $\dfrac{3}{8}, D = 24 \Rightarrow \dfrac{3}{8}\cdot\dfrac{3}{3} = \dfrac{9}{24}$

36. $\dfrac{4}{3x}, D = 12x \Rightarrow \dfrac{4}{3x}\cdot\dfrac{4}{4} = \dfrac{16}{12x}$

37. $\dfrac{3x}{x-2}, D = x^2 - 4 \Rightarrow \dfrac{3x}{x-2}\cdot\dfrac{x+2}{x+2} = \dfrac{3x^2+6}{x^2-4}$

38. $\dfrac{2}{x+1}, D = x^2 + x \Rightarrow \dfrac{2}{x+1}\cdot\dfrac{x}{x} = \dfrac{2x}{x^2+x}$

39. $\dfrac{3}{5x}, D = 5x^2 - 5x \Rightarrow \dfrac{3}{5x}\cdot\dfrac{x-1}{x-1} = \dfrac{3x-3}{5x^2-5x}$

40. $\dfrac{2x}{2x-3}, D = 2x^2 + x - 6 \Rightarrow \dfrac{2x}{2x-3}\cdot\dfrac{x+2}{x+2} = \dfrac{2x^2+4x}{2x^2+x-6}$

41. $\dfrac{5}{8} + \dfrac{1}{6} = \dfrac{5}{8}\cdot\dfrac{3}{3} + \dfrac{1}{6}\cdot\dfrac{4}{4} = \dfrac{15}{24} + \dfrac{4}{24} = \dfrac{19}{24}$

42. $\dfrac{3}{4x} + \dfrac{1}{x} = \dfrac{3}{4x} + \dfrac{1}{x}\cdot\dfrac{4}{4} = \dfrac{3}{4x} + \dfrac{4}{4x} = \dfrac{7}{4x}$

43. $\dfrac{5}{9x} - \dfrac{2}{3x} = \dfrac{5}{9x} - \dfrac{2}{3x}\cdot\dfrac{3}{3} = \dfrac{5}{9x} - \dfrac{6}{9x} = \dfrac{-1}{9x} = -\dfrac{1}{9x}$

44. $\dfrac{7}{x-1} - \dfrac{3}{x} = \dfrac{7}{x-1}\cdot\dfrac{x}{x} - \dfrac{3}{x}\cdot\dfrac{x-1}{x-1} = \dfrac{7x}{x(x-1)} - \dfrac{3x-3}{x(x-1)} = \dfrac{4x-3}{x(x-1)}$

45. $\dfrac{1}{x+1} + \dfrac{1}{x-1} = \dfrac{1}{x+1}\cdot\dfrac{x-1}{x-1} + \dfrac{1}{x-1}\cdot\dfrac{x+1}{x+1} = \dfrac{x-1}{(x+1)(x-1)} + \dfrac{x+1}{(x+1)(x-1)} = \dfrac{2x}{(x-1)(x+1)}$

46. $\dfrac{4}{3x^2} - \dfrac{3}{2x} = \dfrac{4}{3x^2}\cdot\dfrac{2}{2} - \dfrac{3}{2x}\cdot\dfrac{3x}{3x} = \dfrac{8}{6x^2} - \dfrac{9x}{6x^2} = \dfrac{8-9x}{6x^2}$

47. $\dfrac{1+x}{3x} - \dfrac{3}{2x} = \dfrac{1+x}{3x}\cdot\dfrac{2}{2} - \dfrac{3}{2x}\cdot\dfrac{3}{3} = \dfrac{2+2x}{6x} - \dfrac{9}{6x} = \dfrac{2x-7}{6x}$

48. $\dfrac{x}{x^2-1} - \dfrac{1}{x-1} = \dfrac{x}{(x+1)(x-1)} - \dfrac{1}{x-1}\cdot\dfrac{x+1}{x+1} = \dfrac{x}{(x+1)(x-1)} - \dfrac{x+1}{(x+1)(x-1)} = \dfrac{1}{(x-1)(x+1)}$

49. $\dfrac{2}{x-y} - \dfrac{3}{x+y} = \dfrac{2}{x-y} \cdot \dfrac{x+y}{x+y} - \dfrac{3}{x+y} \cdot \dfrac{x-y}{x-y} = \dfrac{2x+2y}{(x-y)(x+y)} - \dfrac{3x-3y}{(x-y)(x+y)} = \dfrac{5y-x}{(x-y)(x+y)}$

50. $\dfrac{2}{x} - \dfrac{1}{2x} + \dfrac{2}{3x} = \dfrac{2}{x} \cdot \dfrac{6}{6} - \dfrac{1}{2x} \cdot \dfrac{3}{3} + \dfrac{2}{3x} \cdot \dfrac{2}{2} = \dfrac{12}{6x} - \dfrac{3}{6x} + \dfrac{4}{6x} = \dfrac{12-3+4}{6x} = \dfrac{12+1}{6x} = \dfrac{13}{6x}$

Section 7.5

51. $\dfrac{\frac{3}{4}}{\frac{7}{11}} = \dfrac{3}{4} \div \dfrac{7}{11} = \dfrac{3}{4} \cdot \dfrac{11}{7} = \dfrac{33}{28}$

52. $\dfrac{\frac{x}{5}}{\frac{2x}{7}} = \dfrac{x}{5} \div \dfrac{2x}{7} = \dfrac{x}{5} \cdot \dfrac{7}{2x} = \dfrac{7x}{10x} = \dfrac{7}{10} \cdot \dfrac{x}{x} = \dfrac{7}{10} \cdot 1 = \dfrac{7}{10}$

53. $\dfrac{\frac{m}{n}}{\frac{2m}{n^2}} = \dfrac{m}{n} \div \dfrac{2m}{n^2} = \dfrac{m}{n} \cdot \dfrac{n^2}{2m} = \dfrac{m}{2m} \cdot \dfrac{n^2}{n} = \left(\dfrac{1}{2} \cdot \dfrac{m}{m}\right) \cdot \left(\dfrac{n}{n} \cdot n\right) = \left(\dfrac{1}{2} \cdot 1\right) \cdot 1 \cdot n = \dfrac{n}{2}$

54. $\dfrac{\frac{3}{p-1}}{\frac{1}{p+1}} = \dfrac{3}{p-1} \div \dfrac{1}{p+1} = \dfrac{3}{p-1} \cdot \dfrac{p+1}{1} = \dfrac{3(p+1)}{p-1}$

55. $\dfrac{\frac{3}{m-1}}{\frac{2m-2}{m+1}} = \dfrac{3}{m-1} \div \dfrac{2m-2}{m+1} = \dfrac{3}{m-1} \cdot \dfrac{m+1}{2m-2} = \dfrac{3}{m-1} \cdot \dfrac{m+1}{2(m-1)} = \dfrac{3(m+1)}{2(m-1)^2}$

56. $\dfrac{\frac{2}{2n+1}}{\frac{8}{2n-1}} = \dfrac{2}{2n+1} \div \dfrac{8}{2n-1} = \dfrac{2}{2n+1} \cdot \dfrac{2n-1}{8} = \dfrac{2}{8} \cdot \dfrac{2n-1}{2n+1} = \dfrac{2n-1}{4(2n+1)}$

57. $\dfrac{\frac{1}{2x} - \frac{1}{3x}}{\frac{2}{3x} - \frac{1}{6x}} = \dfrac{\frac{3}{6x} - \frac{2}{6x}}{\frac{4}{6x} - \frac{1}{6x}} = \dfrac{\frac{1}{6x}}{\frac{3}{6x}} = \dfrac{1}{6x} \div \dfrac{3}{6x} = \dfrac{1}{6x} \cdot \dfrac{6x}{3} = \dfrac{1}{3} \cdot \dfrac{6x}{6x} = \dfrac{1}{3} \cdot 1 = \dfrac{1}{3}$

58. $\dfrac{\frac{2}{xy} - \frac{1}{y}}{\frac{2}{xy} + \frac{1}{y}} = \dfrac{\frac{2}{xy} - \frac{1}{x}}{\frac{2}{xy} + \frac{1}{y}} \cdot \dfrac{xy}{xy} = \dfrac{\frac{2xy}{xy} - \frac{xy}{y}}{\frac{2xy}{xy} + \frac{xy}{y}} = \dfrac{2 \cdot \frac{xy}{xy} - x \cdot \frac{y}{y}}{2 \cdot \frac{xy}{xy} + x \cdot \frac{y}{y}} = \dfrac{2 \cdot 1 - x \cdot 1}{2 \cdot 1 + x \cdot 1} = \dfrac{2-x}{2+x}$

59. $\dfrac{\frac{1}{x} - \frac{1}{x+1}}{\frac{x}{x+1}} = \dfrac{\frac{x+1}{x(x+1)} - \frac{x}{x(x+1)}}{\frac{x}{x+1}} = \dfrac{\frac{1}{x(x+1)}}{\frac{x}{x+1}} = \dfrac{1}{x(x+1)} \div \dfrac{x}{x+1} = \dfrac{1}{x(x+1)} \cdot \dfrac{x+1}{x} = \dfrac{1}{x \cdot x} \cdot \dfrac{x+1}{x+1} = $

$\dfrac{1}{x^2} \cdot 1 = \dfrac{1}{x^2}$

60. $\dfrac{\frac{2}{x-1} - \frac{1}{x+1}}{\frac{1}{x^2-1}} = \dfrac{\frac{2x+2}{(x-1)(x+1)} - \frac{x-1}{(x-1)(x+1)}}{\frac{1}{x^2-1}} = \dfrac{\frac{x+3}{x^2-1}}{\frac{1}{x^2-1}} = \dfrac{x+3}{x^2-1} \div \dfrac{1}{x^2-1} = \dfrac{x+3}{x^2-1} \cdot \dfrac{x^2-1}{1} = $

$\dfrac{x+3}{1} \cdot \dfrac{x^2-1}{x^2-1} = x+3 \cdot 1 = x+3$

Section 7.6

61. $\dfrac{x}{5} = \dfrac{4}{7} \Rightarrow 7x = 20 \Rightarrow x = \dfrac{20}{7}$ Check: $\dfrac{\frac{20}{7}}{5} = \dfrac{4}{7} \Rightarrow 7\left(\dfrac{20}{7}\right) = 20 \Rightarrow 20 = 20$

62. $\dfrac{4}{x} = \dfrac{3}{2} \Rightarrow 3x = 8 \Rightarrow x = \dfrac{8}{3}$ Check: $\dfrac{4}{\frac{8}{3}} = \dfrac{3}{2} \Rightarrow 8 = 3\left(\dfrac{8}{3}\right) \Rightarrow 8 = 8$

63. $\dfrac{3}{z+1} = \dfrac{1}{2z} \Rightarrow 6z = z+1 \Rightarrow 5z = 1 \Rightarrow z = \dfrac{1}{5}$

   Check: $\dfrac{3}{\frac{1}{5}+1} = \dfrac{1}{2(\frac{1}{5})} \Rightarrow \dfrac{3}{\frac{6}{5}} = \dfrac{1}{\frac{2}{5}} \Rightarrow \dfrac{3}{1} \cdot \dfrac{5}{6} = \dfrac{1}{1} \cdot \dfrac{5}{2} \Rightarrow \dfrac{15}{6} = \dfrac{5}{2} \Rightarrow \dfrac{5}{2} = \dfrac{5}{2}$

64. $\dfrac{x+2}{x} = \dfrac{3}{5} \Rightarrow 3x = 5x + 10 \Rightarrow -2x = 10 \Rightarrow x = \dfrac{10}{-2} \Rightarrow x = -5$

Check: $\dfrac{-5+2}{-5} = \dfrac{3}{5} \Rightarrow \dfrac{-3}{-5} = \dfrac{3}{5} \Rightarrow \dfrac{3}{5} = \dfrac{3}{5}$

65. $\dfrac{1}{x+1} = \dfrac{2}{x-2} \Rightarrow x - 2 = 2x + 2 \Rightarrow -x = 4 \Rightarrow x = -4$

Check: $\dfrac{1}{-4+1} = \dfrac{2}{-4-2} \Rightarrow \dfrac{1}{-3} = \dfrac{2}{-6} \Rightarrow -\dfrac{1}{3} = -\dfrac{1}{3}$

66. $\dfrac{x}{3} = \dfrac{-1}{x+4} \Rightarrow x^2 + 4x = -3 \Rightarrow x^2 + 4x + 3 = 0 \Rightarrow (x+1)(x+3) = 0 \Rightarrow x + 1 = 0 \Rightarrow x = -1,$

$x + 3 = 0 \Rightarrow x = -3 \Rightarrow x = -1, -3$

Check: $\dfrac{-1}{3} = \dfrac{-1}{-1+4} \Rightarrow -\dfrac{1}{3} = -\dfrac{1}{3}, \dfrac{-3}{3} = \dfrac{-1}{-3+4} \Rightarrow -1 = \dfrac{-1}{1} \Rightarrow -1 = -1$

67. $\dfrac{1}{5x} + \dfrac{3}{5x} = \dfrac{1}{5} \Rightarrow \dfrac{4}{5x} = \dfrac{1}{5} \Rightarrow 5x = 20 \Rightarrow x = 4$ Check: $\dfrac{1}{5(4)} + \dfrac{3}{5(4)} = \dfrac{1}{5} \Rightarrow \dfrac{4}{20} = \dfrac{1}{5} \Rightarrow \dfrac{1}{5} = \dfrac{1}{5}$

68. $\dfrac{1}{x-1} + \dfrac{2x}{x-1} = 1 \Rightarrow \dfrac{2x+1}{x-1} = 1 \Rightarrow \dfrac{2x+1(x-1)}{x-1} = \dfrac{x-1}{1} \Rightarrow 2x + 1 = x - 1 \Rightarrow x = -2$

Check: $\dfrac{1}{-2-1} + \dfrac{2(-2)}{-2-1} = 1 \Rightarrow \dfrac{-3}{-3} = 1 \Rightarrow 1 = 1$

69. $\dfrac{1}{x} + \dfrac{2}{3x} = \dfrac{1}{3} \Rightarrow \dfrac{1(3)}{3(x)} + \dfrac{2}{3x} = \dfrac{1(x)}{3(x)} \Rightarrow \dfrac{3}{3x} + \dfrac{2}{3x} = \dfrac{x}{3x} \Rightarrow \dfrac{5}{3x} = \dfrac{x}{3x} \Rightarrow 15x = 3x^2 \Rightarrow \dfrac{15}{3} = \dfrac{x^2}{x} \Rightarrow$

$5 = x \Rightarrow x = 5$ Check: $\dfrac{1}{5} + \dfrac{2}{3(5)} = \dfrac{1}{3} \Rightarrow \dfrac{1}{5} + \dfrac{2}{15} = \dfrac{1}{3} \Rightarrow \dfrac{3}{15} + \dfrac{2}{15} = \dfrac{5}{15} \Rightarrow \dfrac{5}{15} = \dfrac{5}{15} \Rightarrow \dfrac{1}{3} = \dfrac{1}{3}$

70. $\dfrac{1}{x+3} + \dfrac{2x}{x+3} = \dfrac{3}{2} \Rightarrow \dfrac{2x+1}{x+3} = \dfrac{3}{2} \Rightarrow \dfrac{2x+1(x+3)(2)}{x+3} = \dfrac{3(x+3)(2)}{2} \Rightarrow$

$\dfrac{(4x+2)(x+3)}{x+3} = \dfrac{(3x+9)(2)}{2} \Rightarrow 4x + 2 = 3x + 9 \Rightarrow x = 7$

Check: $\dfrac{1}{7+3} + \dfrac{2(7)}{7+3} = \dfrac{3}{3} \Rightarrow \dfrac{15}{10} = \dfrac{3}{2} \Rightarrow \dfrac{3}{2} = \dfrac{3}{2}$

71. $\dfrac{5}{x} - \dfrac{3}{x+1} = \dfrac{1}{2} \Rightarrow \dfrac{5(x)(x+1)(2)}{x} - \dfrac{3(x)(x+1)(2)}{x+1} = \dfrac{1(x)(x+1)(2)}{2} \Rightarrow$

$\dfrac{(10x+10)(x)}{x} - \dfrac{6x(x+1)}{x+1} = \dfrac{x^2+x(2)}{2} \Rightarrow 10x + 10 - 6x = x^2 + x \Rightarrow 4x + 10 = x^2 + x \Rightarrow$

$x^2 - 3x - 10 = 0 \Rightarrow (x-5)(x+2) = 0, x - 5 = 0 \Rightarrow x = 5, x + 2 = 0 \Rightarrow x = -2 \Rightarrow x = 5, -2$

Check: $\dfrac{5}{-2} - \dfrac{3}{-2+1} = \dfrac{1}{2} \Rightarrow \dfrac{5}{-2} - \dfrac{3}{-1} = \dfrac{1}{2} \Rightarrow \dfrac{5}{-2} - \dfrac{6}{-2} = \dfrac{1}{2} \Rightarrow \dfrac{-1}{-2} = \dfrac{1}{2} \Rightarrow \dfrac{1}{2} = \dfrac{1}{2}$

Check: $\dfrac{5}{5} - \dfrac{3}{5+1} = \dfrac{1}{2} \Rightarrow \dfrac{5}{5} - \dfrac{3}{6} = \dfrac{1}{2} \Rightarrow 1 - \dfrac{1}{2} = \dfrac{1}{2} \Rightarrow \dfrac{1}{2} = \dfrac{1}{2}$

72. $\dfrac{1}{x-1} - \dfrac{1}{x+1} = \dfrac{1}{4} \Rightarrow \dfrac{1(x-1)(x+1)(4)}{x-1} - \dfrac{1(x-1)(x+1)(4)}{x+1} = \dfrac{1(x-1)(x+1)(4)}{4} \Rightarrow$

$\dfrac{(4x+4)(x-1)}{x-1} - \dfrac{(4x-4)(x+1)}{x+1} = \dfrac{x^2-1(4)}{4} \Rightarrow 4x+4-(4x-4) = x^2-1 \Rightarrow 8 = x^2-1 \Rightarrow$

$9 = x^2 \Rightarrow \pm 3 = x \Rightarrow x = -3, 3$

Check: $\dfrac{1}{-3-1} - \dfrac{1}{-3+1} = \dfrac{1}{4} \Rightarrow \dfrac{1}{-4} - \dfrac{1}{-2} = \dfrac{1}{4} \Rightarrow \dfrac{1}{-4} - \dfrac{2}{-4} = \dfrac{1}{4} \Rightarrow \dfrac{-1}{-4} = \dfrac{1}{4} \Rightarrow \dfrac{1}{4} = \dfrac{1}{4}$

Check: $\dfrac{1}{3-1} - \dfrac{1}{3+1} = \dfrac{1}{4} \Rightarrow \dfrac{1}{2} - \dfrac{1}{4} = \dfrac{1}{4} \Rightarrow \dfrac{2}{4} - \dfrac{1}{4} = \dfrac{1}{4} \Rightarrow \dfrac{1}{4} = \dfrac{1}{4}$

73. $\dfrac{4}{p} - \dfrac{5}{p+2} = 0 \Rightarrow \dfrac{4(p)(p+2)}{p} - \dfrac{5(p)(p+2)}{p+2} = 0(p)(p+2) \Rightarrow \dfrac{(4p+8)(p)}{p} - \dfrac{5p(p+2)}{p+2} = 0 \Rightarrow$

$4p+8-5p = 0 \Rightarrow -p+8 = 0 \Rightarrow -p = -8 \Rightarrow p = 8$

Check: $\dfrac{4}{8} - \dfrac{5}{8+2} = 0 \Rightarrow \dfrac{4}{8} - \dfrac{5}{10} = 0 \Rightarrow \dfrac{1}{2} - \dfrac{1}{2} = 0 \Rightarrow 0 = 0$

74. $\dfrac{1}{x-3} - \dfrac{1}{x+3} = \dfrac{1}{x^2-9} \Rightarrow \dfrac{1}{x-3}\cdot\dfrac{x+3}{x+3} - \dfrac{1}{x+3}\cdot\dfrac{x-3}{x-3} = \dfrac{1}{(x+3)(x-3)} \Rightarrow$

$\dfrac{x+3}{(x-3)(x+3)} - \dfrac{x-3}{(x-3)(x+3)} = \dfrac{1}{(x-3)(x+3)} \Rightarrow 6 = 1$, which is false, so no solution.

75. $\dfrac{2}{x^2-2x} + \dfrac{1}{x^2-4} = \dfrac{1}{x^2+2x} \Rightarrow \dfrac{2(x)(x-2)(x+2)}{x(x-2)} + \dfrac{1(x)(x-2)(x+2)}{(x-2)(x+2)} = \dfrac{1(x)(x-2)(x+2)}{x(x+2)} \Rightarrow$

$\dfrac{(2x+4)(x)(x-2)}{x(x-2)} + \dfrac{x(x^2-4)}{x^2-4} = \dfrac{(x-2)(x)(x+2)}{x(x+2)} \Rightarrow 2x+4+x = x-2 \Rightarrow 3x+4 = x-2 \Rightarrow$

$2x = -6 \Rightarrow x = -3$ Check: $\dfrac{2}{(-3)^2-2(-3)} + \dfrac{1}{(-3)^2-4} = \dfrac{1}{(-3)^2+2(-3)} \Rightarrow \dfrac{2}{15} + \dfrac{1}{5} = \dfrac{1}{3} \Rightarrow$

$\dfrac{2}{15} + \dfrac{3}{15} = \dfrac{5}{15} \Rightarrow \dfrac{5}{15} = \dfrac{5}{15} \Rightarrow \dfrac{1}{3} = \dfrac{1}{3}$

76. $\dfrac{3}{x^2-3x} - \dfrac{1}{x^2-9} = \dfrac{1}{x^2+3x} \Rightarrow \dfrac{3(x)(x-3)(x+3)}{x(x-3)} - \dfrac{1(x)(x-3)(x+3)}{(x-3)(x+3)} = \dfrac{1(x)(x-3)(x+3)}{x(x+3)} \Rightarrow$

$\dfrac{(3x+9)(x)(x-3)}{x(x-3)} - \dfrac{x(x^2-9)}{x^2-9} = \dfrac{(x-3)(x)(x+3)}{x(x+3)} \Rightarrow 3x+9-x = x-3 \Rightarrow 2x+9 = x-3 \Rightarrow$

$x = -12$ Check: $\dfrac{3}{(-12)^2-3(-12)} - \dfrac{1}{(-12)^2-9} = \dfrac{1}{(-12)^2+3(-12)} \Rightarrow \dfrac{3}{180} - \dfrac{1}{135} = \dfrac{1}{108} \Rightarrow$

$\dfrac{9}{540} - \dfrac{4}{540} = \dfrac{5}{540} \Rightarrow \dfrac{5}{540} = \dfrac{5}{540} \Rightarrow \dfrac{1}{108} = \dfrac{1}{108}$

77. $\dfrac{1}{x^2} - \dfrac{5}{x^2+4x} = \dfrac{1}{x^2+4x} \Rightarrow \dfrac{1(x^2)(x^2+4x)}{x^2} - \dfrac{5(x^2)(x^2+4x)}{(x^2+4x)} = \dfrac{1(x^2)(x^2+4x)}{x^2+4x} \Rightarrow$

$\dfrac{(x^2+4x)(x^2)}{x^2} - \dfrac{5x^2(x^2+4x)}{x^2+4x} = \dfrac{x^2(x^2+4x)}{x^2+4x} \Rightarrow x^2+4x-5x^2 = x^2 \Rightarrow -4x^2+4x = x^2 \Rightarrow$

$-5x^2 = -4x \Rightarrow \dfrac{x^2}{x} = \dfrac{-4}{-5} \Rightarrow x = \dfrac{4}{5}$

Check: $\dfrac{1}{\left(\frac{4}{5}\right)^2} - \dfrac{5}{\left(\frac{4}{5}\right)^2+4\left(\frac{4}{5}\right)} = \dfrac{1}{\left(\frac{4}{5}\right)^2+4\left(\frac{4}{5}\right)} \Rightarrow \dfrac{1}{\frac{16}{25}} - \dfrac{5}{\frac{96}{25}} = \dfrac{1}{\frac{96}{25}} \Rightarrow \dfrac{1}{1}\cdot\dfrac{25}{16} - \dfrac{5}{1}\cdot\dfrac{25}{96} = \dfrac{1}{1}\cdot\dfrac{25}{96} \Rightarrow$

$\dfrac{25}{16} - \dfrac{125}{96} = \dfrac{25}{96} \Rightarrow \dfrac{150}{96} - \dfrac{125}{96} = \dfrac{25}{96} \Rightarrow \dfrac{25}{96} = \dfrac{25}{96}$

78. $\dfrac{5}{x^2 - 1} - \dfrac{1}{x^2 + 2x + 1} = \dfrac{3}{x^2 - 1} \Rightarrow$

$\dfrac{5(x + 1)(x + 1)(x - 1)}{(x + 1)(x - 1)} - \dfrac{1(x + 1)(x + 1)(x - 1)}{(x + 1)(x + 1)} = \dfrac{3(x + 1)(x + 1)(x - 1)}{(x + 1)(x - 1)} \Rightarrow$

$\dfrac{(5x + 5)(x^2 - 1)}{(x^2 - 1)} - \dfrac{(x - 1)(x^2 + 2x + 1)}{x^2 + 2x + 1} = \dfrac{(3x + 3)(x^2 - 1)}{x^2 - 1} \Rightarrow 5x + 5 - (x - 1) = 3x + 3 \Rightarrow$

$4x + 6 = 3x + 3 \Rightarrow x = -3$

Check: $\dfrac{5}{(-3)^2 - 1} - \dfrac{1}{(-3)^2 + 2(-3) + 1} = \dfrac{2}{(-3)^2 - 1} \Rightarrow \dfrac{5}{8} - \dfrac{1}{4} = \dfrac{3}{8} \Rightarrow \dfrac{5}{8} - \dfrac{2}{8} = \dfrac{3}{8} \Rightarrow \dfrac{3}{8} = \dfrac{3}{8}$

79. $\dfrac{1}{a} + \dfrac{2}{b} = \dfrac{3}{c}$ for $b \Rightarrow \dfrac{1}{a} \cdot \dfrac{bc}{bc} + \dfrac{2}{b} \cdot \dfrac{ac}{ac} = \dfrac{3}{c} \cdot \dfrac{ab}{ab} \Rightarrow bc + 2ac = 3ab \Rightarrow 2ac = 3ab - bc \Rightarrow$

$2ac = b(3a - c) \Rightarrow b = \dfrac{2ac}{3a - c}$

80. $y = \dfrac{x}{x - 1}$ for $x \Rightarrow y(x - 1) = x \cdot 1 \Rightarrow xy - y = x \Rightarrow xy - x = y \Rightarrow x(y - 1) = y \Rightarrow x = \dfrac{y}{y - 1}$

Section 7.7

81. $\dfrac{x}{6} = \dfrac{1}{3} \Rightarrow 3x = 6 \Rightarrow x = \dfrac{6}{3} = 2$

82. $\dfrac{5}{x} = \dfrac{7}{3} \Rightarrow 15 = 7x \Rightarrow \dfrac{15}{7} = x \Rightarrow x = \dfrac{15}{7}$

83. (a) $\dfrac{6}{x} = \dfrac{13}{20}$

    (b) $\dfrac{6}{x} = \dfrac{13}{20} \Rightarrow 120 = 13x \Rightarrow \dfrac{120}{13} = x \Rightarrow x = \dfrac{120}{13}$

84. (a) $\dfrac{341}{11} = \dfrac{x}{8}$

    (b) $\dfrac{341}{11} = \dfrac{x}{8} \Rightarrow 11x = 2728 \Rightarrow x = \dfrac{2728}{11} \Rightarrow x = \$248$

85. (a) $k = \dfrac{y}{x}, \; y = 8, x = 2 \Rightarrow k = \dfrac{8}{2} \Rightarrow k = 4$

    (b) $y = kx, \; k = 4, x = 5 \Rightarrow y = 4 \cdot 5 \Rightarrow y = 20$

86. (a) $k = \dfrac{y}{x}, \; y = 21, x = 7 \Rightarrow k = \dfrac{21}{7} \Rightarrow k = 3$

    (b) $y = kx, \; k = 3, x = 5 \Rightarrow y = 3 \cdot 5 \Rightarrow y = 15$

87. (a) $k = xy, \; x = 4, y = 2.5 \Rightarrow k = 4 \cdot 2.5 \Rightarrow k = 10$

    (b) $y = \dfrac{k}{x}, \; k = 10, x = 5 \Rightarrow y = \dfrac{10}{5} \Rightarrow y = 2$

88. (a) $k = xy, \; x = 3, y = 7 \Rightarrow k = 3 \cdot 7 \Rightarrow k = 21$

    (b) $y = \dfrac{k}{x}, \; k = 21, x = 5 \Rightarrow y = \dfrac{21}{5}$

89. (a) Inverse, because as x increases y decreases and $k = xy \Rightarrow 2 \cdot 30 = 3 \cdot 20 = 4 \cdot 15$, etc.

(b) $k = xy$, $x = 2$, $y = 30 \Rightarrow k = 2 \cdot 30 \Rightarrow k = 60$; $y = \dfrac{k}{x} \Rightarrow y = \dfrac{60}{x}$

(c) See Figure 89.

Figure 89

Figure 90

Figure 93

90. (a) Direct, because as x increases y also increases and $k = \dfrac{y}{x} \Rightarrow \dfrac{6}{2} = \dfrac{12}{4} = \dfrac{18}{6}$, etc.

(b) $k = \dfrac{y}{x}$, $x = 2$, $y = 6 \Rightarrow k = \dfrac{6}{2} \Rightarrow k = 3$; $y = kx \Rightarrow y = 3x$

(c) See Figure 90.

91. Direct, $k = \dfrac{y}{x}$, $y = 2$, $x = 4 \Rightarrow k = \dfrac{2}{4} \Rightarrow k = \dfrac{1}{2}$

92. Inverse, $k = xy$, $x = 2$, $y = 6 \Rightarrow k = 2 \cdot 6 \Rightarrow k = 12$

Applications

93. (a) $x = 10$, $T = \dfrac{1}{15 - x} \Rightarrow T = \dfrac{1}{15 - 10} = \dfrac{1}{5} = 0.2$, when the rate of arrival is 10 cars/min., the wait is

0.2 minutes or 12 seconds.

(b) $x = 5$, $T = \dfrac{1}{15 - x} \Rightarrow T = \dfrac{1}{15 - 5} = \dfrac{1}{10}$; $x = 10$, $T = \dfrac{1}{15 - x} \Rightarrow T = \dfrac{1}{15 - 10} = \dfrac{1}{5}$;

$x = 13$, $T = \dfrac{1}{15 - x} \Rightarrow T = \dfrac{1}{15 - 13} = \dfrac{1}{2}$; $x = 14$, $T = \dfrac{1}{15 - x} \Rightarrow T = \dfrac{1}{15 - 14} = \dfrac{1}{1} = 1$;

$x = 14.9$, $T = \dfrac{1}{15 - x} \Rightarrow T = \dfrac{1}{15 - 14.9} = \dfrac{1}{0.1} = 10$; See Figure 93.

(c) It increases dramatically.

94. If $r \cdot t = d$, then $50 \cdot t = 150 \Rightarrow t = 3$ and $75t = 150 \Rightarrow t = 2$. The combined $d = 300$ and the combined

$t = 5$. Therefore, $r \cdot 5 = 300 \Rightarrow r = 60 \Rightarrow 60$ mph.

95. $\dfrac{t}{100} + \dfrac{t}{160} = 1 \Rightarrow \dfrac{800t}{100} + \dfrac{800t}{160} = 800 \Rightarrow 8t + 5t = 800 \Rightarrow 13t = 800 \Rightarrow t = \dfrac{800}{13} \Rightarrow t = 61.5$ hrs.

96. Let $x =$ slower jogger speed and $x + 2 =$ faster jogger speed, then $\dfrac{10}{x} - \dfrac{10}{x + 2} = 1 \Rightarrow$

$10x + 20 - 10x = x^2 + 2x \Rightarrow 20 = x^2 + 2x \Rightarrow x^2 + 2x - 20 = 0 \Rightarrow (x - 10)(x + 12) = 0 \Rightarrow$

$x - 10 = 0 \Rightarrow x = 10$, $x + 12 = 0 \Rightarrow x = -12 \Rightarrow x = 10, -12$. Therefore 10 mph and 12 mph.

97. $\dfrac{16}{x-4} = \dfrac{48}{x+4} \Rightarrow 16x + 64 = 48x - 192 \Rightarrow 256 = 32x \Rightarrow \dfrac{256}{32} = x \Rightarrow x = 8$ mph

98. $\dfrac{5}{6} = \dfrac{x}{40} \Rightarrow 6x = 200 \Rightarrow x = \dfrac{200}{6} \Rightarrow x \approx 33.3$ ft.

99. $\dfrac{20}{1} = \dfrac{32}{x} \Rightarrow 20x = 32 \Rightarrow x = \dfrac{32}{20} \Rightarrow x = 1.6$ in.

100. $k = xy,\ x = 0.25,\ y = 400 \Rightarrow k = 0.25 \cdot 400 \Rightarrow k = 100$

$y = \dfrac{k}{x},\ x = 0.50,\ k = 100 \Rightarrow y = \dfrac{100}{0.50} \Rightarrow y = 200$ vehicles

101. $k = xy,\ x = 12,\ y = 30 \Rightarrow k = 12 \cdot 30 \Rightarrow k = 360$

$y = \dfrac{k}{x},\ x = 10,\ k = 360 \Rightarrow y = \dfrac{360}{10} \Rightarrow y = 36$ lbs.

102. $k = \dfrac{y}{x},\ x = 17,\ k = 612 \Rightarrow k = \dfrac{612}{17} \Rightarrow y = 36$

$y = kx,\ k = 36,\ x = 13 \Rightarrow y = 36 \cdot 13 \Rightarrow y = \$468$

103. $30 \cdot 25 = 750$ and $90 \cdot 25 = 2250$, therefore 750 to 2250 sec. or 12.5 to 37.5 min.

Chapter 7 Test

1. $x = 3,\ \dfrac{3x}{2x-1} \Rightarrow \dfrac{3(3)}{2(3)-1} = \dfrac{9}{6-1} = \dfrac{9}{5}$

2. $\dfrac{x-1}{x+2}$, the equation is undefined when $x + 2 = 0 \Rightarrow x = -2$.

3. $\dfrac{x^2-25}{x-5} = \dfrac{(x-5)(x+5)}{x-5} = \dfrac{x-5}{x-5} \cdot x + 5 = 1 \cdot x + 5 = x + 5$

4. $\dfrac{3x^2-15x}{3x} = \dfrac{3x(x-5)}{3x} = \dfrac{3x}{3x} \cdot (x-5) = 1 \cdot (x-5) = x - 5$

5. $\dfrac{x-2}{x+4} \cdot \dfrac{3x+12}{x-2} = \dfrac{x-2}{x-2} \cdot \dfrac{3(x+4)}{x+4} = 1 \cdot 1 \cdot 3 = 3$

6. $\dfrac{z+1}{x+3} \cdot \dfrac{2z+6}{z+1} = \dfrac{z+1}{z+1} \cdot \dfrac{2(z+3)}{z+3} = 1 \cdot 1 \cdot 2 = 2$

7. $\dfrac{x+1}{5x} \div \dfrac{2x+2}{x-1} = \dfrac{x+1}{5x} \cdot \dfrac{x-1}{2x+2} = \dfrac{x+1}{2(x+1)} \cdot \dfrac{x-1}{5x} = \dfrac{x-1}{2(5x)} \cdot 1 = \dfrac{x-1}{10x}$

8. $\dfrac{2}{x^2} \div \dfrac{x+3}{3x} = \dfrac{2}{x^2} \cdot \dfrac{3x}{x+3} = \dfrac{x}{x} \cdot \dfrac{2 \cdot 3}{x(x+3)} = 1 \cdot \dfrac{6}{x(x+3)} = \dfrac{6}{x(x+3)}$

9. $\dfrac{x}{x+4} + \dfrac{3x+1}{x+4} = \dfrac{4x+1}{x+4}$

10. $\dfrac{4t+1}{2t-3} - \dfrac{3t-6}{2t-3} = \dfrac{4t+1-(3t-6)}{2t-3} = \dfrac{t+7}{2t-3}$

11. $\dfrac{1}{y^2+y} - \dfrac{y-1}{y^2-y} = \dfrac{1}{y(y+1)} \cdot \dfrac{y-1}{y-1} - \dfrac{y-1}{y(y-1)} \cdot \dfrac{y+1}{y+1} = \dfrac{y-1}{y(y+1)(y-1)} - \dfrac{y^2-1}{y(y+1)(y-1)} =$

$\dfrac{y-y^2}{y(y+1)(y-1)} = \dfrac{-y(y-1)}{y(y+1)(y-1)} = \dfrac{-1}{y+1} = -\dfrac{1}{y+1}$

12. $\dfrac{1}{xy} + \dfrac{x}{y} - \dfrac{1}{y^2} = \dfrac{y}{xy^2} + \dfrac{x^2 y}{xy^2} - \dfrac{x}{xy^2} = \dfrac{x^2 y - x + y}{xy^2}$

13. $\dfrac{\frac{a}{3b}}{\frac{5a}{b^2}} = \dfrac{a}{3b} \div \dfrac{5a}{b^2} = \dfrac{a}{3b} \cdot \dfrac{b^2}{5a} = \dfrac{a}{a} \cdot \dfrac{b}{b} \cdot \dfrac{b}{15} = 1 \cdot 1 \cdot \dfrac{b}{15} = \dfrac{b}{15}$

14. $\dfrac{1 + \frac{1}{p-1}}{1 - \frac{1}{p-1}} = \dfrac{\frac{p-1}{p-1} + \frac{1}{p-1}}{\frac{p-1}{p-1} - \frac{1}{p-1}} = \dfrac{\frac{p}{p-1}}{\frac{p-2}{p-1}} = \dfrac{p}{p-1} \div \dfrac{p-2}{p-1} = \dfrac{p}{p-1} \cdot \dfrac{p-1}{p-2} = \dfrac{p-1}{p-1} \cdot \dfrac{p}{p-2} = 1 \cdot \dfrac{p}{p-2} =$

$\dfrac{p}{p-2}$

15. $\dfrac{2}{7} = \dfrac{5}{x} \Rightarrow 2x = 35 \Rightarrow x = \dfrac{35}{2}$

16. $\dfrac{x+3}{2x} = 1 \Rightarrow x + 3 = 2x \Rightarrow 3 = x \Rightarrow x = 3$

17. $\dfrac{1}{2x} + \dfrac{2}{5x} = \dfrac{9}{10} = \dfrac{1 \cdot 10x}{2x} + \dfrac{2 \cdot 10x}{5x} = \dfrac{9 \cdot 10x}{10} \Rightarrow 5 + 4 = 9x \Rightarrow 9 = 9x \Rightarrow x = 1$

18. $\dfrac{1}{x-1} + \dfrac{2}{x+2} = \dfrac{3}{2} \Rightarrow \dfrac{2(x-1)(x+2)}{x-1} + \dfrac{2(2)(x-1)(x+2)}{x+2} = \dfrac{3(2)(x-1)(x+2)}{2} \Rightarrow$

$2x + 4 + 4x - 4 = 3x^2 + 3x - 6 \Rightarrow 6x = 3x^2 + 3x - 6 \Rightarrow 3x^2 - 3x - 6 = 0 \Rightarrow$

$3(x+1)(x-2) = 0,\ x + 1 = 0 \Rightarrow x = -1,\ x - 2 = 0 \Rightarrow x = 2 \Rightarrow x = -1, 2$

19. $\dfrac{1}{x^2 - 1} - \dfrac{4}{x+1} = \dfrac{3}{x-1} \Rightarrow \dfrac{1}{(x+1)(x-1)} - \dfrac{4}{x+1} = \dfrac{3}{x-1} \Rightarrow$

$\dfrac{1(x+1)(x-1)}{(x+1)(x-1)} - \dfrac{4(x+1)(x-1)}{x+1} = \dfrac{3(x+1)(x-1)}{x-1} \Rightarrow 1 - (4x - 4) = 3x + 3 \Rightarrow$

$-4x + 5 = 3x + 3 \Rightarrow -7x = -2 \Rightarrow x = \dfrac{-2}{-7} \Rightarrow x = \dfrac{2}{7}$

20. $\dfrac{1}{x^2 - 4x} + \dfrac{2}{x^2 - 16} = \dfrac{2}{x^2 + 4x} \Rightarrow \dfrac{1}{4(x-4)} + \dfrac{2}{(x-4)(x+4)} = \dfrac{2}{x(x+4)} \Rightarrow$

$\dfrac{1(x)(x+4)(x-4)}{x(x-4)} + \dfrac{2(x)(x+4)(x-4)}{(x-4)(x+4)} = \dfrac{2(x)(x+4)(x-4)}{x(x+4)} \Rightarrow x + 4 + 2x = 2x - 8 \Rightarrow$

$3x + 4 = 2x - 8 \Rightarrow x = -12$

21. $y = \dfrac{2}{3x - 5}$ for x, $y(3x - 5) = 2 \Rightarrow 3x - 5 = \dfrac{2}{y} \Rightarrow 3x = \dfrac{2}{y} + 5 \Rightarrow x = \left(\dfrac{2}{y} + 5\right)\dfrac{1}{3} \Rightarrow$

$x = \dfrac{2}{3y} + \dfrac{5}{3} \Rightarrow x = \dfrac{2}{3y} + \dfrac{5y}{3} \Rightarrow x = \dfrac{2 + 5y}{3y}$

22. $\dfrac{a+b}{ab} = 1$ for b, $ab = a + b \Rightarrow ab - b = a \Rightarrow b(a - 1) = a \Rightarrow b = \dfrac{a}{a - 1}$

23. (a) $k = \dfrac{y}{x} \Rightarrow k = \dfrac{14}{4} \Rightarrow k = \dfrac{7}{2}$

   (b) $y = kx \Rightarrow y = \dfrac{7}{2}(6) \Rightarrow y = \dfrac{42}{2} \Rightarrow y = 21$

24. Inversely, as x increases y decreases and for all $k = xy$, $k = 32$.

25. $\dfrac{t}{40} + \dfrac{t}{60} = 1 \Rightarrow \dfrac{120t}{40} + \dfrac{120t}{60} = 120 \Rightarrow 3t + 2t = 120 \Rightarrow 5t = 120 \Rightarrow t = 24$ hours

26. $\dfrac{5}{4} = \dfrac{x}{54} \Rightarrow 4x = 270 \Rightarrow x = 67.5$ ft.

27. $N = \dfrac{x^2}{900 - 30x}$ for $x = 24$, $N = \dfrac{24^2}{900 - 30(24)} \Rightarrow N = \dfrac{576}{900 - 720} \Rightarrow N = \dfrac{576}{180} \Rightarrow N = \dfrac{16}{5}$ or 3.2;

    when the arrival rate is 24 people/hr., there are about 3 people in line.

Chapter 7 Extended and Discovery Exercises

1. (a) $x = 3$, $N = \dfrac{3^2}{225 - 15(3)} = \dfrac{9}{225 - 45} = \dfrac{9}{180} = \dfrac{1}{20} \Rightarrow N = 0.05$;

      $x = 9$, $N = \dfrac{9^2}{225 - 15(9)} = \dfrac{81}{225 - 135} = \dfrac{81}{90} = \dfrac{9}{10} \Rightarrow N = 0.9$;

      $x = 12$, $N = \dfrac{12^2}{225 - 15(12)} = \dfrac{144}{225 - 180} = \dfrac{144}{45} = \dfrac{16}{5} \Rightarrow N = 3.2$;

      $x = 13$, $N = \dfrac{13^2}{225 - 15(13)} = \dfrac{169}{225 - 195} = \dfrac{169}{30} \Rightarrow N = 5.6\overline{3}$;

      $x = 14$, $N = \dfrac{14^2}{225 - 15(14)} = \dfrac{196}{225 - 210} = \dfrac{196}{15} \Rightarrow N = 13.0\overline{6}$ See Figure 1a.

   (b) $x = 15$, because $\dfrac{15^2}{225 - 15(15)} = \dfrac{225}{0}$, which is undefined.

   (c) See Figure 1c.

   (d) See Figure 1d.

   (e) As x approaches 15, the wait increases dramatically.

   (f) The formula is only valid for arrival rates under 15 cars per hour, but it can be inferred that the line of cars will continue to grow.

x	3	9	12	13	14
N	0.05	0.9	3.2	5.6$\overline{3}$	13.0$\overline{6}$

Figure 1a

Figure 1c

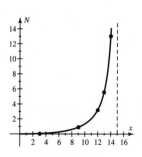

Figure 1d

2. (a) $x = -4$, $y = \dfrac{1}{-4 - 1} \Rightarrow y = -\dfrac{1}{5}$; $x = -3$, $y = \dfrac{1}{-3 - 1} \Rightarrow y = -\dfrac{1}{4}$;

$x = -2$, $y = \dfrac{1}{-2 - 1} \Rightarrow y = -\dfrac{1}{3}$; $x = -1$, $y = \dfrac{1}{-1 - 1} \Rightarrow y = -\dfrac{1}{2}$;

$x = 0$, $y = \dfrac{1}{0 - 1} \Rightarrow y = -\dfrac{1}{1} = -1$; $x = 1$, $y = \dfrac{1}{1 - 1} \Rightarrow y = \dfrac{1}{0} \Rightarrow y =$ undefined;

$x = 2$, $y = \dfrac{1}{2 - 1} \Rightarrow y = \dfrac{1}{1} \Rightarrow y = 1$; $x = 3$, $y = \dfrac{1}{3 - 1} \Rightarrow y = \dfrac{1}{2}$;

$x = 4$, $y = \dfrac{1}{4 - 1} \Rightarrow y = \dfrac{1}{3}$; See Figure 2a.

(b) $x = 1$ yields $\dfrac{1}{0}$ which is undefined.

(c) See Figure 2c-e.

(d) See Figure 2c-e.

(e) See Figure 2c-e.

x	-4	-3	-2	-1	0	1	2	3	4
y	-0.2	-0.25	$-0.\overline{3}$	-0.5	-1	—	1	0.5	$0.\overline{3}$

Figure 2a   Figure 2c-e

3. (a) $x = -4$, $y = \dfrac{1}{-4 + 1} \Rightarrow y = -\dfrac{1}{3}$; $x = -3$, $y = \dfrac{1}{-3 + 1} \Rightarrow y = -\dfrac{1}{2}$;

$x = -2$, $y = \dfrac{1}{-2 + 1} \Rightarrow y = -\dfrac{1}{1} = -1$; $x = -1$, $y = \dfrac{1}{-1 + 1} \Rightarrow y = \dfrac{1}{0} \Rightarrow y =$ undefined;

$x = 0$, $y = \dfrac{1}{0 + 1} \Rightarrow y = \dfrac{1}{1} = 1$; $x = 1$, $y = \dfrac{1}{1 + 1} \Rightarrow y = \dfrac{1}{2}$;

$x = 2$, $y = \dfrac{1}{2 + 1} \Rightarrow y = \dfrac{1}{3}$; $x = 3$, $y = \dfrac{1}{3 + 1} \Rightarrow y = \dfrac{1}{4}$;

$x = 4$, $y = \dfrac{1}{4 + 1} \Rightarrow y = \dfrac{1}{5}$; See Figure 3a.

(b) $x = -1$ yields $\dfrac{1}{0}$ which is undefined.

(c) See Figure 3c-e.

(d) See Figure 3c-e.

(e) See Figure 3c-e.

x	−4	−3	−2	−1	0	1	2	3	4
y	−0.$\overline{3}$	−0.5	−1	—	1	0.5	0.$\overline{3}$	0.25	0.2

Figure 3a

Figure 3c-e

4. (a) $x = -4,\ y = \dfrac{4}{16 + 1} \Rightarrow y = \dfrac{4}{17};\ x = -3,\ y = \dfrac{4}{9 + 1} \Rightarrow y = \dfrac{4}{10};$

   $x = -2,\ y = \dfrac{4}{4 + 1} \Rightarrow y = \dfrac{4}{5};\ x = -1,\ y = \dfrac{4}{1 + 1} \Rightarrow y = \dfrac{4}{2} \Rightarrow y = 2;$

   $x = 0,\ y = \dfrac{4}{0 + 1} \Rightarrow y = \dfrac{4}{1} = 4;\ x = 1,\ y = \dfrac{4}{1 + 1} \Rightarrow y = \dfrac{4}{2} = 2;$

   $x = 2,\ y = \dfrac{4}{4 + 1} \Rightarrow y = \dfrac{4}{5};\ x = 3,\ y = \dfrac{4}{9 + 1} \Rightarrow y = \dfrac{4}{10};$

   $x = 4,\ y = \dfrac{4}{16 + 1} \Rightarrow y = \dfrac{4}{17};$ See Figure 4a.

   (b) No points are undefined.

   (c) See Figure 4c-e.

   (d) See Figure 4c-e.

   (e) See Figure 4c-e.

x	−4	−3	−2	−1	0	1	2	3	4
y	0.235	0.4	0.8	2	4	2	0.8	0.4	0.235

Figure 4a

Figure 4c-e

5. (a) $x = -4$, $y = \dfrac{-4}{-4 + 1} \Rightarrow y = \dfrac{4}{3}$; $x = -3$, $y = \dfrac{-3}{-3 + 1} \Rightarrow y = \dfrac{3}{2}$;

$x = -2$, $y = \dfrac{-2}{-2 + 1} \Rightarrow y = \dfrac{2}{1} = 2$; $x = -1$, $y = \dfrac{-1}{-1 + 1} \Rightarrow y = \dfrac{-1}{0} \Rightarrow y = $ undefined;

$x = 0$, $y = \dfrac{0}{0 + 1} \Rightarrow y = \dfrac{0}{1} = 0$; $x = 1$, $y = \dfrac{1}{1 + 1} \Rightarrow y = \dfrac{1}{2}$;

$x = 2$, $y = \dfrac{2}{2 + 1} \Rightarrow y = \dfrac{2}{3}$; $x = 3$, $y = \dfrac{3}{3 + 1} \Rightarrow y = \dfrac{3}{4}$;

$x = 4$, $y = \dfrac{4}{4 + 1} \Rightarrow y = \dfrac{4}{5}$; See Figure 5a.

(b) $x = -1$ yields $\dfrac{-1}{0}$ which is undefined.

(c) See Figure 5c-e.

(d) See Figure 5c-e.

(e) See Figure 5c-e.

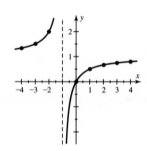

x	-4	-3	-2	-1	0	1	2	3	4
y	$1.\overline{3}$	1.5	2	—	0	0.5	$0.\overline{6}$	0.75	0.8

Figure 5a   Figure 5c-e

6. (a) $x = -4$, $y = \dfrac{-4}{-4 - 1} \Rightarrow y = \dfrac{4}{5}$; $x = -3$, $y = \dfrac{-3}{-3 - 1} \Rightarrow y = \dfrac{3}{4}$;

$x = -2$, $y = \dfrac{-2}{-2 - 1} \Rightarrow y = \dfrac{2}{3}$; $x = -1$, $y = \dfrac{-1}{-1 - 1} \Rightarrow y = \dfrac{1}{2}$;

$x = 0$, $y = \dfrac{0}{0 - 1} \Rightarrow y = \dfrac{0}{-1} = 0$; $x = 1$, $y = \dfrac{1}{1 - 1} \Rightarrow y = \dfrac{1}{0} \Rightarrow y = $ undefined;

$x = 2$, $y = \dfrac{2}{2 - 1} \Rightarrow y = \dfrac{2}{1} = 2$; $x = 3$, $y = \dfrac{3}{3 - 1} \Rightarrow y = \dfrac{3}{2}$;

$x = 4$, $y = \dfrac{4}{4 - 1} \Rightarrow y = \dfrac{4}{3}$; See Figure 6a.

(b) $x = 1$ yields $\dfrac{1}{0}$ which is undefined.

(c) See Figure 6c-e.

(d) See Figure 6c-e.

(e) See Figure 6c-e.

x	-4	-3	-2	-1	0	1	2	3	4
y	0.8	0.75	$0.\overline{6}$	0.5	0	—	2	1.5	$1.\overline{3}$

Figure 6a   Figure 6c-e

Critical Thinking Solutions for Chapter 7

Section 7.1

- With n winning numbers, the number of nonwinners out of 100 is $100 - n$. Therefore the probability of not drawing a winning number is $\dfrac{100 - n}{100}$.

Section 7.2

- $\dfrac{x^2 - 1}{x + 5} \div \dfrac{x - 1}{x + 5} \div x + 1 = \dfrac{(x + 1)(x - 1)}{x + 5} \cdot \dfrac{x + 5}{x - 1} \cdot \dfrac{1}{x + 1} = \dfrac{1}{1} = 1$

Section 7.4

- $x + \dfrac{1}{x} = \dfrac{x}{1} + \dfrac{1}{x} = \dfrac{x^2}{x} + \dfrac{1}{x} = \dfrac{x^2 + 1}{x}$, then the reciprocal is $\dfrac{x}{x^2 + 1}$

Section 7.5

- No, $\dfrac{\frac{a}{b}}{\frac{a}{b} + 1} = \dfrac{\frac{a}{b}}{\frac{a}{b} + \frac{b}{b}} = \dfrac{\frac{a}{b}}{\frac{a + b}{b}} = \dfrac{a}{b} \div \dfrac{a + b}{b} = \dfrac{a}{b} \cdot \dfrac{b}{a + b} = \dfrac{a}{a + b}$, which is not equal to $\dfrac{1}{1 + 1}$.

  Yes, $\dfrac{\frac{a + b}{b}}{\frac{a}{b}} = \dfrac{a + b}{b} \div \dfrac{a}{b} = \dfrac{a + b}{b} \cdot \dfrac{b}{a} = \dfrac{b}{b} \cdot \dfrac{a + b}{a} = 1 \cdot \dfrac{a + b}{a} = \dfrac{a + b}{a} = 1 + \dfrac{b}{a}$, which does equal $1 + \dfrac{b}{a}$.

Section 7.6

- Solving $y = \dfrac{2}{x}$ and $y = x + 1$ by substitution, we get $\dfrac{2}{x} = x + 1 \Rightarrow 2 = x^2 + x \Rightarrow x^2 + x - 2 = 0 \Rightarrow$

  $(x - 1)(x + 2) = 0 \Rightarrow x - 1 = 0 \Rightarrow x = 1$ and $x + 2 = 0 \Rightarrow x = -2$, so $x = 1, -2$, the same answers from

  the graph and table.

- $\dfrac{t}{x} + \dfrac{t}{y} = 1 \Rightarrow \dfrac{txy}{x} + \dfrac{txy}{y} = xy \Rightarrow ty + tx = xy \Rightarrow t(x + y) = xy \Rightarrow t = \dfrac{xy}{x + y}$

Section 7.7

- Using $S = kwt^2$ and width w and thickness t; when width doubles, $w = 2w$, stength $S = k2wt^2 \Rightarrow$ $S = 2kwt^2$ or strength doubles. When thickness t doubles, $t = 2t$, strength $S = kw(2t)^2 \Rightarrow S = 4kwt^2$ or strength quadruples. And when both triple, $w = 3w$ and $t = 3t$, strength $S = k3w(3t)^2 \Rightarrow S = 27kwt^2$ or strength is 27 times greater.

Chapter 8: Radical Expressions

8.1: Introduction to Radical Expressions

Concepts

1. Square root

3. radicand

5. Irrational

7. $\sqrt[3]{64} = 4$

9. $3^2 + 4^2 = c^2 \Rightarrow 9 + 16 = c^2 \Rightarrow 25 = c^2 \Rightarrow \sqrt{c^2} = \sqrt{25} \Rightarrow c = 5$

Square and Cube Roots

11. $\sqrt{4} = \pm\sqrt{4} = \pm 2$

13. $\sqrt{49} = \pm\sqrt{49} = \pm 7$

15. $\sqrt{121} = \pm\sqrt{121} = \pm 11$

17. $\sqrt{400} = \pm\sqrt{400} = \pm 20$

19. $\sqrt{196} = \pm\sqrt{196} = \pm 14$

21. $\sqrt{8} = \pm\sqrt{8} = \pm 2.828$

23. $\sqrt{24} = \pm\sqrt{24} = \pm 4.899$

25. $\sqrt{100} = \pm 10 \Rightarrow$ real, rational

27. $\sqrt{2500} = \pm 50 \Rightarrow$ real, rational

29. $\sqrt{6} = \pm 2.45 \Rightarrow$ real, irrational

31. $\sqrt{150} = \pm 12.28 \Rightarrow$ real, irrational

33. None, no real solution to a square root of a negative number.

35. $\sqrt{144} = 12$

37. $-\sqrt{9} = -(3) = -3$

39. $\sqrt{10} = 3.16$

41. $\sqrt[3]{8} = 2$ because $2^3 = 2 \cdot 2 \cdot 2 = 8$

43. $\sqrt[3]{-125} = -5$ because $(-5)^3 = (-5)(-5)(-5) = -125$

45. $-\sqrt[3]{27} = -(3) = -3$ because $-3^3 = -(3 \cdot 3 \cdot 3) = -(27)$

47. $-\sqrt[3]{-1} = \sqrt[3]{1} = 1$ because $1^3 = 1 \cdot 1 \cdot 1 = 1$

49. $\sqrt[3]{1000} = 10$ because $10^3 = 10 \cdot 10 \cdot 10 = 1000$

51. $\sqrt[3]{-343} = -7$ because $(-7)^3 = (-7)(-7)(-7) = -343$

53. $\sqrt[3]{5} = 1.710$ because $1.710^3 = 1.710 \cdot 1.710 \cdot 1.710 = 5$

55. $\sqrt[3]{-16} = -2.520$ because $(-2.520)^3 = (-2.520)(-2.520)(-2.520) = -16$

57. $\sqrt[3]{-9} = -2.080$ because $(-2.080)^3 = (-2.080)(-2.080)(-2.080) = -9$

Pythagorean Theorem

59. Given $a = 4$ inches, $b = 3$ inches, and using Pythagorean Theorem: $a^2 + b^2 = c^2$, we get $4^2 + 3^2 = c^2 \Rightarrow$ $16 + 9 = c^2 \Rightarrow 25 = c^2 \Rightarrow \sqrt{25} = \sqrt{c^2} \Rightarrow c = 5$ inches.

61. Given $a = 5$ meters, $b = 12$ meters, and using Pythagorean Theorem: $a^2 + b^2 = c^2$, we get $5^2 + 12^2 = c^2 \Rightarrow$ $25 + 144 = c^2 \Rightarrow 169 = c^2 \Rightarrow \sqrt{169} = \sqrt{c^2} \Rightarrow c = 13$ meters.

63. Given $c = 3$ miles, $b = 2$ miles, and using Pythagorean Theorem: $a^2 + b^2 = c^2$, we get $a^2 + 2^2 = 3^2 \Rightarrow$ $a^2 + 4 = 9 \Rightarrow a^2 = 5 \Rightarrow \sqrt{a^2} = \sqrt{5} \Rightarrow a = \sqrt{5}$ miles.

65. Given $a = 6$ feet, $c = 10$ feet, and using Pythagorean Theorem: $a^2 + b^2 = c^2$, we get $6^2 + b^2 = 10^2 \Rightarrow$ $36 + b^2 = 100 \Rightarrow b^2 = 64 \Rightarrow \sqrt{b^2} = \sqrt{64} \Rightarrow b = 8$ feet.

67. Given $a = 5$, $b = 12$, c $= 13$, and using Pythagorean Theorem: $a^2 + b^2 = c^2$, we get $5^2 + 12^2 = 13^2 \Rightarrow$ $25 + 144 = 169 \Rightarrow 169 = 169$, yes a right triangle.

69. Given $a = 6$, $b = 4$, c $= 8$, and using Pythagorean Theorem: $a^2 + b^2 = c^2$, we get $6^2 + 4^2 = 8^2 \Rightarrow$ $36 + 16 = 64 \Rightarrow 52 \neq 64$, no not a right triangle.

71. Given $a = 60$, $b = 11$, c $= 61$, and using Pythagorean Theorem: $a^2 + b^2 = c^2$, we get $60^2 + 11^2 = 61^2 \Rightarrow$ $3600 + 121 = 3721 \Rightarrow 3721 = 3721$, yes a right triangle.

The Distance Formula

73. Using $d = \sqrt{(x_2 - x_1)^2 + (y_2 - y_1)^2}$, for $(-3, -1)$, $(1, 2)$, we get $d = \sqrt{(1 - (-3))^2 + (2 - (-1))^2} \Rightarrow$ $d = \sqrt{(4)^2 + (3)^2} \Rightarrow d = \sqrt{16 + 9} \Rightarrow d = \sqrt{25} \Rightarrow d = 5$

75. Using $d = \sqrt{(x_2 - x_1)^2 + (y_2 - y_1)^2}$, for $(-20, 30)$, $(20, -20)$, we get $d = \sqrt{20 - (-20))^2 + (-20 - 30)^2} \Rightarrow d = \sqrt{(40)^2 + (-50)^2} \Rightarrow d = \sqrt{1600 + 2500} \Rightarrow$ $d = \sqrt{4100} \Rightarrow d = \sqrt{4100} \approx 64.03$

77. Using $d = \sqrt{(x_2 - x_1)^2 + (y_2 - y_1)^2}$, for $(1, 3)$, $(4, 7)$, we get $d = \sqrt{(4 - 1)^2 + (7 - 3)^2} \Rightarrow$ $d = \sqrt{(3)^2 + (4)^2} \Rightarrow d = \sqrt{9 + 16} \Rightarrow d = \sqrt{25} \Rightarrow d = 5.$

79. Using $d = \sqrt{(x_2 - x_1)^2 + (y_2 - y_1)^2}$, for $(4, -4)$, $(-3, 20)$, we get $d = \sqrt{(-3 - 4)^2 + (20 - (-4))^2} \Rightarrow$ $d = \sqrt{(-7)^2 + (24)^2} \Rightarrow d = \sqrt{49 + 576} \Rightarrow d = \sqrt{625} \Rightarrow d = 25.$

81. Using $d = \sqrt{(x_2 - x_1)^2 + (y_2 - y_1)^2}$, for $(-3, 5)$, $(2, -6)$, we get $d = \sqrt{(2 - (-3))^2 + (-6 - 5)^2} \Rightarrow$ $d = \sqrt{(5)^2 + (-11)^2} \Rightarrow d = \sqrt{25 + 121} \Rightarrow d = \sqrt{146} \Rightarrow d = \sqrt{146} \approx 12.083$

83. Using $d = \sqrt{(x_2 - x_1)^2 + (y_2 - y_1)^2}$, for $(-2, -1)$, $(0, -9)$, we get $d = \sqrt{(0 - (-2))^2 + (-9 - (-1))^2} \Rightarrow$ $d = \sqrt{(2)^2 + (-8)^2} \Rightarrow d = \sqrt{4 + 64} \Rightarrow d = \sqrt{68} \Rightarrow d = \sqrt{68} \approx 8.246$

Applications

85. Using Pythagorean Theorem: $a^2 + b^2 = c^2$, for $b = 5$ inches, $c = 13$ inches, we get $a^2 + 5^2 = 13^2 \Rightarrow$ $a^2 + 25 = 169 \Rightarrow a^2 = 144 \Rightarrow \sqrt{a^2} = \sqrt{144} \Rightarrow a = 12$ inches. Therefore the perimeter is $a + b = c \Rightarrow$ $12 + 5 + 13 = 30$ inches.

87. Using Pythagorean Theorem: $a^2 + b^2 = c^2$, for $a = 9$ feet, $b = 12$ feet, we get $9^2 + 12^2 = c^2 \Rightarrow$ $81 + 144 = c^2 \Rightarrow 225 = c^2 \Rightarrow \sqrt{225} = \sqrt{c^2} \Rightarrow c = 15$ feet. Therefore the diagonal is 15 feet.

89. (a) For $h = 3$, $F = \dfrac{0.87}{\sqrt{h}} \Rightarrow F = \dfrac{0.87}{\sqrt{3}} \Rightarrow F = \dfrac{0.87}{\sqrt{3}} \approx 0.502$ steps/second

    (b) For $h = 0.8$, $F = \dfrac{0.87}{\sqrt{h}} \Rightarrow F = \dfrac{0.87}{\sqrt{0.8}} \Rightarrow F = \dfrac{0.87}{\sqrt{0.8}} \approx 0.973$ steps/second

    (c) For $h = 0.6$, $F = \dfrac{0.87}{\sqrt{h}} \Rightarrow F = \dfrac{0.87}{\sqrt{0.6}} \Rightarrow F = \dfrac{0.87}{\sqrt{0.6}} \approx 1.123$ steps/second

91. Using Pythagorean Theorem: $a^2 + b^2 = c^2$, for $a = 20$ inches, $b = 15$ inches, we get $20^2 + 15^2 = c^2 \Rightarrow$ $400 + 225 = c^2 \Rightarrow 625 = c^2 \Rightarrow \sqrt{c^2} = \sqrt{625} \Rightarrow c = 25$ inches.

93. Using Pythagorean Theorem: $a^2 + b^2 = c^2$, for $a = 15$ feet, $c = 40$ feet, we get $15^2 + b^2 = 40^2 \Rightarrow$ $225 + b^2 = 1600 \Rightarrow b^2 = 1375 \Rightarrow \sqrt{b^2} = \sqrt{1375} \Rightarrow b = \sqrt{1375} = 37.1$ feet.

95. Using Pythagorean Theorem: $a^2 + b^2 = c^2$, for $a = 52$ feet, $b = 96$ feet, we get $52^2 + 96^2 = c^2 \Rightarrow$ $2704 + 9216 = c^2 \Rightarrow 11{,}920 = c^2 \Rightarrow \sqrt{c^2} = \sqrt{11{,}920} \Rightarrow c = 109.2$ feet.

97. Using Pythagorean Theorem: $a^2 + b^2 = c^2$, for $a = 25 \cdot 2.5$ miles, $b = 20 \cdot 2.5$ miles $\Rightarrow$ $a = 62.5$ miles, b = 50 miles, we get $62.5^2 + 50^2 = c^2 \Rightarrow 3906.25 + 2500 = c^2 \Rightarrow 6406.25 = c^2 \Rightarrow$ $\sqrt{c^2} = \sqrt{6406.25} \Rightarrow c = 80$ miles.

99. The height h is one leg of a right triangle with hypotenuse a and base $\dfrac{a}{2}$. Using Pythagorean Therem:

$$a^2 + b^2 = c^2 \text{ we get } h^2 + \left(\frac{a}{2}\right)^2 = a^2 \Rightarrow h^2 = a^2 - \frac{a^2}{4} \Rightarrow h^2 = \frac{4a^2}{4} - \frac{a^2}{4} \Rightarrow h^2 = \frac{3a^2}{4} \Rightarrow$$

$$\sqrt{h^2} = \sqrt{\frac{3a^2}{4}} \Rightarrow h = \frac{a\sqrt{3}}{2}$$

8.2: Multiplication and Division of Radical Expressions

Concepts

1. $\sqrt{2} \cdot \sqrt{32} \Rightarrow \sqrt{2 \cdot 32} \Rightarrow \sqrt{64} \Rightarrow 8$

3. $\sqrt{25} = 5$, yes

5. $\sqrt{8} \Rightarrow \sqrt{4} \cdot \sqrt{2} \Rightarrow 2\sqrt{2}$

7. $\dfrac{\sqrt{32}}{\sqrt{2}} \Rightarrow \dfrac{\sqrt{16} \cdot \sqrt{2}}{\sqrt{2}} \Rightarrow 4 \cdot \dfrac{\sqrt{2}}{\sqrt{2}} \Rightarrow 4 \cdot 1 \Rightarrow 4$

Multiplying Square Roots

9. $\sqrt{5} \cdot \sqrt{5} = \sqrt{5 \cdot 5} = \sqrt{25} = 5$

11. $\sqrt{3} \cdot \sqrt{7} = \sqrt{3 \cdot 7} = \sqrt{21}$

13. $\sqrt{\dfrac{1}{2}} \cdot \sqrt{\dfrac{1}{2}} = \sqrt{\dfrac{1}{2} \cdot \dfrac{1}{2}} = \sqrt{\dfrac{1}{4}} = \dfrac{1}{2}$

15. $\sqrt{\frac{3}{5}} \cdot \sqrt{\frac{2}{7}} = \sqrt{\frac{3}{5} \cdot \frac{2}{7}} = \sqrt{\frac{6}{35}}$

17. $\sqrt{2} \cdot \sqrt{8} = \sqrt{2 \cdot 8} = \sqrt{16} = 4$

19. $\sqrt{48} \cdot \sqrt{3} = \sqrt{48 \cdot 3} = \sqrt{144} = 12$

21. $\sqrt{5x} \cdot \sqrt{3} = \sqrt{5x \cdot 3} = \sqrt{15x}$

23. $\sqrt{a} \cdot \sqrt{5b} = \sqrt{a \cdot 5b} = \sqrt{5ab}$

25. 4, because $4 \cdot 5 = 20$

27. 144, because $144 \cdot 1 = 144$

29. 100, because $100 \cdot 2 = 200$

31. 64, because $64 \cdot 2 = 128$

33. $\sqrt{75} = \underline{}\sqrt{3} \Rightarrow \sqrt{75} = \underline{\sqrt{25}} \cdot \sqrt{3} \Rightarrow \sqrt{75} = \underline{5}\sqrt{3}$; therefore 5

35. $\sqrt{24} = \underline{}\sqrt{6} \Rightarrow \sqrt{24} = \underline{\sqrt{4}} \cdot \sqrt{6} \Rightarrow \sqrt{24} = \underline{2}\sqrt{6}$; therefore 2

37. $\sqrt{28} = \underline{}\sqrt{7} \Rightarrow \sqrt{28} = \underline{\sqrt{4}} \cdot \sqrt{7} \Rightarrow \sqrt{28} = \underline{2}\sqrt{7}$; therefore 2

39. $\sqrt{20} = \sqrt{4} \cdot \sqrt{5} = 2\sqrt{5}$

41. $\sqrt{63} = \sqrt{9} \cdot \sqrt{7} = 3\sqrt{7}$

43. $\sqrt{12} = \sqrt{4} \cdot \sqrt{3} = 2\sqrt{3}$

45. $\sqrt{300} = \sqrt{100} \cdot \sqrt{3} = 10\sqrt{3}$

47. $\sqrt{180} = \sqrt{36} \cdot \sqrt{5} = 6\sqrt{5}$

49. $\sqrt{t^3} = \sqrt{t^2} \cdot \sqrt{t} = t\sqrt{t}$

51. $\sqrt{4a^2} = \sqrt{4} \cdot \sqrt{a^2} = 2a$

53. $\sqrt{81x^4} = \sqrt{81} \cdot \sqrt{x^4} = 9x^2$

55. $\sqrt{8x^2} = \sqrt{4x^2} \cdot \sqrt{2} = 2x\sqrt{2}$

57. $\sqrt{125t^3} = \sqrt{25t^2} \cdot \sqrt{5t} = 5t\sqrt{5t}$

59. $\sqrt{x^2y^2} = xy$

61. $\sqrt{16x^2y^3} = \sqrt{16x^2y^2} \cdot \sqrt{y} = 4xy\sqrt{y}$

63. $\sqrt{\frac{4}{49}} = \frac{\sqrt{4}}{\sqrt{49}} = \frac{2}{7}$

65. $\sqrt{\frac{16}{81}} = \frac{\sqrt{16}}{\sqrt{81}} = \frac{4}{9}$

67. $\sqrt{\frac{17}{36}} = \frac{\sqrt{17}}{\sqrt{36}} = \frac{\sqrt{17}}{6}$

69. $\sqrt{\frac{0.01}{0.49}} = \frac{\sqrt{0.01}}{\sqrt{0.49}} = \frac{0.1}{0.7} = \frac{1}{7}$

71. $\frac{\sqrt{72}}{\sqrt{2}} = \frac{\sqrt{36} \cdot \sqrt{2}}{\sqrt{2}} = 6 \cdot \frac{\sqrt{2}}{\sqrt{2}} = 6 \cdot 1 = 6$

73. $\dfrac{\sqrt{75}}{\sqrt{3}} = \dfrac{\sqrt{25} \cdot \sqrt{3}}{\sqrt{3}} = 5 \cdot \dfrac{\sqrt{3}}{\sqrt{3}} = 5 \cdot 1 = 5$

75. $\sqrt{5} \cdot \dfrac{\sqrt{5}}{\sqrt{9}} = \dfrac{\sqrt{5 \cdot 5}}{\sqrt{9}} = \dfrac{\sqrt{25}}{\sqrt{9}} = \dfrac{5}{3}$

77. $\sqrt{\dfrac{2}{3}} \cdot \dfrac{\sqrt{2}}{\sqrt{3}} = \dfrac{\sqrt{2}}{\sqrt{3}} \cdot \dfrac{\sqrt{2}}{\sqrt{3}} = \dfrac{\sqrt{2 \cdot 2}}{\sqrt{3 \cdot 3}} = \dfrac{\sqrt{4}}{\sqrt{9}} = \dfrac{2}{3}$

79. $\sqrt{\dfrac{x^2}{9}} = \dfrac{\sqrt{x^2}}{\sqrt{9}} = \dfrac{x}{3}$

81. $\sqrt{\dfrac{2y^2}{49}} = \dfrac{\sqrt{2y^2}}{\sqrt{49}} = \dfrac{y\sqrt{2}}{7}$

83. $\sqrt{\dfrac{16}{x^3}} = \dfrac{\sqrt{16}}{\sqrt{x^3}} = \dfrac{\sqrt{16}}{\sqrt{x^2} \cdot \sqrt{x}} = \dfrac{4}{x\sqrt{x}}$

85. $\sqrt{\dfrac{20}{y^4}} = \dfrac{\sqrt{20}}{\sqrt{y^4}} = \dfrac{\sqrt{4} \cdot \sqrt{5}}{\sqrt{y^4}} = \dfrac{2\sqrt{5}}{y^2}$

87. $\sqrt{2xy} \cdot \sqrt{2xy} = \sqrt{2xy \cdot 2xy} = \sqrt{4x^2y^2} = 2xy$

89. $\sqrt{2xy} \cdot \sqrt{8xy^3} = \sqrt{2xy \cdot 8xy^3} = \sqrt{16x^2y^4} = 4xy^2$

91. $\sqrt{\dfrac{2}{x^2y^2}} = \dfrac{\sqrt{2}}{\sqrt{x^2y^2}} = \dfrac{\sqrt{2}}{xy}$

93. $\sqrt{\dfrac{x^2y^3}{50}} = \dfrac{\sqrt{x^2y^3}}{\sqrt{50}} = \dfrac{\sqrt{x^2y^2} \cdot \sqrt{y}}{\sqrt{25} \cdot \sqrt{2}} = \dfrac{xy\sqrt{y}}{5\sqrt{2}}$

95. $\dfrac{\sqrt{75x^3}}{\sqrt{3x}} = \dfrac{\sqrt{25x^2} \cdot \sqrt{3x}}{\sqrt{3x}} = 5x \cdot \dfrac{\sqrt{3x}}{\sqrt{3x}} = 5x \cdot 1 = 5x$

97. $\dfrac{\sqrt{50xy}}{\sqrt{2xy}} = \dfrac{\sqrt{25} \cdot \sqrt{2xy}}{\sqrt{2xy}} = 5 \cdot \dfrac{\sqrt{2xy}}{\sqrt{2xy}} = 5 \cdot 1 = 5$

99. $\dfrac{\sqrt{2x}}{\sqrt{3y}} \cdot \dfrac{\sqrt{32xy^2}}{\sqrt{3x^2y}} = \dfrac{\sqrt{2x \cdot 32xy^2}}{\sqrt{3y \cdot 3x^2y}} = \dfrac{\sqrt{64x^2y^2}}{\sqrt{9x^2y^2}} = \dfrac{8xy}{3xy} = \dfrac{8}{3} \cdot \dfrac{xy}{xy} = \dfrac{8}{3} \cdot 1 = \dfrac{8}{3}$

101. $\sqrt{\dfrac{32}{xy}} \cdot \sqrt{\dfrac{x^3y}{2}} = \dfrac{\sqrt{32 \cdot x^3y}}{\sqrt{xy \cdot 2}} = \dfrac{\sqrt{32x^3y}}{\sqrt{2xy}} = \dfrac{\sqrt{16x^2} \cdot \sqrt{2xy}}{\sqrt{2xy}} = 4x \cdot \dfrac{\sqrt{2xy}}{\sqrt{2xy}} = 4x \cdot 1 = 4x$

Applications

103. (a) If $h = 81$ and $T = \sqrt{\dfrac{h}{4}}$, then $T = \sqrt{\dfrac{81}{4}} \Rightarrow T = \dfrac{\sqrt{81}}{\sqrt{4}} \Rightarrow T = \dfrac{9}{2}$ seconds

   (b) $T = \sqrt{\dfrac{h}{4}} \Rightarrow T = \dfrac{\sqrt{h}}{\sqrt{4}} \Rightarrow T = \dfrac{\sqrt{h}}{2}$

105. (a) If $v = 40$mph, $D = 225$ feet, $d = 100$ feet, and $V = \sqrt{\dfrac{v^2 D}{d}}$, then $V = \sqrt{\dfrac{40^2 \cdot 225}{100}} \Rightarrow$

$V = \dfrac{\sqrt{1600 \cdot 225}}{\sqrt{100}} \Rightarrow V = \dfrac{40 \cdot 15}{10} \Rightarrow V = \dfrac{600}{10} \Rightarrow V = 60$mph.

(b) $V = \sqrt{\dfrac{v^2 D}{d}} \Rightarrow V = \sqrt{v^2} \cdot \sqrt{\dfrac{D}{d}} \Rightarrow V = v\sqrt{\dfrac{D}{d}}$

Checking Basic Concepts for Sections 8.1 & 8.2

1. (a) $\sqrt{81} = 9$

   (b) $\pm\sqrt{625} = \pm 25$

2. $\sqrt{7} = 2.646$

3. (a) $\sqrt[3]{8} = 2$ because $2^3 = 2 \cdot 2 \cdot 2 = 8$

   (b) $-\sqrt[3]{-64} = \sqrt[3]{64} = 4$ because $4^3 = 4 \cdot 4 \cdot 4 = 64$

   (c) $\sqrt[3]{-27} = -3$ because $-3^3 = (-3) \cdot (-3) \cdot (-3) = -27$

4. Using the distance formula: $d = \sqrt{(x_2 - x_1)^2 + (y_2 - y_1)^2}$, for $(-3, 4), (5, -2)$, we get

   $d = \sqrt{(5 - (-3))^2 + (-2 - 4)^2} \Rightarrow d = \sqrt{(8)^2 + (-6)^2} \Rightarrow d = \sqrt{64 + 36} \Rightarrow$

   $d = \sqrt{100} \Rightarrow d = 10$.

5. (a) $\sqrt{80} = \sqrt{16} \cdot \sqrt{5} = 4\sqrt{5}$

   (b) $\sqrt{16x^3} = \sqrt{16x^2} \cdot \sqrt{x} = 4x\sqrt{x}$

   (c) $\sqrt{20x^2y^2} = \sqrt{4x^2y^2} \cdot \sqrt{5} = 2xy\sqrt{5}$

6. (a) $\sqrt{8} \cdot \sqrt{2} = \sqrt{8 \cdot 2} = \sqrt{16} = 4$

   (b) $\sqrt{\dfrac{a^3}{100}} = \dfrac{\sqrt{a^3}}{\sqrt{100}} = \dfrac{\sqrt{a^2} \cdot \sqrt{a}}{\sqrt{100}} = \dfrac{a\sqrt{a}}{10}$

   (c) $\sqrt{\dfrac{8}{x^3}} \cdot \sqrt{\dfrac{x}{2}} = \dfrac{\sqrt{8 \cdot x}}{\sqrt{x^3 \cdot 2}} = \dfrac{\sqrt{8x}}{\sqrt{2x^3}} = \dfrac{\sqrt{4} \cdot \sqrt{2x}}{\sqrt{x^2} \cdot \sqrt{2x}} = \dfrac{2}{x} \cdot 1 = \dfrac{2}{x}$

7. Using Pythagorean Theorem: $a^2 + b^2 = c^2$, for $b = 7$ feet, $c = 25$ feet, we get $a^2 + 7^2 = 25^2 \Rightarrow$

   $a^2 + 49 = 625 \Rightarrow a^2 = 576 \Rightarrow \sqrt{a^2} = \sqrt{576} \Rightarrow a = 24$ feet.

8. Using Pythagorean Theorem: $a^2 + b^2 = c^2$, for $a = 20 \cdot 3.5$ miles, $b = 25 \cdot 3.5$ miles $\Rightarrow$

   a = 70 miles, b = 87.5 miles, we get $70^2 + 87.5^2 = c^2 \Rightarrow 4900 + 7656.25 = c^2 \Rightarrow 12556.25 = c^2 \Rightarrow$

   $\sqrt{c^2} = \sqrt{12556.25} \Rightarrow c \approx 112$ miles.

8.3: Addition and Subtraction of Radical Expressions

Concepts

1. $\sqrt{2} + \sqrt{2} = (1 + 1)\sqrt{2} = 2\sqrt{2}$

3. $3\sqrt[3]{b} - 2\sqrt[3]{b} = (3-2)\sqrt[3]{b} = \sqrt[3]{b}$

5. Yes, it simplifies to $3\sqrt{3}$, $\sqrt{3} + \sqrt{12} = \sqrt{3} + (\sqrt{4} \cdot \sqrt{3}) = \sqrt{3} + 2\sqrt{3} = 3\sqrt{3}$.

Like Radicals

7. $\sqrt{2}, \sqrt{8} \Rightarrow \sqrt{2}, \sqrt{4} \cdot \sqrt{2} \Rightarrow \sqrt{2}, 2\sqrt{2}$

9. Not possible

11. $\sqrt{63}, \sqrt{28} \Rightarrow \sqrt{63} = \sqrt{9} \cdot \sqrt{7}, \sqrt{28} = \sqrt{4} \cdot \sqrt{7} \Rightarrow 3\sqrt{7}, 2\sqrt{7}$

13. $\sqrt{5}, \sqrt{125} \Rightarrow \sqrt{5}, \sqrt{125} = \sqrt{25} \cdot \sqrt{5} = \sqrt{5}, 5\sqrt{5}$

Operations on Radical Expressions

15. $2\sqrt{5} + 3\sqrt{5} = (2+3)\sqrt{5} = 5\sqrt{5}$

17. $\sqrt{13} + 8\sqrt{13} = (1+8)\sqrt{13} = 9\sqrt{13}$

19. $2\sqrt{8} + 3\sqrt{8} = 2(\sqrt{4} \cdot \sqrt{2}) + 3(\sqrt{4} \cdot \sqrt{2}) = 2(2)\sqrt{2} + 3(2)\sqrt{2} = 4\sqrt{2} + 6\sqrt{2} = (4+6)\sqrt{2} = 10\sqrt{2}$

21. $4\sqrt{3} + \sqrt{27} + \sqrt{18} = 4\sqrt{3} + (\sqrt{9} \cdot \sqrt{3}) + (\sqrt{9} \cdot \sqrt{2}) = 4\sqrt{3} + 3\sqrt{3} + 3\sqrt{2} =$
    $(4+3)\sqrt{3} + 3\sqrt{2} = 7\sqrt{3} + 3\sqrt{2}$

23. $9\sqrt{72} + \sqrt{32} = 9(\sqrt{36} \cdot \sqrt{2}) + (\sqrt{16} \cdot \sqrt{2}) = 9(6)\sqrt{2} + 4\sqrt{2} = 54\sqrt{2} + 4\sqrt{2} = (54+4)\sqrt{2} =$
    $58\sqrt{2}$

25. $6\sqrt{15} - 2\sqrt{15} = (6-2)\sqrt{15} = 4\sqrt{15}$

27. $5\sqrt{75} - 7\sqrt{75} = 5(\sqrt{25} \cdot \sqrt{3}) - 7(\sqrt{25} \cdot \sqrt{3}) = 5(5)\sqrt{3} - 7(5)\sqrt{3} = 25\sqrt{3} - 35\sqrt{3} =$
    $(25-35)\sqrt{3} = -10\sqrt{3}$

29. $\sqrt{7} - 5\sqrt{28} = \sqrt{7} - 5(\sqrt{4} \cdot \sqrt{7}) = \sqrt{7} - 5(2)\sqrt{7} = \sqrt{7} - 10\sqrt{7} = (1-10)\sqrt{7} = -9\sqrt{7}$

31. $2\sqrt{54} - 2\sqrt{24} = 2(\sqrt{9} \cdot \sqrt{6}) - 2(\sqrt{4} \cdot \sqrt{6}) = 2(3)\sqrt{6} - 2(2)\sqrt{6} = 6\sqrt{6} - 4\sqrt{6} = (6-4)\sqrt{6} =$
    $2\sqrt{6}$

33. $9\sqrt{50} - 3\sqrt{8} + \sqrt{2} = 9(\sqrt{25} \cdot \sqrt{2}) - 3(\sqrt{4} \cdot \sqrt{2}) + \sqrt{2} = 9(5)\sqrt{2} - 3(2)\sqrt{2} + \sqrt{2} =$
    $45\sqrt{2} - 6\sqrt{2} + \sqrt{2} = (45 - 6 + 1)\sqrt{2} = 40\sqrt{2}$

35. $2\sqrt[3]{4} + 5\sqrt[3]{4} = (2+5)\sqrt[3]{4} = 7\sqrt[3]{4}$

37. $\sqrt[3]{20} - 2\sqrt[3]{20} = (1-2)\sqrt[3]{20} = -\sqrt[3]{20}$

39. $3\sqrt{t} + 2\sqrt{t} = (3+2)\sqrt{t} = 5\sqrt{t}$

41. $\sqrt{x} - 5\sqrt{x} = (1-5)\sqrt{x} = -4\sqrt{x}$

43. $\sqrt{9b} + \sqrt{4b} = \sqrt{9} \cdot \sqrt{b} + \sqrt{4} \cdot \sqrt{b} = 3\sqrt{b} + 2\sqrt{b} = (3+2)\sqrt{b} = 5\sqrt{b}$

45. $\sqrt{4t^3} - 8\sqrt{t} - \sqrt{4t} = (\sqrt{4t^2} \cdot \sqrt{t}) - 8\sqrt{t} - (\sqrt{4} \cdot \sqrt{t}) = 2t\sqrt{t} - 8\sqrt{t} - 2\sqrt{t} = (2t - 8 - 2)\sqrt{t} =$
    $(2t - 10)\sqrt{t}$

47. $4\sqrt[3]{x} - 2\sqrt[3]{x} = (4-2)\sqrt[3]{x} = 2\sqrt[3]{x}$

Geometry

49. Using Pythagorean Theorem: $a^2 + b^2 = c^2$, for $a = \sqrt{22}$, $b = \sqrt{33}$, we get $(\sqrt{22})^2 + (\sqrt{33})^2 = c^2 \Rightarrow$

    $22 + 33 = c^2 \Rightarrow 55 = c^2 \Rightarrow \sqrt{55} = c \Rightarrow c = \sqrt{55}$ so the perimeter is $\sqrt{22} + \sqrt{33} + \sqrt{55}$ inches.

8.4: Simplifying Radical Expressions

Concepts

1. $a^2 - b^2$

3. $(1 - \sqrt{2})(1 + \sqrt{2}) = 1^2 - (\sqrt{2})^2 = 1 - 2 = -1$

5. $4 + \sqrt{11}$

7. $\dfrac{\sqrt{11}}{\sqrt{11}}$

Multiplying Radical Expressions

9. $(4 - \sqrt{2})(4 + \sqrt{2}) = 4^2 - (\sqrt{2})^2 = 16 - 2 = 14$

11. $(8 + \sqrt{11})(8 - \sqrt{11}) = 8^2 - (\sqrt{11})^2 = 64 - 11 = 53$

13. $(\sqrt{5} - 7)(\sqrt{5} + 7) = (\sqrt{5})^2 - 7^2 = 5 - 49 = -44$

15. $(\sqrt{15} + 2)(\sqrt{15} - 2) = (\sqrt{15})^2 - 2^2 = 15 - 4 = 11$

17. $(\sqrt{x} - 5)(\sqrt{x} + 5) = (\sqrt{x})^2 - 5^2 = x - 25$

19. $(7 - \sqrt{t})(7 + \sqrt{t}) = 7^2 - (\sqrt{t})^2 = 49 - t$

21. $(\sqrt{y} - 1)(\sqrt{y} - 2) = \sqrt{y} \cdot \sqrt{y} - 1 \cdot \sqrt{y} - 2 \cdot \sqrt{y} + 1 \cdot 2 = (\sqrt{y})^2 - 3\sqrt{y} + 2 = y - 3\sqrt{y} + 2$

23. $(3 - \sqrt{x})(1 + \sqrt{x}) = 3 \cdot 1 - \sqrt{x} \cdot 1 + \sqrt{x} \cdot 3 - \sqrt{x} \cdot \sqrt{x} = 3 + 2\sqrt{x} - (\sqrt{x})^2 = 3 + 2\sqrt{x} - x$

25. $(\sqrt{x} - \sqrt{y})(\sqrt{x} + \sqrt{y}) = (\sqrt{x})^2 - (\sqrt{y})^2 = x - y$

27. $(\sqrt{r} - 3\sqrt{t})(\sqrt{r} + 3\sqrt{t}) = (\sqrt{r})^2 - (3\sqrt{t})^2 = r - 9t$

Rationalizing the Denominator

29. $\sqrt{17} + 3$

31. $20 + \sqrt{5}$

33. $\sqrt{x} + \sqrt{z}$

35. $\dfrac{2}{\sqrt{5}} \cdot \dfrac{\sqrt{5}}{\sqrt{5}} = \dfrac{2\sqrt{5}}{\sqrt{5} \cdot \sqrt{5}} = \dfrac{2\sqrt{5}}{5}$

37. $\dfrac{14}{\sqrt{14}} \cdot \dfrac{\sqrt{14}}{\sqrt{14}} = \dfrac{14\sqrt{14}}{\sqrt{14} \cdot \sqrt{14}} = \dfrac{14\sqrt{14}}{14} = \dfrac{14}{14} \cdot \sqrt{14} = 1 \cdot \sqrt{14} = \sqrt{14}$

39. $-\dfrac{3}{\sqrt{3}} \cdot \dfrac{\sqrt{3}}{\sqrt{3}} = -\dfrac{3\sqrt{3}}{\sqrt{3} \cdot \sqrt{3}} = -\dfrac{3\sqrt{3}}{3} = -\dfrac{3}{3} \cdot \sqrt{3} = -1 \cdot \sqrt{3} = -\sqrt{3}$

41. $\dfrac{5}{\sqrt{10}} \cdot \dfrac{\sqrt{10}}{\sqrt{10}} = \dfrac{5\sqrt{10}}{\sqrt{10} \cdot \sqrt{10}} = \dfrac{5\sqrt{10}}{10} = \dfrac{1\sqrt{10}}{2} = \dfrac{\sqrt{10}}{2}$

43. $-\dfrac{4}{3\sqrt{7}} \cdot \dfrac{\sqrt{7}}{\sqrt{7}} = -\dfrac{4\sqrt{7}}{3\sqrt{7} \cdot \sqrt{7}} = -\dfrac{4\sqrt{7}}{3 \cdot 7} = -\dfrac{4\sqrt{7}}{21}$

45. $\dfrac{1}{\sqrt{3}-1} \cdot \dfrac{\sqrt{3}+1}{\sqrt{3}+1} = \dfrac{\sqrt{3}+1}{(\sqrt{3})^2-1^2} = \dfrac{\sqrt{3}+1}{3-1} = \dfrac{\sqrt{3}+1}{2}$

47. $\dfrac{\sqrt{5}}{\sqrt{5}+2} \cdot \dfrac{\sqrt{5}-2}{\sqrt{5}-2} = \dfrac{(\sqrt{5})^2-2\sqrt{5}}{(\sqrt{5})^2-2^2} = \dfrac{5-2\sqrt{5}}{5-4} = \dfrac{5-2\sqrt{5}}{1} = 5-2\sqrt{5}$

49. $\dfrac{\sqrt{2}+1}{\sqrt{2}-1} \cdot \dfrac{\sqrt{2}+1}{\sqrt{2}+1} = \dfrac{\sqrt{2}\cdot\sqrt{2}+1\cdot\sqrt{2}+1\cdot\sqrt{2}+1\cdot1}{(\sqrt{2})^2-1^2} = \dfrac{(\sqrt{2})^2+2\sqrt{2}+1}{2-1} = \dfrac{2+2\sqrt{2}+1}{1} =$

$\dfrac{2\sqrt{2}+3}{1} = 2\sqrt{2}+3$

51. $\dfrac{5-\sqrt{13}}{5+\sqrt{13}} \cdot \dfrac{5-\sqrt{13}}{5-\sqrt{13}} = \dfrac{5\cdot5-5\cdot\sqrt{13}-5\cdot\sqrt{13}+\sqrt{13}\cdot\sqrt{13}}{5^2-(\sqrt{13})^2} = \dfrac{25-10\sqrt{13}+(\sqrt{13})^2}{25-13} =$

$\dfrac{25-10\sqrt{13}+13}{12} = \dfrac{38-10\sqrt{13}}{12} = \dfrac{19-5\sqrt{13}}{6}$

53. $\dfrac{1}{2\sqrt{x}} \cdot \dfrac{\sqrt{x}}{\sqrt{x}} = \dfrac{1\sqrt{x}}{2\sqrt{x}\cdot\sqrt{x}} = \dfrac{\sqrt{x}}{2x}$

55. $\dfrac{\sqrt{x}-2}{\sqrt{x}+2} \cdot \dfrac{\sqrt{x}-2}{\sqrt{x}-2} = \dfrac{\sqrt{x}\cdot\sqrt{x}-2\cdot\sqrt{x}-2\cdot\sqrt{x}+2\cdot2}{(\sqrt{x})^2-2^2} = \dfrac{(\sqrt{x})^2-4\sqrt{x}+4}{x-4} = \dfrac{x-4\sqrt{x}+4}{x-4}$

57. $\dfrac{\sqrt{a}-2b}{\sqrt{a}+2b} \cdot \dfrac{\sqrt{a}-2b}{\sqrt{a}-2b} = \dfrac{\sqrt{a}\cdot\sqrt{a}-2b\cdot\sqrt{a}-2b\cdot\sqrt{a}+2b\cdot2b}{(\sqrt{a})^2-(2b)^2} = \dfrac{(\sqrt{a})^2-4b\sqrt{a}+4b^2}{a-4b^2} =$

$\dfrac{a-4b\sqrt{a}+4b^2}{a-4b^2}$

59. $\dfrac{\sqrt{a}+\sqrt{b}}{\sqrt{a}-\sqrt{b}} \cdot \dfrac{\sqrt{a}+\sqrt{b}}{\sqrt{a}+\sqrt{b}} = \dfrac{\sqrt{a}\cdot\sqrt{a}+\sqrt{a}\cdot\sqrt{b}+\sqrt{a}\cdot\sqrt{b}+\sqrt{b}\cdot\sqrt{b}}{(\sqrt{a})^2-(\sqrt{b})^2} =$

$\dfrac{\sqrt{a^2}+2\sqrt{ab}+\sqrt{b^2}}{a-b} = \dfrac{a+2\sqrt{ab}+b}{a-b}$

61. $\dfrac{\sqrt{2x}-\sqrt{y}}{\sqrt{2x}+\sqrt{y}} \cdot \dfrac{\sqrt{2x}-\sqrt{y}}{\sqrt{2x}-\sqrt{y}} = \dfrac{\sqrt{2x}\cdot\sqrt{2x}-\sqrt{2x}\cdot\sqrt{y}-\sqrt{2x}\cdot\sqrt{y}+\sqrt{y}\cdot\sqrt{y}}{(\sqrt{2x})^2-(\sqrt{y})^2} =$

$\dfrac{(\sqrt{2x})^2-2\sqrt{2xy}+(\sqrt{y})^2}{2x-y} = \dfrac{2x-2\sqrt{2xy}+y}{2x-y}$

63. $\dfrac{1}{\sqrt{b+1}+\sqrt{b}} \cdot \dfrac{\sqrt{b+1}-\sqrt{b}}{\sqrt{b+1}-\sqrt{b}} = \dfrac{\sqrt{b+1}-\sqrt{b}}{(\sqrt{b+1})^2-(\sqrt{b})^2} = \dfrac{\sqrt{b+1}-\sqrt{b}}{b+1-b} = \dfrac{\sqrt{b+1}-\sqrt{b}}{1} =$

$\sqrt{b+1}-\sqrt{b}$

Geometry

65. Perimeter: If $P = 2l + 2w$ then, $2(\sqrt{91}+2) + 2(\sqrt{91}-2) = (2+2)\sqrt{91}(2-2) = 4\sqrt{91}$

   Area: If $A = l \cdot w$ then, $(\sqrt{91}-2)(\sqrt{91}+2) = (\sqrt{91})^2 - 2^2 = 91 - 4 = 87$

Checking Basic Concepts for Sections 8.3 & 8.4

1. (a) $5\sqrt{6} + 5\sqrt{6} = (5 + 5)\sqrt{6} = 10\sqrt{6}$

   (b) $3\sqrt{75} - 2\sqrt{27} = 3(\sqrt{25} \cdot \sqrt{3}) - 2(\sqrt{9} \cdot \sqrt{3}) = 3(5)\sqrt{3} - 2(3)\sqrt{3} = 15\sqrt{3} - 6\sqrt{3} =$

   $(15 - 6)\sqrt{3} = 9\sqrt{3}$

   (c) $\sqrt{16k} + \sqrt{25k} = (\sqrt{16} \cdot \sqrt{k}) + (\sqrt{25} \cdot \sqrt{k}) = 4\sqrt{k} + 5\sqrt{k} = (4 + 5)\sqrt{k} = 9\sqrt{k}$

2. Perimeter: If $P = 2l + 2w$ then, $2\sqrt{45} + 2\sqrt{125} = 2(\sqrt{9} \cdot \sqrt{5}) + 2(\sqrt{25} \cdot \sqrt{5}) = 2(3)\sqrt{5} + 2(5)\sqrt{5} =$

   $6\sqrt{5} + 10\sqrt{5} = (6 + 10)\sqrt{5} = 16\sqrt{5}$

3. (a) $(5 + \sqrt{2})(5 - \sqrt{2}) = 5^2 - (\sqrt{2})^2 = 25 - 2 = 23$

   (b) $(\sqrt{x} - 3)(\sqrt{x} + 5) = \sqrt{x} \cdot \sqrt{x} - 3 \cdot \sqrt{x} + 5 \cdot \sqrt{x} - 3 \cdot 5 = (\sqrt{x})^2 + 2\sqrt{x} - 15 = x + 2\sqrt{x} - 15$

4. (a) $\dfrac{5}{3\sqrt{5}} \cdot \dfrac{\sqrt{5}}{\sqrt{5}} = \dfrac{5\sqrt{5}}{3\sqrt{5} \cdot \sqrt{5}} = \dfrac{5\sqrt{5}}{3 \cdot 5} = \dfrac{5\sqrt{5}}{15} = \dfrac{1\sqrt{5}}{3} = \dfrac{\sqrt{5}}{3}$

   (b) $\dfrac{3 + \sqrt{7}}{3 - \sqrt{7}} \cdot \dfrac{3 + \sqrt{7}}{3 + \sqrt{7}} = \dfrac{3 \cdot 3 + 3 \cdot \sqrt{7} + 3 \cdot \sqrt{7} + \sqrt{7} \cdot \sqrt{7}}{3^2 - (\sqrt{7})^2} = \dfrac{9 + 6\sqrt{7} + (\sqrt{7})^2}{9 - 7} =$

   $\dfrac{9 + 6\sqrt{7} + 7}{2} = \dfrac{6\sqrt{7} + 16}{2} = \dfrac{3\sqrt{7} + 8}{1} = 3\sqrt{7} + 8$

   (c) $\dfrac{1}{\sqrt{x} + \sqrt{y}} \cdot \dfrac{\sqrt{x} - \sqrt{y}}{\sqrt{x} - \sqrt{y}} = \dfrac{\sqrt{x} - \sqrt{y}}{(\sqrt{x})^2 - (\sqrt{y})^2} = \dfrac{\sqrt{x} - \sqrt{y}}{x - y}$

8.5: Equations Involving Radical Expressions

Concepts

1. Square each side.

3. $\sqrt{x} = 4 \Rightarrow \sqrt{x}^2 = 4^2 \Rightarrow x = 16$ Check: $x = 16 \Rightarrow \sqrt{16} = 4 \Rightarrow 4 = 4$

5. $x = 4$, solution is 4; $x^2 = 16$, solution is 4 and -4, No

Solving Radical Equations

7. $\sqrt{x} = 6 \Rightarrow (\sqrt{x})^2 = 6^2 \Rightarrow x = 36$ Check: $x = 36 \Rightarrow \sqrt{36} \overset{?}{=} 6 \Rightarrow 6 = 6$, so $x = 36$

9. No solution, no square roots can equal a negative number.

11. $\sqrt{x - 7} = 3 \Rightarrow (\sqrt{x - 7})^2 = 3^2 \Rightarrow x - 7 = 9 \Rightarrow x = 16$ Check: $x = 16 \Rightarrow \sqrt{16 - 7} \overset{?}{=} 3 \Rightarrow$

   $\sqrt{9} \overset{?}{=} 3 \Rightarrow 3 = 3$, so $x = 16$

13. $\sqrt{1 - k} = 10 \Rightarrow (\sqrt{1 - k})^2 = 10^2 \Rightarrow 1 - k = 100 \Rightarrow -k = 99 \Rightarrow k = -99$ Check: $k = -99 \Rightarrow$

   $\sqrt{1 - (-99)} \overset{?}{=} 10 \Rightarrow \sqrt{100} \overset{?}{=} 10 \Rightarrow 10 = 10$, so $k = -99$

15. $\sqrt{2t - 3} = 4 \Rightarrow (\sqrt{2t - 3})^2 = 4^2 \Rightarrow 2t - 3 = 16 \Rightarrow 2t = 19 \Rightarrow t = \dfrac{19}{2}$ Check: $t = \dfrac{19}{2} \Rightarrow$

   $\sqrt{2\left(\dfrac{19}{2}\right) - 3} \overset{?}{=} 4 \Rightarrow \sqrt{19 - 3} \overset{?}{=} 4 \Rightarrow \sqrt{16} \overset{?}{=} 4 \Rightarrow 4 = 4$, so $t = \dfrac{19}{2}$

17. $\sqrt{3x} + 1 = 5 \Rightarrow \sqrt{3x} = 4 \Rightarrow (\sqrt{3x})^2 = 4^2 \Rightarrow 3x = 16 \Rightarrow x = \dfrac{16}{3}$ Check: $x = \dfrac{16}{3} \Rightarrow$

$\sqrt{3\left(\dfrac{16}{3}\right)} + 1 \overset{?}{=} 5 \Rightarrow \sqrt{16} + 1 \overset{?}{=} 5 \Rightarrow 4 + 1 \overset{?}{=} 5 \Rightarrow 5 = 5$, so $x = \dfrac{16}{3}$

19. $9 - \sqrt{x} = 1 \Rightarrow -\sqrt{x} = -8 \Rightarrow \sqrt{x} = 8 \Rightarrow (\sqrt{x})^2 = 8^2 \Rightarrow x = 64$ Check: $x = 64 \Rightarrow 9 - \sqrt{64} \overset{?}{=} 1 \Rightarrow$

$9 - 8 \overset{?}{=} 1 \Rightarrow 1 = 1$, so $x = 64$

21. $\sqrt{b + 1} = 2\sqrt{b} \Rightarrow (\sqrt{b + 1})^2 = (2\sqrt{b})^2 \Rightarrow b + 1 = 4b \Rightarrow 1 = 3b \Rightarrow \dfrac{1}{3} = b$ Check: $b = \dfrac{1}{3} \Rightarrow$

$\sqrt{\dfrac{1}{3} + 1} \overset{?}{=} 2\sqrt{\dfrac{1}{3}} \Rightarrow \left(\sqrt{\dfrac{1}{3} + 1}\right)^2 \overset{?}{=} \left(2\sqrt{\dfrac{1}{3}}\right)^2 \Rightarrow \dfrac{1}{3} + 1 \overset{?}{=} 4\left(\dfrac{1}{3}\right) \Rightarrow \dfrac{4}{3} = \dfrac{4}{3}$, so $b = \dfrac{1}{3}$

23. $\sqrt{4z - 2} = \sqrt{3z} \Rightarrow (\sqrt{4z - 2})^2 = (\sqrt{3z})^2 \Rightarrow 4z - 2 = 3z \Rightarrow z = 2$ Check: $z = 2 \Rightarrow$

$\sqrt{4(2) - 2} \overset{?}{=} \sqrt{3(2)} \Rightarrow \sqrt{6} = \sqrt{6}$, so $z = 2$

25. $2\sqrt{x + 1} + 3 = 9 \Rightarrow 2\sqrt{x + 1} = 6 \Rightarrow \sqrt{x + 1} = 3 \Rightarrow (\sqrt{x + 1})^2 = 3^2 \Rightarrow x + 1 = 9 \Rightarrow x = 8$

Check: $2\sqrt{8 + 1} + 3 \overset{?}{=} 9 \Rightarrow 2\sqrt{9} + 3 \overset{?}{=} 9 \Rightarrow 2(3) + 3 \overset{?}{=} 9 \Rightarrow 9 = 9$, so $x = 8$

27. $\sqrt{x + 20} = x \Rightarrow (\sqrt{x + 20})^2 = x^2 \Rightarrow x + 20 = x^2 \Rightarrow 0 = x^2 - x - 20 \Rightarrow 0 = (x - 5)(x + 4) \Rightarrow$

$x = 5, -4$ Check: $\sqrt{5 + 20} \overset{?}{=} 5 \Rightarrow \sqrt{25} \overset{?}{=} 5 \Rightarrow 5 = 5$, and $\sqrt{-4 + 20} \overset{?}{=} -4 \Rightarrow \sqrt{16} \overset{?}{=} -4 \Rightarrow$

$4 \neq -4$, so $x = 5$

29. $5\sqrt{2t - 1} = 3t \Rightarrow \sqrt{2t - 1} = \dfrac{3}{5}t \Rightarrow (\sqrt{2t - 1})^2 = \left(\dfrac{3}{5}t\right)^2 \Rightarrow 2t - 1 = \dfrac{9}{25}t^2 \Rightarrow 25(2t - 1) = 9t^2 \Rightarrow$

$50t - 25 = 9t^2 \Rightarrow 0 = 9t^2 - 50t + 25 \Rightarrow 0 = (9t - 5)(t - 5) \Rightarrow t = \dfrac{5}{9}, 5$ Check:

$5\sqrt{2\left(\dfrac{5}{9}\right) - 1} \overset{?}{=} 3\left(\dfrac{5}{9}\right) \Rightarrow 5\sqrt{\dfrac{10}{9} - 1} \overset{?}{=} \dfrac{5}{3} \Rightarrow 5\sqrt{\dfrac{1}{9}} \overset{?}{=} \dfrac{5}{3} \Rightarrow 5\left(\dfrac{1}{3}\right) \overset{?}{=} \dfrac{5}{3} \Rightarrow \dfrac{5}{3} = \dfrac{5}{3}$, and

$5\sqrt{2(5) - 1} \overset{?}{=} 3(5) \Rightarrow 5\sqrt{9} \overset{?}{=} 15 \Rightarrow 5(3) \overset{?}{=} 15 \Rightarrow 15 = 15$, so $x = \dfrac{5}{9}, 5$

31. $\sqrt{2x + 1} = x - 1 \Rightarrow (\sqrt{2x + 1})^2 = (x - 1)^2 \Rightarrow 2x + 1 = x^2 - 2x + 1 \Rightarrow 0 = x^2 - 4x \Rightarrow$

$0 = x(x - 4) \Rightarrow x = 0, 4$ Check: $\sqrt{2(0) + 1} \overset{?}{=} 0 - 1 \Rightarrow \sqrt{1} \overset{?}{=} -1 \Rightarrow 1 \neq -1$, and

$\sqrt{2(4) + 1} \overset{?}{=} 4 - 1 \Rightarrow \sqrt{9} \overset{?}{=} 3 \Rightarrow 3 = 3$, so $x = 4$

33. $z + 1 = \sqrt{37 + 2z} \Rightarrow (z + 1)^2 = (\sqrt{37 + 2z})^2 \Rightarrow z^2 + 2z + 1 = 37 + 2z \Rightarrow z^2 - 36 = 0 \Rightarrow$

$(z + 6)(z - 6) = 0 \Rightarrow z = -6, 6$ Check: $-6 + 1 \overset{?}{=} \sqrt{37 + 2(-6)} \Rightarrow -5 \overset{?}{=} \sqrt{25} \Rightarrow -5 \neq 5$, and

$6 + 1 \overset{?}{=} \sqrt{37 + 2(6)} \Rightarrow 7 \overset{?}{=} \sqrt{49} \Rightarrow 7 = 7$, so $x = 6$

35. $\sqrt{(x - 1)(x + 2)} = 2 \Rightarrow (\sqrt{(x - 1)(x + 2)})^2 = 2^2 \Rightarrow (x - 1)(x + 2) = 4 \Rightarrow x^2 + x - 2 = 4 \Rightarrow$

$x^2 + x - 6 = 0 \Rightarrow (x + 3)(x - 2) = 0 \Rightarrow x = -3, 2$ Check: $\sqrt{(-3 - 1)(-3 + 2)} \overset{?}{=} 2 \Rightarrow$

$\sqrt{(-4)(-1)} \overset{?}{=} 2 \Rightarrow \sqrt{4} \overset{?}{=} 2 \Rightarrow 2 = 2$, and $\sqrt{(2 - 1)(2 + 2)} \overset{?}{=} 2 \Rightarrow \sqrt{(1)(4)} \overset{?}{=} 2 \Rightarrow \sqrt{4} \overset{?}{=} 2 \Rightarrow$

$2 = 2$, so $x = -3, 2$

37. $T = \sqrt{L}$ for $L \Rightarrow T^2 = (\sqrt{L})^2 \Rightarrow T^2 = L \Rightarrow L = T^2$

39. $b = \sqrt{2a}$ for $a \Rightarrow b^2 = (\sqrt{2a})^2 \Rightarrow b^2 = 2a \Rightarrow \dfrac{1}{2}b^2 = a \Rightarrow a = \dfrac{1}{2}b^2$

41. $D = 4\sqrt{t + 1}$ for $t \Rightarrow \frac{1}{4}D = \sqrt{t + 1} \Rightarrow \left(\frac{1}{4}D\right)^2 = (\sqrt{t + 1})^2 \Rightarrow \frac{1}{16}D^2 = t + 1 \Rightarrow \frac{1}{16}D^2 - 1 = t \Rightarrow$

$t = \frac{1}{16}D^2 - 1$

43. $c = \sqrt{a^2 + b^2}$ for $b \Rightarrow c^2 = (\sqrt{a^2 + b^2})^2 \Rightarrow c^2 = a^2 + b^2 \Rightarrow c^2 - a^2 = b^2 \Rightarrow \sqrt{c^2 - a^2} = \sqrt{b^2} \Rightarrow$

$\sqrt{c^2 - a^2} = b \Rightarrow b = \sqrt{c^2 - a^2}$

45. $k = 4 + \sqrt{d}$ for $d \Rightarrow k - 4 = \sqrt{d} \Rightarrow (k - 4)^2 = (\sqrt{d})^2 \Rightarrow (k - 4)^2 = d \Rightarrow d = (k - 4)^2$

Numerical and Graphical Solutions

47. (a) From the table we see that $\sqrt{x} = 2$ when $x = 4$. See Figure 47a.

    (b) The solution is the x-coordinate of the intersection point, or 4. See Figure 47b.

x	0	1	4	9	16	25
$\overline{x}$	0	1	2	3	4	5

           Figure 47a   Figure 47b

49. (a) From the table we see that $\sqrt{x - 2} = 1$ when $x = 3$. See Figure 49a.

    (b) The solution is the x-coordinate of the intersection point, or 3. See Figure 49b.

x	2	3	6	11	18	27
$x - 2$	0	1	2	3	4	5

           Figure 49a   Figure 49b

51. (a) From the table we see that $\sqrt{x} + 1 = 3$ when $x = 4$. See Figure 51a.

    (b) The solution is the x-coordinate of the intersection point, or 4. See Figure 51b.

x	0	1	4	9	16	25
$\sqrt{x} + 1$	1	2	3	4	5	6

           Figure 51a   Figure 51b

53. (a) From the table we see that $2\sqrt{x} = 2$ when $x = 1$. See Figure 53a.

  (b) The solution is the x-coordinate of the intersection point, or 1. See Figure 53b.

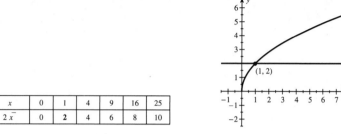

x	0	1	4	9	16	25
$2\overset{-}{x}$	0	2	4	6	8	10

Figure 53a   Figure 53b

Applications

55. (a) If $h = 100$, then $D = 1.22\sqrt{100} \Rightarrow D = 1.22(10) \Rightarrow D = 12.2$ miles.

  (b) f $D = 50$, then $50 = 1.22\sqrt{h} \Rightarrow \dfrac{50}{1.22} = \sqrt{h} \Rightarrow 40.984^2 = (\sqrt{h})^2 \Rightarrow h =$ about 1680 feet.

  (c) If $h = x$, then $D = 1.22\sqrt{x}$, if $4x$, then $D = 1.22\sqrt{4x} \Rightarrow D = 1.22(2)\sqrt{x}$, so the distance to the horizon doubles.

57. (a) Solving Pythagorean Theorem $a^2 + b^2 = c^2$ for b, $b^2 = c^2 - a^2 \Rightarrow \sqrt{b^2} = \sqrt{c^2 - a^2} \Rightarrow$

  $b = \sqrt{c^2 - a^2}$

  (b) $b = \sqrt{(25)^2 - (7)^2} \Rightarrow b = \sqrt{625 - 49} \Rightarrow b = \sqrt{576} \Rightarrow b = 24$ inches

59. (a) $V = v\sqrt{\dfrac{D}{d}}$ for $D \Rightarrow \dfrac{V}{v} = \sqrt{\dfrac{D}{d}} \Rightarrow \left(\dfrac{V}{v}\right)^2 = \left(\sqrt{\dfrac{D}{d}}\right)^2 \Rightarrow \dfrac{V^2}{v^2} = \dfrac{D}{d} \Rightarrow \dfrac{V^2 d}{v^2} = D \Rightarrow D = \dfrac{V^2 d}{v^2}$

  (b) $V = 50$mph, $v = 40$mph, $d = 200$ feet $\Rightarrow D = \dfrac{50^2(200)}{40^2} \Rightarrow D = \dfrac{2500(200)}{1600} \Rightarrow D = \dfrac{500,000}{1600} \Rightarrow$

  $D = 312.5$ feet.

61. If $m = x$, then $R = k\sqrt{x}$ and if $m = 4x$ then $R = k\sqrt{4x} \Rightarrow R = k2\sqrt{x}$ which is two times bigger, so it increases by a factor of 2 or doubles.

63. If $k = 2000$, and $m = 0.09$ then $R = 2000\sqrt{0.09} \Rightarrow R = 2000(0.3) \Rightarrow R = 600$ cfs, it increases to 600 cfs.

8.6: Higher Roots and Rational Exponents

Concepts

1. index, radicand

3. even

5. Negative number

7. $\sqrt[n]{a} \cdot \sqrt[n]{b} = \sqrt[n]{ab}$

9. $a^{1/n} = \sqrt[n]{a}$

Simplifying Expressions

11. $\sqrt[3]{-27} = -3$, because $-3^3 = -27$

13. $\sqrt[5]{243} = 3$, because $3^5 = 243$

15. $\sqrt[4]{16} = 2$, because $2^4 = 16$

17. $\sqrt[4]{10,000} = 10$, because $10^4 = 10,000$

19. $-\sqrt[5]{-32} = \sqrt[5]{32} = 2$, because $2^5 = 32$

21. $-\sqrt[6]{1} = -(1^{1/6}) = -1$

23. $\sqrt[4]{5^4} = 5^{4/4} = 5^1 = 5$

25. $-\sqrt[4]{5^4} = -5^{4/4} = -5^1 = -5$

27. $\sqrt[3]{\dfrac{27}{8}} = \dfrac{\sqrt[3]{27}}{\sqrt[3]{8}} = \dfrac{3}{2}$, because $\dfrac{3^3 = 27}{2^3 = 8}$

29. $\sqrt[4]{\dfrac{20}{81}} = \dfrac{\sqrt[4]{20}}{\sqrt[4]{81}} = \dfrac{\sqrt[4]{20}}{3}$, because $3^4 = 81$

31. $\sqrt[3]{16} \cdot \sqrt[3]{4} = \sqrt[3]{64} = 4$, because $4^3 = 64$

33. $\sqrt[6]{2} \cdot \sqrt[6]{32} = \sqrt[6]{64} = 2$, because $2^6 = 64$

35. $\sqrt[5]{16} \cdot \sqrt[5]{-2} = \sqrt[5]{-32} = -2$, because $(-2)^5 = -32$

37. $\dfrac{\sqrt[3]{3}}{\sqrt[3]{81}} = \sqrt[3]{\dfrac{3}{81}} = \sqrt[3]{\dfrac{1}{27}} = \dfrac{1}{3}$, because $\dfrac{1^3 = 1}{3^3 = 27}$

39. $\dfrac{\sqrt[4]{2}}{\sqrt[4]{32}} = \sqrt[4]{\dfrac{2}{32}} = \sqrt[4]{\dfrac{1}{16}} = \dfrac{1}{2}$, because $\dfrac{1^4 = 1}{2^4 = 16}$

41. $\dfrac{\sqrt[5]{-128}}{\sqrt[5]{4}} = \sqrt[5]{\dfrac{-128}{4}} = \sqrt[5]{-32} = -2$, because $-2^5 = -32$

Rational Exponents

43. $36^{1/2} = \sqrt{36} = 6$

45. $27^{1/3} = \sqrt[3]{27} = 3$

47. $(-1)^{1/3} = \sqrt[3]{-1} = -1$

49. $81^{1/4} = \sqrt[4]{81} = 3$

51. $32^{1/5} = \sqrt[5]{32} = 2$

53. $4^{3/2} = \sqrt{4^3} = (\sqrt{4})^3 = 2^3 = 8$

55. $64^{2/3} = \sqrt[3]{64^2} = (\sqrt[3]{64})^2 = 4^2 = 16$

57. $16^{5/4} = \sqrt[4]{16^5} = (\sqrt[4]{16})^5 = 2^5 = 32$

59. $(-1)^{3/5} = \sqrt[5]{-1^3} = (\sqrt[5]{-1})^3 = (-1)^3 = -1$

61. $49^{-1/2} = \dfrac{1}{\sqrt{49}} = \dfrac{1}{7}$

63. $8^{-2/3} = \dfrac{1}{\sqrt[3]{8^2}} = \dfrac{1}{(\sqrt[3]{8})^2} = \dfrac{1}{2^2} = \dfrac{1}{4}$

65. $625^{-3/4} = \dfrac{1}{\sqrt[4]{625^3}} = \dfrac{1}{(\sqrt[4]{625})^3} = \dfrac{1}{5^3} = \dfrac{1}{125}$

67. $16^{-5/4} = \dfrac{1}{\sqrt[4]{16^5}} = \dfrac{1}{(\sqrt[4]{16})^5} = \dfrac{1}{2^5} = \dfrac{1}{32}$

Applications

69. If $W = 27$, then $A = 100\sqrt[3]{27^2} \Rightarrow A = 100(\sqrt[3]{27})^2 \Rightarrow A = 100(3)^2 \Rightarrow A = 100(9) \Rightarrow A = 900\ \text{in}^2$

71. (a) $r = \sqrt{\dfrac{A}{\pi}} \Rightarrow r = \left(\dfrac{A}{\pi}\right)^{1/2}$

    (b) If $A = 9\pi$, then $r = \sqrt{\dfrac{9\pi}{\pi}} \Rightarrow r^2 = \dfrac{9\pi}{\pi} \Rightarrow r^2 = 9 \cdot \dfrac{\pi}{\pi} \Rightarrow r^2 = 9 \cdot 1 \Rightarrow r^2 = 9 \Rightarrow \sqrt{r^2} = \sqrt{9} \Rightarrow$

    $r = 3$ feet.

Checking Basic Concepts for Sections 8.5 & 8.6

1. (a) $\sqrt{3x + 4} - 2 = 2 \Rightarrow \sqrt{3x + 4} = 4 \Rightarrow (\sqrt{3x + 4})^2 = 4^2 \Rightarrow 3x + 4 = 16 \Rightarrow 3x = 12 \Rightarrow x = 4$

    Check: $x = 4 \Rightarrow \sqrt{3(4)4} - 2 \stackrel{?}{=} 2 \Rightarrow \sqrt{12 + 4} - 2 \stackrel{?}{=} 2 \Rightarrow \sqrt{16} - 2 \stackrel{?}{=} 2 \Rightarrow 4 - 2 \stackrel{?}{=} \Rightarrow 2 = 2$,

    so $x = 4$

    (b) $\sqrt{24 - 2x} = -x \Rightarrow (\sqrt{24 - 2x})^2 = (-x)^2 \Rightarrow 24 - 2x = x^2 \Rightarrow 0 = x^2 + 2x - 24 \Rightarrow$

    $0 = (x + 6)(x - 4)$, so $x = -6, 4$ Check: $x = -6 \Rightarrow \sqrt{24 - 2(-6)} \stackrel{?}{=} -(-6) \Rightarrow \sqrt{24 - (-12)} \stackrel{?}{=} 6 \Rightarrow$

    $\sqrt{36} \stackrel{?}{=} 6 \Rightarrow 6 = 6$, and $\sqrt{24 - 2(4)} \stackrel{?}{=} -4 \Rightarrow \sqrt{16} \stackrel{?}{=} -4 \Rightarrow 4 \neq -4$, so $x = -6$

2. Solve: $S = 4\sqrt{t} - 2$ for t, $S + 2 = 4\sqrt{t} \Rightarrow \dfrac{S + 2}{4} = \sqrt{t} \Rightarrow \left(\dfrac{S + 2}{4}\right)^2 = (\sqrt{t})^2 \Rightarrow \dfrac{(S + 2)^2}{16} = t \Rightarrow$

    $t = \dfrac{(S + 2)^2}{16}$

3. (a) $\sqrt[3]{-27} = -3$, because $-3^3 = -27$

    (b) $\sqrt[4]{16} = 2$, because $2^4 = 16$

4. (a) $\sqrt[4]{9} \cdot \sqrt[4]{9} = \sqrt[4]{81} = 3$, because $3^4 = 81$

    (b) $\sqrt[3]{\dfrac{9}{64}} = \dfrac{\sqrt[3]{9}}{\sqrt[3]{64}} = \dfrac{\sqrt[3]{9}}{4}$, because $4^3 = 64$

    (c) $\dfrac{\sqrt[3]{40}}{\sqrt[3]{5}} = \sqrt[3]{\dfrac{40}{5}} = \sqrt[3]{8} = 2$, because $2^3 = 8$

5. (a) $9^{1/2} = \sqrt{9} = 3$

    (b) $16^{3/4} = \sqrt[4]{16^3} = (\sqrt[4]{16})^3 = 8$

    (c) $1000^{-1/3} = \dfrac{1}{\sqrt[3]{1000}} = \dfrac{1}{10}$

Chapter 8 Review Exercises

Section 8.1

1. $\sqrt{36} = \pm 6$

2. $\sqrt{400} = \pm 20$

3. $\sqrt{7} = \pm 2.646$

4. $\sqrt{12} = \pm 3.464$

5. real, rational

6. real, rational

7. real, irrational

8. None

9. $\sqrt{121} = 11$

10. $\sqrt{400} = 20$

11. $-\sqrt{49} = -7$

12. $-\sqrt{17} = -4.12$

13. $\sqrt[3]{6} = 1.82$ because $1.82^3 = 6$

14. $\sqrt[3]{-125} = -5$ because $-5^3 = -125$

15. Using Pythagorean Theorem: $a^2 + b^2 = c^2$, for $a = 4$ inches, $b = 5$ inches, we get $4^2 + 5^2 = c^2 \Rightarrow$
    $16 + 25 = c^2 \Rightarrow 41 = c^2 \Rightarrow \sqrt{41} = \sqrt{c^2} \Rightarrow c = \sqrt{41}$ inches.

16. Using Pythagorean Theorem: $a^2 + b^2 = c^2$, for $a = 7$ feet, $c = 25$ feet, we get $7^2 + b^2 = 25^2 \Rightarrow$
    $49 + b^2 = 625 \Rightarrow b^2 = 576 \Rightarrow \sqrt{b^2} = \sqrt{576} \Rightarrow b = 24$ feet.

17. Using the distance formula: $d = \sqrt{(x_2 - x_1)^2 + (y_2 - y_1)^2}$, for $(-3, 2), (3, -3)$, we get
    $d = \sqrt{(3 - (-3))^2 + (-3 - 2)^2} \Rightarrow d = \sqrt{(6)^2 + (-5)^2} \Rightarrow d = \sqrt{36 + 25} \Rightarrow d = \sqrt{61} \Rightarrow$
    $d = \sqrt{61} \approx 7.81$.

18. Using Pythagorean Theorem: $a^2 + b^2 = c2$, for $a = \sqrt{20}, b = \sqrt{30}$, we get $(\sqrt{20})^2 + (\sqrt{30})^2 = c^2 \Rightarrow$
    $20 + 30 = c^2 \Rightarrow 50 = c^2 \Rightarrow \sqrt{50} = \sqrt{c^2} \Rightarrow c = \sqrt{50} \Rightarrow c = \sqrt{25} \cdot \sqrt{2} \Rightarrow c = 5\sqrt{2}$. Therefore the
    perimeter is $2\sqrt{20} + 2\sqrt{30} \Rightarrow 2(\sqrt{4} \cdot \sqrt{5}) + 2\sqrt{30} \Rightarrow 2(2)\sqrt{5} + 2\sqrt{30} \Rightarrow 4\sqrt{5} + 2\sqrt{30}$.

19. Using the distance formula: $d = \sqrt{(x_2 - x_1)^2 + (y_2 - y_1)^2}$, for $(2, -5), (7, 7)$, we get
    $d = \sqrt{(7 - 2)^2 + (7 - (-5))^2} \Rightarrow d = \sqrt{(5)^2 + (12)^2} \Rightarrow d = \sqrt{25 + 144} \Rightarrow d = \sqrt{169} \Rightarrow d = 13$.

20. Using the distance formula: $d = \sqrt{(x_2 - x_1)^2 + (y_2 - y_1)^2}$, for $(0, -3), (-1, 2)$, we get
    $d = \sqrt{(-1 - 0)^2 + (2 - (-3))^2} \Rightarrow d = \sqrt{(-1)^2 + (5)^2} \Rightarrow d = \sqrt{1 + 25} \Rightarrow d = \sqrt{26} \Rightarrow$
    $d = \sqrt{26} \approx 5.099$.

21. Using the distance formula: $d = \sqrt{(x_2 - x_1)^2 + (y_2 - y_1)^2}$, for $(6, -4), (-5, -4)$, we get
    $d = \sqrt{(-5 - 6)^2 + (-4 - (-4))^2} \Rightarrow d = \sqrt{(-11)^2 + (0)^2} \Rightarrow d = \sqrt{121 + 0} \Rightarrow d = \sqrt{121} \Rightarrow d = 11$.

22. Using the distance formula: $d = \sqrt{(x_2 - x_1)^2 + (y_2 - y_1)^2}$, for $(20, -30)$, $(5, -10)$, we get

$$d = \sqrt{(5 - 20)^2 + (-10 - (-30))^2} \Rightarrow d = \sqrt{(-15)^2 + (20)^2} \Rightarrow d = \sqrt{225 + 400} \Rightarrow d = \sqrt{625} \Rightarrow$$
$$d = 25.$$

Section 8.2

23. $\sqrt{6} \cdot \sqrt{5} = \sqrt{6 \cdot 5} = \sqrt{30}$

24. $\sqrt{\dfrac{1}{3}} \cdot \sqrt{\dfrac{2}{7}} = \sqrt{\dfrac{1}{3} \cdot \dfrac{2}{7}} = \sqrt{\dfrac{2}{21}}$

25. $\sqrt{4} \cdot \sqrt{64} = 2 \cdot 8 = 16$

26. $\sqrt{2x} \cdot \sqrt{2x} = \sqrt{2x \cdot 2x} = \sqrt{4x^2} = 2x$

27. $\sqrt{3t} \cdot \sqrt{27t} = \sqrt{3t \cdot 27t} = \sqrt{81t^2} = 9t$

28. $\sqrt{7a} \cdot \sqrt{2b} = \sqrt{7a \cdot 2b} = \sqrt{14ab}$

29. $\sqrt{45} = \sqrt{9} \cdot \sqrt{5} = 3\sqrt{5}$

30. $\sqrt{200} = \sqrt{100} \cdot \sqrt{2} = 10\sqrt{2}$

31. $\sqrt{t^5} = \sqrt{t^4} \cdot \sqrt{t} = t^2\sqrt{t}$

32. $\sqrt{5b^2} = \sqrt{b^2} \cdot \sqrt{5} = b\sqrt{5}$

33. $\sqrt{9x^2y} = \sqrt{9x^2} \cdot \sqrt{y} = 3x\sqrt{y}$

34. $\sqrt{49a^3b} = \sqrt{49a^2} \cdot \sqrt{ab} = 7a\sqrt{ab}$

35. $\sqrt{\dfrac{25}{36}} = \dfrac{\sqrt{25}}{\sqrt{36}} = \dfrac{5}{6}$

36. $\sqrt{5} \cdot \sqrt{8} = \sqrt{5 \cdot 8} = \sqrt{40} = \sqrt{4} \cdot \sqrt{10} = 2\sqrt{10}$

37. $\sqrt{\dfrac{3}{x}} \cdot \sqrt{\dfrac{27}{x}} = \sqrt{\dfrac{3}{x} \cdot \dfrac{27}{x}} = \sqrt{\dfrac{81}{x^2}} = \dfrac{\sqrt{81}}{\sqrt{x^2}} = \dfrac{9}{x}$

38. $\dfrac{\sqrt{64}}{\sqrt{4}} = \dfrac{8}{2} = 4$

39. $\dfrac{\sqrt{50}}{\sqrt{2}} = \sqrt{\dfrac{50}{2}} = \sqrt{25} = 5$

40. $\dfrac{\sqrt{3r^3}}{\sqrt{r}} = \dfrac{\sqrt{r^2} \cdot \sqrt{3} \cdot \sqrt{r}}{\sqrt{r}} = r\sqrt{3} \cdot \dfrac{\sqrt{r}}{\sqrt{r}} = r\sqrt{3} \cdot 1 = r\sqrt{3}$

41. $\sqrt{\dfrac{16}{x}} \cdot \sqrt{\dfrac{4}{x^2}} = \sqrt{\dfrac{16}{x} \cdot \dfrac{4}{x^2}} = \sqrt{\dfrac{64}{x^3}} = \dfrac{\sqrt{64}}{\sqrt{x^3}} = \dfrac{8}{\sqrt{x^2} \cdot \sqrt{x}} = \dfrac{8}{x\sqrt{x}}$

42. $\sqrt{3ab^3} \cdot \sqrt{27ab} = \sqrt{3ab^3 \cdot 27ab} = \sqrt{81a^2b^4} = 9ab^2$

43. $\dfrac{\sqrt{75ab}}{\sqrt{3ab}} = \sqrt{\dfrac{75ab}{3ab}} = \sqrt{25} \cdot \dfrac{\sqrt{ab}}{\sqrt{ab}} = 5 \cdot 1 = 5$

44. $\dfrac{\sqrt{8xy^3}}{\sqrt{2xy}} = \sqrt{\dfrac{8xy^3}{2xy}} = \sqrt{4y^2} \cdot \dfrac{\sqrt{xy}}{\sqrt{xy}} = 2y \cdot 1 = 2y$

Section 8.3

45. $8\sqrt{7} - 5\sqrt{7} = (8 - 5)\sqrt{7} = 3\sqrt{7}$

46. $\sqrt{15} + 2\sqrt{15} = (1 + 2)\sqrt{15} = 3\sqrt{15}$

47. $2\sqrt{2} + \sqrt{8} = 2\sqrt{2} + (\sqrt{4} \cdot \sqrt{2}) = 2\sqrt{2} + 2\sqrt{2} = (2 + 2)\sqrt{2} = 4\sqrt{2}$

48. $3\sqrt{45} - 2\sqrt{20} = 3(\sqrt{9} \cdot \sqrt{5}) - 2(\sqrt{4} \cdot \sqrt{5}) = 3(3)\sqrt{5} - 2(2)\sqrt{5} = 9\sqrt{5} - 4\sqrt{5} = (9 - 4)\sqrt{5} = 5\sqrt{5}$

49. $5\sqrt[3]{9} - 2\sqrt[3]{9} = (5 - 2)\sqrt[3]{9} = 3\sqrt[3]{9}$

50. $9\sqrt[3]{10} + \sqrt[3]{10} = (9 + 1)\sqrt[3]{10} = 10\sqrt[3]{10}$

51. $\sqrt{4t} + \sqrt{9t} = (\sqrt{4} \cdot \sqrt{t}) + (\sqrt{9} \cdot \sqrt{t}) = 2\sqrt{t} + 3\sqrt{t} = (2 + 3)\sqrt{t} = 5\sqrt{t}$

52. $2\sqrt{ab} - \sqrt{4ab} = 2\sqrt{ab} - (\sqrt{4} \cdot \sqrt{ab}) = 2\sqrt{ab} - 2\sqrt{ab} = 0$

Section 8.4

53. $(9 - \sqrt{6})(9 + \sqrt{6}) = 9^2 - (\sqrt{6})^2 = 81 - 6 = 75$

54. $(2 + \sqrt{t})(2 - \sqrt{t}) = 2^2 - (\sqrt{t})^2 = 4 - t$

55. $\dfrac{5}{\sqrt{5}} = \dfrac{5}{\sqrt{5}} \cdot \dfrac{\sqrt{5}}{\sqrt{5}} = \dfrac{5\sqrt{5}}{\sqrt{5} \cdot \sqrt{5}} = \dfrac{5\sqrt{5}}{5} = \dfrac{5}{5} \cdot \sqrt{5} = 1 \cdot \sqrt{5} = \sqrt{5}$

56. $-\dfrac{9}{3\sqrt{11}} = -\dfrac{9}{3\sqrt{11}} \cdot \dfrac{\sqrt{11}}{\sqrt{11}} = -\dfrac{9\sqrt{11}}{3\sqrt{11} \cdot \sqrt{11}} = -\dfrac{3\sqrt{11}}{11}$

57. $\dfrac{1}{\sqrt{5} - 2} = \dfrac{1}{\sqrt{5} - 2} \cdot \dfrac{\sqrt{5} + 2}{\sqrt{5} + 2} = \dfrac{\sqrt{5} + 2}{\sqrt{5}^2 - 2^2} = \dfrac{\sqrt{5} + 2}{5 - 4} = \dfrac{\sqrt{5} + 2}{1} = \sqrt{5} + 2$

58. $\dfrac{4 - \sqrt{b}}{4 + \sqrt{b}} = \dfrac{4 - \sqrt{b}}{4 + \sqrt{b}} \cdot \dfrac{4 - \sqrt{b}}{4 - \sqrt{b}} = \dfrac{4^2 - 8\sqrt{b} + \sqrt{b}^2}{4^2 - \sqrt{b}^2} = \dfrac{16 - 8\sqrt{b} + b}{16 - b}$

Section 8.5

59. $\sqrt{x} = 5 \Rightarrow \sqrt{x}^2 = 5^2 \Rightarrow x = 25$ Check: $x = 25 \Rightarrow \sqrt{25} \stackrel{?}{=} 5 \Rightarrow 5 = 5$

60. No solution, a radical cannot equal a negative number.

61. $\sqrt{2 - t} = 5 \Rightarrow (\sqrt{2 - t})^2 = 5^2 \Rightarrow 2 - t = 25 \Rightarrow -t = 23 \Rightarrow t = -23$ Check: $t = -23 \Rightarrow$

   $\sqrt{2 - (-23)} \stackrel{?}{=} 5 \Rightarrow \sqrt{25} \stackrel{?}{=} 5 \Rightarrow 5 = 5$

62. $\sqrt{3b + 1} = 5 \Rightarrow (\sqrt{3b + 1})^2 = 5^2 \Rightarrow 3b + 1 = 25 \Rightarrow 3b = 24 \Rightarrow b = 8$ Check: $b = 8 \Rightarrow$

   $\sqrt{3(8) + 1} \stackrel{?}{=} 5 \Rightarrow \sqrt{25} \stackrel{?}{=} 5 \Rightarrow 5 = 5$

63. $\sqrt{x + 4} - 1 = 5 \Rightarrow \sqrt{x + 4} = 6 \Rightarrow (\sqrt{x + 4})^2 = 6^2 \Rightarrow x + 4 = 36 \Rightarrow x = 32$ Check: $x = 32 \Rightarrow$

   $\sqrt{32 + 4} - 1 \stackrel{?}{=} 5 \Rightarrow \sqrt{36} - 1 \stackrel{?}{=} 5 \Rightarrow 6 - 1 \stackrel{?}{=} 5 \Rightarrow 5 = 5$

64. $\sqrt{8x} = 4\sqrt{x - 4} \Rightarrow \dfrac{\sqrt{8x}}{4} = \sqrt{x - 4} \Rightarrow \left(\dfrac{\sqrt{8x}}{4}\right)^2 = (\sqrt{x - 4})^2 \Rightarrow \dfrac{8x}{16} = x - 4 \Rightarrow \dfrac{x}{2} = x - 4 \Rightarrow$

   $x = 2x - 8 \Rightarrow 0 = x - 8 \Rightarrow x = 8$ Check: $x = 8 \Rightarrow \sqrt{8(8)} \stackrel{?}{=} 4\sqrt{8 - 4} \Rightarrow \sqrt{64} \stackrel{?}{=} 4\sqrt{4} \Rightarrow$

   $8 \stackrel{?}{=} 4(2) \Rightarrow 8 = 8$

65. $\dfrac{1}{2}\sqrt{2b+4}+4=b \Rightarrow \sqrt{2b+4}=2(b-4) \Rightarrow (\sqrt{2b+4})^2=(2b-8)^2 \Rightarrow$

$2b+4=4b^2-32b+64 \Rightarrow 0=4b^2-34b+60 \Rightarrow 2(2b^2-17b+30)=0 \Rightarrow$

$2(2b-5)(b-6)=0 \Rightarrow 2b-5=0 \Rightarrow 2b=5 \Rightarrow b=\dfrac{5}{2}$, and $b-6=0 \Rightarrow b=6$ Check: $b=6 \Rightarrow$

$\dfrac{1}{2}\sqrt{2(6)+4}+4 \overset{?}{=} 6 \Rightarrow \dfrac{1}{2}\sqrt{16}+4 \overset{?}{=} 6 \Rightarrow \dfrac{1}{2}(4)+4 \overset{?}{=} 6 \Rightarrow 2+4 \overset{?}{=} 6 \Rightarrow 6=6$, and $b=\dfrac{5}{2} \Rightarrow$

$\dfrac{1}{2}\sqrt{2\left(\dfrac{5}{2}\right)+4}+4 \overset{?}{=} \dfrac{5}{2} \Rightarrow \dfrac{1}{2}\sqrt{5+4}+4 \overset{?}{=} \dfrac{5}{2} \Rightarrow \dfrac{1}{2}\sqrt{9}+4 \overset{?}{=} \dfrac{5}{2} \Rightarrow \dfrac{1}{2}(3)+4 = \dfrac{5}{2} \Rightarrow \dfrac{3}{2}+\dfrac{8}{2} \overset{?}{=} \dfrac{5}{2} \Rightarrow$

$\dfrac{11}{2} \neq \dfrac{5}{2}$, so $b=6$

66. $x-7=\sqrt{2x+1} \Rightarrow (x-7)^2=(\sqrt{2x+1})^2 \Rightarrow x^2-14x+49=2x+1 \Rightarrow x^2-16x+48=0 \Rightarrow$

$(x-12)(x-4)=0 \Rightarrow x-12=0 \Rightarrow x=12 \Rightarrow$, and $x-4=0 \Rightarrow x=4$ Check: $x=12 \Rightarrow$

$12-7 \overset{?}{=} \sqrt{2(12)+1} \Rightarrow 5 \overset{?}{=} \sqrt{25} \Rightarrow 5=5$, and $x=4 \Rightarrow 4-7 \overset{?}{=} \sqrt{2(4)+1} \Rightarrow -3 \overset{?}{=} \sqrt{9} \Rightarrow$

$-3 \neq 3$, so $x=12$

67. $A=\sqrt{4P}$ for $P \Rightarrow A^2=4P \Rightarrow \dfrac{A^2}{4}=P \Rightarrow P=\dfrac{A^2}{4}$

68. $P=2\pi\sqrt{\dfrac{L}{g}}$ for $g \Rightarrow \dfrac{P}{2\pi}=\sqrt{\dfrac{L}{g}} \Rightarrow \left(\dfrac{P}{2\pi}\right)^2=\left(\sqrt{\dfrac{L}{g}}\right)^2 \Rightarrow \dfrac{P^2}{4\pi^2}=\dfrac{L}{g} \Rightarrow \dfrac{P^2}{4\pi^2L}=\dfrac{1}{g} \Rightarrow g=\dfrac{4\pi^2L}{P^2}$

69. (a) From the table we see that $\sqrt{x}+2=2$ when $x=0$. See Figure 69a.

    (b) The solution is the x-coordinate of the intersection point, or 0. See Figure 69b.

x	0	1	4	9	16	25
$\sqrt{x}+2$	2	3	4	5	6	7

Figure 69a   Figure 69b

70. (a) From the table we see that $\sqrt{x-1}=4$ when $x=17$. See Figure 70a.

    (b) The solution is the x-coordinate of the intersection point, or 17. See Figure 70b.

x	1	2	5	10	17	26
$\sqrt{x-1}$	0	1	2	3	4	5

Figure 70a   Figure 70b

Section 8.6

71. $\sqrt[3]{64} = 4$, because $4^3 = 64$

72. $\sqrt[3]{-1000} = -10$, because $(-10)^3 = -1000$

73. $-\sqrt[4]{81} = -3$, because $-(3^4) = -(81)$

74. $\sqrt[5]{32} = 2$, because $2^5 = 32$

75. $\sqrt[4]{7^4} = 7^{4/4} = 7^1 = 7$

76. $-\sqrt[6]{\dfrac{1}{64}} = -\dfrac{\sqrt[6]{1}}{\sqrt[6]{64}} = -\dfrac{1}{2}$, because $-\dfrac{1^6}{2^6} = -\dfrac{1}{64}$

77. $\sqrt[3]{-4} \cdot \sqrt[3]{16} = \sqrt[3]{-4 \cdot 16} = \sqrt[3]{-64} = -4$, because $(-4)^3 = -64$

78. $\sqrt[4]{3} \cdot \sqrt[4]{27} = \sqrt[4]{3 \cdot 27} = \sqrt[4]{81} = 3$, because $3^4 = 81$

79. $\dfrac{\sqrt[3]{2}}{\sqrt[3]{16}} = \sqrt[3]{\dfrac{2}{16}} = \sqrt[3]{\dfrac{1}{8}} = \dfrac{\sqrt[3]{1}}{\sqrt[3]{8}} = \dfrac{1}{2}$, because $\dfrac{1^3}{2^3} = \dfrac{1}{8}$

80. $\dfrac{\sqrt[4]{2}}{\sqrt[4]{32}} = \sqrt[4]{\dfrac{2}{32}} = \sqrt[4]{\dfrac{1}{16}} = \dfrac{\sqrt[4]{1}}{\sqrt[4]{16}} = \dfrac{1}{2}$, because $\dfrac{1^4}{2^4} = \dfrac{1}{16}$

81. $25^{3/2} = \sqrt{25^3} = (\sqrt{25})^3 = 5^3 = 125$

82. $1000^{1/3} = \sqrt[3]{1000} = 10$

83. $16^{-5/4} = \dfrac{1}{\sqrt[4]{16^5}} = \dfrac{1}{(\sqrt[4]{16})^5} = \dfrac{1}{2^5} = \dfrac{1}{32}$

84. $(-8)^{-2/3} = \dfrac{1}{\sqrt[3]{(-8)^2}} = \dfrac{1}{(\sqrt[3]{-8})^2} = \dfrac{1}{-2^2} = \dfrac{1}{4}$

Applications

85. $a^2 + b^2 = c^2 \Rightarrow a = 400, b = 300$, we get $400^2 + 300^2 = c^2 \Rightarrow 160{,}000 + 90{,}000 = c^2 \Rightarrow$
    $250{,}000 = c^2 \Rightarrow \sqrt{250{,}000} = \sqrt{c^2} \Rightarrow 500 = c \Rightarrow c = 500$ feet.

86. $a^2 + b^2 = c^2 \Rightarrow a = 30 \cdot 2.5, b = 16 \cdot 2.5 \Rightarrow a = 75, b = 40$, we get $75^2 + 40^2 = c^2 \Rightarrow$
    $5625 + 1600 = c^2 \Rightarrow 7225 = c^2 \Rightarrow \sqrt{7225} = \sqrt{c^2} \Rightarrow 85 = c \Rightarrow c = 85$ miles.

87. $R = 150$ bpm $\Rightarrow 150 = \dfrac{885}{\sqrt{W}} \Rightarrow \dfrac{150}{885} = \dfrac{1}{\sqrt{W}} \Rightarrow \sqrt{W} = \dfrac{885}{150} \Rightarrow (\sqrt{W})^2 = 5.9^2 \Rightarrow W = $ about 35 lb

88. $T = 4$ seconds $\Rightarrow 4 = \sqrt{\dfrac{h}{4}} \Rightarrow 4^2 = \left(\sqrt{\dfrac{h}{4}}\right)^2 \Rightarrow 16 = \dfrac{h}{4} \Rightarrow 64 = h \Rightarrow h = 64$ feet

89. (a) $T = D^{3/2} \Rightarrow T = \sqrt{D^3} \Rightarrow T = (\sqrt{D})^3$

    (b) $D = 1.52 \Rightarrow T = (\sqrt{1.52})^3 \Rightarrow T = 1.233^3 \Rightarrow T = 1.87$ years

90. $V = v\sqrt{\dfrac{D}{d}}$ for $d \Rightarrow \dfrac{V}{v} = \sqrt{\dfrac{D}{d}} \Rightarrow \left(\dfrac{V}{v}\right)^2 = \left(\sqrt{\dfrac{D}{d}}\right)^2 \Rightarrow \dfrac{V^2}{v^2} = \dfrac{D}{d} \Rightarrow \dfrac{V^2}{v^2D} = \dfrac{1}{d} \Rightarrow d = \dfrac{v^2D}{V^2}$

91. $P = 2(100 - \sqrt{98}) + 2(100 + \sqrt{98}) = (200 - 2\sqrt{98}) + (200 + 2\sqrt{98}) = 400 + 0 = 400$
    $A = (100 - \sqrt{98})(100 + \sqrt{98}) = 100^2 - (\sqrt{98})^2 = 10{,}000 - 98 = 9902$

92. $D = 10 \Rightarrow 10 = 1.22\sqrt{h} \Rightarrow \dfrac{10}{1.22} = \sqrt{h} \Rightarrow 8.19 = \sqrt{h} \Rightarrow 8.19^2 = \sqrt{h}^2 \Rightarrow h = $ about 67 feet

93. (a) $L = 8 \Rightarrow P = 2\pi\sqrt{\dfrac{8}{32}} \Rightarrow P = 2\pi\sqrt{\dfrac{1}{4}} \Rightarrow P = 2\pi\left(\dfrac{1}{2}\right) \Rightarrow P = \dfrac{2}{2}\cdot\pi \Rightarrow P = 1\cdot\pi \Rightarrow$

 $P = \pi$ seconds

 (b) $P = 2 \Rightarrow 2 = 2\pi\sqrt{\dfrac{L}{32}} \Rightarrow \dfrac{2}{2\pi} = \sqrt{\dfrac{L}{32}} \Rightarrow \left(\dfrac{2}{2\pi}\right)^2 = \left(\sqrt{\dfrac{L}{32}}\right)^2 \Rightarrow \dfrac{4}{4\pi^2} = \dfrac{L}{32} \Rightarrow \dfrac{128}{4\pi^2} = L \Rightarrow$

 $L =$ about 3.24 feet

94. (a) $L = 27.5\sqrt[3]{W} \Rightarrow L = 27.5W^{1/3}$

 (b) $W = 8 \Rightarrow L = 27.5\sqrt[3]{8} \Rightarrow L = 27.5(2) \Rightarrow L = 55$ inches

Chapter 8 Test

1. $\sqrt{64} = \pm 8$

2. real, irrational

3. $\sqrt{81} = 9$, because $9^2 = 81$

4. $\sqrt[3]{-64} = -4$, because $-4^3 = -64$

5. $\sqrt[5]{32} = 2$, because $2^5 = 32$

6. $25^{3/2} = \sqrt{25^3} = (\sqrt{25})^3 = 5^3 = 125$

7. Using Pythagorean Theorem: $a^2 + b^2 = c^2$, for $a = 5$ inches, $b = 7$ inches, we get $5^2 + 7^2 = c^2 \Rightarrow$

 $25 + 49 = c^2 \Rightarrow 74 = c^2 \Rightarrow \sqrt{74} = \sqrt{c^2} \Rightarrow \sqrt{74} = c \Rightarrow c = \sqrt{74}$ inches.

8. Using the distance formula: $d = \sqrt{(x_2 - x_1)^2 + (y_2 - y_1)^2}$, for $(-3, -2)$, $(3, 1)$, we get

 $d = \sqrt{(3 - (-3))^2 + (1 - (-2))^2} \Rightarrow d = \sqrt{(6)^2 + (3)^2} \Rightarrow d = \sqrt{36 + 9} \Rightarrow d = \sqrt{45}$.

9. $D = a^2 + b^2 = c^2$, for $a = \sqrt{8}$, $b = \sqrt{32}$, we get $(\sqrt{8})^2 + (\sqrt{32})^2 = c^2 \Rightarrow 8 + 32 = c^2 \Rightarrow 40 = c^2 \Rightarrow$

 $\sqrt{40} = \sqrt{c^2} \Rightarrow \sqrt{40} = c \Rightarrow c = \sqrt{4}\cdot\sqrt{10} \Rightarrow c = 2\sqrt{10}$

 $P = 2\sqrt{8} + 2\sqrt{32} = 2(\sqrt{4}\cdot\sqrt{2}) + 2(\sqrt{16}\cdot\sqrt{2}) = 2(2)\sqrt{2} + 2(4)\sqrt{2} = 4\sqrt{2} + 8\sqrt{2} = (4 + 8)\sqrt{2} =$

 $12\sqrt{2}$

10. Using $d = \sqrt{(x_2 - x_1)^2 + (y_2 - y_1)^2}$, for $(5, -4)$, $(-2, 3)$, we get $d = \sqrt{(-2 - 5)^2 + (3 - (-4))^2} \Rightarrow$

 $d = \sqrt{(-7)^2 + (7)^2} \Rightarrow d = \sqrt{49 + 49} \Rightarrow d = \sqrt{98} \Rightarrow d = \sqrt{49}\cdot\sqrt{2} \Rightarrow d = 7\sqrt{2} \approx 9.899$.

11. $\sqrt{54} = \sqrt{9}\cdot\sqrt{6} = 3\sqrt{6}$

12. $\sqrt{9t^3} = \sqrt{9t^2}\cdot\sqrt{t} = 3t\sqrt{t}$

13. $\sqrt{6}\cdot\sqrt{24} = \sqrt{6\cdot 24} = \sqrt{144} = 12$

14. $\dfrac{\sqrt{90}}{\sqrt{10}} = \sqrt{\dfrac{90}{10}} = \sqrt{9} = 3$

15. $\sqrt{3a}\cdot\sqrt{27a} = \sqrt{3a\cdot 27a} = \sqrt{81a^2} = 9a$

16. $\dfrac{\sqrt{4r^5}}{\sqrt{r^3}} = \dfrac{\sqrt{4r^2}\cdot\sqrt{r^3}}{\sqrt{r^3}} = 2r\dfrac{\sqrt{r^3}}{\sqrt{r^3}} = 2r\cdot 1 = 2r$

17. $\sqrt{\dfrac{x}{3}} \cdot \sqrt{\dfrac{x}{3}} = \sqrt{\dfrac{x}{3} \cdot \dfrac{x}{3}} = \sqrt{\dfrac{x^2}{9}} = \dfrac{x}{3}$

18. $\sqrt{8ab^2} \cdot \sqrt{2a^2b} = \sqrt{8ab^2 \cdot 2a^2b} = \sqrt{16a^3b^3} = \sqrt{16a^2b^2} \cdot \sqrt{ab} = 4ab\sqrt{ab}$

19. $7\sqrt{5} - 2\sqrt{5} = (7-2)\sqrt{5} = 5\sqrt{5}$

20. $3\sqrt{8} - \sqrt{18} = 3(\sqrt{4} \cdot \sqrt{2}) - (\sqrt{9} \cdot \sqrt{2}) = 3(2)\sqrt{2} - 3\sqrt{2} = 6\sqrt{2} - 3\sqrt{2} = (6-3)\sqrt{2} = 3\sqrt{2}$

21. $2\sqrt[3]{11} - 3\sqrt[3]{11} = (2-3)\sqrt[3]{11} = -\sqrt[3]{11}$

22. $\sqrt{25ab} + \sqrt{9ab} = (\sqrt{25} \cdot \sqrt{ab}) + (\sqrt{9} \cdot \sqrt{ab}) = 5\sqrt{ab} + 3\sqrt{ab} = (5+3)\sqrt{ab} = 8\sqrt{ab}$

23. $\dfrac{4}{2\sqrt{3}} = \dfrac{4}{2\sqrt{3}} \cdot \dfrac{\sqrt{3}}{\sqrt{3}} = \dfrac{4\sqrt{3}}{2\sqrt{3} \cdot \sqrt{3}} = \dfrac{4\sqrt{3}}{2(3)} = \dfrac{4\sqrt{3}}{6} = \dfrac{2\sqrt{3}}{3}$

24. $\dfrac{2-\sqrt{x}}{2+\sqrt{x}} = \dfrac{2-\sqrt{x}}{2+\sqrt{x}} \cdot \dfrac{2-\sqrt{x}}{2-\sqrt{x}} = \dfrac{2^2 - 4\sqrt{x} + \sqrt{x^2}}{2^2 - \sqrt{x^2}} = \dfrac{4 - 4\sqrt{x} + x}{4 - x}$

25. $\sqrt{2x-5} = 5 \Rightarrow (\sqrt{2x-5})^2 = 5^2 \Rightarrow 2x - 5 = 25 \Rightarrow 2x = 30 \Rightarrow x = 15$ Check: $x = 15 \Rightarrow$
$\sqrt{2(15)-5} \overset{?}{=} 5 \Rightarrow \sqrt{30-5} \overset{?}{=} = 5 \Rightarrow \sqrt{25} \overset{?}{=} 5 \Rightarrow 5 = 5$, so $x = 15$

26. $\sqrt{x+30} = x \Rightarrow (\sqrt{x+30})^2 = x^2 \Rightarrow x + 30 = x^2 \Rightarrow x^2 - x - 30 = 0 \Rightarrow 0 = (x-6)(x+5)$
Check: $x = 6 \Rightarrow \sqrt{6+30} \overset{?}{=} 6 \Rightarrow \sqrt{36} \overset{?}{=} = 6 \Rightarrow 6 = 6$, so $x = 6$

27. $b = \sqrt{c^2 - a^2}$ for $c \Rightarrow b^2 = (\sqrt{c^2 - a^2})^2 \Rightarrow b^2 = c^2 - a^2 \Rightarrow a^2 + b^2 = c^2 \Rightarrow \sqrt{a^2 + b^2} = \sqrt{c^2} \Rightarrow$
$c = \sqrt{a^2 + b^2}$

28. $a^2 + b^2 = c^2$ for $a = 60 \cdot \dfrac{3}{4}, b = 40 \cdot \dfrac{3}{4} \Rightarrow a = 45, b = 30$, we get $45^2 + 30^2 = c^2 \Rightarrow$
$2025 + 900 = c^2 \Rightarrow 2925 = c^2 \Rightarrow \sqrt{2925} = \sqrt{c^2} \Rightarrow 54 \approx c \Rightarrow c \approx 54$ miles.

29. (a) $W = 64 \Rightarrow R = \dfrac{885}{\sqrt{64}} \Rightarrow R = \dfrac{885}{8} \Rightarrow R \approx 111$ bpm

(b) $R = 177 \Rightarrow 177 = \dfrac{885}{\sqrt{W}} \Rightarrow \dfrac{177}{885} = \dfrac{1}{\sqrt{W}} \Rightarrow \sqrt{W} = \dfrac{885}{177} \Rightarrow (\sqrt{W})^2 = 5^2 \Rightarrow W = 25$ pounds

(c) $R = \dfrac{885}{\sqrt{W}} \Rightarrow R = 885W^{-1/2}$

(d) $R = \dfrac{885}{\sqrt{W}}$ for $W \Rightarrow \dfrac{R}{885} = \dfrac{1}{\sqrt{W}} \Rightarrow \sqrt{W} = \dfrac{885}{R} \Rightarrow (\sqrt{W})^2 = \left(\dfrac{885}{R}\right)^2 \Rightarrow W = \left(\dfrac{885}{R}\right)^2$

Chapter 8 Extended and Discovery Exercises

1. $\sqrt{2x} - 1 = \sqrt{x+1} \Rightarrow (\sqrt{2x} - 1)^2 = (\sqrt{x+1})^2 \Rightarrow 2x - 2\sqrt{2x} + 1 = x + 1 \Rightarrow -2\sqrt{2x} = -x \Rightarrow$
$\sqrt{2x} = \dfrac{x}{2} \Rightarrow (\sqrt{2x})^2 = \left(\dfrac{x}{2}\right)^2 \Rightarrow 2x = \dfrac{x^2}{4} \Rightarrow 8x = x^2 \Rightarrow 0 = x^2 - 8x \Rightarrow x(x-8) = 0 \Rightarrow$
$x = 0$, or $x - 8 = 0 \Rightarrow x = 8$ Check: $x = 0 \Rightarrow \sqrt{2(0)} - 1 = \sqrt{0+1} \Rightarrow -1 \neq 1$, and $x = 8 \Rightarrow$
$\sqrt{2(8)} - 1 = \sqrt{8+1} \Rightarrow \sqrt{16} - 1 = \sqrt{9} \Rightarrow 4 - 1 = 3 \Rightarrow 3 = 3$, so $x = 8$

2. $\sqrt{x} = \sqrt{x-7} + 1 \Rightarrow \sqrt{x} - 1 = \sqrt{x-7} \Rightarrow (\sqrt{x} - 1)^2 = (\sqrt{x-7})^2 \Rightarrow x - 2\sqrt{x} + 1 = x - 7 \Rightarrow$
$-2\sqrt{x} = -8 \Rightarrow \sqrt{x} = 4 \Rightarrow (\sqrt{x})^2 = 4^2 \Rightarrow x = 16$ Check: $x = 16 \Rightarrow \sqrt{16} = \sqrt{16-7} + 1 \Rightarrow$
$4 = \sqrt{9} + 1 \Rightarrow 4 = 3 + 1 \Rightarrow 4 = 4$, so $x = 16$

3. $\sqrt{t-2} = \sqrt{t+3} - 1 \Rightarrow (\sqrt{t-2})^2 = (\sqrt{t+3}-1)^2 \Rightarrow t-2 = t+3 - 2\sqrt{t+3} + 1 \Rightarrow$
   $-6 = -2\sqrt{t+3} \Rightarrow 3 = \sqrt{t+3} \Rightarrow 3^2 = (\sqrt{t+3})^2 \Rightarrow 9 = t+3 \Rightarrow t = 6$ Check:
   $\sqrt{6-2} = \sqrt{6+3} - 1 \Rightarrow \sqrt{4} = \sqrt{9} - 1 \Rightarrow 2 = 3 - 1 \Rightarrow 2 = 2$, so $t = 6$

4. $\sqrt{2t-2} + \sqrt{t} = 7 \Rightarrow \sqrt{2t-2} = -\sqrt{t} + 7 \Rightarrow (\sqrt{2t-2})^2 = (-\sqrt{t}+7)^2 \Rightarrow$
   $2t - 2 = t - 14\sqrt{t} + 49 \Rightarrow t - 51 = -14\sqrt{t} \Rightarrow (t-51)^2 = (-14\sqrt{t})^2 \Rightarrow t^2 - 102t + 2601 = 196t \Rightarrow$
   $t^2 - 298t + 2601 = 0 \Rightarrow (t-9)(t-289) = 0 \Rightarrow t = 9$ or 289 Check: $t = 9 \Rightarrow$
   $\sqrt{2(9)-2} + \sqrt{9} = 7 \Rightarrow \sqrt{16} + \sqrt{9} = 7 \Rightarrow 4 + 3 = 7 \Rightarrow 7 = 7$, and $t = 289 \Rightarrow$
   $\sqrt{2(289)-2} + \sqrt{289} = 7 \Rightarrow \sqrt{578-2} + \sqrt{289} = 7 \Rightarrow \sqrt{576} + \sqrt{289} = 7 \Rightarrow 24 + 17 = 7 \Rightarrow$
   $41 \neq 7$, so $t = 9$

5. $\sqrt{b+1} - \sqrt{b-6} = 1 \Rightarrow \sqrt{b+1} = \sqrt{b-6} + 1 \Rightarrow (\sqrt{b+1})^2 = (\sqrt{b-6}+1)^2 \Rightarrow$
   $b + 1 = b - 6 + 2\sqrt{b-6} + 1 \Rightarrow 6 = 2\sqrt{b-6} \Rightarrow 3 = \sqrt{b-6} \Rightarrow (\sqrt{b-6})^2 \Rightarrow$
   $9 = b - 6 \Rightarrow b = 15$ Check: $b = 15 \Rightarrow \sqrt{15+1} - \sqrt{15-6} = 1 \Rightarrow \sqrt{16} - \sqrt{9} = 1 \Rightarrow$
   $4 - 3 = 1 \Rightarrow 1 = 1$, so $b = 15$

6. $\sqrt{b-7} = \sqrt{b} - 1 \Rightarrow (\sqrt{b-7})^2 = (\sqrt{b}-1)^2 \Rightarrow b - 7 = b - 2\sqrt{b} + 1 \Rightarrow -8 = -2\sqrt{b} \Rightarrow$
   $4 = \sqrt{b} \Rightarrow 4^2 = (\sqrt{b})^2 \Rightarrow b = 16$ Check: $b = 16 \Rightarrow \sqrt{16-7} = \sqrt{16} - 1 \Rightarrow \sqrt{9} = \sqrt{16} - 1 \Rightarrow$
   $3 = 4 - 1 \Rightarrow 3 = 3$, so $b = 16$

7. $\sqrt[3]{x} = 3 \Rightarrow (\sqrt[3]{x})^3 = 3^3 \Rightarrow x = 27$ Check: $x = 27 \Rightarrow \sqrt[3]{27} = 3 \Rightarrow 3 = 3$, so $x = 27$

8. $\sqrt[3]{2x} + 1 = 3 \Rightarrow \sqrt[3]{2x} = 2 \Rightarrow (\sqrt[3]{2x})^3 = 2^3 \Rightarrow 2x = 8 \Rightarrow x = 4$ Check: $x = 4 \Rightarrow \sqrt[3]{2(4)} + 1 = 3 \Rightarrow$
   $\sqrt[3]{8} + 1 = 3 \Rightarrow 2 + 1 = 3 \Rightarrow 3 = 3$, so $x = 4$

9. $\sqrt[3]{2x-2} + 1 = 4 \Rightarrow \sqrt[3]{2x-2} = 3 \Rightarrow (\sqrt[3]{2x-2})^3 = 3^3 \Rightarrow 2x - 2 = 27 \Rightarrow 2x = 29 \Rightarrow x = \dfrac{29}{2}$
   Check: $x = \dfrac{29}{2} \Rightarrow \sqrt[3]{2\left(\dfrac{29}{2}\right) - 2} + 1 = 4 \Rightarrow \sqrt[3]{29 - 2} + 1 = 4 \Rightarrow \sqrt[3]{27} + 1 = 4 \Rightarrow 3 + 1 = 4 \Rightarrow$
   $4 = 4$, so $x = \dfrac{29}{2}$

10. $\sqrt[4]{t} = 2 \Rightarrow (\sqrt[4]{t})^4 = 2^4 \Rightarrow t = 16$ Check: $t = 16 \Rightarrow \sqrt[4]{16} = 2 \Rightarrow 2 = 2$, so $t = 16$

11. $\sqrt[4]{4x} + 2 = 4 \Rightarrow \sqrt[4]{4x} = 2 \Rightarrow (\sqrt[4]{4x})^4 = 2^4 \Rightarrow 4x = 16 \Rightarrow x = 4$ Check: $x = 4 \Rightarrow$
    $\sqrt[4]{4(4)} + 2 = 4 \Rightarrow \sqrt[4]{16} + 2 = 4 \Rightarrow 2 + 2 = 4 \Rightarrow 4 = 4$, so $x = 4$

12. $\sqrt[5]{5x-3} = 2 \Rightarrow (\sqrt[5]{5x-3})^5 = 2^5 \Rightarrow 5x - 3 = 32 \Rightarrow 5x = 35 \Rightarrow x = 7$ Check: $x = 7 \Rightarrow$
    $\sqrt[5]{5(7)-3} = 2 \Rightarrow \sqrt[5]{35-3} = 2 \Rightarrow \sqrt[5]{32} = 2 \Rightarrow 2 = 2$, so $x = 7$

13. Raise each side to the sixth power: $\sqrt[3]{3x} = \sqrt{x} \Rightarrow (\sqrt[3]{3x})^6 = (\sqrt{x})^6 \Rightarrow (3x)^2 = x^3 \Rightarrow 9x^2 = x^3 \Rightarrow$
    $x^3 - 9x^2 = 0 \Rightarrow x^2(x-9) = 0 \Rightarrow x = 0, 9$

14. Perfect squares between 10 and 99 are: 16, 25, 36, 49, 64 and 81. The perfect cubes are: 27 and 64 $\Rightarrow$ 64 is
    the only perfect square and cube between 10 and 99.

15. Perfect cubes between 100 and 999 are: 125, 216, 343, 512 and 729. The only perfect square of those numbers
    is 729 $\Rightarrow$ 729 is the only perfect square and cube between 100 and 999.

Critical Thinking Solutions for Chapter 8

Section 8.2

- $\sqrt{x^{2n}} = \left(\sqrt{x^n}\right)^2 = x^n$, so $\sqrt{x^{16}} = \left(\sqrt{x^8}\right)^2 = x^8$, so $\sqrt{x^{16}} \neq x^4$ but $\sqrt{x^{16}} = x^8$

Section 8.4

- $\dfrac{\sqrt{x} - \sqrt{y}}{\sqrt{x} + \sqrt{y}} = \dfrac{\sqrt{x} - \sqrt{y}}{\sqrt{x} + \sqrt{y}} \cdot \dfrac{\sqrt{x} + \sqrt{y}}{\sqrt{x} + \sqrt{y}} = \dfrac{\left(\sqrt{x}\right)^2 - \left(\sqrt{y}\right)^2}{\left(\sqrt{x}\right)^2 + 2\sqrt{x \cdot y} + \left(\sqrt{y}\right)^2} = \dfrac{x - y}{x + 2\sqrt{xy} + y}$

Section 8.5

- First divide each side by 2 and then cube each side: $2\sqrt[3]{x} = 6 \Rightarrow \sqrt[3]{x} = 3 \Rightarrow \left(\sqrt[3]{x}\right)^3 = 3^3 \Rightarrow x = 27$

- Using $P = 2\pi\sqrt{\dfrac{L}{32}}$ and quadrupling L gives us $P = 2\pi\sqrt{\dfrac{4L}{32}} \Rightarrow P = 2\pi\sqrt{4 \cdot \dfrac{L}{32}} \Rightarrow P = 2\pi(2)\sqrt{\dfrac{L}{32}}$ which is (2) times the original, so it doubles.

Chapter 9: Quadratic Equations

9.1: Parabolas

Concepts

1. parabola

3. axis of symmetry

5. See Figure 5. *Answers may vary.*

Figure 5

Figure 23

Figure 25

7. narrower

9. $ax^2 + bx + c$ with $a \neq 0$

11. The equation is in the form $y = ax^2 + bx + c$ with $a = 5$. Since $a > 0$, the parabola opens upward.

13. Rewrite the equation as $y = -4x^2 + 3x - 7$ with $a = -4$. Since $a < 0$, the parabola opens downward.

15. Rewrite the equation as $y = -x^2 - 12x - 36$ with $a = -1$. Since $a < 0$, the parabola opens downward.

17. Rewrite the equation as $y = x^2 - 4x + 4$ with $a = 1$. Since $a > 0$, the parabola opens upward.

Graphs of Quadratic Equations

19. The vertex is $(1, -2)$. The axis of symmetry is $x = 1$. The parabola opens upward.

    The graph is increasing when $x \geq 1$ and decreasing when $x \leq 1$.

21. The vertex is $(-2, 3)$. The axis of symmetry is $x = -2$. The parabola opens downward.

    The graph is increasing when $x \leq -2$ and decreasing when $x \geq -2$.

23. (a) See Figure 23.

    (b) The vertex is $(0, -2)$. The axis of symmetry is $x = 0$.

25. (a) See Figure 25.

    (b) The vertex is $(0, 1)$. The axis of symmetry is $x = 0$.

27. (a) See Figure 27.

(b) The vertex is $(1, 0)$. The axis of symmetry is $x = 1$.

29. (a) See Figure 29.

(b) The vertex is $(-0.5, -2.25)$. The axis of symmetry is $x = -0.5$.

Figure 27

Figure 29

Figure 31

31. (a) See Figure31.

(b) The vertex is $(0, -3)$. The axis of symmetry is $x = 0$.

33. (a) See Figure 33.

(b) The vertex is $(1, 1)$. The axis of symmetry is $x = 1$.

35. (a) See Figure 35.

(b) The vertex is $(1, 1)$. The axis of symmetry is $x = 1$.

Figure 33

Figure 35

Figure 37

37. (a) See Figure 37.

(b) The vertex is $(2, 4)$. The axis of symmetry is $x = 2$.

39. $x = -\dfrac{b}{2a} = -\dfrac{(-4)}{2(1)} = 2, y = (2)^2 - 4(2) - 2 = 4 - 8 - 2 = -6$; The vertex is $(2, -6)$.

41. $x = -\dfrac{b}{2a} = -\dfrac{(-2)}{2(-\frac{1}{3})} = -3, y = -\dfrac{1}{3}(-3)^2 - 2(-3) + 1 = -3 + 6 + 1 = 4$; The vertex is $(-3, 4)$.

43. $x = -\dfrac{b}{2a} = -\dfrac{(0)}{2(-2)} = 0, y = 3 - 2(0)^2 = 3 - 0 = 3$; The vertex is $(0, 3)$.

45. $x = -\dfrac{b}{2a} = -\dfrac{(0.6)}{2(-0.3)} = 1, y = -0.3(1)^2 + 0.6(1) + 1.1 = -0.3 + 0.6 + 1.1 = 1.4$; The vertex is $(1, 1.4)$.

47. See Figure 47. Compared to $y = x^2$, the graph is reflected across the x-axis.

Figure 47

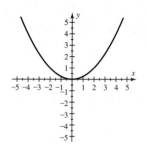

Figure 49

Figure 51

49. See Figure 49. Compared to $y = x^2$, the graph is narrower.

51. See Figure 51. Compared to $y = x^2$, the graph is wider.

53. See Figure 53. Compared to $y = x^2$, the graph is reflected across the x-axis and is wider.

Figure 53

55. Because $-\dfrac{b}{2a} = -\dfrac{2}{2(1)} = -1$ and $y = (-1)^2 + 2(-1) - 1 = -2$, the vertex is $(-1, -2)$.

The graph is increasing when $x \geq -1$ and decreasing when $x \leq -1$.

57. Because $-\dfrac{b}{2a} = -\dfrac{-5}{2(1)} = \dfrac{5}{2}$ and $y = \left(\dfrac{5}{2}\right)^2 - 5\left(\dfrac{5}{2}\right) = -\dfrac{25}{4}$, the vertex is $\left(\dfrac{5}{2}, -\dfrac{25}{4}\right)$.

The graph is increasing when $x \geq \dfrac{5}{2}$ and decreasing when $x \leq \dfrac{5}{2}$.

59. Because $-\dfrac{b}{2a} = -\dfrac{2}{2(2)} = -\dfrac{1}{2}$ and $y = 2\left(-\dfrac{1}{2}\right)^2 + 2\left(-\dfrac{1}{2}\right) - 3 = -\dfrac{7}{2}$, the vertex is $\left(-\dfrac{1}{2}, -\dfrac{7}{2}\right)$.

The graph is increasing when $x \geq -\dfrac{1}{2}$ and decreasing when $x \leq -\dfrac{1}{2}$.

61. Because $-\dfrac{b}{2a} = -\dfrac{2}{2(-1)} = 1$ and $y = -(1)^2 + 2(1) + 5 = 6$, the vertex is $(1, 6)$.

The graph is increasing when $x \leq 1$ and decreasing when $x \geq 1$.

63. Because $-\dfrac{b}{2a} = -\dfrac{4}{2(-1)} = 2$ and $y = 4(2) - (2)^2 = 4$, the vertex is $(2, 4)$.

The graph is increasing when $x \leq 2$ and decreasing when $x \geq 2$.

65. Because $-\dfrac{b}{2a} = -\dfrac{1}{2(-2)} = \dfrac{1}{4}$ and $y = -2\left(\dfrac{1}{4}\right)^2 + \left(\dfrac{1}{4}\right) - 5 = -\dfrac{39}{8}$, the vertex is $\left(\dfrac{1}{4}, -\dfrac{39}{8}\right)$.

The graph is increasing when $x \le \dfrac{1}{4}$ and decreasing when $x \ge \dfrac{1}{4}$.

Applications

67. (a) Because $-\dfrac{b}{2a} = -\dfrac{64}{2(-16)} = 2$ and $y = -16(2)^2 + 64(2) + 2 = 66$, the vertex is $(2, 66)$.

(b) The maximum height of 66 feet is reached after 2 seconds.

9.2: Introduction to Quadratic Equations

Concepts

1. $x^2 + 3x - 2 = 0$; *Answers may vary.* A quadratic equation can have 0, 1 or 2 solutions.

3. Factoring and square root property.

5. See Figure 5. *Answers may vary.*

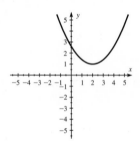

Figure 5

7. Yes

9. No, there is no x^2 term.

11. Yes

13. No, the term $\sqrt{x}$ is not allowed in a quadratic equation.

Solving Quadratic Equations

15. The solutions are the x-intercepts, $-2, 1$.

17. Since there are no x-intercepts, there are no real solutions.

19. The solutions are the x-values where $Y_1 = 0$: $-2, 3$.

21. The solutions are the x-values where $Y_1 = 0$: -0.5.

23. $x^2 - 4x - 5 = 0 \Rightarrow (x + 1)(x - 5) = 0 \Rightarrow x + 1 = 0$ or $x - 5 = 0 \Rightarrow x = -1$ or 5

A graph of $y = x^2 - 4x - 5$ (not shown) intersects the x-axis at -1 and 5.

25. $x^2 + 2x = 3 \Rightarrow x^2 + 2x - 3 = 0 \Rightarrow (x + 3)(x - 1) = 0 \Rightarrow x + 3 = 0$ or $x - 1 = 0 \Rightarrow x = -3$ or 1

A graph of $y = x^2 + 2x - 3$ (not shown) intersects the x-axis at -3 and 1.

27. $x^2 = 9 \Rightarrow x^2 - 9 = 0 \Rightarrow (x + 3)(x - 3) = 0 \Rightarrow x + 3 = 0$ or $x - 3 = 0 \Rightarrow x = -3$ or 3

    A graph of $y = x^2 - 9$ (not shown) intersects the x-axis at -3 and 3.

29. $x^2 + 2x - 35 = 0 \Rightarrow (x + 7)(x - 5) = 0 \Rightarrow$ Either $x + 7 = 0 \Rightarrow x = -7$ or $x - 5 = 0 \Rightarrow x = 5$

31. $6x^2 - x - 1 = 0 \Rightarrow (3x + 1)(2x - 1) = 0 \Rightarrow$ Either $3x + 1 = 0 \Rightarrow x = -\dfrac{1}{3}$ or $2x - 1 = 0 \Rightarrow x = \dfrac{1}{2}$

33. $2x^2 - 5x + 3 = 0 \Rightarrow (x - 1)(2x - 3) = 0 \Rightarrow$ Either $x - 1 = 0 \Rightarrow x = 1$ or $2x - 3 = 0 \Rightarrow x = \dfrac{3}{2}$

35. $x^2 = 144 \Rightarrow x = \pm\sqrt{144} \Rightarrow x = \pm 12$

37. $5x^2 - 64 = 0 \Rightarrow 5x^2 = 64 \Rightarrow x^2 = \dfrac{64}{5} \Rightarrow x = \pm\sqrt{\dfrac{64}{5}} \Rightarrow x = \pm\dfrac{8}{\sqrt{5}}$

39. $(x + 1)^2 = 25 \Rightarrow x + 1 = \pm\sqrt{25} \Rightarrow x + 1 = \pm 5 \Rightarrow x = -1 \pm 5 \Rightarrow x = -6$ or 4

41. $(x - 1)^2 = 64 \Rightarrow x - 1 = \pm\sqrt{64} \Rightarrow x - 1 = \pm 8 \Rightarrow x = 1 \pm 8 \Rightarrow x = -7$ or 9

Solving Equations by More Than One Method

43. (a) $x^2 - 3x - 18 = 0 \Rightarrow (x + 3)(x - 6) = 0 \Rightarrow$ Either $x + 3 = 0 \Rightarrow x = -3$ or $x - 6 = 0 \Rightarrow x = 6$

    (b) Graph $Y_1 = X^2 - 3X - 18$ in $[-5, 8, 1]$ by $[-25, 5, 5]$. See Figures 43a & 43b.

        The solutions are the x-intercepts, $x = -3$ or $x = 6$.

    (c) Table $Y_1 = X^2 - 3X - 18$ with TblStart = -6 and ΔTbl = 3. See Figure 43c.

        Since $Y_1 = 0$ when $x = -3$ or when $x = 6$, the solutions are $x = -3$ or $x = 6$.

$[-5, 8, 1]$ by $[-25, 5, 5]$ $[-5, 8, 1]$ by $[-25, 5, 5]$

    Figure 43a   **Figure 43b**   **Figure 43c**

45. (a) $x^2 - 8x + 15 = 0 \Rightarrow (x - 3)(x - 5) = 0 \Rightarrow$ Either $x - 3 = 0 \Rightarrow x = 3$ or $x - 5 = 0 \Rightarrow x = 5$

    (b) Graph $Y_1 = X^2 - 8X + 15$ in $[-10, 0, 1]$ by $[-5, 10, 1]$. See Figures 45a & 45b.

        The solutions are the x-intercepts, $x = 3$ or $x = 5$.

    (c) Table $Y_1 = X^2 - 8X + 15$ with TblStart = 1 and ΔTbl = 1. See Figure 45c.

        Since $Y_1 = 0$ when $x = 3$ or when $x = 5$, the solutions are $x = 3$ or $x = 5$.

$[-10, 0, 1]$ by $[-5, 10, 1]$ $[-10, 0, 1]$ by $[-5, 10, 1]$

    Figure 45a   **Figure 45b**   **Figure 45c**

47. (a) $4(x^2 + 35) = 48x \Rightarrow x^2 + 35 = 12x \Rightarrow x^2 - 12x + 35 = 0 \Rightarrow (x - 5)(x - 7) = 0 \Rightarrow$

    Either $x - 5 = 0 \Rightarrow x = 5$ or $x - 7 = 0 \Rightarrow x = 7$

    (b) Graph $Y_1 = 4(X^2 + 35) - 48X$ in $[-2, 10, 1]$ by $[-6, 6, 1]$. See Figures 47a & 47b.

    The solutions are the x-intercepts, $x = 5$ or $x = 7$.

    (c) Table $Y_1 = 4(X^2 + 35) - 48X$ with TblStart = 3 and ΔTbl = 1. See Figure 47c.

    Since $Y_1 = 0$ when $x = 5$ or when $x = 7$, the solutions are $x = 5$ or $x = 7$.

[-3, 3, 1] by [-3, 3, 1]   [-3, 3, 1] by [-3, 3, 1]

Figure 47a   Figure 47b   Figure 47c

Applications

49. (a) $\dfrac{1}{2}x^2 = 450 \Rightarrow x^2 = 900 \Rightarrow x = \pm\sqrt{900} \Rightarrow x = 30$ mph ($x = -30$ has no physical meaning)

    (b) $\dfrac{1}{2}x^2 = 800 \Rightarrow x^2 = 1600 \Rightarrow x = \pm\sqrt{1600} \Rightarrow x = 40$ mph ($x = -40$ has no physical meaning)

51. $60 - 16t^2 = 0 \Rightarrow -16t^2 = -60 \Rightarrow t^2 = \dfrac{60}{16} \Rightarrow t = \pm\sqrt{\dfrac{60}{16}} \Rightarrow t = \dfrac{\sqrt{60}}{4} \approx 1.9$ seconds. The value

    $t \approx -1.9$ seconds has no physical meaning. The toy takes about 1.9 seconds to hit he ground. This is not

    twice the time it takes to fall from a height of 30 feet.

53. Let x represent the height of the triangle. Then $x + 3$ represents the base and $\dfrac{1}{2}x(x + 3)$ represents the area.

    $\dfrac{1}{2}x(x + 3) = 35 \Rightarrow x(x + 3) = 70 \Rightarrow x^2 + 3x - 70 = 0 \Rightarrow (x - 7)(x + 10) = 0 \Rightarrow x = 7$ or -10

    Since the value -10 has no physical meaning, the height is 7 inches and the base is $7 + 3 = 10$ inches.

Checking Basic Concepts for Sections 9.1 & 9.2

1. (a) See Figure 1a. The vertex is $(0, -2)$, and the axis of symmetry is $x = 0$.

   (b) See Figure 1b. The vertex is $(1, -3)$, and the axis of symmetry is $x = 1$.

Figure 1a   Figure 1b

2. The graph of y_1 opens upward whereas y_2 opens downward. Also, y_1 is narrower than y_2.

3. Because $-\dfrac{b}{2a} = -\dfrac{12}{2(-3)} = 2$ and $y = -3(2)^2 + 12(2) - 5 = 7$, the vertex is $(2, 7)$.

   The graph is increasing when $x \leq 2$ and decreasing when $x \geq 2$.

4. Symbolical:

   $$2x^2 - 7x + 3 = 0 \Rightarrow (2x - 1)(x - 3) = 0 \Rightarrow \text{Either } 2x - 1 = 0 \Rightarrow x = \frac{1}{2} \text{ or } x - 3 = 0 \Rightarrow x = 3$$

   Graphical: Graph $Y_1 = 2X^2 - 7X + 3$ in $[-5, 5, 1]$ by $[-5, 5, 1]$. See Figures 4a & 4b. $x = \dfrac{1}{2}$ or $x = 3$

   $[-5, 5, 1]$ by $[-5, 5, 1]$ $[-5, 5, 1]$ by $[-5, 5, 1]$

   Figure 4a   Figure 4b

5. $x^2 = 5 \Rightarrow x = \pm\sqrt{5}$

9.3: Solving by Completing the Square

Concepts

1. The constant term equals the square of half the coefficient of the x-term.

3. The square of half the coefficient of the x-term is 9.

Perfect Square Trinomials

5. No, because $20 \neq \left(\dfrac{-10}{2}\right)^2$.

7. Yes, because $4 = \left(\dfrac{4}{2}\right)^2$.

9. Yes, because $64 = \left(\dfrac{-16}{2}\right)^2$.

11. No, because $\dfrac{81}{2} \neq \left(\dfrac{-9}{2}\right)^2$.

13. The term needed to complete the square is $\left(\dfrac{-8}{2}\right)^2 = (-4)^2 = 16$. The resulting perfect square is $(x - 4)^2$.

15. The term needed to complete the square is $\left(\dfrac{9}{2}\right)^2 = \dfrac{81}{4}$. The resulting perfect square is $\left(x + \dfrac{9}{2}\right)^2$.

Completing the Square

17. $\left(\dfrac{4}{2}\right)^2 = 2^2 = 4$

19. $\left(\dfrac{-5}{2}\right)^2 = \dfrac{25}{4}$

21. $x^2 - 2x = 24 \Rightarrow x^2 - 2x + 1 = 24 + 1 \Rightarrow (x-1)^2 = 25 \Rightarrow x - 1 = \pm\sqrt{25} \Rightarrow x - 1 = \pm 5 \Rightarrow$

$x = 1 \pm 5 \Rightarrow x = -4$ or 6

23. $x^2 + 6x - 2 = 0 \Rightarrow x^2 + 6x + 9 = 2 + 9 \Rightarrow (x+3)^2 = 11 \Rightarrow x + 3 = \pm\sqrt{11} \Rightarrow x = -3 \pm \sqrt{11}$

25. $x^2 - 3x = 5 \Rightarrow x^2 - 3x + \dfrac{9}{4} = 5 + \dfrac{9}{4} \Rightarrow \left(x - \dfrac{3}{2}\right)^2 = \dfrac{29}{4} \Rightarrow x - \dfrac{3}{2} = \pm\sqrt{\dfrac{29}{4}} \Rightarrow$

$x = \dfrac{3}{2} \pm \dfrac{\sqrt{29}}{2} = \dfrac{3 \pm \sqrt{29}}{2}$

27. $x^2 - 5x + 1 = 0 \Rightarrow x^2 - 5x = -1 \Rightarrow x^2 - 5x + \dfrac{25}{4} = -1 + \dfrac{25}{4} \Rightarrow \left(x - \dfrac{5}{2}\right)^2 = \dfrac{21}{4} \Rightarrow$

$x - \dfrac{5}{2} = \pm\sqrt{\dfrac{21}{4}} \Rightarrow x = \dfrac{5}{2} \pm \dfrac{\sqrt{21}}{2} = \dfrac{5 \pm \sqrt{21}}{2}$

29. $x^2 - 4 = 2x \Rightarrow x^2 - 2x = 4 \Rightarrow x^2 - 2x + 1 = 4 + 1 \Rightarrow (x-1)^2 = 5 \Rightarrow x - 1 = \pm\sqrt{5} \Rightarrow$

$x = 1 \pm \sqrt{5}$

31. $2x^2 - 3x = 4 \Rightarrow x^2 - \dfrac{3}{2}x = 2 \Rightarrow x^2 - \dfrac{3}{2}x + \dfrac{9}{16} = 2 + \dfrac{9}{16} \Rightarrow \left(x - \dfrac{3}{4}\right)^2 = \dfrac{41}{16} \Rightarrow x - \dfrac{3}{4} = \pm\sqrt{\dfrac{41}{16}} \Rightarrow$

$x = \dfrac{3}{4} \pm \dfrac{\sqrt{41}}{4} = \dfrac{3 \pm \sqrt{41}}{4}$

33. $4x^2 - 8x - 7 = 0 \Rightarrow x^2 - 2x - \dfrac{7}{4} = 0 \Rightarrow x^2 - 2x + 1 = \dfrac{7}{4} + 1 \Rightarrow (x-1)^2 = \dfrac{11}{4} \Rightarrow$

$x - 1 = \pm\sqrt{\dfrac{11}{4}} \Rightarrow x = 1 \pm \dfrac{\sqrt{11}}{2} \Rightarrow x = \dfrac{2 \pm \sqrt{11}}{2}$

35. $36x^2 + 18x + 1 = 0 \Rightarrow 36\left(x^2 + \dfrac{1}{2}x + \dfrac{1}{16}\right) = -1 + \dfrac{36}{16} \Rightarrow 36\left(x + \dfrac{1}{4}\right)^2 = \dfrac{20}{16} \Rightarrow$

$\left(x + \dfrac{1}{4}\right)^2 = \dfrac{20}{576} \Rightarrow x + \dfrac{1}{4} = \pm\sqrt{\dfrac{20}{576}} \Rightarrow x = -\dfrac{1}{4} \pm \dfrac{\sqrt{20}}{24} = \dfrac{-6 \pm 2\sqrt{5}}{24} = \dfrac{-3 \pm \sqrt{5}}{12}$

Applications

37. Let x represent the width of the rectangle. Then the length is represented by $x + 4$. Since the area is 16,

$x(x + 4) = 16 \Rightarrow x^2 + 4x = 16 \Rightarrow x^2 + 4x + 4 = 16 + 4 \Rightarrow (x+2)^2 = 20 \Rightarrow x + 2 = \pm\sqrt{20} \Rightarrow$

$x = -2 + \sqrt{20} \approx 2.47$ inches (The value $-2 - \sqrt{20} \approx -6.47$ has no physical meaning in this problem.)

9.4: The Quadratic Formula

Concepts

1.   We use the quadratic formula to solve equations of the form $ax^2 + bx + c = 0$.

3. $b^2 - 4ac$

5.   Factoring, square root property, completing the square and the quadratic formula.

The Quadratic Formula

7. $x = \dfrac{-11 \pm \sqrt{(11)^2 - 4(2)(-6)}}{2(2)} = \dfrac{-11 \pm \sqrt{169}}{4} = \dfrac{-11 \pm 13}{4} \Rightarrow x = -6 \text{ or } x = \dfrac{1}{2}$

Graph $Y_1 = 2X^2 + 11X - 6$ in $[-10, 5, 1]$ by $[-25, 10, 5]$. See Figures 7a & 7b. $x = -6 \text{ or } x = \dfrac{1}{2}$

Table $Y_1 = 2X^2 + 11X - 6$ with TblStart $= -7.3$ and ΔTbl $= 1.3$. See Figure 7c. $x = -6 \text{ or } x = \dfrac{1}{2}$

$[-10, 5, 1]$ by $[-25, 10, 5]$ $[-10, 5, 1]$ by $[-25, 10, 5]$

Figure 7a   Figure 7b   Figure 7c

9. $x = \dfrac{-2 \pm \sqrt{(2)^2 - 4(-1)(-1)}}{2(-1)} = \dfrac{-2 \pm \sqrt{0}}{-2} = \dfrac{-2}{-2} \Rightarrow x = 1$

Graph $Y_1 = -X^2 + 2X - 1$ in $[-5, 5, 1]$ by $[-5, 5, 1]$. See Figure 9a. $x = 1$

Table $Y_1 = -X^2 + 2X - 1$ with TblStart $= -2$ and ΔTbl $= 1$. See Figure 9b. $x = 1$

$[-5, 5, 1]$ by $[-5, 5, 1]$

Figure 9a   Figure 9b

11. $x = \dfrac{-(-6) \pm \sqrt{(-6)^2 - 4(1)(-16)}}{2(1)} = \dfrac{6 \pm \sqrt{100}}{2} = \dfrac{6 \pm 10}{2} \Rightarrow x = -2 \text{ or } x = 8$

13. $x = \dfrac{-(-1) \pm \sqrt{(-1)^2 - 4(4)(-1)}}{2(4)} = \dfrac{1 \pm \sqrt{17}}{8}$

15. $x = \dfrac{-2 \pm \sqrt{(2)^2 - 4(-3)(-1)}}{2(-3)} = \dfrac{-2 \pm \sqrt{-8}}{-6} \Rightarrow \text{No real solutions.}$

17. $x = \dfrac{-(-36) \pm \sqrt{(-36)^2 - 4(36)(9)}}{2(36)} = \dfrac{36 \pm \sqrt{0}}{72} = \dfrac{36}{72} = \dfrac{1}{2}$

19. $x = \dfrac{-(-6) \pm \sqrt{(-6)^2 - 4(2)(-2)}}{2(2)} = \dfrac{6 \pm \sqrt{52}}{4} = \dfrac{6 \pm 2\sqrt{13}}{4} = \dfrac{2(3 \pm \sqrt{13})}{2(2)} = \dfrac{3 \pm \sqrt{13}}{2}$

21. $x = \dfrac{-(-4) \pm \sqrt{(-4)^2 - 4(1)(1)}}{2(1)} = \dfrac{4 \pm \sqrt{12}}{2} = \dfrac{4 \pm 2\sqrt{3}}{2} = \dfrac{2(2 \pm \sqrt{3})}{2} = 2 \pm \sqrt{3}$

23. $x = \dfrac{-(-\frac{1}{2}) \pm \sqrt{(-\frac{1}{2})^2 - 4(\frac{3}{2})(-\frac{3}{2})}}{2(\frac{3}{2})} = \dfrac{\frac{1}{2} \pm \sqrt{\frac{37}{4}}}{3} = \dfrac{\frac{1}{2} \pm \frac{\sqrt{37}}{2}}{3} = \dfrac{1 \pm \sqrt{37}}{6}$

25. $x = \dfrac{-(-2) \pm \sqrt{(-2)^2 - 4(2)(-7)}}{2(2)} = \dfrac{2 \pm \sqrt{60}}{4} = \dfrac{2 \pm 2\sqrt{15}}{4} = \dfrac{2(1 \pm \sqrt{15})}{4} = \dfrac{1 \pm \sqrt{15}}{2}$

27. $x = \dfrac{-10 \pm \sqrt{(10)^2 - 4(-3)(-5)}}{2(-3)} = \dfrac{-10 \pm \sqrt{40}}{-6} = \dfrac{-10 \pm 2\sqrt{10}}{-6} = \dfrac{-2(5 \pm \sqrt{10})}{-6} = \dfrac{5 \pm \sqrt{10}}{3}$

The Discriminant

29. (a) Since the parabola opens upward, $a > 0$.

    (b) The solutions are the x-intercepts, $x = -1$ or $x = 2$

    (c) Since there are two real solutions, the discriminant is positive.

31. (a) Since the parabola opens upward, $a > 0$.

    (b) Since there are no x-intercepts, there are no real solutions.

    (c) Since there are no real solutions, the discriminant is negative.

33. (a) Since the parabola opens downward, $a < 0$.

    (b) The solution is the x-intercept, $x = 2$

    (c) Since there is one real solution, the discriminant is zero.

35. (a) $(1)^2 - 4(3)(-2) = 25$

    (b) Since the discriminant is positive, there are two real solutions.

    (c) Graph $Y_1 = 3X^2 + X - 2$ in $[-3, 3, 1]$ by $[-3, 3, 1]$. See Figure 35. There are two x-intercepts.

37. (a) $(-4)^2 - 4(1)(4) = 0$

    (b) Since the discriminant is zero, there is only one real solution.

    (c) Graph $Y_1 = X^2 - 4X + 4$ in $[0, 4, 1]$ by $[-3, 3, 1]$. See Figure 37. There is one x-intercept.

[−3, 3, 1] by [−3, 3, 1]

Figure 35

[0, 4, 1] by [−3, 3, 1]

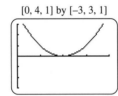

Figure 37

[−10, 10, 1] by [0, 10, 1]

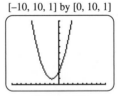

Figure 39

[−5, 5, 1] by [−8, 5, 1]

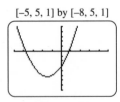

Figure 41

39. (a) $\left(\dfrac{3}{2}\right)^2 - 4\left(\dfrac{1}{2}\right)(2) = -\dfrac{7}{4}$

    (b) Since the discriminant is negative, there are no real solutions.

    (c) Graph $Y_1 = (1/2)X^2 - (3/2)X + 2$ in $[-10, 10, 1]$ by $[0, 10, 1]$. See Figure 39. There are no x-intercepts.

41. (a) $(3)^2 - 4(1)(-3) = 21$

    (b) Since the discriminant is positive, there are two real solutions.

    (c) Graph $Y_1 = X^2 + 3X - 3$ in $[-5, 5, 1]$ by $[-8, 5, 1]$. See Figure 41. There are two x-intercepts.

43. $x = \dfrac{-(-2) \pm \sqrt{(-2)^2 - 4(1)(-1)}}{2(1)} = \dfrac{2 \pm \sqrt{8}}{2} = \dfrac{2 \pm 2\sqrt{2}}{2} = \dfrac{2(1 \pm \sqrt{2})}{2} = 1 \pm \sqrt{2}$

45. $x = \dfrac{-(-1) \pm \sqrt{(-1)^2 - 4(-2)(3)}}{2(-2)} = \dfrac{1 \pm \sqrt{25}}{-4} = \dfrac{1 \pm 5}{-4} = -\dfrac{3}{2} \text{ or } 1$

47. $x = \dfrac{-1 \pm \sqrt{(1)^2 - 4(1)(5)}}{2(1)} = \dfrac{-1 \pm \sqrt{-19}}{2} \Rightarrow$ No real solutions. No x-intercepts.

49. $x = \dfrac{-(0) \pm \sqrt{(0)^2 - 4(1)(9)}}{2(1)} = \dfrac{0 \pm \sqrt{-36}}{2} \Rightarrow$ No real solutions. No x-intercepts.

51. $x = \dfrac{-4 \pm \sqrt{(4)^2 - 4(3)(-2)}}{2(3)} = \dfrac{-4 \pm \sqrt{40}}{6} = \dfrac{-4 \pm 2\sqrt{10}}{6} = \dfrac{2(-2 \pm \sqrt{10})}{6} = \dfrac{-2 \pm \sqrt{10}}{3}$

Applications

53. $\dfrac{1}{9}x^2 + \dfrac{11}{3}x - 42 = 0 \Rightarrow x^2 + 33x - 378 = 0 \Rightarrow x = (x - 9)(x + 42) = 0 \Rightarrow x = 9$ mph

The value $x = -42$ has no physical meaning.

55. $\dfrac{1}{9}x^2 + \dfrac{11}{3}x - 390 = 0 \Rightarrow x^2 + 33x - 3510 = 0 \Rightarrow x = (x - 45)(x + 78) = 0 \Rightarrow x = 45$ mph

The value $x = -78$ has no physical meaning.

57. $2.39x^2 + 5.04x + 5.1 = 200 \Rightarrow 2.39x^2 + 5.04x - 194.9 = 0$

$x = \dfrac{-5.04 \pm \sqrt{(5.04)^2 - 4(2.39)(-194.9)}}{2(2.39)} = \dfrac{-5.04 \pm \sqrt{1888.6456}}{4.78} \Rightarrow x \approx 8.04; \text{ about } 1992$

The value $x \approx -10.15$ has no meaning in this problem. Our answer agrees with the graph.

Checking Basic Concepts for Sections 9.3 & 9.4

1. (a) No, because $12 \neq \left(\dfrac{6}{2}\right)^2$.

    (b) Yes, because $1 = \left(\dfrac{2}{2}\right)^2$.

2. (a) $x^2 - 4x = -1 \Rightarrow x^2 - 4x + 4 = -1 + 4 \Rightarrow (x - 2)^2 = 3 \Rightarrow x - 2 = \pm\sqrt{3} \Rightarrow x = 2 \pm \sqrt{3}$

    (b) $x^2 - 6x = -4 \Rightarrow x^2 - 6x + 9 = -4 + 9 \Rightarrow (x - 3)^2 = 5 \Rightarrow x - 3 = \pm\sqrt{5} \Rightarrow x = 3 \pm \sqrt{5}$

3. (a) $2x^2 = 3x + 1 \Rightarrow 2x^2 - 3x - 1 = 0 \Rightarrow x = \dfrac{-(-3) \pm \sqrt{(-\ \ \ ) - 4(2)(-1)}}{2(2)} = \dfrac{3 \pm \sqrt{17}}{4}$

    (b) $9x^2 - 24x + 16 = 0 \Rightarrow x = \dfrac{-(-24) \pm \sqrt{(-24)^2 - 4(9)(16)}}{2(9)} = \dfrac{24 \pm \sqrt{0}}{18} = \dfrac{24}{18} = \dfrac{4}{3}$

4. (a) $(-5)^2 - 4(1)(5) = 5$; Since the discriminant is positive, there are two real solutions.

    (b) $(-5)^2 - 4(2)(4) = -7$; Since the discriminant is negative, there are no real solutions.

    (c) $(-56)^2 - 4(49)(16) = 0$; Since the discriminant is zero, there is one real solution.

9.5: Complex Solutions

Concepts

1. $2 + 3i$; *Answers may vary.*

3. i

5. $i\sqrt{a}$

7. 4

Complex Numbers

9. $\sqrt{-5} = i\sqrt{5}$

11. $\sqrt{-100} = i\sqrt{100} = i \cdot 10 = 10i$

13. $\sqrt{-144} = i\sqrt{144} = i \cdot 12 = 12i$

15. $\sqrt{-12} = i\sqrt{12} = i \cdot \sqrt{4 \cdot 3} = i \cdot \sqrt{4} \cdot \sqrt{3} = i \cdot 2 \cdot \sqrt{3} = 2i\sqrt{3}$

17. $\sqrt{-18} = i\sqrt{18} = i \cdot \sqrt{9 \cdot 2} = i \cdot \sqrt{9} \cdot \sqrt{2} = i \cdot 3 \cdot \sqrt{2} = 3i\sqrt{2}$

19. $(5 + 3i) + (-2 - 3i) = (5 + (-2)) + (3 + (-3))i = 3 + 0i = 3$

21. $(2i) + (-8 + 5i) = (0 + (-8)) + (2 + 5)i = -8 + 7i$

23. $(2 - 7i) - (1 + 2i) = (2 - 1) + (-7 - 2)i = 1 - 9i$

25. $(5i) - (10 - 2i) = (0 - 10) + (5 - (-2))i = -10 + 7i$

27. $4(5 - 3i) = 20 - 12i$

28. $(-3 - 4i)(5 - 4i) = -15 + 12i - 20i + 16i^2 = -15 - 8i + 16(-1) = -15 - 8i - 16 = -31 - 8i$

31. $(-4i)(5i) = -4 \cdot 5 \cdot i^2 = -20(-1) = 20$

33. $3i + (2 - 3i) - (1 - 5i) = 3i + 2 - 3i - 1 + 5i = 1 + 5i$

35. $(2 + i)^2 = 4 + 4i + i^2 = 4 + 4i - 1 = 3 + 4i$

37. $2i(-3 + i) = -6i + 2i^2 = -6i + 2(-1) = -2 - 6i$

39. $i(1 + i)^2 = i(1 + 2i + i^2) = i(1 + 2i - 1) = i(2i) = 2i^2 = 2(-1) = -2$

Complex Solutions

41. $x^2 + 9 = 0 \Rightarrow x^2 = -9 \Rightarrow x = \pm\sqrt{-9} \Rightarrow x = \pm 3i$

43. $x^2 + 80 = 0 \Rightarrow x^2 = -80 \Rightarrow x = \pm\sqrt{-80} \Rightarrow x = \pm\sqrt{-16 \cdot 5} \Rightarrow x = \pm 4i\sqrt{5}$

45. $x^2 + \dfrac{1}{4} = 0 \Rightarrow x^2 = -\dfrac{1}{4} \Rightarrow x = \pm\sqrt{-\dfrac{1}{4}} \Rightarrow x = \pm\dfrac{1}{2}i$

47. $16x^2 + 9 = 0 \Rightarrow 16x^2 = -9 \Rightarrow x^2 = -\dfrac{9}{16} \Rightarrow x = \pm\sqrt{-\dfrac{9}{16}} \Rightarrow x = \pm\dfrac{3}{4}i$

49. $x^2 = -6 \Rightarrow x = \pm\sqrt{-6} \Rightarrow x = \pm i\sqrt{6}$

51. $x^2 - 3 = 0 \Rightarrow x^2 = 3 \Rightarrow x = \pm\sqrt{3}$

53. $x^2 + 2 = 0 \Rightarrow x^2 = -2 \Rightarrow x = \pm\sqrt{-2} \Rightarrow x = \pm i\sqrt{2}$

55. $x = \dfrac{-(-1) \pm \sqrt{(-1)^2 - 4(1)(2)}}{2(1)} = \dfrac{1 \pm \sqrt{-7}}{2} = \dfrac{1 \pm i\sqrt{7}}{2} = \dfrac{1}{2} \pm i\dfrac{\sqrt{7}}{2}$

57. $x = \dfrac{-3 \pm \sqrt{3^2 - 4(2)(4)}}{2(2)} = \dfrac{-3 \pm \sqrt{-23}}{4} = \dfrac{-3 \pm i\sqrt{23}}{4} = -\dfrac{3}{4} \pm i\dfrac{\sqrt{23}}{4}$

59. $x = \dfrac{-(-4) \pm \sqrt{(-4^2) - 4(1)(1)}}{2(1)} = \dfrac{4 \pm \sqrt{12}}{2} = \dfrac{4 \pm 2\sqrt{3}}{2} = 2 \pm \sqrt{3}$

You Decide the Method

61. $x^2 - 3x + 2 = 0 \Rightarrow (x - 1)(x - 2) = 0 \Rightarrow x = 1$ or $x = 2$; *Answers may vary.*

63. Multiply both sides of the equation by 4 to obtain the following result. *Answers may vary.*

$0.5x^2 - 1.75x - 1 = 0 \Rightarrow 2x^2 - 7x - 4 = 0 \Rightarrow (2x + 1)(x - 4) = 0 \Rightarrow x = -\dfrac{1}{2}$ or $x = 4$

64. $x = \dfrac{-(-5) \pm \sqrt{(-5)^2 - 4(1)(2)}}{2(1)} = \dfrac{5 \pm \sqrt{17}}{2}$; Quadratic formula or completing the square.

67. $x = \dfrac{-1 \pm \sqrt{(1)^2 - 4(2)(8)}}{2(2)} = \dfrac{-1 \pm \sqrt{-63}}{4} = \dfrac{-1 \pm 3i\sqrt{7}}{4} = -\dfrac{1}{4} \pm \dfrac{3}{4}i\sqrt{7}$; Quadratic formula.

Applications

69. $V = IZ = (2 + 3i)\left(\dfrac{290}{13} + \dfrac{20}{13}i\right) = \dfrac{580}{13} + \dfrac{40}{13}i + \dfrac{870}{13}i + \dfrac{60}{13}i^2 = \dfrac{520}{13} + \dfrac{910}{13}i = 40 + 70i$

Checking Basic Concepts for Section 9.5

1. (a) $\sqrt{-64} = i\sqrt{64} = i(8) = 8i$

   (b) $\sqrt{-17} = i\sqrt{17}$

2. (a) $(2 - 3i) + (1 - i) = (2 + 1) + (-3 + (-1))i = 3 - 4i$

   (b) $4i - (2 + i) = (0 - 2) + (4 - 1)i = -2 + 3i$

   (c) $(3 - 2i)(1 + i) = 3 + 3i - 2i - 2i^2 = 3 + i - 2(-1) = 3 + i + 2 = 5 + i$

3. (a) $x^2 + 25 = 0 \Rightarrow x^2 = -25 \Rightarrow x = \pm\sqrt{-25} \Rightarrow x = \pm 5i$

   (b) $x = \dfrac{6 \pm \sqrt{(-6)^2 - 4(1)(13)}}{2(1)} = \dfrac{6 \pm \sqrt{-16}}{2} = \dfrac{6 \pm 4i}{2} = \dfrac{6}{2} \pm \dfrac{4}{2}i = 3 \pm 2i$

   (c) $x = \dfrac{-1 \pm \sqrt{1^2 - 4(1)(2)}}{2(1)} = \dfrac{-1 \pm \sqrt{-7}}{2} = -\dfrac{1}{2} \pm i\dfrac{\sqrt{7}}{2}$

Chapter 9 Review Exercises

Section 9.1

1. Vertex: $(-3, 4)$; Axis of symmetry: $x = -3$; Opens downward; Increasing: $x \leq -3$; Decreasing: $x \geq -3$

2. Vertex: $(1, 0)$; Axis of symmetry: $x = 1$; Opens upward; Increasing: $x \geq 1$; Decreasing: $x \leq 1$

3. (a) See Figure 3.

    (b) The vertex is $(0, -2)$. The axis of symmetry is $x = 0$.

4. (a) See Figure 4.

    (b) The vertex is $(2, 1)$. The axis of symmetry is $x = 2$.

Figure 3

Figure 4

Figure 5

5. (a) See Figure 5.

    (b) The vertex is $(1, 2)$. The axis of symmetry is $x = 1$.

6. (a) See Figure 6.

    (b) The vertex is $(-2, -3)$. The axis of symmetry is $x = -2$.

7. $x = -\dfrac{b}{2a} = -\dfrac{(-4)}{2(1)} = 2, y = (2)^2 - 4(2) - 2 = -6$; The vertex is $(2, -6)$.

8. $x = -\dfrac{b}{2a} = -\dfrac{(0)}{2(-1)} = 0, y = 5 - (0)^2 = 5$; The vertex is $(0, 5)$.

9. $x = -\dfrac{b}{2a} = -\dfrac{(1)}{2(-\frac{1}{4})} = 2, y = -\dfrac{1}{4}(2)^2 + (2) + 1 = 2$; The vertex is $(2, 2)$.

10. $x = -\dfrac{b}{2a} = -\dfrac{(2)}{2(1)} = -1, y = 2 + 2(-1) + (-1)^2 = 1$; The vertex is $(-1, 1)$.

Section 9.2

11. The solutions are the x-intercepts: $-2, 3$.

12. The solution is the x-intercept: -1.

13. There are no x-intercepts: No real solutions.

14. The solutions are the x-intercepts: $-4, 6$.

15. The solutions are the x-values where $Y_1 = 0$: $-10, 5$

16. The solutions are the x-values where $Y_1 = 0$: $-0.5, 0.25$

17. (a) Graph $Y_1 = X^2 - 5X - 50$ in $[-10, 20, 5]$ by $[-100, 20, 10]$. See Figures 17a & 17b.

   The solutions are the x-intercepts, $x = -5$ or $x = 10$.

(b) Table $Y_1 = X^2 - 5X - 50$ with TblStart $= -10$ and ΔTbl $= 5$. See Figure 17c.

   Since $Y_1 = 0$ when $x = -5$ or when $x = 10$, the solutions are $x = -5$ or $x = 10$.

$[-10, 20, 5]$ by $[-100, 20, 10]$ $[-10, 20, 5]$ by $[-100, 20, 10]$

Figure 17a   Figure 17b   Figure 17c

18. (a) Graph $Y_1 = (1/2)X^2 + X - (3/2)$ in $[-5, 5, 1]$ by $[-5, 5, 1]$. See Figures 18a & 18b.

   The solutions are the x-intercepts, $x = -3$ or $x = 1$.

(b) Table $Y_1 = (1/2)X^2 + X - (3/2)$ with TblStart $= -4$ and ΔTbl $= 1$. See Figure 18c.

   Since $Y_1 = 0$ when $x = -3$ or when $x = 1$, the solutions are $x = -3$ or $x = 1$.

$[-5, 5, 1]$ by $[-5, 5, 1]$ $[-5, 5, 1]$ by $[-5, 5, 1]$

Figure 18a   Figure 18b   Figure 18c

19. (a) Graph $Y_1 = (1/4)X^2 + (1/2)X - 2$ in $[-5, 5, 1]$ by $[-3, 3, 1]$. See Figures 19a & 19b.

   The solutions are the x-intercepts, $x = -4$ or $x = 2$.

(b) Table $Y_1 = (1/4)X^2 + (1/2)X - 2$ with TblStart $= -8$ and ΔTbl $= 2$. See Figure 19c.

   Since $Y_1 = 0$ when $x = -4$ or when $x = 2$, the solutions are $x = -4$ or $x = 2$.

$[-5, 5, 1]$ by $[-3, 3, 1]$ $[-5, 5, 1]$ by $[-3, 3, 1]$

Figure 19a   Figure 19b   Figure 19c

20. (a) Graph $Y_1 = (1/4)X^2 - (1/2)X - (3/4)$ in $[-5, 5, 1]$ by $[-3, 3, 1]$. See Figures 20a & 20b.

   The solutions are the x-intercepts, $x = -1$ or $x = 3$.

(b) Table $Y_1 = (1/4)X^2 - (1/2)X - (3/4)$ with TblStart $= -2$ and ΔTbl $= 1$. See Figure 20c.

   Since $Y_1 = 0$ when $x = -1$ or when $x = 3$, the solutions are $x = -1$ or $x = 3$.

$[-5, 5, 1]$ by $[-3, 3, 1]$ $[-5, 5, 1]$ by $[-3, 3, 1]$

Figure 20a   Figure 20b   Figure 20c

21. $x^2 + x - 20 = 0 \Rightarrow (x + 5)(x - 4) = 0 \Rightarrow x = -5$ or $x = 4$

22. $x^2 + 11x + 24 = 0 \Rightarrow (x + 8)(x + 3) = 0 \Rightarrow x = -8$ or $x = -3$

23. $15x^2 - 4x - 4 = 0 \Rightarrow (5x + 2)(3x - 2) = 0 \Rightarrow x = -\dfrac{2}{5}$ or $x = \dfrac{2}{3}$

24. $7x^2 - 25x + 12 = 0 \Rightarrow (7x - 4)(x - 3) = 0 \Rightarrow x = \dfrac{4}{7}$ or $x = 3$

25. $x^2 = 100 \Rightarrow x = \pm\sqrt{100} \Rightarrow x = \pm 10$

26. $3x^2 = \dfrac{1}{3} \Rightarrow x^2 = \dfrac{1}{9} \Rightarrow x = \pm\sqrt{\dfrac{1}{9}} \Rightarrow x = \pm\dfrac{1}{3}$

27. $4x^2 - 6 = 0 \Rightarrow x^2 = \dfrac{6}{4} \Rightarrow x = \pm\sqrt{\dfrac{6}{4}} \Rightarrow x = \pm\dfrac{\sqrt{6}}{2}$

28. $5x^2 = x^2 - 4 \Rightarrow 4x^2 = -4 \Rightarrow x^2 = -1 \Rightarrow x = \pm\sqrt{-1} \Rightarrow$ No real solutions.

Section 9.3

29. No, because $8 \neq \left(\dfrac{-8}{2}\right)^2$.

30. Yes, because $4 = \left(\dfrac{-4}{2}\right)^2$.

31. Yes, because $100 = \left(\dfrac{20}{2}\right)^2$.

32. No, because $2 \neq \left(\dfrac{-2}{2}\right)^2$.

33. $x^2 + 6x = -2 \Rightarrow x^2 + 6x + 9 = -2 + 9 \Rightarrow (x + 3)^2 = 7 \Rightarrow x + 3 = \pm\sqrt{7} \Rightarrow x = -3 \pm \sqrt{7}$

34. $x^2 - 4x = 6 \Rightarrow x^2 - 4x + 4 = 6 + 4 \Rightarrow (x - 2)^2 = 10 \Rightarrow x - 2 = \pm\sqrt{10} \Rightarrow x = 2 \pm \sqrt{10}$

35. $x^2 - 2x - 5 = 0 \Rightarrow x^2 - 2x + 1 = 5 + 1 \Rightarrow (x - 1)^2 = 6 \Rightarrow x - 1 = \pm\sqrt{6} \Rightarrow x = 1 \pm \sqrt{6}$

36. $2x^2 + 6x - 1 = 0 \Rightarrow x^2 + 3x + \dfrac{9}{4} = \dfrac{1}{2} + \dfrac{9}{4} \Rightarrow \left(x + \dfrac{3}{2}\right)^2 = \dfrac{11}{4} \Rightarrow x + \dfrac{3}{2} = \pm\sqrt{\dfrac{11}{4}} \Rightarrow x = \dfrac{-3 \pm \sqrt{11}}{2}$

Section 9.4

37. $x = \dfrac{-(-9) \pm \sqrt{(-9)^2 - 4(1)(18)}}{2(1)} = \dfrac{9 \pm \sqrt{9}}{2} = \dfrac{9 \pm 3}{2} \Rightarrow x = 3$ or $x = 6$

38. $x = \dfrac{-(-24) \pm \sqrt{(-24)^2 - 4(1)(143)}}{2(1)} = \dfrac{24 \pm \sqrt{4}}{2} = \dfrac{24 \pm 2}{2} \Rightarrow x = 11$ or $x = 13$

39. $x = \dfrac{-1 \pm \sqrt{(1)^2 - 4(6)(-1)}}{2(6)} = \dfrac{-1 \pm \sqrt{25}}{12} = \dfrac{-1 \pm 5}{12} \Rightarrow x = -\dfrac{1}{2}$ or $x = \dfrac{1}{3}$

40. $x = \dfrac{-(-5) \pm \sqrt{(-5)^2 - 4(5)(1)}}{2(5)} = \dfrac{5 \pm \sqrt{5}}{10}$

41. $x = \dfrac{-(-8) \pm \sqrt{(-8)^2 - 4(1)(-5)}}{2(1)} = \dfrac{8 \pm \sqrt{84}}{2} = \dfrac{8 \pm 2\sqrt{21}}{2} = \dfrac{2(4 \pm \sqrt{21})}{2} = 4 \pm \sqrt{21}$

42. $x = \dfrac{-(-6) \pm \sqrt{(-6)^2 - 4(2)(3)}}{2(2)} = \dfrac{6 \pm \sqrt{12}}{4} = \dfrac{6 \pm 2\sqrt{3}}{4} = \dfrac{2(3 \pm \sqrt{3})}{2(2)} = \dfrac{3 \pm \sqrt{3}}{2}$

43. (a) Since the parabola opens upward, $a > 0$.

   (b) The solutions are the x-intercepts, $x = -2$ or $x = 3$.

   (c) Since there are two unique solutions, the discriminant is positive.

44. (a) Since the parabola opens upward, $a > 0$.

   (b) The solution is the x-intercept, $x = 2$.

   (c) Since there is one solution, the discriminant is zero.

45. (a) Since the parabola opens downward, $a < 0$.

   (b) There are no x-intercepts. No real solutions

   (c) Since there are no real solutions, the discriminant is negative.

46. (a) Since the parabola opens downward, $a < 0$.

   (b) The solutions are the x-intercepts, $x = -4$ or $x = 2$.

   (c) Since there are two unique solutions, the discriminant is positive.

47. (a) $(-3)^2 - 4(2)(1) = 1$

   (b) Since the discriminant is positive, there are two real solutions.

   (c) Graph $Y_1 = 2X^2 - 3X + 1$ in $[0, 2, 1]$ by $[-1, 1, 1]$. See Figure 47. There are two x-intercepts.

48. (a) $(2)^2 - 4(7)(-5) = 144$

   (b) Since the discriminant is positive, there are two real solutions.

   (c) Graph $Y_1 = 7X^2 + 2X - 5$ in $[-2, 2, 1]$ by $[-10, 5, 1]$. See Figure 48. There are two x-intercepts.

$[0, 2, 1]$ by $[-1, 1, 1]$	$[-2, 2, 1]$ by $[-10, 5, 1]$	$[-3, 3, 1]$ by $[-5, 10, 1]$	$[0, 3, 1]$ by $[-5, 10, 1]$
Figure 47	Figure 48	Figure 49	Figure 50

49. (a) $(1)^2 - 4(3)(2) = -23$

   (b) Since the discriminant is negative, there are no real solutions.

   (c) Graph $Y_1 = 7X^2 + 2X - 5$ in $[-3, 3, 1]$ by $[-5, 10, 1]$. See Figure 49. There are no x-intercepts.

50. (a) $(-12.6)^2 - 4(4.41)(9) = 0$

   (b) Since the discriminant is zero, there is one real solution.

   (c) Graph $Y_1 = 7X^2 + 2X - 5$ in $[0, 3, 1]$ by $[-5, 10, 1]$. See Figure 50. There is one x-intercepts.

Section 9.5

51. $(1 - 2i) + (-3 + 2i) = (1 + (-3)) + (-2 + 2)i = -2 + 0i = -2$

52. $(1 + 3i) - (3 - i) = (1 - 3) + (3 - (-1))i = -2 + 4i$

53. $(1 - i)(2 + 3i) = 2 + 3i - 2i - 3i^2 = 2 + i - 3(-1) = 2 + i + 3 = 5 + i$

54. $(1 - i)^2(1 + i) = (1 - 2i + i^2)(1 + i) = (1 - 2i - 1)(1 + i) = -2i(1 + i) = -2i - 2i^2 = 2 - 2i$

55. $x = \dfrac{-1 \pm \sqrt{(1)^2 - 4(1)(5)}}{2(1)} = \dfrac{-1 \pm \sqrt{-19}}{2} = -\dfrac{1}{2} \pm i\dfrac{\sqrt{19}}{2}$

56. $2x^2 + 8 = 0 \Rightarrow 2x^2 = -8 \Rightarrow x^2 = -4 \Rightarrow x = \pm\sqrt{-4} \Rightarrow x = \pm 2i$

57. $x = \dfrac{-(-1) \pm \sqrt{(-1)^2 - 4(2)(1)}}{2(2)} = \dfrac{1 \pm \sqrt{-7}}{4} = \dfrac{1}{4} \pm i\dfrac{\sqrt{7}}{4}$

58. $x = \dfrac{-(-2) \pm \sqrt{(-2)^2 - 4(7)(5)}}{2(7)} = \dfrac{2 \pm \sqrt{-136}}{14} = \dfrac{2 \pm 2\sqrt{-34}}{14} = \dfrac{2(1 \pm \sqrt{-34})}{14} = \dfrac{1}{7} \pm i\dfrac{\sqrt{34}}{7}$

Applications

59. (a) $\dfrac{x^2}{12} = 144 \Rightarrow x^2 = 1728 \Rightarrow x = \sqrt{1728} \approx 41.6$ mph $(-\sqrt{1728}$ mph has no meaning).

   (b) $\dfrac{x^2}{12} = 300 \Rightarrow x^2 = 3600 \Rightarrow x = \sqrt{3600} = 60$ mph $(-60$ mph has no meaning).

60. (a) $x(x + 2) = 143$ or $x^2 + 2x - 143 = 0$

   (b) $x^2 + 2x - 143 = 0 \Rightarrow (x + 13)(x - 11) = 0 \Rightarrow x = -13$ or 11. There are two possible number pairs.

   Either $x = -13$, and the other number is -11, or $x = 11$, and the other number is 13.

61. $\sqrt{123} \approx 11.1$; the screen is about 11.1 inches by 11.1 inches.

62. $x^2 + (x + 70)^2 = 130^2 \Rightarrow x^2 + x^2 + 140x + 4900 = 16,900 \Rightarrow 2x^2 + 140x - 12,000 = 0 \Rightarrow$

   $2(x - 50)(x + 120) = 0 \Rightarrow x = 50$ or $x = -120$. The solution is $x = 50$ feet $(x = -120$ has no meaning).

Chapter 9 Test

1. $x = -\dfrac{b}{2a} = -\dfrac{1}{2(-\frac{1}{2})} = \dfrac{1}{1} = 1,\ y = -\dfrac{1}{2}(1)^2 + (1) + 1 = \dfrac{3}{2}$; Vertex: $\left(1, \dfrac{3}{2}\right)$; Axis of symmetry: $x = 1$.

2. The solutions are the x-intercepts, $x = -1$ or $x = 2$.

3. $3x^2 + 11x - 4 = 0 \Rightarrow (x + 4)(3x - 1) = 0 \Rightarrow x = -4$ or $x = \dfrac{1}{3}$

4. $2x^2 = 2 - 6x^2 \Rightarrow 8x^2 = 2 \Rightarrow x^2 = \dfrac{1}{4} \Rightarrow x = \pm\sqrt{\dfrac{1}{4}} \Rightarrow x = -\dfrac{1}{2}$ or $x = \dfrac{1}{2}$

5. $x^2 - 5x = 1 \Rightarrow x^2 - 5x + \dfrac{25}{4} = 1 + \dfrac{25}{4} \Rightarrow \left(x - \dfrac{5}{2}\right)^2 = \dfrac{29}{4} \Rightarrow x - \dfrac{5}{2} = \pm\sqrt{\dfrac{29}{4}} \Rightarrow x = \dfrac{5 \pm \sqrt{29}}{2}$

6. $x = \dfrac{-3 \pm \sqrt{(3)^2 - 4(-2)(1)}}{2(-2)} = \dfrac{-3 \pm \sqrt{17}}{-4} = \dfrac{3 \pm \sqrt{17}}{4}$

7. (a) Since the parabola opens downward, $a < 0$.

   (b) The solutions are the x-intercepts, $x = -3$ or $x = 1$.

   (c) Since there are two real solutions, the discriminant is positive.

8. (a) $(4)^2 - 4(-3)(-5) = -44$

   (b) Since the discriminant is negative, there are no real solutions.

   (c) Graph $Y_1 = -3X^2 + 4X - 5$ in $[-5, 5, 1]$ by $[-20, 10, 5]$. See Figure 8. It does not intersect the x-axis.

[−5, 5, 1] by [−20, 10, 5]

Figure 8

9. $(-5 + i) + (7 - 20i) = (-5 + 7) + (1 - 20)i = 2 - 19i$

10. $(3i) - (6 - 5i) = 3i - 6 + 5i = -6 + (3 + 5)i = -6 + 8i$

11. $2i(2 + 3i) = (2i)(2) + (2i)(3i) = 4i + 6i^2 = 4i + 6(-1) = 4i - 6 = -6 + 4i$

12. $\left(\frac{1}{2} - i\right)\left(\frac{1}{2} + i\right) = \left(\frac{1}{2}\right)^2 - i^2 = \frac{1}{4} - (-1) = \frac{5}{4}$

13. $x^2 + 11 = 0 \Rightarrow x^2 = -11 \Rightarrow x = \pm\sqrt{-11} \Rightarrow x = \pm i\sqrt{11}$

14. $x = \dfrac{8 \pm \sqrt{(-8)^2 - 4(1)(25)}}{2(1)} = \dfrac{8 \pm \sqrt{-36}}{2} = \dfrac{8 \pm 6i}{2} = \dfrac{8}{2} \pm \dfrac{6}{2}i = 4 \pm 3i$

15. $\dfrac{x^2}{9} = 250 \Rightarrow x^2 = 2250 \Rightarrow x = \sqrt{2250} \approx 47.4$ mph (the value $x \approx -47.4$ mph has no physical meaning).

Chapter 9 Extended and Discovery Exercises

1. (a) For the first 3 years of life, the likelihood of survival increases with age. After 3 years of life, it decreases with age.

   (b) Plot the data in $[0, 10, 1]$ by $[0, 75, 5]$. See Figure 1b. A parabola could model this data.

   (c) Graph $Y_1 = -3.57X + 71.1$ in $[0, 10, 1]$ by $[0, 75, 5]$. See Figure 1c.

   Graph $Y_2 = -2.07X^2 + 17.1X + 33$ in $[0, 10, 1]$ by $[0, 75, 5]$. See Figure 1d.

   The equation y_2 models the data better.

   (d) Let $x = 6.5$ to find the likelihood of a 5.5-year-old sparrowhawk living 1 more year.

   $y_2 = -2.07(6.5)^2 + 17.1(6.5) + 33 \approx 56.7\%$

[0, 10, 1] by [0, 75, 5]   [0, 10, 1] by [0, 75, 5]   [0, 10, 1] by [0, 75, 5]

Figure 1b   Figure 1c   Figure 1d

2. The discriminant is $(-1)^2 - 4(10)(-3) = 121 = 11^2$. The trinomial factors as $(2x + 1)(5x - 3)$.

3. The discriminant is $(-3)^2 - 4(4)(-6) = 105$. The trinomial will not factor.

4. The discriminant is $(2)^2 - 4(3)(-2) = 28$. The trinomial will not factor.

5. The discriminant is $(1)^2 - 4(2)(3) = -23$. The trinomial will not factor.

Cumulative Review Exercises for Chapters 1-9

1. Prime factors of $360 = 2 \cdot 2 \cdot 2 \cdot 3 \cdot 3 \cdot 5 \Rightarrow 2^3 \cdot 3^2 \cdot 5$.

2. $2n + 7 = n - 2$, then $2n + 7 = n - 2 \Rightarrow n + 7 = -2 \Rightarrow n = -9$

3. $\dfrac{2}{3} + \dfrac{4}{7} \cdot \dfrac{21}{28} = \dfrac{2}{3} + \dfrac{84}{196} = \dfrac{392}{588} + \dfrac{252}{588} = \dfrac{644}{588} = \dfrac{23}{21}$

4. $\dfrac{3}{5} \div \dfrac{6}{5} - \dfrac{2}{3} = \dfrac{3}{5} \times \dfrac{5}{6} - \dfrac{2}{3} = \dfrac{1}{2} - \dfrac{2}{3} = \dfrac{3}{6} - \dfrac{4}{6} = -\dfrac{1}{6}$

5. $30 - 4 \div 2 \cdot 6 = 30 - (4 \div 2) \cdot 6 = 30 - (2) \cdot 6 = 30 - (2 \cdot 6) = 30 - 12 = 18$

6. $\dfrac{3^2 - 2^3}{20 - 5 \cdot 2} = \dfrac{9 - 8}{20 - 10} \Rightarrow \dfrac{1}{10}$

7. $2(x + 1) - 6x = x - 4 \Rightarrow 2x + 2 - 6x = x - 4 \Rightarrow -5x + 2 = -4 \Rightarrow -5x = -6 \Rightarrow x = \dfrac{6}{5}$

8. $x = 2$. See Figure 8. Checking: $4 - 3(2) = -2 \Rightarrow 4 - 6 = -2 \Rightarrow -2 = -2$, yes.

Figure 8

Figure 13

Figure 14

9. $124\% = \dfrac{124}{100}$, which reduced $= \dfrac{31}{25}$ and 1.24.

10. When $A = 30$ miles^2 and $h = 10$ miles then for $A = \dfrac{1}{2}bh$, $30 = \dfrac{1}{2}b(10) \Rightarrow 30 = 5b \Rightarrow b = 6$ miles.

11. $A = \dfrac{h}{2}(a + b)$ then $A = \dfrac{h}{2}a + \dfrac{h}{2}b \Rightarrow A - \dfrac{h}{2}a = \dfrac{h}{2}b \Rightarrow \dfrac{2}{h}\left(A - \dfrac{ha}{2}\right) = b \Rightarrow b = \dfrac{2a}{h} - a$

12. $bt - 1 < 3 - t$, $7t < 4 \Rightarrow t < \dfrac{4}{7} \Rightarrow \left\{t \,\middle|\, t < \dfrac{4}{7}\right\}$

13. See Figure 13.

14. See Figure 14. x-intercept: 4; y-intercept: 2.

15. See Figure 15. x-intercept: -4; y-intercept: 3.

16. See Figure 16. x-intercept: -2; y-intercept: none.

Figure 15

Figure 16

Figure 23

17. x-intercept: 2; y-intercept: 4; Therefore $m = \dfrac{4-0}{0-2} \Rightarrow m = -2 \Rightarrow y = -2x + 4$.

18. Using point-slope form: $y - 3 = -2(x+1) \Rightarrow y - 3 = -2x - 2 \Rightarrow y = -2x + 1$

19. First find slope: $m = \dfrac{8-5}{2-(-3)} = \dfrac{3}{5}$. Now use point-slope form: $y - 8 = \dfrac{3}{5}(x-2) \Rightarrow y - 8 = \dfrac{3}{5}x - \dfrac{6}{5} \Rightarrow$

$y = \dfrac{3}{5}x + \dfrac{34}{5}$.

20. First put $x + 2y = 5$ into slope-intercept form: $x + 2y = 5 \Rightarrow 2y = -x + 5 \Rightarrow y = -\dfrac{1}{2}x + \dfrac{5}{2} \Rightarrow m = -\dfrac{1}{2}$.

The slope of a line perpendicular to this would be $\dfrac{2}{1}$ or 2. Now using slope-intercept form

$y - 1 = 2(x+1) \Rightarrow y - 1 = 2x + 2 \Rightarrow y = 2x + 3$.

21. $P = 500x + 4000$

22. Using substitution; $-2a + b = -5 \Rightarrow b = 2a - 5$ and so $4a - 3(2a - 5) = 0, 4a - 6a + 15 = 0,$

$-2a + 15 = 0 \Rightarrow a = 7.5$, and $-2(7.5) + b = -5 \Rightarrow b = 10 \Rightarrow (7.5, 10)$.

23. See Figure 23.

24. See Figure 24.

25. See Figure 25.

Figure 24

Figure 25

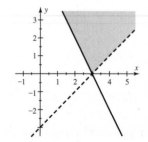

Figure 26

26. See Figure 26.

27. $(ab - bb^2) - (4b^2 + 8ab + 2) \Rightarrow -7ab - 10b^2 - 2$

28. $5 - 3^4 = 5 - 81 \Rightarrow -76$

29. $4(4^{-2})(3^{-1})(3^4) = \frac{4}{1} \cdot \frac{1}{4^2} \cdot \frac{1}{3} \cdot \frac{3^4}{1} = \frac{4}{1} \cdot \frac{1}{16} \cdot \frac{1}{3} \cdot \frac{81}{1} = \frac{27}{4}$

30. $\frac{2^{-4}}{4^{-2}} = \frac{4^2}{2^4} = \frac{16}{16} = 1$

31. $(8t^{-3})(3t^2)(t^5) = (8 \cdot 3)(t^{-3+2+5}) = 24t^4$

32. $2(rt)^4 \Rightarrow 2r^4t^4$

33. $(2t^3)^{-2} = \frac{1}{(2t^3)^2} \Rightarrow \frac{1}{2^2 \cdot t^{3 \cdot 2}} = \frac{1}{4t^6}$

34. $(4a^2b^3)^2(2ab)^{-3} = (4^2 \cdot a^{2 \cdot 2} \cdot b^{3 \cdot 2})\left(\frac{1}{2^3a^3b^3}\right) = \frac{16a^4b^6}{8a^3b^3} = 2a^{4-3}b^{6-3} = 2ab^3$

35. $\left(\frac{2rt^{-1}}{3r^{-2}t^3}\right)^4 = \frac{2^4 \cdot r^4 \cdot t^{-1 \cdot 4}}{3^4 \cdot r^{-2 \cdot 4} \cdot t^{3 \cdot 4}} = \frac{16r^4y^{-4}}{81r^{-8}t^{12}} = \frac{16r^{4-(-8)}t^{-4-12}}{81} = \frac{16r^{12}t^{-16}}{81} = \frac{16r^{12}}{81t^{16}}$

36. $\left(\frac{2a^{-1}}{ab^{-2}}\right)^{-3} = \frac{2^{-3} \cdot a^{-1 \cdot (-3)}}{a^{-3}b^{-2 \cdot (-3)}} = \frac{2^{-3}a^3}{a^{-3}b^6} = \frac{a^{3-(-3)}}{2^3b^6} = \frac{a^6}{8b^6}$

37. $2a^2(a^2 - 2a + 3) = 2a^4 - 4a^3 + 6a^2$

38. $(a + b)(a^2 - ab + b^2) = a^3 - a^2b + ab^2 + a^2b - ab^2 + b^3 = a^3 + b^3$

39. $(5x + 1)(x - 7) = 5x^2 - 35x + x - 7 = 5x^2 - 34x - 7$

40. $(y - 3)(2y + 3) = 2y^2 + 3y - 6y - 9 = 2y^2 - 3y - 9$

41. $(a + b)(a - b) = a^2 - ab + ab - b^2 = a^2 - b^2$

42. $(2x + 3y)^2 = 4x^2 + 6xy + 6xy + 9y^2 = 4x^2 + 12xy + 9y^2$

43. Move the decimal point five places to the left, $1.5 \times 10^{-5} = 0.000015$.

44. Move the decimal point six places to the left, $2,130,000 = 2.13 \times 10^6$.

45. $\frac{4x^3 - 8x^2 + 6x}{2x} = \frac{4x^3}{2x} - \frac{8x^2}{2x} + \frac{6x}{2x} = 2x^2 - 4x + 3$

46.
$$
\begin{array}{r}
x^3 - 4x^2 + 3x - 2 + \dfrac{1}{x - 5} \\
x - 5\overline{)x^4 - 9x^3 + 23x^2 - 17x + 11} \\
\underline{x^4 - 5x^3} \qquad\qquad\qquad\qquad \\
-4x^3 + 23x^2 \qquad\qquad \\
\underline{-4x^3 + 20x^2} \qquad\qquad \\
3x^2 - 17x \qquad \\
\underline{3x^2 - 15x} \qquad \\
-2x + 11 \\
\underline{-2x + 10} \\
1
\end{array}
$$

47. $10ab^2 - 25a^3b^5 = 5ab^2(2 - 5a^2b^3)$

48. $y^3 - 3y^2 + 2y - 6 = (y^3 - 3y^2) + (2y - 6) = y^2(y - 3) + 2(y - 3) = (y - 3)(y^2 + 2)$

49. $6z^2 + 7z - 3 = (2z + 3)(3z - 1)$

50. $4z^2 - 9 = (2z)^2 - 3^2 = (2z - 3)(2z + 3)$

51. $4y^2 - 20y + 25 = (2y - 5)(2y - 5) = (2y - 5)^2$

52. $a^3 - 27 = a^3 - 3^3 = (a - 3)(a^2 + 3a + 9)$

53. $4z^4 - 17z + 15 = (z^2 - 3)(4z^2 - 5)$

54. $2a^3b + a^2b^2 - ab^3 = ab(2a^2 + ab - b^2) = ab(2a - b)(a + b)$

55. $x - 1 = 0 \Rightarrow x = 1$ and $x + 2 = 0 \Rightarrow x = -2$. Therefore $x = -2, 1$.

56. Factor $x^2 - 9x = 0 \Rightarrow x(x - 9) = 0$, so $x = 0$ and $x - 9 = 0 \Rightarrow x = 9$. Therefore $x = 0, 9$.

57. Set $6y^2 - 7y = 3$ equal to zero $\Rightarrow 6y^2 - 7y - 3 = 0$. Now factor: $6y^2 - 7y - 3 = 0 \Rightarrow$

   $(3y + 1)(2y - 3) = 0$. So $3y + 1 = 0 \Rightarrow 3y = -1 \Rightarrow y = -\dfrac{1}{3}$ and $2y - 3 = 0 \Rightarrow 2y = 3 \Rightarrow y = \dfrac{3}{2}$.

   Therefore $y = -\dfrac{1}{3}, \dfrac{3}{2}$.

58. Set $x^3 = 4x$ equal to zero $\Rightarrow x^3 - 4x = 0$. Now factor: $x^3 - 4x = 0 \Rightarrow x(x^2 - 4) \Rightarrow$

   $x(x + 2)(x - 2) = 0$. So $x + 2 = 0 \Rightarrow x = -2$, and $x - 2 = 0 \Rightarrow x = 2$. Therefore $x = -2, 0, 2$.

59. $\dfrac{x^2 - 16}{x + 4} = \dfrac{(x + 4)(x - 4)}{x + 4} = x - 4$

60. $\dfrac{2x^2 - 11x - 6}{6x^2 - 5x - 4} = \dfrac{(2x + 1)(x - 6)}{(2x + 1)(3x - 4)} = \dfrac{x - 6}{3x - 4}$

61. $\dfrac{x - 3}{16 - x^2}$ will be undefined when $16x^2 = 0$. $x^2 - 16 = 0 \Rightarrow (x + 4)(x - 4) = 0$. So $x + 4 = 0 \Rightarrow$

   $x = -4$ and $x - 4 = 0 \Rightarrow x = 4$. Therefore it will be undefined when $x = -4, 4$.

62. $\dfrac{4(-2) + 1}{(-2) - 1} = \dfrac{-8 + 1}{-3} = \dfrac{-7}{-3} = \dfrac{7}{3}$

63. $\dfrac{x^2 - 3x + 2}{x + 7} \div \dfrac{x - 2}{2x + 14} = \dfrac{(x - 2)(x - 1)}{x + 7} \div \dfrac{x - 2}{2(x + 7)} = \dfrac{(x - 2)(x - 1)}{x + 7} \cdot \dfrac{2(x + 7)}{x - 2} = \dfrac{2(x - 1)}{1} = 2(x - 1)$

64. $\dfrac{x}{2x + 3} + \dfrac{x + 3}{2x + 3} = \dfrac{x + x + 3}{2x + 3} = \dfrac{2x + 3}{2x + 3} = 1$

65. $\dfrac{5x}{x^2 - 1} - \dfrac{3}{x + 1} = \dfrac{5x}{(x + 1)(x - 1)} - \dfrac{3}{x + 1} = \dfrac{5x}{(x + 1)(x - 1)} - \dfrac{3(x - 1)}{(x + 1)(x - 1)} = \dfrac{5x - 3x + 3}{(x + 1)(x - 1)} =$

   $\dfrac{2x + 3}{(x - 1)(x + 1)}$

66. $\dfrac{\frac{2}{x} - \frac{2}{y}}{\frac{2}{x} + \frac{2}{y}} = \dfrac{\frac{2y}{xy} - \frac{2x}{xy}}{\frac{2y}{xy} + \frac{2x}{xy}} = \dfrac{\frac{2y - 2x}{xy}}{\frac{2y + 2x}{xy}} = \dfrac{2y - 2x}{xy} \cdot \dfrac{xy}{2y + 2x} = \dfrac{2y - 2x}{2y + 2x} = \dfrac{2(y - x)}{2(y + x)} = \dfrac{y - x}{y + x}$

67. $\dfrac{x + 2}{5} = \dfrac{x}{4} \Rightarrow 4(x + 2) = 5x \Rightarrow 4x + 8 = 5x \Rightarrow x = 8$

68. $\dfrac{1}{3x} + \dfrac{5}{2x} = 2 \Rightarrow \dfrac{2}{6x} + \dfrac{15}{6x} = \dfrac{12x}{6x}$, so $2 + 15 = 12x \Rightarrow 17 = 12x \Rightarrow x = \dfrac{17}{12}$

69. $\dfrac{1}{x - 2} + \dfrac{2}{x + 2} = \dfrac{1}{x^2 - 4} \Rightarrow \dfrac{1}{x - 2} + \dfrac{2}{x + 2} = \dfrac{1}{(x + 2)(x - 2)} \Rightarrow \dfrac{x + 2}{(x + 2)(x - 2)} + \dfrac{2(x - 2)}{(x + 2)(x - 2)} =$

   $\dfrac{1}{(x + 2)(x - 2)}$, so $x + 2 + 2(x - 2) = 1 \Rightarrow x + 2 + 2x - 4 = 1 \Rightarrow 3x - 2 = 1 \Rightarrow 3x = 3 \Rightarrow x = 1$

70. If y is inversely proportional to x then $y = \dfrac{k}{x}$. If $y = 25$ when $x = 4$ then $25 = \dfrac{k}{4} \Rightarrow k = 100$.

So if $x = 10$ then $y = \dfrac{100}{10} \Rightarrow y = 10$.

71. $8^2 + 3^2 = c^2 \Rightarrow 64 + 9 = c^2 \Rightarrow c^2 = 73 \Rightarrow c = \sqrt{73}$ feet

72. $a^2 + 24^2 = 25^2 \Rightarrow a^2 + 576 = 625 \Rightarrow a^2 = 49 \Rightarrow a = \sqrt{49} \Rightarrow a = 7$ miles

73. $d = \sqrt{(-2-4)^2 + (3-7)^2} = \sqrt{36 + 16} = \sqrt{52} = 2\sqrt{13}$

74. $d = \sqrt{(3-(-1))^2 + (-8-(-8))^2} = \sqrt{16 + 0} = \sqrt{16} = 4$

75. $\dfrac{\sqrt{80}}{\sqrt{5}} = \sqrt{\dfrac{80}{5}} = \sqrt{16} = 4$

76. $\sqrt{2x^3 y} \cdot \sqrt{32xy} = \sqrt{2 \cdot 32 x^3 xyy} = \sqrt{64 x^4 y^2} = 8x^2 y$

77. $8\sqrt[3]{7} - 3\sqrt[3]{7} = (8-3)\sqrt[3]{7} = 5\sqrt[3]{7}$

78. $\dfrac{\sqrt[4]{64}}{\sqrt[4]{4}} = \sqrt[4]{\dfrac{64}{4}} = \sqrt[4]{16} = 2$

79. $\sqrt{4-x} = 7 \Rightarrow (\sqrt{4-x})^2 = 7^2 \Rightarrow 4 - x = 49 \Rightarrow x = -45$

Check: $\sqrt{4-(-45)} = \sqrt{49} = 7$

80. $x - 1 = \sqrt{2x+1} \Rightarrow (x-1)^2 = (\sqrt{2x+1})^2 \Rightarrow x^2 - 2x + 1 = 2x + 1 \Rightarrow x^2 - 4x = 0 \Rightarrow$

$x(x-4) = 0 \Rightarrow x = 0, 4$

Check: $0 - 1 \overset{?}{=} \sqrt{2(0)+1} \Rightarrow -1 \overset{?}{=} \sqrt{1} \Rightarrow -1 \neq 1$ (This answer does not check)

Check: $4 - 1 \overset{?}{=} \sqrt{2(4)+1} \Rightarrow 3 \overset{?}{=} \sqrt{9} \Rightarrow 3 = 3$. The only solution is 4.

81. $x = -\dfrac{b}{2a} = -\dfrac{(-6)}{2(1)} = 3, y = (3)^2 - 6(3) + 14 = 5$; The vertex is $(3, 5)$.

82. $x = -\dfrac{b}{2a} = -\dfrac{(-4)}{2(2)} = 1, y = 2(1)^2 - 4(1) - 1 = -3$; The vertex is $(1, -3)$.

83. $x^2 + 3x = 18 \Rightarrow x^2 + 3x - 18 = 0 \Rightarrow (x+6)(x-3) = 0 \Rightarrow x = -6, 3$

84. $x^2 - 2x = 2 \Rightarrow x^2 - 2x + 1 = 2 + 1 \Rightarrow (x-1)^2 = 3 \Rightarrow x - 1 = \pm\sqrt{3} \Rightarrow x = 1 \pm \sqrt{3}$

85. $3x^2 - 4 = 11 \Rightarrow 3x^2 = 15 \Rightarrow x^2 = 5 \Rightarrow x = \pm\sqrt{5}$

86. $x = \dfrac{12 \pm \sqrt{(-12)^2 - 4(4)(7)}}{2(4)} = \dfrac{12 \pm \sqrt{32}}{8} = \dfrac{12 \pm 4\sqrt{2}}{8} = \dfrac{4(3 \pm \sqrt{2})}{8} = \dfrac{3 \pm \sqrt{2}}{2}$

87. $x = \dfrac{4 \pm \sqrt{(-4)^2 - 4(1)(29)}}{2(1)} = \dfrac{4 \pm \sqrt{-100}}{2} = \dfrac{4 \pm 10i}{2} = \dfrac{4}{2} \pm \dfrac{10}{2}i = 2 \pm 5i$

88. $x = \dfrac{6 \pm \sqrt{(-6)^2 - 4(9)(17)}}{2(9)} = \dfrac{6 \pm \sqrt{-576}}{18} = \dfrac{6 \pm 24i}{18} = \dfrac{6}{18} \pm \dfrac{24}{18}i = \dfrac{1}{3} \pm \dfrac{4}{3}i$

89. Since the constant change is 325 and since when $t = 0, d = 0$. Then $d = 325t$.

90. (a) $I = \dfrac{1}{2}x + 4$

(b) $\dfrac{1}{2}$

(c) Snow is falling at the rate of $\dfrac{1}{2}$ inch per hour.

(d) $I = \dfrac{1}{2}(4) + 4 \Rightarrow f(4) = 2 + 4 \Rightarrow f(4) = 6$ inches of snow.

91. See Figure 91.

Figure 91

92. Let x = number of adults and let y = number of children. Then $x + y = 8$ and $25x + 15y = 170$. Multiplying the first equation by (-15) and adding it to the second equation yields: $10x = 50 \Rightarrow x = 5$, so $5 + y = 8 \Rightarrow y = 3$. Therefore there are 5 adults and 3 children.

93. If rate $\cdot$ time $= 1$ job, then the two rates are: $r \cdot 2 = 1 \Rightarrow r = \dfrac{1}{2}$ and $r \cdot (1.5) = 1 \Rightarrow r = \dfrac{2}{3}$. Now working together we add the rates so, $\dfrac{1}{2}t + \dfrac{2}{3}t = 1 \Rightarrow \dfrac{7}{6}t = 1 \Rightarrow t = \dfrac{6}{7}$. Therefore they can do the job together in $\dfrac{6}{7}$ hour.

94. (a) $h = 88(2) - 16(2)^2 \Rightarrow h = 176 - 16(4) \Rightarrow h = 176 - 64 \Rightarrow h = 112$ feet.

(b) $0 = 88t - 16t^2 \Rightarrow 16t^2 - 88t = 0 \Rightarrow 8t(2t - 11) = 0$. So $8t = 0 \Rightarrow t = 0$ at contact and

$2t - 11 = 0 \Rightarrow 2t = 11 \Rightarrow t = \dfrac{11}{2} \Rightarrow t = 5.5$ seconds.

95. $\dfrac{7}{4} = \dfrac{x}{35} \Rightarrow 4x = 245 \Rightarrow x = 61.25$ feet.

96. (a) $T = \dfrac{1}{20 - 15} \Rightarrow T = \dfrac{1}{5}. \dfrac{1}{5}$ min.; the average wait is $\dfrac{1}{5}$ min. or 12 sec. when vehicles arrive at 15/min.

(b) See Figure 97.

x	5	10	15	19	19.9
T	$\frac{1}{15}$	$\frac{1}{10}$	$\frac{1}{5}$	1	10

Figure 97

(c) The wait time increases dramatically.

97. For $A = 74, -0.005 \le \dfrac{L - A}{A} \le 0.005 \Rightarrow -0.37 \le L - 74 \le 0.37 \Rightarrow 73.63 \le L \le 74.37$.

Critical Thinking Solutions for Chapter 9

Section 9.1

*   If the point (x, y) is reflected across the y-axis, the resulting point is $(-x, y)$.

Section 9.3

*   If we write the equation in $x^2 + kx = d$ form, it would become $x^2 + 0x = 7$. To complete the square we would add zero to both sides of the equation. Completing the square will not work in this case. The square root property should be used for this equation.

Section 9.4

*   Both expressions equal zero because these values of x are the solutions to $2x^2 - 3x - 1 = 0$.

Section 9.5

*   Both expressions equal zero because these values of x are the solutions to $2x^2 + x + 3 = 0$.